VISUAL QUICKSTA

MACROMEDIA FREEHAND 10

FOR WINDOWS AND MACINTOSH

Sandee Cohen

Visual QuickStart Guide

Macromedia FreeHand 10 for Windows and Macintosh

Peachpit Press

1249 Eighth Street
Berkeley, CA 94710
800 283-9444 • 510 524 2178
fax 510 524 2221
Find us on the Web at http://www.peachpit.com

Published by Peachpit Press in association with Macromedia Press
Peachpit Press is a division of Pearson Education

Cover Design: The Visual Group
Interior Design: Sandee Cohen
Production: Sandee Cohen
Illustrations: Sandee Cohen

Notice of Liability

Trademarks

ISBN 0-201-74965-3

0 9 8 7 6 5 4 3

Printed and bound in the United States of America

DEDICATED TO

Jim Alley, my favorite editor, FreeHand compatriot, dinner companion, and co-worker.

Your contributions to our field through your teaching and writing will be sorely missed.

THANKS TO

Jim Alley, who did a great job copy editing, under the most daunting of circumstances, as well as providing insights as to working with FreeHand.

Maje Alley, who helped Jim with the copy-editing.

Toby Malina, who did a great technical edit.

Nancy Ruenzel, publisher of Peachpit Press.

Majorie Baer, managing editor of Peachpit Press.

Kate Reber, production coordinator.

Steve Rath, who creates the best index in the business.

Ian Kelleigh, creator of **freehandsource.com,** for his help describing how the Flash action scripting works. His Web sit is one of the best resources for FreeHand tips, techniques, history, and bug reports.

Keith Hutchinson, FreeHand 10 product manager.

Olav Martin Kvern, who may have gone on to other programs, but still is a FreeHander at heart.

Michael Randazzo and the staff of the New School Computer Instruction Center.

Pixel, my cat. She did absolutely nothing to help me with this book. However, she gets very snippy if she isn't mentioned.

Terry DuPrât, who helped me enormously during the last weeks of production when my leg was in a cast.

All my students at the New School Computer Instruction Center who remind me how little I really know.

Colophon

This book was created using Macromedia FreeHand 10 and Adobe Photoshop 6 for illustrations; Adobe InDesign 1.5 for layout; and Ambrosia SW Snapz Pro for screen shots. The computers used were a 450 MHz G4 Power Macintosh and a G3 PowerBook.
FreeHand 10 for Windows ran on Virtual PC from Connectix. (No Intel inside.)

The fonts used were Minion and Futura from Adobe and two specialty fonts that I created myself.
A single cable modem Web connection was shared between computers using the miraculous Xsense XRouter Pro.

TABLE OF CONTENTS

INTRODUCTION

Welcome to learning Macromedia FreeHand. If you are like most people who are just starting out with the program, you may find it a little overwhelming. This Visual QuickStart Guide has been written to help you sort out the many different features.

FreeHand is one of the most versatile graphics programs for the computer. At its simplest, FreeHand is a vector drawing program. It allows you to create varied artwork such as drawings, logos, and illustrations.

FreeHand also lets you add scanned artwork from programs such as Macromedia Fireworks or Adobe Photoshop. This makes it an excellent layout program to create ads, book covers, posters, and so on. FreeHand has a multiple-page feature that allows you to create newsletters and flyers, as well as multi-page presentations with differently sized pages.

Finally, FreeHand uses the newest Flash technology to turn FreeHand artwork into animations. FreeHand also lets you save your files in formats that can be posted directly onto the World Wide Web.

Using This Book

The first few chapters provide overviews of the program. You may find that you do not create any artwork in those chapters. Do not skip them. They contain information that will help you later.

The middle chapters of the book contain the most artistic information. This is where you can see how easy it is to create sophisticated artwork using FreeHand.

The final chapters are about printing, preferences, and using your artwork with other applications and the Web. Some of this information refers to technical printing terms. If you are not familiar with these terms, speak to the print shop that will be printing your artwork.

Using the Exercises

If you have used any of the Visual QuickStart Guides, you will find this book very similar. Each of the chapters consists of numbered exercises that deal with a specific technique or feature of the program. As you work through each exercise, you gain an understanding of the technique or feature. The illustrations for each of the exercises help you judge if you are following the steps correctly.

Instructions

Working with a book such as this, it is vital that you understand the terms I am using. This is especially important since some books use terms somewhat incorrectly. Therefore, here are the terms I use in the book and explanations of what they mean.

Click refers to pressing down and releasing the mouse button on the Macintosh, and the left mouse button on Windows. You must release the mouse button or it is not a click.

Press means to hold down the mouse button, or the keyboard key.

Press and drag means to hold the mouse button down and then move the mouse. In later chapters, I use the shorthand term *drag*; just remember that you have to press and hold as you drag the mouse.

Menu commands

FreeHand has menu commands that you follow to open dialog boxes, change artwork, and invoke certain commands. These menu commands are listed in bold type. The typical direction to choose a menu command might be written as **Window > Panels > Style**. This means that you should first choose the Window menu, then choose the Panels submenu, and then choose the Style command.

Keyboard shortcuts

Most of the menu commands for FreeHand 10 have keyboard shortcuts that help you work faster. For instance, instead of choosing New from the File menu, it is faster and easier to press the keys on the keyboard. On the Macintosh, the keys are Cmd-N. On Windows, the keys are Ctrl-N.

Keyboard shortcuts are sometimes listed in different orders by different software companies or authors. For example, I always list the Command or Ctrl keys first, then the Option or Alt key, and then the Shift key. Other people may list the Shift key first. The order that you press those modifier keys is not important. However, it is very important that you always add the last key (the letter or number key) after you are holding the other keys.

Learning keyboard shortcuts

While keyboard shortcuts help you work faster, you really do not have to start using them right away. In fact, you will most likely learn more about FreeHand by using the menus. As you look for one command, you may see others that you would like to explore.

Once you feel comfortable working with FreeHand, you can start adding keyboard shortcuts to your repertoire. My suggestion is to look at which menu commands you use a lot. Then each day choose one of those shortcuts.

For instance, if you do a lot of blends, you might decide to learn the shortcut for the Blend command. For the rest of that day use the Blend shortcut every time you need to make a blend. Even if you have to look at the menu to refresh your memory, still use the keyboard shortcut to actually apply the blend. By the end of the day you will have memorized the Blend shortcut. The next day you can learn a new one.

Onscreen element appearances

Some of the onscreen elements, such as the toolbars, may look different in this book from your settings. That's because I changed those panels to make them easier to read. For more information on customizing the toolbars, see Chapter 32.

Cross-platform issues

One of the great strengths of FreeHand is that it is almost identical on both the Macintosh and Windows platforms. In fact, at first glance it is hard to tell which platform you are working on. However, because there are some differences between the platforms, there are some things you should keep in mind.

Modifier keys

Modifier keys are always listed with the Macintosh key first and then the Windows key second. So a direction to hold the Command/Ctrl key as you drag means to hold the Command key on the Macintosh platform or the Ctrl key on the Windows platform. When the key is the same on both computers, such as the Shift key, only one key is listed.

Generally the Command key on the Macintosh (sometimes called the Apple key) corresponds to the Ctrl key on Windows. The Option key on the Macintosh corresponds to the Alt key on Windows. The Control key on the Macintosh platform does not have an equivalent on the Windows platform. Notice that the Control key for the Macintosh is always spelled out while the Ctrl key for Windows is not.

Platform-specific features

A few times in the book, I have written separate exercises for the Macintosh and Windows platforms. These exercises are indicated by (Mac) and (Win).

Most of the time this is because the procedures are so different that they need to be written separately. Sometimes features exist only on one platform. Those features are then labeled as to their platform.

Mac OS X

Macromedia FreeHand is one of the first applications to take advantage of the new Mac OS X (ten) operating system. If you are learning FreeHand on a computer that uses OS X, you will find much of the interface to look different. Don't worry, though. The differences are cosmetic. There is nothing that FreeHand running in OS X can do that can't be done in Mac OS 9 or Windows.

Learning FreeHand

With a program as extensive as FreeHand, there will be many features that you never use. For instance, if you are an illustrator, you may never need any of FreeHand's text or layout features. Or you may never need to create charts or graphs. And if you are strictly a print person, you may never need to do any exporting as Web animations. Do not worry. It may be hard to believe but even the experts do not use all of FreeHand's features.

Find the areas you want to master, then follow the exercises. If you are patient, you will find yourself creating your own work in no time.

And don't forget to have fun!

Sandee Cohen (SandeeC@vectorbabe.com)
July 2001

FREEHAND BASICS 1

Ever wonder why houses are built from the ground up? After all, the basement is so dull, so basic. Why not start with something more flashy like the windows, the front door, or the roof? The reason is that if you don't have a firm foundation as you start building, your house will not last very long.

The same is true when you learn a computer graphics program. As excited as you must be to learn Macromedia FreeHand, there are a few basics that we need to cover before we can go on to the fun stuff.

This chapter covers those basics: the onscreen panels and toolbars, menus, and window elements. And although you may be tempted to skip ahead to the fun stuff in the other chapters, please take a moment to look at what's here.

Think of this chapter as a set of road signs that will help you navigate through the rest of FreeHand.

Setting up FreeHand

You need to make sure your computer has the minimum hardware and system requirements necessary to run FreeHand properly. You can then install and launch FreeHand.

System Requirements (Win)

- An Intel Pentium processor or equivalent running Microsoft Windows 98, Windows 2000, Windows NT version 4, or Windows ME.
- RAM sufficient to meet your operating system's requirements plus 64 MB application memory.
- 70 MB available hard disk space.
- A CD-ROM drive.
- A color monitor capable of 800-by-600-pixel resolution and 256-color display (1024 x 768 and millions of colors recommended).
- Adobe Type Manager version 4 or later with Type 1 fonts (recommended).
- A PostScript Level 2-compatible printer or later.

To check memory (Win):

◆ Choose System Properties from the Control Panels directory to view the amount of installed memory and the available memory ❶.

To check hard disk space (Win):

1. Open the My Computer icon on the desktop.
2. Select the hard disk, usually named a letter such as C.
3. Click with the right mouse button to open the contextual menu.
4. Choose Properties from the contextual menu. This opens the Properties dialog box that contains the disk information ❷.

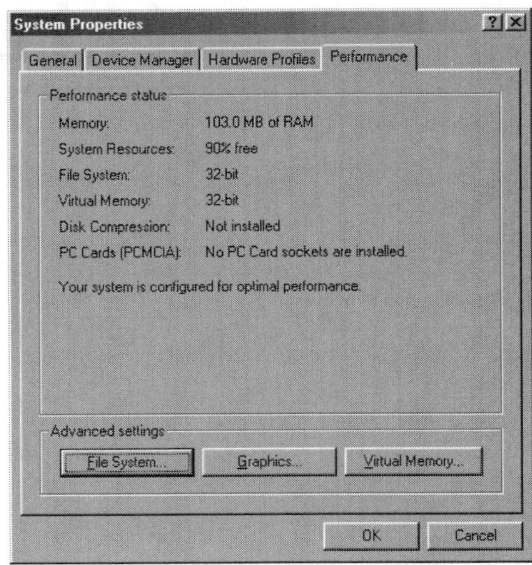

❶ *The* **Windows System Properties** *display shows that this computer has 103 megabytes of memory.*

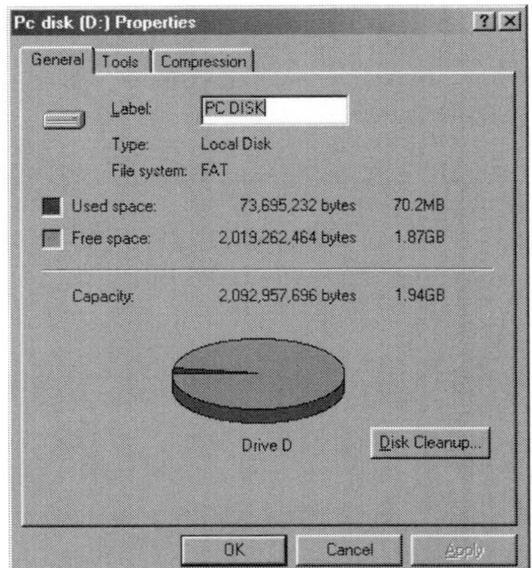

❷ *The* **Windows Hard Disk Properties** *display shows that this computer has 1.87 gigabytes of free disk space.*

❸ *The* Macintosh Memory display *shows that this computer is operating under Mac OS 9.1 and has 640 megabytes of memory.*

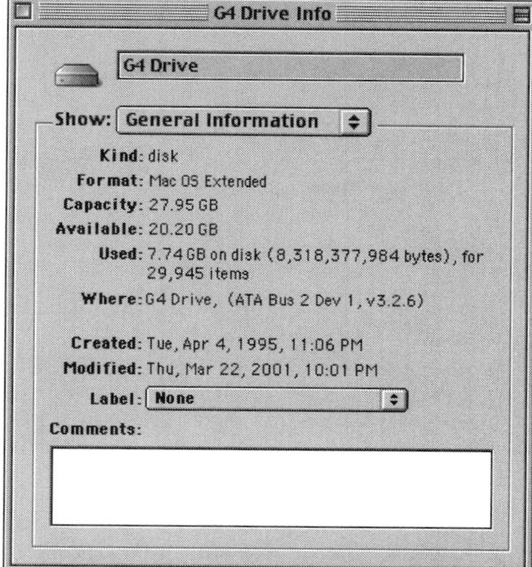

❹ *The* Macintosh Hard Disk space display *shows that this computer has 20.20 gigabytes of storage space available.*

Sytem Requirements (Mac)

- PowerPC processor running System 8.6, 9.1, or OS X.
- RAM sufficient to meet your operating system's requirements plus 32 MB application memory.
- 70 MB available hard disk space.
- A CD-ROM drive.
- A color monitor capable of 800-by-600-pixel resolution and 256-color display (1024 x 768 and millions of colors recommended).
- Adobe Type Manager version 4 or later with Type 1 fonts (recommended).
- A PostScript Level 2-compatible printer or later.

To check memory (Mac):

- Choose About This Computer from the Apple menu to view the version of the operating system, the built-in memory, and the amount of virtual memory ❸.

To check hard disk space (Mac):

1. Select the hard disk.
2. Choose **File > Get Info > General Information.** The panel displays the available space for the disk ❹.

To install FreeHand (Win)

1. Disable any virus-protection programs and clear the TEMP directory before installing the software.
2. Insert the FreeHand CD-ROM in your CD-ROM drive.
3. Follow the onscreen instructions ❺.
4. After installation, restart the computer.

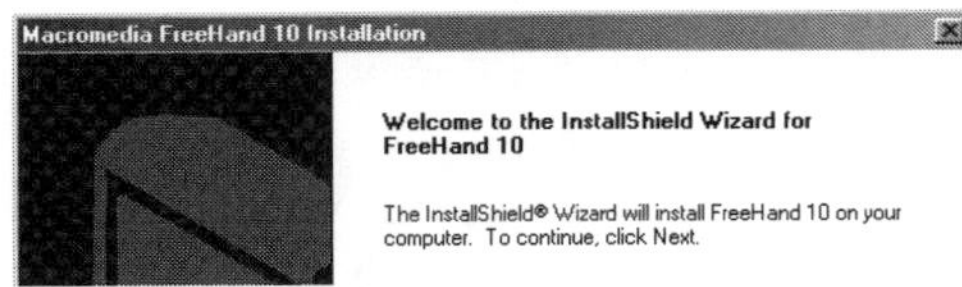

❺ *The* **Windows FreeHand 10 Installation screen** *takes you through all the steps of the installation.*

To install FreeHand (Mac)

1. Disable any virus-protection extensions.
2. Insert the FreeHand CD-ROM in your CD-ROM drive.
3. Open the FreeHand 10 folder on the CD-ROM.
4. Double-click the FreeHand 10 Installer icon ❻.
5. When the FreeHand installer screen displays, follow the onscreen instructions.
6. After installation, restart the computer.

❻ *Double-click the* **Macintosh FreeHand Installer icon** *to start the installation process.*

To launch FreeHand (Win)

◆ Choose **Start > Programs > Macromedia FreeHand 10 > FreeHand 10** ❼.

TIP You can double-click the icon for a previously saved FreeHand document. This launches FreeHand and brings you directly to that document.

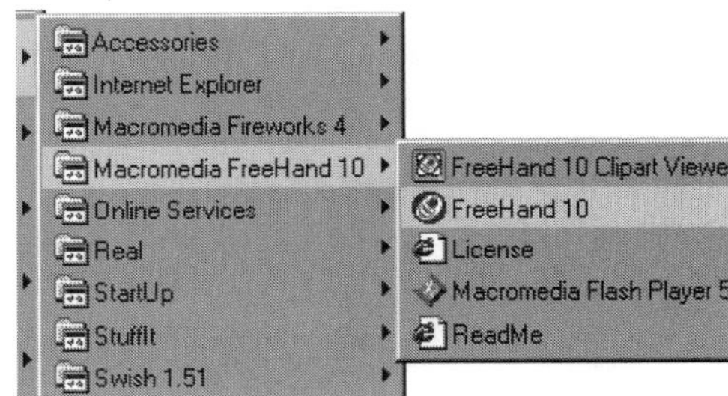

❼ *You can launch FreeHand from the* **Windows Start menu.**

To launch FreeHand (Mac)

◆ Double-click the FreeHand 10 application icon ❽.

TIP You can double-click the icon for a previously saved FreeHand document. This launches FreeHand and brings you directly to that document.

❽ *You can also launch FreeHand by double-clicking the* **FreeHand application icon.**

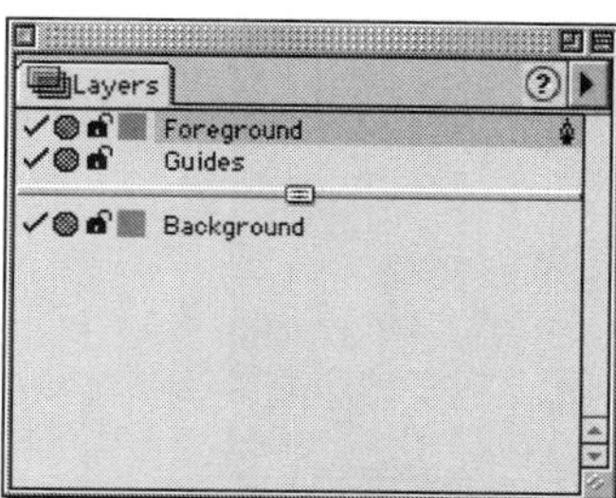

❾ The **Layers panel** *controls the order in which objects appear.*

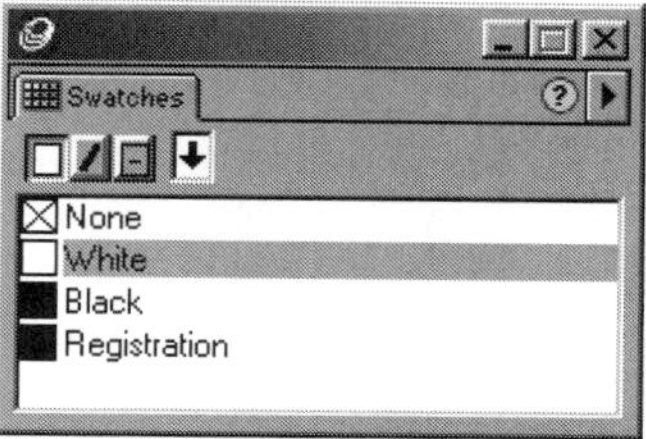

❿ The **Swatches panel** *stores the colors used in your documents.*

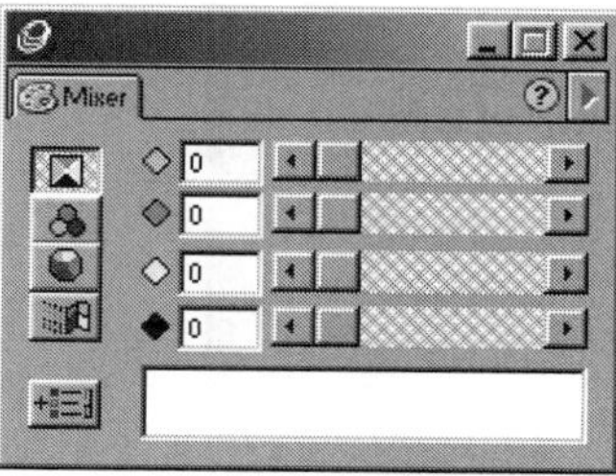

⓫ The **Color Mixer panel** *lets you define specific colors.*

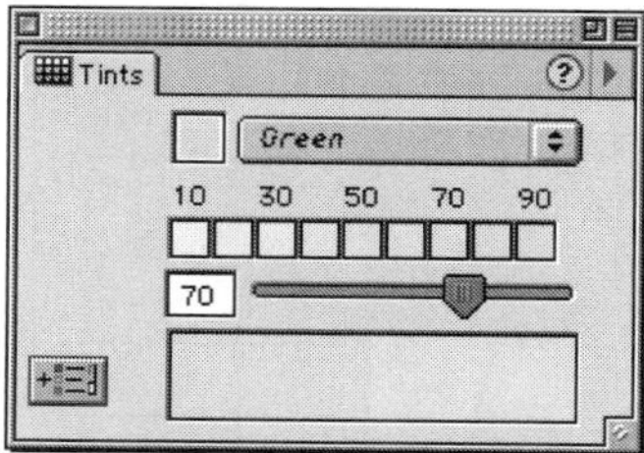

⓬ The **Tints panel** *is where you can make tints of colors.*

Onscreen Elements

When you launch FreeHand, you see various FreeHand onscreen elements called panels, inspectors, and toolbars. These elements control different aspects of the program. They can be closed, opened, resized, or moved around the screen to suit your own work habits.

TIP FreeHand remembers the layout of the onscreen elements when you quit the program. The next time you open FreeHand, the panels are arranged in the same position.

Layers panel

The Layers panel (**Window > Panel > Layers**) allows you to control the order in which objects appear onscreen ❾. *(For more information on the Layers panel, see Chapter 12, "Layers and Layering.")*

Swatches panel

The Swatches panel (**Window > Panel > Swatches**)lets you store colors and apply them to objects ❿. *(For more information on the Swatches panel, see Chapter 13, "Working in Color.")*

Color Mixer panel

The Color Mixer panel (**Window > Panel > Color Mixer**)allows you to define colors according to four different modes: CMYK, RGB, HLS, and the system color picker ⓫. *(For more information on the Color Mixer panel, see Chapter 13, "Working in Color.")*

Tints panel

The Tints panel (**Window > Panel > Tints**)lets you create tints of colors and apply them to objects ⓬. *(For more information on the Tints panel, see Chapter 13, "Working in Color.")*

Onscreen Elements

Styles panel

The Styles panel (**Window > Panel > Styles**) lets you store the appearance of graphics and text as styles that can be easily reapplied to other objects ⓭. *(For more information on the Styles panel, see Chapter 21, "Styles.")*

⓭ *The* **Styles panel** *lets you store graphic and text styles.*

Halftones panel

The Halftones panel (**Window > Panel > Halftones**) is used to set custom screens for objects such as tints, gradients, blends, and scanned images ⓮. *(For more information on the Halftones panel, see Chapter 31, "Advanced Printing.")*

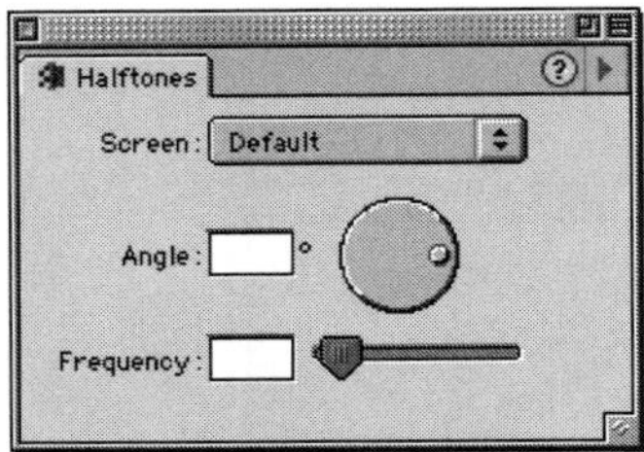

⓮ *The* **Halftones panel** *lets you apply custom screens.*

Transform panel

The Transform panel (**Window > Panel > Transform**) allows you to move, rotate, scale, skew, or reflect objects by numerical input ⓯. *(For more information on the Transform panel, see Chapter 10, "Move and Transform.")*

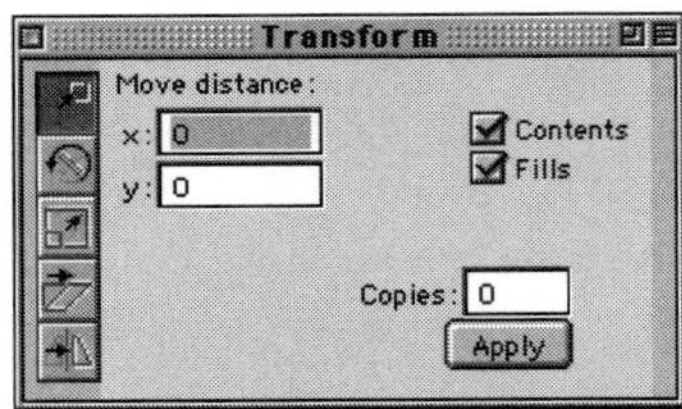

⓯ *The* **Transform panel** *lets you numerically move, rotate, scale, skew, or reflect objects.*

Navigation panel

The Navigation panel (**Window > Panel > Navigation**) is used to add navigational elements and Flash commands to FreeHand documents ⓰. *(For more information on the Navigation panel, see Chapter 29, "Flash Animations.")*

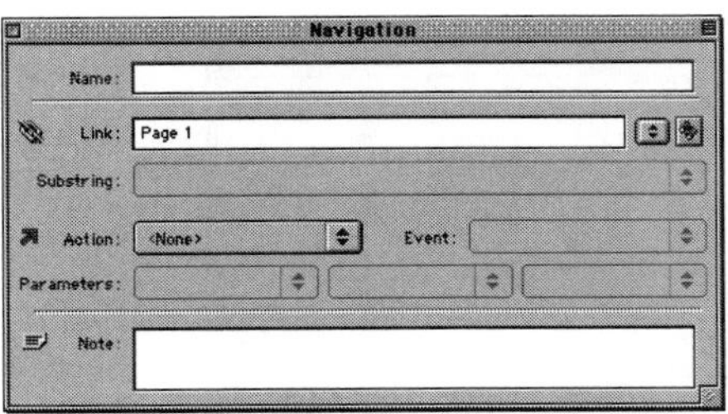

⓰ *The* **Navigation panel** *is used to add navigational elements that are part of HTML, SWF, and PDF files.*

Onscreen Elements

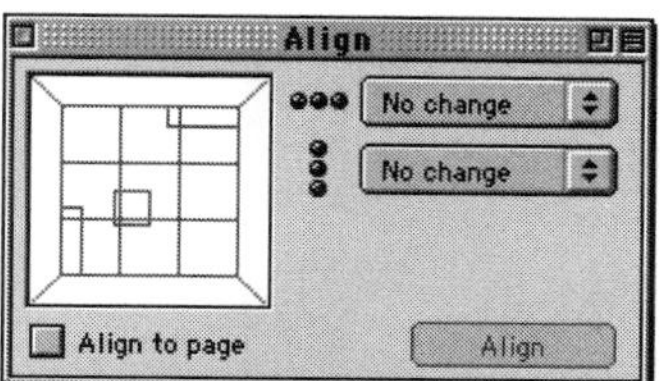

⓱ *The* **Align panel** *lets you align or distribute objects.*

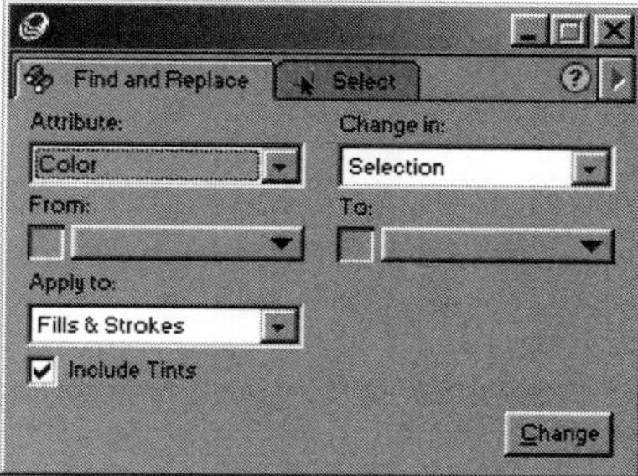

⓲ *The* **Find and Replace Graphics panel** *lets you make global changes to graphics in your documents.*

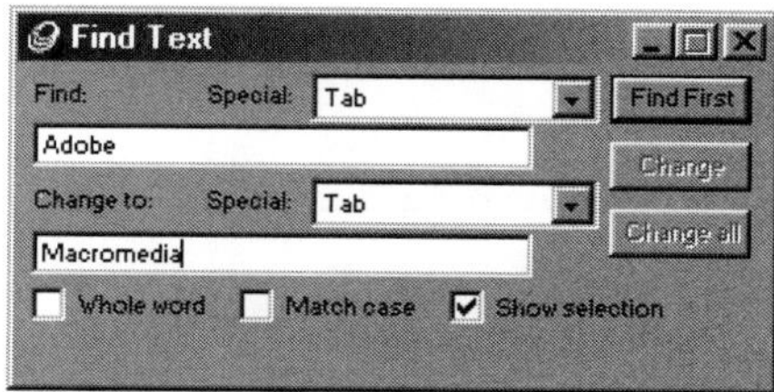

⓳ *The* **Find Text panel** *lets you make global changes to text in your documents.*

Align panel

The Align panel (**Window > Panel > Align**) is used to align or distribute selected objects on their sides, tops, bottoms, and, centers ⓱. *(For more information on the Align panel, see Chapter 10, "Move and Transform.")*

Find & Replace Graphics panel

The Find & Replace Graphics panel (**Edit > Find & Replace > Graphics**) is used to make changes to many objects in a document ⓲ at the same time. *(For more information on the Find and Replace Graphics panel, see Chapter 23, "Automating FreeHand.")*

TIP Although the Find and Replace Graphics panel has tabs, it cannot be grouped with any of the other tabbed panels. Also, the two tabs of the panel cannot be separated into two different panels.

Find Text panel

The Find Text panel (**Edit > Find & Replace > Graphics**) is used to make changes to all the text in a document ⓳. *(For more information on the Find Text panel, see Chapter 19, "Text Tools.")*

Object inspector

The Object inspector (**Window > Inspector > Object**) lets you set specific attributes for selected objects ⓴. The attributes change depending on the object selected. *(The Object inspector is covered in chapters 5 and 8.)*

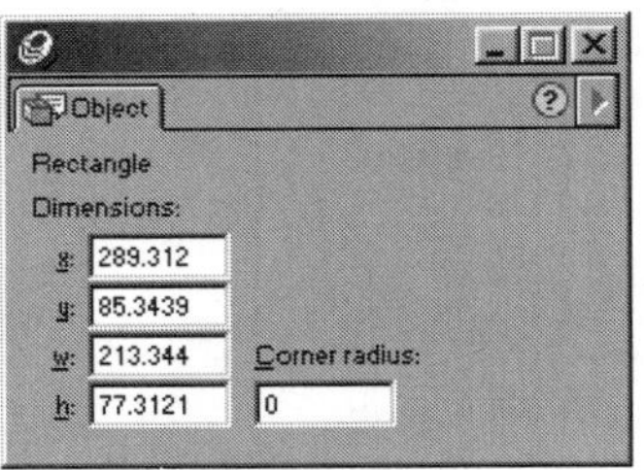

⓴ *The* **Object inspector** *changes its display depending on the object that is selected.*

Fill inspector

The Fill inspector (**Window > Inspector > Fill**) is used to set the type of fill applied inside objects ㉑. There are eight different types of fills that include a basic color fill or a gradient that changes from one color to another. *(For more information on the Fill inspector, see Chapter 14, "Fills.")*

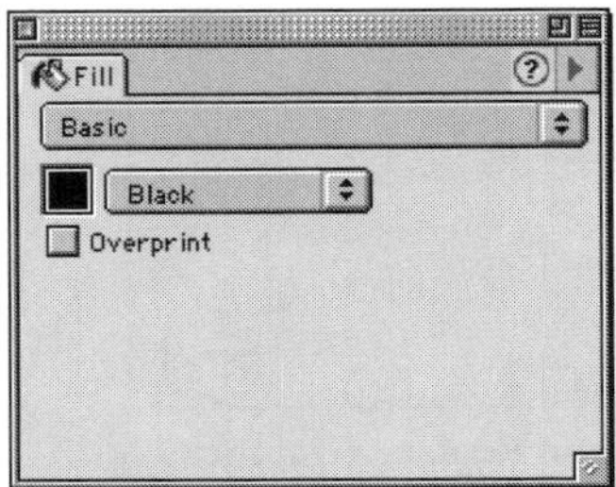

㉑ *The* **Fill inspector** *controls the colors and effects applied inside objects.*

Stroke inspector

The Stroke inspector (**Window > Inspector > Stroke**) is used to set the type of stroke applied to objects ㉒. There are five different types of strokes that include a basic color stroke or a brush stroke that wraps artwork around an object. *(For more information on the Stroke inspector, see Chapter 15, "Strokes.")*

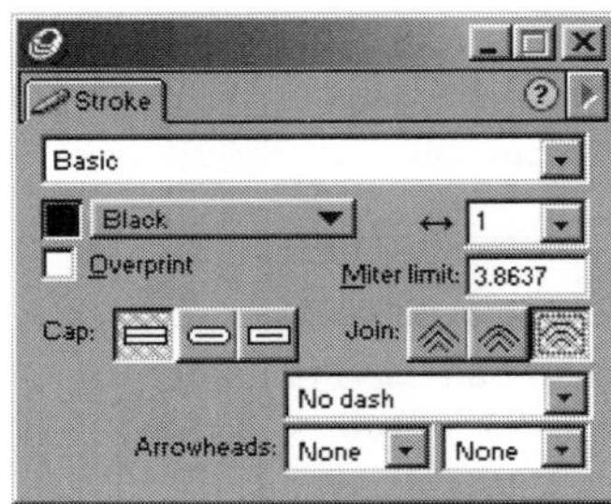

㉒ *The* **Stroke inspector** *controls the colors and effects applied to an object's outside edge.*

Panels or Inspectors: What's the difference?

I wish I knew. Many years ago there were differences between the two types of onscreen elements. But those differences were lost with each new version of FreeHand.

In fact, you can even group panels with inspectors.

The only real difference I can see is that inspectors are found under the **Window > Inspectors** and panels are under **Window > Panels.**

Perhaps the real reason to keep the two different names is to avoid confusing old-time users like me.

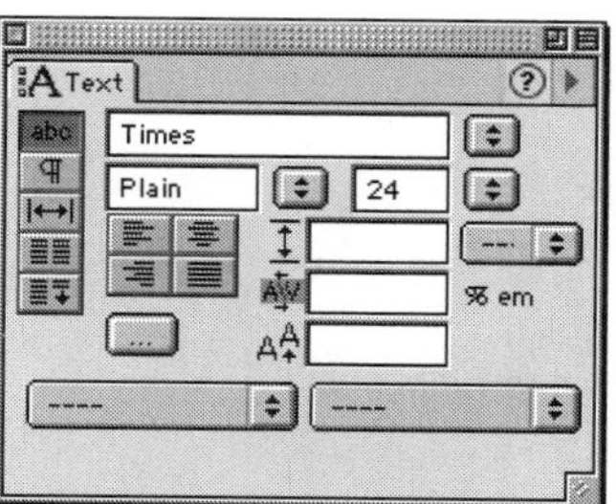

㉓ *The* **Text inspector** *controls five different categories of text attributes.*

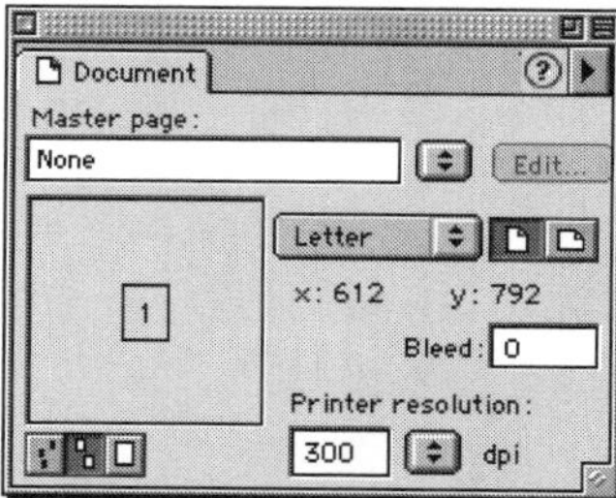

㉔ *The* **Document inspector** *controls the document's pages and printer resolution.*

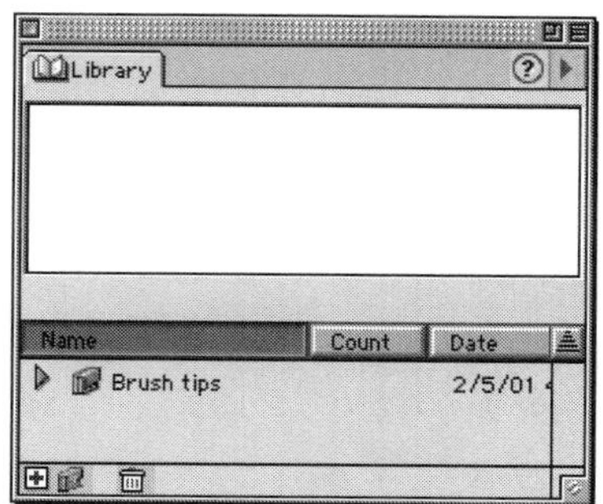

㉕ *The* **Library** *stores symbols that help you automate changes, use brushes, and create Flash (SWF) animations.*

Text inspector

The Text inspector (**Window > Inspector > Text**) is used to control the various attributes applied to text ㉓. There are five different settings for the Text inspector. *(For more information on the Text inspector, see Chapter 18, "Basic Text.")*

Document inspector

The Document inspector (**Window > Inspector > Document**) controls various attributes of the entire FreeHand document including pages ㉔. *(For more information on the Document inspector, see Chapter 4, "Working with Pages.")*

Library

The Library (**Window > Library**) stores the graphic symbols that are used to help automate working with FreeHand ㉕. These symbols are also used when working with brushes and when exporting as Flash (SWF) animations. *(For more information on the Library, see Chapter 21, "Styles.")*

TIP Technically, the Library looks like—and can be used like—a panel. But it is such an important onscreen element that it is found under its own listing: **Window > Library**. So it is named simply as Library, not Library panel or Library inspector.

Main toolbar

The Main toolbar (**Window > Toolbars > Main**) contains icons that let you apply the most commonly used commands in FreeHand such as Save, Copy, Paste, Undo, and so on ㉖. *(For information on the basic commands, see Chapter 2, "Document Basics.")*

TIP You can customize the toolbars so they contain your own set of commands. *(For information on customizing the toolbars, see Chapter 32, "Customizing FreeHand.")*

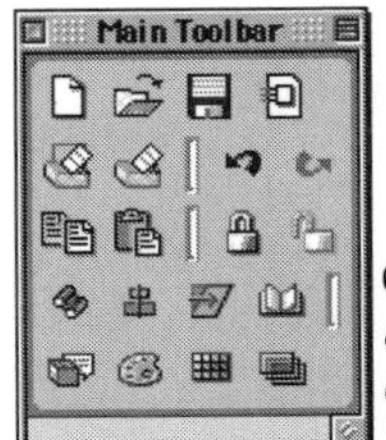

㉖ *The* **Main toolbar** *contains icons for commands such as New, Open, and Save.*

Text toolbar

The Text toolbar (**Window > Toolbars > Text**) contains some of the most commonly used attributes for working with text ㉗. This makes the Text toolbar a quick alternative to using the five different modes of the Text inspector. *(For information on styling text, see Chapter 18, "Basic Text.")*

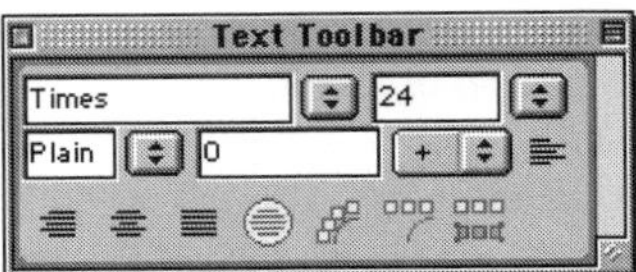

㉗ *The* **Text toolbar** *lets you apply text attributes such as font, point size, and alignment.*

Xtra Tools toolbar

The Xtra Tools toolbar (**Window > Toolbars > Xtra Tools**) contains specialized tools ㉘. These tools may not appear in the Tools panel *(covered on page 19)*. The Xtra tools include the Arc, Smudge, and Graphic Hose tools. *(For information on the Xtra tools, see Chapter 24, "Xtra Tools.")*

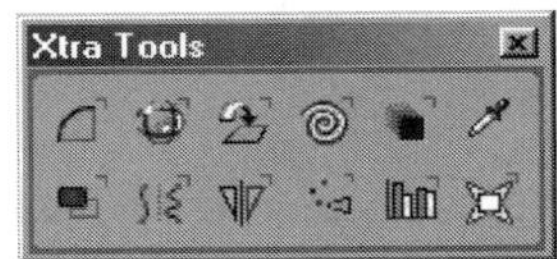

㉘ *The* **Xtra Tools toolbar** *contains added tools that are not in the Tools panel.*

Xtra Operations toolbar

The Xtra Operations toolbar (**Window > Toolbars > Xtra Operations**) contains icons that let you apply Xtra Operations such as Emboss ㉙. *(For information on the Xtra operations, see Chapter 9, "Path Operations.")*

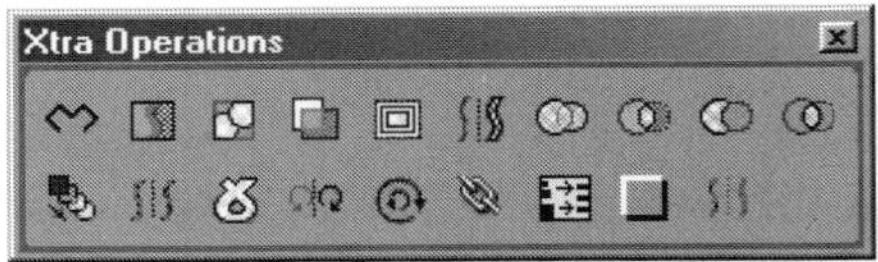

㉙ *The* **Xtra Operations toolbar** *contains commands for working with objects.*

Controller toolbar

The Controller toolbar (**Window > Toolbars > Controller**)is used to work with the preview of Flash (SWF) movies ㉚. *(For information on creating Flash (SWF) movies, see Chapter 29, "Flash Animations.")*

㉚ *The* **Controller toolbar** *is used when previewing Flash (SWF) movies.*

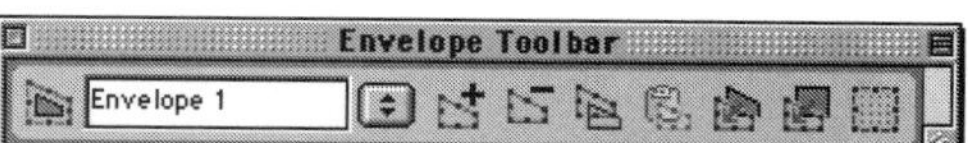

(31) The **Envelope toolbar** *contains the controls for distorting objects within specific shapes.*

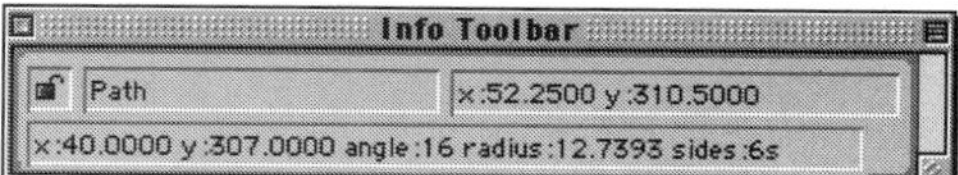

(32) The **Info toolbar** *displays information about the objects as they are drawn.*

(33) *The Windows* **Status toolbar** *controls the views and units of your document.*

Customize your FreeHand Experience

When you first install FreeHand you will notice the toolbars, panels, and inspectors are all arranged in certain orders. These are the default settings.

If you want to restore the onscreen elements to their default settings, you can trash the Preferences file which is located in Macromedia FreeHand: English: Settings.

However, if you have made any customization settings to the toolbars, you will need to reinstall a fresh copy of the toolbars file which is located in Macromedia FreeHand: English: Settings: Toolbars.

A backup copy of these settings is on the FreeHand application CD.

Envelope toolbar

The Envelope toolbar (**Window > Toolbars > Envelope**) lets you assign the features of FreeHand's envelopes to distort text (31). *(For information on the envelope commands, see Chapter11, "Envelopes and Perspectives.")*

Info toolbar

The Info toolbar (**Window > Toolbars > Info**) shows the size, position, and other attributes of objects as they are created and manipulated (32). *(For information on using the Info toolbar, see Chapter 10, "Move and Transform.")*

Status toolbar (Win)

The Status toolbar (**Window > Toolbars > Status**) controls various attributes of the document such as the preview mode and magnification (33). The Status toolbar is only available in Windows. On the Macintosh it is permanently fixed to the bottom of the document window. *(For details on the using the parts of the Status toolbar, see Chapter 3, "Display Options.")*

TIP Although it is not labeled as a toolbar, the Tools panel *(covered on page 19)* can also be modified like the toolbars.

Working with Onscreen Elements

When you first install FreeHand, some of the panels and inspectors are grouped into the arrangements that the Macromedia engineers thought you would like to work with. You can change these groups as well as resize the panels into whatever arrangements suit you.

TIP Only those panels and inspectors that have tabs can be grouped together. The other panels and toolbars cannot be grouped.

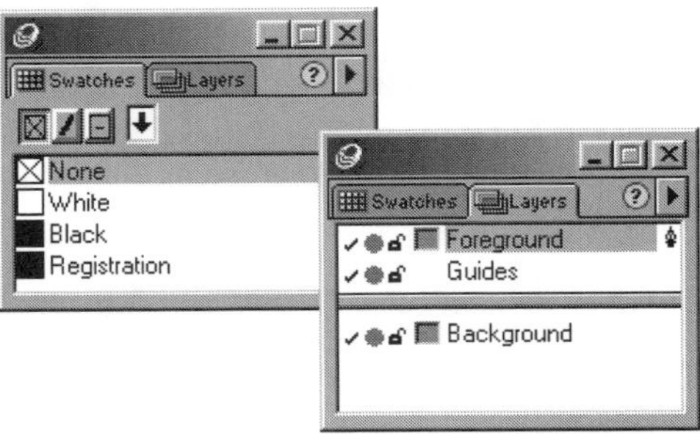

34 *Click the tab of one panel to switch to a second panel in the group. Here the Layers panel moves in front of the Swatches panel.*

To change the active panel in a group:

- Click the tab for a panel. That panel will become the active panel and will be displayed in front of the other panels in the group 34.

To combine panels into a group:

1. Drag a panel by its tab onto the area of another panel.
2. Release the mouse to allow the panel to join the group 35.

To release a panel from a group:

1. Drag a panel by its tab outside the area of the panel.
2. When the panel is outside the area of the group, release the mouse 36. The panel is separated from the group.

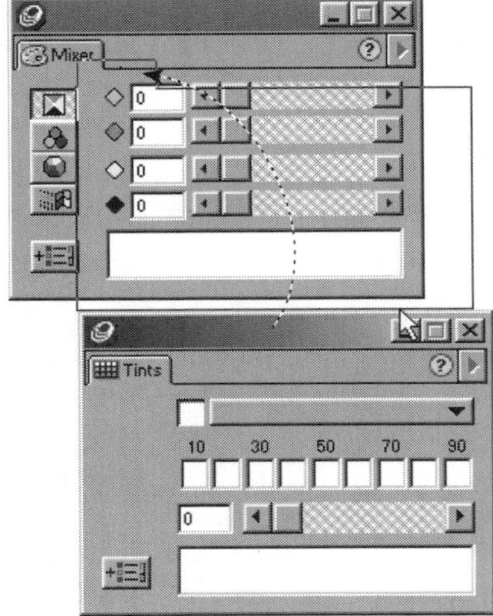

35 **Drag the panel tab into a panel** *to add it to the panel group.*

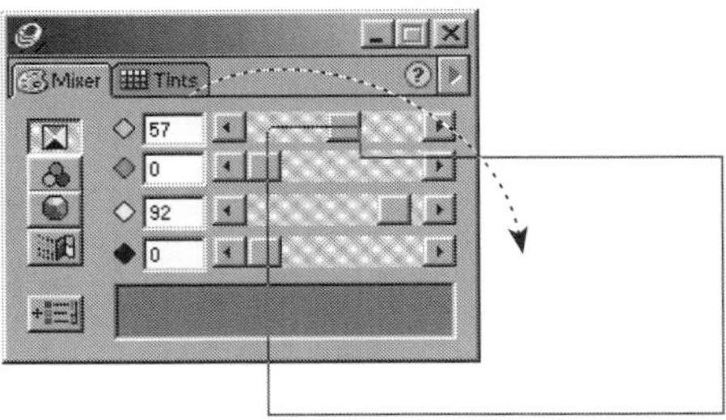

36 **Drag the panel tab out of a panel** *to detatch it from a group.*

Working with Onscreen Elements

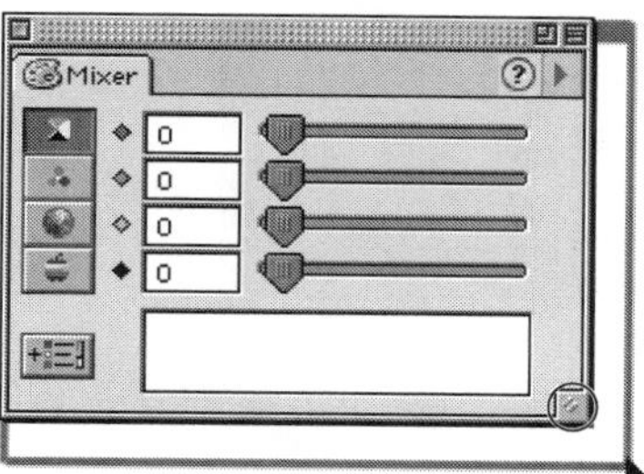

37 **Drag the resize control** (Mac) *to change the size of a panel.*

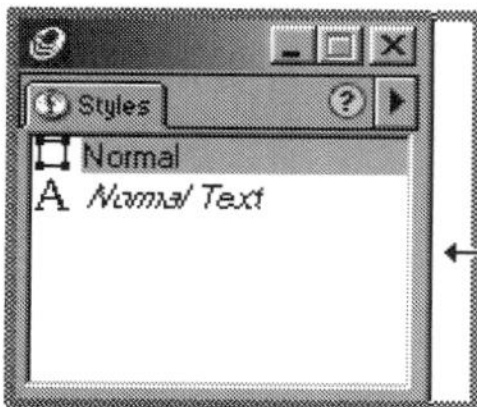

38 **Drag the double-headed arrow** (Win) *on any side or corner to change the size of a panel.*

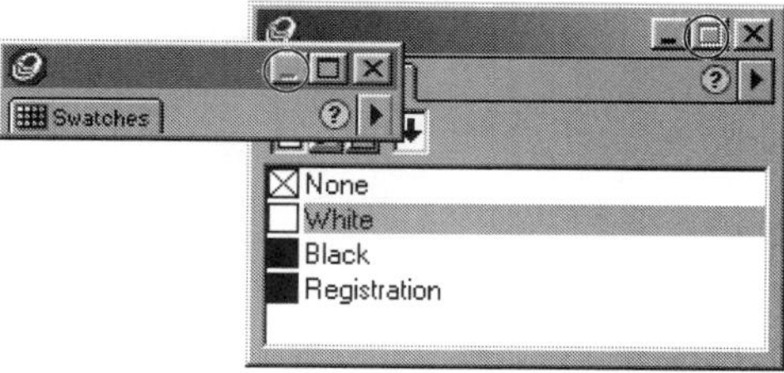

39 *(Win) Click the* **minimize icon** *(left) to collapse a panel. Click the* **maximize icon** *(right) to expand a panel.*

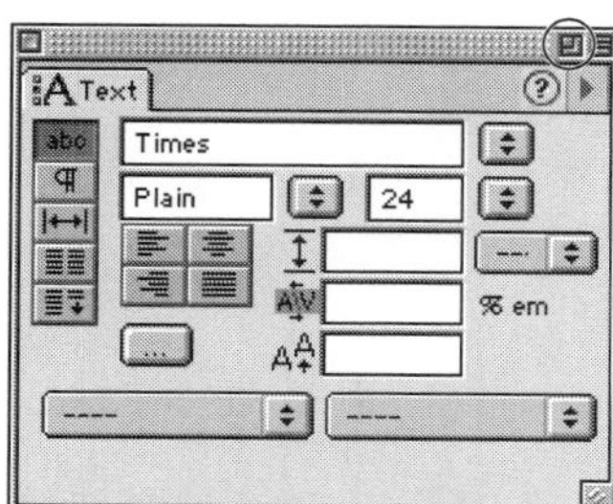

40 *(Mac) Click the* **minimize control** *(circled) to expand and contract a panel.*

You can also change the size of some of the panels, inspectors, and toolbars. This is helpful for panels such as the Layers and Swatches panels that may contain many items.

To resize onscreen elements (Mac):

- Drag the resize control in the lower right-hand corner of the panel or inspector **37**.

To resize panels (Win):

1. Move the cursor over the sides or corners of the panel. A double-headed arrow appears.
2. Drag the double-headed arrow to change the size of the panel **38**.

To minimize and maximize panels (Win):

- Click the minimize icon of a panel to display only the title bar of the panel **39**.

  or

  Click the maximize icon of a minimized panel to expand it to its full size.

To minimize and maximize panels (Mac):

- Click the minimize icon of a panel to display only the title bar of the panel **40**.

  or

  Click the minimize icon of a minimized panel to expand it to its full size.

FreeHand has another way to group panels together called *docking*. Docking lets you group panels and inspectors so that they act as a unit. Even the non-tabbed panels that can't be grouped can still be docked to other panels.

TIP You can dock panels from top to bottom or side to side. (When many panels are docked together they are called barges!)

TIP Once panels are docked, they are minimized and maximized as a single unit. This makes it easy to quickly open and close panels.

To dock panels:

1. Hold the Control (Mac) or Ctrl (Win) key as you drag the panel by its title bar next to the panel you want to dock it to.
2. Release the mouse button. A filled area between the panels indicates that the panels are docked to each other **41**.

To release docked panels:

- Click the filled area between the docked panels.

  or

  Hold the Control (Mac) or Ctrl (Win) key and drag the panel away from the other.

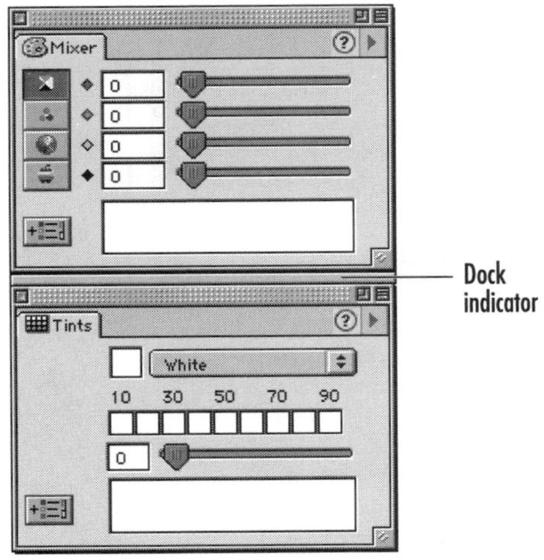

41 **Docked panels** *move and act as a unit.*

> **Adding Screen Real Estate**
>
> I like to spread out all my panels into individual elements. Unfortunately that takes up a lot of room on my monitor.
>
> Fortunately, I found it very easy to add a second monitor to my system. So all my panels and inspectors are on one screen and my artwork is on my main screen.
>
> I already had an old monitor in my office, but it's not too expensive to buy a second monitor.
>
> Of course if you've got three thousand dollars lying around, you can always buy one of those incredible Apple Cinema Displays.

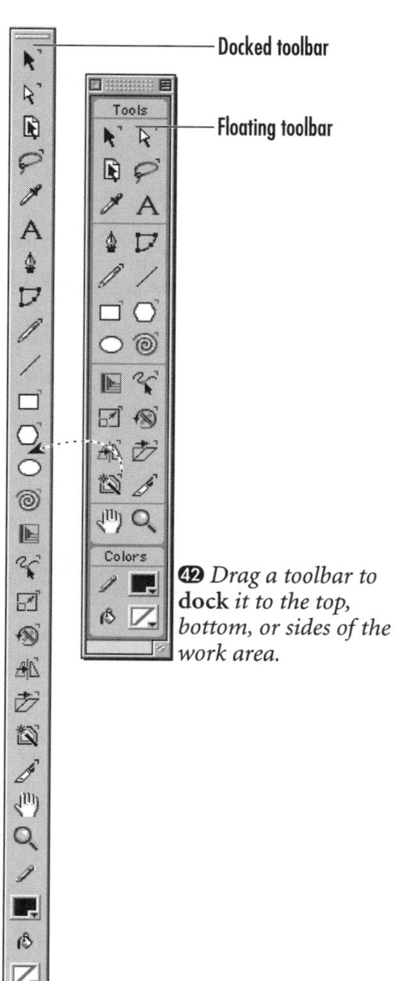

42 *Drag a toolbar to* **dock** *it to the top, bottom, or sides of the work area.*

Unfortunately, toolbars cannot be docked or grouped with either panels or inspectors. However, there is a special type of docking that allows you to fix toolbars so that they stick to the top, bottom, or sides of your work area.

TIP Even though it is called a panel, the Tools panel can also be docked like the toolbars.

To dock a toolbar to the work areas:

1. Drag the toolbar towards the edge of the work area.
2. When you see the outline of the toolbar, release the mouse. The toolbar appears inside a gray area that is part of the work area 42.

To released a docked toolbar:

1. Drag the toolbar out from the gray docking area.
2. When you see the outline of the toolbar, release the mouse button. The docked toolbar will be converting into a floating toolbar.

TIP You can also customize toolbars so they display the exact commands and tools that you want. For instance, you can move the tools from the Xtra Tools toolbar over to the Tools panel. *(See Chapter 32, "Customizing FreeHand," for more information on customizing toolbars.)*

Using the Interface Elements

As you work with FreeHand there are many different interface elements that you click, drag, and otherwise manipulate. Although you most likely know how these work from other applications, FreeHand does have a few unique elements.

Tabbed panels

- Tabbed panels allow you to choose between different features. Click the tabbed panel to make those features active 43.

Fields

- Fields allow you to enter specific information that might not appear in a menu. Click to insert the cursor into the field and then being typing 44.

TIP Use the Tab key to jump from one field to another. Type Shift-Tab to move backward from one field to another.

Buttons

- Buttons allow you to apply settings or commands. Click to apply the command indicated on the button 45.

Icons

- Icons are graphic symbols applied to buttons. Many icons change their display depending if they are on or off. Click to choose the icon 46.

Checkboxes

- Checkboxes are options that when chosen display a small check next to their description. Click to turn the checkbox command on or off 47.

43 *Click to choose a* **tabbed panel.**

44 *Click inside to enter text into a* **field.**

45 *Click to activate a* **button.**

46 *Click to choose an* **icon.**

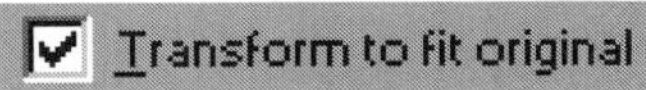

47 *Click inside a* **checkbox** *to turn it on or off.*

First selected paragraph
Shared attributes

(48) *Click to turn a* **radio button** *on or off.*

(49) *Type the* **underlined letter** *to apply the keyboard prompt.*

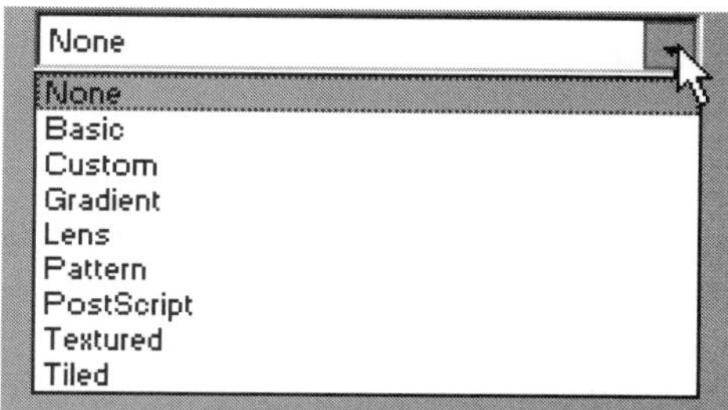

(50) *Click to open a* **pop-up menu**.

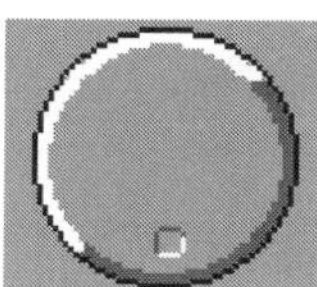

(51) *Drag to rotate a* **wheel** *to change its values.*

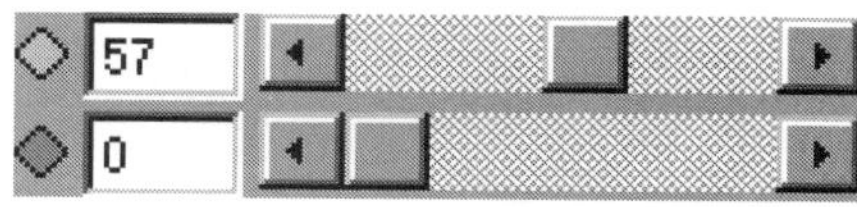

(52) *Drag the square box to change the values controlled by a* **slider**.

Radio Buttons

- Radio buttons are similar to checkboxes. However, when one radio button is on, the other option is automatically turned off. Click to turn the radio button on or off (48).

Keyboard Prompts (Win)

- An underlined letter in an element or a dialog box means you can press that letter on your keyboard to go to that command (49).

Pop-up Menus

- Pop-up menus can pop up or down depending on their position on the screen. Click to open the menu (50). Once the menu is open, you can move the mouse to choose a specific entry.

Wheels

- Wheels are dragged around to change a value (51). Most wheels are used to set amounts such as rotation angles.

Sliders

- Sliders are dragged to set a specific value (52). Most sliders also have fields that you can enter the values in directly.

Plus/Minus Signs (Win)

- Plus/minus signs are used to open and close lists in the Windows version of FreeHand ⓹③.

Twist triangles (Mac)

- Twist triangles are used to open and close lists in the Macintosh version of FreeHand ⓹④.

Panel menus

- Some panels, such as the Layers panel, also have their own menus with commands that apply to the panel. Click the small triangle on the top-right corner to open the panel menu ⓹⑤.

Sub-menus

- Sub-menus are adjuncts of the main application menus. Move the mouse over to choose the items in a sub-menu ⓹⑥.

53 *Click the* **plus/minus sign** *(Win) to open or close a list entry.*

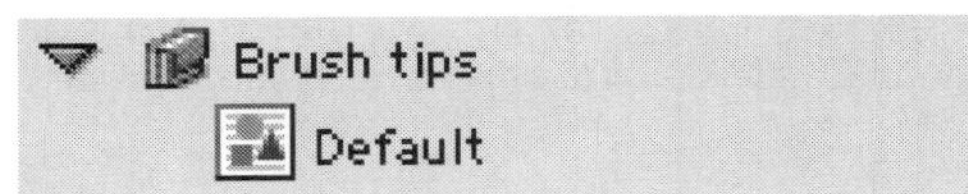

54 *Click the* **twist triangle** *(Mac) to open or close a list entry.*

55 *Click the triangle in the upper right corner of a panel to open the* **panel menu.**

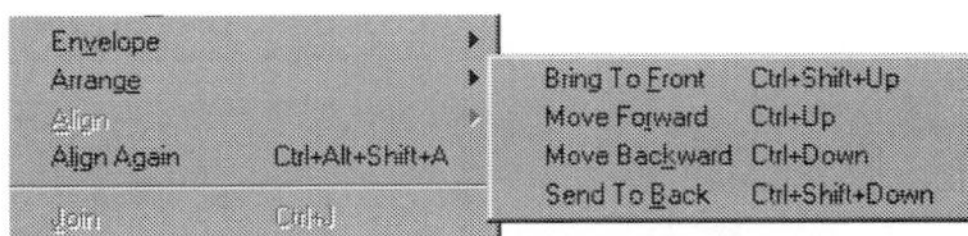

56 *Click to choose an item in a* **sub-menu.**

Using the Interface Elements

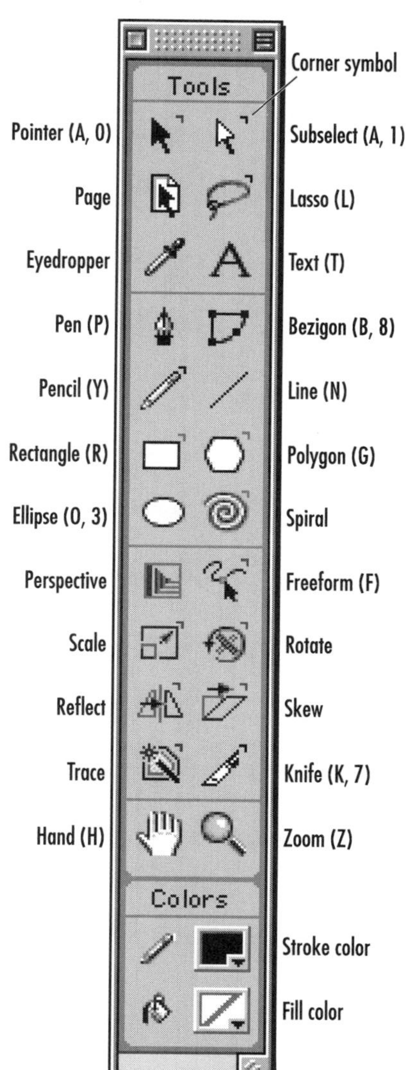

57 *The* **Tools panel** *in its default setting with the keyboard shortcuts for each tool.*

Tools Panel and Tools Shortcuts

The most vital part of FreeHand is the Tools panel (**Window > Tools**) which contains the program's 24 primary tools. The Tools panel also contains the controls for the fill and stroke colors for objects 57.

Strictly speaking the Tools panel is much more like a toolbar than a panel. It doesn't group with the other panels and it adheres to the sides of the work area like a toolbar. Perhaps since Tools toolbar sounds silly, Macromedia calls it the Tools panel.

TIP You don't have to work with the Tools panel in the arrangement that Macromedia created. You can customize the Tools panel by adding tools from the Xtras Tools and Xtras Operations toolbars. You can also delete tools from the Tools panel. *(See Chapter 32, "Customizing FreeHand.")*

To use a tool:

1. Click the tool you want to use.

   or

   Type the keyboard character of the tool.
2. Move your cursor to the page and use the tool.

TIP The corner symbol indicates that there are additional controls you can set to change how the tool works. Double-click the corner symbol to access the dialog box for the tool. If you change the setting for the Pencil and Freeform tools, you change the icons for those tools in the Tools panel.

DOCUMENT BASICS 2

When I first started teaching computer graphics, my students didn't come in to learn just Macromedia FreeHand. For many of them it was their first time using a computer. So not only did they need to learn how to create artwork, they had to grasp the concepts of opening documents, saving files, creating new versions of those files, and so on.

These days I doubt that you're sitting down to learn FreeHand without ever having used a computer before. Even if you've only used a word processing program and surfed the Internet, you'll find many of the basic commands the same from one program to the next. (That's why they call them basics.)

In fact, there are some features that are unique to FreeHand—not even other Macromedia applications have them. So don't skip this chapter completely.

Basic Menu Commands

The basic menu commands are used to start new documents, open existing documents, and save your work. You can also use a basic command to go back to the last saved version of a file. There are also commands that undo your most recent actions. Finally, the basic commands are also used to quit working with FreeHand.

To create a new document:

- Choose **File > New.**

  or

  Click the New icon in the Main toolbar. This creates a new untitled document ❶.

TIP Each new untitled document has the temporary name Untitled followed by a number.

TIP (Win) When you first launch FreeHand, you see the Wizard screen that helps you choose different actions. *(See page 26 for more information on working with the Wizard.)*

To open an existing document:

1. Choose **File > Open.**

   or

   Click the Open icon in the Main toolbar.
2. Use the operating system navigation controls to find the document you want to open.
3. Click Open. The document opens in a new window.

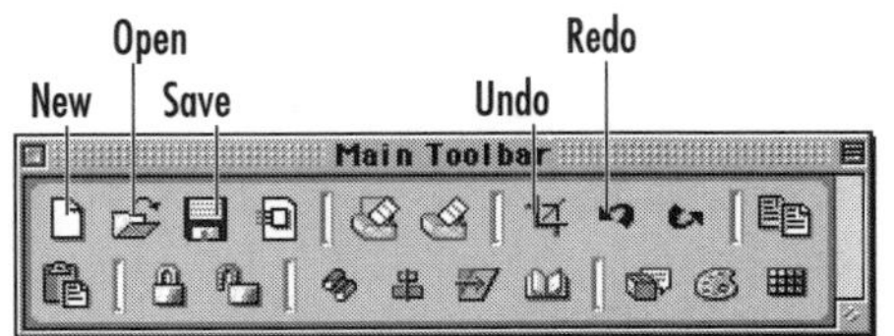

❶ *The* **Main toolbar** *contains some of the basic menu commands.*

Menus, Icons or Keyboard Commands?

FreeHand offers you different ways to activate commands. For instance, to open a new document you can choose the command from the menu bar (**File > New**), use a keyboard command (Cmd/Ctrl-N), or click the command on a toolbar.

So which is the best way to work? It depends.

If my fingers are already on my keyboard, I use a keyboard command.

If I'm working with the mouse, I usually go to the menu command.

Finally, I find it's easiest to click the icon on a toolbar when I use a stylus and pressure-sensitive tablet.

As you work, you will discover the way that's best for you.

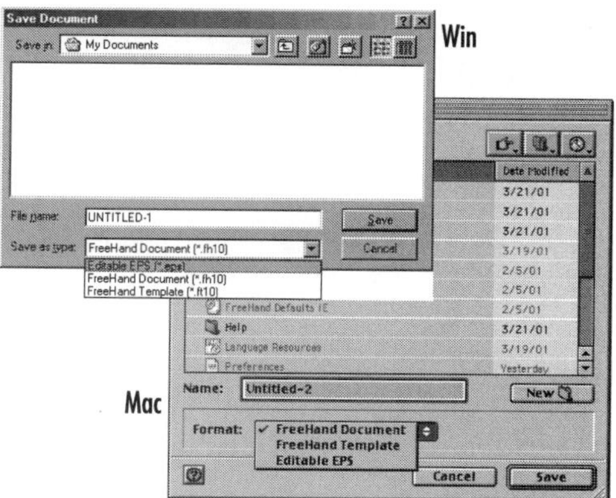

❷ *The* **Save dialog box** *lets you choose FreeHand Document, FreeHand Template, or Editable EPS.*

❸ *The difference between the icons for a document, a template, and an editable EPS.*

Save or Save As?

If you are working on an untitled document, there is no difference between the Save or Save As commands. Both open the Save dialog box where you can name the file.

However, once you have named and saved a document, there is a difference between the two commands. **File > Save** saves the changes to the file without opening the Save dialog box.

File > Save As re-opens the Save dialog box so you can save the document under a new name. The original file is left unchanged. This lets you save various versions of your file.

Once you have named a document, the Save command saves the changes without opening the Save dialog box.

As you work in a new document, the current state of your document only exists in the computer's RAM. This means that if your computer crashes you will lose that work. So, you need to save your work as a file that exists on a disk.

To save an untitled document:

1. Choose **File > Save** or **File > Save As.** The Save dialog box appears ❷.
2. From the Format (Mac) or Save as Type (Win) pop-up menu, choose the type of document:
   - **FreeHand Document** is the native file format for FreeHand files.
   - **FreeHand Template** is used to protect the file from inadvertent changes. If you save the file as a template, it will always open as an untitled file.
   - Choose **Editable EPS** if you want to place the file in a layout program such as QuarkXPress, Adobe InDesign, or Adobe PageMaker. *(For exporting files in other formats, see Chapter 27, "Exporting.")*

TIP You can tell the difference between a document, a template, and an editable EPS by their icons ❸.

3. Use the Name (Mac) or File Name (Win) field to enter a name for the document.
4. Use the operating system navigation controls to find the location where the file should be saved.
5. Click Save to save the file.

TIP To make changes to a template, open it and make the changes. Use the Save As command to save the document with the same name as the original template.

As you work, any additional changes you make to the document also need to be saved.

To save additional work:

- Choose **File > Save**. The previous version of the file is replaced by the current version.

You can also save a document under a new name. This allows you to make incremental versions of each change of the document.

To save a document under a new name:

- Choose **File > Save As**. This opens the Save dialog box. Follow the steps on page 23 to rename and save the file.

To close a document:

1. Choose **File > Close**.

   or

   Click the Close box ❹.
2. If you have not saved the document, an alert box asks if you want to save the document ❺.
   - Click Save/Yes to save your changes.
   - Click Don't Save/No to close the document in the last saved version.
   - Click Cancel to leave the document open.

As you work on a document, the Undo command makes it easy to step back through the actions you have taken.

To undo previous actions:

- Choose **Edit > Undo**.

  or

  Click the Undo icon in the Main toolbar ❶.

To redo an action you have undone:

- Choose **Edit > Redo**.

  or

  Click the Redo icon in the Main toolbar ❶.

❹ *The* **Close box** *for a Windows window (top) and a Macintosh window (bottom).*

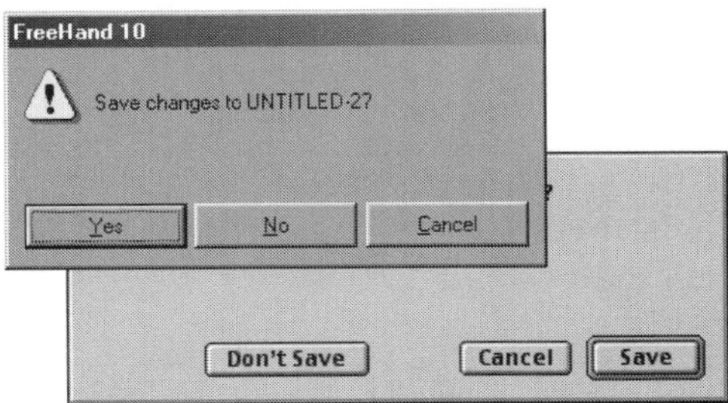

❺ *The* **Save changes alert box** *for Windows (top) and Macintosh (bottom).*

> **The Price of Undos**
>
> The number of actions you can undo is set in the General Preferences.
>
> The default setting is ten, which I think is a little low. However, don't go crazy and set a huge number. The higher the number you set, the greater the amount of RAM that is needed to run FreeHand.
>
> I like a setting of 30. If I need more than that, I can use the **File > Revert** command. *(See Appendix C for more information on setting the preferences.)*

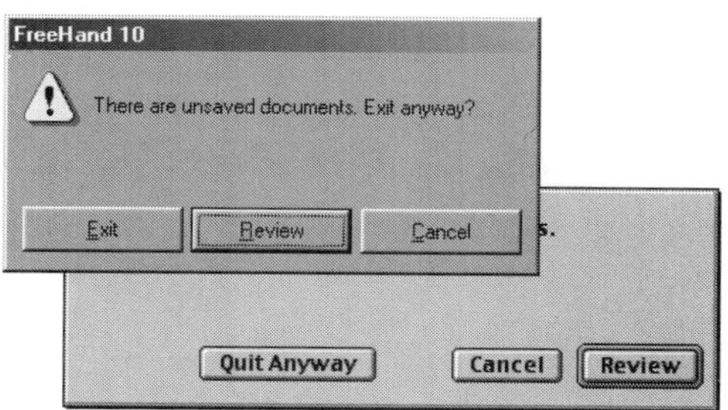

❻ *The* **Review dialog box** *prompts you to save or discard any changes you have made in your documents before quitting/exiting FreeHand.*

To revert to the last saved version:

1. Choose **File > Revert**. An alert box appears asking you to confirm your command.
2. Click the Revert button to restore your document to the last saved version.

TIP You can also revert to the last saved version by closing the document without saving any changes and then reopening it.

To quit FreeHand:

1. Choose **File > Quit** (Mac) or **File > Exit** (Win). If there are no unsaved documents, the application will close.
2. If there are unsaved documents, the Review dialog box opens ❻.
   - Click Review to see each of the open documents along with the Save Changes dialog box.
   - Click Quit Anyway (Mac) or Exit (Win) to close all documents, discarding any unsaved work.
   - Click Cancel to remain in the application.

TIP You can turn the Review feature on or off by changing the Preferences settings *(see Appendix C)*.

Using the Windows Wizards

FreeHand for Windows has Wizards that make it easy to create new documents with particular settings.

To use the Wizards:

1. Choose **Help >Wizards**. The Choose a Wizard screen appears ❼.
2. Click the icon for the Wizard you want to use.
   - **Welcome** opens the Welcome to FreeHand 10 Wizard.
   - **Setup** helps you arrange the document with a specific unit of measurement, page size, orientation, and colors.
   - **Screen-based** helps you set up a document for publication on the internet or in multimedia projects.
   - **Stationery** sets up a document for use as a letterhead, business card, and envelope.
   - **Publication** sets up a document with one or more pages.
3. Follow the instructions for the Wizard.

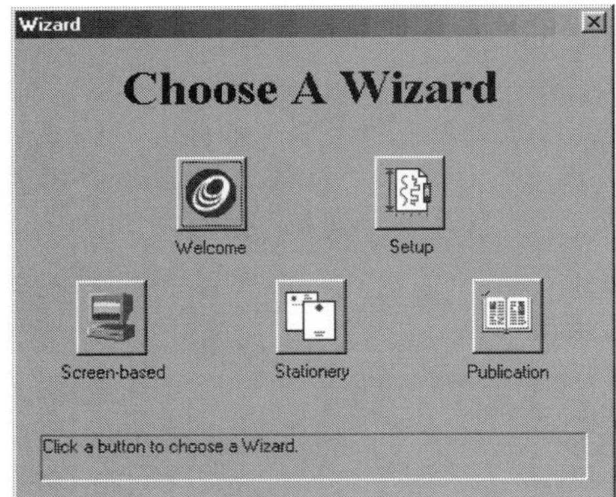

❼ *The* **Choose a Wizard screen** *takes you through the steps to create different types of documents.*

To use the Welcome to FreeHand 10 Wizard:

1. Launch FreeHand. The Welcome to FreeHand 10 Wizard appears ❽.

   or

   Click Welcome in the Choose a Wizard screen.
2. Click the icon for what you want to do.
   - **New** opens a new document.
   - **Previous File** opens the last file you worked on.
   - **Open** opens the dialog box that lets you open a previously saved document.
   - **Template** opens one of the templates that ship with FreeHand.
   - **FreeHand Help** opens the FreeHand online Help information.

TIP Deselect the checkbox if you do not want to see the Wizard again.

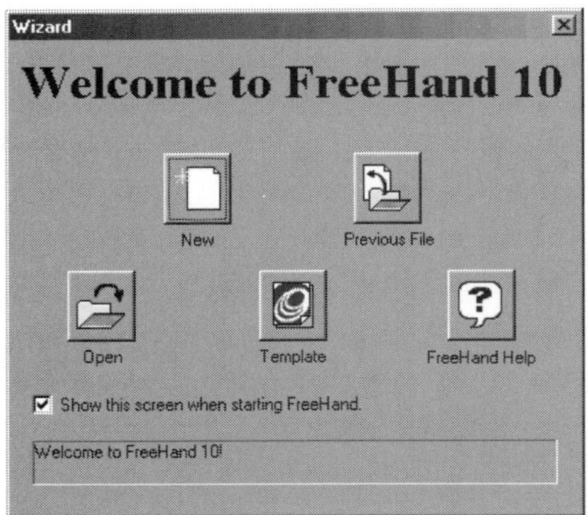

❽ *The* **Welcome to FreeHand 10 Wizard** *makes it easy to perform various commands when you first launch the program.*

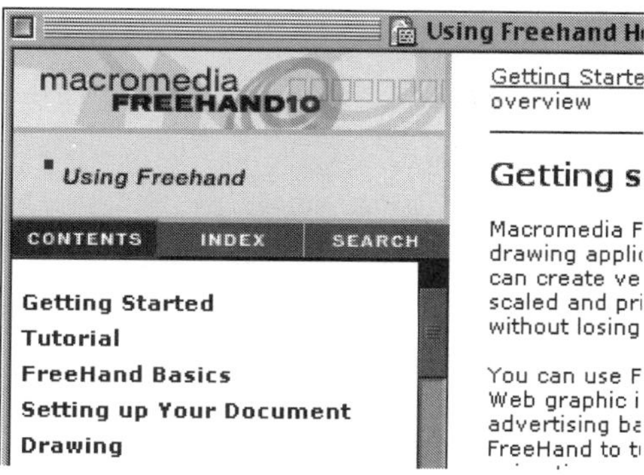

❾ *The* **Help Contents** *displays various FreeHand topics.*

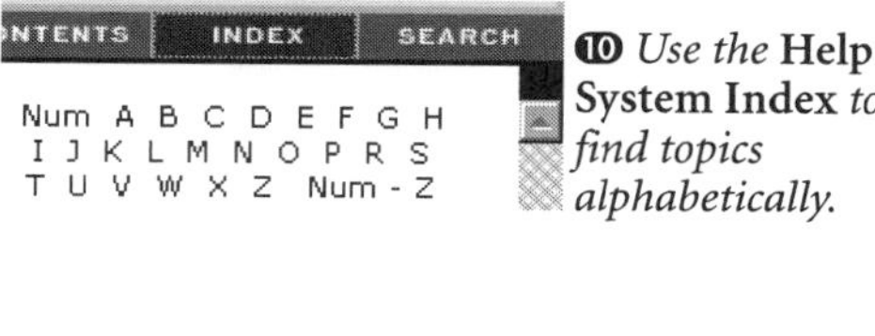

❿ *Use the* **Help System Index** *to find topics alphabetically.*

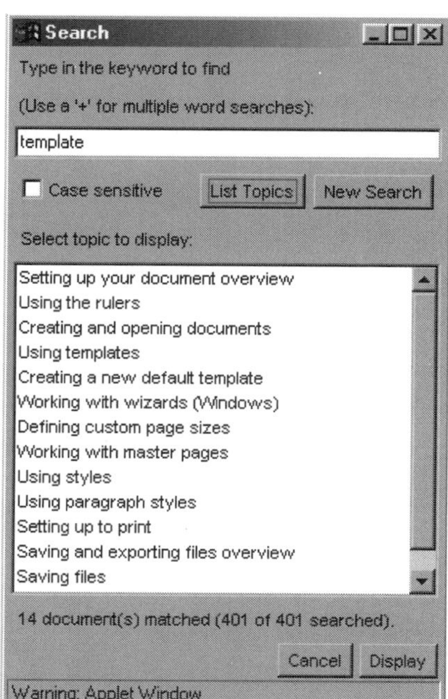

⓫ *The* **Help Search Applet** *lets you search for specific terms.*

Getting Help

As far as I'm concerned there is no reason why you should need to use the Using FreeHand electronic help files. In my dreams, this book is all you need to understand Free-Hand's features. However, the reality is that there may be times when the electronic help files can explain an esoteric feature that is beyond the scope of this book. The help files also offer electronic searches that make it easy to find specific features.

To use the Using FreeHand Help system:

1. Choose **Help > Using FreeHand**. This launches your internet browser and opens the opening screen of the Using FreeHand files.
2. Click the navigation buttons on the left side to access the help files.
   - **Contents** displays a list of topics on the left side of the screen ❾.
   - **Index** lets you choose topics alphabetically ❿.
   - **Search** opens an Applet window that lets you enter a specific search term ⓫.

To use the Search Applet:

1. Enter the search term in the keyword field.
2. Click the List Topics button. This displays all the topics with that search term.
3. Choose the topic that should contain the information you need.
4. Click the Display button. The topic you chose will be shown in the main browser window.

DISPLAY OPTIONS 3

Billions of years ago, people used to create artwork on stiff boards called *mechanicals*. If they wanted to see tiny details, they moved their head closer to the mechanical. If they wanted to see the whole picture, they held the mechanical farther away.

Creating computer artwork is different. Although you may want to move in on your monitor, it is actually easier to use the magnification controls to zoom in or out.

However, unlike the primitive board mechanicals, Macromedia FreeHand offers many more features for how your artwork is displayed. You can create guides and grids that make it easy to align objects. You can show rulers to help you judge the size of objects. And you can control how colors and images appear on the screen.

Athough these features do not affect the final output or printing of your artwork, they are important in how quickly and efficiently you work.

Setting the Artwork View Modes

You don't have to view your files exactly as they will finally print. FreeHand offers different options for how artwork is displayed onscreen. Some options show more details of the artwork, but take longer to be displayed. Other options display faster, but show less detail.

The Preview mode shows the best representation possible of how your artwork will print ❶. However, very complicated artwork may take a long time to display in the Preview mode.

To view artwork in the Preview mode:

- Choose **View > Preview.** If Preview is checked, you are already in the Preview mode.

  or

  Choose Preview from the menu at the bottom of the document window ❷. The menu shows the mode you are currently working in.

In the Fast Preview mode, you see basic colors but blends and gradients are shown with less detail ❸. This makes the screen redraw faster than the Preview mode.

To view artwork in the Fast Preview mode:

- Choose **View > Fast Mode.** If you are in the Preview mode you switch to the Fast Preview mode.

  or

  Choose Fast Preview from the pop-up menu at the bottom of the document window.

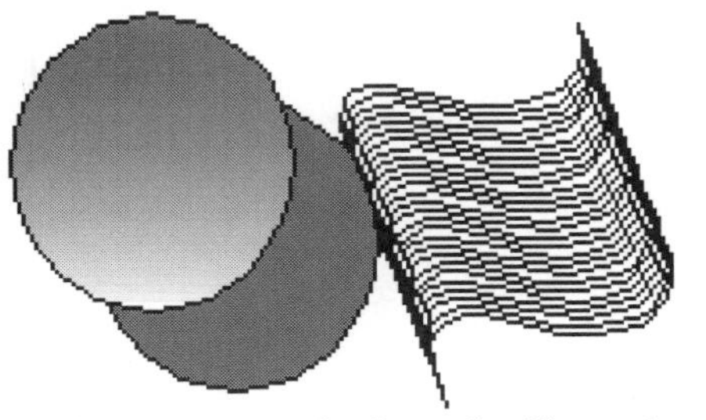

❶ *The* **Preview mode** *shows the fills, strokes, and other elements that will print.*

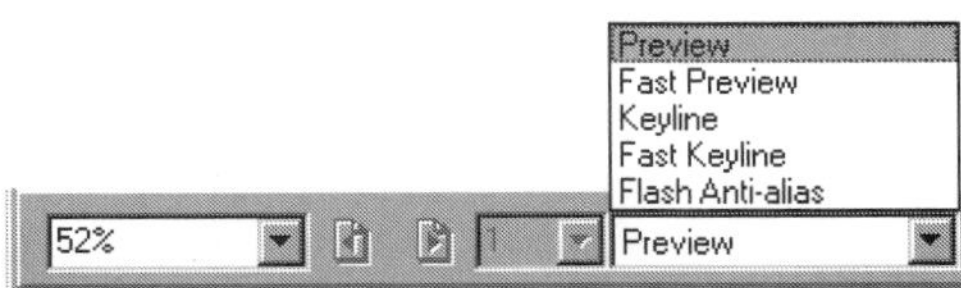

❷ *The* **View mode menu** *switches between the view modes.*

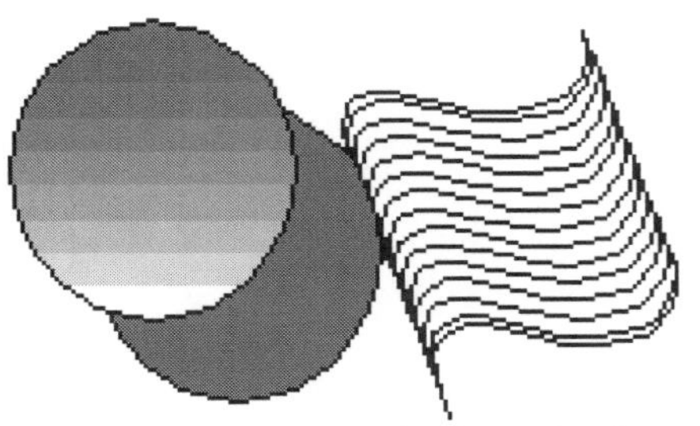

❸ *The* **Fast Preview mode** *shows the elements without smooth blends and gradients.*

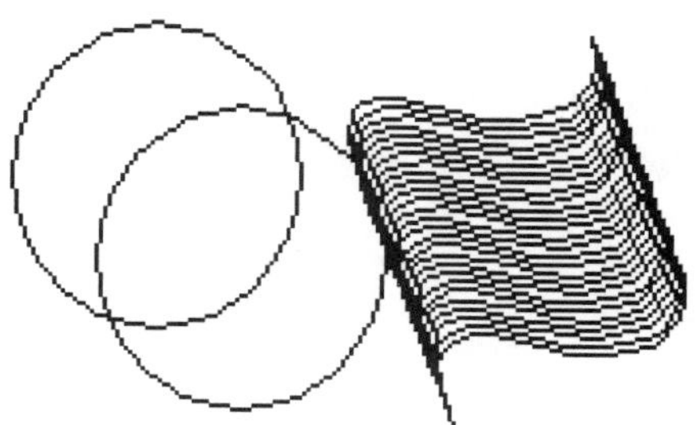

❹ *The* **Keyline mode** *shows only the outlines that define the shape of objects.*

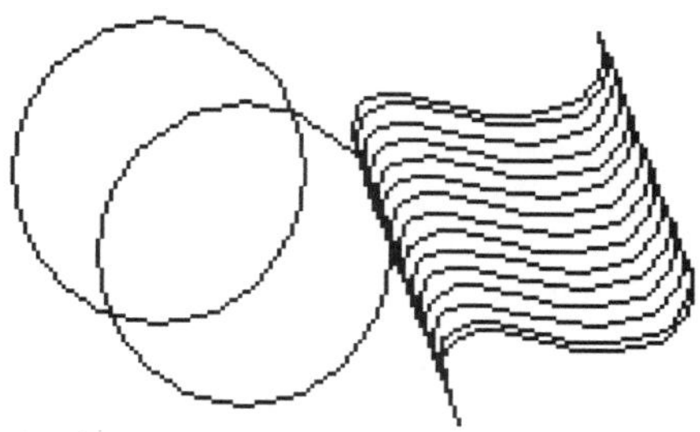

❺ *The* **Fast Keyline mode** *shows fewer steps between blends.*

In Keyline mode, you see only the outlines that define the shapes of paths ❹. The keyline mode makes it easier to select objects and speeds up the screen redraw.

To view artwork in the Keyline mode:

◆ If there is a checkmark next to the Preview command, choose **View > Preview**. This changes the setting from the Preview to the Keyline mode.

TIP If there is no checkmark, you are already in the Keyline mode and choosing the command switches to the Preview mode.

or

Choose Keyline from the pop-up menu at the bottom of the document window.

In the Fast Keyline mode, you see fewer steps between blends ❺.

To view artwork in the Fast Keyline mode:

◆ Choose **View > Fast Mode.** If you are in the Keyline mode you switch to the Fast Keyline mode.

or

Choose Fast Keyline from the pop-up menu at the bottom of the document window.

The Flash Anti-alias mode shows you how artwork will look when exported to Macromedia Flash or as SWF movies. For most artwork this adds a slight blur to the edges of objects ❻.

TIP Because the artwork looks smoother onscreen, you may be tempted to work in the Flash Anti-alias mode even if you are not going to export your artwork to Flash. Be careful—you may find your artwork looks different when you print it than it did in the Flash Anti-alias mode.

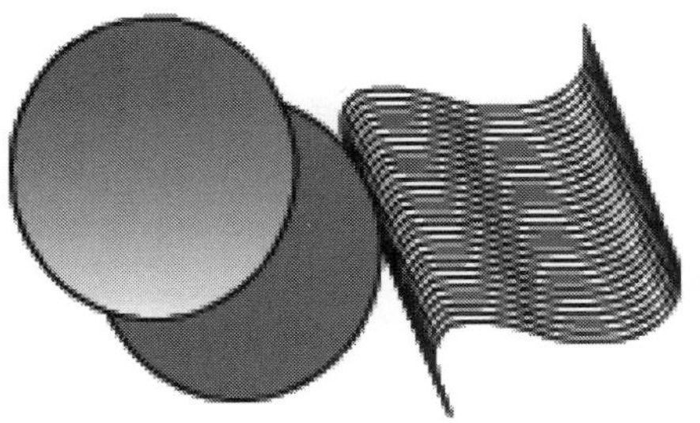

❻ *The* **Flash Anti-alias mode** *smooths the edges of the objects.*

To view artwork in Flash anti-alias mode:

- Choose **View > Flash Anti-alias.**

  or

  Choose Flash Anti-alias from the pop-up menu at the bottom of the document window.

TIP The Flash Anti-alias mode changes the onscreen display of the artwork. It does not change how the file prints.

Screen Redraw Obsession

Why so many different settings for displaying objects? Well, part of the reason has to do with the the speed of the screen redraw.

When you move around the screen to see new parts of your artwork, FreeHand has to redraw what is on the screen.

If you have many objects or complicated gradients and blends, that redraw can take time.

If you're just starting out creating simple graphics, you most likely will not need to use the Fast Mode to improve screen redraw.

However, as your artwork becomes more sophisticated, you may want to take advantage of the improved screen redraw.

Also, there are techniques that use hiding artwork on layers that can also help you improve your screen redraw.

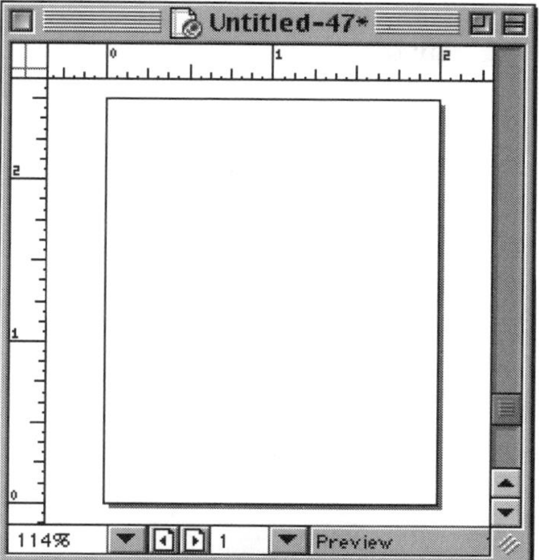

❼ *The* **page rulers** *run along the left and top sides of the document window.*

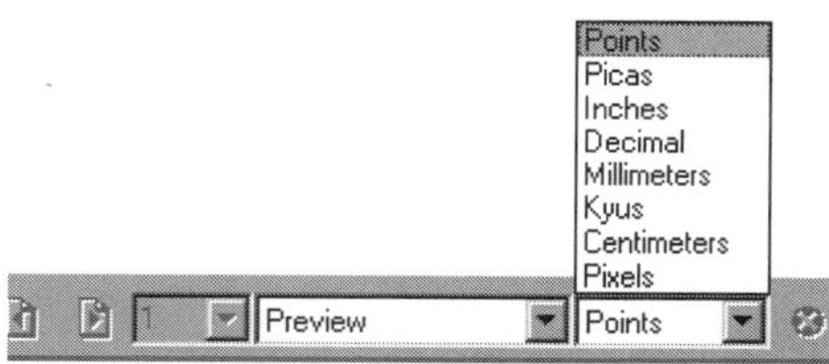

❽ *Use the* **Units of Measurement menu** *to change the measurements for the document.*

Working with Rulers

Just as in real life, you can use FreeHand's rulers to see how big things are. FreeHand has two rulers that extend along the top and left sides of your document window ❼.

To see the page rulers:

◆ To make the rulers visible, choose **View > Page Rulers > Show.** If Page Rulers is checked the rulers are visible. If you choose Page Rulers when it is checked, you turn off the rulers.

FreeHand's electronic rulers are much more flexible than the ones in real life. You can easily change the unit of measurement in FreeHand's electronic rulers. Changing the units of measurement also changes the units in dialog boxes and panels.

To change the unit of measurement:

◆ Choose one of the eight units of measurement from the menu at the bottom of the document window ❽.

TIP Although your document may be in one unit of measurement, you can still enter sizes in other units and FreeHand will convert them into the chosen units.

- For picas, type **p** after the number.
- For inches, type **i** after the number.
- For millimeters, type **m** after the number.
- For kyus, type **k** after the number.
- For centimeters, type **c** after the number.
- For pixels, type **x** after the number.
- Type **p** before the number for points.

or

- Type **pt** after the number for points.

The zero point of the rulers is usually located at the lower-left corner of the page. However, you can change that position to help measure objects on your page.

To change the zero-point position:

◆ Drag the zero point crosshairs out from the top-left corner of the rulers ❾.

TIP Double-click the zero point crosshairs in the rulers to reset the zero point to the lower-left corner of the page.

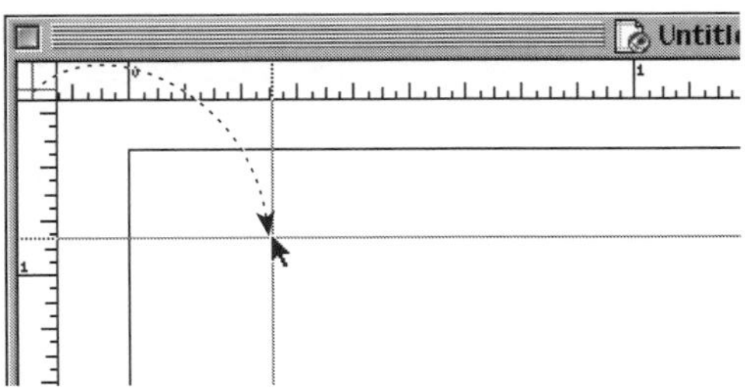

❾ *Drag the* **zero point crosshairs** *to change the position of the zero point on the rulers.*

In addition to the basic units of measurement, you can create custom units. For instance, you can create a custom unit where one inch equals six feet. This is helpful if you create large-scale artwork such as blueprints.

To define custom ruler units:

1. Choose **View > Page Rulers > Edit**. This opens the Edit Units dialog box ❿.
2. Enter a descriptive name for the custom unit in the Unit field.
3. Use the first pop-up menu to choose one of FreeHand's basic units of measurement.
4. Enter a number in the field for how many of these units will be used.
5. Use the second pop-up menu to choose what the amount should equal. In addition to the basic units you can choose feet, yards, miles, nautical miles, meters, kilometers, ciceros, and didots.
6. Enter a number in the field for how many of these units will be used.
7. Click Accept to accept this custom unit.
8. Select Add as unit of measurement to add this custom unit to the pop-up menu at the bottom of the document window ⓫.
9. Click the Close button to close the Edit Units dialog box.

TIP Click the plus or minus buttons to add or delete the custom units.

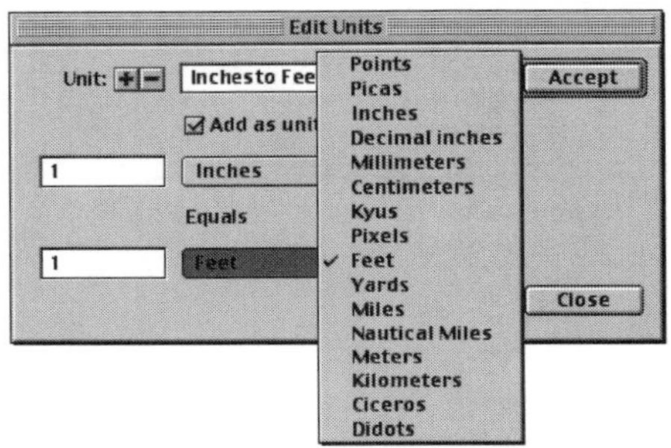

❿ *Use the* **Edit Units** *dialog box to create your own custom units of measurement.*

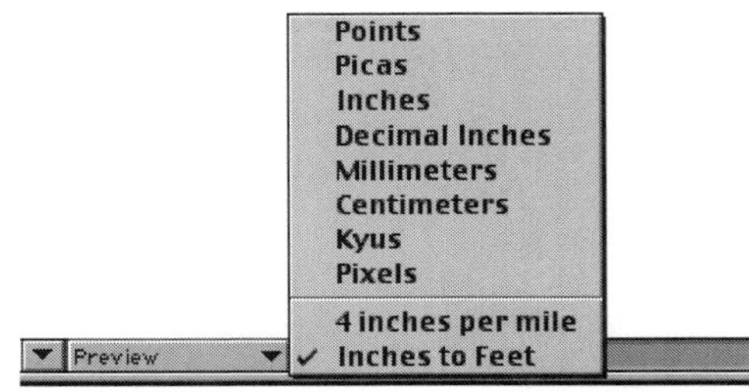

⓫ **Custom units** *appear in the units of measurement pop-up menu.*

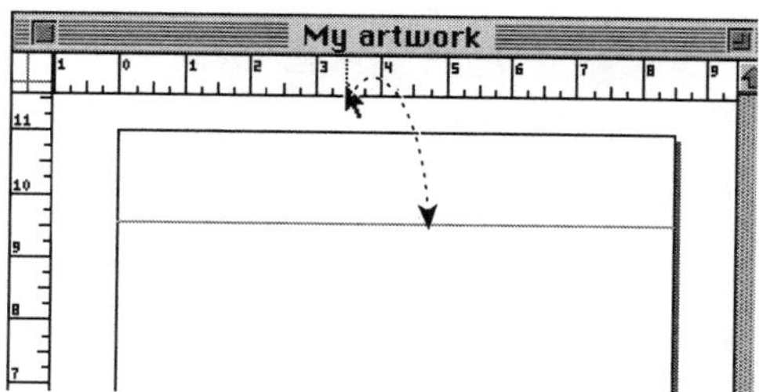

⓬ *To create a* **horizontal guide,** *place your pointer on the top ruler and drag down into the page area.*

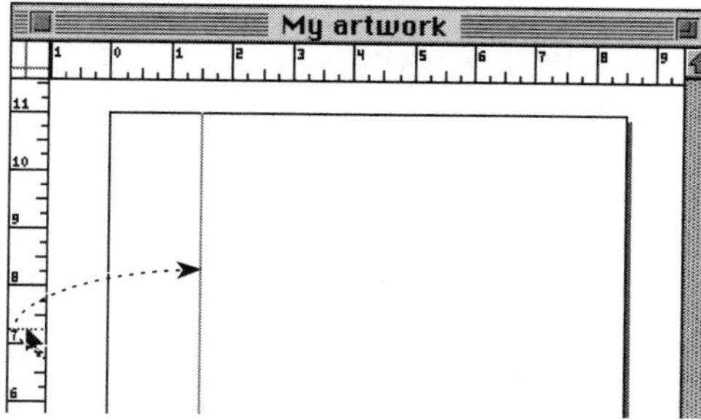

⓭ *To make a* **vertical guide,** *place your pointer on the left ruler and drag to the right.*

Working with Guides

Once the rulers are visible, you can use them to create guides on your page. Guides can be used to divide pages into different areas as well as to help you align objects.

To create guides by dragging:

1. Choose **View > Guides > Show.** (If Show is checked, the command is selected.)
2. Move your pointer so that it touches either the top (horizontal) ruler or the left (vertical) ruler.
3. For a horizontal guide, press and drag the arrow from the top ruler down into the page ⓬.

   or

   For a vertical guide, press and drag the arrow from the left ruler onto the page ⓭.

TIP Drag your arrow from the ruler onto the page, not the pasteboard.

TIP As you drag from the rulers a line appears that shows where your guide will be when you release the mouse.

4. Release the mouse to set the guide.

TIP To turn a path into a guide, you need to place the path on the Guides layer *(see page 156)*.

To move a guide to a new position:

- Use the Pointer or Subselect tool to drag the guide into the new position.

To delete a single guide:

- Use the Pointer or Subselect tool to drag the guide off the page onto the pasteboard.

If you want to work with many guides at once, you should use the Guides dialog box.

To add guides at numerical positions:

1. Double-click any guide or choose **View > Guides > Edit**. The Guides dialog box appears ⓮.
2. Click Add to open the Add Guides dialog box ⓯.
3. Choose Horizontal or Vertical.
4. To set a specific number of equally spaced guides, click Count and enter the number.
5. To set a specific distance between guides, click Increment and enter the spacing.
6. Use the First and Last fields to specify where the guides should start and end.
7. Use the Page range to set the pages on which the guides should appear.
8. Click Add to return to the Guides dialog box.
9. Click OK in the Guides dialog box. The new guides are listed in the Guides dialog box and inserted on the page.

TIP If you want the guides in front of the artwork, you need to change the order of the Guides layer *(see page 154)*.

To reposition guides using the Guides dialog box:

1. Double-click the guide or choose **View > Guides > Edit** to open the Guides dialog box.
2. Select the guide from the list.
3. Click Edit. This opens the Guide Position dialog box ⓰.
4. Enter a new location in the field and click OK to return to the Guides dialog box.
5. Click OK to close the Guides dialog box and institute the changes.

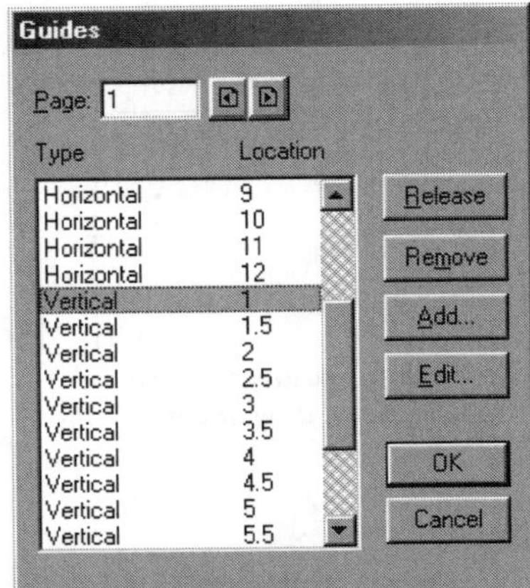

⓮ *The* **Guides dialog box** *lists all the guides on each of the pages as well as their positions.*

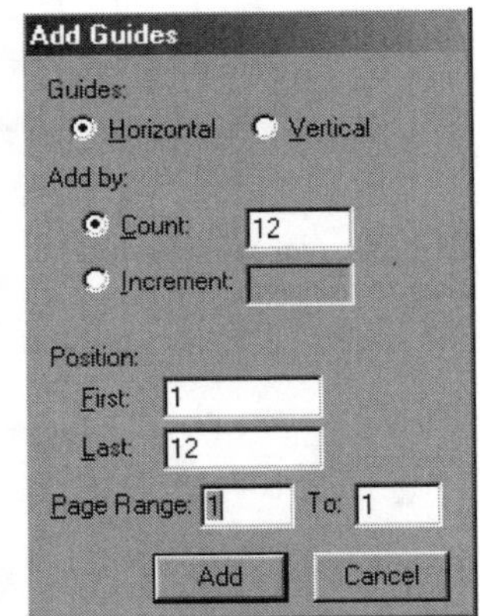

⓯ *The* **Add Guides dialog box** *allows you to create multiple guides at regular intervals.*

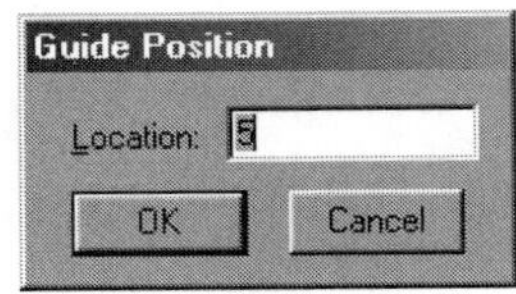

⓰ *The* **Guide Position dialog box** *allows you to relocate guides precisely.*

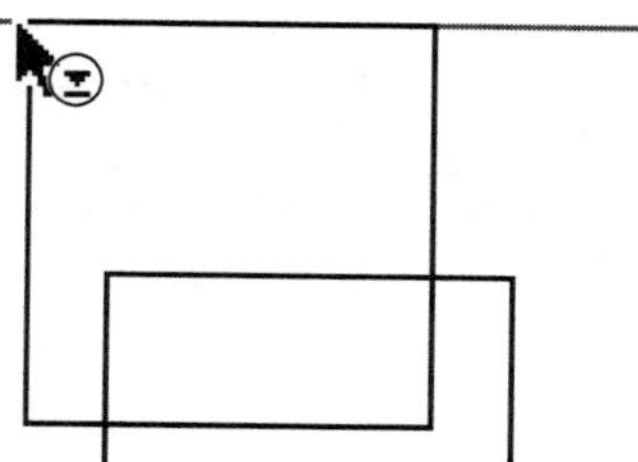

⓱ *The* **Snap To Guide cursor** *(circled) indicates that the object being moved will jump into place along a guide.*

Don't Cover Your Page With Guides

You may be tempted to cover your page with many guides. Try to avoid that. Each guide you create adds to the size of the file. You may also find it distracting to work with all those guides.

Any time you find yourself about to create many guides, think about using FreeHand's automatic grids *(see the following page)*.

Unlike guides, they don't add to the file size, and they can be automatically changed to new increments.

To delete guides using the Guides dialog box:

1. Double-click the guide or choose **View > Guides > Edit** to open the Guides dialog box.
2. Select the guide or guides from the list.
3. Click Delete/Remove.
4. When you have finished, click OK.

TIP Hold Cmd/Ctrl to select multiple non-contiguous guides or hold Shift to select contiguous guides in the Guides dialog box.

TIP Any path can be turned into a guide by selecting it and then double-clicking the Guides layer in the Layers panel. *(See Chapter 12, "Layers and Layering.")*

TIP The Release button in the Guides dialog box turns the selected guide into a regular path.

You can lock guides to prevent them from being moved.

To lock the guides:

- Choose **View > Guides > Lock.** If you choose Lock when it is checked, you unlock the guides.

TIP You can also lock guides using the Layers panel *(see page 158)*.

As you move objects, you may want them to jump so that they align with guides. This is called snapping to guides. The Snap To Guide cursor indicates that the object has jumped into alignment with a guide ⓱.

To turn on Snap To Guides:

- Choose **View > Snap To Guides.** If Snap To Guides is checked, the feature is already on.

TIP The Preferences let you control the snap to distance—how close the object has to be before it will jump to the guide *(see Appendix C)*.

Working with Grids

I grew up using guides, but then I discovered the power of FreeHand's grids. Grids are much more powerful and versatile than guides. If you change your design, grids are much easier to modify than guides. You can also use one object to be the starting point of the grid for other objects.

To view the document grid:

◆ Choose **View > Grid > Show.** If you choose Show when it is checked, you turn off the grid.

TIP Although the grid is displayed as dots ⓲, the actual grid is created from lines that intersect those dots. So the grid is active along the lines that connect the dots ⓳.

To change the document grid intervals:

1. Choose **View > Grid > Edit.** The Edit Grid dialog box appears ⓴.
2. In the Grid size field, type the distance you want between the imaginary lines of your grid.

TIP The Relative grid checkbox is described on the next page.

3. Click OK or press Return.

TIP You can change the size of the grid at any time.

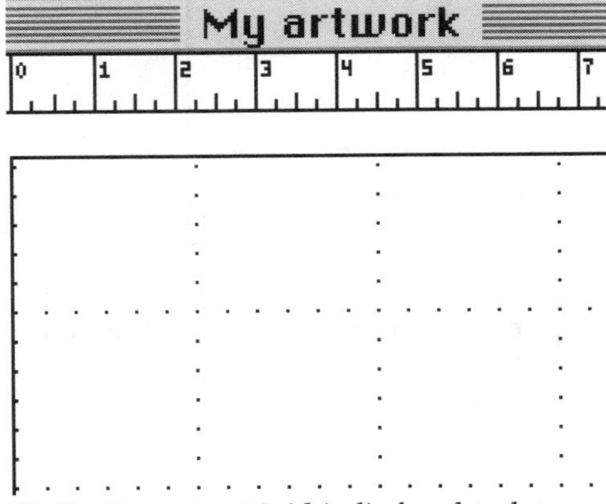

⓲ *The* **Document Grid** *is displayed as dots evenly spaced along the page.*

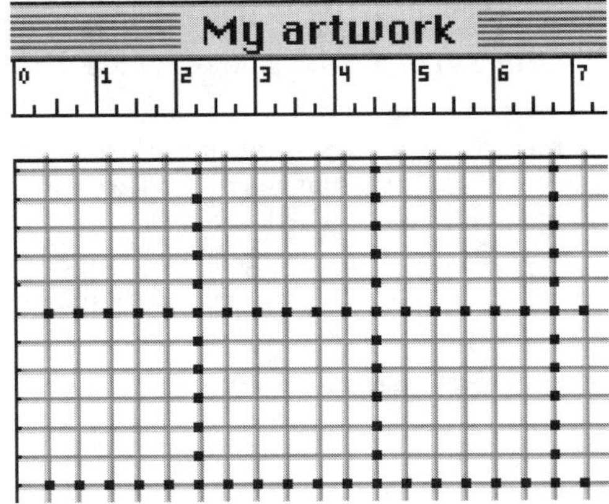

⓳ *The* **actual grid** *is a series of lines that connect the dots of the visible document grid.*

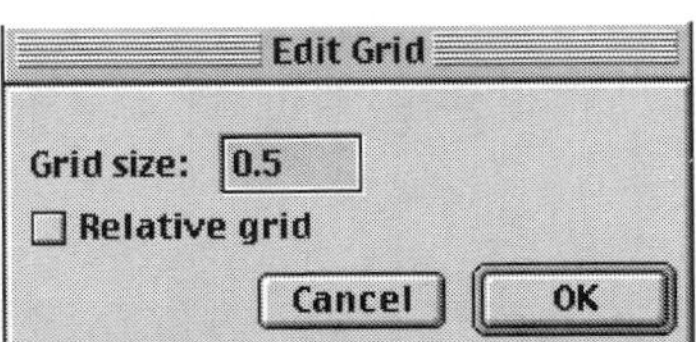

⓴ *The* **Edit Grid dialog box** *lets you change the increments of the document grid.*

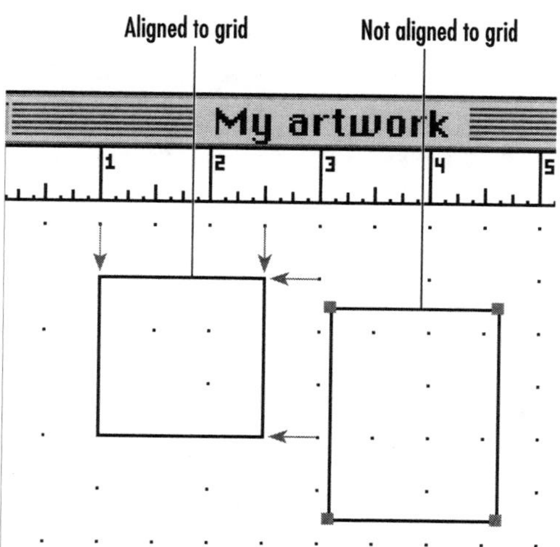

㉑ *When an object is drawn with* **Snap To Grid** *on, its sides stay on the grid. When Snap To Grid is off, the sides fall between the intervals.*

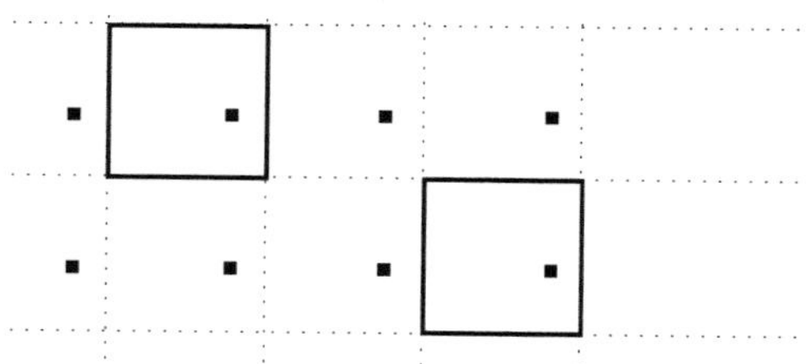

㉒ *Turning on the* **Relative grid** *means that when the object is duplicated, it stays aligned to the object's relative grid (dotted lines) rather than the document grid square dots).*

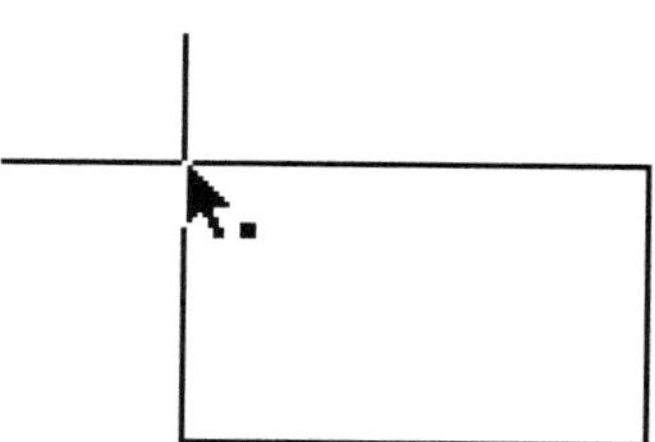

㉓ *The* **Snap to Point dot** *next to the pointer indicates that the object being moved will snap to a point on the other object.*

You can work with objects so that their edges always fall on the grid. This is called setting an object to *snap to* the grid ㉑.

To turn on Snap To Grid:

- Choose **View > Grid > Snap To Grid.** If you choose Snap To Grid when it is checked, you turn off the feature.

TIP The grid does not have to be visible for objects to snap to it.

TIP If Snap To Grid is on, you cannot draw objects between the grid intervals.

You can also work with a relative grid. Instead of the grid starting at the edge of the page, a relative grid uses the selected object as the start of the document grid. When the relative grid is turned on, if you copy one object, the copy is aligned to the original ㉒.

To work with a Relative Grid:

- Check Relative Grid in the Edit Grid dialog box *(see previous page).*

FreeHand also lets you snap to points ㉓. This lets you use the points of one object as a type of grid so you can align other objects.

To turn on Snap To Point:

- Choose **View > Snap To Point.** If Snap To Point is already checked, you turn off the feature when you select the command.

TIP Snap To Point overrides Snap to Guides, which in turn overrides Snap to Grid.

TIP FreeHand (Mac) offers sounds that play when the object snaps to a guide, the grid, or a point. The sounds are set in the Preferences *(see page 398).*

Setting the Magnification Options

When working in your document, you may find that you need to see different magnifications. There are many ways to zoom in and out of your document.

To zoom using the View menu:

- You can use one of the View menu commands to change the magnification of your document.
  - **View > Fit All** adjusts the magnification so you can see all the pages in your document ㉔.
  - Choose **View > Fit to Page** to adjust the magnification so you can see the entire page you are working on ㉕.
  - **View > Fit Selection** adjusts the magnification so that the selected item fills the window ㉖.
  - **View > Magnification** lets you choose one of the magnification settings in the submenu. These are the same as the settings in the Magnification pop-up menu *(next exercise)*.

To use the Magnification pop-up menu:

- Choose one of the preset magnification settings from the Magnification menu at the bottom of the document window ㉗.

To enter exact magnification amounts:

1. Double-click or drag across the number in the Magnification menu ㉘.
2. Type in the percentage at which you would like to view your page. (You do not need to type the % character.)
3. Press the Return/Enter key.

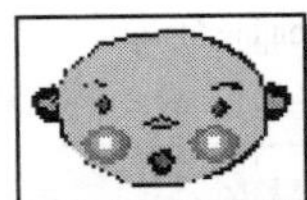

㉔ *The* **Fit All command** *changes the magnification so you can see all the pages in the document.*

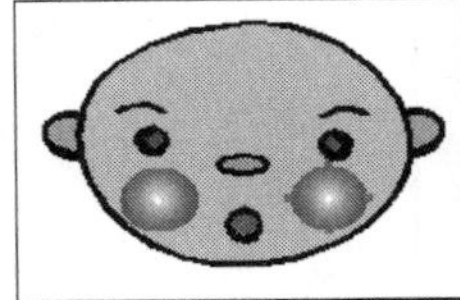

㉕ *The* **Fit To Page command** *changes the magnification so you can see all the items on the current page.*

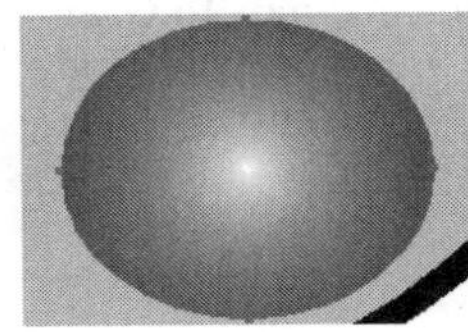

㉖ *The* **Fit Selection command** *changes the magnification to zoom in on the selected item.*

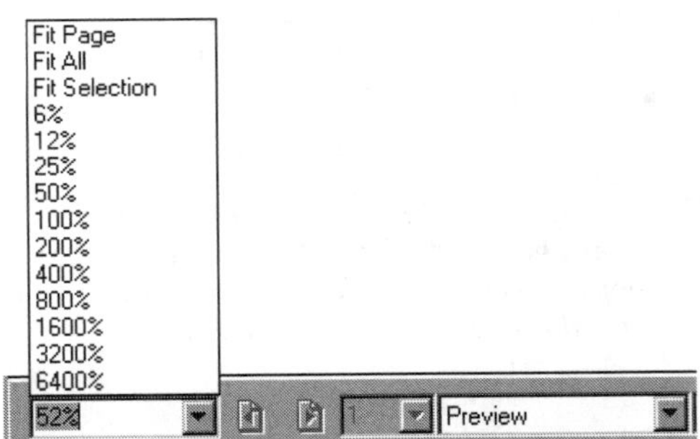

㉗ *The* **Magnification menu** *lets you choose one of the preset magnifications.*

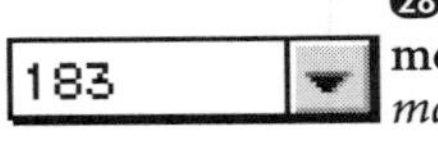

㉘ *Use the* **Magnification menu field** *to enter an exact magnification.*

㉙ *The* **Zoom tool** *in the Tools panel.*

㉚ *Use the Zoom tool to increase the magnification of a specific object by* **dragging a marquee** *around that object. The dashed-line marquee shows the area being selected.*

㉛ *Hold the* **Opt/Alt key** *while in the Zoom tool to zoom out from an object.*

To use the Zoom tool:

1. Click the Zoom tool in the Tools panel ㉙.
2. Click the Zoom tool on the object you want to zoom in on. Click as many times as you need to get as close as necessary to the objects you are working on.

   or

   Click and drag the Zoom tool diagonally across the area you want to zoom in on. When you release the mouse button, you zoom in on the area ㉚.

TIP Press the Cmd/Ctrl key and Spacebar to get the Zoom tool without leaving the tool that is currently selected in the Tools panel.

TIP Hold the Opt/Alt key to zoom out from objects. The icon changes from a plus sign (+) to a minus sign (-) ㉛.

Moving Around

One of the easiest ways to spot a novice computer user is to watch them use the document window scroll bars to move up and down or from side to side on the page. While they will eventually get to where they want to be, most experienced users use the Hand tool which lets you move up, down, left, right, and diagonally—all without ever touching the sides of your window.

㉜ *The* **Hand tool** *in the Tools panel.*

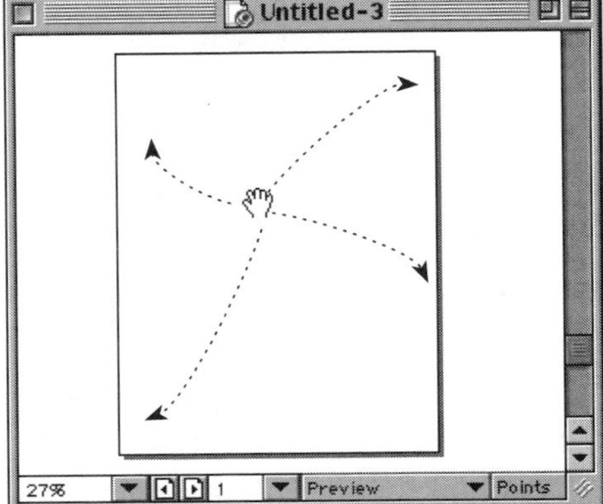

㉝ *The* **Hand tool** *lets you drag any which way you want to move around the page.*

To use the Hand tool:

1. Click the Hand tool in the Tools panel ㉜.
2. Drag the Hand tool inside the document window ㉝.

TIP Press the Spacebar to temporarily use the Hand tool without leaving the tool that is currently selected in the Tools panel.

TIP Do not press the Spacebar to access the Hand tool while you are within a text block or you will insert many spaces into your text.

Use the Zoom Tool and Hand Tool Shortcuts!

I haven't chosen the Zoom or Hand tools in the Tools panel in years. So how do I zoom in and out on my artwork? I use the Zoom and Hand tool keyboard shortcuts. And the sooner you learn them the better your FreeHand experience will be.

While you are using any tool, hold the Spacebar. This gives you the Hand tool that lets you move around the screen.

Then add the Cmd/Ctrl key to access the Zoom tool. You can now click or drag to zoom in on objects.

Now add the Opt/Alt key to zoom out from objects.

This is why the really efficient designers always have their fingers moving up and down on those three keys. (Sharon Steuer, author of *The Illustrator Wow! Book,* calls this a "Finger Dance.")

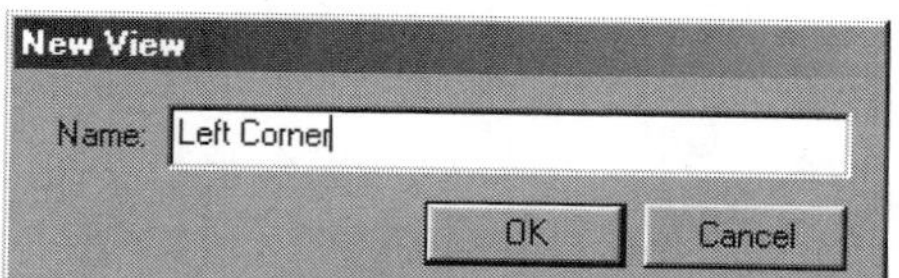

34 *The* **New View dialog box** *is where you can name a custom view.*

35 *The* **Edit Views dialog box** *is where you can redefine or delete custom views.*

Setting Custom Views

This is, in my opinion, one of the most overlooked features in FreeHand. Instead of relying on the preset magnifications and view commands, you can set your own custom views. A custom view remembers the magnification and the position of the screen. Custom views are very helpful anytime you find yourself zooming and moving into the same area over and over.

To create a custom view:

1. Choose the magnification and page position you want for the view.
2. Choose **View > Custom > New**. The New View dialog box appears 34.
3. Type a name for the view.
4. Click OK to close the dialog box.

To use a custom view:

- Choose **View > Custom** and choose one of the custom views listed at the bottom of the submenu.

  or

  Choose the custom view listed at the bottom of the magnification pop-up menu at the bottom of the document window.

To edit a custom view:

1. Change your magnification and position to the way you want your new view to appear.
2. Choose **View > Custom > Edit**. The Edit Views dialog box appears 35.
3. Select the view you want to change and click Redefine.
4. Click OK. This closes the dialog box and sets the new view.

WORKING WITH PAGES 4

What is a page? In word processing programs, a page is the space designated by the size of the paper in the printer.

But in programs such as Macromedia FreeHand, a page can be used to designate the size of the paper in the printer, or the size of the Web page, or the size of the Flash movie.

FreeHand offers more flexibility than many page layout and vector drawing programs. Not only can you have multiple pages, but each page can have its own size. This makes FreeHand an excellent choice for creating a wide variety of layouts such as envelopes, business cards, and letterheads.

Some people work with FreeHand for years, and never use anything more than one page for each document. Others could not exist without FreeHand's multiple pages to create booklets and other small documents.

Adjusting Page Size and Orientation

Inside the document window is the page on which you create your work. An area called the *pasteboard* surrounds the page ❶. You use the Document inspector to adjust the size and orientation of the page.

To display the Document inspector:

- To open the Document inspector, choose **Window > Inspectors > Document.**

As you create documents, you may need to change your page to a different size.

To set a page size in the Document inspector:

- Use the page size pop-up menu in the Document inspector ❷.

If none of the preset sizes is right for your job, you need to create a page with custom measurements. For instance, if you create business cards, you would want your page to match the trim size of the cards.

To create a custom-size page:

1. Choose Custom from the Page Size pop-up menu of the Document inspector.
2. Enter the horizontal measurement in the x field ❸.
3. Enter the vertical measurement in the y field ❸.
4. Press Return/Enter on the keyboard to apply the sizes to the page.

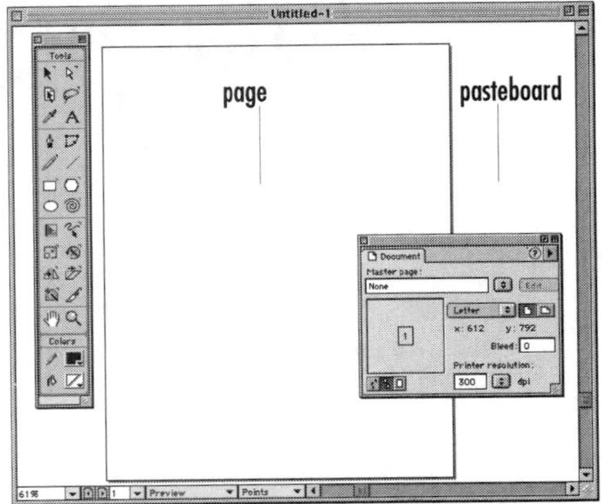

❶ *The* **page** *sits inside the* **pasteboard area.**

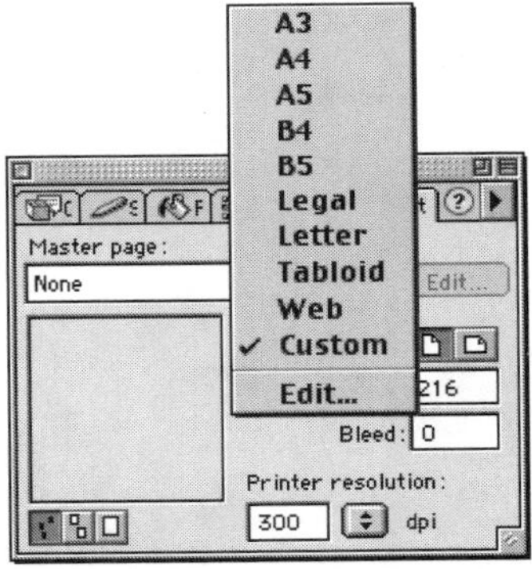

❷ *There are* **nine preset page sizes,** *plus Custom, which lets you enter the exact measurements for any size page.*

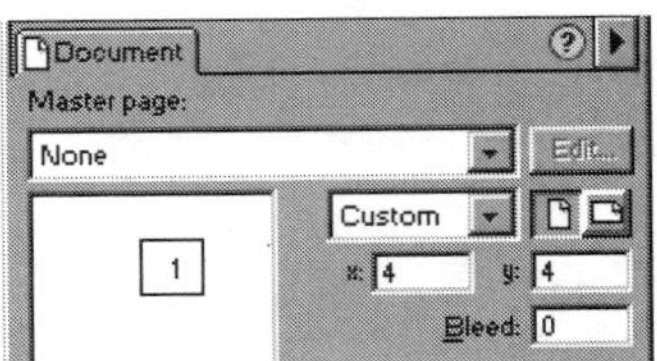

❸ *Use the* **x and y fields** *to set the dimensions of a custom page.*

❹ *Choose the* **Page tool** *in the Tools panel to visually manipulate pages on the artboard.*

❺ *Use the Page tool to drag the handles around a page to change the size of the page.*

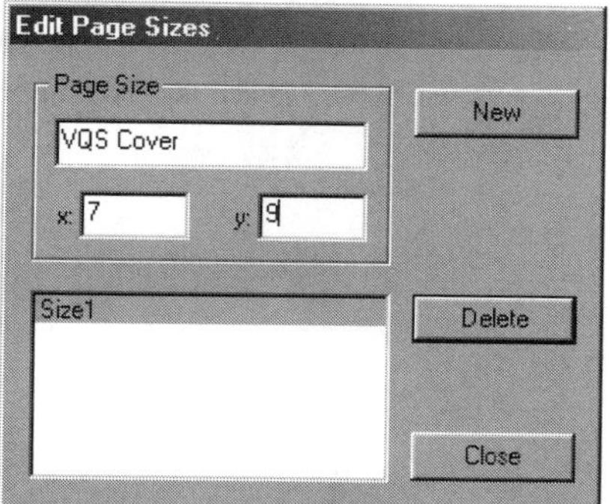

❻ *The* **Edit Page Sizes dialog box** *lets you set custom page sizes that are displayed in the Page Size pop-up menu.*

Instead of changing the size of the page numerically, you can use the Page tool to visually drag the page so that it is the same size as your artwork.

To use the Page tool to create a custom-size page:

1. Choose the Page tool in the Tools panel ❹.
2. Click the page you want to change. A set of handles appears around the edges of the page.
3. Drag one of the arrows to change the size of the page ❺.

TIP Keep an eye on the Info toolbar to see the dimensions of the page as you drag.

If you create many custom-size pages, you can save those sizes as part of the page size list. This makes it easier to select those page sizes later on.

To add custom page sizes to the page size list:

1. Choose edit from the page size list. The Edit Page Sizes dialog box appears ❻.
2. Click the New button to create a new page size entry.
3. Enter a descriptive name for the custom size.
4. Enter the horizontal size in the x field.
5. Enter the vertical size in the y field.
6. To enter additional custom sizes, click the New button.

   or

   Click the Delete button to delete any sizes.

   or

   Click the Close button to close the dialog box. The custom sizes appear in the Document inspector menu.

You may want to reverse the horizontal and vertical sizes of your document. You can do this using the Document inspector or the Page tool.

TIP Changing the orientation or rotating a page changes only the position of the artboard. It does not rotate any artwork on the page.

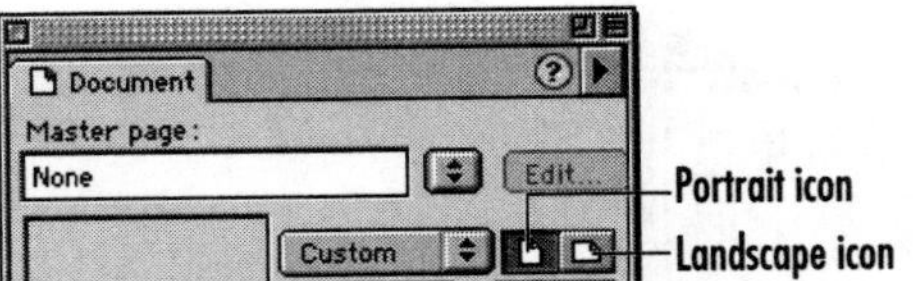

❼ *Click the* **Portrait or Landscape icons** *to change the orientation of a page.*

To set the orientation in the Document inspector:

- To make the page wider than it is tall, click the Landscape icon in the Document inspector ❼.

  or

  To make the page taller than it is wide, click the Portrait icon in the Document inspector ❼.

TIP If the Portrait is selected, FreeHand does not accept measurements that would make a page wider than it is tall. Similarly, if the Landscape icon is selected, you can never specify a page that is taller than it is wide.

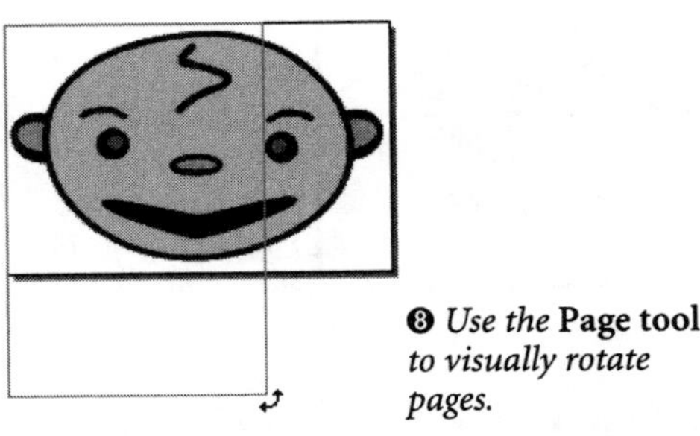

❽ *Use the* **Page tool** *to visually rotate pages.*

To rotate a page using the Page tool:

1. Choose the Page tool in the Tools panel.
2. Click the page you want to change. A set of handles appears around the edges of the page.
3. Move the cursor outside a handle so that a curved arrow appears.
4. Drag the curved arrow to rotate the page ❽.

❾ *Choosing* Duplicate *from the Document inspector menu creates a new page the same size as the selected page.*

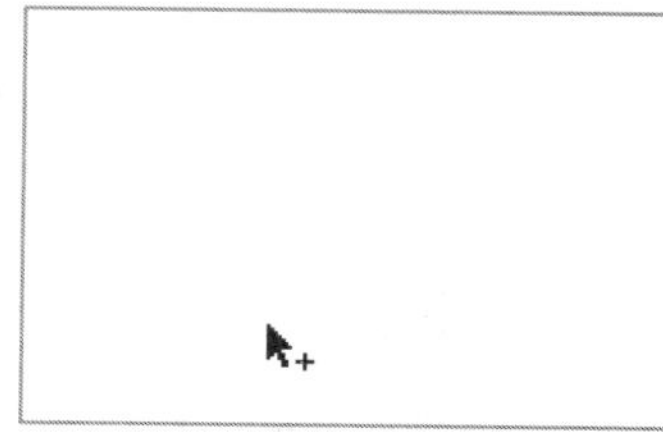

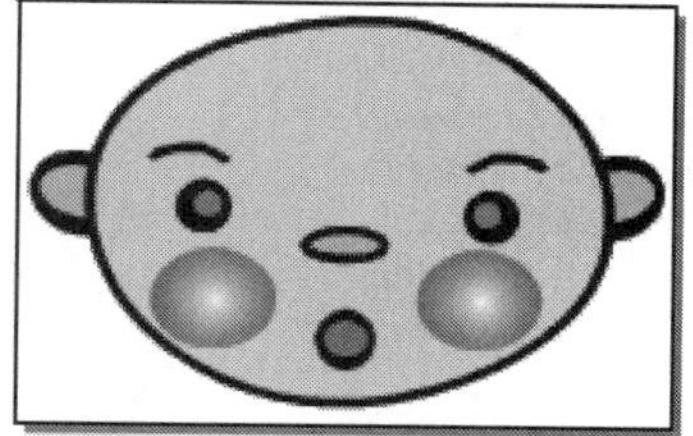

❿ *Hold the Opt/Alt key as you drag with the Page tool to duplicate pages.*

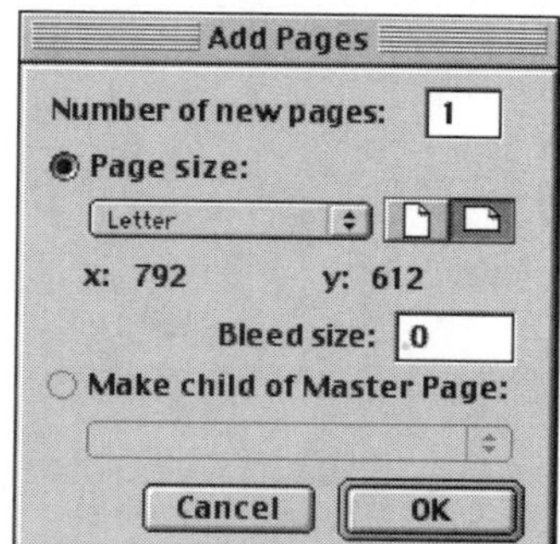

⓫ *Use the* Add Pages dialog box *to add multiple pages.*

Duplicating and Adding Pages

If you are creating a series of layouts for your client to choose from, you may want additional pages for different versions of the art. You can add new empty pages, or duplicate the current pages that may contain artwork.

To duplicate pages using the Document inspector:

- Choose Duplicate from the Document inspector menu. This creates a new page exactly the same size as the first page ❾.

TIP The new page also contains the same artwork as the original page.

To duplicate pages using the Page tool:

1. Choose the Page tool in the Tools panel.
2. Hold the Opt/Alt key ❿.
3. Drag the page to a new position.
4. Release the mouse button when the new page appears.

TIP Use the Shift key to select multiple pages. Then use the Opt/Alt key to duplicate the pages as you drag with the Page tool.

To add blank pages:

1. Choose Add Pages from the Document inspector menu. This opens the Add Pages dialog box ⓫.
2. Enter a number in the Number of new pages field.
3. Choose a size from the Page size pop-up menu.
4. Click the icon for orientation.
5. Set a Bleed size *(see page 53)*.
6. Set a master page *(see page 54)*.
7. Click OK to create the new pages.

TIP See the sidebar, *Where Are My New Pages?* on page 51, for information as to where the new or duplicate pages may be added.

Organizing Pages

You might want pages to touch so that you can spread artwork across the pages. Or you may want a page to come before another. You can move pages using the Page tool or the page thumbnails in the Document inspector.

To move pages with the Page tool:

1. Choose the Page tool in the Toolbox.
2. Click to select a page. The handles indicate the page is selected.
3. If needed, hold the Shift key to select additional pages.
4. Press and drag inside the handles to move the pages ⓬.
5. Release the mouse button when the pages are in position.

TIP Hold the Shift key to constrain the motion to 45-degree angles.

To move pages with the page thumbnails:

- Drag the page thumbnail in the Document inspector ⓭.

TIP If thumbnail is too small, change the thumbnail magnification *(see below)*.

TIP Hold the Spacebar to switch to a Hand tool that can scroll around the thumbnail area in the Document inspector.

To change the page icon magnification:

- Click the Magnification icons in the Document inspector as follows ⓮:
  - The Small icon shrinks the thumbnails to their smallest size.
  - The Medium icon expands the thumbnails to their second size.
  - The Large icon expands the thumbnails to their largest size.

TIP Double-click a thumbnail in the Document inspector to go to that page and fit the page in the window in one step.

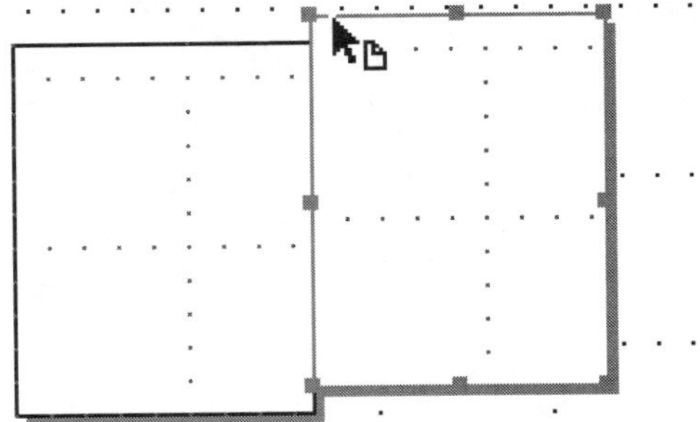

⓬ *The Page tool lets you select pages directly on the pasteboard and move them into position. The page icon shows that you are moving the page.*

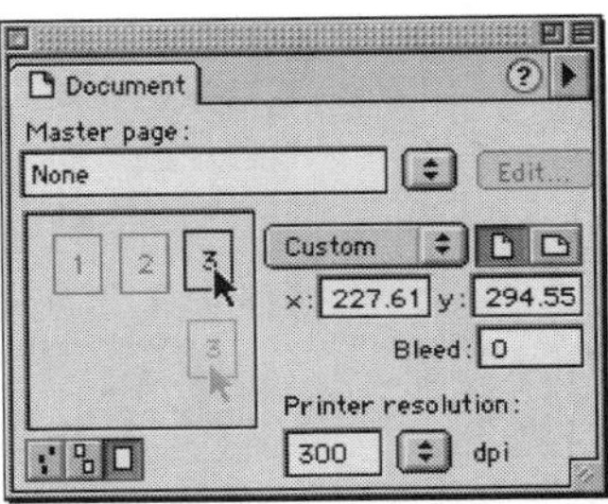

⓭ *As you move the page thumbnails in the Document inspector you also change the arrangement of the pages icon the pasteboard.*

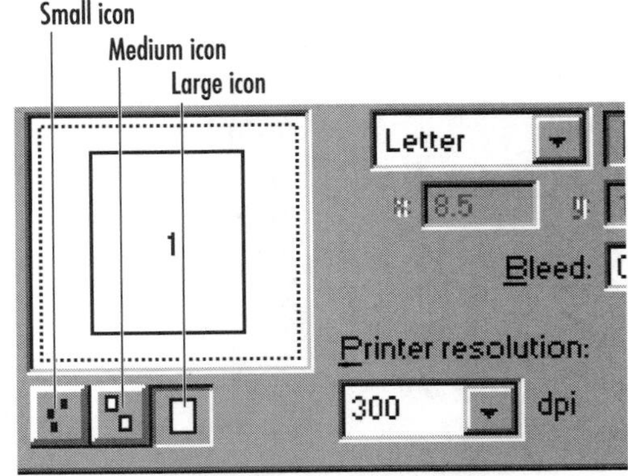

⓮ *The* **three magnification icons** *change the size of the page display in the preview area of the Document inspector.*

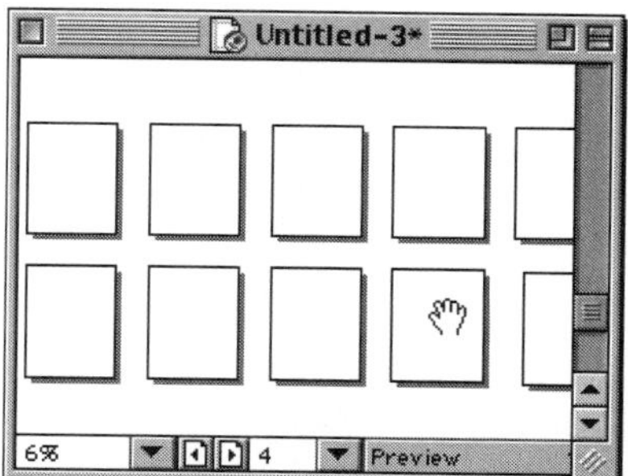

⓯ *Use the Hand tool to move from one page to another in the document window.*

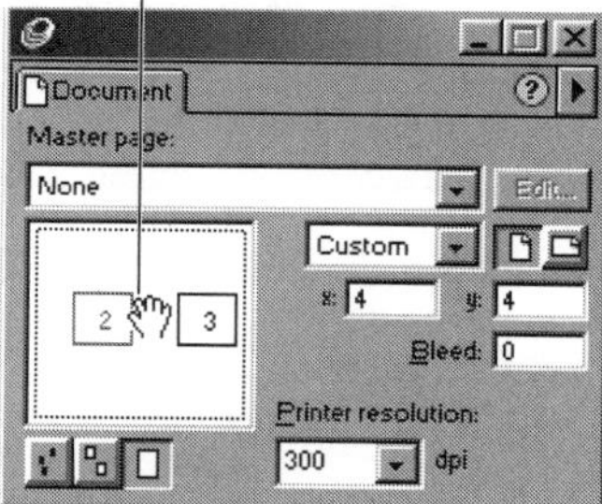

⓰ *Use the Hand tool to scroll within the Preview Area of the Document inspector.*

Moving Between Pages

With multiple pages in your document, you will need to move from one page to another. You can move between pages in the document window or by using the Document inspector.

To move between pages in the window area:

1. Choose the Hand tool.

   or

   Hold the Spacebar to temporarily access the Hand tool.
2. Drag to move from one page to another ⓯.

To move between pages in the Document inspector:

1. Position the cursor inside the Preview Area of the Document inspector.
2. Hold the Spacebar to temporarily access the Hand tool.
3. Drag within the Preview Area to move from one page to another ⓰.

Where Are My New Pages?

In theory, each new page you add or duplicate should appear just to the right of the current page. Unfortunately this doesn't always happen. (The technical name for something like this is called a *bug.*)

You may find that you add or duplicate pages, but you don't see the new pages on the pasteboard. If this happens, use the Hand tool to move all the way to the top-left corner of the pasteboard. You should see your missing pages there.

Why does this happen? The best reason I've been able to discover is that if you have changed the magnification icon to either the middle or large icon, there may not be enough room to add pages in the Document inspector. In that case, FreeHand creates new pages all the way in the top-left corner of the pasteboard.

If your pages do appear in the wrong position, you can use the Page tool *(see the previous page)* or the Document inspector to move the pages into the correct position.

Selecting and Deleting Pages

A FreeHand document must contain at least one page. That means you can never delete the only page in a document. However, if you have added pages to a document, you can delete one page at a time.

Before you delete a page, you need to select the page you want to delete.

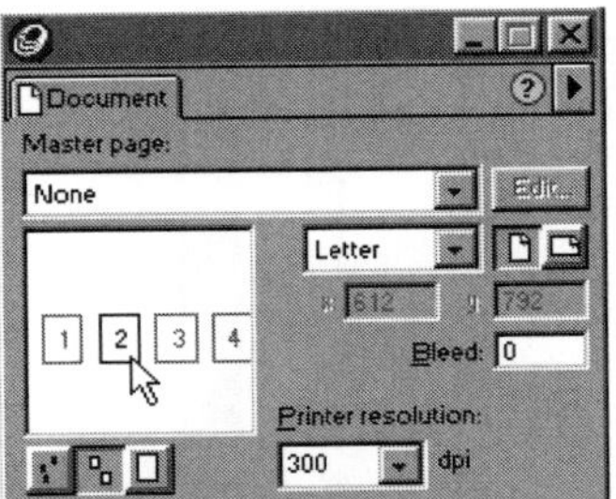

(17) *A selected page appears with a dark outline in the Preview Area of the Document inspector.*

To select a page in the Document inspector:

- Click the page you want to select in the Preview Area of the Document inspector. The selected page is indicated by a dark outline in the Preview Area (17).

To select a page in the FreeHand document window:

- Click the page you want to select in the document window.

  or

  Scroll through the document window so that the page you want to select is in the center of the window area.

  or

  Use the Page tool to select the page you want to delete.

TIP Although you can select multiple pages with the Page tool, only one page will be selected in the Document inspector.

To delete a selected page:

- Choose Remove from the Document inspector menu (18).

(18) *Use the Remove command to delete a selected page.*

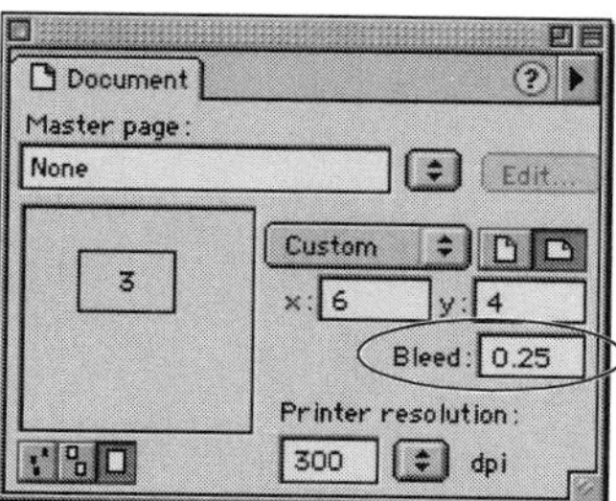

⓳ *Use the* **Bleed field** *(circled) to set the extra area around a page where artwork is printed.*

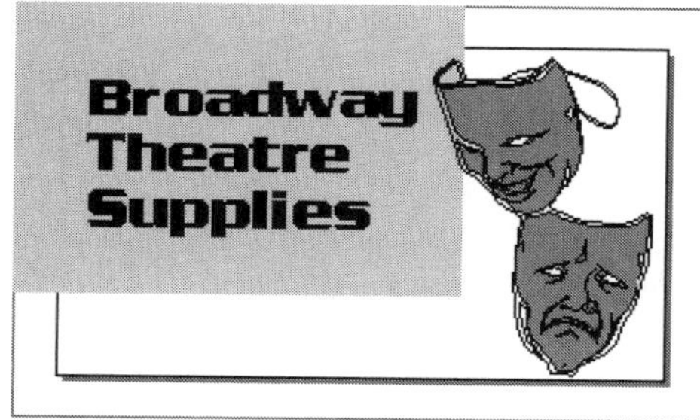

⓴ *The light gray line outside the work page indicates the bleed area.*

Setting a Page Bleed

Ordinarily, FreeHand doesn't print any part of an image that lies outside the page. If you want the artwork to print right to the edge of a page, you need to extend or bleed the artwork outside the edge of the page. (See the sidebar on this page *Why do I need to bleed?*)

To set a bleed size:

1. Enter the desired bleed size in the Bleed field of the Document inspector ⓳.
2. Press Return or Enter. A light gray line appears around your work page. This is the bleed area ⓴.

TIP Use the bleed area to hold elements that should print outside the live area of your artwork.

Why do I need to bleed?

The reason is that the people who cut paper don't always trim pages exactly evenly. Take a look at the thumbtabs on the sides of this book. If you flip from page to page you will see that the gray area isn't always the same size. That's because when the paper for the book is cut to the final trim size, some of the pages will be cut slightly differently from others. (Yes, I know this will happen, even before the book is printed.)

If I had laid out the page so the gray area stopped right at the edge of the page, there might be some pages where the trim showed the white outside the page.

So instead of trusting that the trim position would always be perfect, I set a bleed to extend the gray area outside the size of the page. That way I don't have to worry if the trim is slightly off. I know that the gray area will still be visible outside the trim.

Unless your print shop is trying to trim pages in the middle of an earthquake, you shouldn't need more than a quarter-inch bleed. However, if you are in doubt, ask your print shop for the size they would like for a bleed.

Using Master Pages

If you have used a page layout program such as QuarkXPress or Adobe InDesign, you may be familiar with the concept of master pages. A master page is a page that can be applied to ordinary document pages. Then any change you make to the master page is automatically applied to the document pages that are governed by the master page. The benefit of this is that you can make changes to many pages by making changes to a single master page.

FreeHand lets you create master pages that can then be applied to document pages.

To create and style a master page:

1. Choose New Master Page from the Document inspector menu ㉑.

   or

   Choose New Master Page from the Library menu ㉒. A new window that contains the master page appears.

TIP You can tell you are on the master page because the title bar shows the name of the document followed by the name of the master page. Also, the Document inspector shows the Master Page label ㉓.

2. Add any items to the master page that you want to appear on the document pages.
3. Close the window containing the master page. This returns you to the document pages.

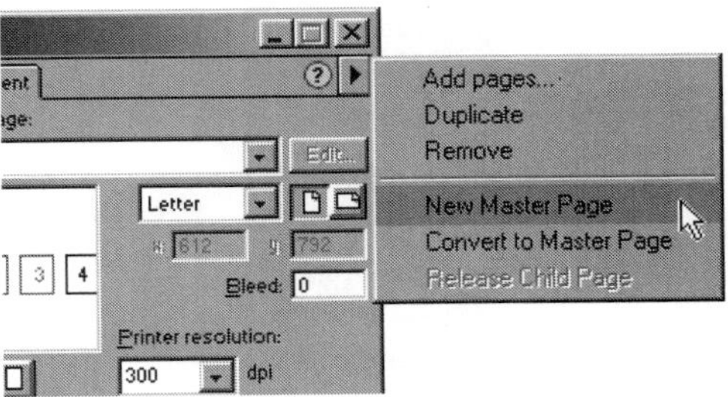

㉑ *Choose* **New Master Page** *from the Document inspector to add a new master page.*

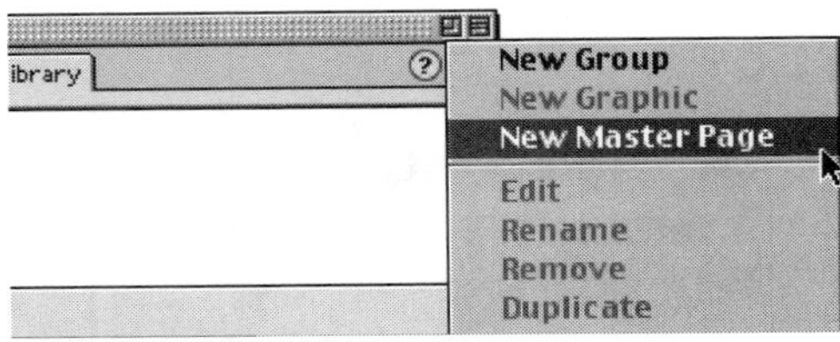

㉒ *Choose* **New Master Page** *from the Library menu to add a new master page.*

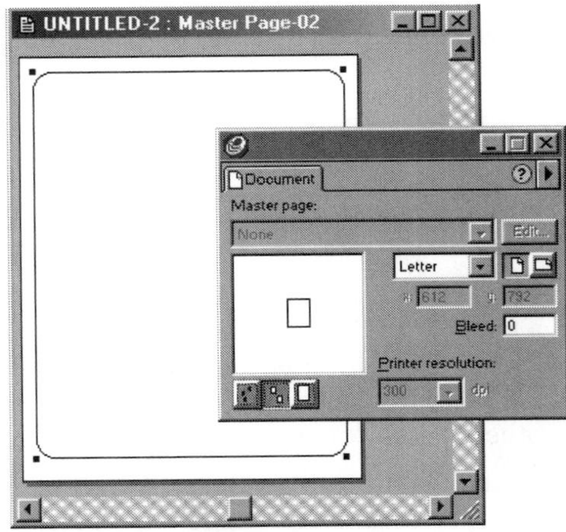

㉓ *The* **master page window** *is indicated in the title bar of the window and by the un-numbered page in the Document inspector.*

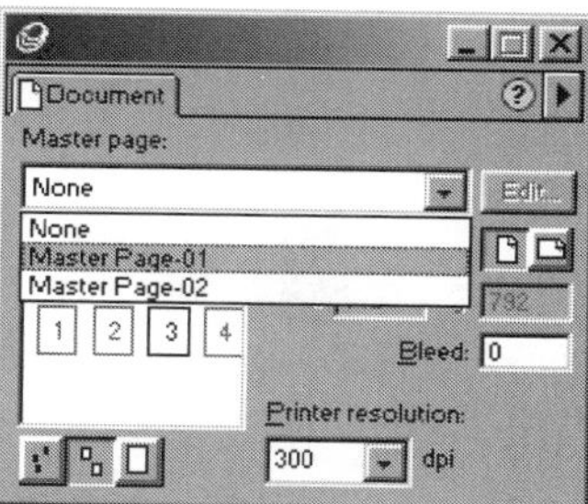

㉔ *You can apply a master page by choosing it from the Master page list in the Document inspector.*

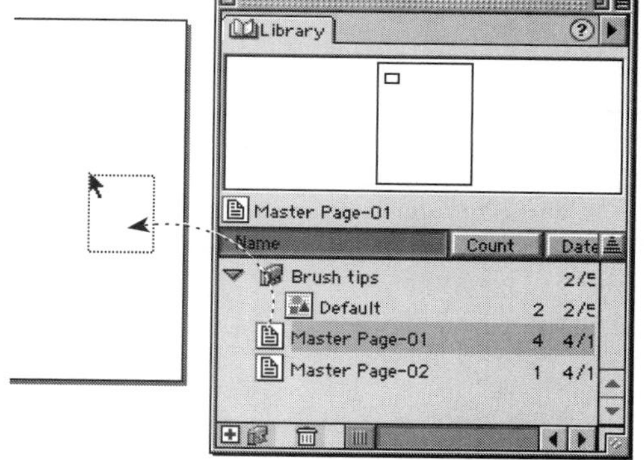

㉕ *Drag the icon of a master page from the Library onto a document page to apply that master page to the document page.*

As you work, you may realize that you would like a document page to act as a master page. Fortunately, it is easy to convert a document page into a master page.

To convert a document page into a master page:

1. Select the page you would like to have as a master page.
2. Choose Convert to Master Page from the Document inspector menu. A new master page is created from the elements on the document page.

TIP When you convert a document page to a master page, the items on the document page are deleted and the master page is applied to the document page.

Once you have created a master page, you can apply it to document pages. You can use either the Document inspector or the Library.

To apply master pages using the Document inspector:

1. Select the page or pages using the Page tool, the Document inspector, or click in the document window.
2. Choose the master page from the Master Page list in the Document inspector ㉔. The master page elements appear on the page.

To apply master pages using the Library:

- Drag the icon of the master page from the Library onto the page ㉕. The master page elements appear on the page.

TIP You can apply a new master page to a document page at any time.

You can remove the master page elements by removing the master page applied to a document page.

To remove the master page from a document page:

1. Select the page or pages that you want to change.
2. Choose None from the Master Page list in the Document inspector. The master page elements disappear from the page.

Master pages appear with a default name. However, you can rename a master page at any time.

To rename a master page:

1. Double-click the name of the master page in the Library ㉖.
2. Type the new name of the master page.
3. Press Return/Enter to apply the new name.

To edit a master page using the Library:

1. Double-click the icon of the master page in the Library. This opens the master page window.
2. Make whatever changes you want to the master page.
3. Close the master page window. The changes to the master page appear on those document pages that have the master page applied to them.

To edit a master page using the Document inspector:

1. Select the master page in the Master Page list in the Document inspector.
2. Click the Edit button ㉗.
3. Make whatever changes you want on the master page.
4. Close the master page window. The changes to the master page appear on those document pages that have the master page applied to them.

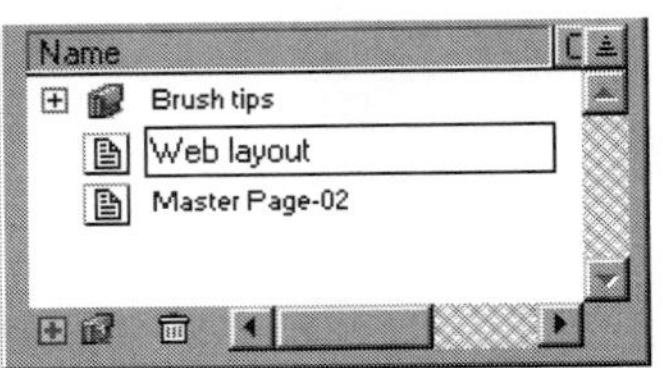

㉖ *Double-click the name of a master page in the Library to rename the master page.*

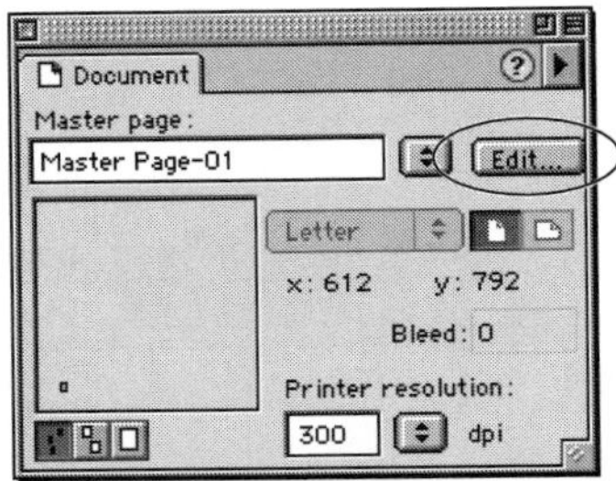

㉗ *The* **Edit button** *in the Document inspector allows you to make changes to the master page.*

Items that are on the master page are not editable when they appear on the document pages. If you want to modify those items on the document pages, you need to release those items from the master page.

To release master page items on document pages:

1. Select the document page that you want to release.
2. Choose Release Child Page from the Document inspector menu. The items on the document page are no longer governed by the master page and can be freely edited.

PATH CREATION TOOLS 5

One of the best ways to learn a vector drawing program is to start by creating basic shapes. Rather than create these shapes from scratch, it is much easier to use FreeHand's many different tools that make all sorts of different objects.

For instance, if you want to draw a daisy, you can easily draw a few ovals around a circle using the ellipse tool. A house is easily created from several rectangles with a triangle on the top.

You can also use tools to create complicated mathematical shapes such as spirals and arcs. Finally, FreeHand lets you mimic the look of traditional pen and ink drawing tools.

Of course, you can also create paths with very defined shapes using two specialized tools called the Pen and Bezigon. Those tools are covered in Chapter 6.

Understanding Paths

Almost all the objects you create within FreeHand are vector paths. Vector paths consist of anchor points that define the shape of the path and segments that join the points together.

For instance, in a vector-drawing program a circle is defined by placing four anchor points in position and joining them with curved segments ❶.

In a pixel-drawing program, each individual dot that creates the circle must be defined ❷.

To change the shape of a vector path, the anchor points or segments are modified. To change the shape of a pixel image, the original pixels must be erased and the new pixels placed into position.

Vector paths are usually used to create line artwork or illustration images ❸. Pixel-images are used to capture scanned photographs and the images taken by digital cameras ❹.

One of the most important reasons to create objects using vector paths is that the size of the file is much smaller than the same image created using pixels. Also, unlike pixels, vector images can be scaled up with no loss of resolution.

Most people feel it is much easier to create photorealistic images using pixel-drawing programs. However, if you have the patience, you can create realistic images using vector objects. This includes special effects such as blends and gradients.

For more information on the differences between vector and pixel images and working with resolution, see *The Non-Designer's Scan and Print Book* by Sandee Cohen and Robin Williams.

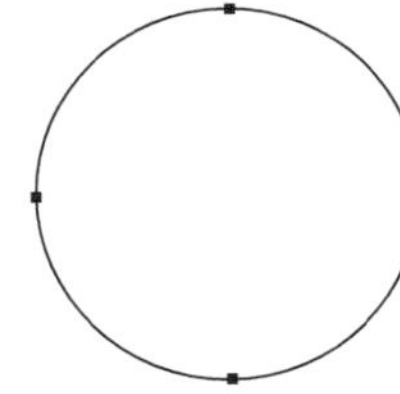

❶ *A vector-drawing program defines shapes using anchor points (indicated by squares) connected by segments.*

❷ *A pixel-drawing program creates shapes using pixels (indicated by black and white squares).*

❸ *In this* **example of vector artwork,** *each shape is created by a separate vector path.*

❹ *In this* **scanned pixel image** *the artwork consists of millions of tiny, colored pixels.*

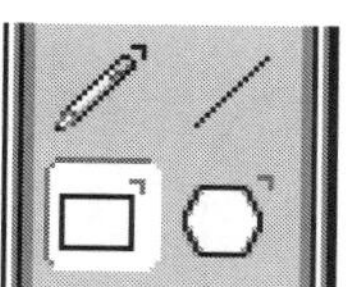

❺ *The* **Rectangle tool** *selected in the Tools panel.*

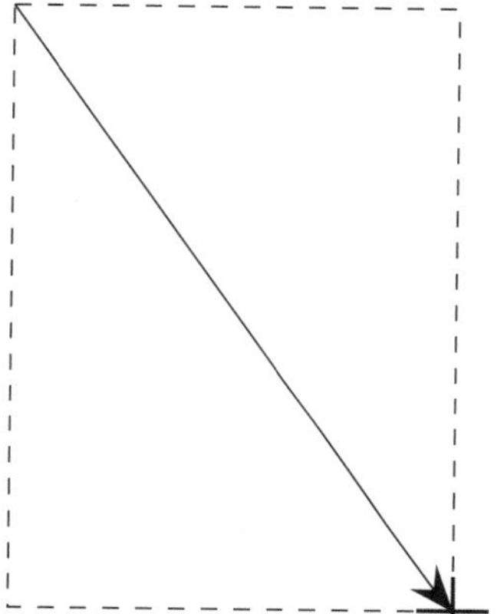

❻ *To* **draw a rectangle,** *drag the cursor along the diagonal line between two corners.*

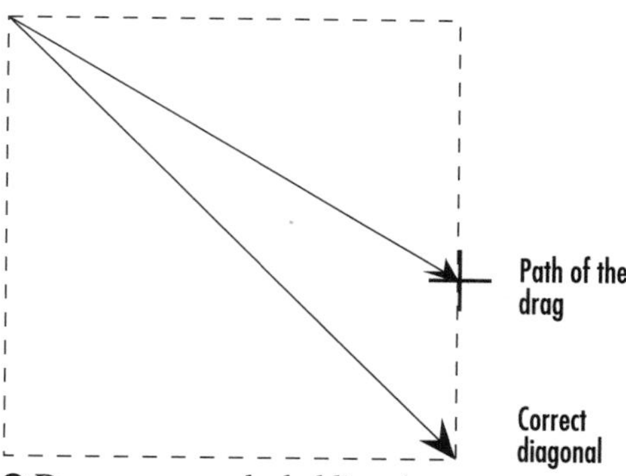

❼ **Draw a square** *by holding the Shift key while you drag with the Rectangle tool.*

Using the Rectangle Tool

One of the most basic objects you can create is a rectangle. This includes plain rectangles, squares, and rounded-corner rectangles.

To draw a rectangle:

1. Click the Rectangle tool in the Tools panel ❺.
2. Position the plus sign cursor (+) where you want one corner of the rectangle and press to start the rectangle.
3. Drag diagonally to the opposite corner ❻.
4. Release the mouse button when you are satisfied with the size of the rectangle.

TIP Hold the Opt/Alt key to draw a rectangle outward from the center point.

TIP Once you draw the rectangle, you can still change its dimensions *(see page 62)*.

You may think of a square as different from a rectangle, but FreeHand doesn't make the distinction. The Rectangle tool creates squares.

To draw a square:

1. Follow the steps to start creating a rectangle.
2. As you drag, hold Shift key. This forces, or *constrains,* your rectangle into a square even if you do not follow the proper diagonal ❼.

TIP Whenever you hold a modifier, such as the Shift key, always release the mouse button first, then the modifier second.

TIP Hold both the Opt/Alt and the Shift keys to draw a square outward from the center point.

Another type of rectangle has curved or rounded corners. The amount of the curve depends on the corner radius ❽.

To set the corner radius for a rectangle:

1. Double-click the Rectangle tool in the Tools panel to open the Rectangle Tool dialog box ❾.
2. In the Corner radius field, type the amount or drag the slider to set the number for the corner radius.
3. Click OK and draw your rectangle.

You can change the size and shape of a rectangle using the Object inspector. This includes changing the corner radius.

To change the dimensions of a rectangle:

1. Select the rectangle.
2. In the Object inspector, change the settings as follows ❿:
   - The **x** field controls the horizontal position of the left-corner of the rectangle on the artboard.
   - The **y** field controls the vertical position of the left-corner of the rectangle on the artboard.
   - The **w** field controls the width of the rectangle.
   - The **h** field controls the height of the rectangle.
   - The **Corner radius** field controls the amount of curve applied to the corners of the rectangle.
3. Press Return/Enter to apply the change.

TIP Do not ungroup the rectangle or you will no longer be able to enter a corner radius for the rectangle.

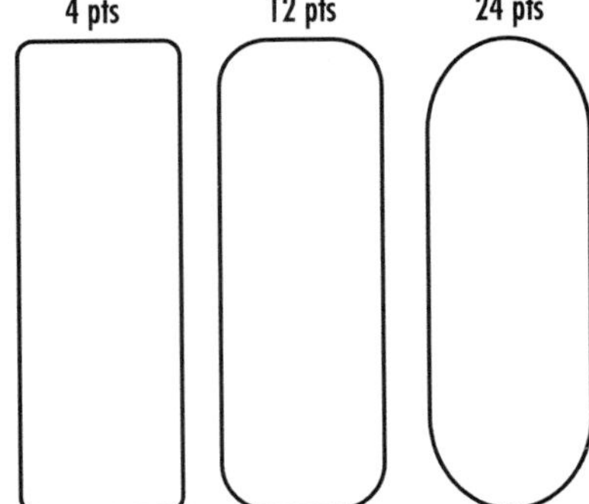

❽ *Different* **Corner radius settings** *change the shape of rounded-corner rectangles.*

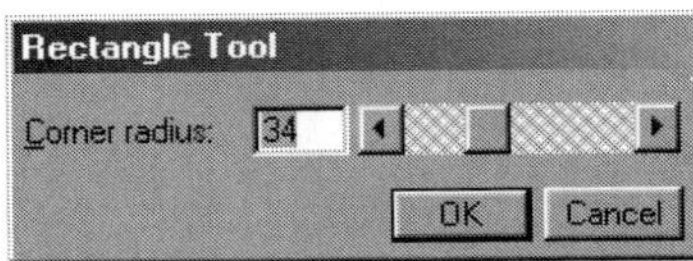

❾ *The* **Rectangle Tool dialog box** *lets you set the amount of the Corner radius.*

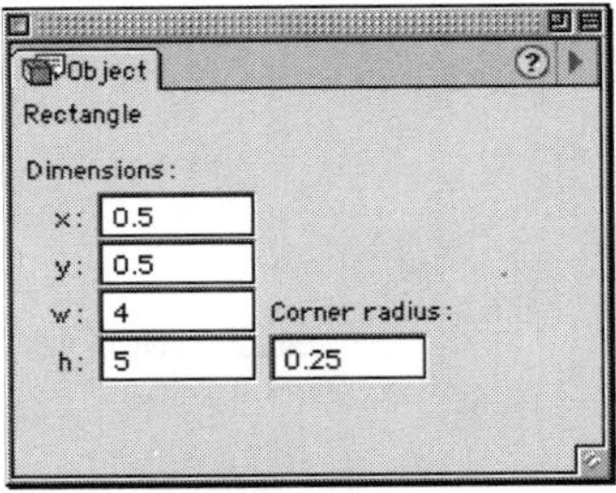

❿ *Use the settings in the Object inspector to change the attributes of a rectangle.*

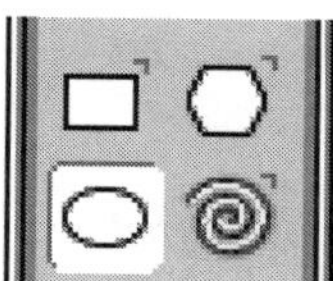

⓫ *The* **Ellipse tool** *selected in the Tools panel.*

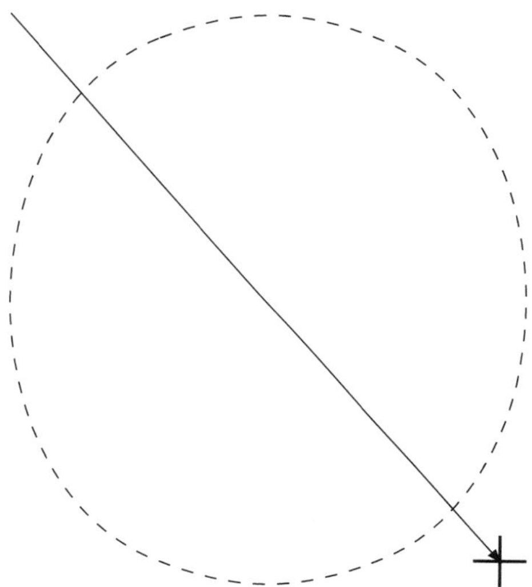

⓬ *To* **draw an ellipse**, *drag the cursor along the diagonal line between two sides.*

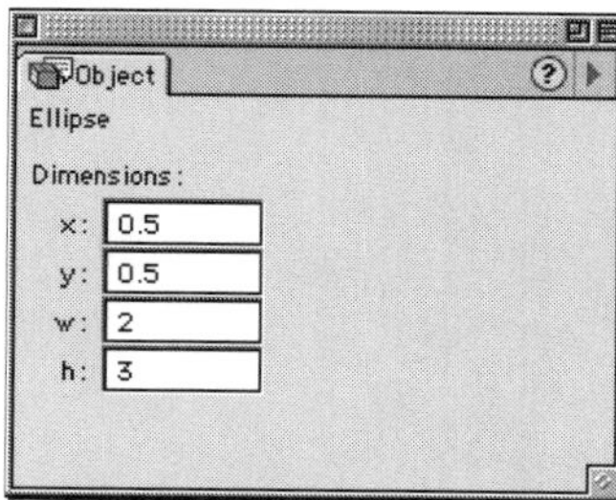

⓭ *Use the settings in the Object inspector to change the attributes of a ellipse.*

Using the Ellipse Tool

Another type of object you can create is the ellipse. The Ellipse tool also creates circles.

To draw an ellipse or circle:

1. Click the Ellipse tool in the Tools panel ⓫.
2. Position the cursor where you want one "corner" of the ellipse.
3. Press and drag to the opposite "corner" ⓬.

TIP Hold the Shift key as you drag to constrain the ellipse to a circle.

TIP Hold the Opt/Alt key to draw the ellipse from the center outward.

TIP Combine both the Opt/Alt and Shift keys to draw a circle outward from the center point.

To change the dimensions of an ellipse:

1. Select the ellipse.
2. In the Object inspector, change the settings as follows ⓭:
   - The **x** field controls the horizontal position of the left-corner of the ellipse on the artboard.
   - The **y** field controls the vertical position of the left-corner of the ellipse on the artboard.
   - The **w** field controls the width of the ellipse.
   - The **h** field controls the height of the ellipse.
3. Press Return/Enter to apply the change.

Using the Line Tool

FreeHand is definitely the program for anyone who has said they cannot even draw a straight line. The Line tool makes it easy!

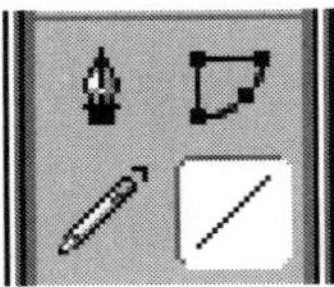

14 *The* **Line tool** *selected in the Tools panel.*

To draw a straight line:

1. Click the Line tool in the Tools panel 14.
2. Position the cursor where you want the line to start.
3. Press and drag along the direction the line should follow.
4. Release the mouse button where you want the line to end 15.

TIP If you press the Shift key as you use the Line tool, your lines will be constrained to 45° or 90° increments of the Constrain axis *(see page 138)*.

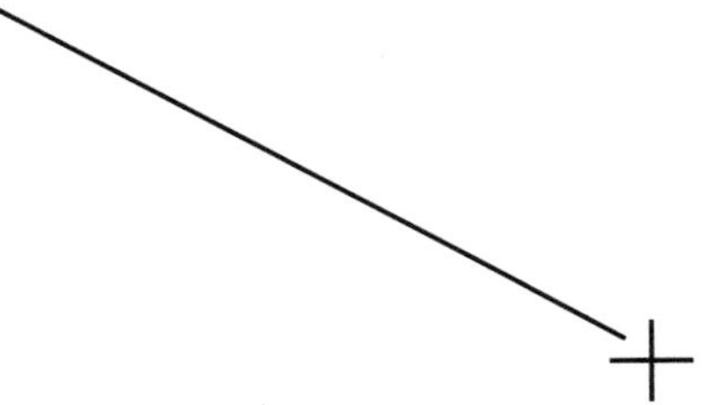

15 *A* **straight line** *drawn with the Line tool.*

Unlike the rectangle and ellipse tools, you can't use the Object inspector to change the settings of the path created by the Line tool. However, you can check the attributes of the line as you draw using the Info Toolbar.

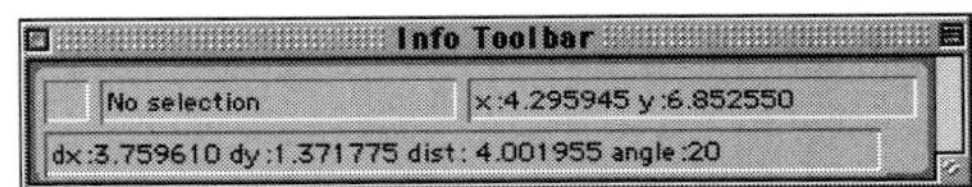

16 *Watch the values in the Info Toolbar to see the angles as you draw a line.*

To see the attibutes of a line as you draw:

1. Start the drag to create the line.
2. Without releasing the mouse button, note the attributes in the Info Toolbar 16:
   - The **x** shows the horizontal position of the first point of the line on the artboard.
   - The **y** shows the vertical position of the first point of the line on the artboard.
   - The **dx** shows the horizontal distance to the second point of the line.
   - The **dy** shows the vertical distance to the second point of the line.
   - The **distance** shows the actual length of the line.
   - The **angle** shows the angle of the line.

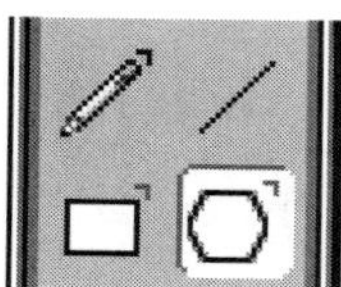

⓱ *The* **Polygon tool** *in the Tools panel.*

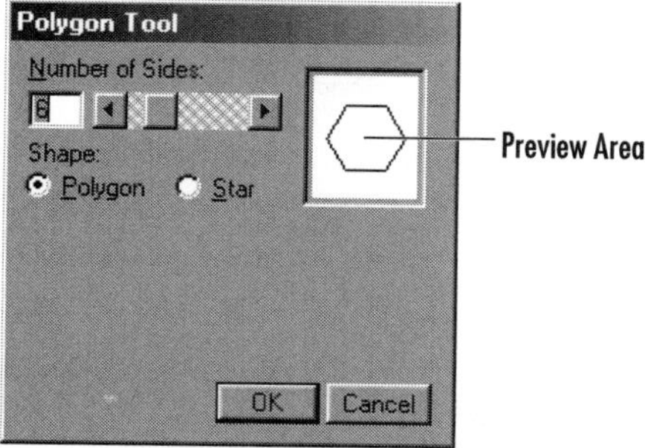

⓲ *The* **Polygon Tool dialog box.**

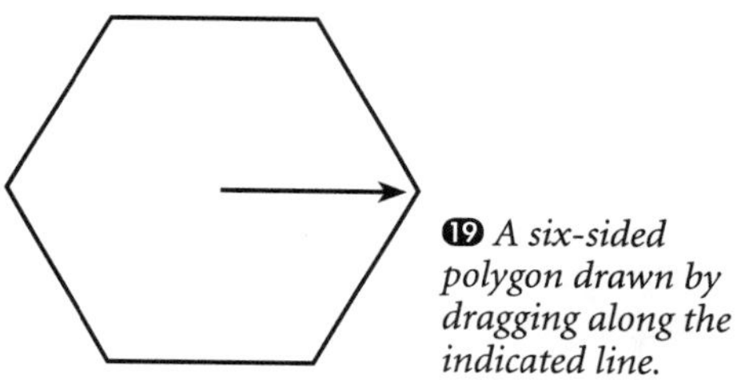

⓳ *A six-sided polygon drawn by dragging along the indicated line.*

Using the Polygon Tool

There are two types of objects you can create with the Polygon tool: polygons and stars. Before you draw a polygon you have to set its attributes.

To set the attributes for a polygon:

1. Double-click the Polygon tool in the Tools panel ⓱. This opens the Polygon Tool dialog box.
2. If it is not already selected, choose Polygon from the Shape choices. The Polygon settings appear ⓲.
3. Use the Number of Sides field or slider to enter the the number of sides for your polygon. The Preview Area shows a representation of the polygon.
4. Click OK. The settings for the polygon are kept until the next time you change the dialog box.

To draw a polygon:

1. Position the cursor where you want the center of your shape.
2. Drag outward ⓳. As you drag, you will see the shape that defines your polygon.
3. Move the mouse to rotate the polygon to the position you want.
4. Release the mouse button when you are satisfied with the size and position of the polygon.

TIP If you set the Polygon tool to four sides, you can draw a rectangle that you can rotate as you drag.

Stars are the second type of object that you can draw with the Polygon tool.

To set the attributes to create a star:

1. Double-click the Polygon tool in the Tools panel. This opens the Polygon Tool dialog box.
2. If it is not already selected, choose Star from the Shape coices. The Star settings appear ⑳.
3. Use the Number of Sides field or slider to control the number of points of the star. The Preview Area shows a representation of the star.

TIP Strictly speaking, the Number of Sides label is incorrect. A star has twice the number of sides than it does points. The label should read Number of Outside Points when defining a star.

4. Set the Star Points as follows:
   - **Automatic** creates a star that has its segments automatically aligned.
   - **Manual** lets you set your own angle for the alignment of the star sides.
5. If you have chosen the Manual setting for Star points, drag the slider between actute and obtuse settings ㉑. The preview window shows how your changes affect the star.

To draw a star:

1. Position the cursor where you want the center of your star.
2. Drag outward. As you drag, you will see the shape that defines your star.
3. Move the mouse to rotate the star to the position you want.
4. Release the mouse button when you are satisfied with the size and position of the star.

TIP Once you have drawn a polygon or a star, you cannot use the settings to change its size or shape.

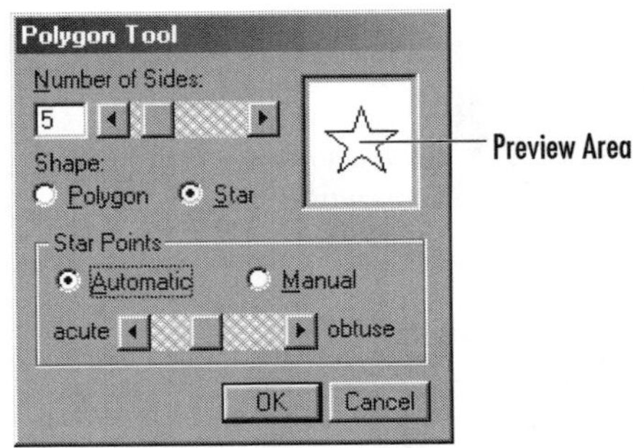

⑳ **Star choices** *in the Polygon Tool dialog box.*

㉑ *Stars set for Automatic alignment (top), an Acute angle (middle), and an Obtuse angle (bottom).*

Using the Polygon Tool

㉒ *Pencil tool modes:* **Freehand** *(top),* **Variable stroke** *(middle), and* **Calligraphic pen** *(bottom).*

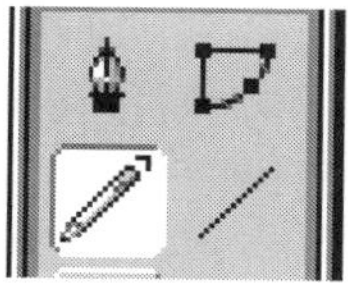

㉓ *The icon for the* **Pencil tool,** *when set for the Freehand mode.*

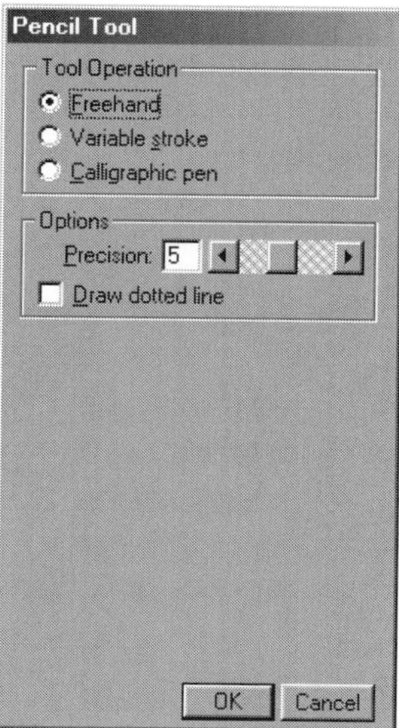

㉔ *The* **Pencil Tool dialog box** *set for the* **Freehand mode.**

Using the Pencil Tool

The Pencil tool has three different tool modes: Freehand, Variable stroke, and Calligraphic pen. Each of these modes creates a different look ㉒.

The Freehand mode is useful for tracing over scanned images. The Variable stroke resembles a brushstroke. The Calligraphic pen resembles the stroke of an angled pen used in calligraphy.

Both Variable stroke and Calligraphic pen are especially effective if you are working with a pressure-sensitive drawing tablet and pen instead of a mouse. These tablets allow you to vary the width of the stroke, depending on how much or how little pressure you exert.

To set the Pencil tool to the Freehand mode:

1. Double-click the Pencil tool in the Tools panel ㉓. This opens the Pencil tool dialog box.

TIP The icon for the Pencil tool changes depending on the settings in the Pencil tool dialog box.

2. Choose Freehand as the Tool Operation. This displays the settings for the Freehand mode ㉔.
3. Set Precision to a high value to have your path follow any minor variables as you drag.

   or

   Choose a low value to smooth out any minor variables as you drag.
4. Click OK, which returns you to the page.

TIP If you drag too quickly, your stroke may not fill in correctly. Check the box for Draw dotted line. This creates a dotted line that follows your path. FreeHand then fills in that line with the actual path.

To draw in the Freehand mode:

1. Drag the cursor along the path you want to create.
2. Release the mouse button when you have completed your line ㉕.

TIP As you draw, you can erase part of the path created with any of the Freehand modes by holding down the Cmd/Ctrl key and dragging backward over the path.

TIP If you want part of the path you are drawing with the Freehand tool to be straight, press the Opt/Alt key as you drag. Release the Opt/Alt key (but not the mouse button) to continue the path ㉖.

To close a path drawn in the Freehand mode:

1. Bring the line back to its origin and watch for a little square to appear next to the cursor.
2. Release the mouse button and the path will be closed.

㉕ *The* **Pencil tool** *creates a line that follows the path you dragged.*

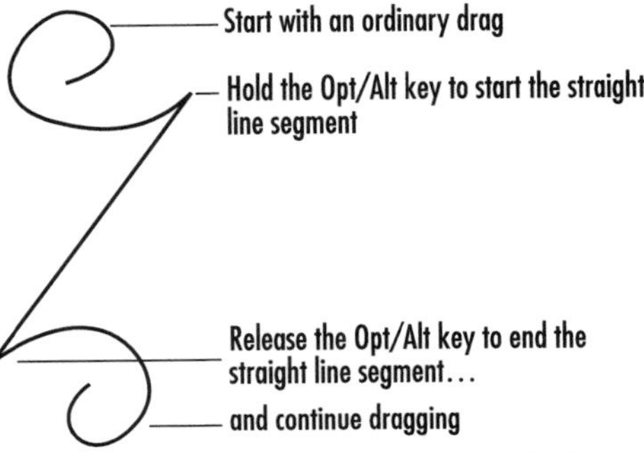
Start with an ordinary drag
Hold the Opt/Alt key to start the straight line segment
Release the Opt/Alt key to end the straight line segment...
and continue dragging

㉖ *Hold the Opt/Alt key to create straight lines with the Pencil tool in the Freehand mode.*

Working with a Pressure-Sensitive Tablet

Many years ago I heard the statement that "drawing with a mouse is like drawing with a bar of soap." The solution to that cumbersome idea is to get a pressure-sensitive tablet such as the Wacom tablets. I can't think of a better investment for any computer artist or graphic designer.

In FreeHand, the Variable stroke and the Calligraphic pen modes of the Pencil tool will respond to pressure exerted on the tablet's surface. This helps these two tools create more natural-looking brush strokes. However, there's more than just artistic reasons to use a tablet.

Using a stylus keeps your hand in a more comfortable position than working with a mouse. This means you are less likely to develop hand strain or other problems.

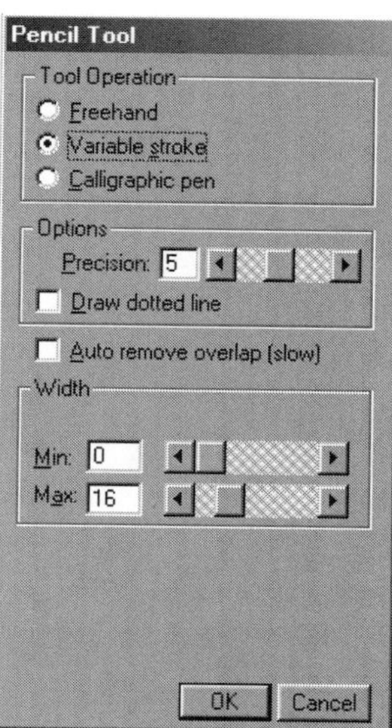

㉗ *The* **Pencil tool** *dialog box set for the* **Variable stroke mode.**

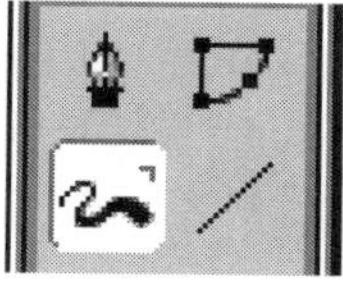

㉘ *The icon for the* **Pencil tool,** *when set in the* **Variable stroke mode.**

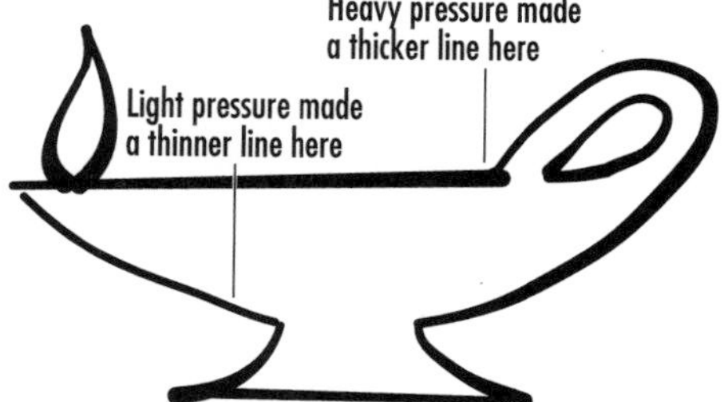

㉙ *Changing the pressure while drawing in the* **Variable stroke mode** *(and a pressure-sensitive tablet) changes the thickness of the line created.*

To set the Variable stroke mode:

1. Double-click the Pencil tool in the Tools panel. This opens the Pencil Tool dialog box.
2. Choose Variable stroke as the Tool Operation ㉗. This displays the settings for the Variable stroke.
3. Set Precision to a high value to have your path follow any minor variables as you drag.

   or

   Choose a low value to smooth out any minor variables as you drag.
4. In the Min field, enter the size for the thinnest part of your brush stroke (any size from 1 to 72 points).
5. In the Max field, enter the size for the thickest part of your brush stroke (any size from 1 to 72 points).
6. Choose Auto remove overlap (slow) to eliminate overlapping parts of the path. This makes it easier to reshape the path and avoid printing problems.
7. Click OK to return to your work page.

To draw in the Variable stroke mode:

1. If you have chosen the Variable stroke tool operation in the Pencil dialog box, you should see its icon in the Tools panel ㉘.
2. Drag to create the path.
3. If you have a pressure-sensitive tablet, any changes in the pressure you exert will change the thickness of your stroke ㉙.

TIP Use the fill color to set the color of the object created in the Variable stroke and Calligraphic pen modes.

To set the Calligraphic pen mode:

1. Double-click the Pencil tool in the Tools panel. This opens the Pencil tool dialog box.
2. Choose Calligraphic pen as the Tool Operation ㉚. This displays the settings for the Calligraphic pen.
3. Set Precision to a high value to have your path follow any minor variables as you drag.

   or

   Choose a low value to smooth out any minor variables as you drag.
4. Set the Width to Fixed to have a single width for the stroke.

   or

   Set the Width to Variable to be able to set a minimum and maximum width for the stroke.
5. If you have chosen a Fixed width, use the slider or type in the amount in the field.

   or

   If you have chose a Variable width, use the slider for the Min field to enter the size for the thinnest part of your brush stroke (any size from 1 to 72 points).

   In the Max field, enter the size for the thickest part of your brush stroke (any size from 1 to 72 points).
6. Use the Angle wheel or type in the field to set the angle that the stroke uses for its calligraphic lines.
7. Click OK to return to your page.

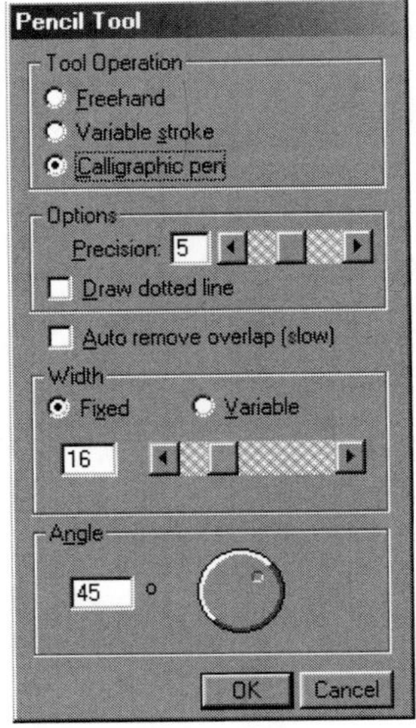

㉚ *The* **Pencil tool** *dialog box set for the* **Calligraphic pen mode.**

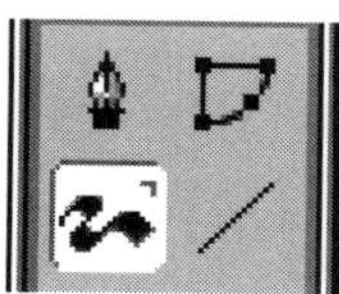

㉛ *The icon for the* **Pencil tool,** *when set in the Calligraphic pen mode.*

㉜ *Changing* **the angle for the Calligraphic pen** *changes the shape of the curves.*

To draw with the Calligraphic pen tool:

1. If you have chosen the Calligraphic pen tool operation in the dialog box, you should see its icon in the Tools panel ㉛.
2. Drag to create the path.

TIP As you change the direction of the path the angle determines the shape of the path ㉜. Pressure-sensitive tablets such as the Wacom Intuos™ will also respond to the changes in the angle that you hold the pen as you draw.

Varying the Pressure with a Mouse

Even if you don't use a tablet, you can still vary your stroke for the Pencil tool in either the Variable stroke or the Calligraphic pen modes.

To increase the thickness, press the right arrow or the number 2 key as you drag with the mouse.

To decrease the thickness, press the left arrow or the number 1 key as you drag with the mouse.

If you draw with a mouse rather than a pressure-sensitive tablet, the Pencil tool uses the Min setting as the default width of the stroke.

Using the Spiral Tool

FreeHand's Spiral tool provides you with more than enough options for creating all sorts of spirals.

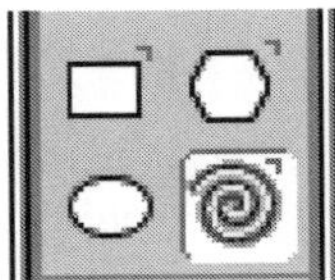

33 *The* **Spiral tool** *in the Tools panel.*

To set the Spiral tool mode:

1. Double-click the Spiral tool in the Tools panel or Xtra Tools toolbar 33. This opens the Spiral dialog box 34.
2. Choose between the Non-expanding and Expanding type.

TIP An Expanding spiral opens up as it moves out from the center. Non-expanding spirals are evenly spaced.

3. If you choose Expanding, use the slider or enter a number in the Expansion field. The higher the number, the greater the expansion rate 35.
4. Choose one of the following from the Draw by list:
   - **Rotations** lets you specify the Number of rotations in your spiral.
   - **Increments** lets you specify the amount of space between the curls in non-expanding spirals or the starting radius for expanding spirals.
5. Choose one of the following from the Draw from list:
   - **Center** starts at the center of the spiral.
   - **Edge** starts from the edge of the spiral.
   - **Corner** starts from the corner of the bounding box that holds the spiral 36.
6. Click one of the Direction icons to choose either a counterclockwise or a clockwise spiral.
7. Click OK to implement your settings.

To create a spiral:

- Drag with the Spiral tool to create the spiral on the page.

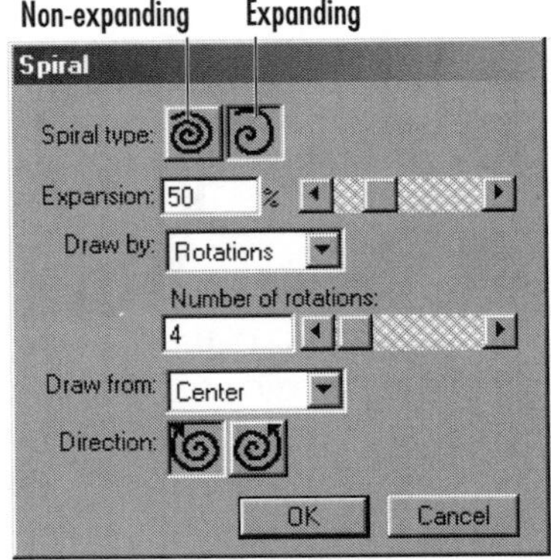

34 *The* **Spiral dialog box.**

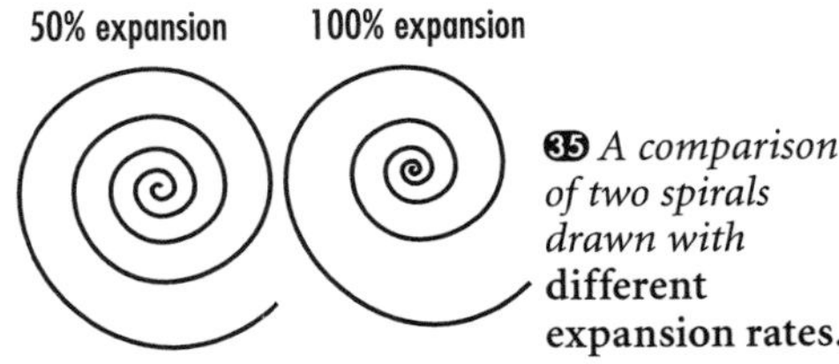

35 *A comparison of two spirals drawn with* **different expansion rates.**

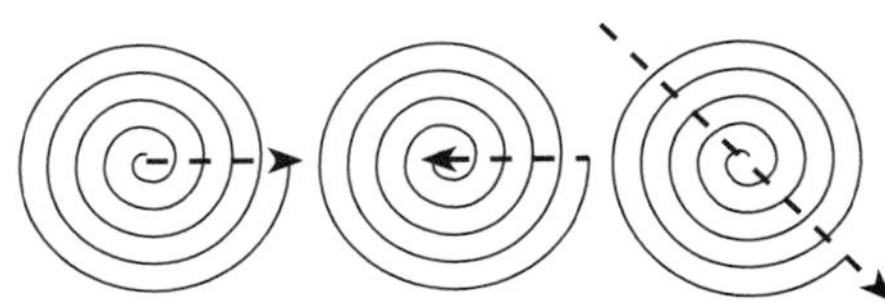

36 *Spirals drawn from the* **Center** *(left), the* **Edge** *(middle), and the* **Corner** *(right). The dashed lines show the length and direction of the drags.*

Using the Spiral Tool

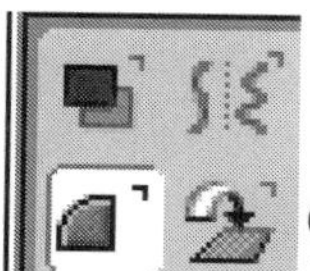
37 *The* **Arc tool** *selected in the Xtra Tools toolbar.*

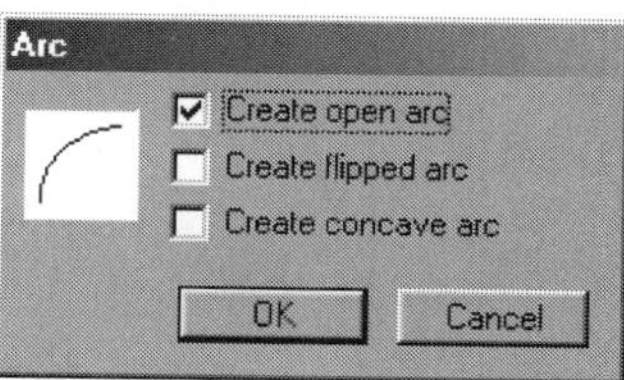

38 *The* **Arc dialog box** *allows you to choose from open, flipped, or concave arc settings.*

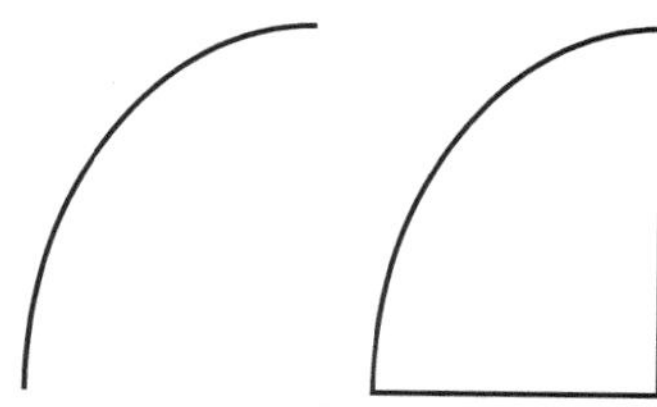
39 *Notice the difference between an* **open arc** *(left) and a* **closed arc** *(right).*

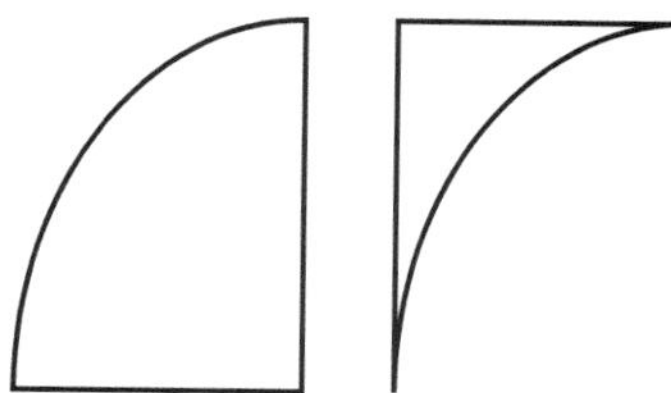
40 *Closed arcs can be either* **convex** *(left) or* **concave** *(right).*

Using the Arc Tool

Here's the tool for Indiana Jones—the Arc tool.

To choose settings for the Arc tool:

1. Choose **Window > Toolbars > Xtra Tools** to open the Xtra Tools toolbar.
2. Double-click the Arc tool in the Xtra Tools panel 37. This opens the Arc dialog box 38.
3. Choose Create open arc if you want a simple arc. Deselect this option if you want your arc to form a wedge shape 39.
4. Choose Create flipped arc to reflect the arc from one direction to another.
5. Choose Create concave arc to create an arc that curves inside a corner.
6. Click OK to return to the work page.

To draw with the Arc tool:

1. With the Arc tool selected, drag to create the arc on the page.
2. Release the mouse button when you are satisfied with the arc.

TIP Hold the Cmd/Ctrl key after you start the drag to close or open the arc 40.

TIP Hold the Opt/Alt key after you start the drag to flip the arc horizontally or vertically.

TIP Hold the Control key (Mac) to switch between either concave or convex settings.

TIP Hold the Shift key to constrain the arc to quarter circles.

Using the Trace Tool

You may have scanned artwork that you want to convert into FreeHand paths. The Trace tool can recognize the different shapes in the artwork and convert them into vector paths. Before you use the Trace tool you need to import the scanned artwork into your FreeHand document.

To import artwork for tracing:

1. With your document open, choose **File > Import**.
2. Use the navigational tools to find the PICT, TIFF, or EPS file you want to trace. After the file is imported, your cursor changes to a corner symbol.
3. Click with the corner symbol to place the image on the page ㊶.

TIP Though you can trace art on any layer, most people put imported images on layers below the horizontal line of the Layers panel. This lightens the image so it is easier to work with and ensures that it does not print *(see page 156)*.

TIP For best results using the Trace tool, set the preference for Smart image preview resolution to Full Resolution *(see page 397)*.

㊶ *An imported image appears on the page with four anchor points.*

Realistic Expectations for Using the Trace Tool

FreeHand's Trace tool is one of the best in the business—much better than its nearest competitor, and just about as good as the stand-alone tracing product, Adobe Streamline.

However, no automatic tracing tool or dedicated tracing program can do it all! Most likely, when you trace, you will have to manually clean up the image to get it to look good.

This is especially true if you are tracing company logos, text, or other artwork that has very graphic shapes.

You may find that it is easier to use FreeHand's other creation tools to manually trace that type of artwork. For instance, it is easier to use the Ellipse tool to trace a circle than try to get the Trace tool to create a perfect circle.

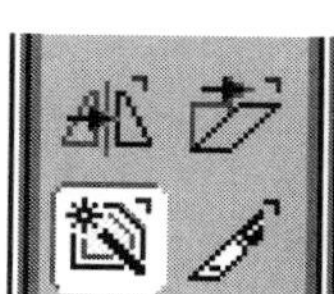

42 *The* **Trace tool** *in the Tools panel.*

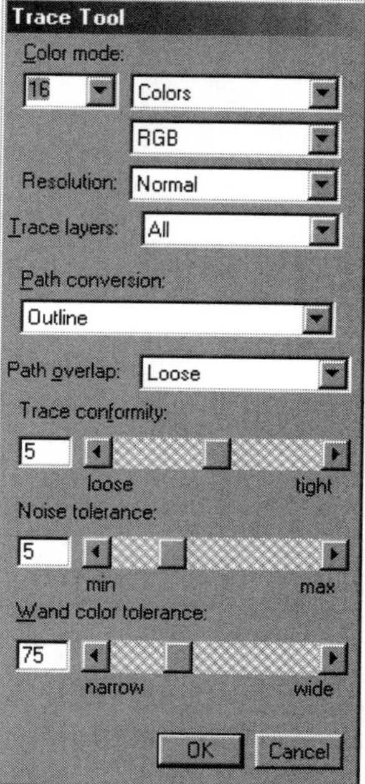

43 *The* **Trace Tool dialog box** *lets you set the controls for how the Trace tool follows the shapes and colors of scanned images.*

Before you can use the Trace tool, you need to set its options, such as how many colors should be created, what kind of image you are working on, and so on.

To set the trace options:

1. Double-click the Trace tool in the Tools panel 42. This opens the Trace Tool dialog box 43.
2. Set the Color mode, Resolution, Trace layers, Path conversion, Trace conformity, Noise tolerance, and Wand color tolerance as detailed in the following exercises.
3. Click OK to apply the settings.

To set the Trace tool Color modes:

1. Use the pop-up list or type the number of colors or shades of gray that you want in the final image.
2. Choose between Colors or Grays for the final objects.
3. If you have chosen Colors, use the second pop-up list to select RGB or CMYK colors.

To set the Trace tool Resolution options:

◆ Set the Resolution options as follows:
  - **High** sets the Trace tool to look at the most details in the image.
  - **Normal** sets the Trace tool to look for less details.
  - **Low** sets the Trace tool to look for the fewest details.

TIP High resolution traces take longer and require more memory.

To set the layers to be traced:

◆ Set the Trace layers options as follows:
  - **All** uses all the layers in the document.
  - **Foreground** uses just the foreground layers.
  - **Background** uses only those layers in the background of the Layers panel.

To set the how the paths are converted:

◆ Set the Path Conversions as follows:

- **Outline** traces the ouside border of the image to create closed, filled paths. This is the option most often used to trace scanned images.
- **Centerline** traces the center of graphic strokes. Use this option if you have an image that has many lines, but few filled areas.
- **Centerline/Outline** uses both options together.
- **Outer Edge** traces only the outside contours of the image. Use this option if you want to mask the silhouette of an image against a background.

To set the sensitivity of the Trace tool:

◆ Set the three sensitivity sliders as follows:

- **Trace conformity** controls how close the traced objects follow the original. Set the value from 0 (lowest conformity) to 10 (highest conformity).
- **Noise tolerance** lets you eliminate any stray pixels, such as dirt or paper grain, in the scan. Set the value from 0 (more noise kept) to 10 (more noise eliminated).
- Wand color lets you set how broad a range of colors the Trace tool recognizes as one final color. Set the value from 0 (narrow range) to 255 (broadest range).

To trace an image:

1. Use the Trace tool to drag a marquee around the part of the image you want to trace 44.
2. Release the mouse button to finish tracing the artwork. The traced objects appear on top of the original image 45.

TIP When tracing photographic images, the Trace tool may create many objects. Choose **Modify > Group** to join the objects into an easily selected group.

44 **Drag a marquee** *with the Trace tool to trace an imported image.*

45 *A comparison of the original scanned image (top) and the traced image (bottom). Notice the small differences in the traced objects.*

46 *Click with the Trace tool to create a selection based on the color of the underlying image.*

47 *The Wand Options dialog box lets you choose how to convert the area selected with the Trace tool.*

48 *An example of how individual elements can be traced by clicking with the Trace tool.*

Rather than draw a marquee around the image, you can also use the Trace tool to select individual areas of a scanned image. This makes it easy to isolate a particular area from the rest of the scan.

To trace specific areas of an image:

1. Click the Trace tool on the area you want to capture. A blue line appears around the area that has been selected 46.
2. If you want to add to the selection, hold the Shift key and click in another area of the image. Continue as many times as necessary to select all the areas you want.
3. Release the Shift key and click the Trace tool inside the selected area. The Wand Options dialog box appears 47.
4. Choose Trace Selection to trace the selected areas as if they had been part of a marquee selection.

   or

   Choose Convert Selection Edge to merge all the selected areas into one selection with a default color of black 48.

Using the Pen and Bezigon Tools

There are two other creation tools in the the Tools panel: the Pen and Bezigon tools. Both allow you much greater control over the shape of the path, especially when you compare them to the Pencil tool ㊾.

However, these tools are not as simple to use as the other creation tools. Therefore I've given them their own chapter *(that follows immediately)* to cover how they work in exquisite detail.

㊾ *Compare the same object drawn with the Pencil tool (top) and the Pen tool (bottom). Notice the uneven areas (circled) in the Pencil tool object. The Pen tool makes it easier to draw smooth paths.*

PEN AND BEZIGON 6

I remember the first time I tried to use the Pen tool in a vector-drawing program. I clicked the tool and dragged across the screen in a way that I thought would create a curve. Instead, I got a wild series of lines that shot out in different directions.

When I tried to change the shape of the lines, things got worse. I was so startled I closed up the program and didn't use the Pen tool again for a long, long, time.

When I finally got up enough nerve to try the Pen, it took a lot of trial and error but eventually I got it! I saw that the principles of using the Pen are actually quite simple.

I just wish someone had written out easy to understand, step-by-step instructions. So, think of this chapter as the instructions on the Pen and Bezigon tools that I wish I had back then.

> This chapter contains everything you should need to master the Pen tool in FreeHand. However, if you would like to learn the Pen tool using movies and audio narration, may I suggest you visit **www.zenofthepen.org**. They have an online tutorial you can purchase that can help you learn the Pen tool in FreeHand as well as other programs such as Adobe Phtoshop.

Working with the Pen Tool

Learning FreeHand's Pen tool makes it easier to learn the Pen tool in Macromedia Fireworks, Macromedia Flash, Adobe Photoshop, QuarkXPress, or Adobe InDesign.

❶ *The* **Pen tool** *in the Tools panel.*

❷ *Clicking with either the Pen or the Bezigon creates a* **corner point** *shown as a hollow square.*

To create straight sides with the Pen:

1. Choose the Pen tool from the Tools panel ❶.
2. Position the cursor where you want the path to start and click. A corner point appears as a white square ❷.
3. Position the cursor for the next point of the object and click. A line extends from the first point to the second point.
4. Continue clicking until you have created all the sides of your object ❸.
5. Create a closed path by clicking the first point again.

TIP Once you finish a path, press Tab to deselect the path. This lets you start a new path instead of continuing the old one.

TIP Hold the Shift key to constrain your lines to 45° increments relative to the constrain axis.

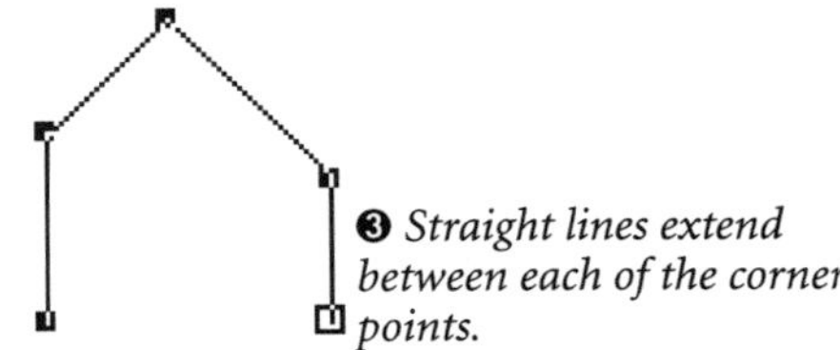

❸ *Straight lines extend between each of the corner points.*

The difference between the Pen and Bezigon tools

Both the Pen and the Bezigon tools allow you to draw much more precisely than the Freehand tool. So what is the difference between the two tools? At first glance, there is very little difference. In fact, once a path has been created, there is no way to tell which tool created it.

The main difference is that the Pen tool allows you to manipulate handles as you place points. The Bezigon tool allows you to quickly click to place points, but all the point handles are set automatically. After you place points with the Bezigon tool, you must then go back to adjust the point handles. This makes the Bezigon tool easier to learn but makes the Pen tool faster when truly mastered.

These days I find find few people who use the Bezigon tool. However, mastering one or the other is vital to working with FreeHand.

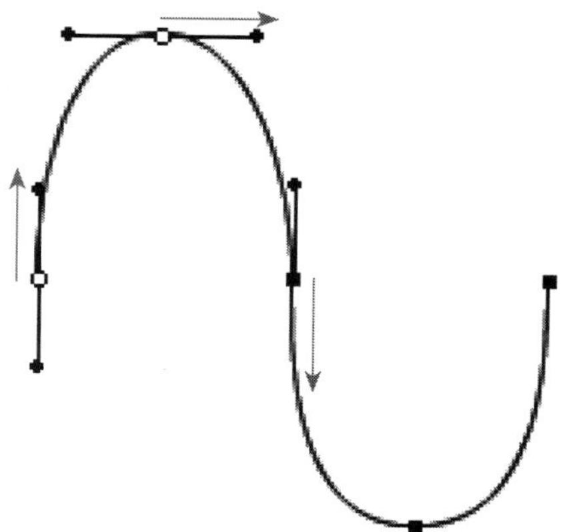

❹ *To draw a smooth curved path with the Pen tool,* **drag to place curve points** *at each spot where the path changes direction.*

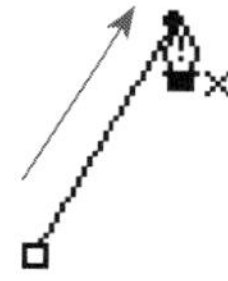

❺ *To start the* **bumpy curved path,** *press the Opt/Alt key and drag with the Pen tool. This creates a corner point with a handle.*

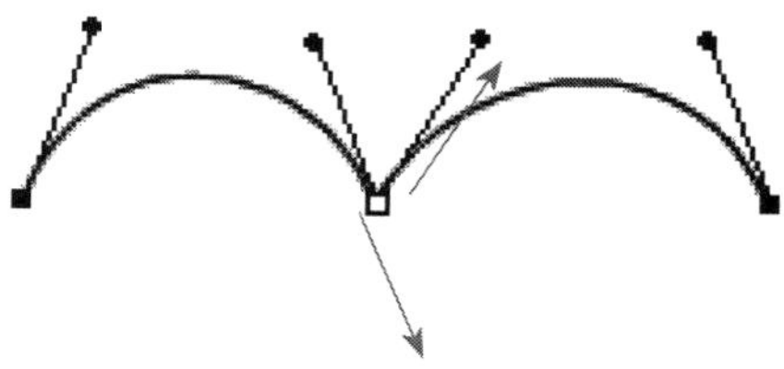

❻ *To create a* **corner point with two handles,** *drag down. When the handle extends backward enough, hold the Opt/Alt key and then drag in the direction of the second arrow.*

The Pen tool helps you draw smooth curves. A smooth curve makes the transition from one direction to another with no abrupt changes, like the curve created by a roller-coaster.

To draw a smooth curved path with the Pen:

1. Choose the Pen tool.
2. Click the first point and drag up. Do not release the mouse until you have created a handle that extends about a third of the way up the curve you want to create ❹.
3. Continue dragging to place curve points at each spot where the path changes direction.
4. Press the Tab key to deselect the path when you have finished creating the path.

TIP You can modify a path by changing both the lengths of the point handles and their directions.

Life is not all smooth, and neither are paths. So, there may be times you need a bumpy curved path—a curved path that makes an abrupt change. Think of a bumpy curve as the path a bouncing ball takes.

To draw a bumpy curved path with the Pen:

1. Hold the Opt/Alt key as you drag with the Pen tool to create a corner point with a handle ❺.
2. Drag down at the second point. Two point handles extend out from the sides of the point. Do not release the mouse button.
3. When the point handle in the back has extended out enough, press the Opt/Alt key. Then rotate the front point handle so that it aligns properly ❻. You may then release the mouse button.
4. Drag to create the final point.

Imagine you are riding in a car, and suddenly there is a bump in the road. As your car travels up and down the bump it follows the shape of a straight-to-bumpy path.

To draw a straight-to-bumpy path with the Pen:

1. Click to place the first corner point.
2. Click to create the next corner point.
3. To add a handle to this point, hold the Opt/Alt key and then drag ❼.
4. Drag to create a curve point at the end of the bump.
5. To add a straight line from the third point, hold the Opt/Alt key and move the Pen tool over the point. A small caret appears next to the Pen cursor.
6. Click on the point. This converts the point into a corner point and retracts the second handle ❽.

FreeHand has a special kind of point—the connector point—that is not found in most other vector-drawing programs. Connector points provide a smooth transition between straight lines and curves. Connector points ensure that the handle that defines the curve always stays aligned with the direction of the straight line ❾.

To create connector points using the Pen:

◆ (Mac) Hold the Control key (Mac) and click to create a connector point.

(Win) Hold the Alt key and click with the right mouse button.

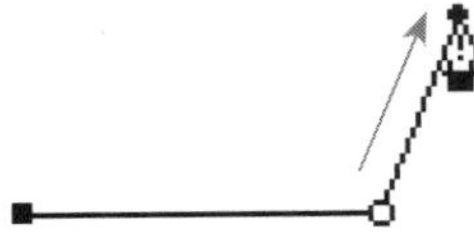

❼ *To* **add a handle to a corner point,** *hold the Opt/Alt key and then drag on the point.*

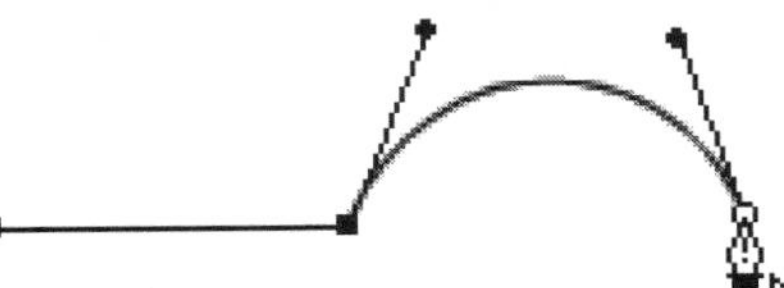

❽ *To retract a handle from a curve point, press the Opt/Alt key and click the point again.*

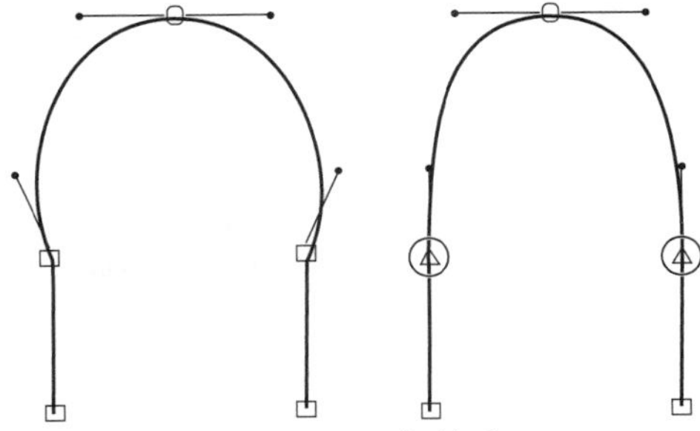

❾ *Unlike the curve points (left) the* **connector points** *(circled) always stay aligned to the straight lines they are connected to.*

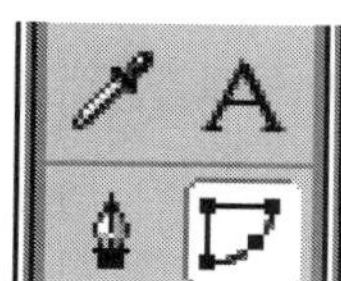

(10) *The* **Bezigon tool** *in the Tools panel.*

(11) *Clicking with the Bezigon creates a* **corner point** *shown as a hollow square.*

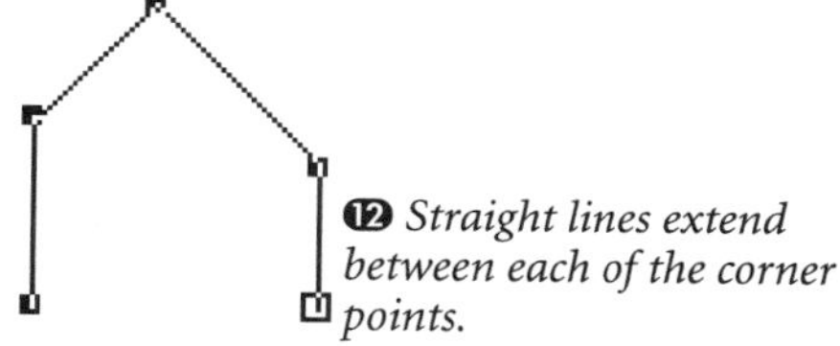

(12) *Straight lines extend between each of the corner points.*

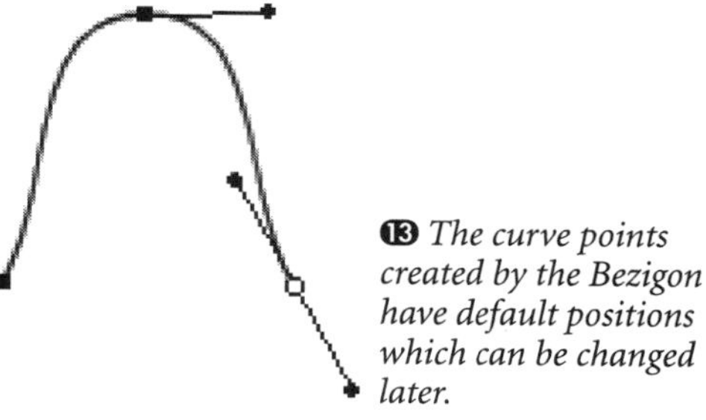

(13) *The curve points created by the Bezigon have default positions which can be changed later.*

Creating Paths with the Bezigon Tool

If you find it difficult to remember all the moves with the Pen, you may find it easier to create objects with the Bezigon.

To create straight sides with the Bezigon tool:

1. Choose the Bezigon tool from the Tools panel (10).
2. Position the cursor where you want the path to start and click. A corner point appears as a white square (11).
3. Position the cursor for the next point of the object and click. A line extends from the first point to the second point.
4. Continue clicking until you have created all the sides of your object (12).
5. Create a closed path by clicking the first point again.

TIP Once you finish a path, press Tab to deselect the path. This lets you start a new path instead of continuing the old one.

When you place curve points with the Bezigon, you only plot the position of each point. After you are done, you reshape the points to the exact shape of the curve.

To draw a smooth curved path with the Bezigon:

1. Choose the Bezigon tool and place your first curve point holding down the Opt/Alt key.
2. Hold the Opt/Alt key and click to create a second curve point. Although the segment between the points may not look correct, don't worry.
3. Keep holding the Opt/Alt key and click to create all the curve points.
4. Use the Pointer tool to adjust the point handles so the curve is the proper shape (13).

When you use the Bezigon tool to create a bumpy path, you need an extra point at the top of the bump.

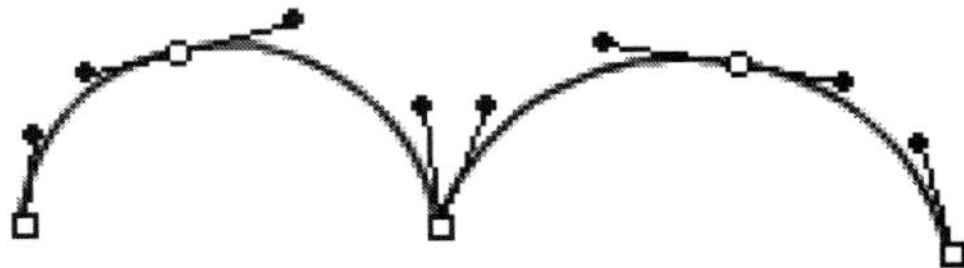

⓮ The Bezigon tool requires a curve point at the top of the bump to create a bumpy path.

To draw a bumpy path with the Bezigon:

1. Click to create the first point, which is a corner point.
2. Hold the Opt/Alt key and click to add a curve point at the top of the bump. This adds a handle to the first corner point.
3. Click to create a corner point. A handle is added because this point is connected to a curve point.
4. Hold the Opt/Alt key and click to add a curve point at the top of the second bump. A handle is added to the previous corner point ⓮.
5. Click to create the final corner point. A handle is added because this point is connected to a curve point.

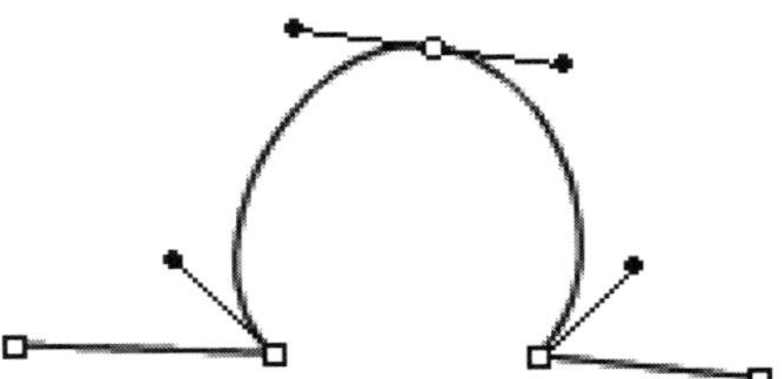

⓯ The Bezigon tool automatically add handles to the corner points that are connected to the top curve point.

To draw a straight-to-bumpy path with the Bezigon:

1. Click to create a corner point.
2. Click again to create a corner point. The two points are connected by a line.
3. Hold the Opt/Alt key and click where the top of the bump should be. This creates a curve point. It also adds a handle to the corner point created in Step 2.
4. Click to create the next corner point ⓯. This adds a handle to the corner point that is connected to the curve point.
5. Click to create the final corner point that creates the straight line.

You create connector points with the Bezigon the same way as you do with the Pen.

To create connector points using the Bezigon:

- (Mac) Hold the Control key (Mac) and click to create a connector point.

  (Win) Hold the Alt key and click with the right mouse button.

⓰ *The slash next to the cursor indicates that you can click or drag to add points to the path.*

Adding Points to a Path

You may finish creating a path and later realize you want to add more segments to it. You then add points to the end of the path. (This only works with open paths. Closed paths have no endpoints.)

To add points to the end of a path:

1. Move the Pen or Bezigon over the endpoint that you want to continue. A slash appears next to the cursor ⓰.
2. Click to create a corner point.

   or

   Drag to extend a handle out from the point.
3. Click to add more points to the path.

WORKING WITH POINTS 7

As you have seen in the previous chapters, all the objects created by the creation tools are called paths. And all paths consist of points that are joined by segments.

As soon as you start to change the shape of objects, it is necessary to understand what the different types of points are and how they can be modified. You also need to understand how to work with the handles that extend out from points.

Fortunately, Macromedia FreeHand gives you a wealth of powerful tools for working with points—either manually or automatically.

Understanding the Types of Points

If you are familiar with programs such as Macromedia Fireworks, or Adobe Illustrator, you should understand the basic aspects of working with points.

The basics of points

There are three elements to working with points (also called anchor points). There is the point itself, the line segment that connects the point to other points on the path, and point handles that may extend out from the point ❶.

TIP Points and point handles are displayed in the highlight color of the layer that they are on *(see page 158)*.

Handles are nonprinting lines that control the direction along which any path curves. Changing the direction of the handle changes the shape of the path ❷.

Point handles are also called Bézier (pronounced Bay-zee-ay) handles. They were named after the French mathematician Pierre Bézier. He invented the mathematical principles that control handles.

Three different types of points make up FreeHand objects: corner points, curve points, and connector points. In order to have a complete understanding of FreeHand, it is vital to understand how these points work.

Corner points

Corner points are anchor points that allow paths to have an abrupt change in direction. Depending on how they were created, there are three different types of corner points: points with no handles, points with two handles, and points with one handle ❸.

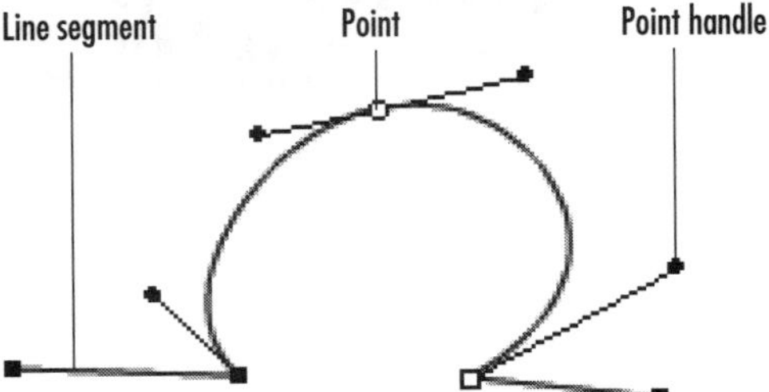

❶ *The different elements that combine to create a path.*

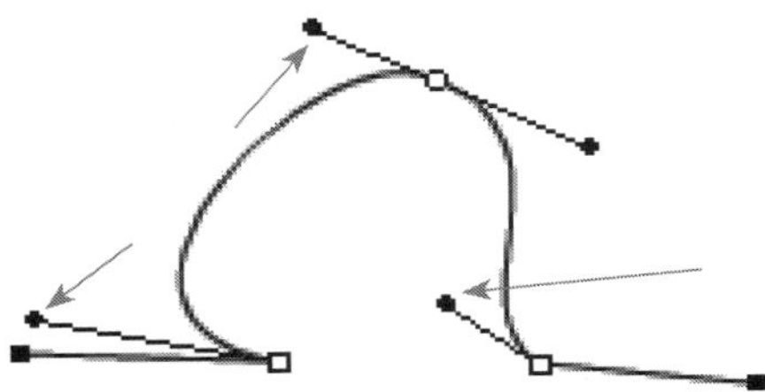

❷ *The results of moving the point handles in the directions indicated.*

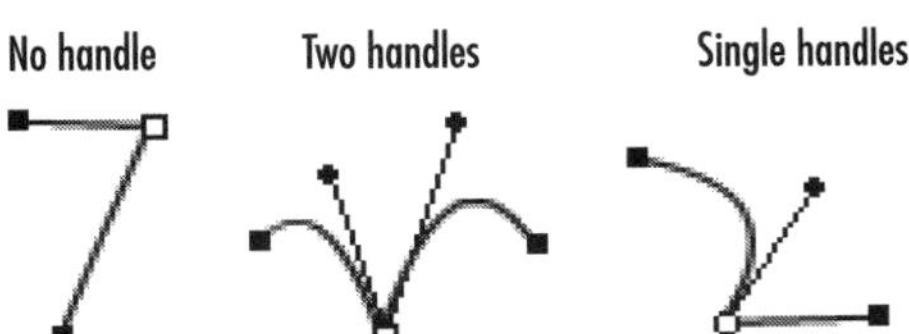

❸ **Corner points** *are indicated by white squares and can have no handles (left), two handles (middle), or one handle (right).*

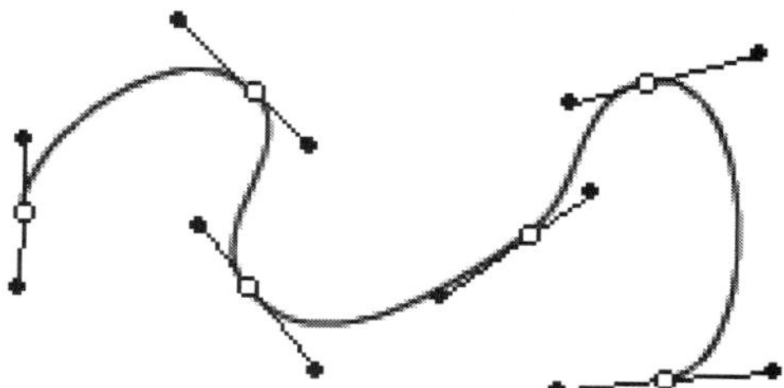

❹ **Curve points** *are indicated by round dots and always have two point handles that govern the shape of the curve.*

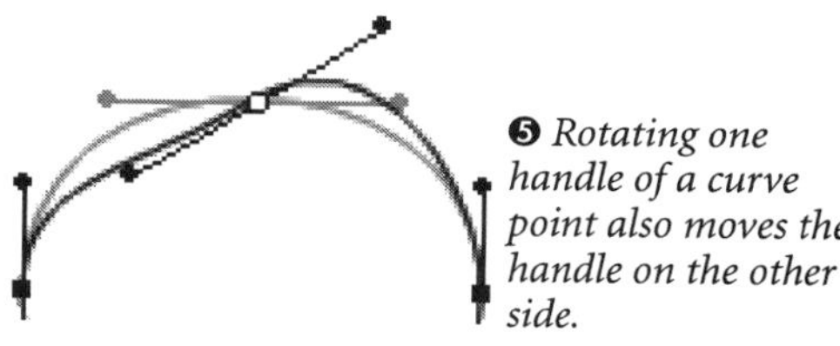

❺ *Rotating one handle of a curve point also moves the handle on the other side.*

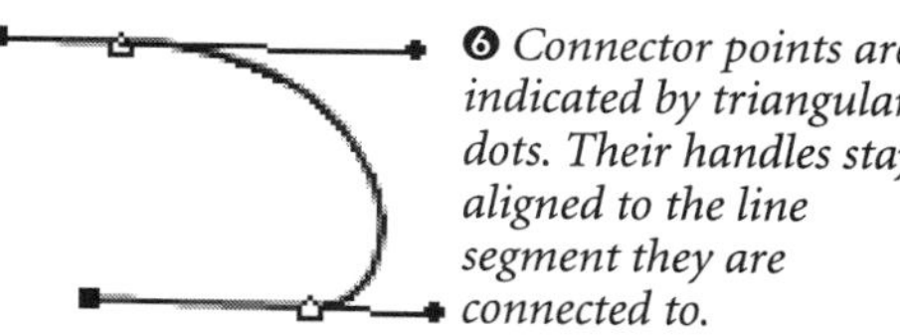

❻ *Connector points are indicated by triangular dots. Their handles stay aligned to the line segment they are connected to.*

> **The one-third rule**
>
> The one-third rule says to limit the length of the point handles for any segment to no more than one-third of the length of that segment.
>
> What happens if you break the one-third rule? Well, no one will come to arrest you, but you will find it difficult to edit your curves with long point handles that pivot all over the place.

Curve points

Curve points are anchor points that make a smooth, curved transition along the direction of the path. A curve point has two handles that extend out from both sides of the point. However, unlike corner points that may have two handles, the handles on curve points are linked so that as the handle on one side moves, the handle on the other side also moves. The length of the handle governs the shape of the curve ❹.

TIP If you rotate the point handle on one sids of a curve point, the handle on the opposite side also moves. It is this "lever" action that makes the curve transition smooth ❺.

Connector points

The purpose of connector points is to constrain the transition between segments so that they cannot be moved out of alignment with their line segments ❻. Connector points are indicated by triangular dots and always have point handles.

Connector points can have one or two point handles. When a connector point occurs between a straight-line segment and a curved segment, there is only one point handle, which runs along the same direction as the straight line. When a connector point is between two curved segments, there are two point handles which are constrained by the position of the points on either side of the connector point.

TIP FreeHand provides two types of handles on the levers that come out of the points. The illustrations in this book show the small handles. You can work with the large handles by switching the Preferences settings *(see Appendix C)*.

Selecting Points

Anchor points define the shape of paths. So when you select and work with the points on a path, you also change the shape of the path. This is how great artwork begins.

FreeHand has two tools that select and move points: the Pointer tool and the Subselect tool. However, as you shall see, the Subselect tool can be found as an option when working with the Pointer tool.

To select points by clicking:

1. Click the Pointer tool in the Tools panel ❼.
2. Move the tip of the arrow of the Pointer tool on the path and click. This selects the path with its anchor points visible ❽. Although the anchor points are visible, they are not individually selected.

TIP Do not use a path drawn with the Rectangle or Ellipse tools unless you have first ungrouped the objects *(see pages 103–104 for more information on grouping and ungrouping objects)*.

3. Move the tip of the arrow over one of the points and click. The point is now selected and is shown as a hollow dot ❾. If it has point handles, they will be visible.
4. Hold the Shift key and click with the Pointer tool to select additional points.

TIP If you need to deselect a point, hold the Shift key and click on the selected point. This deselects the point without deselecting the path or other points.

❼ *The* **Pointer tool** *in the Tools panel.*

❽ *The* **anchor points of a path** *show up as dark squares when the entire path is selected.*

❾ *A* **point on a path** *is displayed as a hollow dot when that single point is selected.*

For Adobe Illustrator Fans

Selected points on a path are usually displayed as hollow dots. Unselected points are usually solid. However, you can reverse this by choosing Show Solid Points in the FreeHand General Preferences *(see Appendix C)*.

This setting displays selected points as solid dots and unselected points as hollow dots. This is how Adobe Illustrator displays points. Those who move from Illustrator to FreeHand may feel more comfortable working this way. (Sadly Adobe is not as welcoming for those moving from FreeHand to Illustrator.)

Selecting Points

⑩ **Drag a marquee** *with the Pointer tool to select the points inside the marquee rectangle.*

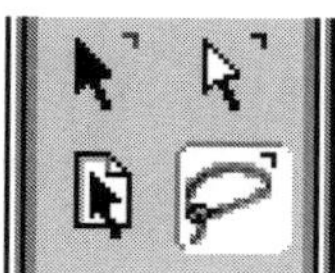

⑪ *The* **Lasso tool** *in the Tools panel.*

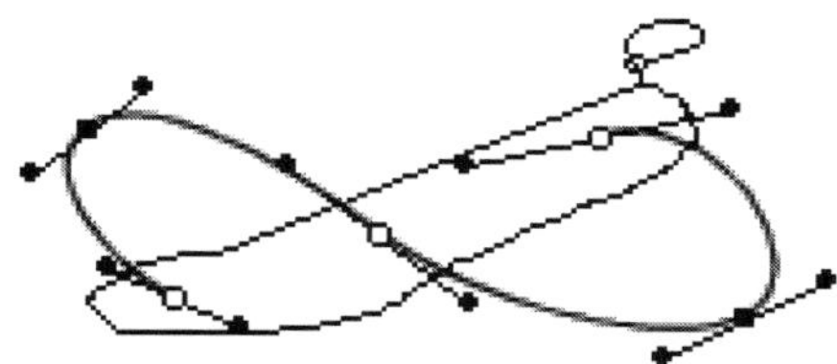

⑫ *Use the* **Lasso tool** *to select points within a non-rectangular area.*

Another way to select points is by using the Pointer to marquee an area around the points you want to select.

To select points with a marquee:

1. Place the Pointer tool outside the point or points you want to select.
2. Press and drag to create a rectangle that surrounds the points you want selected ⑩. The area inside the rectangle is the *marquee.*
3. Release the mouse button. This selects all points inside the marquee.

TIP To select points in more than one area, create your first selection marquee. Then press the Shift key and create your next selection marquee.

TIP Hold the Cmd/Ctrl key to temporarily switch from another tool to the Pointer tool.

Sometimes creating a marquee may select points you don't want selected. In that case you may want to use the Lasso tool, which can select points in a non-rectangular area.

To select points within a non-rectangular area:

1. Choose the Lasso tool in the Tools panel ⑪.
2. Place the Lasso tool outside the point or points you want to select.
3. Press and drag to create an area that surrounds the points you want selected ⑫.
4. Release the mouse button. This selects all points inside the marquee.

To deselect points that are selected:

- Click elsewhere on the work page to deselect points.

Modifying Points and Handles

The shape of a path depends on the types of points on the path. You can change the shape of a path by changing the type of point or changing the point handles.

To modify points using the Object inspector:

1. Use the Pointer tool to select one of the points on a path.
2. In the Object inspector, click the Point type icons for Curve point, Corner point, or Connector point ⓭.
3. Click the Handles icons to retract the handles going into and out of the point.

TIP The left icon retracts the handle going into a point. The right icon retracts the handle coming out of a point.

4. With a curve point selected, choose the Automatic setting. This sets the point handles to the position and length that is best suited for the shape of the path ⓮.

TIP The Bezigon tool creates points with the Automatic setting turned on.

5. Use the Point location **x** field to set the horizontal position of the point.
6. Use the Point location **y** field to set the vertical position of the point.

TIP If you select multiple points on a path, you can change all the point attributes except their Point location.

To retract handles manually:

1. Select a point so that its handles are visible.
2. Place the Pointer tool or Subselect tool on the dot at the end of the handle.
3. Drag the handle into the anchor point ⓯.

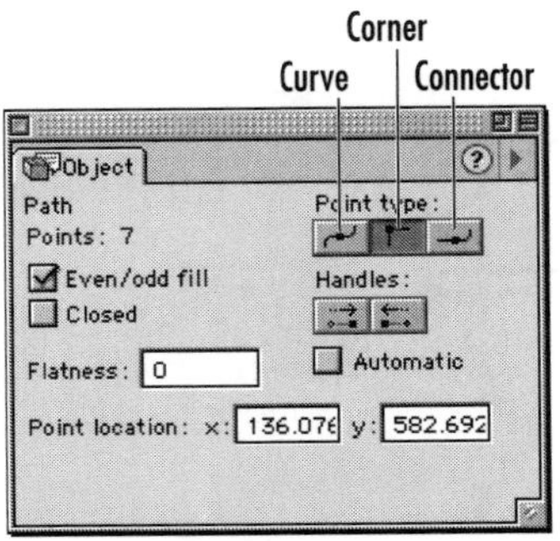

⓭ *With a point selected, you can use the Object inspector to modify points and their handles.*

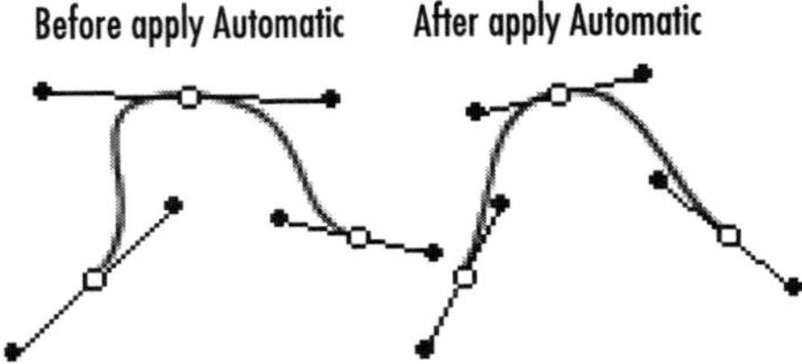

⓮ *A comparison of how the Automatic setting changes the position and length of point handles.*

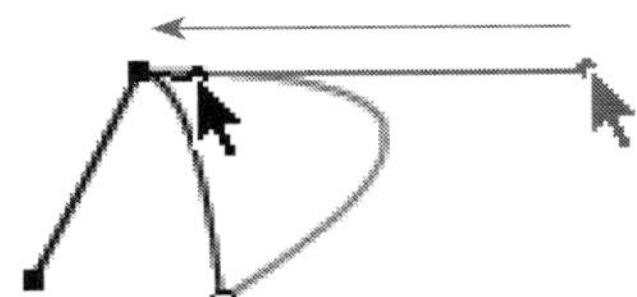

⓯ *You can* **manually drag a point handle** *back into its anchor point.*

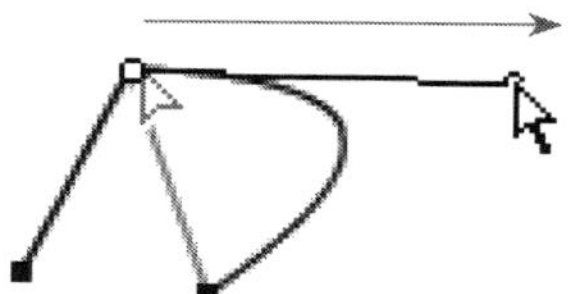

⓰ *Use the Subselect tool to* **manually extend a point handle** *out from a point.*

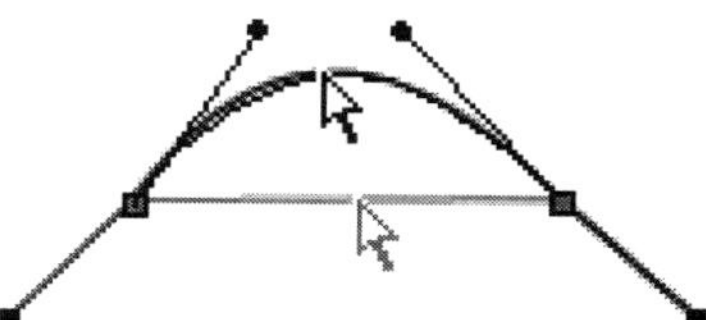

⓱ *Drag with the Subselect tool to* **manually extend point handles** *from both ends of the segment.*

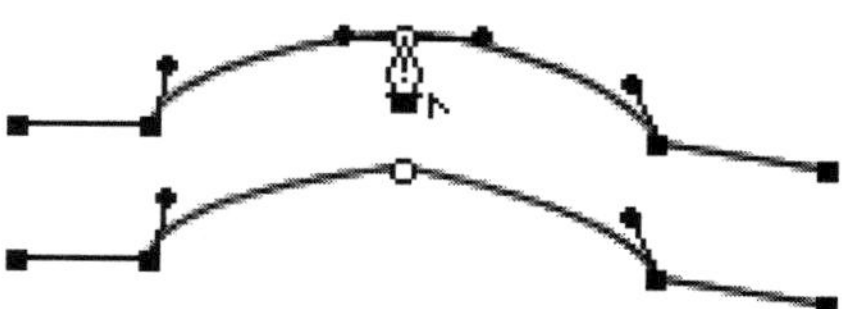

⓲ *Place the Pen over a point (top) and click to* **retract the handles** *(bottom).*

⓳ *Drag with the Pen over a point to extend handles out from the point.*

To extend a single handle manually:

1. Use the Subselect tool to select the point from which you want to extend the handles.
2. Position the pointer over the selected point. A white curved arrowhead appears.
3. Drag to extend the handle out from the point ⓰.

TIP You can hold the Opt/Alt key while in the Pointer tool to access the Subselect tool.

You can also extend two handles at once from the points at either end of a segment. (This technique is sometimes called the "Bend-O-Matic.")

To extend two handles manually:

1. Use the Subselect tool to select the line segment between two points.
2. Drag the line segment. A handle extends out from each of the points on either side of the segment ⓱.

TIP If you use the Pointer tool, hold the Opt/Alt key to access the Subselect tool.

To retract handles with the Pen:

1. Move the Pen tool over the point. A small caret (^) symbol appears next to the cursor ⓲.
2. Click. The handles of the point are automatically retracted.

To extend handles with the Pen:

1. Move the Pen tool over the point. A minus sign (–) appears next to the cursor ⓳.
2. Drag but do not click. The point is converted to a curve point and handles extend out.

TIP If you click instead of drag, you will delete the point *(see the next page)*.

Points on a Path

As you create paths, you may need to delete or add points to make other modifications to the path.

⑳ *When you delete a point, you reshape the path.*

To delete selected point from a path:

1. Select the point or points you want to delete.
2. Press the Delete key. The point is deleted and the path reshapes ⑳.

TIP If you delete an endpoint from a path, the path is reshaped, and the next endpoint is selected. You can then continue to delete each point along the path ㉑.

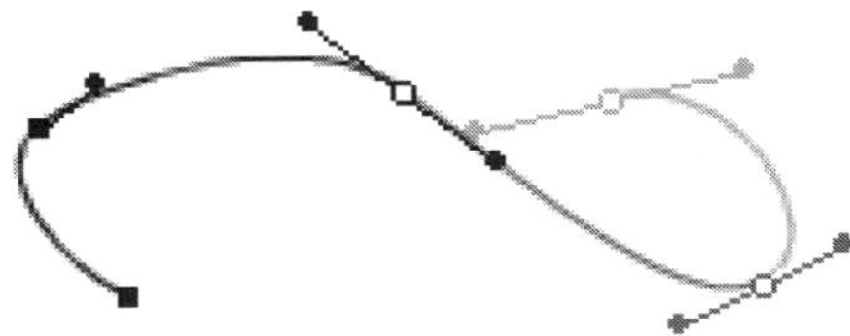

㉑ *When you delete an endpoint, the next point along the path is selected. This point can then be deleted and so on.*

You can also use the Pen or Bezigon tools to delete points from a path. This is helpful if you do not have your hands near the delete key on the keyboard.

To delete a point using the Pen or Bezigon tools:

1. Select the path.
2. Move the Pen or Bezigon tool over the point you want to delete. If the point has no handles, a minus sign (–) appears next to the cursor ㉒.
3. If the minus sign appears, click to delete the point.

   or

   Click to retract the handles. You can then click again to delete the point.

TIP You can't use the Pen or Bezigon to delete an endpoint from a path.

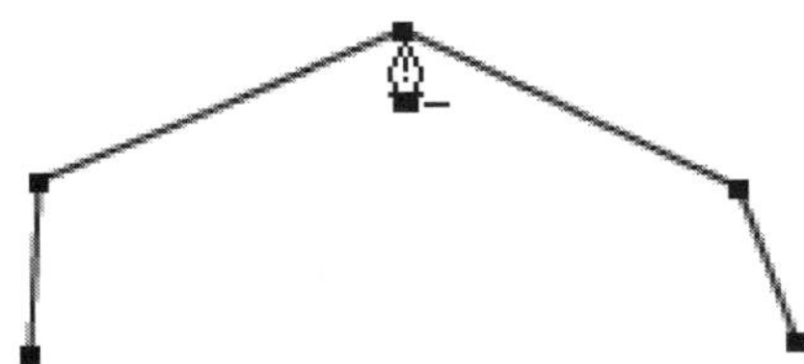

㉒ *Click with the Pen or Bezigon tools to* **delete a point** *from a path.*

Open or Closed Paths

There are two types of paths: open and closed. Open paths have points at the end of the path called *endpoints.* A piece of string is an example of an open path.

Closed paths do not have endpoints. A rubber band is an example of a closed path.

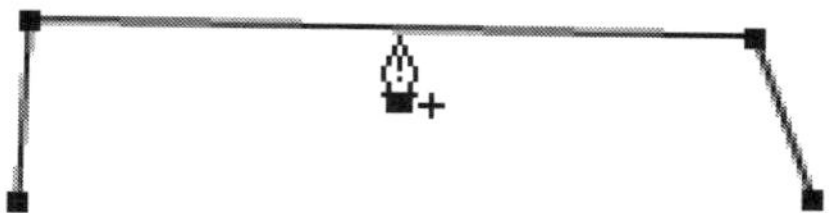

❷❸ *To* **add a point to a path**, *click with the Pen or the Bézigon tool on the path.*

❷❹ *The* **Join command** *automatically created a new line segment connecting the points.*

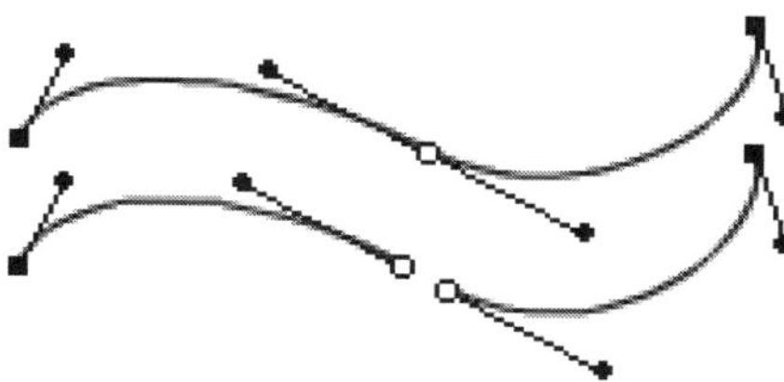

❷❺ *A point on the top path was selected and the* **Split command** *was applied. This created the bottom two paths. (Points were moved to show the separation.)*

You can also use the Pen or Bezigon tools to add points to a path.

To add a point to a path:

1. Select the path.
2. Move the Pen or Bezigon tool where you want the new point. A plus sign (+) appears next to the cursor ❷❸.
3. Click. A point appears where you clicked.

TIP If you click too far away from the path, you create a new point that is not part of the path.

To connect points:

1. Choose two open paths.
2. Choose **Modify > Join**. FreeHand creates a path between the two closest endpoints of the paths ❷❹. If the two points are on top of each other, FreeHand merges them into one point.

To split a point:

1. Choose a single point on a path.
2. Choose **Modify > Split**. FreeHand splits the point into two points on top of each other ❷❺.

TIP There is no indication that the points separate; select the points and then move one manually to see the split.

WORKING WITH PATHS 8

Sometimes I think of anchor points as the atomic particles of graphics. Think about it—the point is the nucleus and the handle contains the electrons that circle the nucleus.

Paths are the next level up from anchor points. In fact, you could think of paths as the molecules that string individual atoms together. Two curved points joined with a single corner point create one path. Three corner points joined together create another.

When you work with paths you do not change the attributes of the individual points, but you manipulate the path as a whole. This gives you more control over the look of your artwork.

Selecting and Moving Objects

Selecting and moving objects are vital in making changes to artwork.

To select and move an object:

1. Press with the Pointer tool on the objects. A four-headed arrow appears.
2. Pause a moment, and then drag to see a preview as you move the object ❶.

   or

   Drag immediately if you do not need to see the object. Instead you see a bounding box which shows the size of the object ❷.

TIP If you do not see the preview when you drag objects, change the Redraw preferences setting for Preview drag field *(see page 397)*.

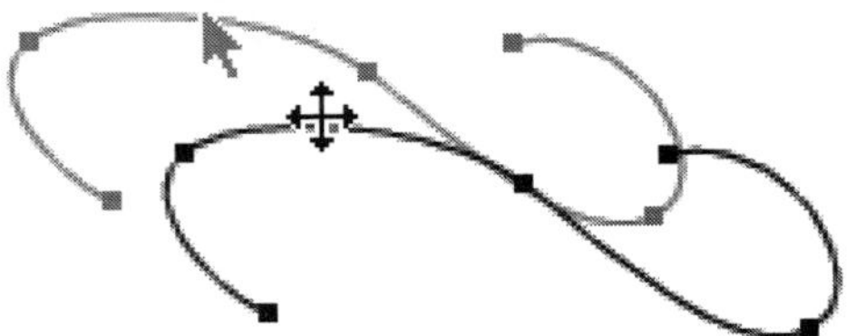

❶ *A path dragged with a* **preview.**

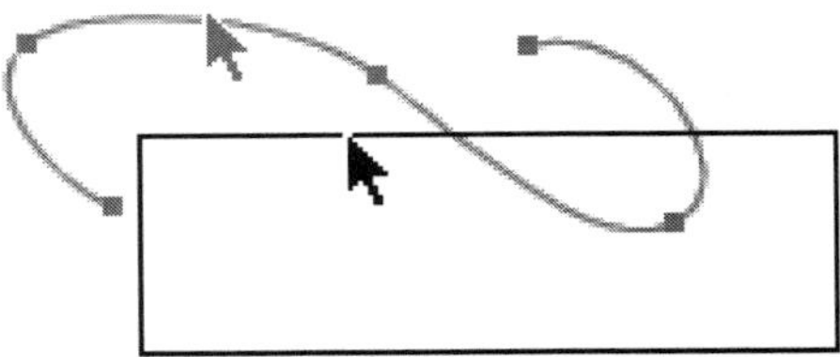

❷ *A path dragged with a* **bounding box.**

Ordinarily you move a path by dragging a line segment. But what if you want to move a path so that one point lies exactly on another point or guide? There is a special technique to move a path by dragging its point.

To move a path by dragging its point:

1. (Win) Deselect the path. (This step is not necessary on the Mac.)
2. Hold the Control key (Mac) or Ctrl key (Win).
3. Using the Pointer tool, position the arrow over the point you want to drag. A dot appears next to the arrow. This indicates you are over a point ❸.
4. Drag the path to the new position. If you drag to another point, a black dot appears next to the cursor. If you drag to a guide, a hollow dot appears.

❸ *A path dragged by its point.*

❹ *When you move a selected point, you also change the shape of the path.*

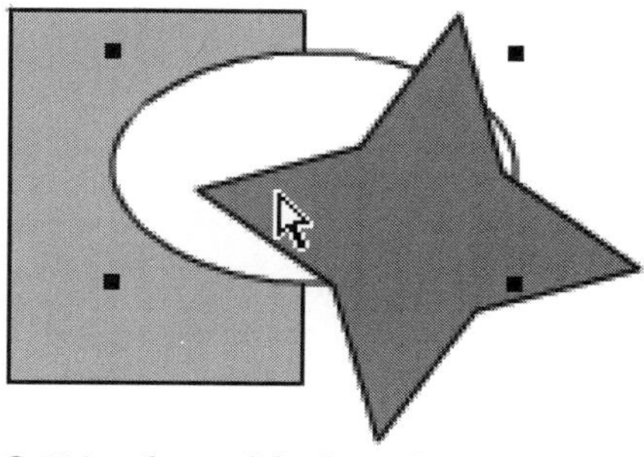

❺ *Using the modifier keys, the circle was selected by clicking twice. The first click selected the star, the second click selected the ellipse.*

To move points on a path:

1. Select the points you want to move.
2. Move the Pointer tool over one of the selected points.
3. Drag the point to the new position. This changes the shape of the path.
4. To change the shape of the path, drag the point you have selected ❹.

To delete an object:

1. Choose the object so that all its anchor points are visible or its group anchor points *(see page 103)* are visible.
2. Press the Delete key or choose **Edit > Clear** to delete the object.

You may find that you want to select objects positioned behind others. Rather than move your mouse to a new position, you can use a modifier key to select behind objects.

(Mac) To select behind objects:

1. Position the cursor over the area where you want to select an object.
2. Hold down Control+Opt keys.
3. Click as many times as necessary to select through to the object behind the others ❺.

(Win) To select behind objects:

1. Position the cursor over the area where you want to select an object.
2. Hold down Control+Alt keys.
3. Right-mouse click as many times as necessary to select through to the object behind the others ❺.

To select all the objects on a page:

◆ Choose **Edit > Select > All.** This selects all objects that touch the page. Objects on other pages or on the pasteboard are not selected ❻.

The above command only selects the objects on the page you are working on. However, you can also select all the objects on all the pages of the document.

To select all the objects in a document:

◆ Choose **Edit > Select > All in Document.** This selects all the objects on all the pages and any objects on the pasteboard ❼.

If you have many objects that you want to select, sometimes it is easier to select the one or two objects that you don't want selected and then invert the selection.

To swap the selected and unselected objects:

1. Select the objects that you ultimately do not want selected.
2. Choose **Edit > Select > Invert Selection.** This deselects the objects that were selected and selects all the other objects on the page.

To deselect an object:

◆ Click with the Pointer, Subselect, or Lasso tools anywhere else in the window.

or

Choose **Edit > Select > None.**

or

If you are not working in a text block press the Tab key.

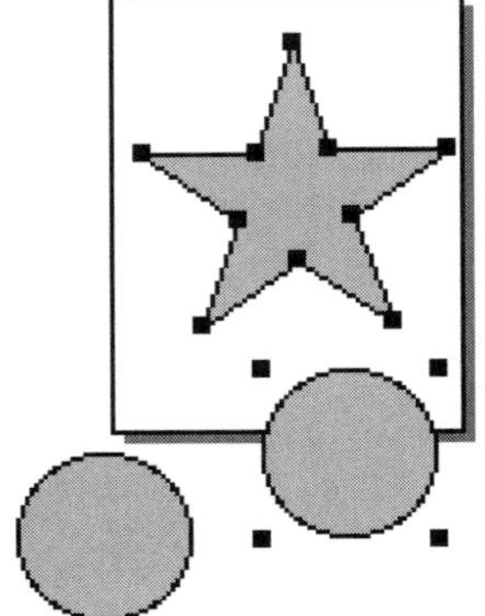

❻ *The* **Select > All** *command selects all the objects on or touching the currently active page.*

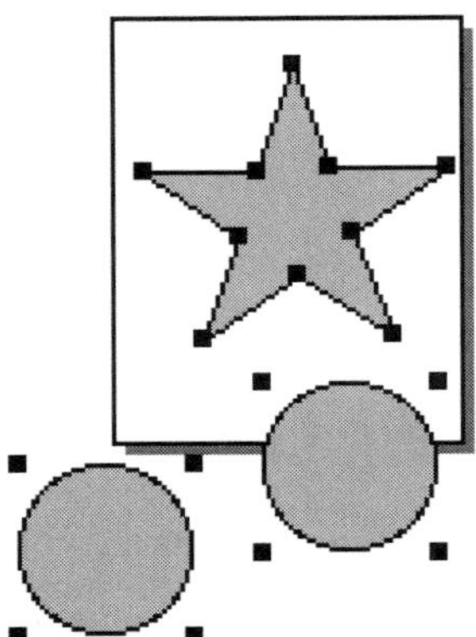

❼ *The* **Select > All in Document** *command selects all the objects on all the pages and the pasteboard.*

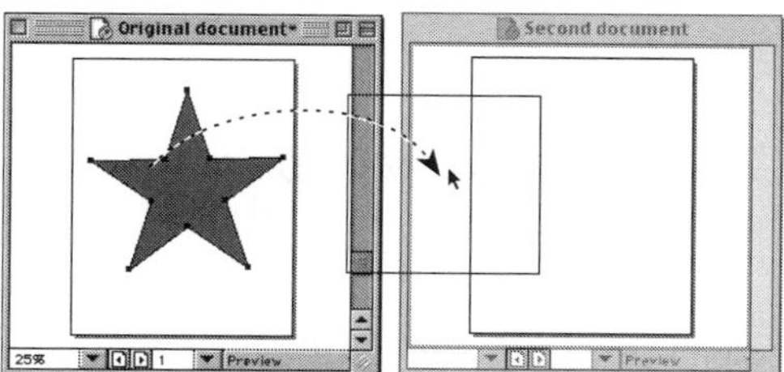

❽ *You can drag and drop objects from one document to another.*

The Computer Clipboard

The Copy and Cut commands place the selected objects into an area of the computer memory called the clipboard. The contents of the clipboard stay within the memory until a new Copy or Cut command is executed or if the computer is turned off. You can even copy objects in FreeHand and paste them into other programs such as Macromedia Fireworks, Macromedia Flash, or Adobe Photoshop.

The clipboard can hold only one set of information at a time. So if you copy one object, and then later copy another, the first object is flushed from the clipboard and replaced by the second.

Using the Clone, Duplicate, Drag and Drop, and Opt/Alt-drag techniques allows you to make copies of objects without losing the current contents of the clipboard.

Copying and Duplicating Objects

One of the conveniences of working in a computer graphics application is that you can make infinite copies of objects.

To copy and paste an object on a page:

1. Select the object (or objects) that you want to copy.
2. Choose **Edit > Copy.** This copies the object to the clipboard.
3. If desired, move to a new position on the page, a new page, or a new document.
4. Choose **Edit > Paste.** A duplicate of the object appears in the middle of the window.

When you copy an object, you leave behind the original. When you cut and paste, it moves from one position to another.

To cut and paste an object:

1. Select the object you want to cut.
2. Choose **Edit > Cut.** This deletes the object and copies it to the clipboard.
3. If desired, move to a new position on the page, a new page, or a new document.
4. Choose **Edit > Paste.** A duplicate of the object appears in the middle of the window.

To drag and drop from one document to another:

1. Position the document windows so you can see both documents.
2. Using the Pointer tool, drag the object from one window across to the other.
3. When the bounding box is inside the second window, release the mouse button. The object appears in the second window ❽.

TIP You can drag and drop from FreeHand to other applications such as Flash or Fireworks.

FreeHand also gives you a command that duplicates objects. This command is useful if you don't want to change the previous contents of the clipboard.

To duplicate an object:

1. Select the object.
2. Choose **Edit > Duplicate.** The new object appears offset from the original ❾.

TIP FreeHand's Clone command also duplicates an object, but the duplicate is positioned right on top of the original. The Clone command is useful when working with the transform commands *(see Chapter 10, "Move and Transform")*.

When you copy to the clipboard, FreeHand uses the best format from the ones set in the Preferences *(see Appendix C)*. The Copy Special command forces FreeHand to copy the selection as a specific file format.

To copy objects to a specific file format:

1. Select the object.
2. Choose **Edit > Copy Special.** The Copy Special dialog box appears ❿.
3. Choose the file format from the list.
4. Click OK. The specified format is copied to the clipboard.

TIP Some file formats in the Copy Special dialog box are available only on the Macintosh or Windows platforms.

You can also force objects copied in other applications to be pasted in a specific format into FreeHand.

To paste objects from other applications:

1. Copy the object in the application.
2. Switch to FreeHand and choose **Edit > Paste Special.** The Paste Special dialog box appears ⓫.
3. Choose the file format from the list and click OK.

❾ *The* **Duplicate** *command makes a copy of the original object and positions it away from the original.*

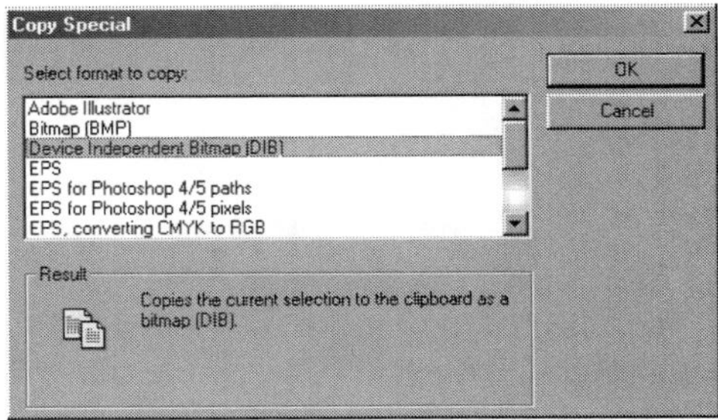

❿ *The* **Copy Special dialog box** *forces FreeHand to copy objects in specific formats.*

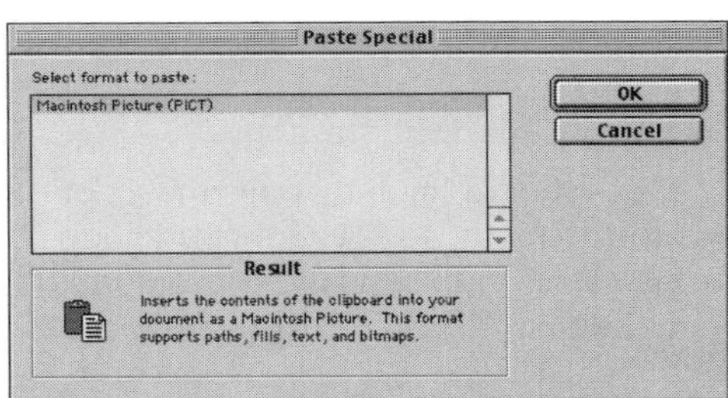

⓫ *The* **Paste Special dialog box** *lets you paste information from other applications.*

⓬ *The anchor points of the selected objects are visible before the objects are grouped.*

⓭ *After the objects are grouped, the group displays* **four anchor points** *when selected.*

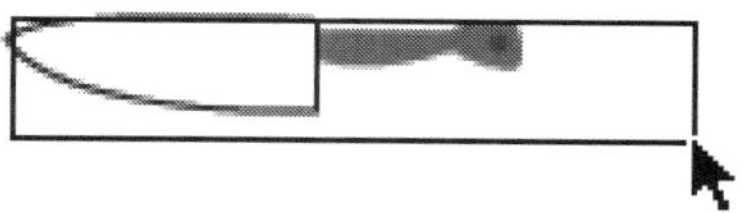

⓮ *Drag one of the group anchor points to resize a grouped object.*

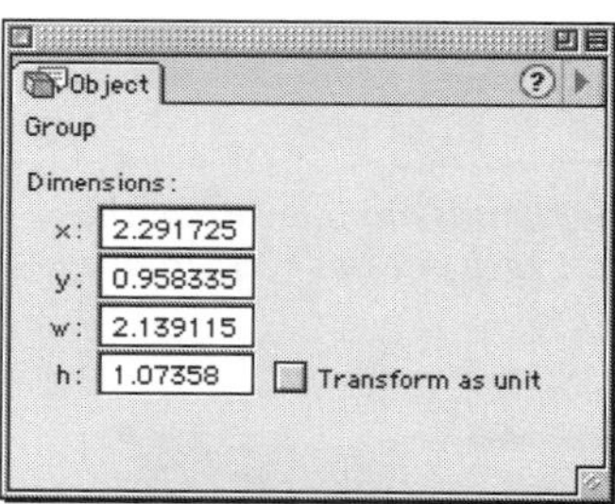

⓯ *When a group is selected, the Object inspector shows the coordinates and dimensions of the group.*

Automatic Groups

Objects drawn with the Rectangle and Ellipse tools are automatically grouped when you draw them.

However, unlike regular groups, you can't use the Subselect tool to select their points.

You must ungroup those objects to select and modify their individual points.

Working with Groups

In order to protect the shape of an object, or to make it easier to select objects, you can group the points on the path or the multiple objects.

To group paths:

1. Select the path or objects you want to group ⓬.
2. Choose **Modify>Group**. Instead of individual points, four group anchor points designate the corners of the path or paths ⓭.

To work with grouped objects:

1. To select a grouped object, click the Pointer tool on the object.
2. To resize a grouped object, drag on one of the four group anchor points that surround the object ⓮.
3. To resize the object without distorting its shape, hold the Shift key as you drag one of the group anchor points.

Once you group objects, they are displayed in the Object inspector as a group. This allows you to make changes to the group as a whole.

To modify a group in the Object inspector:

1. Select the group.
2. Set the attributes in the Object inspector as follows ⓯:
   - Use the **x** field to change the horizontal position of the upper-left corner.
   - Use the **y** field to change the vertical position of the upper-left corner.
   - Use the **w** field to change the width of the group.
   - Use the **h** field to change the height of the group.
3. Press Enter/Return to apply the changes to the group.

To select individual points in a group:

1. Choose the Subselect tool in the Tools panel ⑯.

TIP Instead of the Subselect tool, you can use the Pointer tool while holding the Opt/Alt key.

2. Click one of the objects in the group. The individual points of the object appear.
3. Click the point you want to select. The point is displayed as a hollow dot ⑰.
4. To select additional points, hold the Shift key and click those points.

⑯ *The* **Subselect tool** *in the Tools panel.*

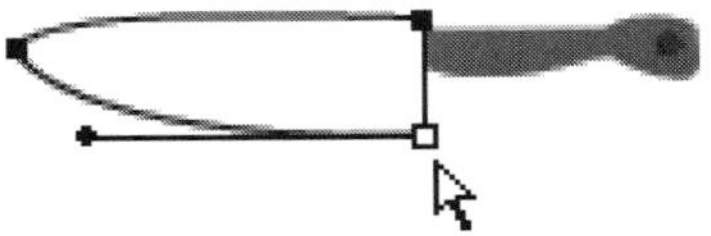

⑰ *Use the Subselect tool to* **select individual points** *of a grouped object.*

You can create levels of groups to make it easier to select objects. This is called nesting.

To nest grouped objects:

1. Select and group the first object.
2. After the object is grouped, deselect it.
3. Group any additional objects ⑱.
4. Select all the individual groups and group them together as a single unit ⑲.

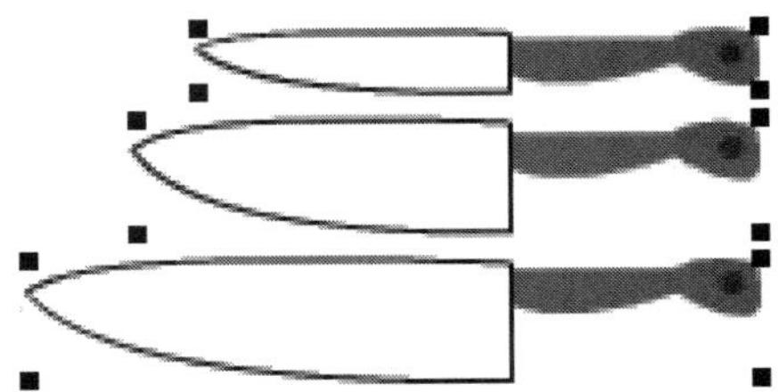

⑱ *The four anchor points around each of the knives indicate that each one has been grouped.*

Once you have taken the time to nest groups, you can easily select the individual groups within the nested group.

To work with nested groups:

1. Use the Subselect tool to select an object or point in a nested group.
2. Press the tilde (~) key. This selects up to the next level of the nest.
3. Continue to press the tilde key until you have selected all the levels you want.

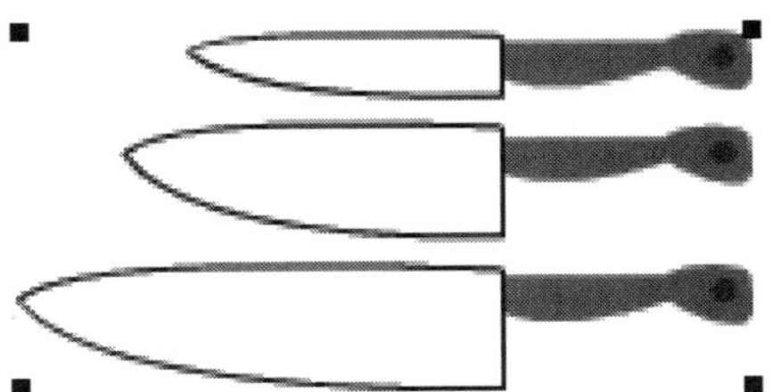

⑲ *The four anchor points around all the knives indicate that they are all part of one group.*

To ungroup an object:

1. Select the grouped object.
2. Choose **Modify > Ungroup**. This ungroups the object.
3. If the object was part of a nested group, choose the Ungroup command again until you have completely ungrouped all the objects.

> **Grouping Techniques**
>
> There is a limit of eight levels for nested objects. And even if you don't exceed that number, numerous nesting levels can cause problems when it comes to printing your file.

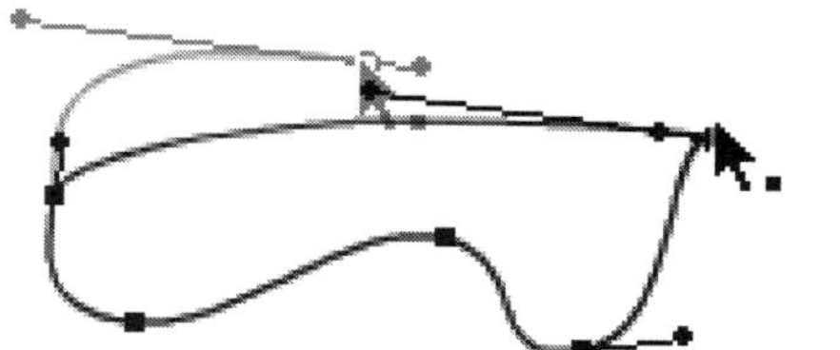

⓴ *To* **close a previously drawn path,** *drag one of the endpoints over the other.*

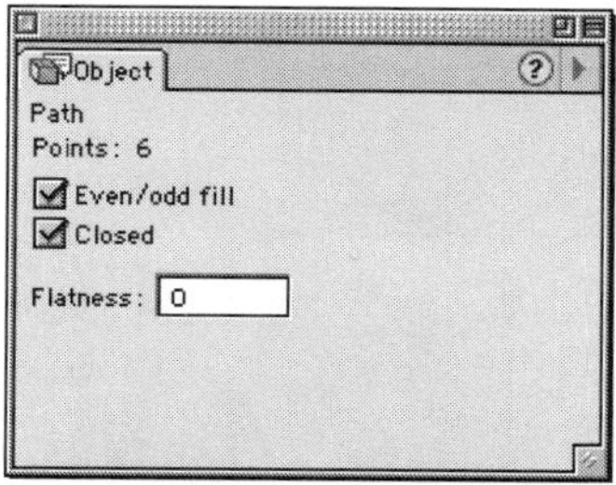

㉑ *A checkmark next to Closed in the Object Inspector indicates a closed path.*

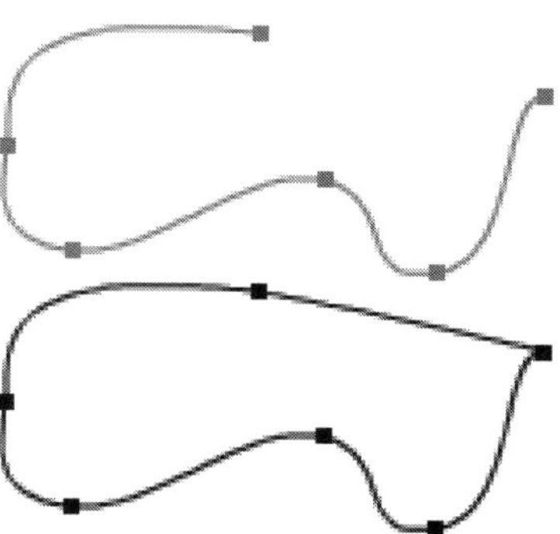

㉒ *Closing an open path (top) adds a segment between the two endpoints (bottom).*

Closing and Opening Paths

When I first started using FreeHand there were times it was absolutely vital to close an open path. For instance, you couldn't fill an object with a color unless it was a closed path. These days it isn't necessary to close a path to see its fill. However, you still may want to close the opening between the endpoints of a path.

To close a previously drawn path:

- Use the Pointer tool to drag one of the endpoints onto the other. As soon as the points touch, the path closes ⓴.

TIP If Snap to Point is turned on, you see a small square next to the cursor when you are close enough to release the mouse button.

To open or close a path using the Object Inspector:

1. Select the path using the Pointer tool.
2. Click the checkbox next to the word Closed in the Object inspector ㉑. A line segment is extended between the endpoints of the path ㉒.

Using the Contact Sensitive Settings

When you use the Pointer or Lasso tools, ordinarily you have to completely encircle the object in order to select it. However, you can change the setting for those tools so that you can circle just a portion of the object and it will be selected. This is called the contact sensitive mode.

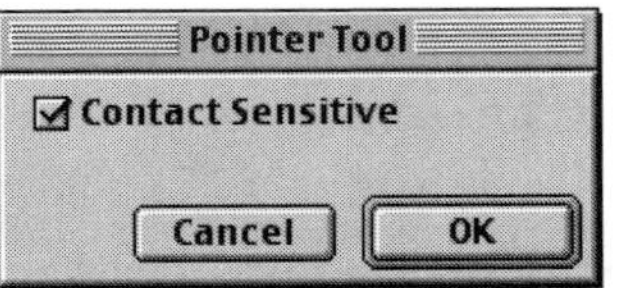

㉓ *The* **Pointer tool** *dialog box lets you turn on the options for the Contact Sensitive mode.*

To set the Pointer to be Contact Sensitive:

1. Double-click the Pointer tool in the Tools panel. This opens the Pointer Tool dialog box ㉓.
2. Click the Contact Sensitive control.
3. Click OK to apply the setting.

To work with the Contact Sensitive Pointer:

- Drag a marquee around a portion of the object you wish to select. When you release the mouse button, the entire object will be selected ㉔.

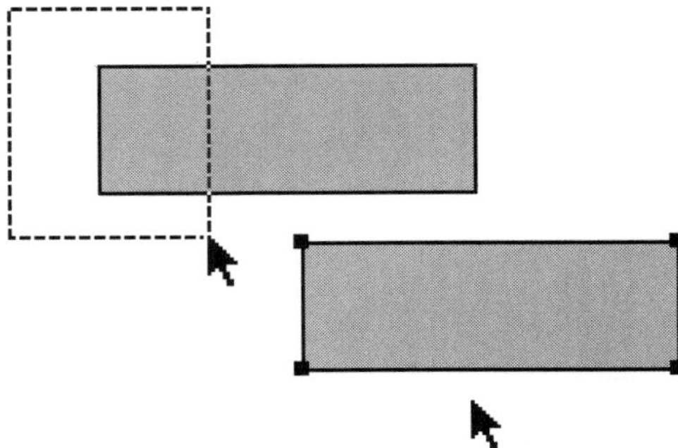

㉔ *When the* **Contact Sensitive mode** *is turned on for the Pointer tool, you can marquee just a portion of an object to select it.*

To set the Lasso to be Contact Sensitive:

1. Double-click the Lasso tool in the Tools panel. This opens the Contact Sensitive dialog box.
2. Click the Contact Sensitive control.
3. Click OK to apply the setting.

To work with the Contact Sensitive Lasso:

- Lasso an area around a portion of the object you wish to select. When you release the mouse button, the entire object will be selected ㉕.

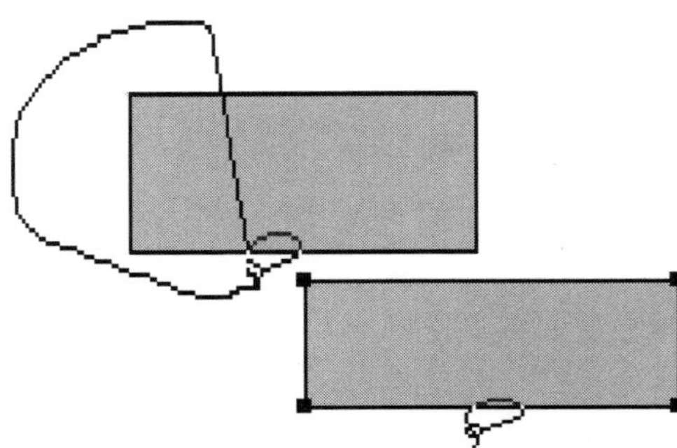

㉕ *When the* **Contact Sensitive mode** *is turned on for the Lasso tool, you can lasso just a portion of an object to select it.*

PATH OPERATIONS 9

Once you have created paths using any of the creation tools, you can modify those paths in a wide variety of ways. These modifications are called *path operations.*

Path operations are actions that start with one or more paths and combine or manipulate them into new shapes. For instance, you can use one shape, like a star, to punch a hole in the side of another shape, such as a circle. This is much faster and simpler than trying to manually draw a circle with a star cut out of its side.

This chapter looks at the majority of path operations. Some specialized path operations such as blends are covered in other chapters.

Joining Paths

Imagine you have created an illustration of a doughnut with a hole in the center. You need a special type of path to see through the hole. In FreeHand, these are called joined paths or composite paths.

TIP This type of effect is sometimes called compound paths in other programs.

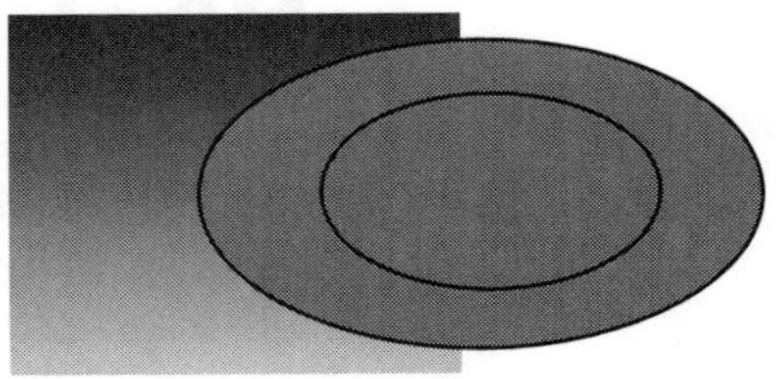

❶ *Two objects before they are joined to make a composite path.*

To create joined paths:

1. Select the objects that you want to join ❶.
2. Choose **Modify > Join.** This creates a hole in the object that you can see through ❷.

TIP If the second object is not completely contained inside the first, the hole will appear where both objects overlap ❸.

TIP After you apply the Join command, the objects have the same fill and stroke attributes.

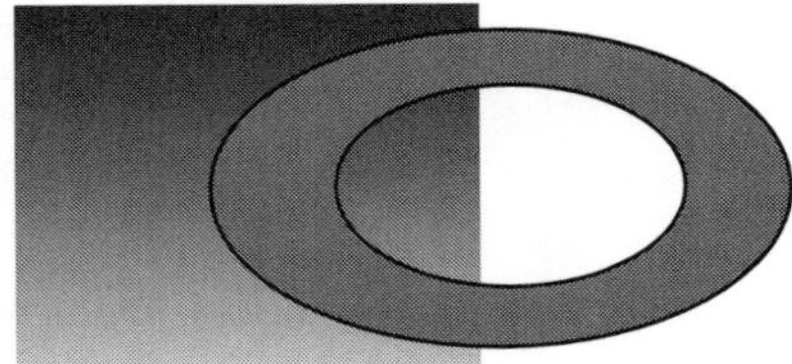

❷ *Two objects after they have been joined to make a* **joined or composite path.**

To split joined objects:

1. Select the entire joined object.
2. Choose **Modify > Split.** This releases the paths into separate objects.

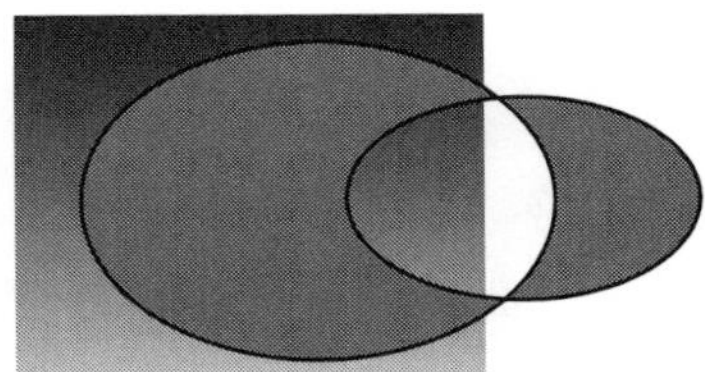

❸ *The transparency between composite paths is visible where the two objects overlap.*

To modify the paths of a joined object:

1. Use the Subselect tool to select the path. The anchor points appear.
2. Move or modify the path as you would work with a grouped object *(see pages 103–104).*

❹ *A* **clipping path** *is needed so that the rectangles are not visible outside the edges of the star.*

❺ *When the rectangles are* **pasted inside** *the star, the star acts as a clipping path.*

❻ *Drag the* **paste inside handle** *(circled) to reposition the objects pasted inside a clipping path.*

Masking

Have you ever seen those posters that show celebrity photos inside star shapes? Rather than cut the photo into the star shape, a mask is used to hide the parts of the image that are outside the star. Pasting an object inside another allows you to fill objects so that anything outside the objects will not be seen. The object that is filled is called a clipping path or mask.

To mask objects:

1. Position the objects to be masked over the object that is to act as the clipping path ❹.
2. Select the objects and choose **Edit > Cut** to put those objects on the clipboard.
3. Select the object to be used as the clipping path and choose **Edit > Paste Inside**. The objects pasted from the clipboard are visible only inside the clipping path ❺.

TIP Use the Subselect tool to select objects pasted inside the clipping path.

To move masked objects:

1. Select the clipping path; a diamond-shaped paste inside handle appears.
2. Drag the paste inside handle to move the objects within the clipping path ❻.

TIP To transform just the clipping path without affecting the objects pasted inside, make sure the Contents box in the Transform panel is not checked. *(See Chapter 10, "Move and Transform" for information on working with the Transform panel.)*

To release masked objects:

◆ Select the clipping path and choose **Edit > Cut Contents.**

Masking

Setting Path Direction

As you create paths, the path direction comes from the order that you create the anchor points. The first point you create is considered the start of the path and the last point the end. Even closed paths such as the rectangles and ellipses that FreeHand creates have a direction. Ordinarily it doesn't make too much difference what direction is applied to a path. However, there are sometimes when the path direction does matter.

To change the direction of a path:

1. Select the path you want to change.
2. Choose **Modify > Alter Path > Reverse Direction.**

   or

   Choose **Xtras > Cleanup > Reverse Direction.**

TIP The Reverse Direction command is obvious when applied to paths that are part of a blend ❼ *(see Chapter 17, "Blends")* or applied to the path that has text attached to a path ❽ *(see Chapter 20, "Text Effects)*.

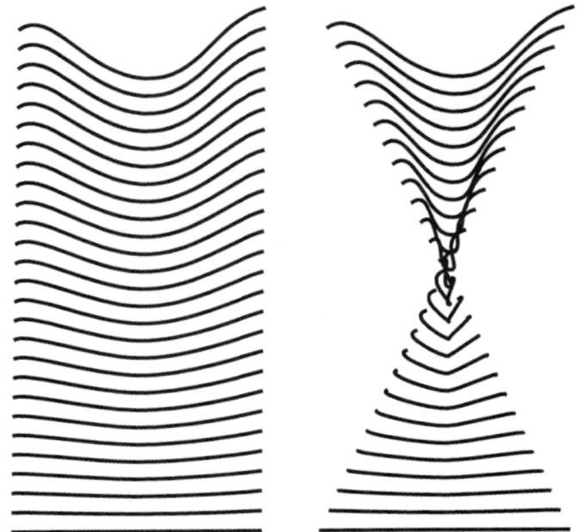

❼ *When objects with the same direction are blended (on the left), the blend is smooth. When the direction of the top object (on the right) is reversed, the shape of the blend changes.*

❽ *The text on a path (top) is positioned on the top of the path and flows to the right. When the direction of the path is reversed (bottom), the text changes position and flows to the left.*

❾ *The* **Knife tool** *in the Tools panel.*

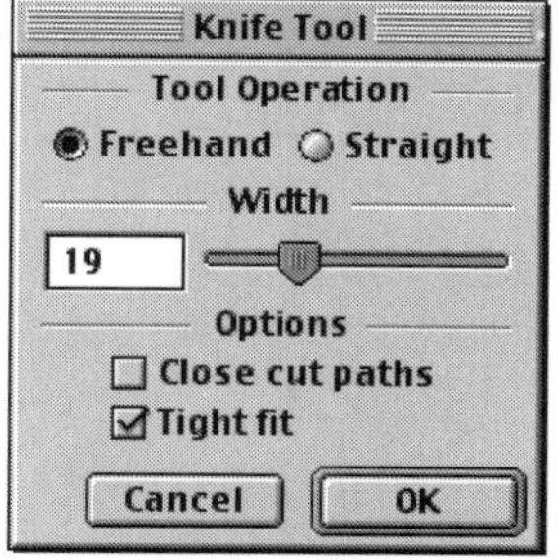

❿ *The* **Knife tool dialog box.**

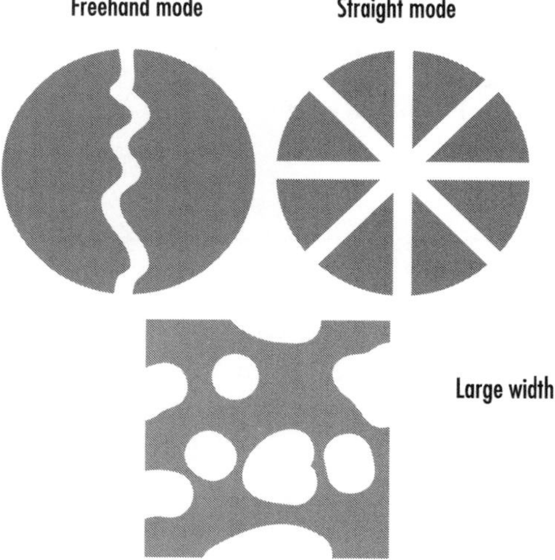

⓫ *Different effects that can be created with the Knife tool.*

Using the Knife Tool

FreeHand's Knife tool is truly a Swiss-army knife. With the Knife tool, you can open paths, slice objects into parts, punch holes in objects, and even erase parts of objects.

To set the Knife tool attributes:

1. Double-click the Knife tool ❾ in the Tools panel. This opens the Knife Tool dialog box ❿.
2. Set the Tool Operation modes as follows:
   - **Freehand** allows you to create curved or wavy line cuts.
   - **Straight** constrains you to creating only straight-line cuts.

TIP Hold the Opt/Alt key as you drag with the Knife to temporarily set the Knife for straight cuts.

TIP As you draw at the straight setting, hold down the Shift key to constrain your cuts to 45° angles.

3. Set the width to control the space between the cuts. A width of 0 leaves no space between the objects created by the cuts. As you increase the width, the Knife acts as an eraser that erases portions of the object.
4. Choose Close cut paths so that the objects created by the Knife are closed paths.
5. Choose Tight fit so that the Knife tool follows the movements of your mouse precisely.
6. Click OK to apply the settings to the Knife tool.

To use the Knife tool:

1. Select the object you wish to cut.
2. Drag the Knife tool across the selected objects ⓫.

Using the Freeform Tool

As a self-proclaimed "vectorbabe," I love Bézier handles. In case you don't share my enthusiasm, the Freeform tool allows you to reshape paths without modifying points or handles. There are two modes to the Freeform tool: Push/Pull and Reshape Area.

The Push/Pull tool allows you to pull to add new segments to a path or push to distort the shape of the segment.

To set the Push/Pull tool operation:

1. Double-click the Freeform tool in the Tools panel ⓬. The Freeform Tool dialog box appears.
2. Set the Tool Operation to Push/Pull. This displays the Push/Pull options ⓭.
3. Set the Size field to control the size of the area pushed by the tool.
4. Set the Precision field to control the precision amount—the greater the amount, the more sensitive the tool is to minor movements of the mouse.
5. Choose one of the following from the Pull Setting list:
   - **Bend By Length** pulls anywhere along a path
   - **Bend Between Points** restricts the pull to only between existing anchor points.
6. Set the Length field to control how much the Pull will alter the path.
7. If you have a pressure-sensitive tablet, check the Size and/or Length boxes to set how the pressure on the tablet affects the tool.
8. Click OK to apply the settings.

⓬ *The* **Freeform tool** *set for the Push/Pull mode.*

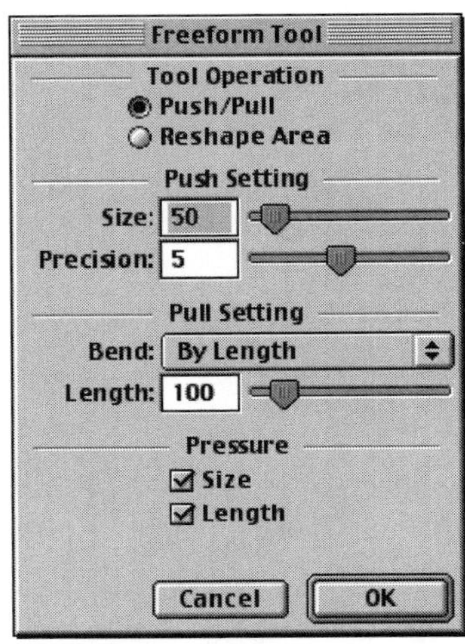

⓭ *The* **Push/Pull settings** *of the Freeform tool dialog box.*

> **Understanding the Freeform tool**
>
> There are subtle differences in the modes of the Freeform tool.
>
> The Push effect of the Push/Pull mode acts like a rolling pin that changes the shape of the object.
>
> The Pull effect of the Push/Pull mode acts like a magnet that draws out the shape of the object.
>
> The Reshape Area mode changes the shape of the object as if it were taffy that can be stretched into thin wisps.

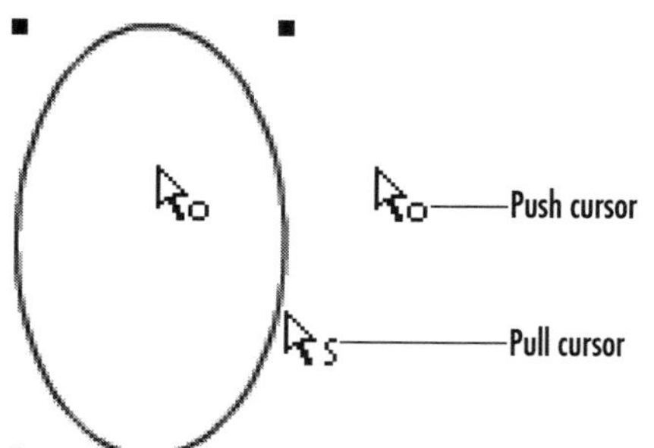

⓮ *The Freeform tool has* **two different cursors** *in the Push/Pull mode.*

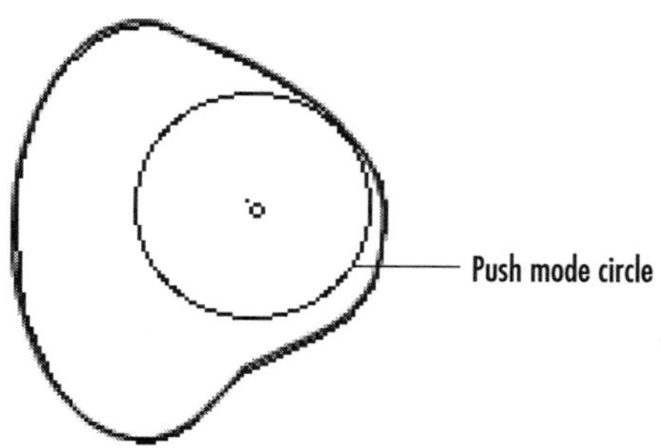

⓯ *The* **Push mode circle** *indicates the size of the area that is distorted.*

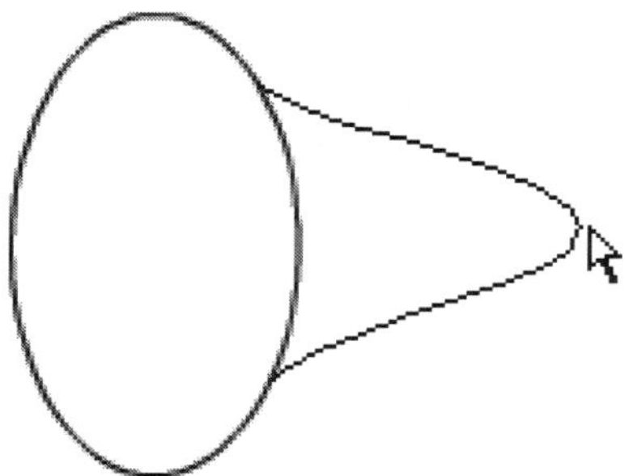

⓰ *The* **Pull arrow** *indicates that the Freeform tool adds a segment where the path is pulled.*

To modify objects in the Push/Pull mode:

1. Select the object you want to modify.
2. Position the cursor as follows ⓮:
   - Move the cursor directly next to the object. A small **s** shape appears next to the cursor. This indicates you are in the pull mode.
   - Move the cursor inside or outside the object. A small **o** shape appears next to the cursor. This indicates you are in the push mode.
3. Drag to modify the object. In the push mode a circle appears that indicates the size of the area being modified ⓯. An arrow indicates you are working in the pull mode ⓰.
4. If you do not have a pressure-sensitive tablet you can modify the area as you drag as follows:
   - Press the 1, [, or left arrow keys as you drag to decrease the size of the Freeform tool effect.
   - Press the 2,], or right arrow keys as you drag to increase the size of the Freeform tool effect.

In the Reshape mode, you distort the path by pulling out new segments to a path. The amount of distortion is set in the Reshape Area settings of the Freeform tool.

⑰ *The* **Reshape Area tool** *in the Tools panel.*

To set the Reshape Area tool operation:

1. Double-click the Freeform tool in the Tools panel ⑰. The Freeform Tool dialog box appears ⑱.
2. Set the Tool Operation to Reshape Area. This displays the Reshape Area options.
3. Set the Size field to control the size of the Reshape Area tool.
4. Set the Strength field to control how long the tool will work during a drag—the greater the amount, the longer the tool distorts the path.
5. Set the Precision field to control the precision amount—the greater the amount, the more sensitive the tool is to minor movements of the mouse.
6. Click OK to apply the settings.

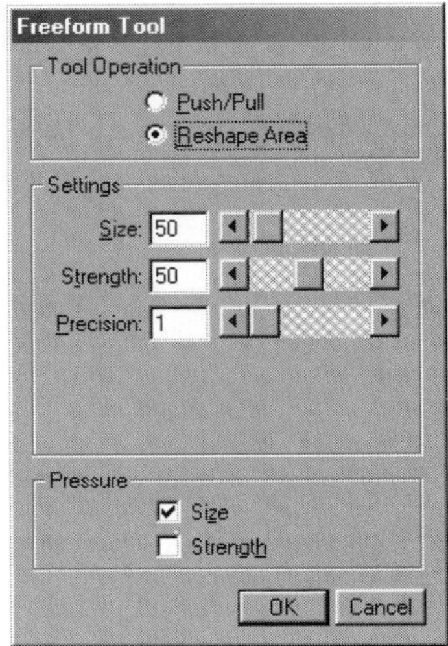

⑱ *The* **Reshape Area settings** *of the Freeform Tool dialog box.*

To modify objects in the Reshape Area mode:

1. Select the object you want to modify.
2. Drag to modify the object ⑲.
3. If you do not have a pressure-sensitive tablet you can modify the area as you drag as follows:
   - Press the 1, [, or left arrow keys as you drag to decrease the size of the Freeform tool effect.
   - Press the 2,], or right arrow keys as you drag to increase the size of the Freeform tool effect.

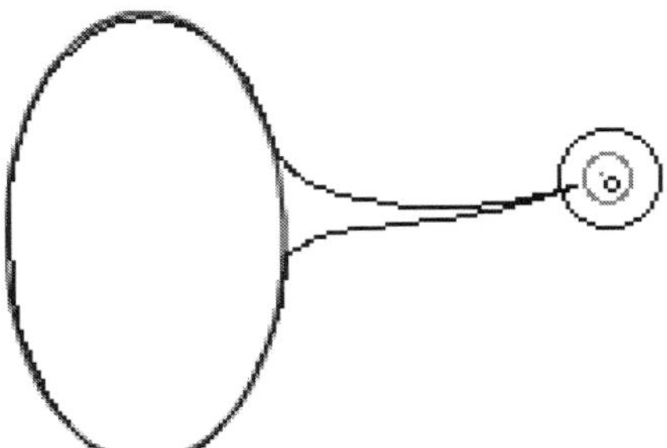

⑲ *The Reshape Area tool distorts a path into a new shape.*

Path Commands

Instead of using a tool such as the Pointer or Knife to modify a path, you can also use commands. The Remove Overlap command changes a path so that areas that overlap each other are eliminated. This is very helpful when working with the Pencil tool.

To use the Remove Overlap command:

1. Select the object.
2. Click the Remove Overlap icon in the Xtra Operations toolbar (20).

   or

   Choose **Modify > Alter Path > Remove Overlap.**

   or

   Choose **Xtras > Cleanup > Remove Overlap.** Notice that the overlapping areas are eliminated (21).

Too many points on a path makes it difficult to reshape and work with paths. The Simplify command lets you remove excess points.

To use the Simplify command:

1. Select the object.
2. Click the Simplify icon in the Xtra Operations toolbar (22).

   or

   Choose **Modify > Alter Path > Simplify.**

   or

   Choose **Xtras > Cleanup > Simplify.** The Simplify dialog box appears (23).
3. Drag the slider to change the value in the Amount field. The greater the number, the more points will be eliminated (24).
4. Click the Apply button to see the effects of the setting.
5. Click OK to apply the command.

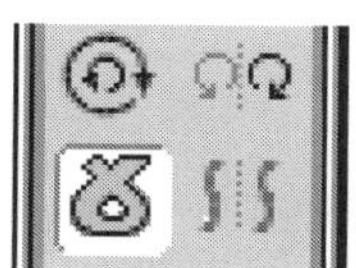

(20) *The* **Remove Overlap icon** *in the Xtra Operations toolbar.*

(21) *The effects of applying the* **Remove Overlap** *command.*

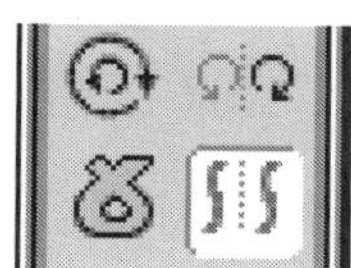

(22) *The* **Simplify icon** *in the Xtra Operations toolbar.*

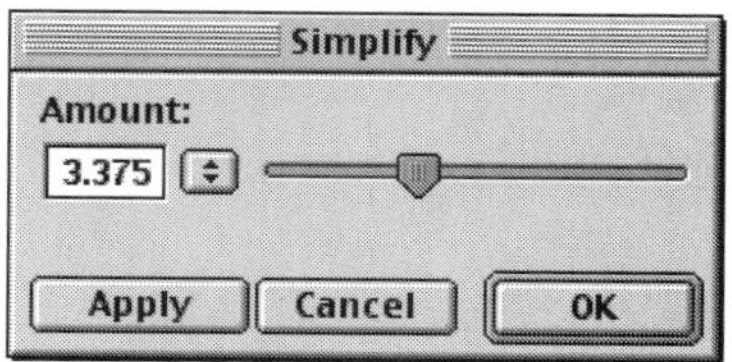

(23) The **Simplify** dialog box.

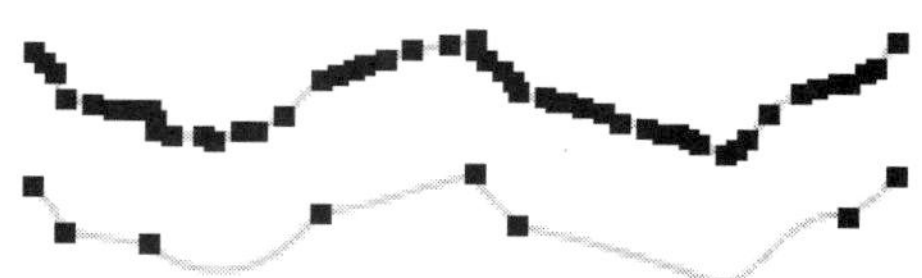

(24) *The effects of the* **Simplify** *command.*

Certain effects need additional points on the path to look good. For instance, more points create a different look when the Bend effect *(see page 296)* is applied. The Add Points command lets you add extra points to a path.

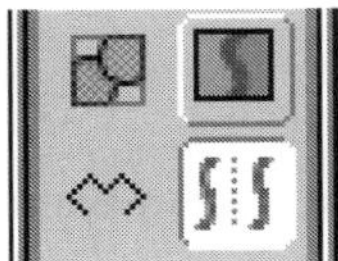

㉕ *The* **Add Points icon** *in the Xtra Operations toolbar.*

To use the Add Points command:

1. Select an object.
2. Click the Add Points icon in the Xtras Operations toolbar ㉕.

   or

   Choose **Xtras > Distort > Add Points.**
3. Each time you choose the command, a new point is added between each existing pair of points ㉖.

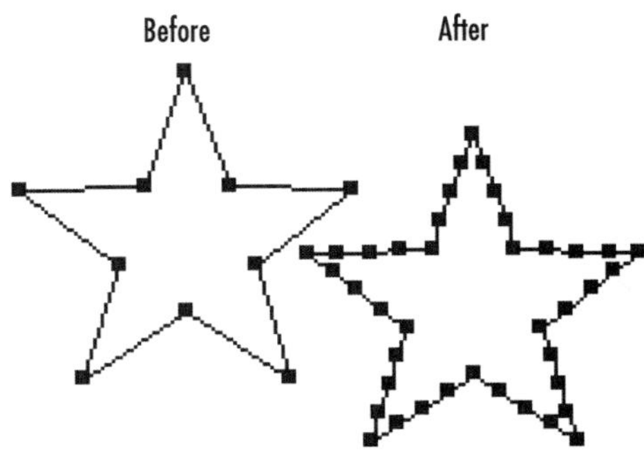

㉖ *The results of the* **Add Points** *command.*

The Intersect command creates a new object from the area where two objects overlap.

To use the Intersect command:

1. Select two or more paths that overlap each other.
2. Click the Intersect icon in the Xtras Operations toolbar ㉗.

   or

   Choose **Modify > Combine > Intersect.**

   or

   Choose **Xtras > Path Operations > Intersect.**
3. A new path is created that is the shape of the overlapping area ㉘.

TIP The Intersect command deletes from the selection any objects that do not overlap.

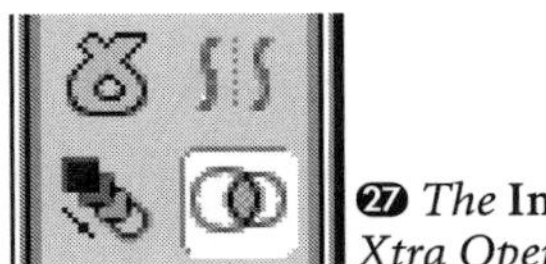

㉗ *The* **Interset icon** *in the Xtra Operations toolbar.*

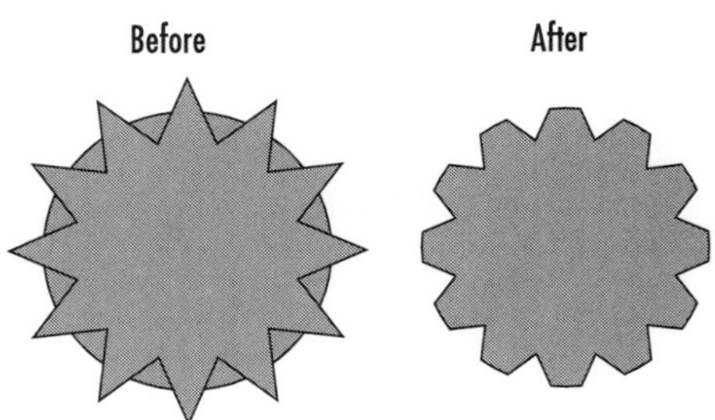

㉘ *The effects of the* **Intersect** *command.*

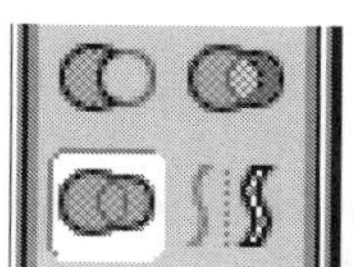

㉙ *The* **Union icon** *in the Xtra Operations toolbar.*

㉚ *The effects of the* **Union** *command.*

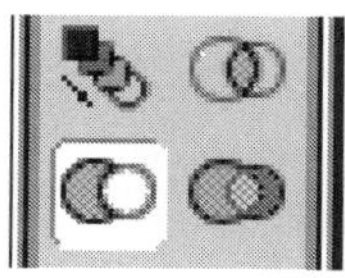

㉛ *The* **Punch icon** *in the Xtra Operations toolbar.*

㉜ *The effects of the* **Punch** *command.*

The Union command allows you to take many objects and turn them into one path.

To use the Union command:

1. Select two or more objects that overlap each other.
2. Click the Union icon in the Xtras Operations toolbar ㉙.

   or

   Choose **Modify > Combine > Union.**

   or

   Choose **Xtras > Path Operations > Union.**
3. The multiple paths join into one ㉚.

TIP If the selected objects for the Union, Intersect, or Punch commands have different attributes, the final object takes on the attributes of the backmost object.

The Punch command allows you to use one object to punch a hole in another.

To use the Punch command:

1. Select two or more objects that overlap each other.
2. Click the Punch icon in the Xtras Operations toolbar ㉛.

   or

   Choose **Modify > Combine > Punch.**

   or

   Choose **Xtras > Path Operations > Punch.**
3. The top object punches through the bottom object ㉜.

TIP To have multiple objects act as the punch, first apply the Union command.

TIP To save the original objects while creating new ones, hold the Shift key as you apply the Intersect or Punch commands or change the Preferences setting for Path operations consume original paths *(see page 391)*.

The Divide command creates new paths from the overlapping areas of objects.

To use the Divide command:

1. Select two or more objects that overlap each other.
2. Click the Divide icon in the Xtra Operations toolbar ㉝.

   or

   Choose **Modify > Combine > Divide.**

   or

   Choose **Xtras > Path Operations > Divide.**
3. The paths divide into new paths wherever they overlapped ㉞.

㉝ *The* **Divide icon** *in the Xtra Operations toolbar.*

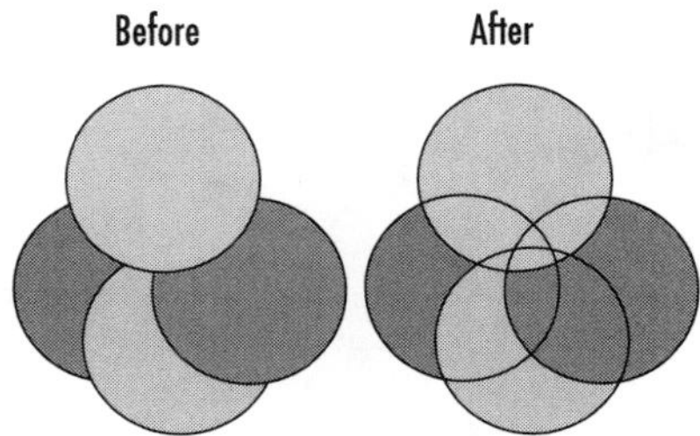

㉞ *The effects of the* **Divide** *command.*

The Crop command allows you to use the top object as a cookie cutter that trims away parts of the path that are outside the top object.

To use the Crop command:

1. Select various objects with one object on top.
2. Click the Crop icon in the Xtra Operations toolbar ㉟.

   or

   Choose **Modify > Combine > Crop.**

   or

   Choose **Xtras > Path Operations > Crop.**
3. All the objects at the bottom are trimmed so that only those portions that were under the topmost object remain ㊱.

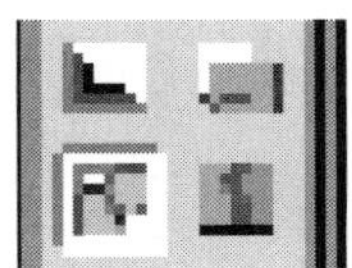

㉟ *The* **Crop icon** *in the Xtra Operations toolbar.*

㊱ *The effects of the* **Crop** *command.*

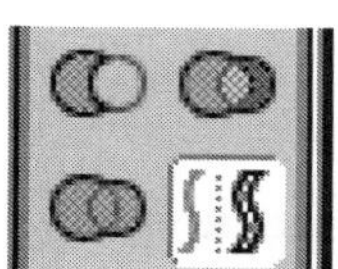

37 *The* **Expand Stroke icon** *in the Xtra Operations toolbar.*

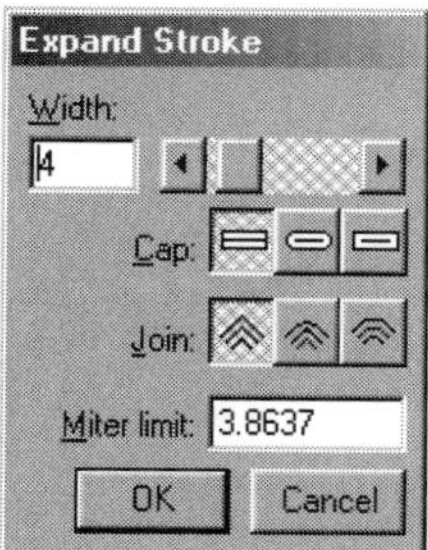

38 *The* **Expand Stroke** *dialog box.*

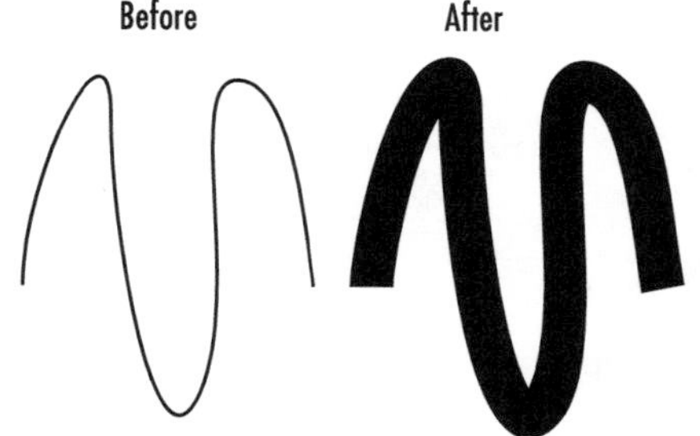

39 *The effects of the* **Expand Stroke** *command.*

FreeHand offers you a way to convert lines or open paths to closed paths by using the Expand Stroke command. This allows you to convert stroked paths into closed paths that can have fills such as the Lens or Gradient fills. *(See Chapter 15, "Strokes" for more information on creating stroked paths.)*

To use the Expand Stroke command:

1. Select the stroked path you wish to convert.
2. Click the Expand Stroke icon in the Xtra Operations toolbar 37.

   or

   Choose **Modify > Alter Path > Expand Stroke.**

   or

   Choose **Xtras > Path Operations > Expand Stroke.** The Expand Stroke dialog box appears 38.
3. Enter the width you want for the final object.
4. Choose one of the Cap settings for the end of the path. *(See page 197 for details of the Cap settings.)*
5. Choose one of the Join settings for the corners of the path. *(See page 198 for details of the Join settings.)*
6. Enter an amount for the Miter limit for the corners of the path. *(See page 198 for details of the Miter limit settings.)*

TIP Note that while these settings are the same as the settings for a stroke, the final object will actually be a filled path.

7. Click OK to create a new filled path 39.

Using the Repeat Xtra Command

Although many path operations are under the Modify menu, you have an extra feature if you choose the commands via the Xtras menu or the Operations toolbar. That command will be listed at the top of the Xtras menu as the Repeat [Xtra] command. This means that if you want to apply the command again, you can choose it from the top of the menu.

The Inset Path command allows you to make multiple copies of an object. These copies can be smaller or larger than the original.

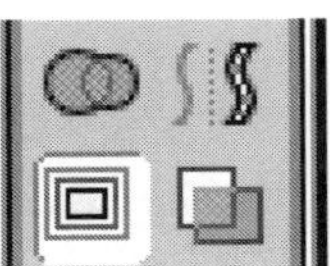

40 *The* **Inset Path icon** *in the Xtra Operations toolbar.*

To use the Inset Path command:

1. Select a closed path.
2. Click the Inset Path icon in the Xtra Operations toolbar **40**.

   or

   Choose **Modify > Alter Path > Inset Path.**

   or

   Choose **Xtras > Path Operations > Inset Path.** The Inset Path dialog box appears **41**.
3. In the Steps field, enter the number of copies you want to create.
4. If the number of steps is greater than 1, choose one of the following from the list:
   - **Uniform** spaces each copy the same distance from the previous object.
   - **Farther** spaces each copy slightly closer than the previous object.
   - **Nearer** spaces each copy slightly further away from the previous object.
5. Use the slider to set the size of the new objects as follows:
   - **Positive numbers** place the new objects inside the original.
   - **Negative numbers** place the new object outside the original.
6. Click OK. This creates copies of the object inset from the original **42**.

TIP Multiples created by the Inset Path command are created as grouped objects.

41 *The* **Inset Path** *dialog box.*

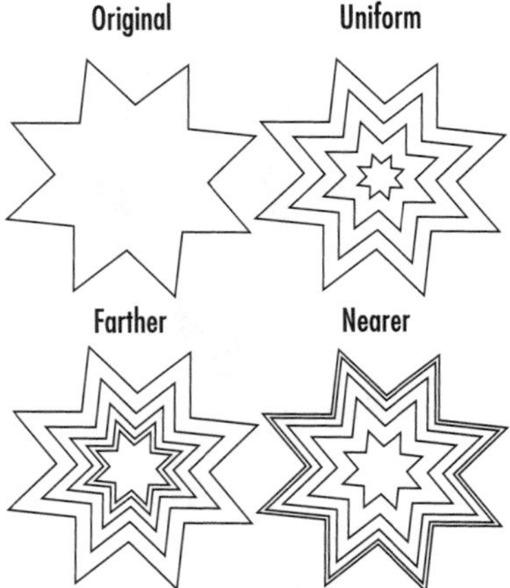

42 *The results of applying the* **Inset Path** *command at the different settings.*

Path Commands

㊸ *The* **Emboss icon** *in the Xtra Operations toolbar.*

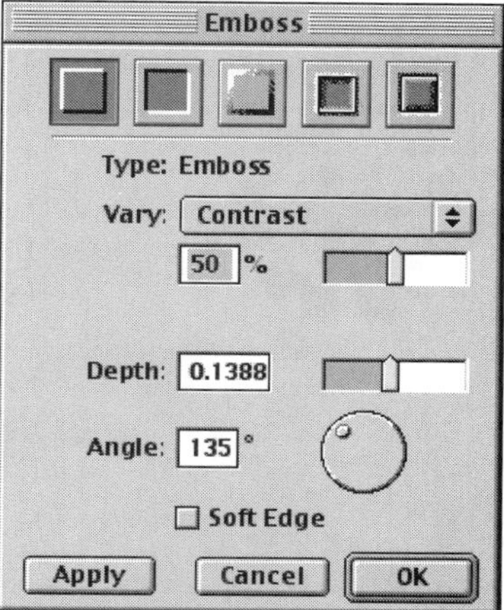

㊹ *The* **Emboss dialog box.**

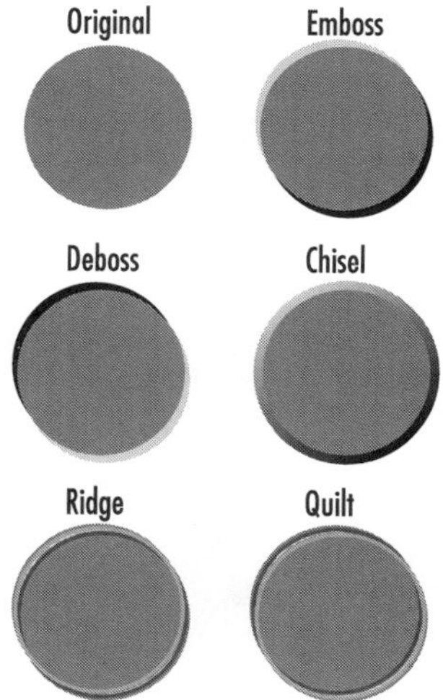

㊺ *The results of applying the* **Emboss** *command at the different settings.*

The Emboss command allows you to create the look of raised or depressed areas on a background.

To use the Emboss command:

1. Select one or more objects.
2. Click the Emboss icon in the Xtra Operations toolbar ㊸.

   or

   Choose **Xtras > Create > Emboss.** This opens the Emboss dialog box ㊹.
3. Click one of the top icons to choose from the five types of embossing effects: emboss, deboss, chisel, ridge, or quilt.
4. Set the Vary controls as follows:
   - **Contrast** lets you use the slider to control how much to change the existing colors in the object to create the light and dark portions of the emboss.
   - **Color** lets you set the color for the highlight and shadows of the emboss.
5. Set the Depth field for how obvious the embossing should be.
6. Set the angle to control where the light and dark areas of the emboss should be.
7. Click the Soft Edge box to make the transition less abrupt.
8. Click Apply to see how the settings affect the object.
9. Click OK when you are satisfied to view the results ㊺.

I admit that not all commands are as useful as others. It takes a lot of creativity to find any practical uses for the Fractalize command. But it does create interesting snowflake effects.

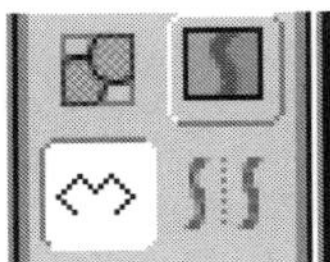

46 *The* **Fractalize icon** *in the Xtra Operations toolbar.*

To use the Fractalize command:

1. Select the object.
2. Make sure the Even/Odd fill box is checked in the Object Inspector.
3. Click the Fractalize icon in the Xtra Operations toolbar 46.

   or

   Choose **Xtras > Distort > Fractalize.**
4. Repeat the command until you are satisfied with the effect 47.

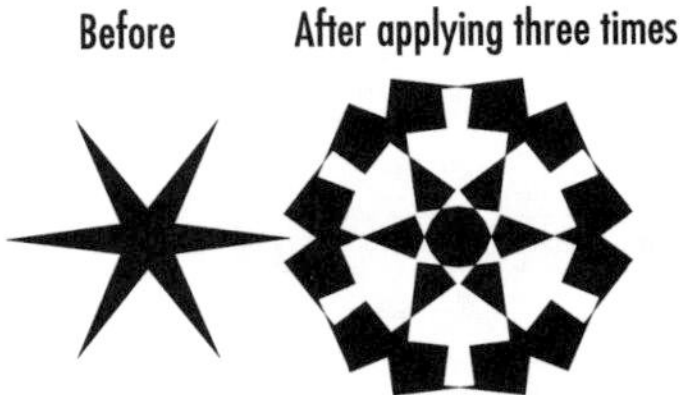

47 *The effects of the* **Fractalize** *command.*

The Transparency command lets you simulate a see-through effect. It doesn't actually make the objects transparent and is not as important now that FreeHand has transparency in the lens fills *(see page 184).*

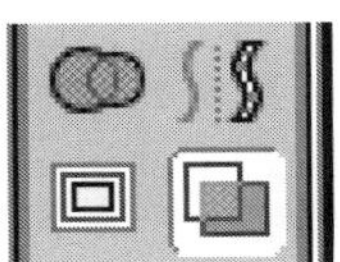

48 *The* **Transparency icon** *in the Xtra Operations toolbar.*

To use the Transparency command:

1. Create two or more overlapping objects filled with different colors.
2. Click the Transparency icon in the Xtra Operations toolbar 48.

   or

   Choose **Xtras > Path Operations > Transparency.** This opens the Transparency dialog box 49.
3. Set the amount of the transparency.

TIP If the amount is less than 50%, the front color is more obvious. If it is more than 50%, the back color looks more obvious.

4. Click OK to see the transparency effect 50.

TIP The Transparency command creates a new object that simulates the transparency effect.

49 *The* **Transparency dialog box.**

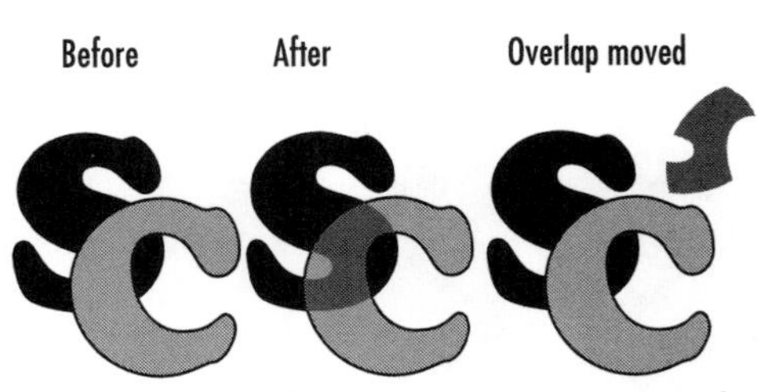

50 *The effects of the* **Transparency** *command.*

MOVE AND TRANSFORM 10

Once you have created an object, most likely you will want to transform it at some other time. It is by moving and transforming objects that you can convert simple shapes into dramatic and sophisticated artwork.

Perhaps you will want to enlarge an object, or rotate it on an angle, or skew its shape, or flip it so it is facing another direction. All those actions—scaling, rotating, skewing, and reflecting—are transformations. In fact, even moving an object from one position to another is considered a transformation.

FreeHand provides many different ways to transform objects. Some techniques let you view the results as you work. Other techniques let you enter numerical values for more precise results.

Viewing Transformations

As you transform an object you can see the details about the transformation in the Info Toolbar ❶.

❶ *The* **Info Toolbar.**

The Info Toolbar readings

The Info Toolbar readings change depending on the position of your cursor, the tool chosen, or the action taken. The Info Toolbar has four fields: Object ❷, Position ❸, Info ❸, and Lock ❺.

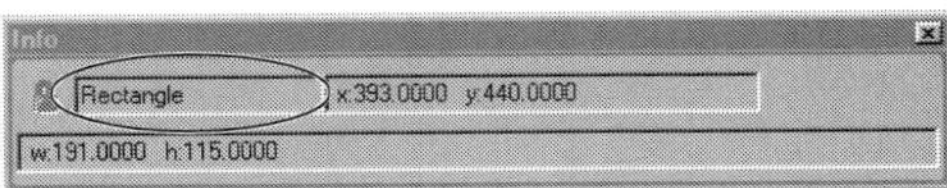

❷ *The* **Object field** *(circled) shows the type of object or the number of objects selected.*

The following are the various categories seen on the Info Toolbar.

- **x** (Position field) position of the cursor along the horizontal axis
- **y** (Position field) position of the cursor along the vertical axis
- **dx** horizontal distance an object is moved
- **dy** vertical distance an object is moved
- **dist** total distance along any angle an object is moved
- **angle** angle along which any object is moved, created, or transformed
- **x** (Info field)horizontal location of the centerpoint around which any object is being created or transformed
- **y** (Info field) vertical location of the center point that any object is being created or transformed around.
- **xscale** horizontal scale or skew of an object expressed as a ratio to an object's original size (e.g., 1.00 = 100%)
- **yscale** vertical scale or skew of an object expressed as a ratio to an object's original size (e.g., 1.00 = 100%)
- **width** width of a rectangle or ellipse.
- **height** height of a rectangle or ellipse
- **radius** size of a radius of a polygon
- **sides** number of sides of a polygon
- **open padlock** (Mac) **grey padlock** (Win) indicates the object is not locked
- **closed padlock** (Mac) **red padlock** (Win) indicates the object is locked

TIP The Info Toolbar does not allow you to enter numbers directly into it.

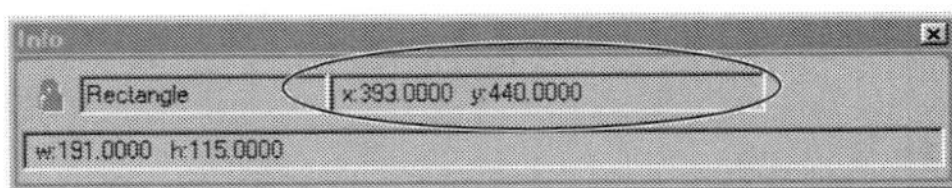

❸ *The* **Position field** *(circled) shows the x and y coordinates of the cursor position.*

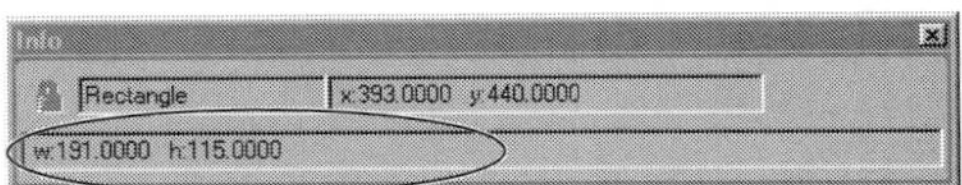

❹ *The* **Info field** *(circled) shows the various attributes of objects as they are created or manipulated.*

❺ *The* **Lock field** *(circled) shows if a selected object is locked or not.*

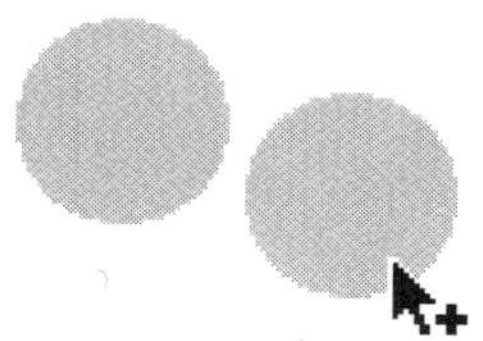

❻ *Hold the Opt/Alt key to* **move and copy** *an object. The plus sign (+) next to the arrow indicates you are creating a copy.*

❼ *Choose* **Edit > Duplicate** *as many times as necessary to create additional copies of the object.*

Moving Objects

As mentioned before, when you move an object you are actually transforming it. There are some special transformation techniques you can use when moving objects.

To move an object:

1. Select the object you want to move.
2. Use the Pointer tool to drag the object to a new position.

TIP When you move an object, the horizontal and vertical distances are recorded in the Move settings of the Transform panel. These settings can then be used to move other objects.

To move and copy an object:

1. Select the object you want to copy.
2. Start to drag the object to a new position.
3. Press the Opt/Alt key as you drag. The plus sign (+) next to the arrow indicates that you are creating a copy of the object.
4. When the object is in the correct position, release the mouse button first and then the Opt/Alt key. A copy of the original object is created at the point where you released the mouse ❻.

Once you have moved and made a copy of an object, you can continue to make copies of the object, each positioned the same distance away from the previous copy.

To Duplicate the previous Move and Copy:

- With the object created in the previous exercise still selected, choose **Edit > Duplicate.** FreeHand duplicates the new object ❼.

TIP You can repeat this command over and over to create as many copies as you want.

In addition to moving manually, you can use the Transform panel to move objects numerically. You can also use the panel to make copies, each spaced the same distance from the previous copy.

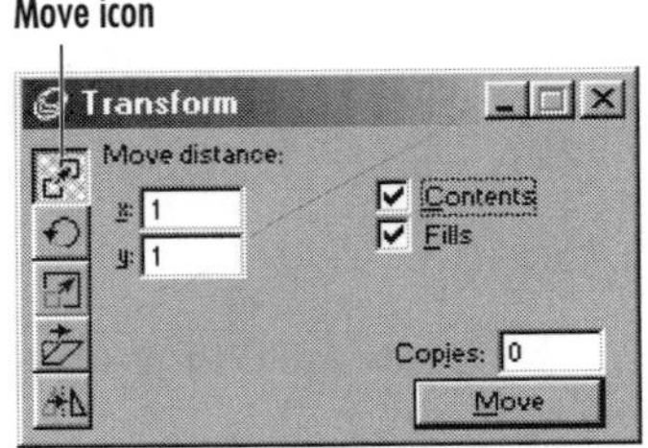

❽ *The Transform dialog box set to the* **Move controls.**

To move using the Transform panel:

1. Select the object you want to move.
2. In the Transform panel, click the Move icon. This switches to the move controls ❽.
3. Set the Move distance as follows:
   - The x field controls the horizontal movement. Positive numbers move the object to the right. Negative numbers move the object to the left.
   - The y field controls the vertical movement. Positive numbers move the object up. Negative numbers move the object down.
4. Select Contents to move any items pasted inside along with the object *(see page 109)* ❾.
5. Select Fills to move any fills such as tiled fills *(see page 188)*.
6. Click the Apply button (Mac) or Move button (Win) or press Return or Enter to apply the move.

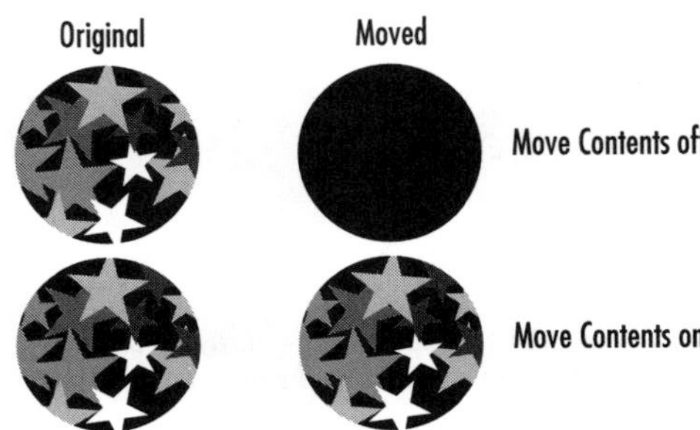

❾ *When* **Move Contents is off** *(top) the stars pasted in do not move with the circle. When* **Move Contents is on** *(bottom) the stars pasted in move along with the circle.*

To copy and move using the Transform panel:

1. Select the object you want to copy and move.
2. Use the steps in the previous exercise to set the distance and attributes of the move.
3. Enter the number of copies in the Copies field.
4. Click the Apply button (Mac) or Move button (Win) or press Return or Enter to copy and move the object.

⑩ *The* **Rotate tool** *in the Tools panel.*

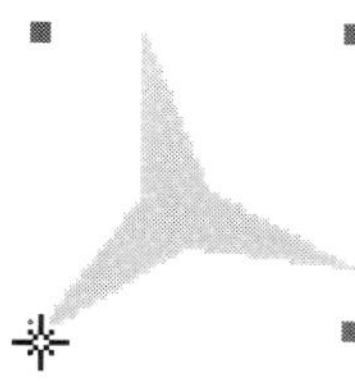

⑪ *Position the* **Rotate tool cursor** *to create the transformation point. The object will rotate around this point.*

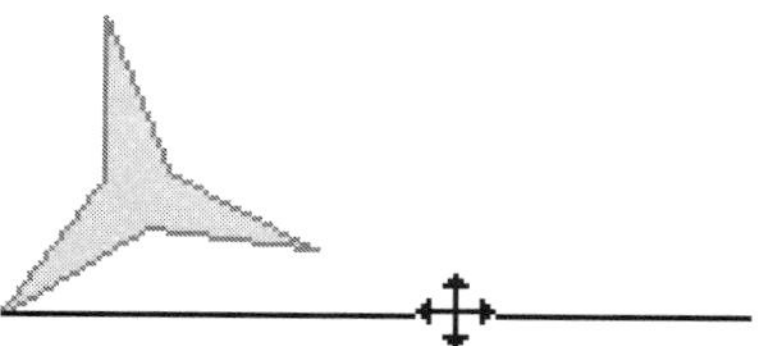

⑫ *Press with the Rotate tool to see the rotation axis—the line that will rotate the object.*

⑬ *The rotation axis and the preview show the position to which the object will be rotated.*

Rotating Objects

Another type of transformation is rotation. Rotation allows you to change the orientation of an object.

To rotate an object by eye:

1. Select the object you want to rotate.
2. Choose the Rotate tool in the Tools panel ⑩.
3. Move your cursor to the page. Your cursor turns into a star.
4. Position the star on the spot around which you would like the object to rotate ⑪. This is the transformation point.
5. Press on the point you have chosen. *Do not release the mouse button.* A line extends out from the transformation point. This is the rotation axis ⑫.

TIP You can transform an object around a point anywhere in the document.

6. Still pressing, drag the cursor away from the transformation point. Then move the rotation axis. The object rotates as you move the rotation axis ⑬.

TIP Hold the Shift key to constrain the rotation to 45° increments.

7. Release the mouse button when you are satisfied with the position of the object.

TIP The farther you drag your cursor away from the transformation point during rotation or reflection, the easier it is to control the transformation.

To copy as you rotate an object:

1. Hold the Opt/Alt key as you drag to rotate the object. A plus sign (+) appears next to the star cursor.
2. Release the mouse button first and then the Opt/Alt key to create a copy of the object rotated to the position you chose.

To rotate using the Transform panel:

1. Choose the object you want to rotate.
2. Click the Rotate icon in the Transform panel ⓮.
3. Enter the number of degrees you want to rotate the object in the Rotation angle field.
4. To change the Center of the rotation, enter the coordinates you want in the **x** and y fields.

   or

   With the Rotate tool active, hold the Opt/Alt key and click to select a transformation point.
5. Select Contents to rotate any items pasted inside along with the object *(see page 109)* ⓯.
6. Select Fills to rotate any fills such as tiled fills *(see page 188)*.
7. Click the Apply (Mac) or Rotate (Win) button or press Return or Enter to apply the rotation.

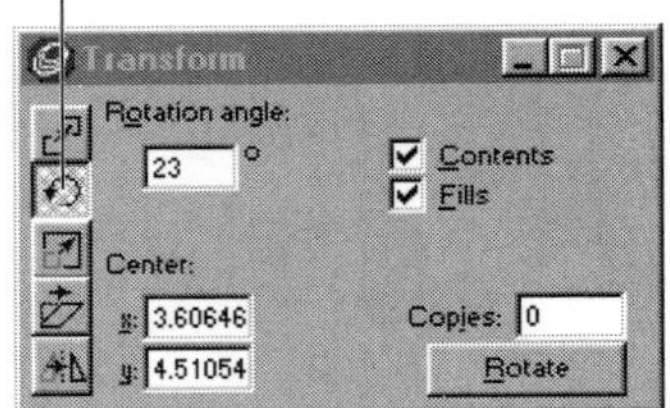

⓮ *The Transform dialog box set to the* **Rotate controls.**

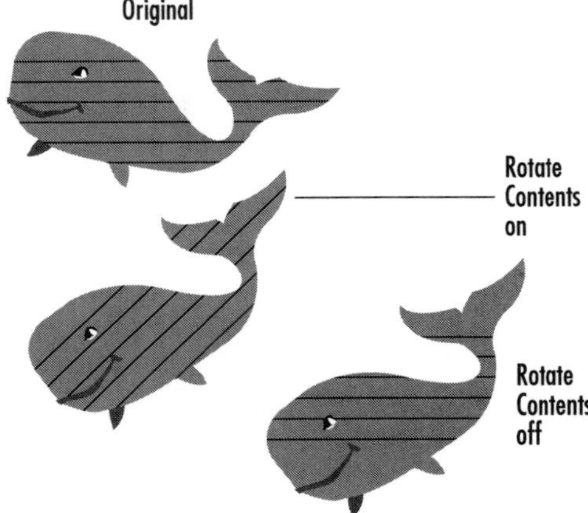

⓯ *When* **Rotate Contents is on** *the lines pasted in rotate along with the whale. When* **Rotate Contents is off** *the horizontal lines pasted in do not rotate with the whale.*

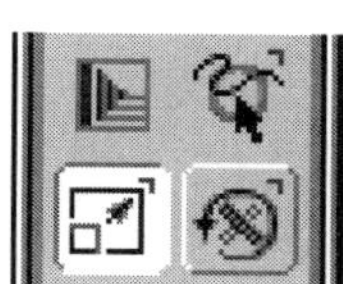

⑯ *The* **Scale tool** *in the Tools panel.*

⑰ *Position the* **Scale tool cursor** *on the point you want the object to scale from.*

⑱ *Drag with the Scale tool to scale the object up or down.*

Scaling Objects

If an object is too big or too small, it is a simple matter to scale it to a new size.

To scale an object by eye:

1. Choose the object you want to scale.
2. Choose the Scale tool in the Tools panel ⑯.
3. Move your cursor to the page. Your cursor turns into a star ⑰.
4. Position the star on the spot from which you would like the object to scale. This is the transformation point.
5. Press down on the point you have chosen. *Do not release the mouse button.*
6. Drag the cursor away from the transformation point. An outline of the object changes to show how the object is being scaled ⑱.

   TIP Hold the Shift key if you want to constrain the scale to a proportional change.
7. Release the mouse button when you are satisfied with the size of the scaled object. Your object scales into position.

To copy as you scale an object:

1. Hold the Opt/Alt key as you drag to scale the object. A plus sign (+) appears next to the star cursor.
2. Release the mouse button first and then the Opt/Alt key to create a copy of the original object scaled to the position you chose.

To scale using the Transform panel:

1. Select the object you want to scale.
2. Click the Scale icon in the Transform panel ⓳.
3. Enter the percent you want to change the object.
4. For a proportional scale, keep the Uniform box checked.

   or

   To scale the object nonproportionally, deselect Uniform ⓴. This opens additional fields to enter the percentages to scale the object.
5. For a uniform scale, enter an amount in the Scale % field.

   or

   For a non-uniform scale, enter values in the **x** (horizontal) and **y** (vertical) (Mac) or **h** (horizontal) and **v** (vertical) (Win) fields.
6. To change the point of transformation from the center, enter the coordinates in the x and y fields.

   or

   With the Scale tool active, hold the Opt/Alt key and click to select a transformation point.
7. Check Contents to scale any items pasted inside along with the object *(see page 109)* ㉑.
8. Check Fills to scale any fills such as tiled fills *(see page 188)*.
9. Check Strokes to scale the size of strokes along with the path.
10. Click the Apply (Mac) or Scale (Win) button or press Return or Enter to apply the scale.

Scale icon

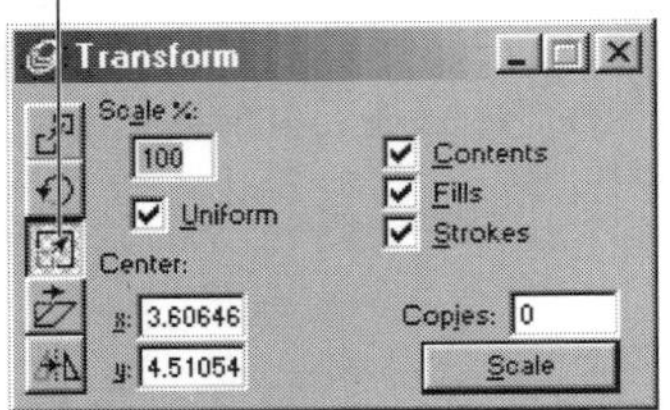

⓳ *The Transform dialog box set to the* **Scale controls.**

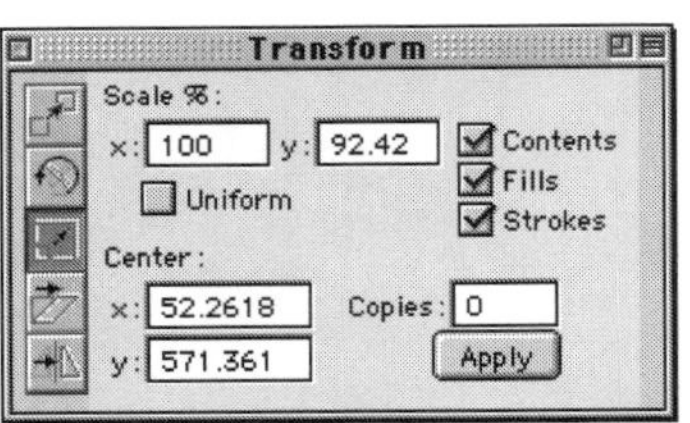

⓴ *The Transform dialog box set to a* **Non-Uniform scale.**

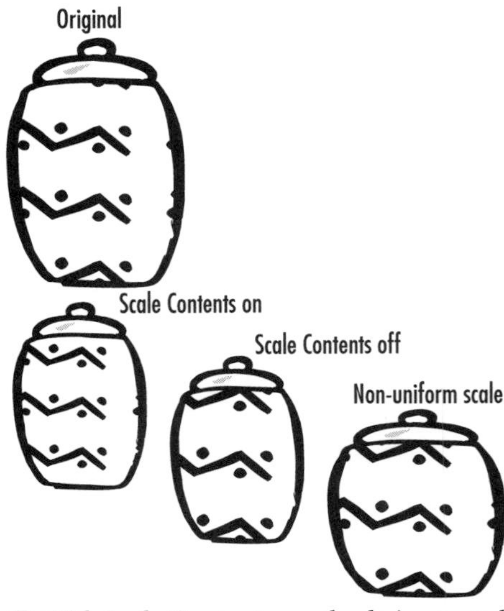

㉑ *With* **Scale Contents on** *the design pasted in scales along with the urn. With* **Scale Contents off** *the design does not scale with the urn.*

Sacling Objects

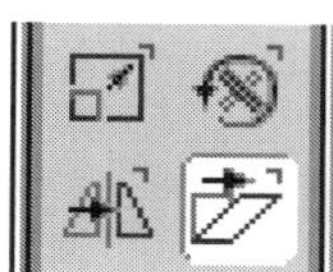

㉒ *The* **Skew tool** *in the Tools panel.*

㉓ *Position the* **Skew tool cursor** *on the point you want the object to skew from.*

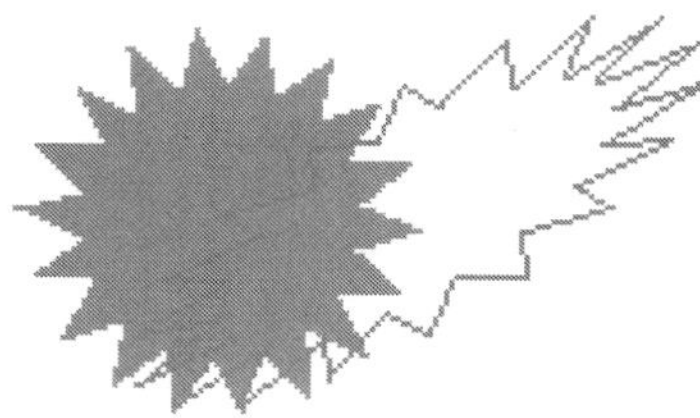

㉔ *Press with the* **Skew tool** *to create a sheared or skewed image of the object.*

Skewing Objects

Skewing (sometimes called shearing) is a way of distorting an object along an axis. This type of distortion is very common when making shadows.

To skew an object by eye:

1. Select the object you want to skew.
2. Choose the Skewing tool in the Tools panel ㉒.
3. Move your cursor to the page. Your cursor turns into a star.
4. Position the star on the point around which you want the object to skew ㉓. This is the transformation point.
5. Press down on the point you have chosen. *Do not release the mouse button.*
6. Drag the cursor away from the transformation point. The outline of the object changes its shape as you move the cursor ㉔.

TIP Hold the Shift key to constrain the skew. Drag horizontally to constrain the skew to the horizontal axis. Drag in a vertical direction to constrain the skew to the vertical axis.

7. Release the mouse button when you are satisfied with the position of the skewed object. Your object skews into position.

To copy as you skew an object:

1. Hold the Opt/Alt key as you drag to skew the object. A plus sign (+) appears next to the star cursor.
2. Release the mouse button first and then the Opt/Alt key to create a copy of the original object skewed to the position you chose.

To skew using the Transform panel:

1. Choose the object you want to skew. Click the Skew icon in the Transform panel ㉕.
2. Enter the horizontal angle amount of the skew in the **h** field. Enter the vertical amount of the skew in the the **v** field.
3. To change the point of transformation from the center, enter the coordinates you want in the **x** and **y** fields.

   or

   With the Skew tool active, hold the Opt/Alt key and click to select a transformation point.
4. Check Contents to skew any items pasted inside along with the object *(see page 109)* ㉖.
5. Check Fills to skew any fills such as tiled fills *(see page 188)*.
6. Click the Apply (Mac) or Skew (Win) button, or press Return or Enter to apply the skew.

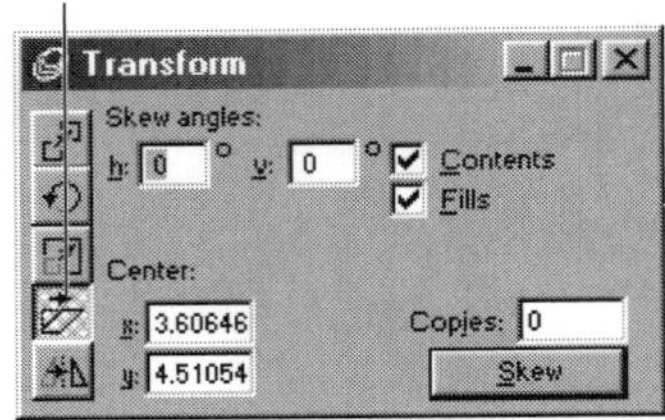

㉕ *The Transform dialog box set to the* **Skew controls.**

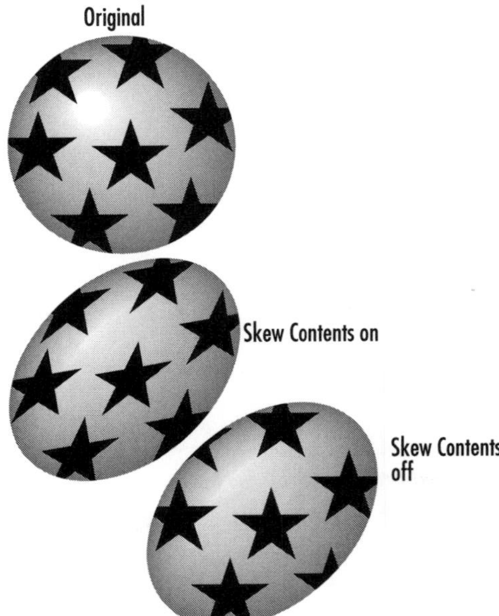

㉖ *With* **Skew Contents on** *the design pasted in skews along with the oval. With* **Skew Contents off** *the design does not skew with the oval.*

㉗ *The* **Reflect tool** *in the Tools panel.*

㉘ *Position the* **Reflect tool cursor** *on the point you want the object to reflect around.*

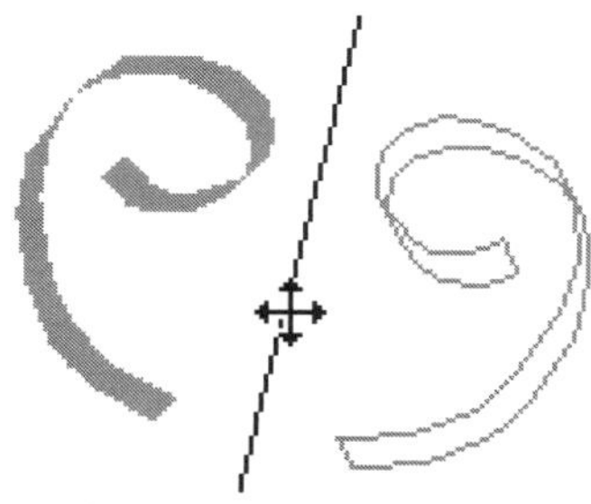

㉙ *The reflection axis and the preview show the position to which the object will be reflected.*

Reflecting Objects

As the Wicked Queen in Snow White knew, reflecting allows you to create a mirror image of an object.

To reflect an object by eye:

1. Select the object you want to reflect.
2. Choose the Reflect tool in the Tools panel ㉗.
3. Move your cursor to the page. Your cursor turns into a star.
4. Position the star on the point around which you want the object to reflect ㉘. This is the transformation point.
5. Press on the point you have chosen. *Do not release the mouse button.* A line extends out from the star. This line is the reflection axis. (Think of the reflection axis as the mirror in which your object is being reflected.)
6. Drag the cursor away from the transformation point. The outline of the object changes its position and shape as you move the cursor ㉙.

TIP Hold the Shift key to constrain your reflection to 45° increments.

7. Release the mouse button when you are satisfied with the position of the reflected object. Your object is reflected into position.

To copy as you reflect an object:

1. Hold the Opt/Alt key as you drag to reflect the object. A plus sign (+) appears next to the star cursor.
2. Release the mouse button first and then the Opt/Alt key to create a copy of the original object reflected to the position you chose.

To reflect using the Transform panel:

1. Select the object you want to reflect.
2. Click the Reflect icon in the Transform panel ㉚.
3. In the Reflect axis field, enter the angle amount that you want the object to reflect around.
4. To change the point of transformation from the center, enter the coordinates you want in the x and y fields.

   or

   With the Scale tool active, hold the Opt/Alt key and click to select a transformation point.
5. Check the Contents to skew any items pasted inside along with the object *(see page 109)* ㉛.
6. Check Fills to skew any fills such as tiled fills *(see page 188)*.
7. Click the Apply (Mac) or Reflect (Win) button or press Return or Enter to apply the reflection.

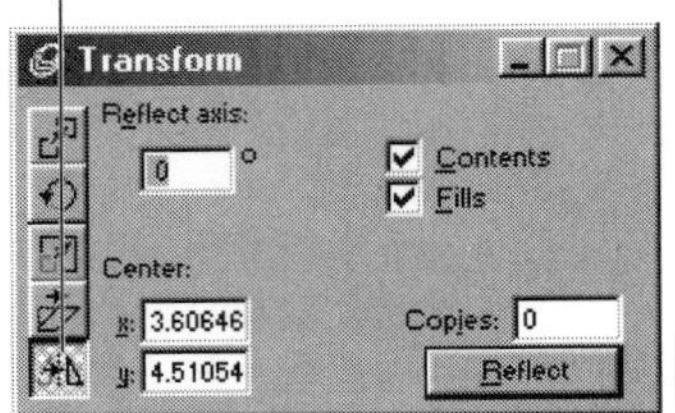

㉚ *The Transform dialog box set to the* **Reflect controls.**

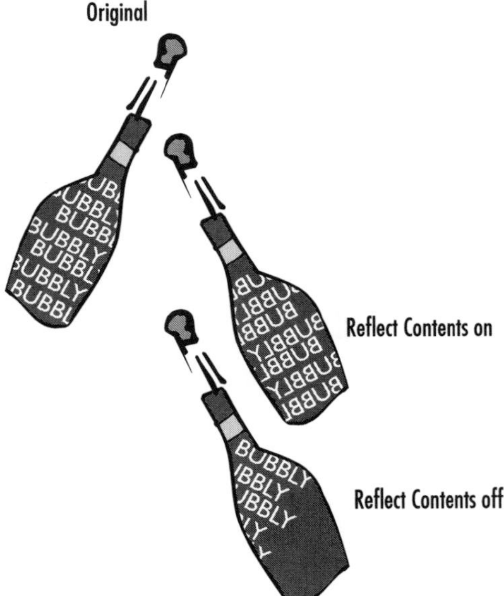

㉛ *With* **Reflect Contents on** *the text pasted in reflects along with the bottle. With* **Reflect Contents off** *the text does not reflect with the bottle.*

Reflecting Objects

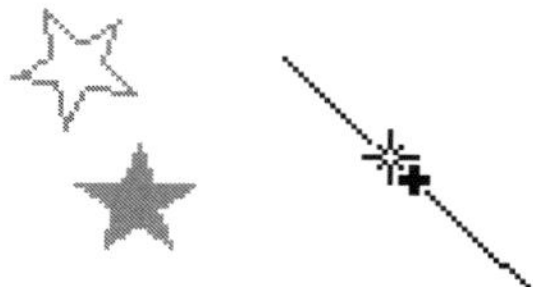

㉜ *The plus sign indicates that a copy of the object is being made as part of the transformation.*

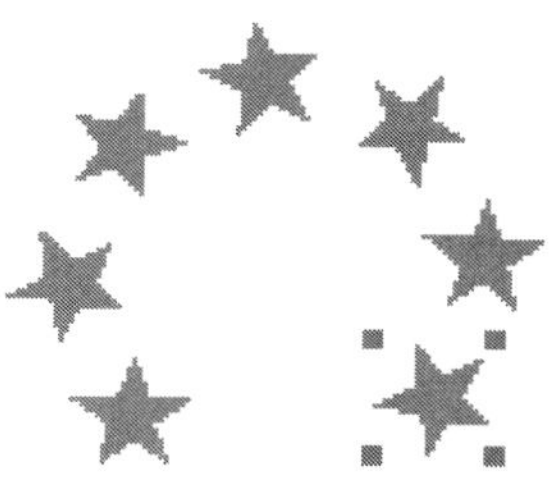

㉝ *The Duplicate command creates additional copies of a rotated object.*

㉞ **Power Duplicating** *allows you to store transformations and reapply them to copies. In this case, the star is both rotated and scaled.*

Using Power Duplicating

FreeHand offers two techniques for copying and transforming objects. The first technique allows you to transform a copy of an object. You can then create additional transformed copies.

To create multiple transformed copies:

1. Hold the Opt/Alt key as you begin the transformation. A plus sign (+) appears next to the star cursor.
2. Release the mouse button first and then the Opt/Alt key to create a transformed copy of the original object ㉜.

TIP If you do not see the plus sign (+), check that the Object Preference for Opt/Alt-dragging to create copies is selected*(see page 391)*.

3. Choose **Edit > Duplicate** to create additional transformed copies ㉝.

The second technique allows you to store up to five transformations. You can then apply all the transformations as you make copies.

To combine transformations into Power Duplicating:

1. Select the object you want to transform.
2. Choose **Edit > Clone.** This creates a copy of the object on top of the original.
3. Move the clone or use any of the transformation tools to modify it.
4. Apply any of the other transformations. Each of the transformations is now stored.
5. Choose **Edit > Duplicate.** The object is copied and modified according to the stored transformations.
6. Choose **Edit > Duplicate** as many times as needed. Each command creates a new object transformed according to the stored transformation settings ㉞.

Using the Transformation Handles

At times it may be cumbersome to stop working on artwork to choose the scale or rotation tools. The Transformation handles let you modify objects directly on the page without needing to change tools.

To use the Transformation handles:

1. With the Pointer tool active, double-click the selected object. A rectangular box with eight Transformation handles appears 35.

TIP Hold the Cmd/Ctrl key to temporarily switch to the Pointer tool.

2. Move the cursor near the handles to transform the selection as described in the following exercises.
3. Move the cursor inside the box. The four-headed arrow indicates you can move the objects to a new position 36.
4. Drag the Transformation point icon away from the center of the object. This changes the point around which the transformation occurs 37.
5. Double-click outside the box to clear the Transformation handles.

TIP Hold the Opt/Alt key as you drag with the Transformation handles to copy the object as it is transformed.

TIP As you use the Transformation handles, the information about the transformation is stored in the Transform panel 38. You can then apply that numerical value to other objects.

TIP If you find the Transformation handles interfere with your work, turn them off using the Preferences *(see page 390)*.

35 *The* **Transformation handles** *around a grouped object.*

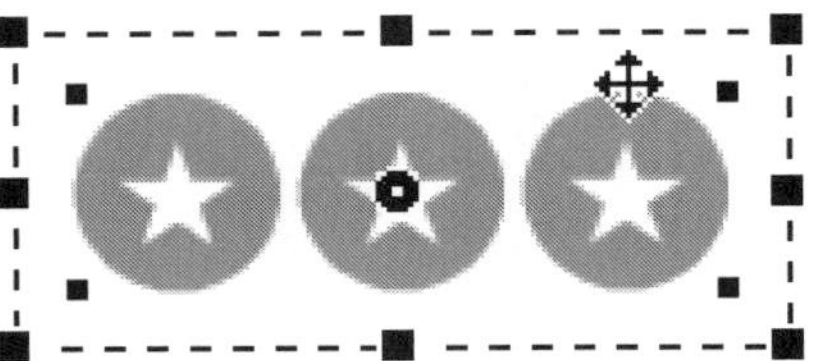

36 *The* **Move cursor** *indicates that you can move the objects and the Transformation handles.*

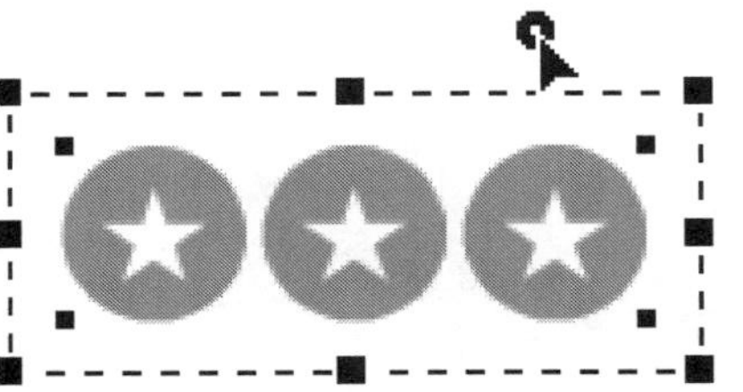

37 *Move the* **Transformation point icon** *to change the point around which the transformation occurs.*

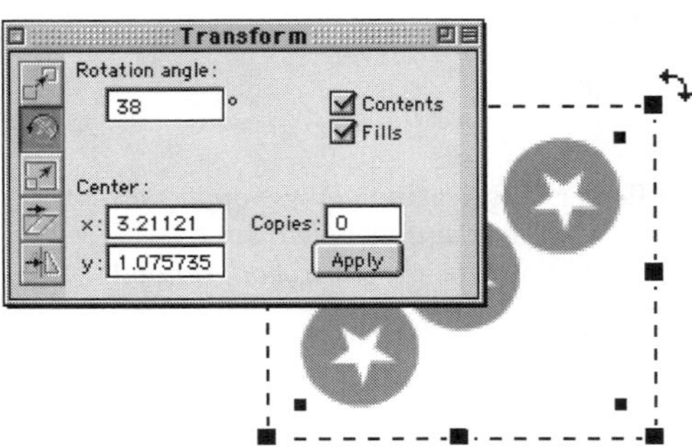

38 *As you use the Transformation handles, the information about the transformation is stored in the Transform panel.*

Using the Transformation Handles

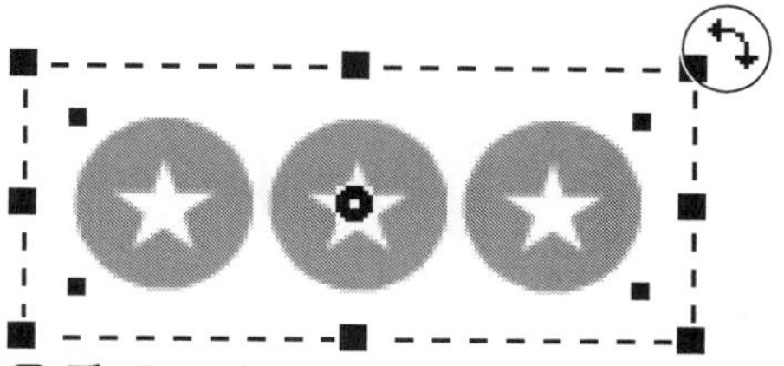

39 *The* **Rotation icon** *(circled) lets you use the Transformation handles to rotate an object.*

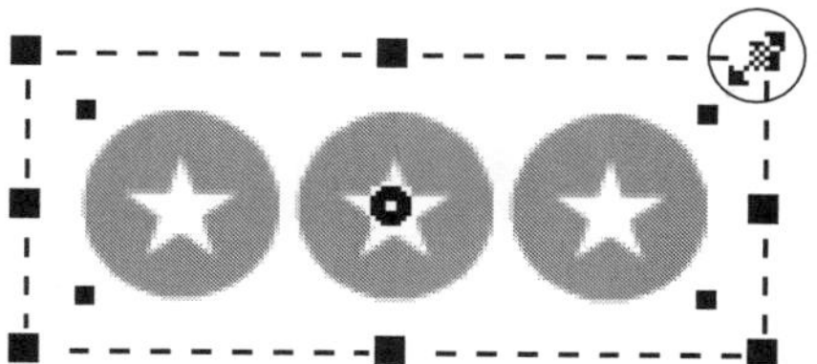

40 *The* **Scale icon** *(circled) lets you use the Transformation handles to scale an object.*

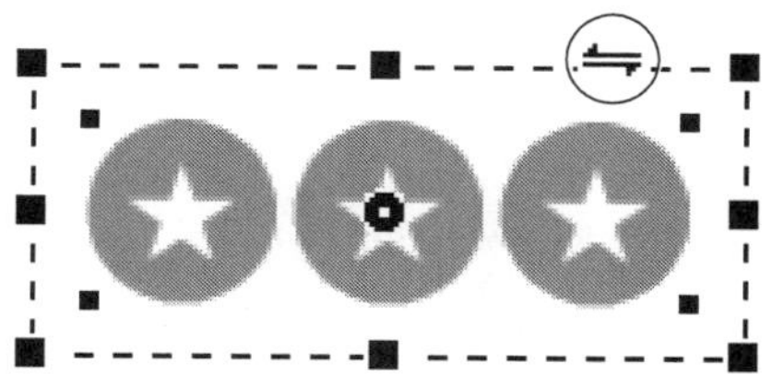

41 *The* **Skew icon** *(circled) lets you skew the object around the Transformation point.*

To rotate using the Transformation handles:

1. Move the cursor near one of the handles. The curved arrow Rotation icon appears **39**.
2. Drag to rotate the object around the transformation point.

To scale using the Transformation handles:

1. Move the cursor directly onto one of the handles. The double-headed arrow Scale icon appears **40**.
2. Drag to scale the object from the transformation point.

To skew using the Transformation handles:

1. Place the cursor between the handles. The split arrow Skew icon appears **41**.
2. Drag to skew the object from the transformation point.

Constraining Transformations

As you draw, move, or transform objects, the objects are positioned along an invisible line called the Constrain axis. The default setting of this axis is 0°. This means that your objects line up in an ordinary horizontal fashion. However, by changing the Constrain axis, you can make all your objects automatically align along any angle you choose.

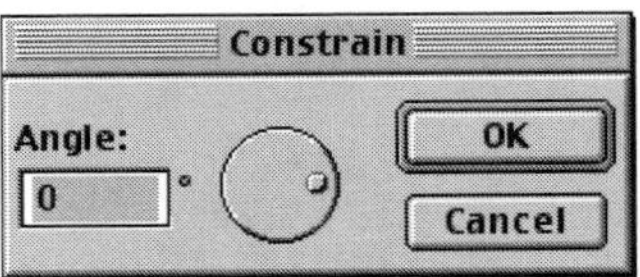

42 *Use the* **Constrain dialog box** *to change the horizontal axis along which objects are drawn.*

To change the Constrain axis:

1. Choose **Modify > Constrain.** The Constrain dialog box appears 42.
2. Enter the angle you want for the Constrain axis in the Angle field.

   or

   Rotate the wheel to enter an angle in the field.
3. Click OK. All objects will be drawn along the angle you have just set 43.

TIP Changing the Constrain axis only affects those objects created from that point on. It does not affect previously created objects.

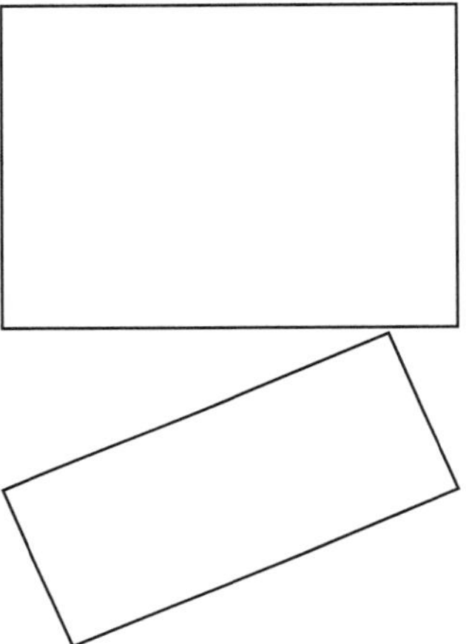

43 *The top rectangle was drawn with a Constrain axis of 0°. The bottom rectangle had a Constrain axis of 23°.*

44 *The Align panel lets you align or distribute objects.*

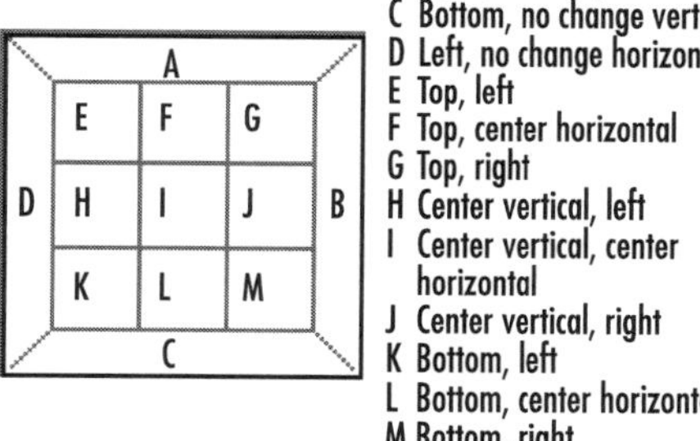

45 *Click each portion of the* **Alignment graphic controller** *to set different alignment options.*

Aligning Objects

You may want to move objects so that their tops, bottoms, sides, or centers are in alignment. You may also want to move objects so they are distributed equally. FreeHand gives you several ways to align and distribute objects.

To align using the Align menu:

1. Select the objects you want to align.
2. Choose one of the following from the Modify > Align menu:
   - **Top** aligns the objects along the top edge of their bounding boxes.
   - **Bottom** aligns the objects along the bottom edge of their bounding box.
   - **Center Horizontal** aligns the objects along the horizontal center of their bounding boxes.
   - **Center Vertical** aligns the objects along the vertical center of their bounding boxes.
   - **Left** aligns the objects along the left edge of their bounding boxes.
   - **Right** aligns the objects along the right edge of their bounding boxes.

To align using the Align panel:

1. Select the objects you want to align.
2. In the Align panel, use the Horizontal menu to set the horizontal alignment of the objects 44.

   or

   Use the Vertical menu to set the vertical alignment of the objects.

   or

   Click inside the Alignment graphic controller to choose an alignment setting 45.
3. Click the Align to page option if you want the objects to align to the page.
4. Click the Align button to move the objects into position.

Aligning Objects

To distributes objects using the Align panel:

1. Select the objects you want to distribute.
2. In the Align panel, use the Horizontal menu to set the horizontal distribution of the objects.

   or

   Use the Vertical menu to set the vertical distribution of the objects.

TIP You can use a combination of the align commands and the distributes commands at once.

ENVELOPES & PERSPECTIVES

Perhaps the most sophisticated path operations are the changes you can make to objects created using the Envelope command and Perspective Grid.

Enveloping is when you use the shape of one object to warp another. The logo of the rock group The Monkees is a perfect example of enveloping. (If you are too young to remember, the Monkees logo consists of the word Monkees in the shape of a guitar.)

FreeHand's Perspective Grid allows you to automatically reshape objects as they would appear in perspective. As someone who has spent hundreds of hours manually creating perspective grid lines and aligning objects, I can assure you the Perspective Grid is a real benefit.

Working with Envelopes

Enveloping starts with 21 ready-made preset shapes that are stored in the Envelope toolbar. These shapes can be applied to either objects or text.

To apply an envelope to a graphic:

1. Select the object or text block you want to distort.
2. In the Envelope toolbar, select the envelope preset you want from the pop-up menu ❶.
3. Click the Create envelope icon to distort the selected object ❷.

   or

   Choose **Modify > Envelope > Create.** This uses the preset currently active in the Envelope toolbar ❸.

TIP Although you can apply envelopes to text objects, you may find you get better results if you first convert the text to paths *(see page 258)*.

TIP You may also find that some envelope shapes look better when they are applied a second time to an object ❹.

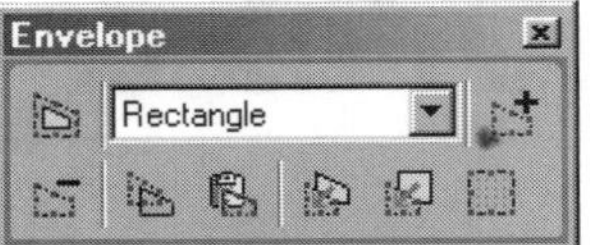

❶ *The* **Envelope toolbar** *contains preset shapes you can choose among to distort an object.*

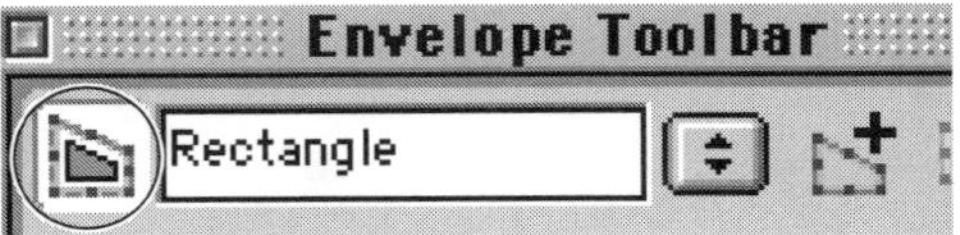

❷ *The* **Create icon** *lets you apply the currently selected preset as an envelope shape.*

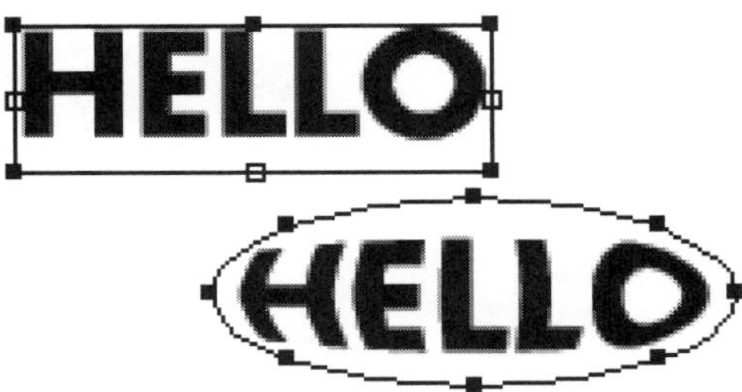

❸ *Applying the circle envelope preset to an elongated object creates an elliptical text object.*

❹ *The Circle preset was applied twice to text to create this elliptical shape.*

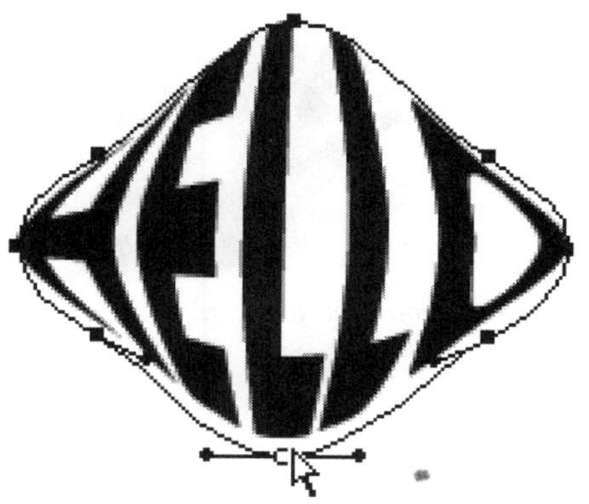

❺ *You can modify the points on the envelope path.*

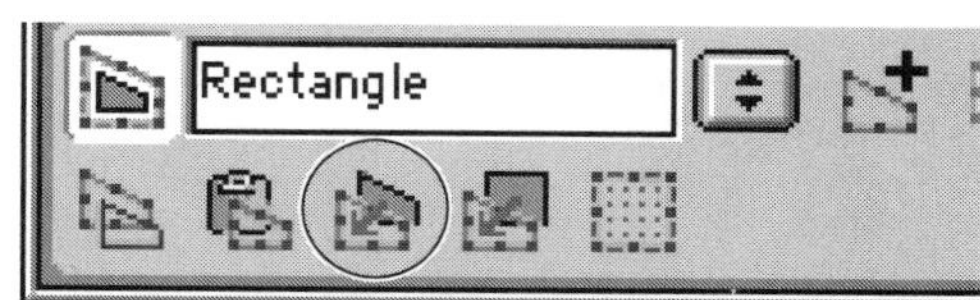

❻ *The* **Release icon** *(circled) applies the envelope shape to the graphic and then removes the envelope path.*

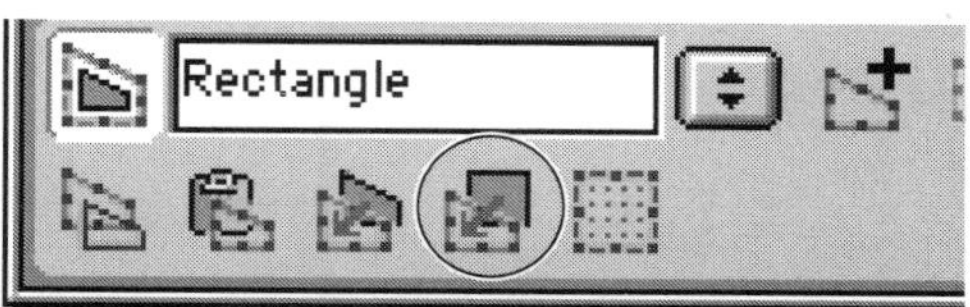

❼ *The* **Remove icon** *(circled) removes the envelope shape from the graphic.*

To modify the envelope applied to a graphic:

1. Use any of the selection tools to select the graphic. The envelope shape appears as a path.
2. Use any of the techniques that modify paths to change the shape of the envelope ❺. This includes moving the points on the path, adding and deleting points, and using the transform tools.

TIP To edit text inside an envelope, Opt/Alt double-click with the Pointer tool. This opens the Text Editor where you can make your changes.

There are some limits to what you can do when an envelope is applied to a graphic. For instance, you can't use the graphic in a blend or apply a second envelope to the graphic. So you may want to release the envelope after you apply it to a graphic.

To release an envelope from a graphic:

◆ Choose **Modify > Envelope > Release.**

or

Click the Release icon in the Envelope toolbar ❻.

TIP When you release an envelope a path will return to being a path; a text block will become a group and the individual letters will have been converted to paths.

You may also want to remove an envelope so that it no longer distorts a graphic.

To remove an envelope from a graphic:

◆ Choose **Modify > Envelope > Remove.**

or

Click the Remove icon in the Envelope toolbar ❼.

You can also create your own custom envelope shapes from paths.

To use a path as an envelope:

1. Select the path you want to use as an envelope ❽.
2. Choose **Edit > Copy** to copy the path to the clipboard.
3. Select the object to which you want to apply the envelope.
4. Choose **Modify > Envelope > Paste as Envelope.**

   or

   Click the Paste as Envelope icon on the Envelope toolbar ❾. The envelope is applied to the object ❿.

Once you have a new envelope shape, you may want to save it to use it on other objects. This includes shapes you have pasted as custom envelopes as well as preset paths you have modified.

To save a custom envelope:

1. Select the object that contains the envelope you wish to save.
2. Choose **Modify > Envelope > Save as Preset.**

   or

   Click the Save as Preset icon on the Envelope toolbar ⓫. The New Envelope dialog box appears ⓬.
3. Name the envelope shape and click OK. The envelope is listed in the preset list.

❽ *Create a path you want to use as an envelope preset.*

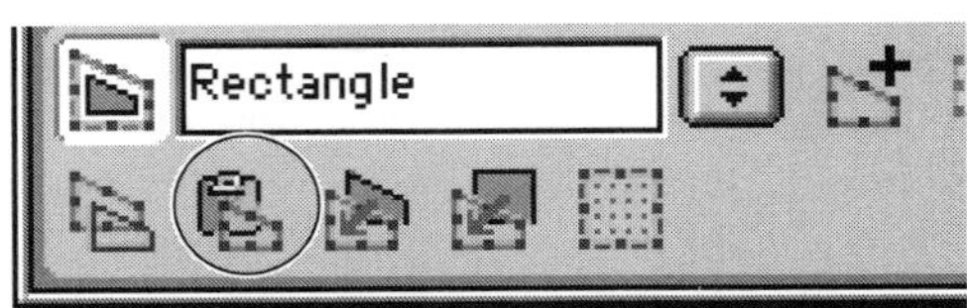

❾ *The* **Paste as Envelope icon** *(circled) applied the contents of the clipboard as an envelope.*

❿ *The results of pasting a path as an envelope.*

⓫ *The* **Save as Preset icon** *(circled) lets you save a custom shape as an envelope preset.*

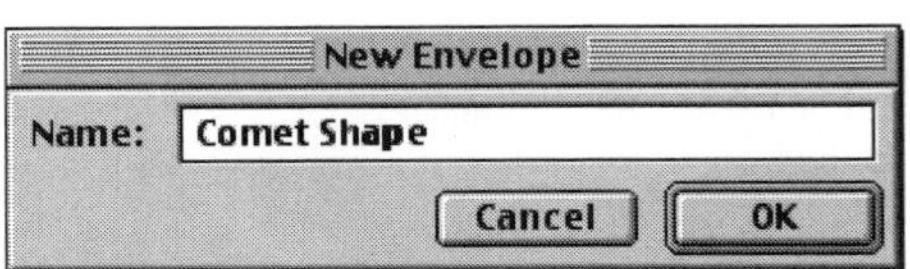

⓬ *The* **New Envelope dialog box** *lets you name a custom preset shape.*

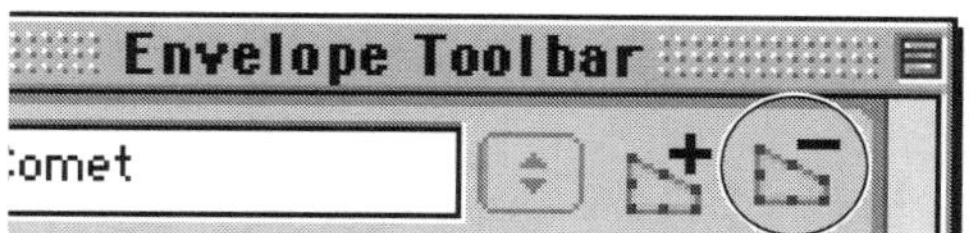

⓭ *The* **Delete Preset icon** *(circled) lets you delete any presets from the envelope preset list.*

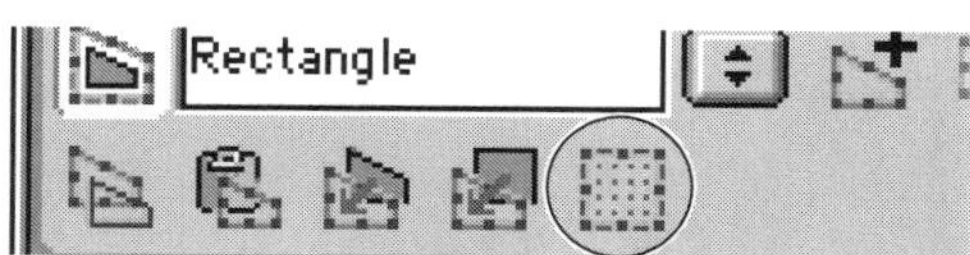

⓮ *The* **Show Map icon** *(circled) lets you reveal or hide the grid used in the envelope distortion.*

⓯ *The* **Envelope Map** *displays the grid of lines used in the envelope.*

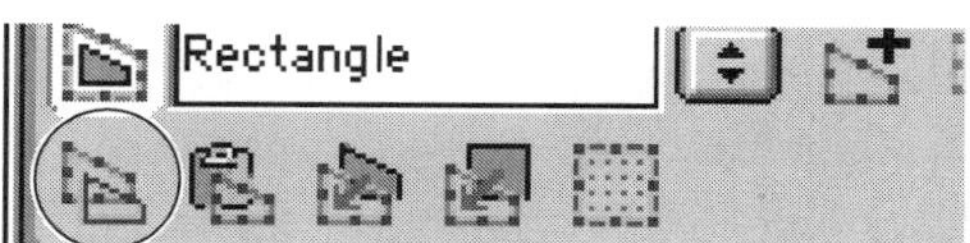

⓰ *The* **Copy as Path icon** *(circled) converts the envelope path into a path on the clipboard*

⓱ *Copy the envelope as a path and put it behind the original envelope to put a fill behind the text.*

To delete an envelope preset:

1. Select the envelope you wish to remove from the pop-up menu on the Envelope toolbar.
2. Choose **Modify > Envelope > Delete Preset.**

   or

   Click the Delete Preset icon on the Envelope toolbar ⓭.

FreeHand also lets you see the envelope map. This is the grid of lines that is used by the envelope as part of the distortion.

To see the envelope grid:

- Choose **Modify > Envelope > Show Map.**

  or

  Click the Show Map icon on the Envelope toolbar ⓮. The map appears inside the envelope ⓯.

After you have created an envelope to modify a path or a text block, you can convert it to a path for use in your document.

TIP Converting an envelope to a path is very helpful since you cannot apply fills or strokes to the paths used as envelopes.

To paste an envelope as a path:

1. Select the graphic that has the envelope you want to copy.
2. Choose **Modify > Envelope > Copy As Path.**

   or

   Click the Copy as Path icon on the Envelope toolbar ⓰.
3. Choose **Edit > Paste** to paste the shape into the document. You can add a fill or stroke to the path ⓱.

Using the Perspective Grid

The perspective grid gives you a very powerful set of tools for quickly and easily creating graphics that maintain a consistent perspective. Essentially, it allows you to create perspective envelopes that automatically adjust as they are moved around the page.

To view the Perspective grid:

◆ Choose **View > Perspective Grid > Show**. The grid appears on the page.

To attach objects to the Perspective grid:

1. Choose the Perspective tool from the Tools panel ⓲.
2. Use the Perspective tool to drag an object to the desired place on the grid.
3. Tap one of the arrow keys on the keyboard as follows:
   - **Left arrow** attaches the object to the left grid.
   - **Right arrow** attaches the object to the right grid.
   - **Down arrow** attaches the object to the floor grid, oriented to the right vanishing point.
   - **Up arrow** attaches the object to the floor grid, oriented to the left vanishing point.

⓲ *The* **Perspective tool** *in the Tools panel.*

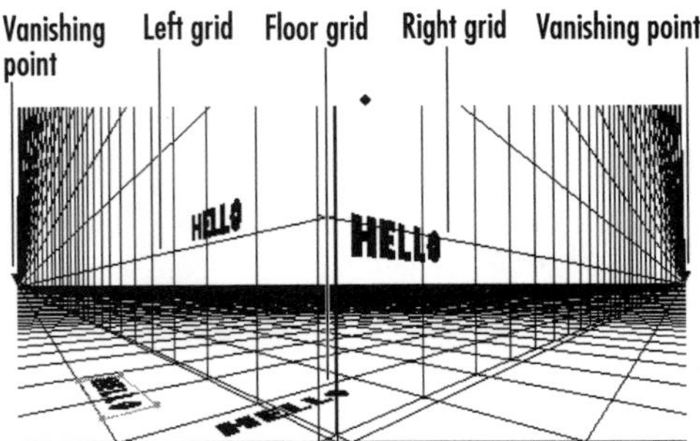

⓳ *Use the* **Units of Measurement** *pop-up menu to change the units of measurement.*

Understanding the Perspective Grids

Perspective is the attempt to portray the appearance of a three-dimensional world in a two-dimensional graphic ⓳.

If you look straight at a book, the cover is a rectangle, but if you put the book on an angle, the lines of the book change. Obviously the book itself doesn't change its shape—its appearance does. The angle that you slant the book is similar to the *left grid* or the *right grid* that the perspective grid aligns objects to. If you lay the book down, that is similar to aligning objects to a *floor grid.*

When you look down a road, objects seem to get smaller as they move away. The point where the objects are too small to be seen is called the *vanishing point.*

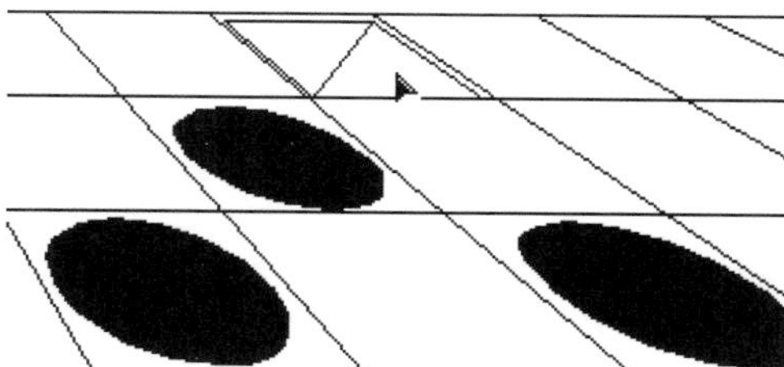

⑳ *As a circle is copied to different places on the perspective grid, it changes its shape.*

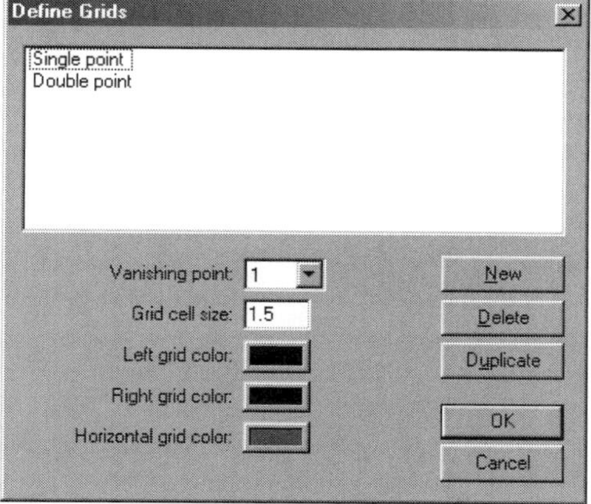

㉑ *The* **Define Grids** *dialog box sets the attributes of the Perspective grids in the document.*

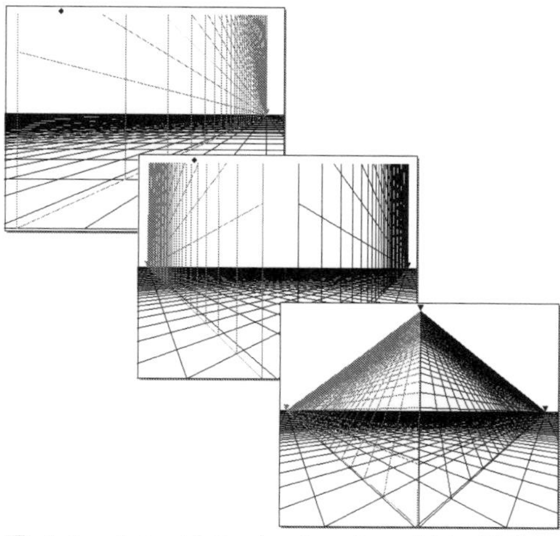

㉒ *A 1-point grid (top), a 2-point grid (middle), and a 3-point grid (bottom).*

To move an object on the Perspective grid:

- Use the Perspective tool to move the object around the grid. As the object changes position it changes its shape to conform to the perspective grid ⑳.

TIP Hold the Opt/Alt key to copy an object while dragging it on the grid with the Perspective tool.

TIP Hold the Shift key to constrain its movement to the grid axes.

To define a Perspective grid:

1. Choose **View > Perspective Grid > Define Grids.** This opens the Define Grids dialog box ㉑.
2. Click New to add a new grid to the list.
3. Double click to change the name of the grid.
4. Use the Vanishing Point list to set the number of vanishing points in the grid ㉒.
5. Use the grid cell size to set how large the cells should be. A larger cell size creates fewer grid lines on the page.
6. Click the color wells to set the color for each portion of the grid.
7. Use the Delete button to delete grids.
8. Use the Duplicate button to make a copy of each grid.
9. Click OK to accept the setting and return to the document. The grids you define can be selected from the bottom of the **View > Perspective Grid** submenu.

To modify the page characteristics of a grid:

- Choose the Perspective tool. Modify the elements of the grid as follows ㉓:
  - To change the height of the grid, drag the diamond control up or down.
  - To change the position of the vanishing point, drag the point to the right or left.
  - To change the angle of a grid, drag the grid lines.
  - To hide or show a left or right grid, double-click the grid's vanishing point.
  - To hide or show the floor grid, double-click the horizon line.

TIP To protect a grid configuration, duplicate the grid in the Define Grid dialog box before you make changes.

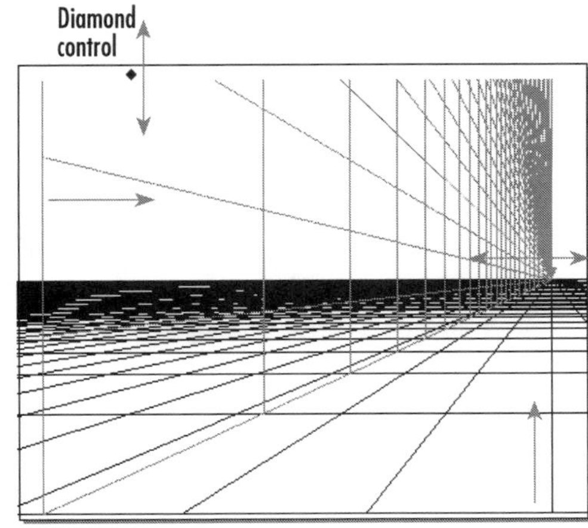

㉓ *Drag the* **Elements of a grid** *to change the characteristics of the grid on the page.*

To keep objects aligned as you modify a grid:

1. Select the objects.
2. Hold the Shift key as you modify the grid.

Objects aligned to a grid are inside envelopes. As with other envelopes, you can release an object leaving it distorted.

To release objects from the grid:

1. Select the object you want to release.
2. Choose **View > Perspective Grid > Release Perspective.**

You can also remove an object from the grid and return it to its original shape.

To remove objects from the grid:

1. Select the object you want to release and restore to its original shape.
2. Choose **View > Perspective Grid > Remove Perspective.**

TIP You can also choose **Modify > Envelope > Release** or **Modify > Envelope > Remove** as well as the Release and Remove buttons on the Envelope toolbar to release or remove objects from the grid.

LAYERS AND LAYERING 12

There were no computers when I started working in advertising. (Amazingly, we still managed to create artwork, logos, ads, and brochures even without any computers.) Instead, we pasted type and artwork on stiff mechanical boards that we sent to the printer to convert into printed materials.

If we needed to change the artwork, we would simply paste a new illustration or text on top of the old one. After a few weeks, we had many layers of paper on the board.

We also had acetate sheets that we would paste the artwork or text onto. This allowed us to flip the acetate over to see one version of the ad or cover it up with a second version.

Although it is electronic, Macromedia FreeHand works very similarly to the old boards. As soon as you put more than one path on your page, you already have layers of the artwork.

And you can also organize your artwork into electronic acetate sheets that can display different versions of the artwork.

Using the Arrange Commands

Objects are layered in the same order they were created. Though you may not see this when the objects are side by side, it is apparent when they overlap ❶–❷.

❶ *Although it may not be obvious, one object is in front of the other.*

❷ *When two objects overlap, it is obvious which object is in front of the other.*

To move objects to the front of a layer:

1. Select an object in your artwork.
2. Choose **Modify > Arrange > Bring To Front** ❸–❹ to move the object to the front of the other objects in its layer.

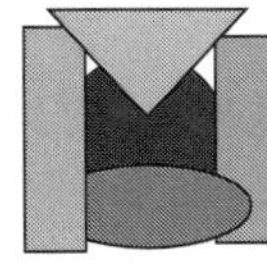

❸ *If you want to move an object to the foreground…*

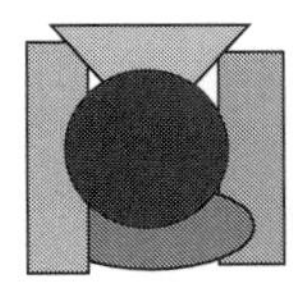

❹ *…select it and use the* **Bring To Front command.**

To move objects to the back of a layer:

1. Select an object in your artwork.
2. Choose **Modify > Arrange > Send To Back** to move the object to the back of its layer.

TIP If you choose Bring To Front or Send To Back on a subselected object of a group, the object moves to the front or back of the group rather than the layer.

Sometimes you want to move an object in the middle of a layer. To do that, you use a different set of commands.

To move objects forward in a layer:

1. Select an object in your artwork.
2. Choose **Modify > Arrange > Move Forward** to move the object forward in its layer. This moves the object in front of the first object it was behind.
3. Repeat until the object is in the correct position in the layer ❺–❻.

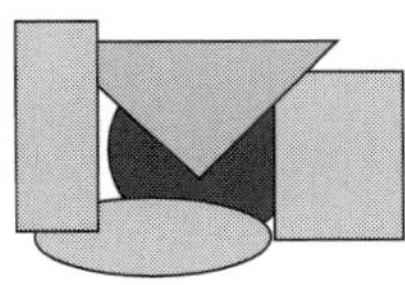

❺ *In this illustration, the circle needs to be in front of the triangle and square.*

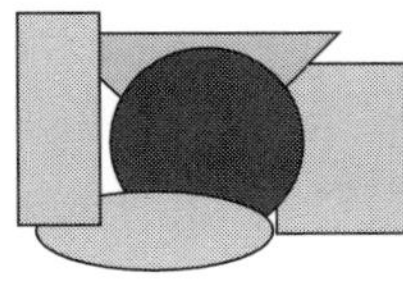

❻ *The same illustration after the* **Move Forward command** *was applied twice to the circle.*

To move objects backward in a layer:

1. Select an object in your artwork.
2. Choose **Modify > Arrange > Move Backward.** This moves the object backward in its layer.
3. Repeat until the object is in the correct position in the layer.

Using Paste in Front or Back

Since it may be tedious to choose Move Backward or Move Forward over and over, FreeHand offers two other ways to move objects within their layer.

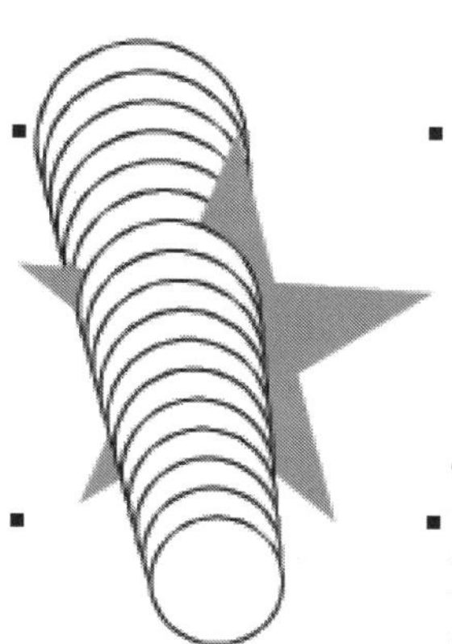

❼ *To move an object using* **Paste Behind**, *select the object you want to move and then choose Cut.*

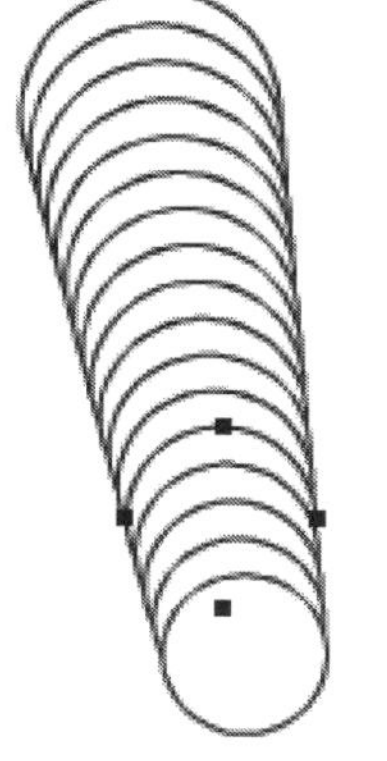

❽ *Select the object that you want the object to be behind, in this case, the fifth circle.*

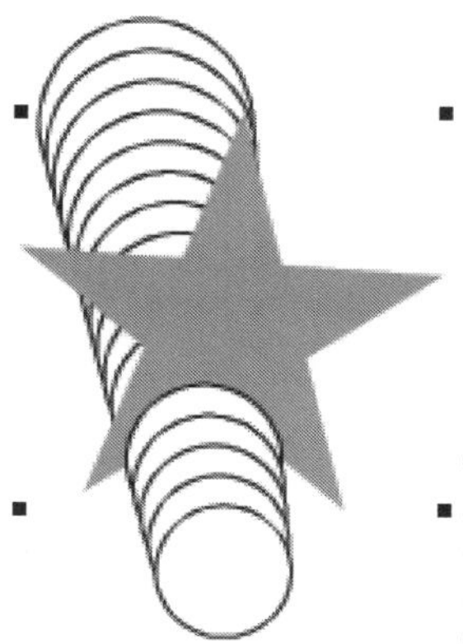

❾ *Choose* **Paste Behind.** *The cut object appears behind the selected object.*

To move objects using Paste Behind:

1. Select the object that you want to move.
2. Choose **Edit > Cut** ❼.
3. Select the object that you want in front of the original object ❽.
4. Choose **Edit > Paste Behind.** The original object is pasted behind the object you chose ❾.

To move objects using Paste In Front:

1. Select the object that you want to move.
2. Choose **Edit > Cut.**
3. Select the object that you want behind the original object.
4. Choose **Edit > Paste In Front.** The original object is pasted in front of the object you chose.

Locking and Unlocking Objects

As you work, there may be times when you want to lock an object on a layer. This may be to avoid moving the object or to make sure it is not transformed.

To lock an object:

1. Select the object or objects you want to lock.
2. Choose **Modify > Lock.** The Lock icon in the Info toolbar indicates that the object is locked ⑩.

To unlock an object:

1. Select the object you want to unlock.
2. Choose **Modify > Unlock.**

If you have used programs such as Adobe Illustrator, you will find FreeHand treats locked objects differently. In Illustrator locked objects can not be selected or modified. However, FreeHand does let you make some changes to locked objects. The chart on the right gives you a list of what you can—and can not—do with locked objects.

⑩ *The* **Lock icon** *of the Info Toolbar indicates that an object is locked.*

Working with Locked Objects

Select	**Yes**	
Modify fill	**Yes**	
Modify stroke	**Yes**	
Move		**No**
Resize		**No**
Transform		**No**
Delete		**No**
Copy	**Yes**	
Cut		**No**
Edit text	**Yes**	
Modify text formatting	**Yes**	

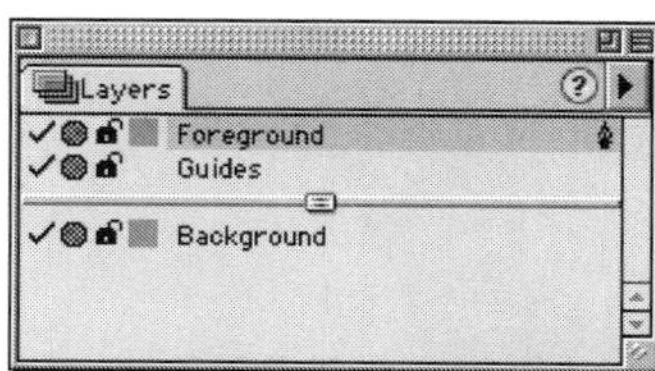

⓫ *The* **Layers panel** *shows the three default layers: Foreground, Guides, and Background.*

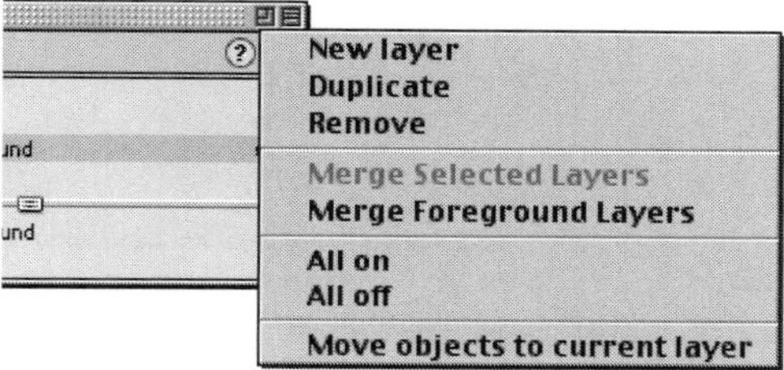

⓬ *The* **Layers panel menu** *lets you add, delete, duplicate, or hide or show the layers.*

Working with Layers

As your artwork becomes more complex, you may find that you need other ways of organizing objects. For instance, you may have many objects that overlap each other and you need to hide some objects while working on others. In that case, you will need to use FreeHand's Layers panel.

To view the Layers panel:

1. If you do not see the Layers panel on your screen, choose **Window > Panels > Layers.**
2. If you have not changed the default layers for your document, you should see three layers: Foreground, Guides, and Background ⓫.

Once you have created a new layer, you may want to rename it so that it reflects the items on that layer.

To rename a layer:

1. In the Layers panel, double-click the name of the layer you want to rename.
2. Type the new name of the layer.
3. Press Return or Enter, or click the Layers panel with the mouse.

To duplicate a layer:

1. Click the name of the layer you want to duplicate.
2. Choose Duplicate from the Layers panel menu ⓬. The layer and all of the objects on it will be duplicated.

TIP The Guides layer cannot be renamed or duplicated.

To remove a layer:

1. Click the name of the layer you want to remove.
2. Choose Remove from the Layers panel menu. The layer and the objects on it are removed.

TIP You cannot delete the Guides layer or the very last drawing layer of a document.

TIP An alert box warns you if you try to remove a layer that has objects on it.

The layer at the top of the Layers panel is in front of the other layers. Layers do not have to remain in the order in which you created them. You use the Layers panel to reorder layers.

⓭ *In this illustration, the layer containing the Moon artwork is above the Earth.*

To reorder layers:

1. In the Layers panel, select the name of the layer you want to reorder ⓭.
2. Drag the name of the layer to the spot on the list that represents where you would like the layer to be.

TIP (Win) A double-headed arrow cursor appears as you drag layers to new positions in the Layers panel.

3. Release the mouse button. The name of the layer disappears from where it was and reappears in its new position in the Layers panel. All objects on the layer are repositioned in the document ⓮.

TIP If you want guides to appear in front of your artwork, drag the Guides layer above the layer that contains the artwork.

⓮ *The Earth layer is dragged above the Moon which changes the position of the artwork.*

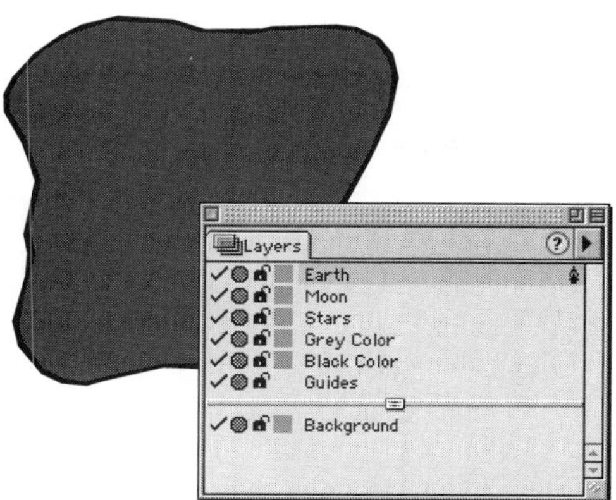

⓯ *In this illustration, the gray color is on the same layer as the Earth.*

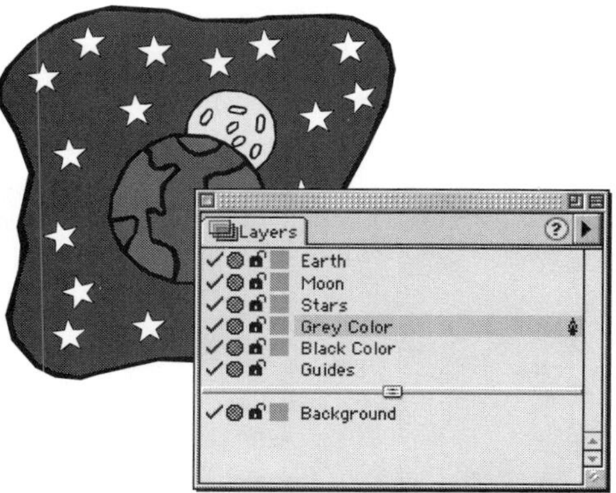

⓰ *The same illustration after clicking the name of the Grey Color layer.*

When you are working, the objects you create go on the active layer, the one that has the pen icon on the Layers panel. You may want to move artwork from one layer to another.

To manually move objects between layers:

1. Select the artwork you want to move to a new layer. The layer to which it belongs is highlighted ⓯.
2. Click the name of the layer that is the destination for the artwork. The artwork moves to that new layer ⓰.

TIP To convert a path into a guide, move the guide onto the Guides layer.

TIP You cannot move artwork onto a locked layer *(see page 158)*.

Some people do not like how easy it is to move objects from one layer to another. FreeHand lets you set a Preference that turns off the ability to move objects by clicking the name of a layer *(see Appendix C)*.

If you turn off the default setting, you must use the Layers panel menu to move objects between layers.

To use the menu to move objects between layers:

1. Select the artwork you want to move to a new layer.
2. Click the name of the layer that is the destination for the artwork.
3. Choose Move objects to current layers from the Layers panel menu. The artwork moves to the selected layer.

A horizontal line divides the Layers panel. The layers above the line appear normal and print. The layers below the line appear dimmed and do not print. You may find you want to move layers from the printing to nonprinting areas of the list.

To create a nonprinting layer:

1. Drag the layer below the dividing line in the Layers panel.
2. Release the mouse button. The layer moves below the line, and any objects on the layer are dimmed and do not print ⑰.

TIP Use nonprinting layers to hold images that have been placed for tracing *(see pages 74–77)*.

To create a printing layer:

1. Drag the name of the layer above the dividing line in the Layers panel.
2. Release the mouse button. The layer moves above the dividing line, and any objects on the layer will print.

TIP Objects on the Guides layer do not ever print, regardless of where the Guides layer is, either above or below the line.

To convert objects to guides:

1. Select the object you want to convert to a guide.
2. Click the Guides layer. The artwork is converted to a guide ⑱.

TIP You must use the Guides dialog box *(see page 36)* to convert guides back into artwork.

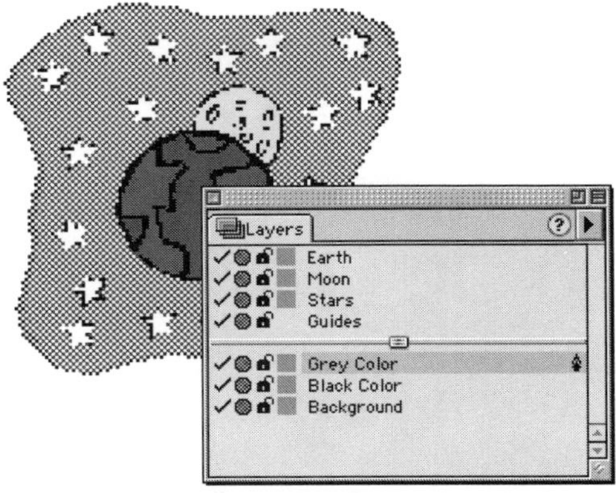

⑰ *To make a* **nonprinting layer,** *drag the name of the layer below the horizontal line.*

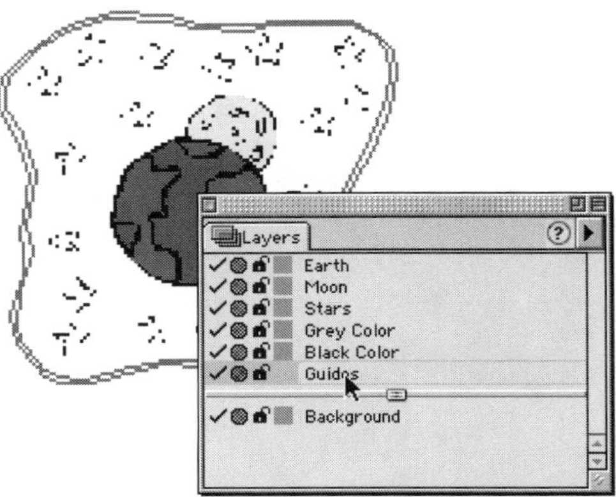

⑱ *Click the Guides layer to* **convert the selected objects to guides.**

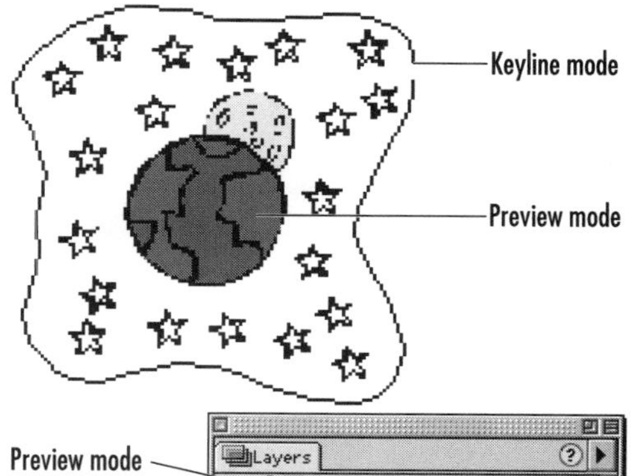

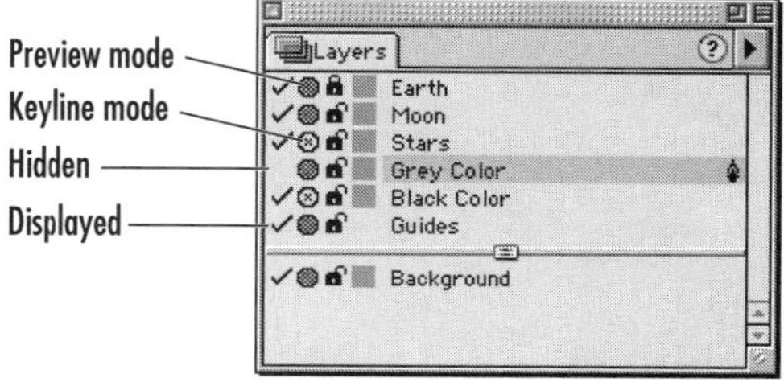

⓳ *Use the Layers panels to control how artwork appears onscreen.*

You can also use the Layers panel to change the preview for the objects on each layer. This is especially helpful if you work with very complicated illustrations and need to select just certain elements.

To hide a layer:

- Click the check mark to the left of the layer name ⓳. The check mark disappears, making the layer invisible.

To show a layer:

- Click the empty space for the check mark to make the layer visible ⓳.

TIP Hold the Opt/Ctrl key as you click a check mark to show or hide all the layers.

TIP Use the *All on* or *All off* commands in the Options pop-up menu to quickly show or hide all layers.

To set a layer to the Keyline mode:

- Click the gray dot to the left of the layer name ⓳. This creates a hollow dot that indicates the layer is in the Keyline mode *(see page 31)*.

To set a layer to the Preview mode:

Click the hollow dot to the left of the layer name ⓳. This creates a gray dot that indicates the layer is in the Preview mode *(see page 30)*.

TIP Hold the Opt/Ctrl key as you click a dot to switch the preview for all the layers.

There may be times when you want to see the objects on a layer, but you do not want to be able to select those objects. In this case, you need to lock the layer.

To lock a layer:

- Click the open padlock icon. This changes the icon to the closed position and locks all objects on the layer ⑳.

To unlock a layer:

- Click the closed padlock icon. This changes the padlock to the open position and unlocks all objects on the layer ⑳.

TIP Objects on locked layers cannot be selected, modified, or moved.

When you select an object, the points and path outlines for that object are displayed in a color *(see Chapter 7, "Working with Points")*. You can change that display color by using the Layers panel.

To change the display color of a layer:

- Drag a color swatch from the Swatches or Mixer onto the color box for the layer ㉑. The color box next to the name changes. All selected objects on that layer have their paths displayed in that color. *(For information on working with Swatches or the Mixer, see Chapter 13, "Working in Color".)*

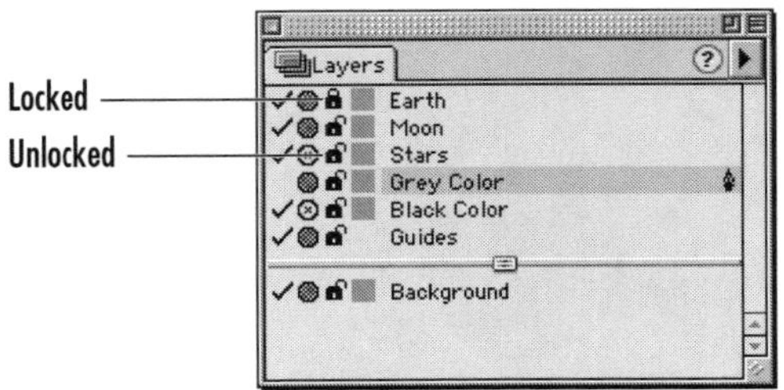

⑳ *Click an open padlock to lock a layer. Click a closed padlock to unlock a layer.*

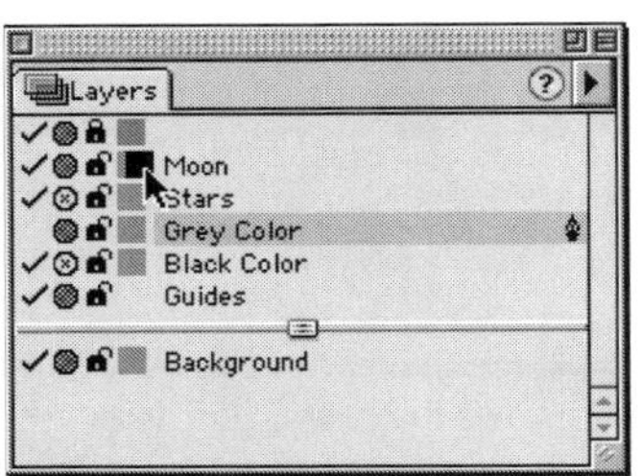

㉑ *To change the* **path display color** *of a layer, drag a color swatch onto the color box of that layer.*

WORKING IN COLOR 13

My first computer was a Macintosh SE which is currently serving as a bookend under my desk. It has a built-in screen that is even smaller than a page of this book. The screen only displays black and white images.

Still, I used it to create all sorts of full-color illustrations and designs. I just defined all my colors using numerical values and used my vivid imagination to visualize what the artwork would look like when it was finally printed.

I doubt you're using anything as primitive as my old computer. Today it's hard to even find a black and white monitor.

Interestingly, though, there are few differences in the principles of working in color from the old days to now. In fact, the basics of working in color aren't computer specific; they come from years and years of print shops printing color images.

Defining Colors

TIP Even though the panel tab says Mixer, the full name of the panel used to define colors is the Color Mixer.

The CMYK mode defines the color according to the four process colors used by most commercial printers—cyan, magenta, yellow, and black. This is the most common and best-known color system used by graphic artists and designers.

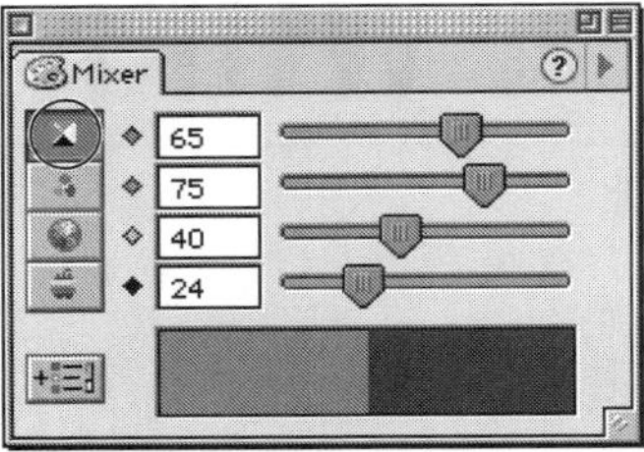

❶ *Click the* **CMYK icon** *(circled) to display the Color Mixer in CMYK mode.*

To define a CMYK color:

1. Click the CMYK icon in the Color Mixer ❶.
2. Click the cyan, magenta, yellow, or black fields and enter values for the color.

   or

   Drag the cyan, magenta, yellow, or black sliders to enter values for the color.

The RGB mode defines the color according to red, green, and blue components. This is primarily a video color system and is the system used by your own monitor. Many people who design for multimedia and the Web use RGB to define colors.

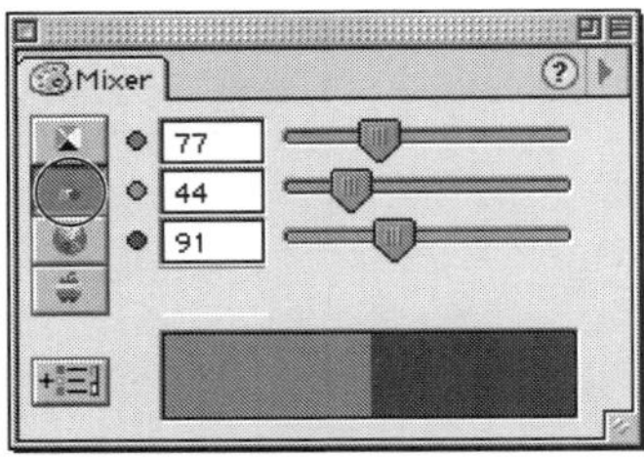

❷ *Click the* **RGB icon** *(circled) to display the Color Mixer in RGB mode.*

To define an RGB color:

1. Click the RGB icon in the Color Mixer ❷.
2. Click the red, green, or blue fields and enter values for the color.

   or

   Drag the red, green, or blue sliders to enter values for the color.

> **The 300% Ink Rule**
>
> When you define process colors, try to limit the total amount of ink to less than 300%. For instance, to make a dark brown, don't create a color of cyan: 75%, magenta: 100%, yellow: 100%, and black: 50%. When all those inks (325%) combine on the page, it can cause problems during the printing and drying of the pages.
>
> If you are defining dark colors, try reducing the amount of cyan, magenta, and yellow inks, and increase the amount of black ink.
>
> However, check with your print shop if you are going to have a lot of dark colors covering a page. They may ask you to limit the amount of ink even further.

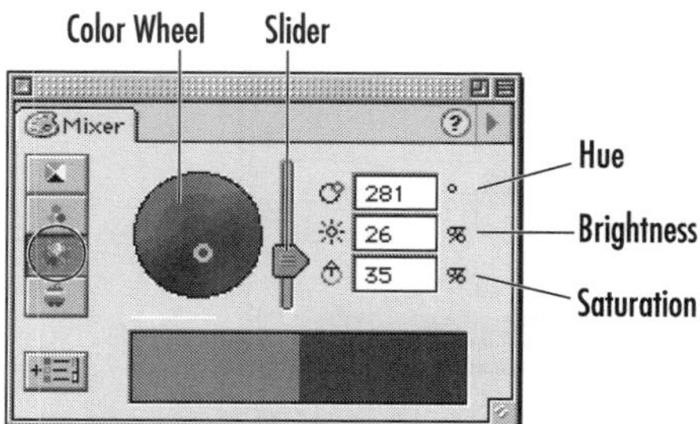

❸ *Click the* **HLS icon** *(circled) to display the Color Mixer in HLS mode.*

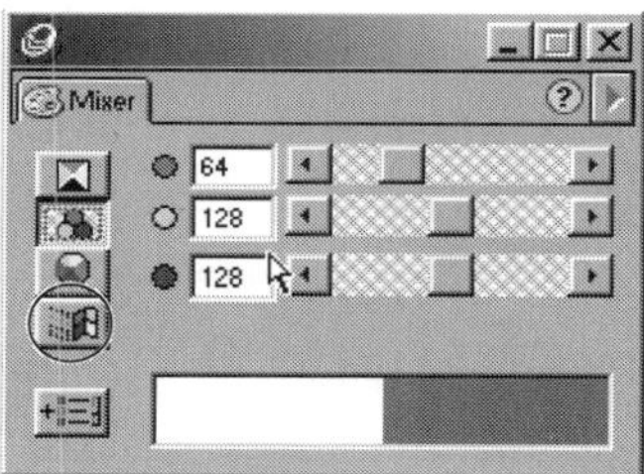

❹ *Click the* **Windows icon** *(circled) to display the Windows Colors.*

❺ *The* **Windows Basic Colors** *choices.*

The HLS system defines the color according to *hue, lightness,* and *saturation* components. The HLS system lets you pick different colors with similar values. For example, if you keep the lightness and saturation values the same, you can choose a red hue and green hue that belong together.

To define an HLS color:

1. Click the HLS icon.
2. Find the hue and saturation you want on the color wheel and click it ❸.

   or

   Enter the hue values (from 0 to 360 degrees) or the saturation amount (from 0 to 100 percent) in the fields.
3. Use the slider to adjust the brightness.

   or

   Enter the brightness value (from 0 to 100 percent) in the field.

The Color Mixer (Win) also has a Windows button that opens the Windows colors where you can pick from the colors installed in the Windows operating system.

To define using the Windows Colors (Win):

1. Click the Windows icon ❹. This opens the Windows Colors dialog box ❺.
2. Select one of the colors displayed.
3. Click the OK button.

The Apple button opens the Macintosh color picker where you can pick colors according to a number of different models installed in the Mac OS.

To define using the Apple Color Picker (Mac):

1. Click the Apple icon ❻. This opens the Apple Color Picker dialog box ❼.
2. Select one of the color systems on the left.
3. Define the color using the onscreen elements.
4. Click OK.

TIP The Apple Color Picker offers several different ways of choosing colors including the 216 Web-safe colors.

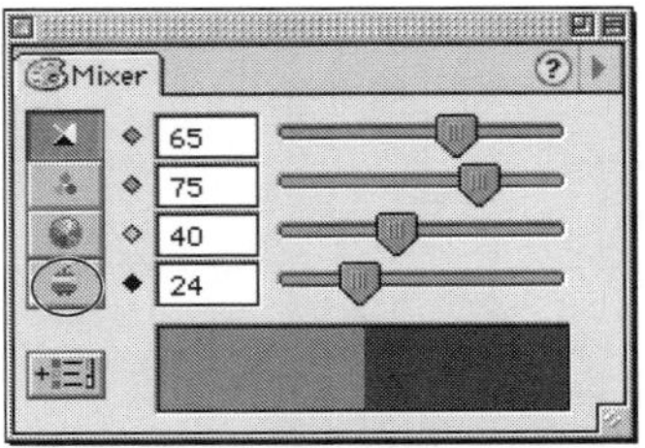

❻ *Click the* **Apple button** *(circled) to open the Macintosh Color Picker.*

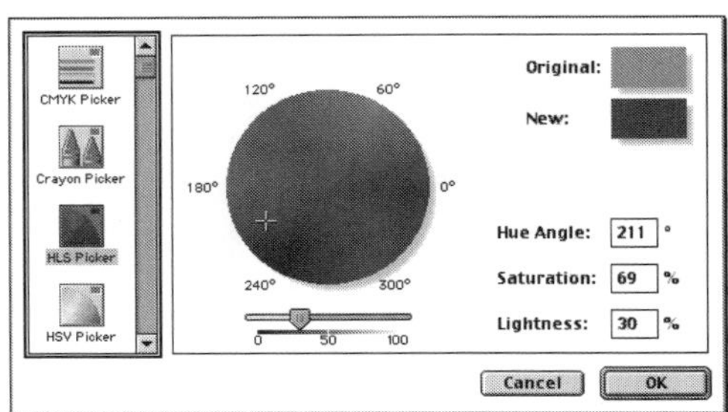

❼ *The* **Macintosh color picker** *lets you choose colors in a variety of systems.*

Which color system should you use?

If you are defining a color for artwork that will be printed in a four-color printing process, the CMYK color system will most likely be the best choice. When you define the CMYK values, you are choosing the exact percentage of cyan, magenta, yellow, and black ink that will be used to create the color. CMYK colors are also called four-color or process colors.

Rather than try to judge what your CMYK colors look like onscreen, you should refer to a printed process color book such as the Trumatch Color Guide, the Agfa Process Color Guide, or the Pantone Process Color Guide.

If you are creating Web graphics or multimedia work, you will most likely want to use the RGB colors. This is because the RGB system is based on the colors that are available on your monitor screen—the same way that Web pages and multimedia projects are displayed. Also, there are some colors that are available in RGB that are not found in CMYK.

HLS is a variation of the RGB color system. I don't know too many designers who use it. However, Sharon Steuer, author of the *Illustrator Wow! Books* suggests using HLS if you are trying to match the saturation or lightness of colors. Once you set one color, you can switch to HLS and then change only the hue value to get complimentary colors.

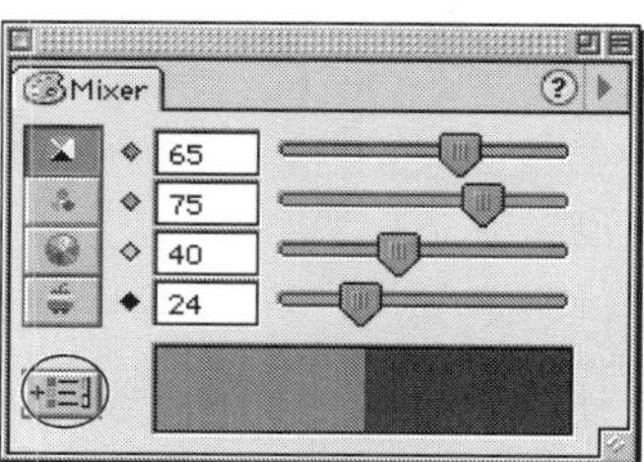

❽ *Click the* **Add to Swatches button** *(circled) to add a color from the Color Mixer to the Swatches panel.*

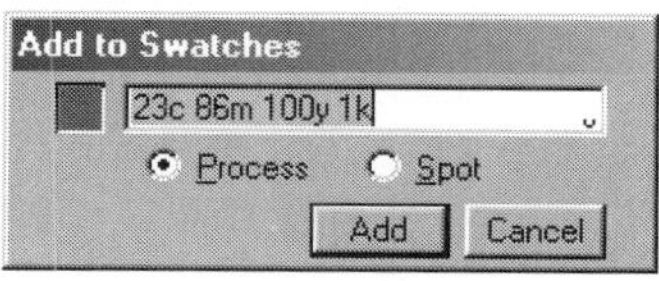

❾ *The* **Add to Swatches** *dialog box allows you to rename the color and set it as process or spot.*

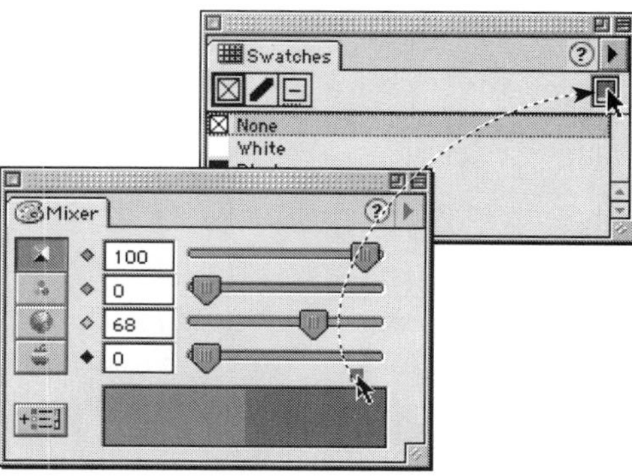

❿ *You can drag a swatch from the Color Mixer and drop it on the Swatches panel* **drop box.**

Using the Swatches Panel

Once you have defined a color in the Color Mixer, you need to store that color so you can define other colors. To do that, you use the Swatches panel.

To add a color to the Swatches panel:

1. Define the color in the Color Mixer.
2. Click the Add to Swatches panel button in the Color Mixer ❽. The Add to Swatches dialog box appears ❾.
3. Name the color.
4. Set the color as process or spot. *(See the sidebar, "Process or Spot?" on page 164.)*
5. Click OK. The color is added to the Swatches panel.

TIP The Add to Swatches panel button works even if the Swatches panel is not visible onscreen.

TIP Hold the Cmd/Ctrl key to bypass the Add to Swatches dialog box.

To drag colors to the Swatches panel:

1. Press and drag the color at the bottom of the Color Mixer.
2. Move to the drop box in the Swatches panel ❿.
3. Release the mouse button. The color appears in the Swatches list.

To rename a color:

1. Double-click or drag across the name of the color in the Swatches panel. This highlights the name, indicating that it is selected ⓫.
2. Type the new name for the color.
3. Press Return/Enter to complete the process of renaming the color.

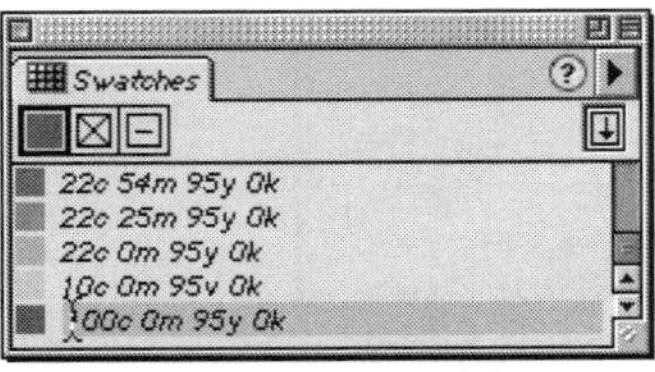

⓫ *Double-click or drag across a color name to rename the color.*

You can change any color from process to spot color, which is separated onto its own plate.

To convert process to spot color:

1. Select the color you want to convert in the Swatches panel ⓬.
2. Choose Make spot from the Swatches panel menu.

⓬ *The Swatches panel displays process colors in italics, spot colors in roman.*

To convert spot to process color:

1. Select the color you want to convert from the Swatches panel.
2. Choose Make process from the Swatches panel menu.

Process or Spot?

Process colors are colors printed using small dots of the four process inks, cyan, magenta, yellow, and black. Spot colors are printed using special inks that are mixed to match a certain color.

For example, if you look at the process color green printed in a magazine, that color is actually a combination of cyan and yellow printed together in a series of dots. However, a spot color green is printed using actual green ink.

The benefit of spot colors is that you can exactly match a special color or use a specialty color such as fluorescents or metallics that could never be created using just process inks.

When you define a color as spot, you are designating that color to be separated on its own printing plate. When you define a color as process, you are designating that color to be broken down into its CMYK values.

Some people use spot colors instead of process colors for one- or two-color jobs. Others use spot colors in addition to process colors for five- or six-color printing.

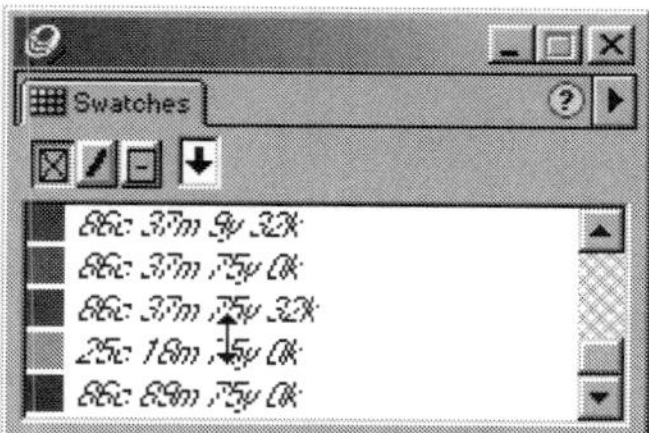

⓭ *You can drag colors from one position to another in the Swatches panel.*

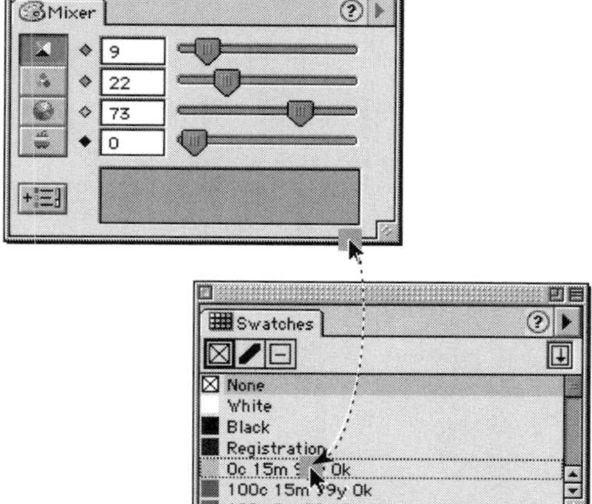

⓮ *Drag a color from the Color Mixer onto an existing color to redefine the color.*

When you add colors to the Swatches panel, they appear in the order that they were added. You may want to move the colors in the Swatches panel to different positions.

To change the order of the colors on the list:

1. Select the color you want to move.
2. Drag it to the new position and then release the mouse button ⓭.

TIP In Windows, a double-headed arrow indicates you are moving the color to a new position.

Once you have added a color to the Swatches panel, you can still change the color values. If you have used the color in your document, the changes will be applied to all the objects that use that color.

To redefine colors:

1. Use the Color Mixer to define the new color.
2. Drag the color swatch from the Color Mixer directly onto the name of the existing color ⓮. All objects that use the color will be redefined.

TIP If you have used the values to name the color, the color name is changed to reflect the new definition.

To duplicate colors:

1. Click the name of the color you want to duplicate.
2. Choose Duplicate from the Swatches panel menu. The duplicate color appears on the Swatches panel with the name "Copy of [Color Name]."

You can remove colors from the Swatches panel.

To remove colors:

1. Click the name of the color you want to remove. The name highlights.
2. If you want to remove a group of adjacent colors, click the top name. Then hold the Shift key and click the bottom name. All the names between highlight.
3. Choose Remove from the Swatches panel menu. All the highlighted colors are deleted.

TIP If the color you remove is in use one of the following happens:

- Process colors are kept in use but are not listed in the Swatches panel.
- Spot colors are converted to process and then kept in use as un-named colors.

You can also direct FreeHand to replace one color with another.

To replace colors:

1. Click the name of the color you want to replace. The name highlights.
2. Choose Replace from the Swatches panel menu. The Replace Color dialog box appears ⓯.
3. Choose a replacement color from the current Swatches panel.

   or

   Choose a replacement from one of the Color Libraries *(see pages 169)*.
4. Click OK. The original color is replaced by the new one throughout the document.

⓯ *The* **Replace Color dialog box** *lets you substitute one color in the Swatches panel for another.*

The Registration Color

You may notice that one of the default colors in the Swatches panel is called Registration. Registration is a color that has been specially defined so that it will print on all plates.

You should not use the Registration color for ordinary artwork. It will create objects that have much too much ink.

Use Registration for items such as crop marks or notes to the printer that you want to see on all the separations.

Registration is usually shown as black, but you can change its appearance by dragging a swatch onto the name.

You can also add colors from objects or imported images to the Swatches panel.

⓰ *The* Eyedropper icon *in the Tools panel.*

To drag colors from objects to the Swatches panel:

1. Choose the Eyedropper tool from the Tools panel ⓰.
2. Press and drag on an area of color. A swatch appears ⓱.
3. Drag the swatch to the drop box of the Swatches panel.

TIP You can also use the Eyedropper tool to move colors directly from one object to another.

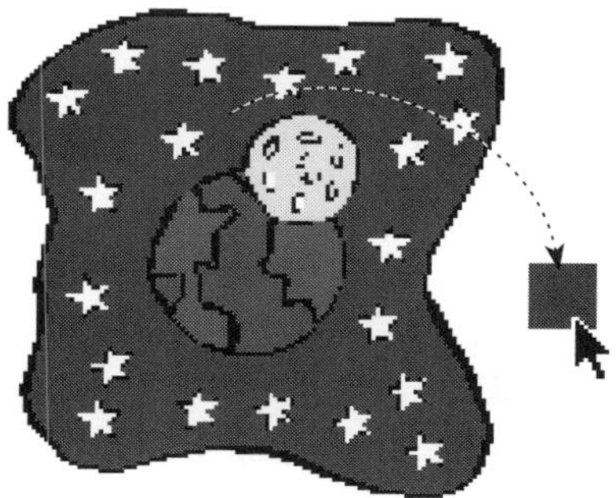

⓱ *Use the Eyedropper to drag colors from artwork and drop them into the Swatches panel.*

If it is difficult to scroll through a long list of color names. FreeHand lets you hide the names of the colors in the Swatches panel.

To hide the color names:

- Choose Hide names from the Swatches panel menu ⓲.

⓲ *The Swatches panel displays only the color swatches after choosing* Hide names.

To show the color names:

- Choose Show names from the Swatches panel menu to display the names.

FreeHand also lets you switch a color between the CMYK and RGB modes. This can be helpful if you are moving from print to the Web.

To change the color mode:

1. Select the color you want to convert.
2. Choose Make RGB from the Swatches panel menu to change the color from CMYK to RGB.

   or

   Choose Make CMYK to change the color from RGB to CMYK.

TIP RGB colors may shift when converted to the CMYK mode.

TIP Colors defined using either the RGB or HLS mode have a small tricolored icon to the right of their name ⓳.

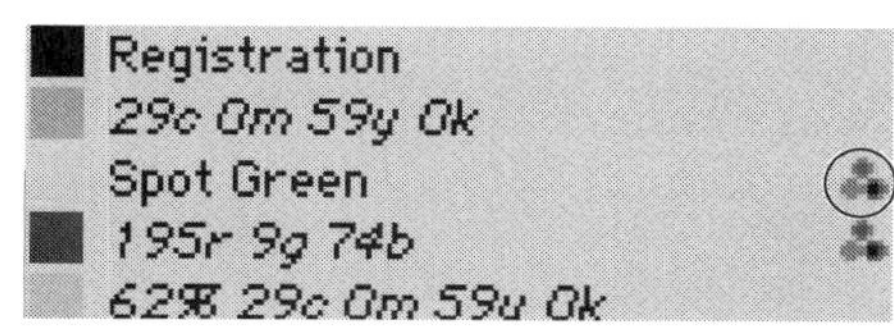

⓳ *Colors defined in the RGB or HLS mode display a small* tricolored icon *(circled) in the list.*

Working with Tints

If you have defined a color, you can use that color as the basis for a tint. This is handy if you are working with spot colors and want to apply tints of those colors.

To define a tint of a color:

1. Define the color in the Color Mixer.

   or

   Add the color to the Swatches panel.
2. If you have not added the color to the Swatches panel, use the pop-up menu in the Tints panel to add the color to the Swatches panel ⑳.

   or

   Choose a color from the pop-up menu in the Tints panel.
3. Choose the tint percentage by one of the following methods:
   - Adjust the tint slider.
   - Type a percentage in the tint field.
   - Click one of the tint swatches.

To Add Tints to the Swatches panel:

1. With a tint percentage defined, click the Add to Swatches panel icon in the Tints panel ㉑. The Add to Swatches panel dialog box appears ㉒.

TIP Hold the Cmd/Ctrl key to bypass the Add to Swatches panel dialog box.

2. The name of the tint is shown as a percentage of the color's name. You can rename the color by typing in the field.
3. Click the Add button to add the tint to the Swatches panel.

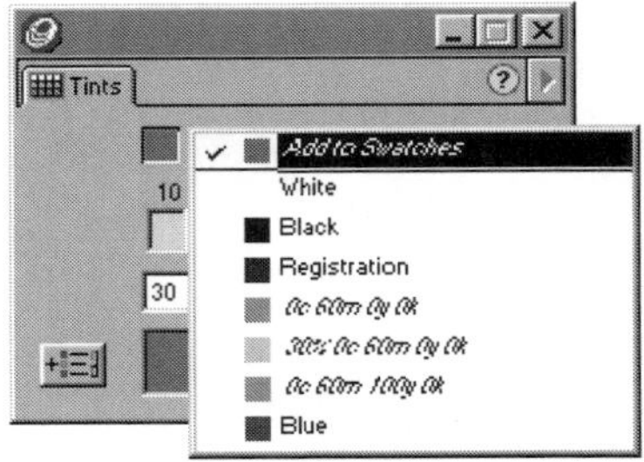

⑳ *The* **Tints panel pop-up list** *lets you choose a color or add the base color of a tint to the Swatches panel.*

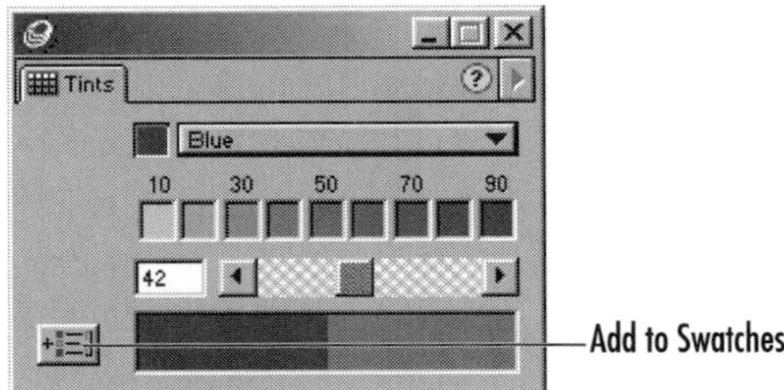

㉑ *Use the* **Add to Swatches button** *to add the current tint setting to the Swatches panel.*

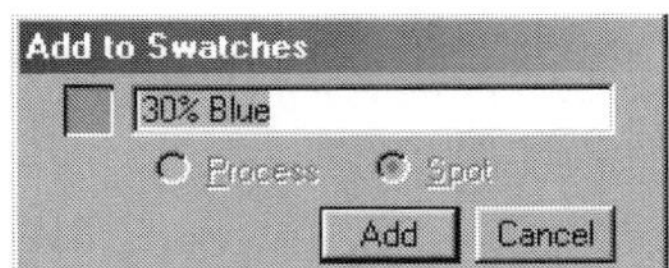

㉒ *The* **Add to Swatches dialog box** *for a tint.*

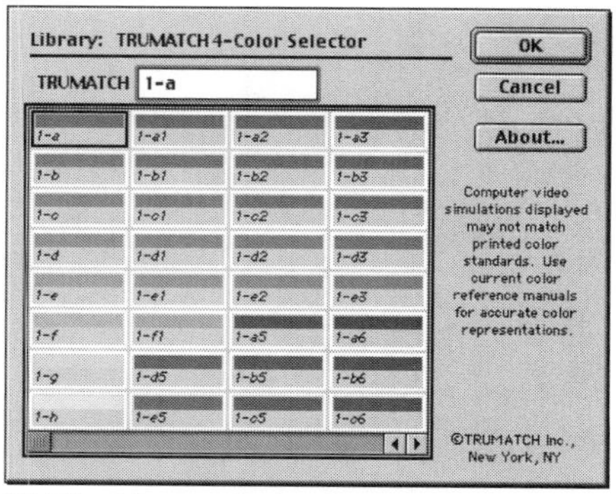

Working with Color Libraries

So far you have been defining your own colors. FreeHand also provides you with libraries of colors that are part of commerical color-matching systems.

To add colors from color-matching system libraries:

1. Choose the name of the color-matching system from the Swatches panel menu. The Library dialog box appears ㉓.
2. Use one of the following techniques to choose a color from the Library:
   - Type in the name or code number of the color in the field.
   - Click a color in the preview area.
3. To select additional colors, hold the Shift key and click in the preview area.

   or

   Hold the Shift key and drag the mouse to select a rangle of colors.
4. Click OK. This adds the selected colors to the Swatches panel.

㉓ *The* **Library dialog box,** *such as this one from Trumatch, lets you choose colors that match those printed in commercial color guides.*

Color-matching system libraries

FreeHand supplies you with various color libraries that are used by commercial printers, artists, and designers. Some of these color libraries are process color, some spot. They are customarily used with printed swatches that allow you to pick a name from the library and compare it to a specific printed color.

The color-matching systems that ship with FreeHand include Pantone (both process and spot), Trumatch (process), Toyo (spot), DIC (spot), Focoltone (process), and Web-safe colors. If you need more information on which color-matching system to use, consult with the print shop that will be printing your work.

FreeHand also supplies two libraries of colors called Crayon and Greys. Neither the Crayon nor the Greys libraries are part of any standard color-matching system. They are included to give you an easy way to import a range of colors.

Once you have created your own list of colors in the Swatches panel, you can export those colors as your own custom color library, which appears in the Swatches panel menu.

To export a custom color library:

1. Choose Export from the Swatches panel menu. The Export Colors dialog box appears.
2. Select a single color.

   or

   Hold down the Shift key to select a continuous range of colors from the Export Colors list (24).
3. Click OK. This opens the Create color library dialog box (25).
4. Enter the Library name.
5. Enter the File name.
6. Under Preferences do the following:
   - Set the number of Colors per column.
   - Set the number of Colors per row.
7. Choose Save to place your custom color library in the Color folder located in the FreeHand application folder. The Library name appears in the Swatches panel menu along with the other color libraries.

   or

   Choose Save As which lets you save the file to a different folder or disk.

TIP To delete custom color libraries from the Swatches panel menu, remove the file from the FreeHand: English: Color folder.

TIP To have a set of colors appear in all new documents, add those colors to the FreeHand Defaults file. *(To create a new defaults file, see page 374.)*

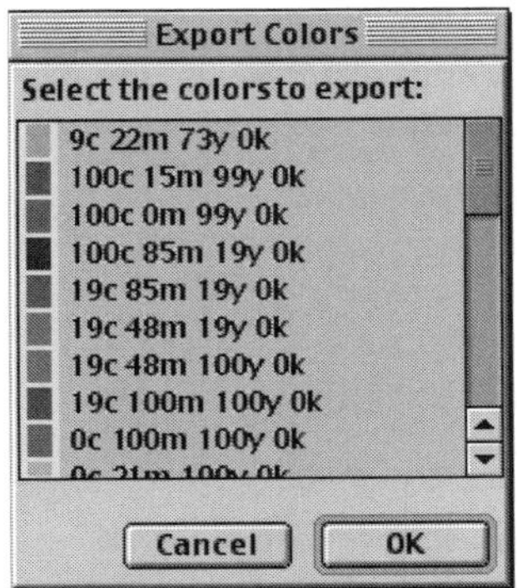

(24) *Use the Shift key in the* **Export Colors dialog box** *to select the colors to be exported.*

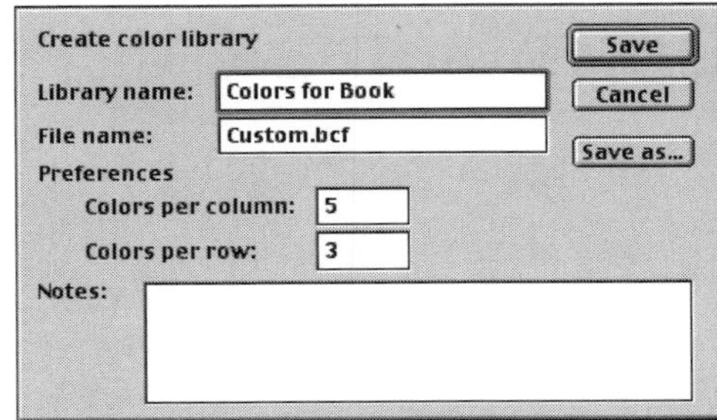

(25) *The* **Create color library dialog box** *allows you to group your own colors into a custom library.*

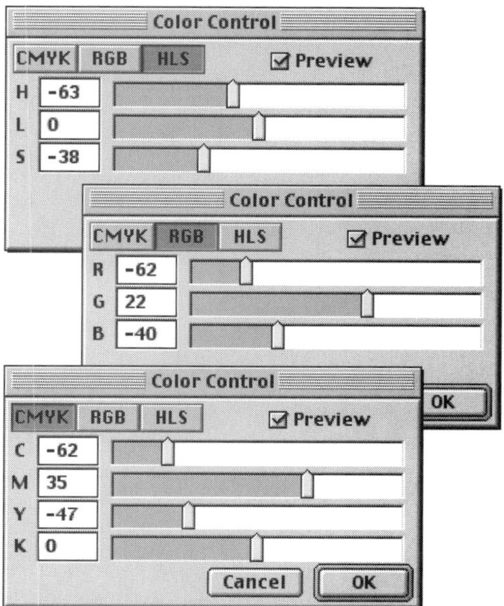

㉖ *The three different settings for the Color Control dialog box (from top to bottom): HLS, RGB, and CMYK.*

㉗ *The Color Control dialog box in the HLS mode was applied to the original artwork to create the other two variations.*

Using the Xtra Color Commands

Once you have created and used colors, the Color commands under the Xtras menu provide many ways you can adjust the colors in your documents. The Color Control Xtra lets you shift the colors in selected objects.

To use the Color Control dialog box:

1. Select the objects you want to adjust.
2. Choose **Xtras > Colors > Color Control.** This opens the Color Control dialog box ㉖.
3. Choose which color mode to use to adjust the colors:
   - **CMYK** lets you adjust the cyan, magenta, yellow, or black components of the color.
   - **RGB** lets you adjust the red, green, or blue components of the color.
   - **HLS** lets you adjust the hue, lightness or saturation components of the color.

   TIP The color can be defined in one color mode but adjusted in another.
4. Use the sliders or the fields to add or subtract color from the selected objects.
   - Positive numbers add color.
   - Negative numbers subtract color.
5. Check the Preview box to see how your adjustments affect the selected objects without actually applying the changes.
6. When you are satisfied with the color changes, click OK. Your changes are applied to the objects ㉗.

TIP The Color Control dialog box only works on objects that have been colored with process colors, not spot colors.

To darken or lighten colors:

1. Select the object or objects you want to change.
2. Choose **Xtras > Colors > Darken Colors** or **Lighten Colors** ㉘.
   - Darken Colors decreases the Lightness value of the color in 5% increments.
   - Lighten Colors increases the Lightness value of the color in 5% increments.
3. To continue to darken or lighten the colors, repeat the command as many times as necessary *(see page 297)*.

Original

Darken Lighten

㉘ *The results of using the Darken Colors and Lighten Colors commands.*

To saturate or desaturate colors:

1. Select the object or objects you want to change.
2. Choose **Xtras > Colors > Saturate Colors** or **Desaturate Colors.**
   - Saturate Colors increases the saturation value of the color in 5% increments. This makes muted colors more vibrant.
   - Desaturate Colors decreases the saturation value of the color in 5% increments. This makes colors less vibrant.
3. To continue to saturate or desaturate the colors, repeat the command as many times as necessary *(see page 297)*.

To convert colors to grayscale:

1. Select the object or objects you want to change.
2. Choose **Xtras > Colors > Convert to Grayscale.** All colors are converted to grays with the equivalent tonal value.

TIP Convert artwork to grayscale to be printed as one-color black. For instance, all the artwork created in FreeHand for this book was converted to grayscale.

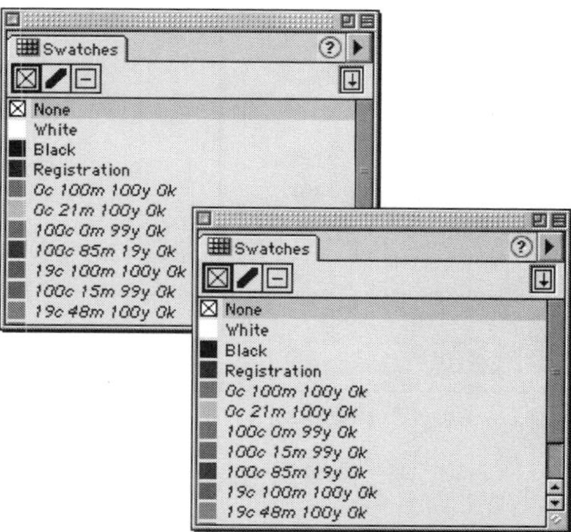

㉙ *The results of applying the* **Sort Color List by Name** *command.*

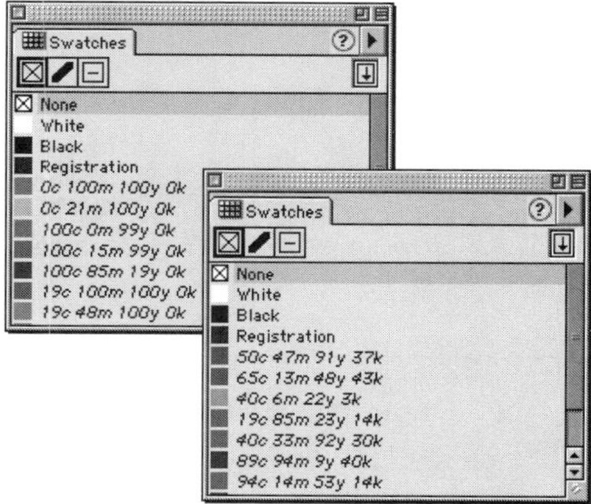

㉚ *The results of applying the Randomize Named Colors command.*

FreeHand offers several Xtras that help you manage colors in the Swatches panel and in your document.

To name all colors:

- Choose **Xtras > Colors > Name All Colors.** All colors used by objects in your document that are not named appear on the Swatches panel, with their names showing their CMYK percentages.

To sort the Swatches panel by name:

- Choose **Xtras > Colors > Sort Color List By Name.** This rearranges the Swatches panel. The default colors appear first, followed by the colors named by their CMYK and RGB compositions, and then named colors ㉙.

To delete unused named colors:

- Choose **Xtras > Delete > Unused Named Colors.** Colors that are not applied to an object or a style are deleted. The default colors are not deleted even if they are not used.

TIP Delete unused colors before exporting artwork to layout programs such as Adobe PageMaker or QuarkXPress.

To use the Randomize Named Colors Xtra:

- Choose **Xtras > Colors > Randomize Named Colors.** This command changes the values of the named colors in the Swatches panel. All objects with named colors applied to them are changed ㉚.

TIP While there aren't too many uses for this command for ordinary graphics, it does create interesting effects when applied to abstract art.

Trapping Colors

Trapping is a technique printers use to compensate for misregistration of color plates in the printing process. FreeHand lets you create traps with the Trap Xtra. Although the Trap Xtra is very easy to apply, setting the proper values takes years of experience.

㉛ *The* **Trap dialog box.**

To use the Trap Xtra:

1. Select two or more objects in your illustration that you want to trap.
2. Choose **Xtras** > **Create** > **Trap**. The Trap dialog box appears ㉛.
3. Use the sliders or type in the Trap width suggested by your print shop.
4. If your print shop agrees, choose Use maximum value to make the trap color the strongest available.

   or

   Choose the Use tint reduction setting and enter the reduction amount suggested by your print shop.
5. Check the Reverse traps box to change the direction of the trap. (Reverse traps are sometimes called *chokes*.) Consult your print shop as to when you should do this.
6. Click OK. The traps are created ㉜.

TIP When you create traps, you create new objects set to overprint between the original objects. If you move or delete objects later, be careful that you do not leave the trap objects behind.

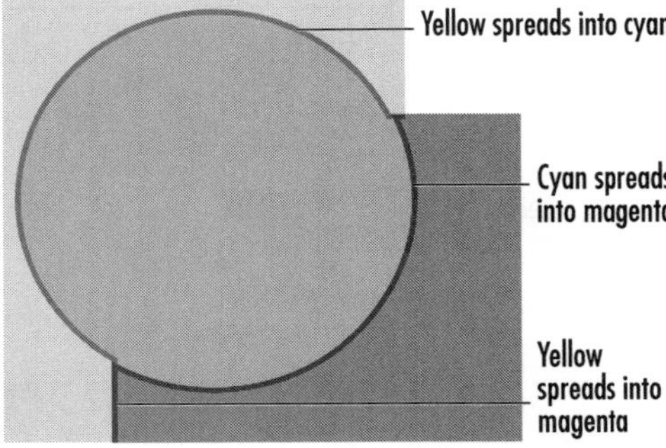

㉜ *The results of* **applying the Trap command.**

> **How to learn about trapping**
>
> Trapping is like buying a boat. If you have to ask the price of a boat, you can't afford it. If you have to ask what trapping is, you shouldn't do it.
>
> If you want to set your own traps, talk to the print shop that will be printing your artwork. They are the best experts to teach you how much to trap, where to trap, and when not to trap.
>
> Most print shops tell you not to trap. They often use their own software that traps automatically.

FILLS 14

Once you have created the outline of a path, it is an empty shell waiting to be filled with a color or some other effect. FreeHand offers a wealth of different ways to fill the empty path.

You can choose one of the solid colors in the Swatches panel. You can also combine those colors into gradients that change one color into another.

You can also apply special effects that fill one object so that it is transparent or it acts like a magnifying glass over other objects.

You can even create small illustrations that can be repeated, like a tiled floor, as the fill inside other objects.

Adding a fill to an object can change it from ordinary to exciting.

Working with Basic Fills

TIP If you do not see the fills for open paths, check the object preferences. *(See Appendix C))*

The most common fill is the Basic fill. This is the equivalent of filling the object with a solid color. FreeHand provides you with many different ways to apply Basic fill.

To apply a Basic fill using the Fill inspector:

1. Select the object.
2. With the Fill inspector displayed, choose Basic from the Fill pop-up menu. This displays the Basic fill settings ❶.
3. Choose a color for the fill from the color list.

To apply a Basic fill using the Tools panel:

1. Select the object.
2. Click the triangle in the Fill color box at the bottom of the Tools panel ❷. This opens the pop-up color palette ❸.
3. Choose a color from the color palette.

The pop-up color palette is set by default to show the 216 Web-safe colors. You can change that setting to display the colors in the Swatches panel.

To change the display of the pop-up color palette:

1. Click the color box to open the pop-up color palette.
2. Click the palette triangle to open the options menu ❹.
3. Choose Swatches to display the colors from the Swatches panel.

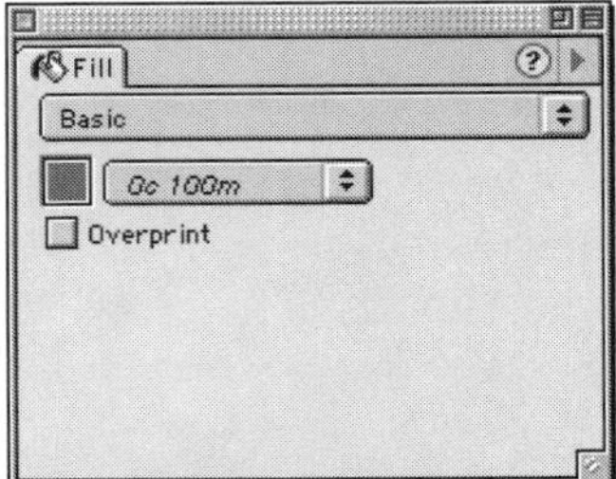

❶ *Choose Basic from the Fill inspector list to display the* **Basic fill options.**

❷ *The* **Fill color box** *in the Tools panel.*

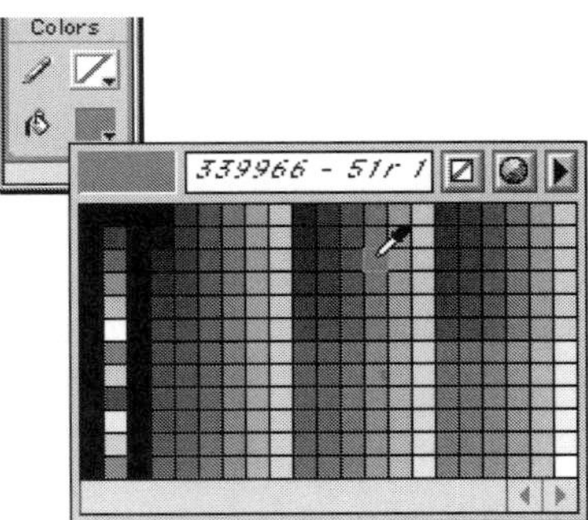

❸ *The* **pop-up color palette** *in the Tools panel lets you choose fill colors.*

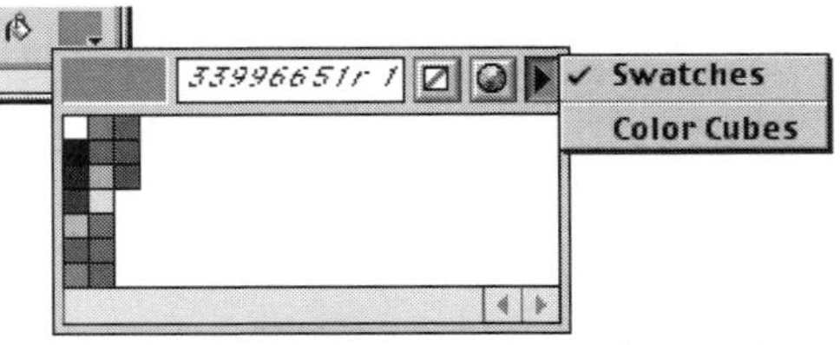

❹ *Use the* **pop-up palette menu** *to display the colors in the Swatches panel.*

❺ *The* **Fill drop box** *(circled) in the Swatches panel indicates the fill color of the selected object.*

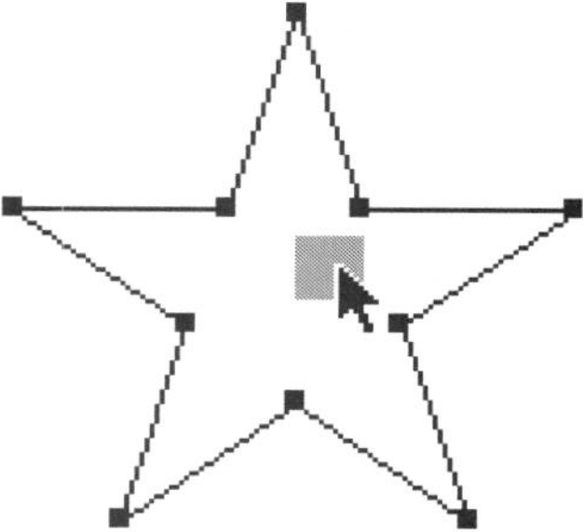

❻ **Drag a color swatch** *onto an object to apply a fill color.*

Setting Overprinting

You may notice the Overprint settings for many of the fills. If you set an object to Overprint, that object will not knock out any colors below. Instead it will mix the colors in that object with the ones below.

You cannot see overprinting on your screen. Depending on the preference setting, objects that have an overprint applied will be displayed with a pattern of white Os on top.

You do not see overprinting in the output of most color printers. You need to make separations of your colors to see where the colors will overprint.

To apply a fill color using the Swatches panel:

1. Select the object.

TIP Make sure that Basic or None is chosen in the Fill inspector. If another type of fill is listed, you may not see the color you choose.

2. Click the Fill drop box in the Swatches panel. A black line appears around the box that indicates that the fill is chosen in the Swatches panel ❺.

3. Click the name of the color you want as the fill in the Swatches panel.

   or

   Drag a color swatch from the Color Mixer onto the Fill drop box in the Swatches panel.

TIP The box next to the Fill drop box controls the stroke color. *(See Chapter 15, "Strokes.")*

TIP If no object is selected, any changes you make to the fill color are applied to the next object you create.

To change a fill color by dragging:

- Drag a color swatch from the Color Mixer or the Swatches panel directly onto the object ❻.

TIP You do not have to select an object to drag a color swatch onto it.

TIP Hold the Shift key as you drag the color swatch onto the object to make sure that only the fill color changes.

In addition to the colors, there is another item in the Swatches panel called *None.* While not a color *per se,* the None fill is very important. When you apply the None fill to an object, the fill of the object becomes transparent ❼. Fortunately you have three different ways to apply the None fill.

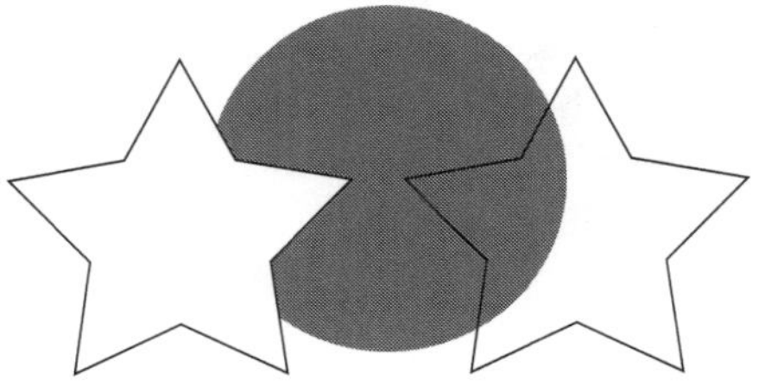

❼ *Selecting a* **fill of None** *lets you see through an object, as seen in the star on the right.*

To change a fill to None:

1. Choose the object you want to become transparent.
2. Make sure the Fill drop box is selected in the Colors panel.
3. Click None in the Swatches panel. An X appears in the Fill drop box, indicating that there is no fill ❽.

   or

   Click the None icon in the Fill color box pop-up palette ❾.

   or

   Choose None from the Fill inspector list ❿.

TIP Objects with no fill color are invisible unless they have a stroke applied. *(See Chapter 15, "Strokes.")*

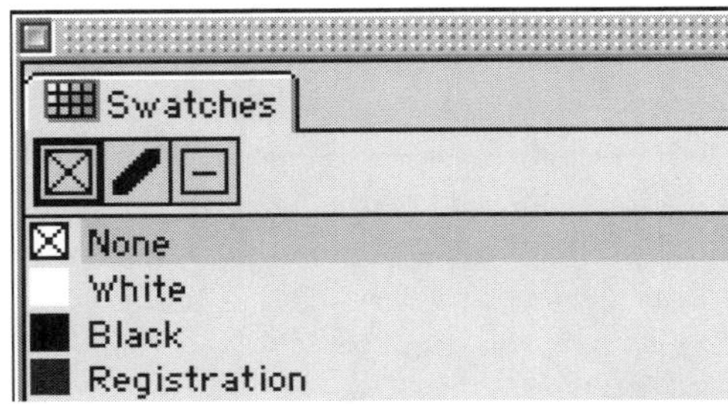

❽ *Choose* **None** *in the Swatches panel to apply a transparent None fill.*

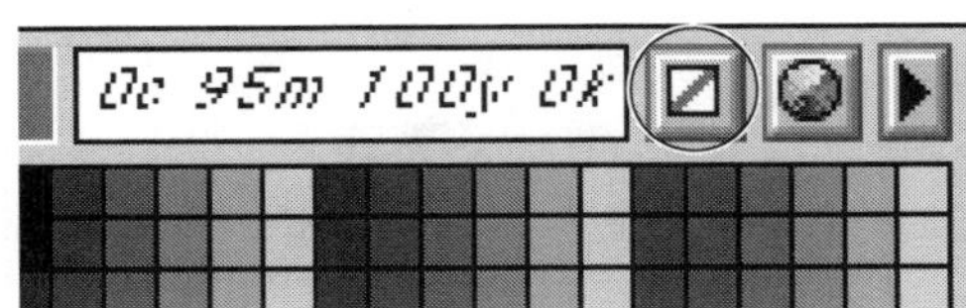

❾ *Click the* **None icon** *(circled) in the Fill color box pop-up palette to apply a transparent fill.*

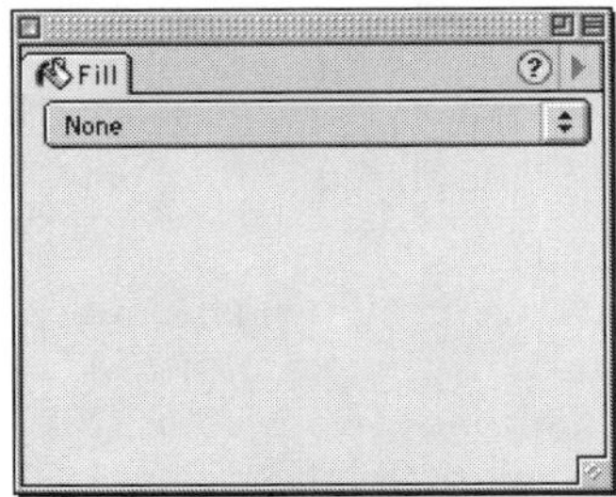

❿ *Choose* **None in the Fill inspector** *to apply a transparent None fill.*

Working with Basic Fills

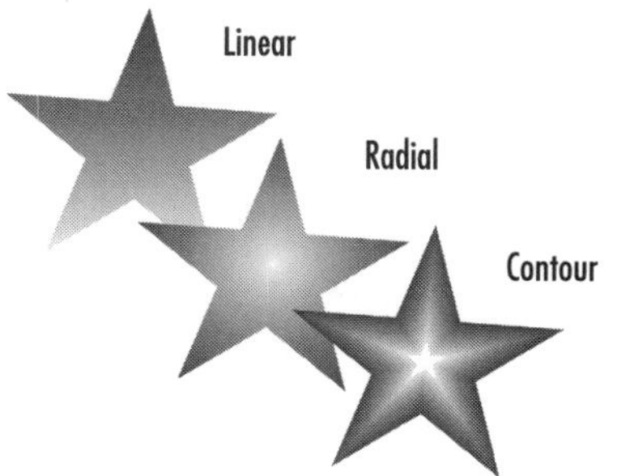

⓫ *The* three different types of gradients.

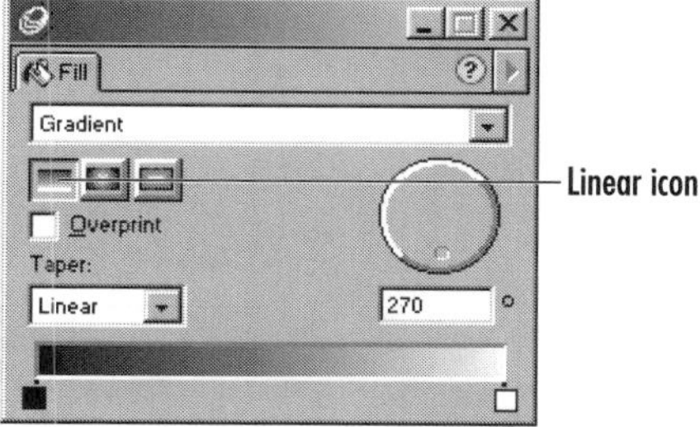

⓬ *The Fill inspector set for a* linear gradient.

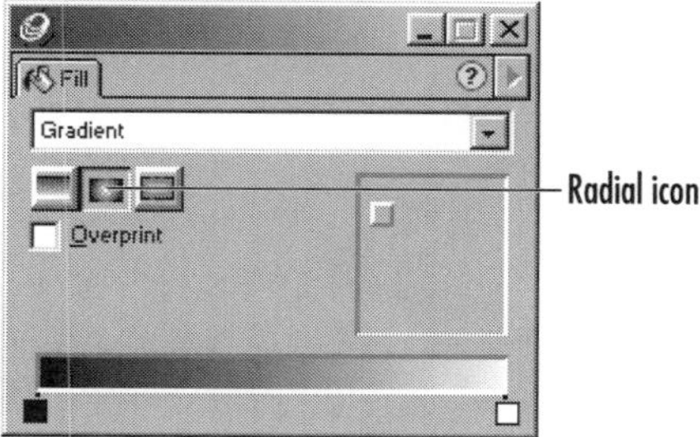

⓭ *The Fill inspector set for a* radial gradient.

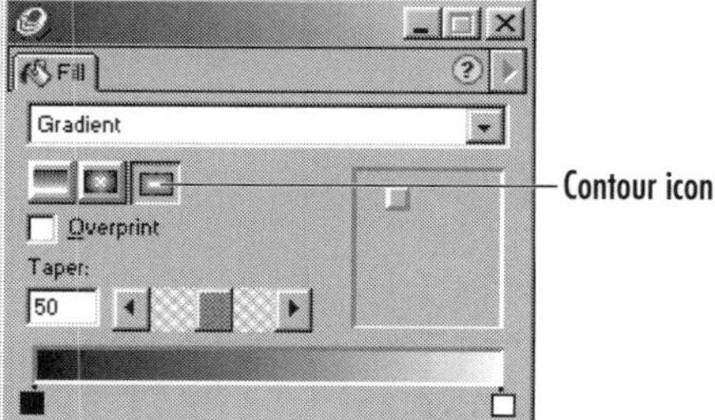

⓮ *The Fill inspector set for a* contour gradient.

Working with Gradient Fills

Gradient fills start with one color and then change into others. There are three types of gradients: linear, radial, and contour ⓫. In a linear gradient, the colors change along a line that can be angled in any direction. A radial gradient is circular. In a contour gradient, the color change is based on the shape of the object.

To choose the type of gradient fill:

1. Choose Gradient from the pop-up menu in the Fill inspector.
2. Click the Linear icon to see the settings for a linear gradient ⓬.

   or

   Click the Radial icon to see the settings for a radial gradient ⓭.

   or

   Click the Contour icon to see the settings for the contour gradient ⓮.
3. Use the other Color pop-up menu to choose the color for the other end of the gradient.

To create a linear gradient fill:

1. With the object selected, click the Linear gradient icon in the Fill inspector ⓯.
2. Click either of the color swatches to choose the colors for each end of the gradient. The pop-up color palette lets you choose a color ⓰.

   or

   Drag a color from the Swatches panel or Color Mixer. The change between the colors is displayed in the Gradient ramp.
3. To add colors in between the end colors, see the exercise on page183.
4. Use the Angle field or rotate the wheel to set the angle for the fill.

TIP Changing the direction of the gradient fills creates the illusion of light reflecting off different surfaces. This creates a 3D effect ⓱.

5. Use the Taper list to choose how fast the gradient changes.
   - Linear changes in uniform increments from one color to another.
   - Logarithmic changes more drastically from one color to another ⓲.

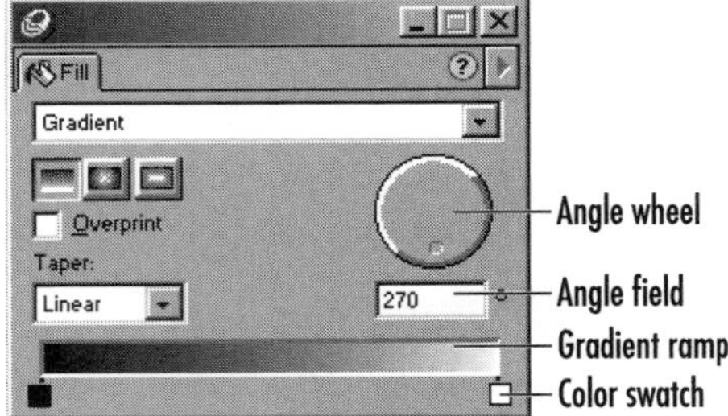

⓯ *The Fill inspector set for a* **linear gradient.**

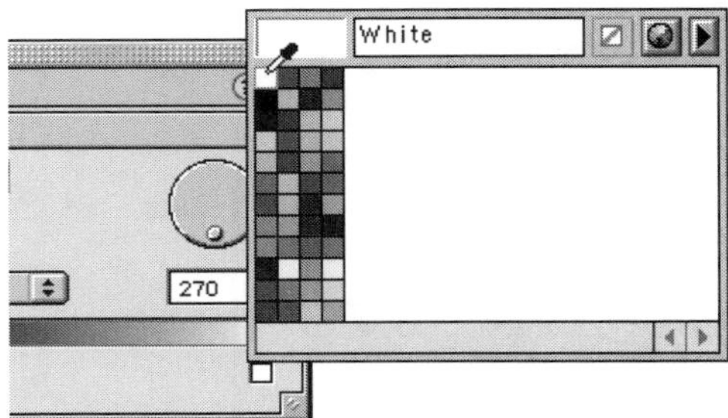

⓰ *The pop-up color palette lets you choose colors for a gradient.*

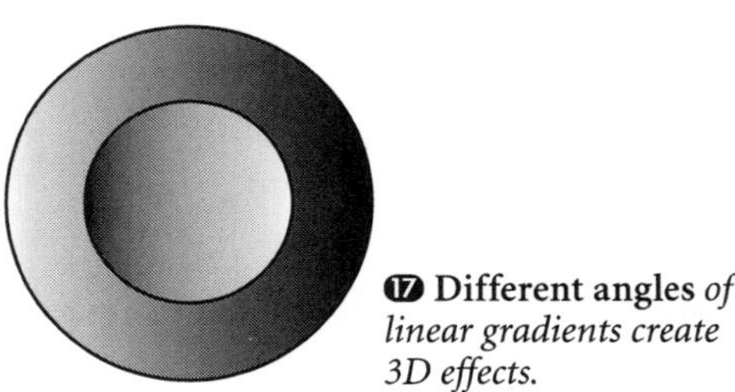

⓱ **Different angles** *of linear gradients create 3D effects.*

⓲ *The difference between a* **Linear taper** *(left) and a* **Logarithmic taper** *(right), both set to 90° angles.*

⑲ *Hold the Control/Ctrl key as you drag a color swatch to apply a linear gradient to an object.*

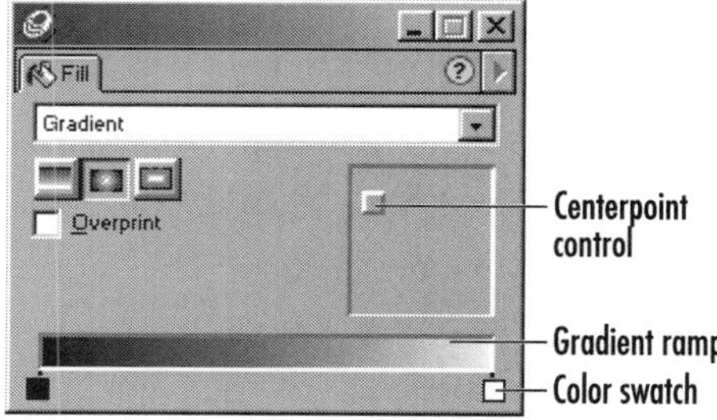

⑳ *The Fill inspector set for a* **radial gradient.**

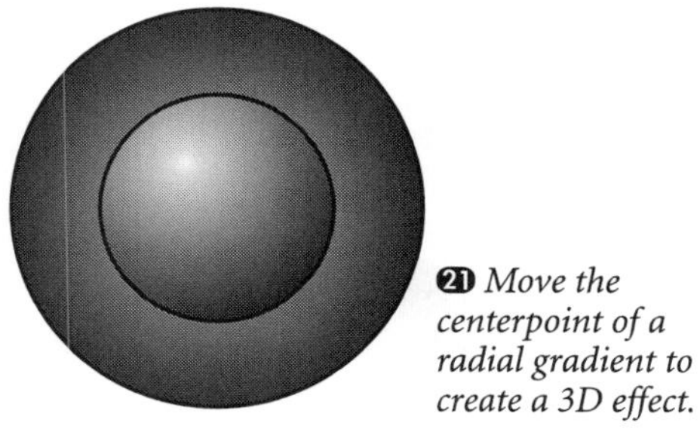

㉑ *Move the centerpoint of a radial gradient to create a 3D effect.*

FreeHand also lets you apply a linear gradient by dragging a color without using the Fill inspector and without selecting the object.

To apply a linear gradient by dragging a color:

1. Press the Control/Ctrl key as you drag a color swatch onto an object that has one color already applied as a Basic fill. A diamond color swatch indicates you are dragging a linear gradient onto the object ⑲.
2. Release the mouse button on the object. A linear gradient fills the object with the color of the swatch applied as the second color.

TIP Where you drop the swatch determines the angle of the fill.

In a radial gradient, the color starts at a center point and moves outward in a circle. A Radial gradient is like a sun radiating colors outward.

To create a radial gradient:

1. With the object selected, click the Radial gradient icon in the Fill inspector ⑳.
2. Choose the color for the outside of the radial fill by changing the color swatch on the left side of the ramp.

   or

   Drag a color from the Swatches panel or Color Mixer. The change between the colors is displayed in the Gradient ramp.
3. Choose the color for the inside of the radial fill by changing the color swatch on the right side of the ramp.
4. Drag the centerpoint control to change the position of the inside color.

TIP Position the centerpoint of a radial gradient off-center to create the effect of a 3D sphere ㉑.

To apply a radial gradient by dragging a color:

1. Press the Opt/Alt key as you drag a color swatch onto an object that already has one color applied as a Basic fill. A circle color swatch indicates you are dragging a radial gradient onto the object.
2. Release the mouse button on the object. A radial gradient fills the object with the color of the swatch applied as the second color ㉒.

TIP The color of the swatch is applied as the inside color of the radial gradient.

TIP Where you drop the swatch determines the center of the radial gradient.

㉒ *Hold the Opt/Alt key as you drag a color swatch to apply a radial gradient to an object.*

To create a contour gradient:

1. With the object selected, click the Contour gradient icon. The settings for the contour gradient appear ㉓.
2. Choose the color for the outside of the contour gradient by changing the color swatch on the left side of the ramp.

   or

   Drag a color from the Swatches panel or Color Mixer. The change between the colors is displayed in the Gradient ramp.
3. Choose the color for the inside of the contour gradient by changing the color swatch on the right side of the ramp.
4. Drag the centerpoint control to change the position of the inside color.
5. Use the Taper controls to adjust the size of the contour gradient. The higher the number, the more the gradient will fill the object ㉔.

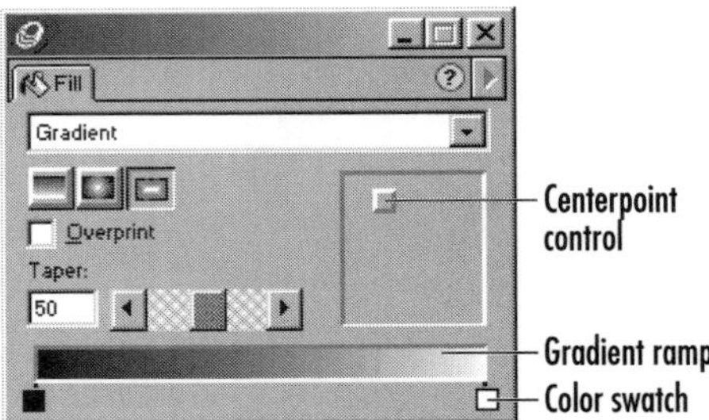

㉓ *The Fill inspector set for a* **linear gradient.**

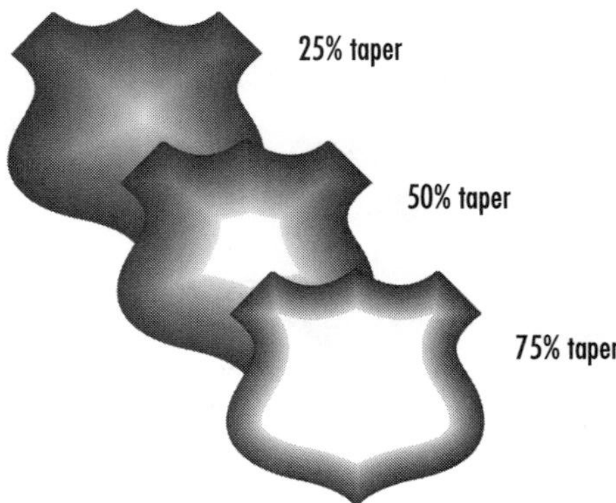

㉔ *Adjusting the* **Taper control** *changes in how much of the object the contour gradient is seen.*

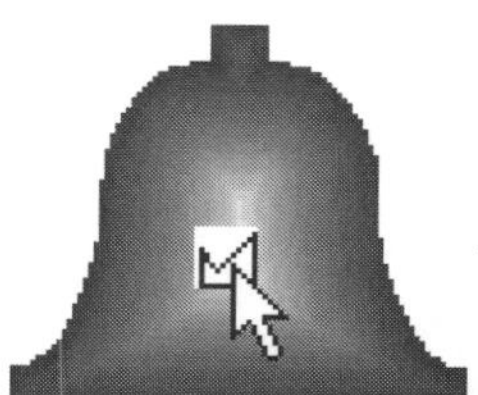

㉕ *Hold the Cmd-Opt key (Mac) or Control-Alt key (Win) as you drag a color swatch to apply a contour gradient to an object.*

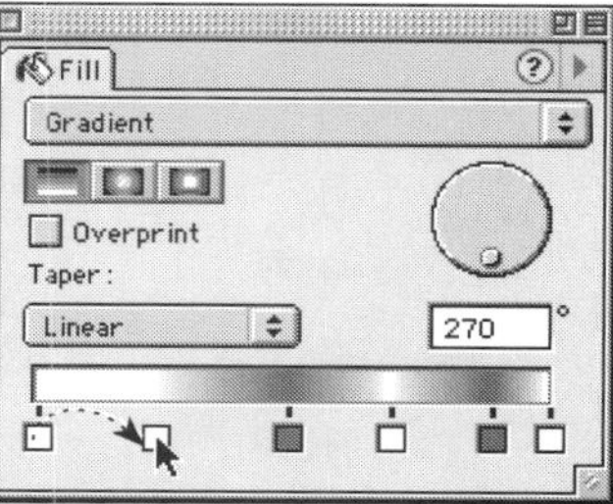

㉖ **Drag a color swatch** *to add colors to a gradient.*

> **Avoiding Banding**
>
> Sometimes gradients print with an effect called banding *(see page 220)*. Here are some tips to avoid banding when printing gradients:
>
> Print at high resolutions. For most work, this is a minimum of 2400 dpi.
>
> Use a lower screen ruling. This is especially helpful when printing to laser printers.
>
> Avoid gradients over 7 inches long. This is especially true if you are outputting to a PostScript Level 1 device. If you are outputting to a higher PostScript device, you may not need to limit the length of your blends.
>
> Examine the difference between the percentages of each of the CMYK colors. If you are getting banding, try increasing the difference between the percentages.

To apply a contour gradient by dragging a color:

1. Press the Cmd-Opt key (Mac) or Control-Alt key (Win) as you drag a color swatch onto an object that has one color already applied as a Basic fill. An irregular-shaped color swatch indicates you are dragging a contour gradient onto the object.
2. Release the mouse button on the object. A contour gradient fills the object with the color of the swatch applied as the second color ㉕.

TIP The color of the swatch is applied as the inside color of the contour gradient.

TIP Where you drop the swatch determines the center of the contour gradient.

Gradient fills can contain more than one color.

To add colors to gradient fills:

1. Drag a color swatch onto the gray area between the top and the bottom colors ㉖. You can drag swatches from the Swatches panel, the Color Mixer, or the color boxes in the Fill inspector.

   or

   Drag a color from either end color swatch.

   or

   Hold the Control/Alt key as you drag to copy the colors of existing color swatches.
2. To delete a color, drag the color box off the gray area. (You can not delete the left or right swatches of a gradient fill.)

Working with Lens Effects

One of the most dramatic features in FreeHand is the set of lens fills. These allow you to create transparency effects and to use one object to magnify others.

To create a transparent lens fill:

1. Choose Lens from the pop-up menu in the Fill inspector.
2. Choose Transparency from the mode pop-up menu ㉗.
3. Choose a color from the color pop-up menu.
4. Use the Opacity slider or the field to set the amount of transparency for the lens ㉘. The lower the opacity, the more you will be able to see through the object.
5. Click Objects Only to have the effects of the lens seen only on objects, not the page ㉙.
6. See the exercise on the facing page for working with the Centerpoint control.
7. Click Snapshot to freeze the lens effect within the object. The object may then be moved to another spot without changing the image within the lens ㉚.

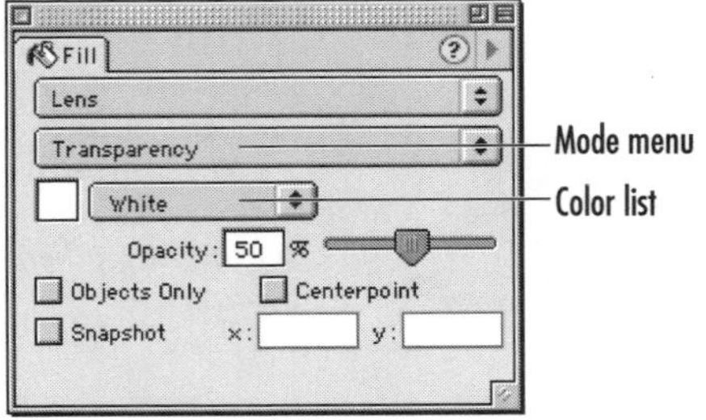

㉗ *The* **Transparency Lens controls** *of the Fill inspector.*

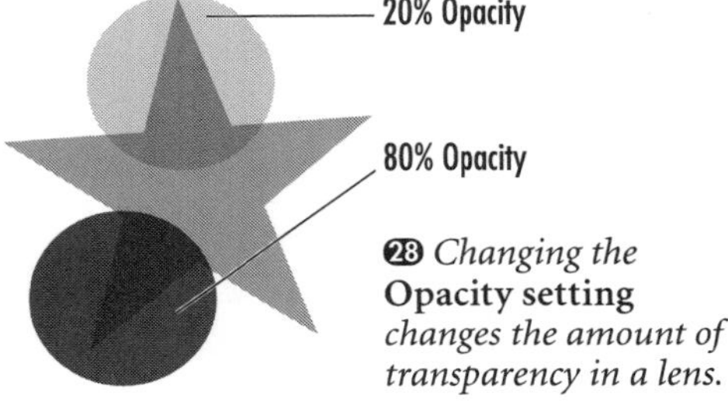

㉘ *Changing the* **Opacity setting** *changes the amount of transparency in a lens.*

㉙ *The* **Objects Only setting** *makes the lens work only on objects, not the page area.*

㉚ *The* **Snapshot setting** *freezes the image in the lens so you can move it.*

> **Working with spot colors**
>
> All of the lens effects convert spot colors to process. When you apply the lens effect, an alert box appears with the message that spot colors viewed through a Lens fill are converted to process colors. This means that if you work with spot colors you most likely will not want to apply any of the lens effects. To turn off the warning, check the Don't Show Again box.

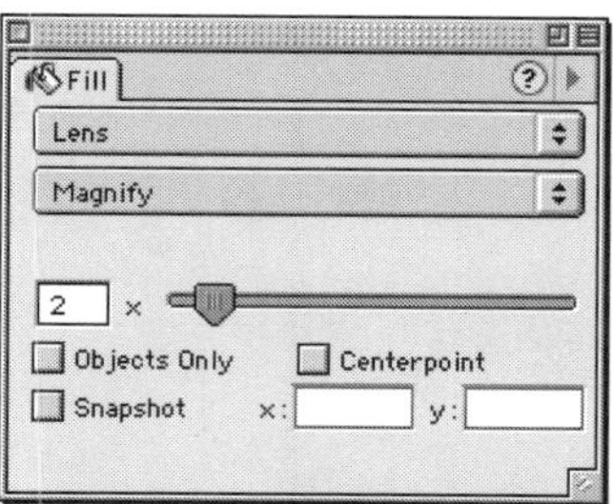

31 *The* **Magnify Lens controls** *of the Fill inspector.*

32 *A* **Magnify lens** *shows a closer view of an object.*

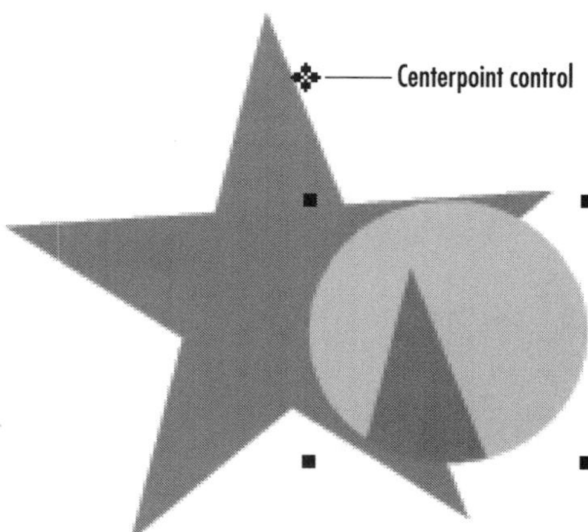

33 *Drag the* **centerpoint control** *to focus a lens over a certain area of the artwork.*

The magnify lens lets one object act as a magnifying glass on whatever objects it covers.

To create a magnify lens fill:

1. With Lens chosen, choose Magnify from the mode pop-up menu.
2. Use the Magnification slider or the field to set the amount of magnification for the lens 31.

TIP Magnification can be set from 1 (actual size) to 20 times bigger.

3. The object appears inside the lens as if it were scaled larger 32.

There may be times when you want the lens object to affect an area that it is not located over. This is especially helpful for callouts of technical drawings or insets of maps. To accomplish this, use the centerpoint control.

To use the centerpoint control:

1. Position the magnify lens where you want it in your image—do not worry yet about what shows in the lens.
2. Check the Centerpoint box in the Fill inspector. A centerpoint control appears.

TIP If the centerpoint is not visible, check to see if the object is part of a group. If so, ungroup it.

3. Drag the centerpoint control to the center of the area you want to be visible within the lens 33.

Stacking lens objects

If you position one lens object over another, you will combine the lens effects. However, there is a limit of eight lens fills stack over each other. If you add more than eight objects, the bottom-most objects will not be active as lens fills.

The Invert lens inverts the colors of objects. This means that black objects turn white, red objects turn green, yellow objects turn blue, and so on.

To use the Invert lens fill:

1. With Lens chosen, choose Invert from the mode pop-up menu ㉞. This causes the selected object to invert the colors in the objects it passes over ㉟.
2. Set the Objects Only control as described on page 184.
3. Set the Snapshot control as described on page 184.
4. Set the Centerpoint control as described on page 185.

To use the Lighten lens fill:

1. With Lens chosen, choose Lighten from the mode pop-up menu. This causes the selected object to lighten the colors in the objects it passes over ㊱. This is similar to adding white to the colors ㊲.
2. Use the Lighten slider or the field to increase or decrease the effect.
3. Set the Objects Only control as described on page 184.
4. Set the Snapshot control as described on page 184.
5. Set the Centerpoint control as described on page 185.

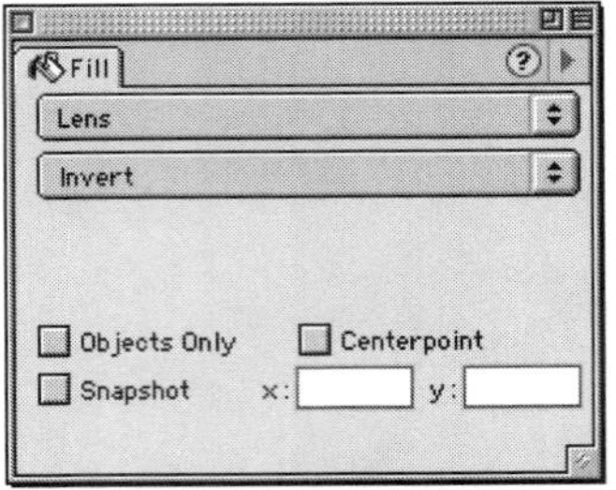

㉞ *The* **Invert Lens controls** *of the Fill inspector.*

㉟ *The* **Invert lens** *reverses the colors of the objects the lens passes over.*

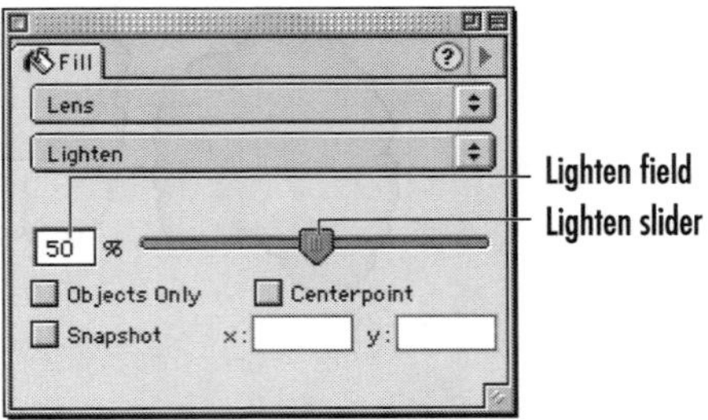

㊱ *The* **Lighten Lens controls** *of the Fill inspector.*

㊲ *The* **Lighten lens** *lightens the colors of the objects the lens passes over.*

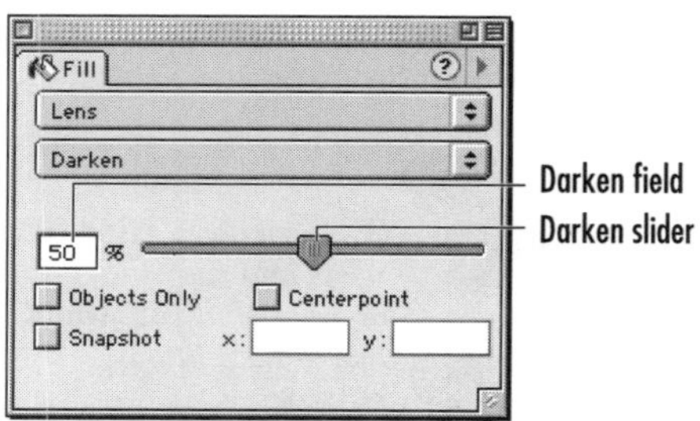

(38) *The* **Darken Lens controls** *of the Fill inspector.*

(39) *The* **Darken lens** *darkens the colors of the objects the lens passes over.*

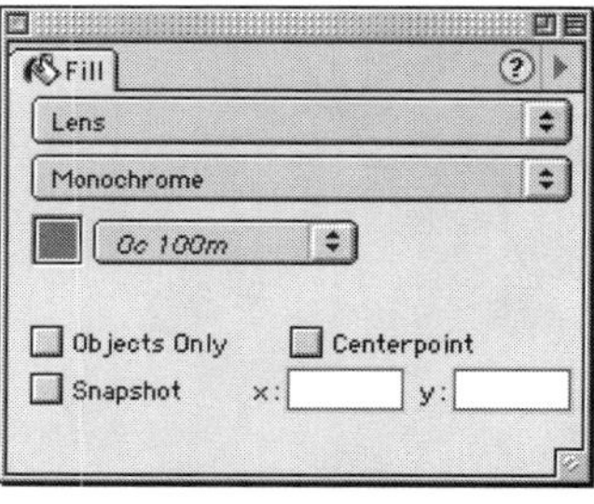

(40) *The* **Monochrome Lens controls** *of the Fill inspector.*

(41) *The* **Monochrome lens** *changes the hue of the colors of the objects the lens passes over.*

To use the Darken lens fill:

1. With Lens chosen, choose Darken from the mode pop-up menu (38). This causes the selected object to Darken the colors in the objects it passes over (39). This is similar to adding black to the colors.
2. Use the Darken slider or the field to increase or decrease the effect.
3. Set the Objects Only control as described on page 184.
4. Set the Snapshot control as described on page 184.
5. Set the Centerpoint control as described on page 185.

To use the Monochrome lens fill:

1. With Lens chosen, choose Monochrome from the mode pop-up menu (40). This causes the selected object to convert all the colors in the objects it passes over to a shade of the monochrome object (41).

TIP The monochrome lens is a great way to tint part of a placed image.

2. Use the Color list to choose the monochrome color.
3. Set the Objects Only control as described on page 184.
4. Set the Snapshot control as described on page 184.
5. Set the Centerpoint control as described on page 185.

Creating and Applying Tiled Fills

You have to create the next kind of fill—called a Tiled fill—by yourself. Other programs may call this a pattern.

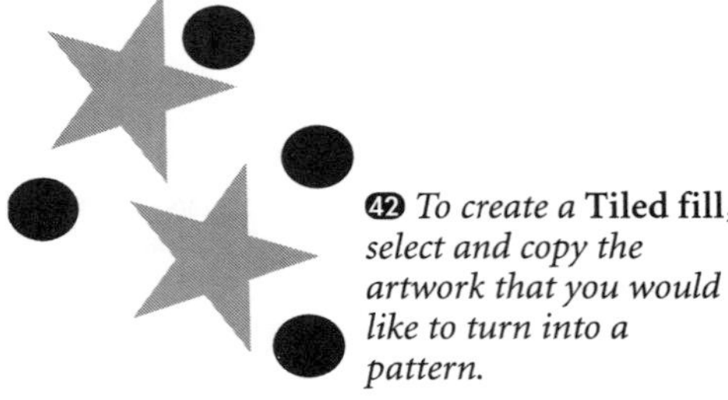

42 *To create a* **Tiled fill**, *select and copy the artwork that you would like to turn into a pattern.*

To create and apply a Tiled fill:

1. Copy the artwork that you want to repeat in other objects 42.
2. Select the object you want to fill with the Tiled fill.
3. Choose Tiled from the Fill inspector pop-up menu.
4. Click Paste in. The artwork you copied appears in the Tiled preview box 43. The selected object displays the Tiled fill 44.

TIP To make the background of the Tiled fill transparent, leave the artwork on an empty area or on a rectangle with no fill.

TIP To give the Tiled fill a white or colored background, place the artwork on a rectangle filled with white or the color. Select the artwork and the rectangle to paste into the Tiled fill box.

TIP The more complex the tiled artwork, the longer it takes for your screen to redraw and for the artwork to print.

TIP Tiled fills cannot contain objects that have Lens fills or Tiled fills applied to them.

TIP Tiled fills cannot contain bitmapped graphics.

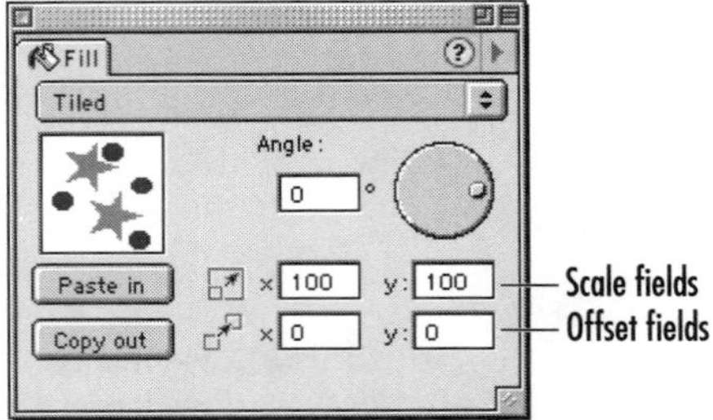

43 *Click* **Paste in** *to transfer the copied artwork into the Tiled fill settings box.*

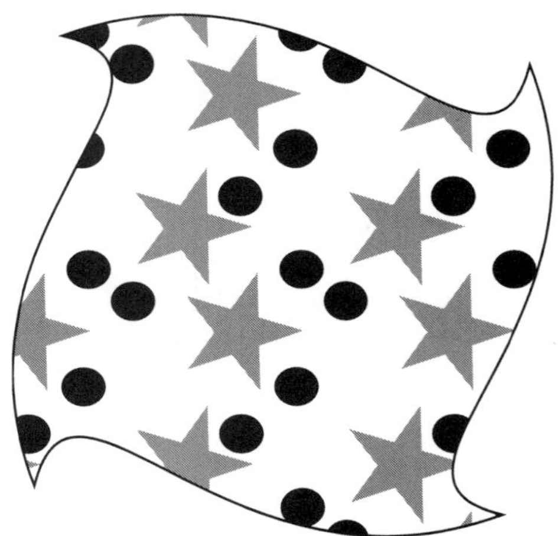

44 *The object selected displays the Tiled fill.*

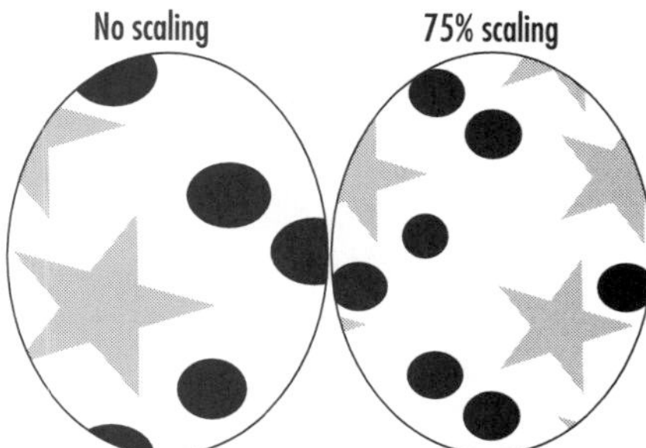

㊺ *The effects of scaling a Tiled fill object.*

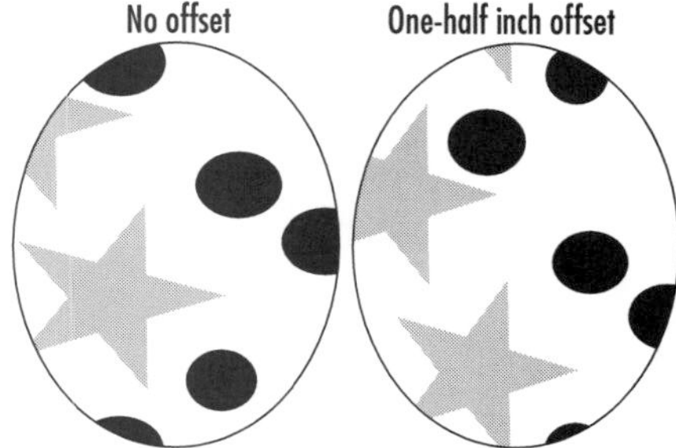

㊻ *The effects of offsetting a Tiled fill object.*

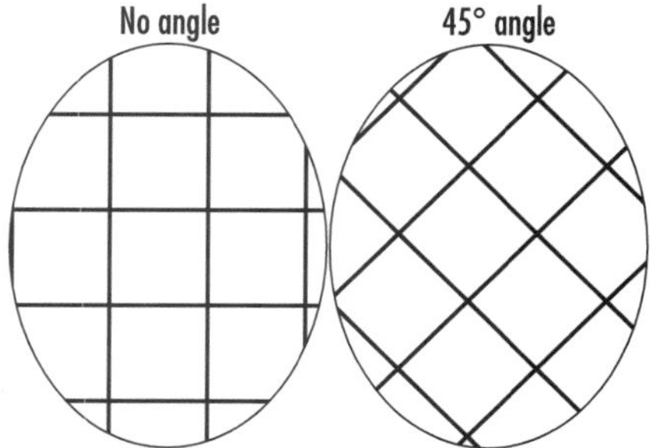

㊼ *The effects of changing the angle of a Tiled fill object.*

To adjust a Tiled fill:

1. With the Fill inspector displayed, select the Tiled fill object.
2. To change the size of the Tiled fill ㊺, use the Scale % **x** and **y** fields. To scale the fill uniformly, use the same amounts for both the **x** and **y** fields.
3. To move a Tiled fill within the object ㊻, enter positive or negative values in the Offset **x** and **y** fields.

TIP Positive **x** values in the Offset field move the fill to the right. Negative **x** values in the Offset field move the fill to the left. Positive **y** values in the Offset field move the fill up. Negative **y** values in the Offset field move the fill down.

4. To angle a Tiled fill within the object ㊼, move the angle wheel or enter the exact angle in the Angle field.

Using Custom and Textured Fills

Custom and Textured fills are premade graphics that simulate the look of various textures. After you choose a Custom or Textured fill, you can still make changes to the texture. *(See Appendix B for a printout of the Custom and Textured fills.)*

To apply a Custom or Textured fill:

1. Choose Custom from the mode menu in the Fill inspector.

   or

   Choose Textured from the mode menu in the Fill inspector.
2. Choose one of the Custom fills from the second pop-up menu that appears ㊽.

   or

   Choose one of the Textured fills from the second pop-up menu that appears ㊾.
3. If applicable, change the color and make any other changes you want to the settings of the fill.
4. Instead of seeing a preview of the fill in the object, you see a series of Cs that fill the object ㊿. You can only see the fill by printing the artwork or placing the artwork in Adobe InDesign ㊿.

TIP Custom and Textured fills cannot be scaled with an object and do not print to non-PostScript printers.

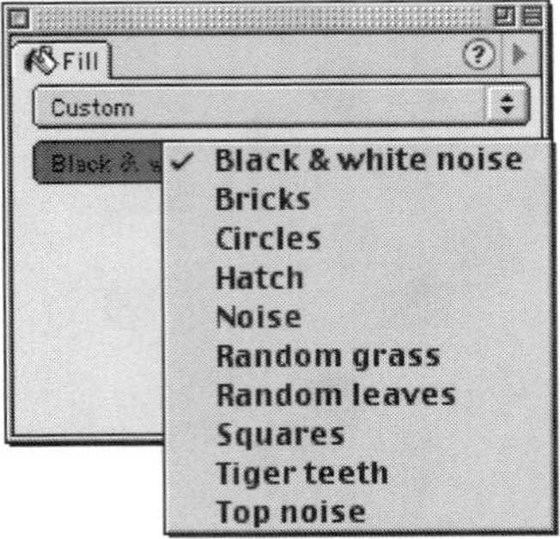

㊽ *The* Custom fill *choices.*

㊾ *The* Textured fill *choices.*

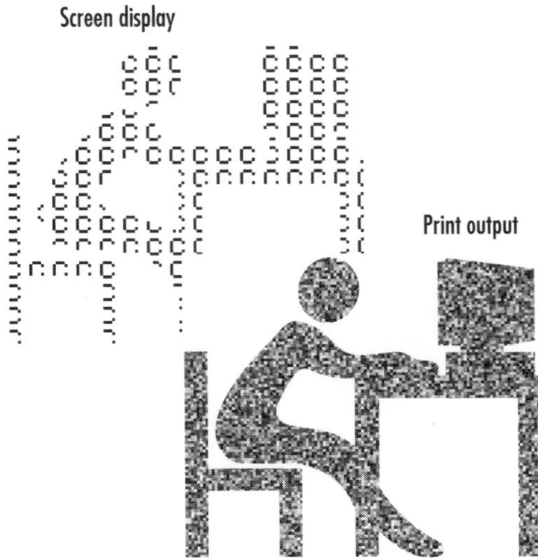

㊿ *The difference between the display and the print output of a Custom or Textured fill.*

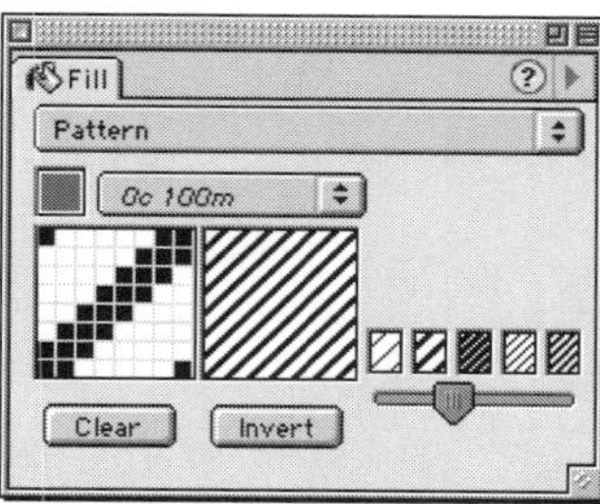

51 *The* **Pattern fill settings** *in the Fill inspector.*

52 *An object filled with a Pattern fill displays and prints that pattern.*

> **Writing PostScript Fills**
>
> When you choose a PostScript fill from the Fill inspector pop-up menu, you see a large box with the word "fill" in it. The purpose of this box is to allow you to type in specific PostScript code to create a pattern. Learning and working with PostScript code is much too advanced to cover here. If you are interested in working with PostScript in FreeHand, find an old edition of *Real World FreeHand* by Olav Martin Kvern (Peachpit Press).

Working with Pattern Fills

Pattern fills are bitmapped patterns that can be edited pixel by pixel. *(See Appendix B for a printout of the default pattern fills.)*

To apply a Pattern fill:

1. Select an object and choose Pattern from the Fill inspector pop-up menu.
2. Use the slider bar to choose one of the Pattern fills from the series of small boxes 51.
3. Use the large preview box on the left to edit the pattern by clicking on each of the pixels. The large preview box on the right shows what your pattern will look like when applied to the object.
4. Use the Clear button to delete all the dark pixels from the large preview boxes to editing a pattern again.
5. Use the Invert button to change the black pixels into white and vice versa.

TIP Objects behind Pattern fills are not visible through the white spaces of the fills.

6. Use the color drop box to apply any color to the dark pixels of a pattern.

TIP Colors are applied to the solid-color portion of the fill. White areas remain white.

TIP Pattern fills appear the same way onscreen as they print 52.

TIP Pattern fills cannot be transformed with an object.

TIP Pattern fills are designed for use on low-resolution printers, not high-resolution imagesetters or film recorders. They may also cause problems when part of Acrobat documents.

STROKES 15

Just as fills occupy the inside of objects, strokes surround the outside of objects. I always think of strokes as the egg shell that surrounds the inside fill. (However, unlike egg shells, the strokes in FreeHand don't crack if you accidentally bump them into another object.)

If you think of strokes as simply thin fill colors, you're very much mistaken. There are so many other things you can do with strokes that you can't do with fills.

You can create dash patterns, add arrowheads, and change the thickness of the stroke color.

However, there is another type of stroke, called Brushes, that is so powerful, I've given it its own chapter.

Setting the Stroke Color

Just like a Basic fill, the most important aspect to setting a Basic stroke is choosing the stroke color.

To apply a stroke color using the Stroke inspector:

1. Select the object.
2. With the Stroke inspector displayed, choose Basic from the Stroke pop-up menu. This displays the Basic stroke settings ❶.
3. Choose a color for the stroke from the color list.

To apply a stroke color using the Tools panel:

1. Select the object.
2. Click the triangle in the Stroke color box at the bottom of the Tools panel ❷. This opens the pop-up color palette ❸.
3. Choose a color from the color palette. *(See page 176 for information on how to change the color palette display.)*

To apply a stroke by dragging:

◆ Hold the Command key (Mac) or Ctrl+Shift keys (Win) after you drag the color swatch onto the object.The cursor changes to a box, indicating that only the stroke will be affected ❹.

To change the color of a stroke by dragging:

◆ If a stroke has already been applied to an object, drag a color swatch from the Color Mixer or Swatches panel directly onto the edge of the object.

TIP If you find it difficult to drag onto the edge, hold the keyboard modifiers mentioned in the previous exercise to ensure that only the stroke color changes.

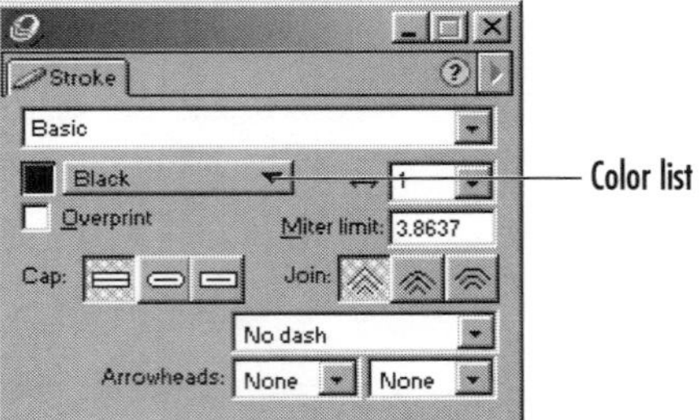

❶ *Choose Basic from the Stroke inspector list to display the* **Basic stroke options.**

❷ *The* **Stroke color box** *in the Tools panel.*

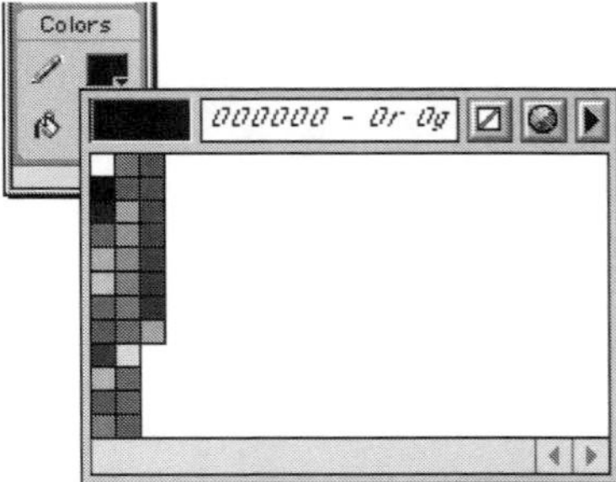

❸ *The* **pop-up color palette** *in the Tools panel lets you choose stroke colors.*

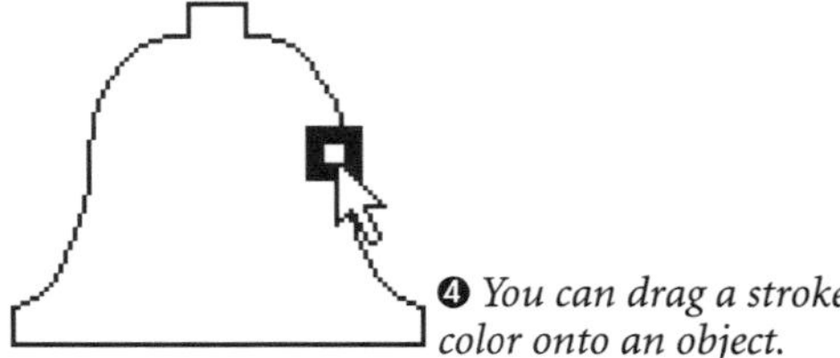

❹ *You can drag a stroke color onto an object.*

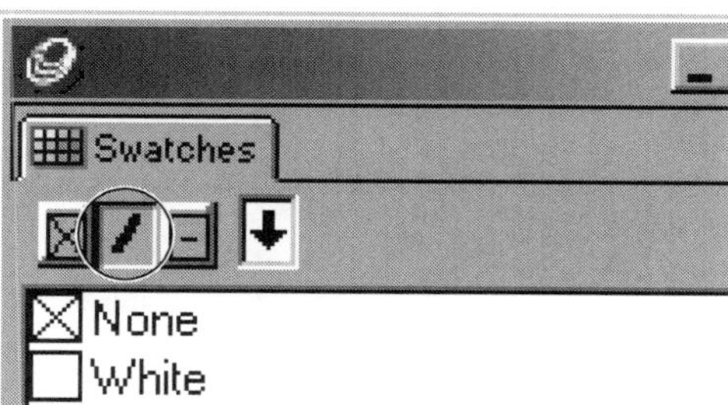

❺ *The* **Stroke drop box** *(circled) in the Swatches panel ndicates the stroke color of the selected object.*

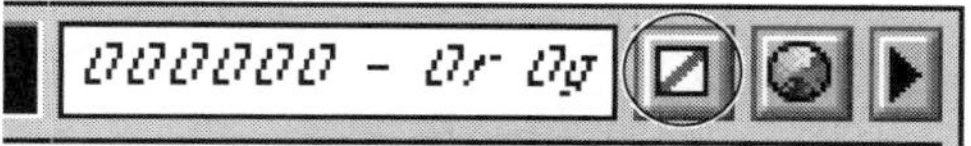

❻ *Click the* **None icon** *circled) in the Stroke color pop-up palette to turn off a stroke.*

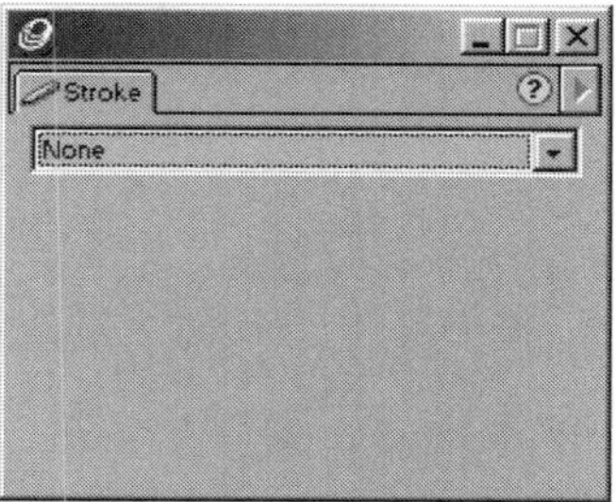

❼ *Choose* **None in the Stroke inspector** *to turn off the stroke.*

To apply a stroke color using the Swatches panel:

1. Select the object.

TIP Make sure that Basic or None is chosen in the Stroke inspector. If another type of stroke is listed, you may not see the color you choose.

2. Click the Stroke drop box in the Swatches panel ❺.
3. Click the name of the color you wish to change the stroke to in the Swatches panel.

   or

   Drag a color swatch from the Swatches panel or the Color Mixer onto the Stroke color drop box.

Just as it does to fills, setting a stroke to None makes the stroke invisible.

To change a stroke to None:

1. Select the object you want to apply the None stroke to.
2. With the Stroke drop box selected, click None in the Swatches panel. An x appears in the Stroke drop box, indicating that there is no stroke.

   or

   Click the None icon in the Stroke color box pop-up palette ❻.

   or

   Choose None from the Stroke inspector list ❼.

TIP Objects with no stroke or fill colors are invisible.

Modifying the Stroke Width

Once you have applied a stroke, you can change the width, or how thick that stroke appears.

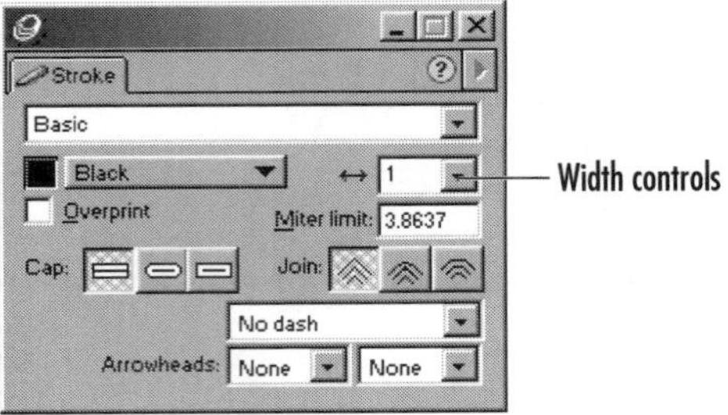

❽ *Use the* **Width field or Width list** *to change the stroke weight or thickness.*

To change a stroke width using the Stroke inspector:

1. Select the object you want to change.
2. With the Stroke inspector set for Basic, type the value for the thickness of the stroke in the Width field ❽.

   or

   Choose a value in points from the pop-up menu next to the field. The thickness of the stroke changes ❾.
3. Press Return/Enter or click anywhere on the Stroke inspector to implement a value in the field.

TIP Half the width of a stroke is applied to the inside of the path. The other half is applied to the outside of the path.

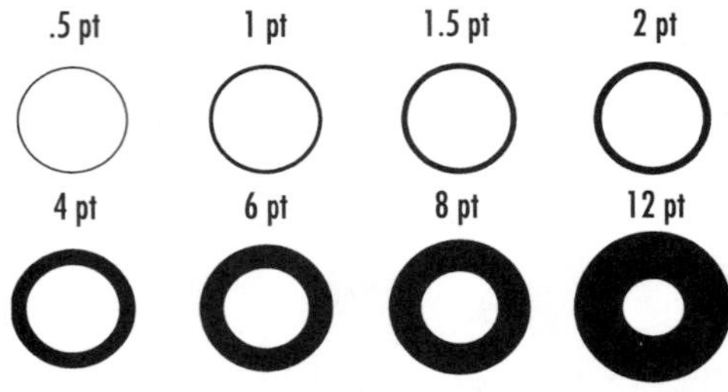

❾ *A sample of the* **stroke weights** *in the Width pop-up list.*

To change a stroke width using keyboard shortcuts:

1. Select the object that has a stroke.
2. (Mac) Press Cmd+Opt+Shift+< to make the stroke weight thinner.

   or

   (Mac) Press Cmd+Opt+Shift+> to make the stroke weight thicker.

   or

   (Win) Press Ctrl+Shift+1 to make the stroke weight thinner.

   or

   (Win) Press Ctrl+Shift+2 to make the stroke weight thicker.

> **Beware the Hairline Stroke**
>
> Unless you absolutely know what you are doing, don't apply the Hairline setting from the Width list.
>
> A hairline stroke is defined as the thinnest possible stroke you can print. If you're printing to the office printer, the hairline will be pretty thin.
>
> If you then send the document out to be printed on a professional imagesetter, the hairline rule turns practically invisible.
>
> As a general rule, you shouldn't specify a stroke width of anything lower than .125 pt—and certainly never specify a hairline!

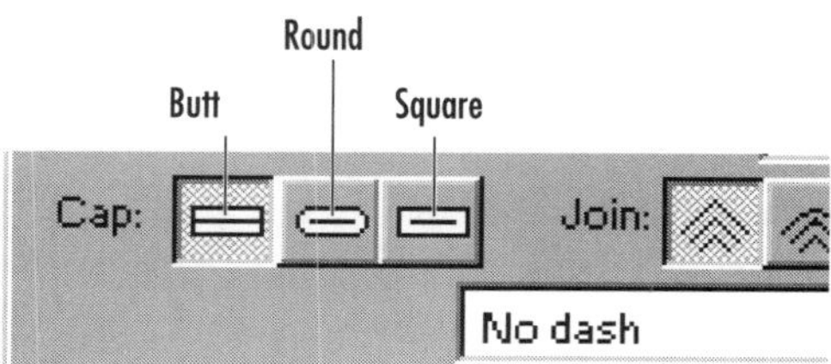

⑩ *Click the icons for the* **three Cap styles.**

⑪ *The three Cap styles applied to open paths. The endpoints are indicated by square white dots.*

> **Exporting Caps and Joins to Flash**
>
> If you export FreeHand files to Macromedia Flash, you may discover that your caps and joins have changed. This is because Flash does not support the caps and joins in FreeHand.
>
> If it is vital to keep the same look of the artwork, you can use the Expand Stroke command *(see page 119)* to convert the stroke to a filled path.
>
> Otherwise, just learn to live with Flash's default Round caps.

Modifying Caps and Joins

If you have an open path, you will want to consider the appearance of the *cap* or the end of the path. If you have a stroke with corner points, you will want to consider the appearance of the *join* or the point where the line segments meet.

To apply a cap to a stroke:

1. Select an open path that has a Basic stroke applied to it.

   TIP If you cannot see the differences in the cap styles, trying zooming in or increasing the stroke width.

2. Choose the cap style as follows ⑩:
   - **Butt** ends the stroke with a straight line that stops exactly on the endpoint of the path ⑪.
   - **Round** ends the stroke with a half-circle that extends past the endpoint of the path ⑪.
   - Square ends the stroke with a square that extends past the endpoint of the path ⑪.

TIP There is no difference between the Butt and Square caps except that the Square cap extends past the endpoints.

To change the join of a stroke:

1. Select an open path that has a Basic stroke applied to it.

TIP If you cannot see the differences in the join styles, trying zooming in or increasing the stroke width.

2. Choose the join style as follows ⓬:
   - **Miter** creates a point where line segments intersect. The sharper the angle, the longer the point extends ⓭.
   - **Round** forms a curve between the two line segments ⓭.
   - **Bevel** creates a line that cuts off the segments at the anchor point that connects the segments ⓭.

TIP My favorite look is to combine a Round cap with the Round join. This creates a look similar to a marker pen.

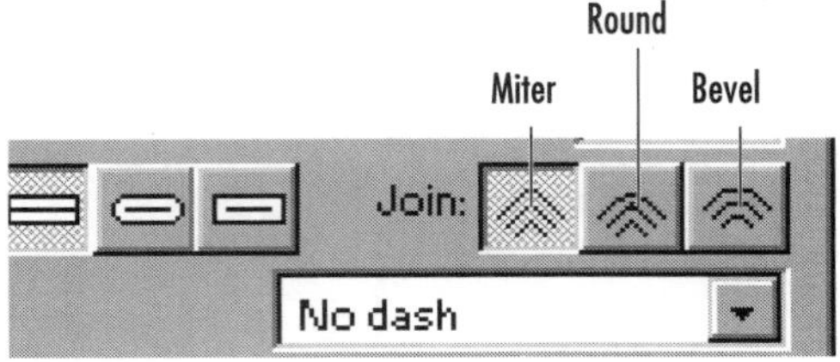

⓬ *Click the icons for the* **three Join styles.**

⓭ *The three Join styles applied to the corner point of a path. The anchor points are indicated by square white dots.*

When you use a Miter join, you can also set the maximum size of the spike that extends out from the join. If the size of the spike exceeds the Miter limit, the join is converted to a Bevel join.

To change the Miter limit:

1. Select a path with a miter join.

TIP In order to see the effects of changing the miter limit, choose a rather thick width such as 24 points and create two line segments with a very acute angle between them. If the miter limit is high enough, the extension should look like a spike.

2. In the Stroke inspector, use the Miter limit field to lower the size of the Miter limit ⓮.

TIP A low number such as 1 or 2 points converts the Miter join to a Bevel join. ⓯.

⓮ *The Miter limit field lets you set the maximum size for the spike of a Miter join.*

⓯ *A Miter limit of 7 points allows the top object to display a spike. A Miter limit of 6 points converts the bottom object's join to a Bevel.*

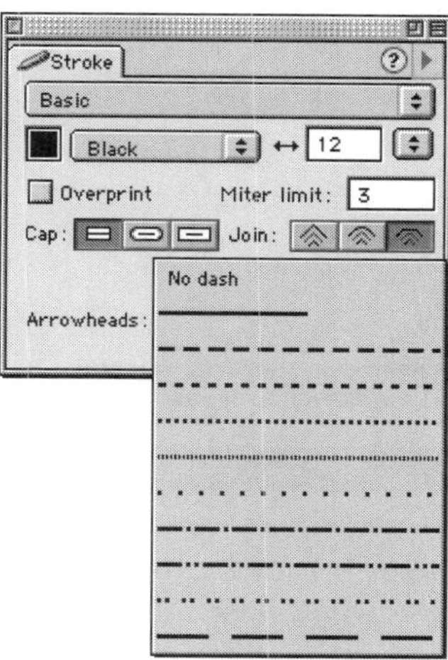

⓰ *The default pop-up list of Dash patterns.*

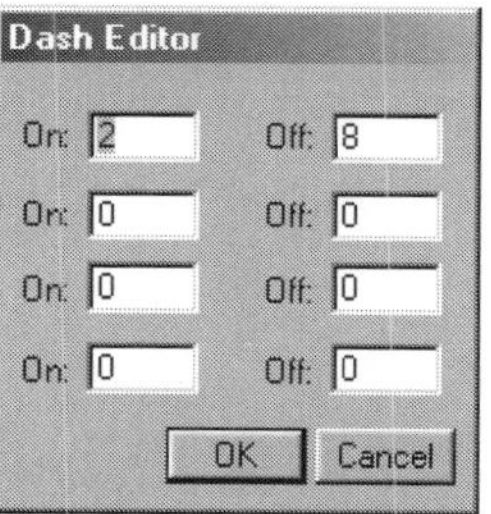

⓱ *The* **Dash Editor dialog box** *lets you create your own dash patterns. Choose up to four sets of On and Off patterns.*

Creating Dashed Strokes

Dashed lines are often used to indicate a coupon that should be cut out of a print ad. (I am always amused when I see a dashed line around a coupon area on a Web page. It's very hard to cut out the coupon on my computer screen.)

To apply a dash pattern:

1. Select a path.

TIP If you cannot see the differences in the dash patterns styles, trying zooming in or increasing the stroke width.

2. In the Stroke inspector, use the Dash pop-up menu to choose from the default list of premade dash patterns ⓰.

TIP The spaces between the dashes of a stroke are transparent, not white. If you lay your dashed stroke over another object, you will see through the spaces to that other object.

You may want to create your own dash patterns for strokes. You do that by using the Dash Editor dialog box.

To edit a dash pattern:

1. With the Stroke inspector displayed, hold down the Opt/Alt key as you click to select one of the dash patterns from the Basic stroke settings. The Dash Editor dialog box appears ⓱.
2. Set the length of the visible portion of the dash by entering a number in the On field.
3. Set the length of the space between the dashes by entering a number in the Off field.
4. You can enter up to four different sets of On and Off values.
5. When you have finished entering the pattern, click OK. The dash pattern is added to the bottom of the dash list.

Although the dashed patterns you can apply to a stroke are limited, you can create very sophisticated effects if you combine several different strokes together. For instance, you can create a multicolored dash by combining two stroked paths together.

⑱ *When two paths are combined, they can simulate the effect of a multicolored dash.*

To create a two-color dashed stroke:

1. Apply a Basic stroke with no dash to a path.
2. Choose **Edit > Clone.** This makes a copy of that line on top of your original line.
3. Change the color of the clone and apply a dash pattern. You now have a dashed line with two colors ⑱.

TIP As a variation, choose a smaller stroke width for the clone. This creates the effect of a dashed line inside a thicker solid ⑲.

TIP You can also create different effects with dashed patterns by setting the caps to Round or Square ⑳.

⑲ *A thinner dashed path creates a different effect when combined with a thicker stroke.*

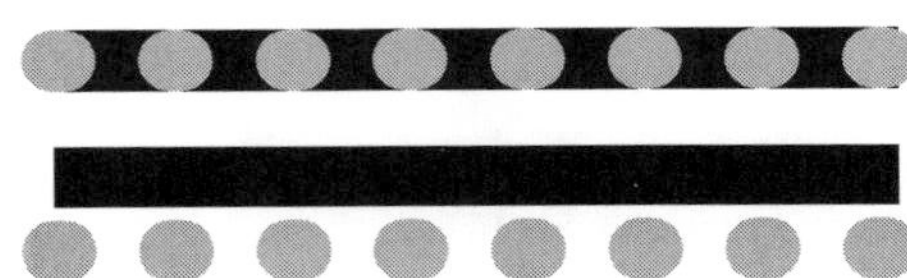

⑳ *A Round cap changes the appearance of a dashed stroke.*

Exporting Dashed Patterns to Flash

Unfortunately Flash does not support the dash patterns FreeHand.

Worse, the Exapnd Stroke command does not convert dashes into filled paths.

The simplest way I know to add dashes to a path, is to add a hyphen as text on a path *(see page 250)*.

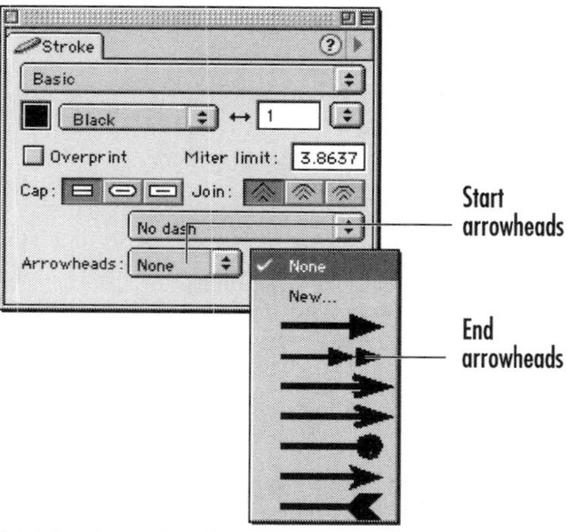

㉑ *The Arrowheads pop-up menu lets you add arrowheads to open paths made with Basic strokes.*

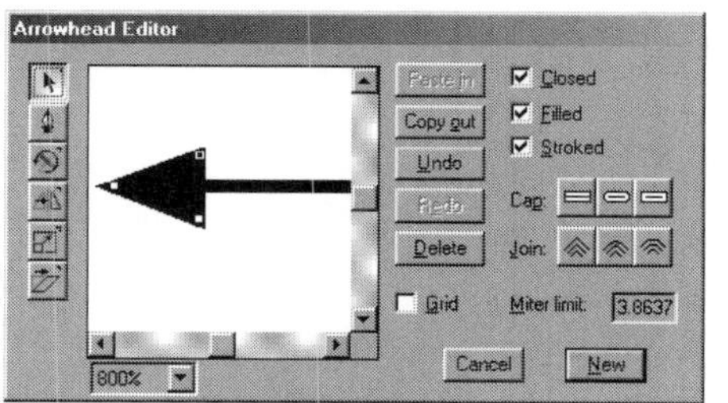

㉒ *The Arrowhead Editor dialog box lets you modify the program's arrowheads or create your own custom arrowheads.*

Working with Arrowheads

The last choice for Basic strokes is arrowheads. You can see arrowheads only on open paths.

To apply arrowheads:

1. Select an open path with a Basic stroke.

   TIP Arrowheads take their size from the point size of the stroke.

2. Choose one of the Arrowheads pop-up menus in the Stroke inspector ㉑. The left menu controls the start of the path, the right menu controls the end of the path.
3. Using the appropriate menu, choose an arrowhead.

   TIP Choose None to remove an arrowhead from a path.

To create new arrowheads:

1. Open either Arrowheads pop-up menu and choose New. The Arrowhead Editor dialog box appears ㉒.
2. Use any of the Arrowhead Editor tools to draw the arrowhead.
3. Click New. The new arrowhead appears at the end of both arrowhead menus.

To edit arrowheads:

1. Hold down the Opt/Alt key as you select one of the arrowheads from the pop-up menu.
2. In the Arrowhead Editor that appears, modify the arrowhead.
3. Click New to complete your edit. The original arrowhead is modified and all objects that use the arrowhead change.

   TIP Use the Paste in and Copy out buttons to transfer arrowheads between the Arrowhead Editor and the work page. This allows you to use all the FreeHand tools to create arrowheads.

Specialty Strokes

Just as there are Custom fills, FreeHand provides Custom stroke patterns. *(See Appendix B for a printout of the Custom stroke patterns.)*

To apply a Custom stroke pattern:

1. Choose Custom from the Stroke pop-up menu of the Stroke inspector ㉓.
2. Choose a stroke effect from the Effect pop-up menu.
3. Choose the color from the Color menu.
4. Use the Width menu or field to set the thickness of the stroke.
5. Enter an amount in the Length field to control the size of the repeating element in the stroke.
6. Enter an amount in the Spacing field to control the space between each repeating element.

TIP FreeHand displays the custom strokes as a solid line. However, you can see them when placed in Adobe InDesign or when printed to a PostScript device ㉔.

TIP You can also use the blend on a path *(see Chapter 17, "Blends")* to create similar effects.

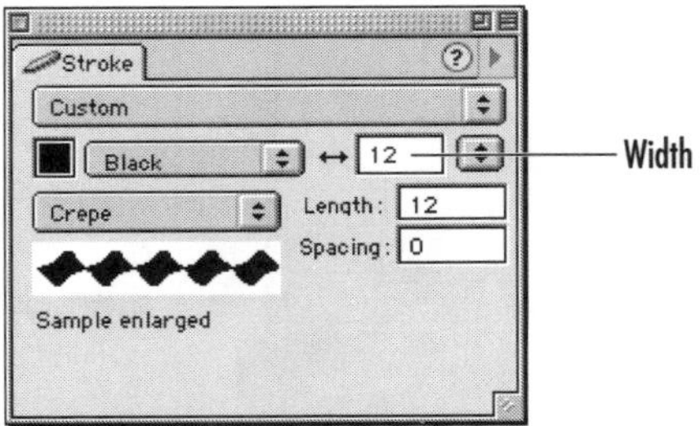

㉓ *The Custom stroke settings in the Stroke inspector.*

㉔ *Three sample custom strokes.*

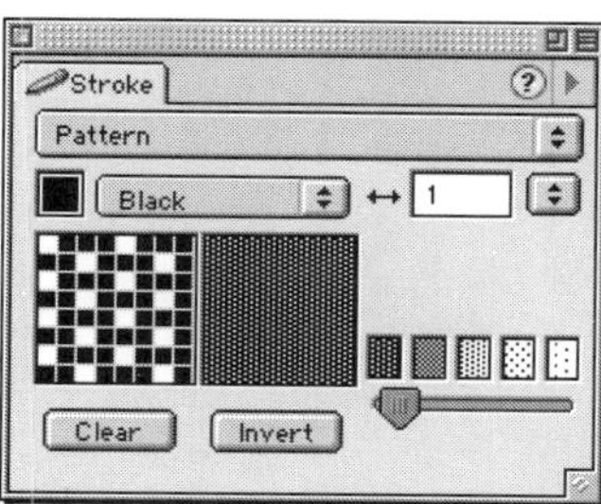

㉕ *The Pattern stroke settings in the Stroke inspector.*

> **Writing PostScript Strokes**
>
> When you choose a PostScript stroke from the Stroke inspector pop-up menu, you see a large box with the word "stroke" in it. Like the PostScript fills, the purpose of this box is to allow you to type in specific PostScript code to create a pattern. Since learning PostScript is beyond the scope of this book, I suggest you find an old edition of *Real World FreeHand* by Olav Martin Kvern (Peachpit Press).

Pattern strokes are bitmapped patterns that can be edited pixel by pixel.

To apply a Pattern stroke:

1. Select the object and choose Pattern from the Stroke inspector.
2. Use the slider bar at the bottom of the palette to choose one of the Pattern strokes ㉕.
3. Use the preview box to edit the pattern by clicking each pixel you want to turn on or off.
4. Use the Clear button to clear all the pixels from the preview boxes.
5. Use the Invert button to change the black pixels into white pixels and vice versa.
6. Use the color drop box to apply a color to the dark pixels.

TIP Pattern strokes are designed for use on low-resolution printers (including non-PostScript devices).

BRUSHES 16

All right, I admit it! I'm a brushes junkie. Ever since I saw my first piece of artwork wrap itself around a path following every twist and turn, I was hooked. If it were up to me, I would have brushes in every graphic I work on. I would have brushes in my page layout programs — even my word processing documents.

Brushes are one of the stroke choices for paths. The basic concept behind brushes is that you define one piece of artwork as the graphic that is used as a brush that is applied to a path.

Macromedia FreeHand offers you two types of brushes. Paint brushes allow you to distort an object so that it scales itself to fit the path. Spray brushes allow you to repeat a graphic over and over along the path.

As you will see, there are many complexities in working with brushes. I only hope that some of my enthusiasm for brushes will spread to you.

Creating Artwork for a Brush

Unlike the strokes covered in the previous chapter, you need to create the artwork that is used in a brush stroke.

To convert selected objects to a brush:

1. Select the object that you want to use as the brush tip.
2. Choose **Modify > Brush > Create Brush.** A dialog box appears asking how you would like to use the selected object ❶.
3. Click the Copy button to create a symbol to be used as the brush. This leaves the selected object unchanged.

   or

   Click the Convert button to create a symbol to be used as the brush, and replace the selected object with an instance of that symbol.
4. In the Edit Brush dialog box, use the Brush Name field to create a name for the brush.

TIP The Include Symbols field automatically uses the symbol that was created from the selected artwork.

5. Set the options as described in the following exercises.
6. Click OK. The brush is available to be applied to paths. *(See page 210 for how to apply a brush to paths.)*

To set the brush mode:

1. Click Paint to create a brush tip that stretches along the length of the path ❷.

   or

   Click Spray to create a brush tip that repeats along the path ❸.
2. If you choose Paint, enter a number from 1 to 500 in the Count field. This sets how many times the brush tip appears along the path.

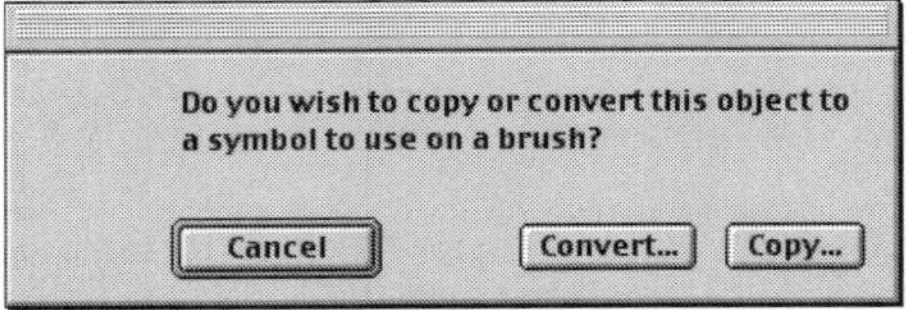

❶ *You have a choice as to how to use the object selected as a brush tip.*

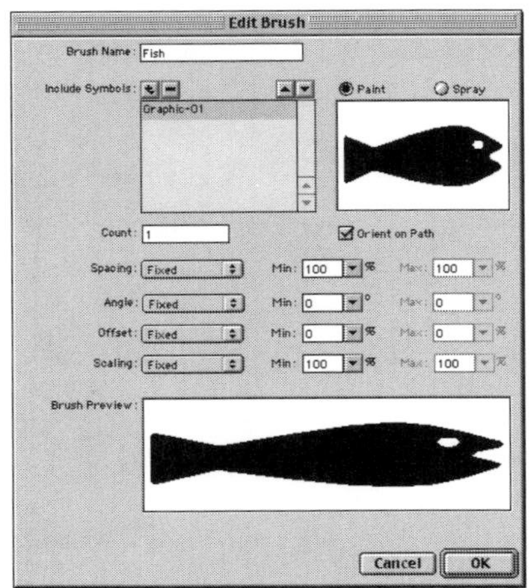

❷ *The* **Edit Brush** *dialog box set for a Paint brush.*

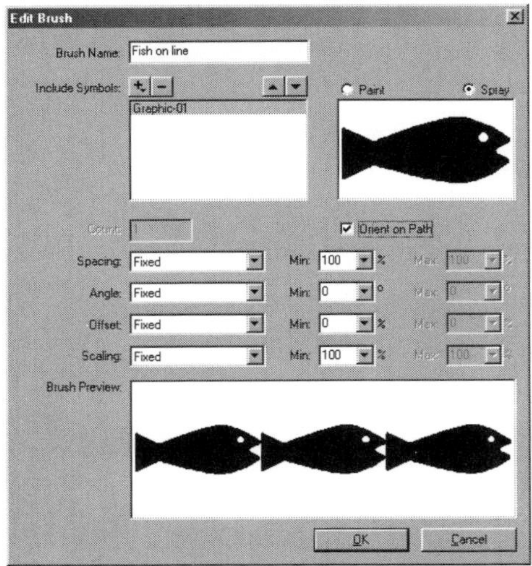

❸ *The* **Edit Brush** *dialog box set for a Spray brush.*

❹ *The* **Orient on Path** *controls how the brush tips align themselves to the path.*

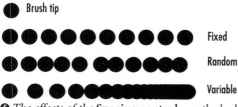

❺ *The effects of the* **Spacing controls** *on the look of a brush.*

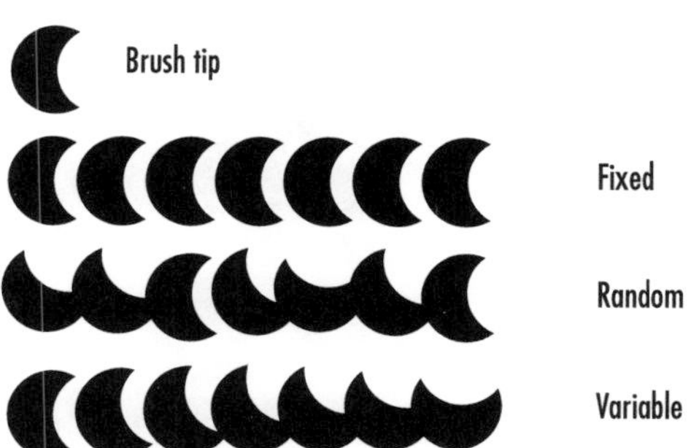

❻ *The effects of the* **Angle controls** *on the look of a brush.*

To control the orientation of the brush:

- Check Orient on Path to have the artwork follow the orientation of the path to which it is applied ❹.

To set the spacing options:

1. Use the Spacing list to choose one of the following options for the space between each instance of the brush tip ❺:
   - **Fixed** sets a specific space.
   - **Random** lets you set minimum and maximum amounts that are applied randomly.
   - **Variable** lets you set the minimum and maximum amounts that are applied linearly.
2. If the Spacing is set for Fixed, enter an amount between 1% to 200% in the Min field.

   or

   If the spacing is set for Random or Variable, set an amount in both the Min and Max fields.

TIP The percentage of spacing is based on the width of the symbol used as the artwork.

To set the angle options:

1. Use the Angle list to choose one of the following options for the rotation of each instance as it is applied to the path ❻:
   - **Fixed** sets a single rotation for all instances.
   - **Random** lets you set minimum and maximum rotations that are applied randomly to each instance.
   - **Variable** lets you set the minimum and maximum amounts that are applied linearly to the instances.
2. If the Angle is set for Fixed, set an amount from 0° to 359° in the Min field.

   or

   If the spacing is set for Random or Variable, set an amount in both the Min and Max fields.

To set the offset options:

1. Use the Offset list to choose one of the following options for the distance of the brush tip from the path ❼:
   - **Fixed** sets a single offset for all instances.
   - **Random** lets you set minimum and maximum amounts that are applied randomly to each instance.
   - **Variable** lets you set the minimum and maximum amounts that are applied linearly to the instances.
   - **Flare** is available for Spray brushes. Flare lets you change the offset amount according to the Scaling amounts.
2. If the Offset is set for Fixed, set an amount from -200% to 200%° in the Min field.

   or

   If the spacing is set for Random or Variable, set an amount in both the Min and Max fields.

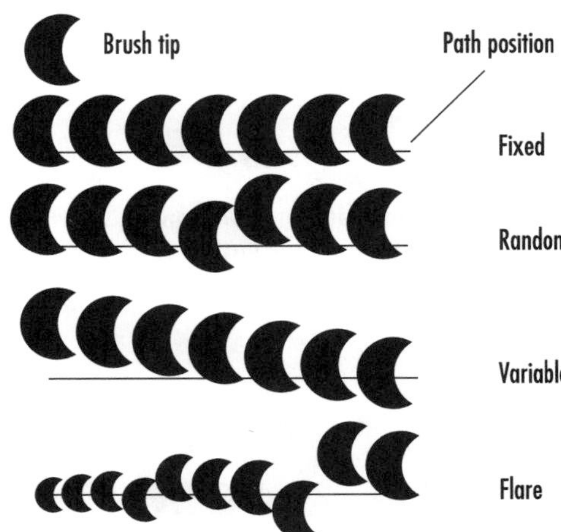

❼ *The effects of the* **Offset controls** *on the look of a brush.*

To set the scaling options:

1. Use the Scaling list to choose one of the following options for the size of the instances ❽:
   - **Fixed** sets a single size for all instances.
   - **Random** lets you set minimum and maximum sizes that are applied randomly to each instance.
   - **Variable** lets you set the minimum and maximum sizes that are applied linearly to the instances.
   - **Flare** is available for Paint brushes. Flare lets you change the scale amount according to the minimum and maximum scaling values ❾.
2. If the Offset is set for Fixed, set an amount from -200% to 200%° in the Min field.

   or

   If the spacing is set for Random or Variable, set an amount in both the Min and Max fields.

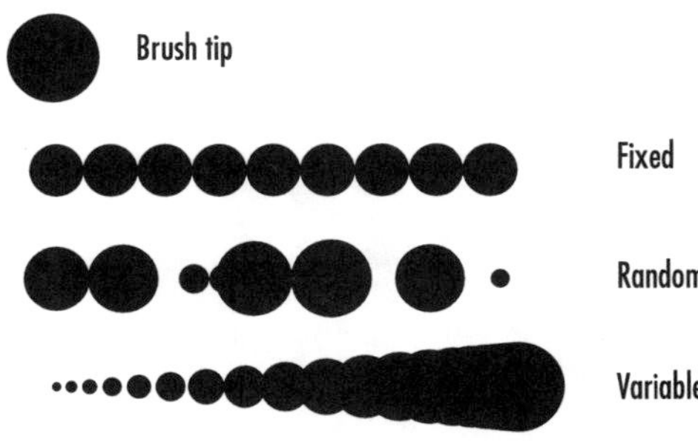

❽ *The effects of the* **Scaling controls** *on the look of a brush.*

❾ *The effects of the* **Scaling controls** *on a Paint brush set for three repetitions.*

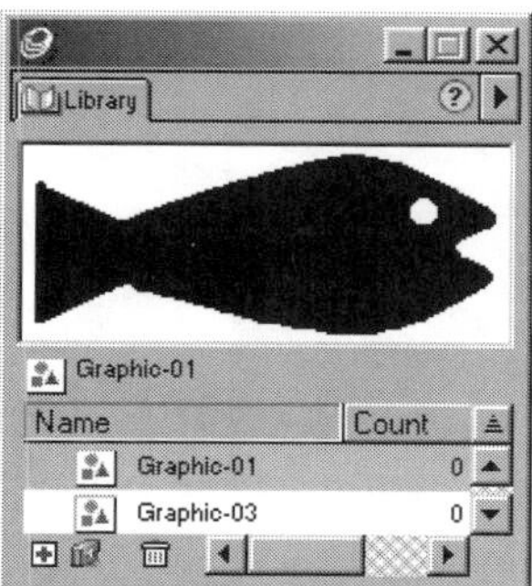

⑩ **Brush symbols** *are stored in the Library.*

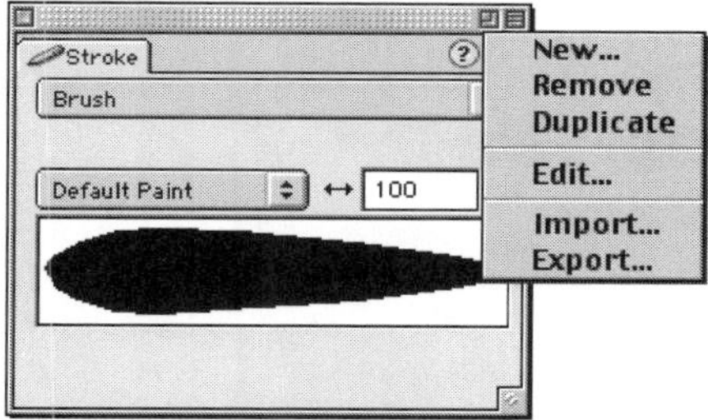

⑪ *The* **Stroke inspector menu** *for the Brush settings.*

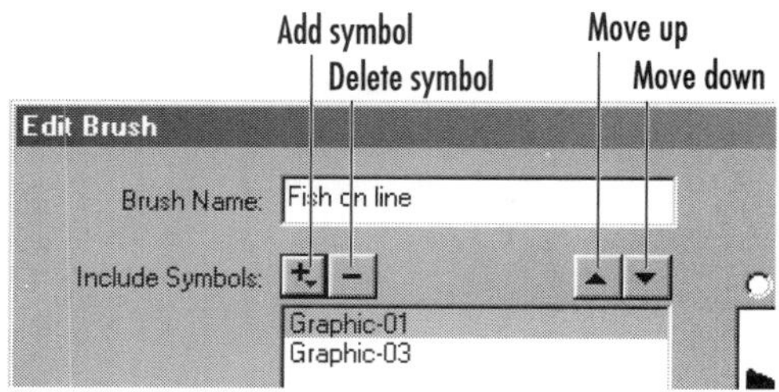

⑫ *You can use multiple symbols for brush tips.*

⑬ *An example of how two symbols (circled) can be combined into a brush tip.*

You're not limited to using only one piece of artwork as a brush tip. FreeHand also lets you create brushes that use more than one graphic.

To create a multi-graphic brush:

1. Select the graphic you want to use as a brush tip.
2. Choose **Modify > Symbol > Copy to Symbol.** This creates a symbol of the artwork that is available in the Library ⑩. *(For more information on working with symbols, see Chapter 22, "Symbols.")*
3. Repeat steps 1 and 2 to create as many symbols as necessary.
4. With the Stroke inspector list set to Brush, choose New from the Stroke inspector menu ⑪. This opens the Edit Brush dialog box.
5. Click the Add Symbol button to choose a symbol from the Library ⑫. The name of the symbol is displayed in the symbol list.
6. Add as many other symbols from the Library.
7. Use the Move up or Move down buttons to change the stacking order of the symbols in the brush.
8. Set the rest of the options in the Edit Brush dialog box as described in the previous exercises.

TIP You can have both Paint and Spray brush tips in the same brush.

9. Click OK. The brush is now available to be used on paths ⑬.

Working with Brushes

Once you have defined brushes, it is relatively simple to apply them to objects.

To apply a brush to a path:

1. Select the object.
2. Choose Brush from the Stroke inspector list.

TIP Each new FreeHand document always contains a default paint brush and a default spray brush ⓮.

3. Enter a number in the Width field to change the size of the brush ⓯.

To release a brush from a path:

1. Select the object.
2. Choose **Modify > Brush > Release Brush.** This converts the brush artwork into discrete instances of the symbol.

TIP The instances can be moved, but not individually modified.

3. If you want to modify an instance, select the instance and choose **Modify > Symbol > Release Instance.** This converts the instances into ordinary paths ⓰.

To delete a brush:

1. Select the brush from the Brush list in the Stroke inspector.
2. Choose Remove from the Stroke inspector menu. If the brush has been applied to a path, a dialog box appears ⓱.
3. Choose Delete to remove the brush from the brush list as well as delete any paths that had the brush applied to them.

   or

   Choose Release to convert the brush to discrete objects and remove the brush from the brush list.

⓮ *The* **default paint brush** *and* **default spray brush** *applied to a spiral path.*

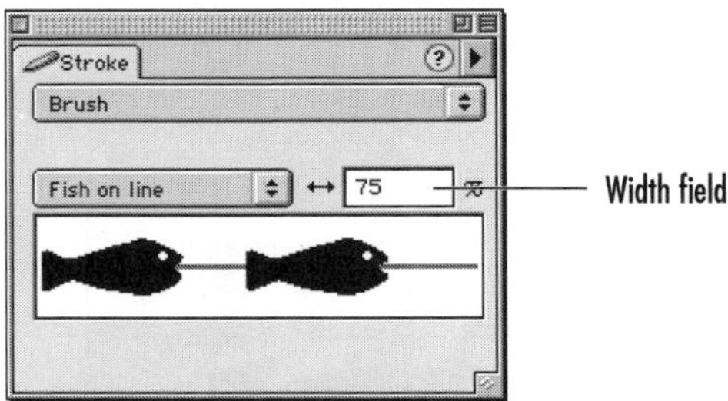

⓯ *Use the* **Width Field** *to change the size of the brush tip applied to a path.*

⓰ *When you use the* **Release Brush** *and* **Release Instance commands,** *you can then modify the individual elements.*

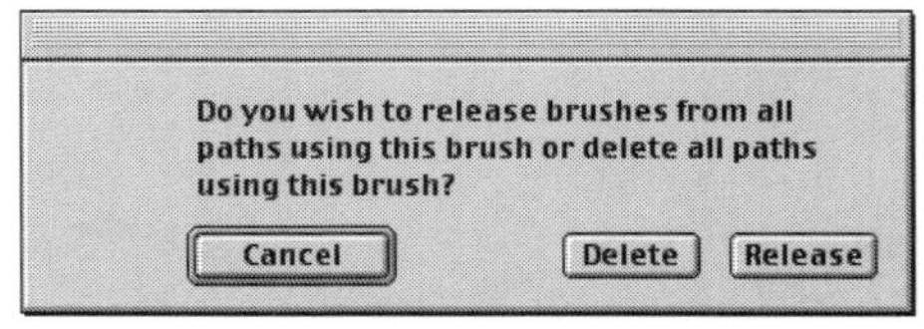

Do you wish to release brushes from all paths using this brush or delete all paths using this brush?

Cancel | Delete | Release

⓱ *You can control what happens to paths when you delete a brush.*

This brush is in use. Do you wish to change all paths using this brush or create a new brush?

Create   Change

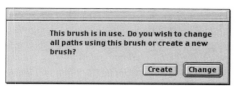

⓲ *You can control what happens when you edit a brush that is is use.*

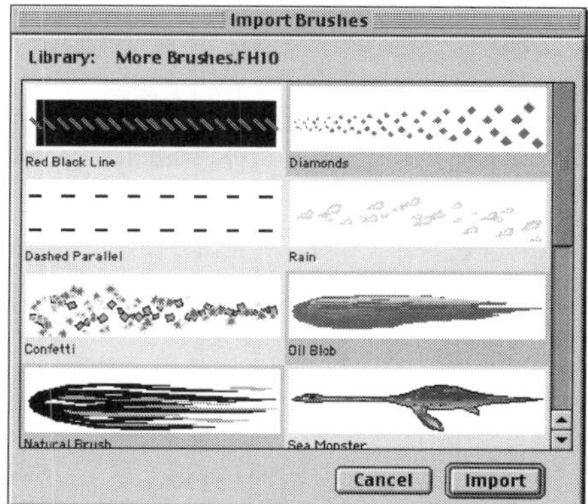

⓳ *The* **Import Brushes** *dialog box lets you choose brushes to import from other documents.*

> **What's Imported with the Brushes?**
>
> When you import a brush into a file, you also import any named colors that are used in the artwork for the brush. You also import any symbols that are used as the brush tip.

To edit a brush:

1. Use the brush list in the Stroke inspector to choose the brush you want to edit.
2. Choose Edit from the Stroke inspector menu. This opens the Edit Brush dialog box.
3. Make whatever changes you want to the brush and click OK. If the brush is in use, a dialog box appears ⓲.
4. Click Change to apply those changes to the existing brush graphic.

   or

   Click Create to create a duplicate of the original brush with the changes. This leaves previously created artwork untouched.

TIP If you want to edit the artwork used to create a brush, you need to edit the symbol for that artwork *(see Chapter 22, "Symbols.")*.

To duplicate a brush:

- Use the brush list in the Stroke inspector to choose the brush you want to duplicate.

To import brushes:

1. With Brush chosen in the Stroke inspector list, choose Import from the Stroke inspector menu.
2. Navigate to find the file you want to import brushes from. The Import Brushes dialog box appears ⓳.

TIP FreeHand ships with a file of additional brushes located in Freehand: Brushes: MoreBrushes.FH10.

3. Select the brushes you want to import.

TIP Use the Shift key to select a range of brushes. Use the Cmd/Ctrl key to select multiple brushes.

4. Click Import. The brushes are added to the document.

To export brushes:

1. With Brush chosen in the Stroke inspector list, choose Export from the Stroke inspector menu. The Export Brushes dialog box appears ⓴.
2. Select the brushes you want to export.

TIP Use the Shift key to select a range of brushes. Use the Cmd/Ctrl key to select multiple brushes.

3. Click Export. The Save dialog box appears.
4. Name and save the file.

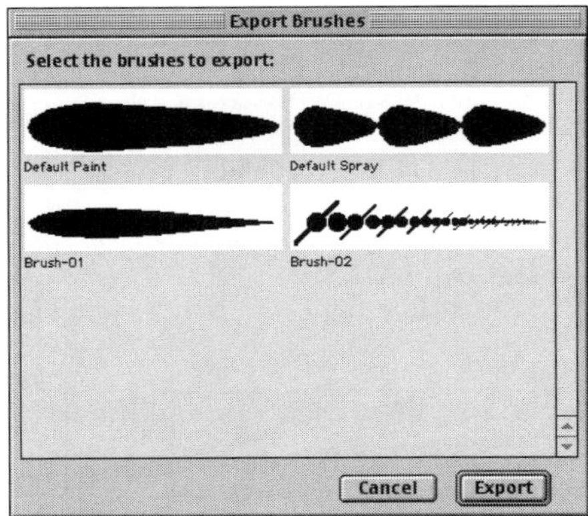

⓴ *Use the* **Export Brushes** *dialog box to choose the brushes to be exported into their own file.*

BLENDS 17

When I first started working with Macromedia FreeHand, blends were the only way we could create certain effects.

Way back then we used blends to create subtle shading and lighting contours. We used blends to create soft edges for shadows. We relied on blends to make one shape morph into another. And we used blends to make a series of objects follow a path.

Today, however, FreeHand has added many new features that are much easier to use than blends. For instance, contour gradients make it much easier to add subtle shading to objects. The spray brushes give you much more control to make objects follow a path.

That's not to say there are no more uses for blends. It's just you don't have to rely on them as much as I did back in the old days.

Understanding Blends

Although there are hundreds of thousands of different looks you can create with blends, they are all variations of three basic effects: color change, shape change, or distributing objects.

Color changes

Color changes are similar to the look of gradients. However, blends give you more control over the look of the color change ❶.

Shape changes

Shape changes create the effect of one object turning into another. Some shape changes use hundreds of intermediate styles which make a subtle change between the objects ❷. Other shape changes use few steps which lets you see how each object changes ❸.

Distributing objects

You can distribute objects by blending one object to an identical copy of itself. The intermediate steps are also identical objects, but they can easily be distributed in a straight line or along a path ❹.

❶ *The top three color changes were created by gradients, but a blend is needed for the more complicated color change on the bottom.*

❷ *The difference between a blend with just a few steps (left) and one with over two hundred steps (right).*

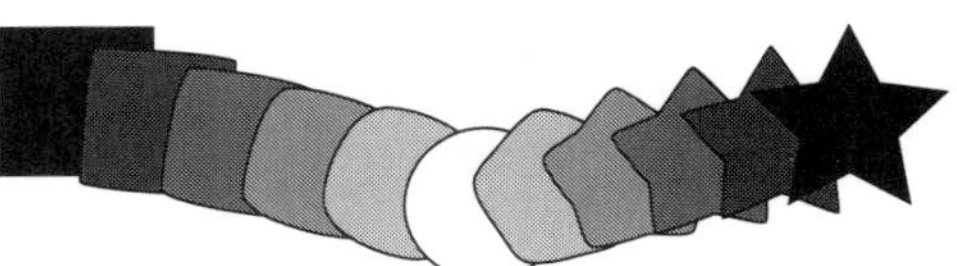

❸ *An example of how a blend can make one object change its shape into another.*

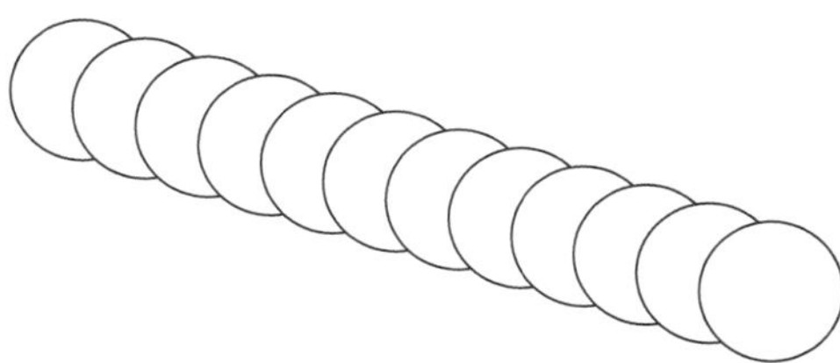

❹ *An example of how a blend between two identical circles creates a distribution of circles.*

❺ *Two objects selected to create a blend.*

❻ *After applying the* **Blend command,** *the objects are blended with intermediate steps.*

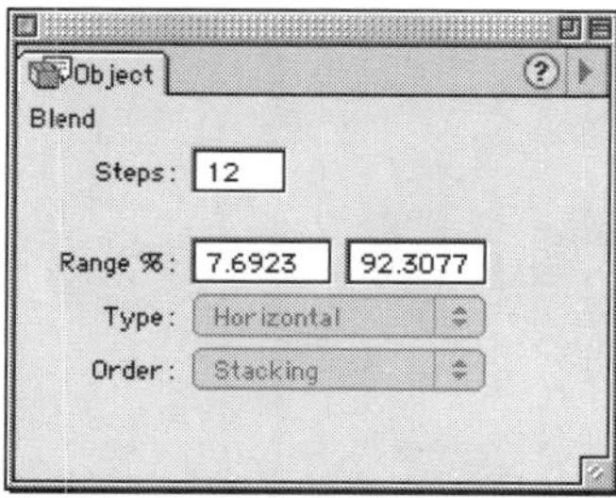

❼ *Use the* **Steps** *field to set the number of steps between the original objects in a blend.*

Blending Paths

No matter what type of blend effect you create, they all start with the same basic blend command.

To create a simple blend:

1. Select two or more shapes you want to blend ❺.
2. Choose **Modify > Combine > Blend.** The objects blend together ❻.

TIP Blends are created in straight lines between objects. To make a blend follow a curve, you align the blend to a path *(see page 219)*.

Once you have a blend, you may want to change the number of steps. You might want to make the blend as smooth as possible or modify it to show the intermediate steps.

To change the number of steps in a blend:

1. Select the blend.
2. In the Object inspector, enter the number of steps between the original objects in the Steps field ❼.
3. Press Return/Enter. The blend re-forms with the new number of steps.

The default number of blend steps

FreeHand calculates the default number of steps in a blend from the Printer resolution in the Document inspector. Higher resolutions give you a greater number of steps.

If you change the resolution you change the number of steps for new blends. Blends made before you changed the resolution do not change.

You can use the Find and Replace Graphics dialog box to find all blends with a certain number of steps and change them to a different number of steps *(see page 276)*.

You may find your blends do not look as smooth as you would like. Or that the objects do not change in the manner you expect. This is because FreeHand automatically calculates the blend using the points from which it wants to blend ❽. You can create a custom blend by forcing FreeHand to use specific points for the blend.

❽ *An* **automatic blend** *between two objects with no points selected.*

To create a custom blend:

1. Use the Pointer tool to select a point on the first of the objects from which you want the blend to begin.
2. Hold the Shift key to select a point on the second object.
3. Continue to select additional points on each of the objects in the blend.
4. Choose **Modify > Combine > Blend.** The intermediate steps of the blend are created by creating shapes between the selected points ❾–❿.

TIP To make blends as smooth as possible, pick points on each object that are in equivalent positions.

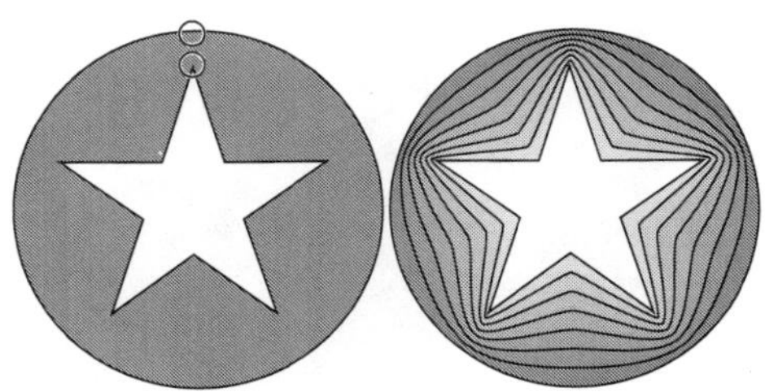

❾ *A* **custom blend** *between two objects created by selecting two points (circled).*

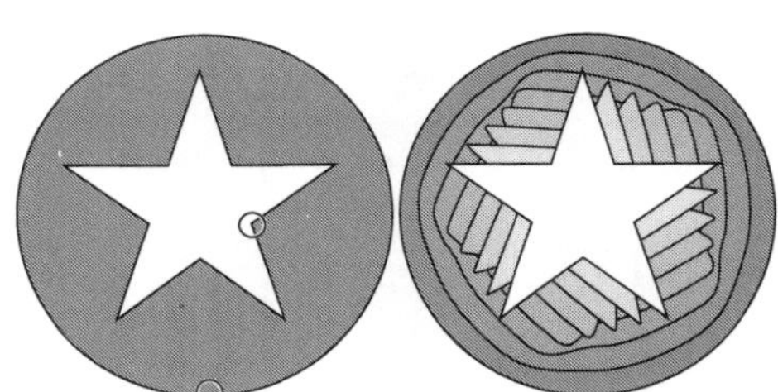

❿ *A* **custom blend** *created by selecting two different points (circled).*

The Rules of Blends

There are limitations to which objects can be used in a blend. The blend command does not work in the following instances:

You cannot blend between paths that have different types of strokes or fill. For example one object cannot contain a basic fill and the other a gradient.

Pattern fills do not blend; they switch abruptly from one to the other. Texture and custom fills must be identical at both ends of the blend. *(See the next page for more rules.)*

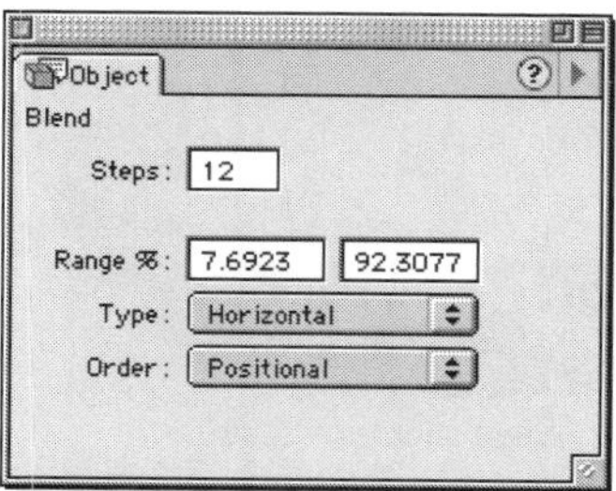

11 *The* **Type and Order controls** *are used to control the appearance of composite shapes in a blend.*

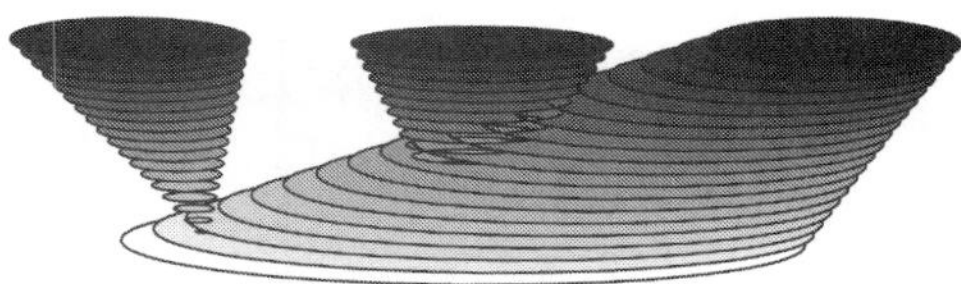

12 *These three composite ovals have been blended to the bottom oval at the settings of* **Type: Normal and Order: Stacking.**

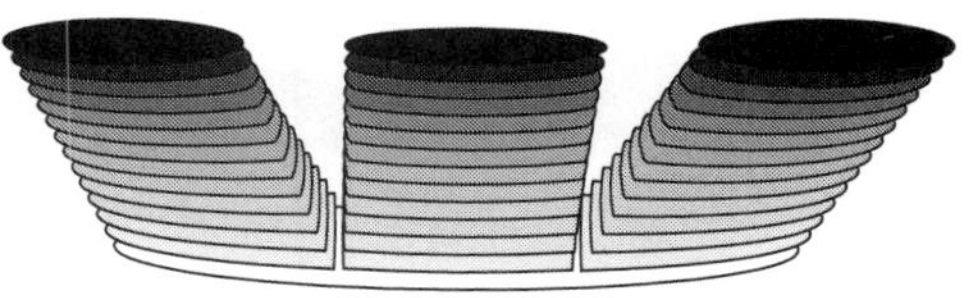

13 *The same composite ovals have been blended to the bottom oval at the settings of* **Type: Horizontal and Order: Position.**

Blending Composite Paths

Composite paths are those objects that have had the Join command applied. If you use composite (joined) paths in a blend, you have some extra controls as to how the blend is drawn. *(For more information on composite paths, see page108.)*

To use composite paths in a blend:

1. Select the composite paths you want to blend.

TIP Some or all of the objects in the blend can be composite.

2. Choose **Modify > Combine > Blend.**
3. Set the Type list options in the Object inspector as follows **11**:
   - **Normal** uses the normal appearance of the composite object for the blend. This is the best setting for most composite paths **12**.
   - **Horizontal** gives the best appearance when the composite paths do not overlap and are arranged in a horizontal alignment.
   - **Vertical** gives the best appearance when the composite paths do not overlap and are arranged in a vertical alignment.
4. Set the Order list options in the Object inspector as follows **11**:
   - **Positional** blends the objects based on their position on the page **13**.
   - **Stacking** blends the objects based on their stacking order.

The Rules of Blends (continued)

Blends between two spot colors must remain grouped in order to mix as spot colors. If you ungroup, the intermediate steps will be converted to process colors.

You cannot blend between objects that have lens fills.

You cannot mix different types of gradient fills. For instance, you cannot blend between a linear and a radial graident. Also the gradients must contain the same number of colors.

Modifying Blends

Once you create a blend, you can still make changes to the objects in the blend. For instance, you may want to change the shape of one of the original objects in the blend.

To modify a blend shape:

1. Use the Subselect tool to select one of the original objects of the blend ⓮.
2. Use the Pointer tool or Subselect tool to make any changes to specific points on the object or move the object into a new position.
3. The blend automatically redraws when you release the mouse button ⓯.

To modify the objects in a blend:

1. Use the Subselect tool to select one of the original objects of the blend.
2. Use any of the onscreen panels, inspectors or tools to change the colors, fills or strokes in the blend.

TIP If you add an attribute to one object in a blend that is not in the other objects, the blend will not redraw.

Blends are actually special types of groups. You use the Ungroup command to release the objects in the blend.

To release a blend:

- With the blend selected, choose **Modify > Ungroup.** The original objects of the blend are released along with the intermediate steps.

TIP The intermediate steps are themselves grouped and can be deleted or modified ⓰.

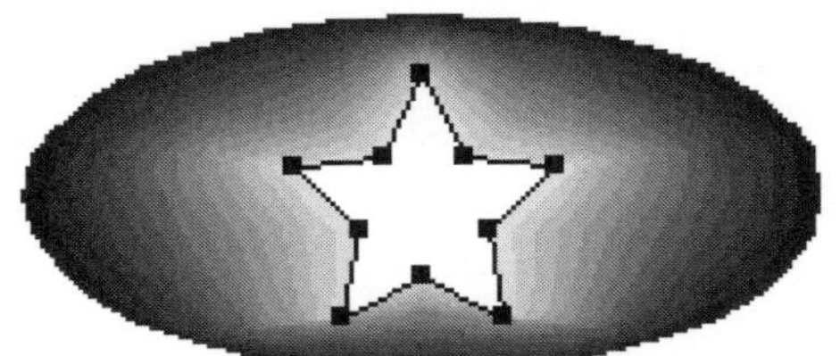

⓮ *To modify an object in a blend, use the Subselect tool to select one of the original objects in the blend.*

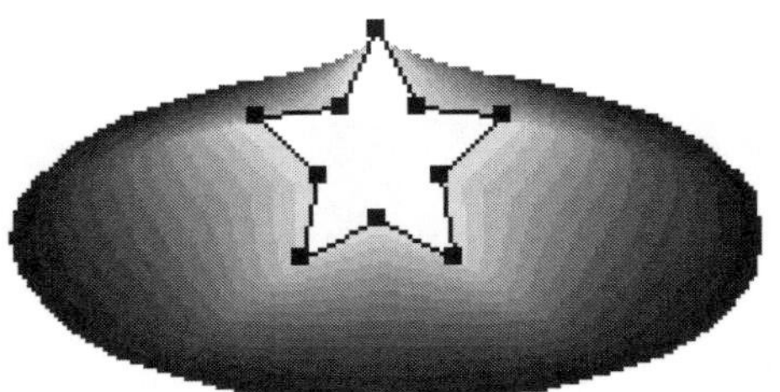

⓯ *Make whatever changes you want to the object. The blend automatically redraws.*

⓰ *When the top blend is ungrouped, the original objects are released. The intermediate steps are grouped together.*

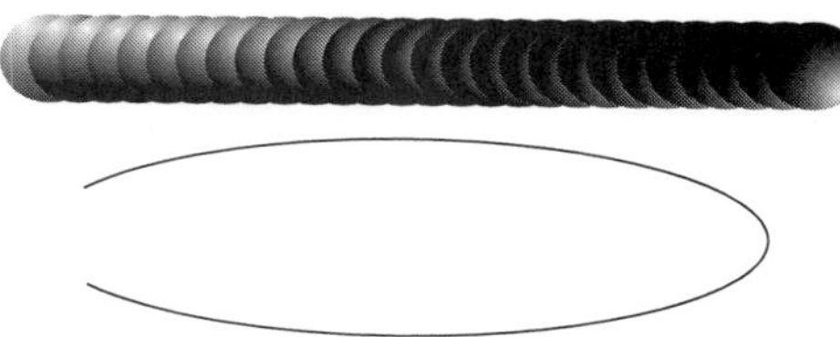

17 *To* **align a blend to a path,** *select the blend and the path to which you want to align it.*

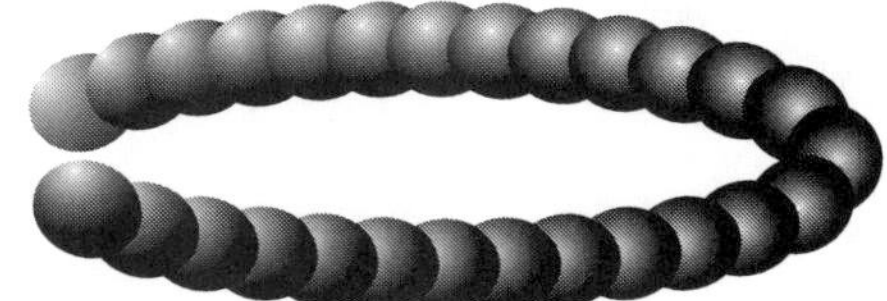

18 *The results of aligning a blend to a path.*

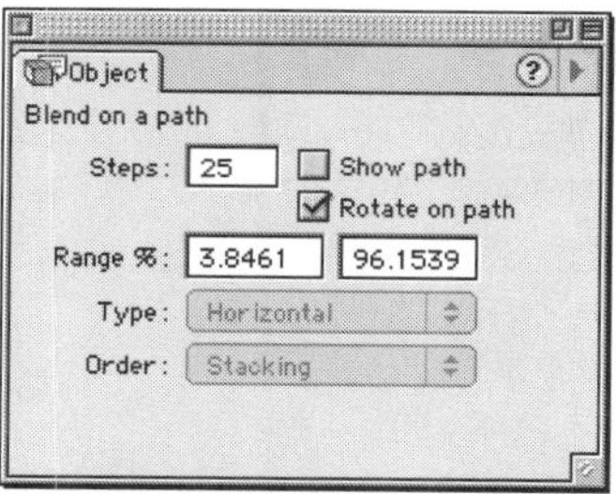

19 *The Blend on a path controls in the Object inspector.*

20 *A blend with Rotate on path selected (top) and unselected (bottom).*

Attaching Blends to a Path

Once you have created a blend, you can then align the blend to a path. This feature allows you to create all sorts of effects, the most exciting of which is the ability to create your own custom strokes.

TIP This feature was much more important before FreeHand added the Spray brushes. If you want to repeat the same object along a path, the Spray brush will probably be easier to use. However, if you want to repeat elements that change color or shape, then you will most likely need to use a blend on a path.

To align a blend to a path:

1. Create a blend and a path. Select both the blend and the path **17**.
2. Choose **Modify > Combine > Join Blend to Path.**
3. The blend automatically aligns to the shape of the path **18**.
4. To see the path, click Show path in the Object Inspector **19**.
5. To change the orientation of the objects in the blend, click Rotate on path in the Inspector palette **20**.

To release a blend from a path:

1. Select a blend that has been aligned to a path.
2. Choose **Modify > Split.**
3. The blend separates from the path.

TIP Blends that have been aligned on a path can still be modified using the Subselect tool *(see previous page).*

Printing Blends

If you are printing to a low-resolution device such as a laser printer, you may not be satisfied with the printout of the blend. That is because those printers cannot reproduce all the tones necessary to create a smooth blend.

If you are printing on a high-resolution device such as an imagesetter, your blend should print smoothly. However, sometimes blends produce an effect called banding ㉑. The following may help you avoid banding when printing on PostScript devices. (*For more information on printing, see Chapters 30 and 31.)*

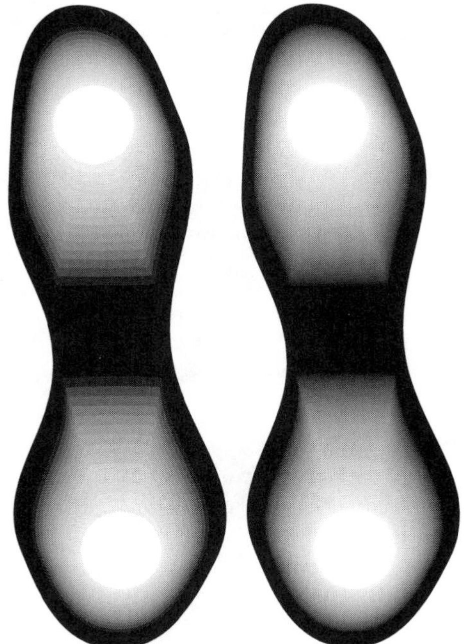

㉑ *A blend with* **banding** *(left). The same blend with more steps to decrease the banding (right).*

To avoid banding in blends when printing

- Print at high resolutions. For most work, this is a minimum of 2400 dpi.
- Lower the screen ruling if you see banding. This is especially helpful when printing to laser printers.
- Avoid blends over 7 inches long. This is especially true if you are outputting to a PostScript Level 1 device. If you are outputting to a PostScript Level 2 device, you may not need to limit the length of your blends.
- Examine the difference between the percentages of each of the CMYK colors. If you are getting banding, try increasing the difference between the percentages.

BASIC TEXT 18

Most people think of Macromedia FreeHand only as a program for creating graphics. However, hidden beneath the graphic tools lies the heart and soul of a full-fledged text layout program.

In fact, FreeHand has text controls that are not found in page layout programs such as QuarkXPress or Adobe PageMaker. For instance, the tab controls in FreeHand allow you to easily format complex data into tables. Also, the copyfitting commands help you automatically balance columns.

And don't let the chapter title "Basic Text" fool you. These may be the basic text features, but they are exceptionally sophisticated and powerful.

Working with Text Blocks

All text in FreeHand starts inside a text block. There are two types of text blocks. Standard text blocks have a fixed height and width.

To create a standard text block:

1. Select the Text tool from the Tools panel ❶.
2. Drag across the page. How far you drag determines the size of the text block.
3. Release the mouse button to see the text block and the text ruler ❷.
4. Start typing. The text automatically wraps within the text block.

TIP If you do not see the text ruler, choose **View > Text Rulers.**

Auto-expanding text blocks shrink or expand depending on the amount of text.

To create an auto-expanding text block:

1. Click with the Text tool. A blinking insertion point and a text ruler appear.
2. Start typing. The text block is set to horizontal auto-expandsion. *(See the sidebar on this page for a description of the auto-expansion settings.)*

TIP If your text does wrap within the box, check your Preferences settings for auto-expansion of text blocks *(see page 392)*.

If you deselect the text block before typing in it, you leave an empty text block on the page. These empty blocks contain font information that may confuse your print shop.

To delete empty text blocks:

- Choose **Xtras > Delete >Empty Text Blocks.** All text blocks with no characters in them are automatically deleted.

❶ *The* **Text tool** *in the Tools panel.*

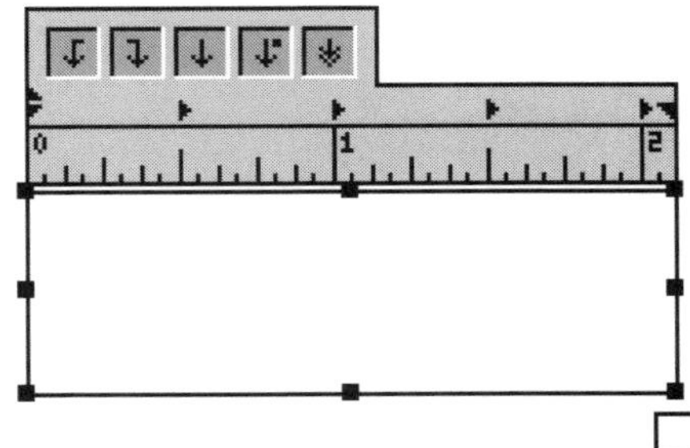

❷ *A* **text block** *with a text ruler.*

Standard or Auto-expanding Text Blocks

A standard text block is a fixed-size container. As you type, the text wraps from one line to another. The text block fills from the top and automatically wraps to the next line until it reaches the bottom.

Auto-expanding text blocks never fill up. If the horizontal control is set to auto-expand, the text block just keeps growing wider. You have to manually type a Return/Enter or Shift-Return/Enter to start a new line.

If the vertical auto-expand feature is selected, the text wraps within the text block, but the height of the text block continues to grow taller and taller. Text blocks set to auto-expand never overflow *(see page 224)*.

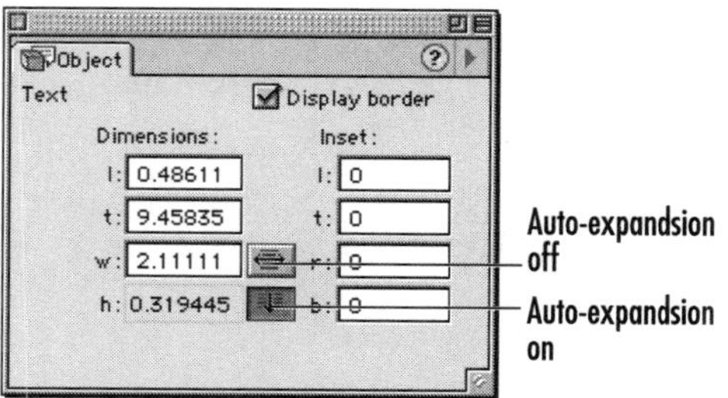

❸ *The* Auto-expansion icons *control the behavior of the text block.*

❹ *To manually* change the size of a text block, *drag one of the corner points of the block.*

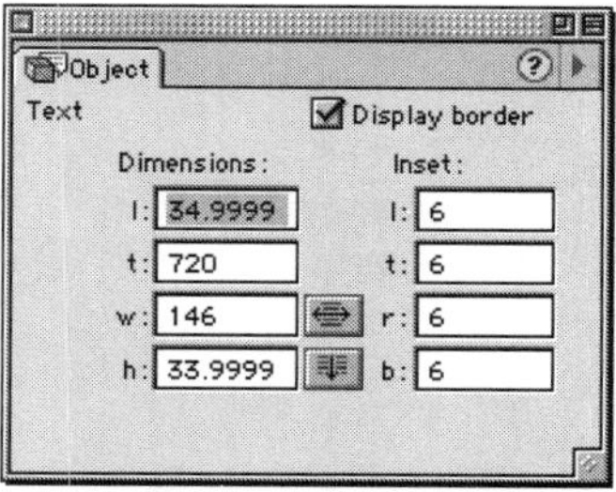

❺ *The* Dimensions fields *let you move a text block to a specific position.*

To change the auto-expansion settings:

1. Select the text block selected.
2. In the Object inspector, click to change the expansion icons as follows ❸:
   - If the icon is light (the up state), the field is not set for auto-expansion.
   - If the icon is dark (the down state), the field is set for auto-expansion as new text is entered.
3. Change the handles on the right and bottom as follows:
   - Double-click a black handle to turn it white. This indicates that auto-expansion is turned on.
   - Double-click a white handle to turn it black. This indicates that auto-expandsion is turned off.

To change the size of a standard text block:

◆ Use the Selection tool and drag one of the corner points of the text block ❹.

or

With the text block selected, open the Object inspector. Under Dimensions, change the measurements in the w (width) or **h** (height) fields ❺.

TIP (Mac) Hold the Control key as you drag horizontally to create a fixed-width text block.

TIP (Mac) Hold the Control key as you drag vertically to create a fixed-height text block.

To position a text block numerically:

1. Select the text block.
2. In the Object inspector set the Dimensions fields as follows:
   - **l** controls the position of the left edge of the text block.
   - **t** controls the position of the top edge of the text block.
3. Press Return or Enter.

The little square at the bottom of the text block is called the Link box. The different states for the Link box convey important information about the text.

To recognize the status of the Link box:

- If the Link box is white, then all the text in the block is visible ❻.
- A black circle inside the Link box means there is more text than can fit inside the text block ❼. This is called an *overflow*.
- Small arrows inside the Link box mean the text block has been linked to another object *(see page 239)* ❽.

Another way to resize a text block is to shrink the block to fit the size of the text.

To automatically shrink a text block:

1. Select a text block that has extra space not filled by text.
2. Using the Selection tool, double-click the Link box of the block ❾. The text block automatically shrinks to fit the text.

TIP If there is no text in a text block, double-clicking the Link box deletes the text block.

❻ *An* **open link box** *indicates that all the text is visible in the text block.*

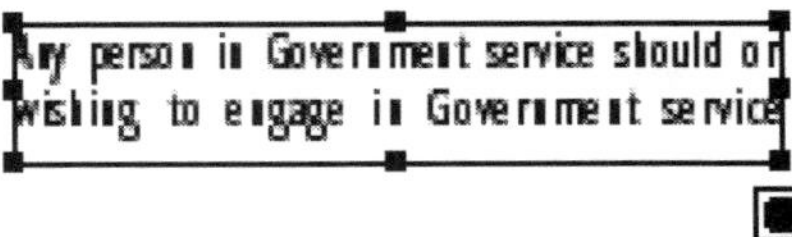

❼ **A circle in the link box** *indicates an overflow.*

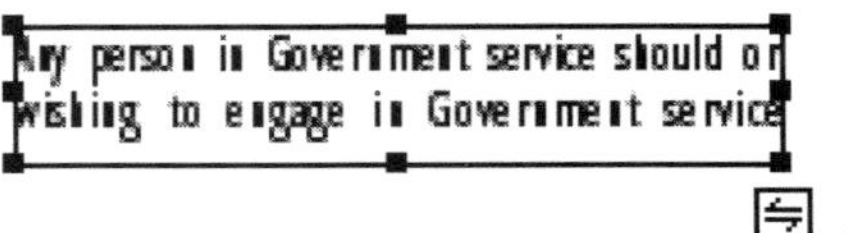

❽ **Two arrows in the link box** *show that the text is continued in another text block.*

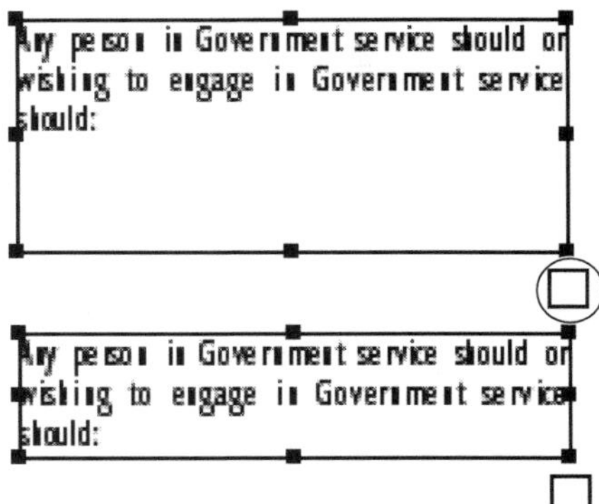

❾ *Double-click the Link box (circled) to shrink a text box with extra space to the actual size of the text.*

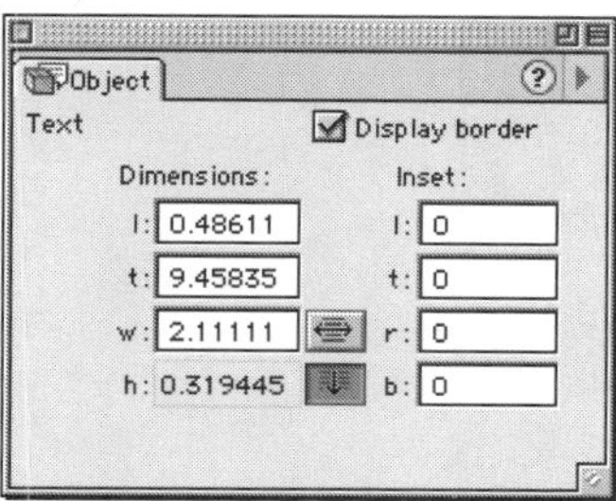

⑩ *Check* **Display border** *to see a stroke applied to a text block.*

Amendment III
No Soldier shall, in time of peace be quartered in any house, without the consent of the Owner, nor in time of war, but in a manner to be prescribed by law.

⑪ *The Stroke inspector applies a border to a text block. Here a dashed line was applied.*

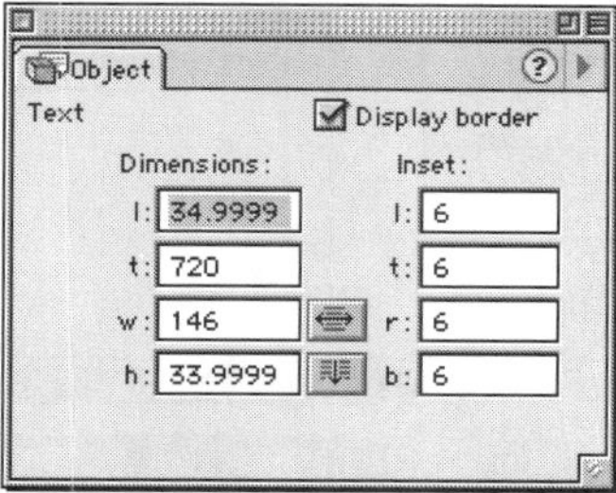

⑫ *The* **Inset fields** *set text away from the edges of a text block.*

Amendment III
No Soldier shall, in time of peace be quartered in any house, without the consent of the Owner, nor in time of war, but in a manner to be prescribed by law.

⑬ *This text is set away from the border by 6 points to make the text more legible.*

Just as in a page layout program, FreeHand lets you stroke or frame the outside border of a text block.

To apply a border to a text block:

1. Select the text block that needs a border.
2. In the Object inspector, click the Display border box ⑩. This allows you to see the border, but it does not create the stroke.
3. To apply a stroke, choose the Stroke Inspector.
4. Apply a stroke using any of the stroke styles. The border appears around the text block ⑪.

Once you have given a text block a border, you will probably want to inset the text to add some white space between the text and the border.

To inset text:

1. Select the text block.
2. In the Object inspector set the Inset fields as follows ⑫:
   - **l** controls inset for the left edge.
   - **t** controls the inset for the top edge.
   - **r** controls the inset for the right edge.
   - **b** controls the inset for the bottom edge.
3. Press Return/Enter to set the amounts ⑬.

TIP Negative values extend the text outside the borders of the block.

Selecting Text

You need to select text to change it. There are several different ways to select text.

To select all the text in a text block:

1. Click with the Text tool inside the text block.
2. Choose **Edit > Select > All.**

TIP Select the text block with the Pointer tool also selects all the text in the text block **14**.

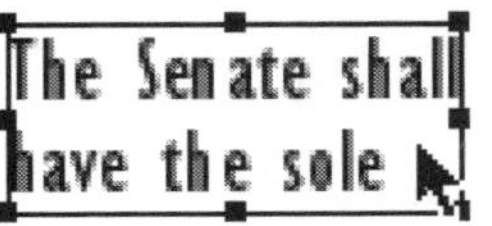

14 *A selected text block also selects all the text inside.*

To select text within a text block:

- Click with the Text tool inside the text block. Use the following techniques to select text:
  - **Double click** to select a word.
  - **Triple click** to select a paragraph.
  - **Drag** to select a range of text **15**.

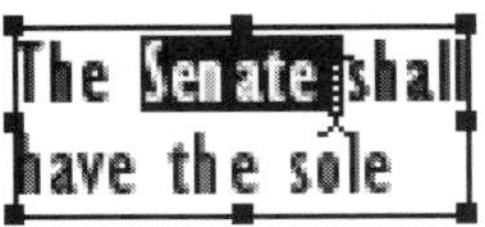

15 *Drag to select text within a text block.*

Although you can drag to select text, it may not be practical to drag to select a long range of text—especially if the text extends over many pages. In that case, you can use the following technique.

To select a range of text:

1. Click with the Text tool to place the insertion point where you want the selection to begin **16**.
2. Hold the Shift key and click where you want the selection to end **17**.

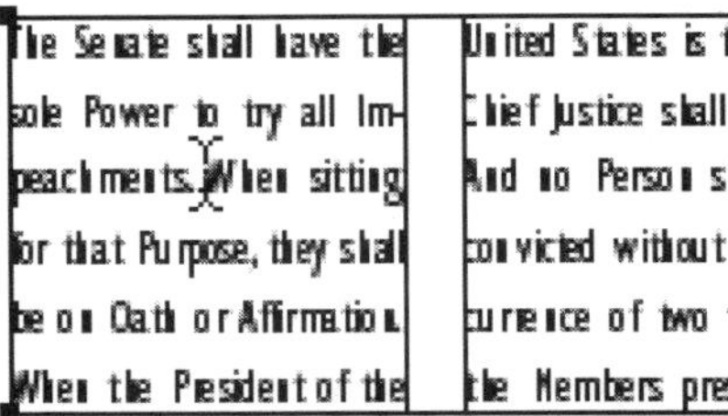

16 *Click to place the insertion point where you want to start the text selection.*

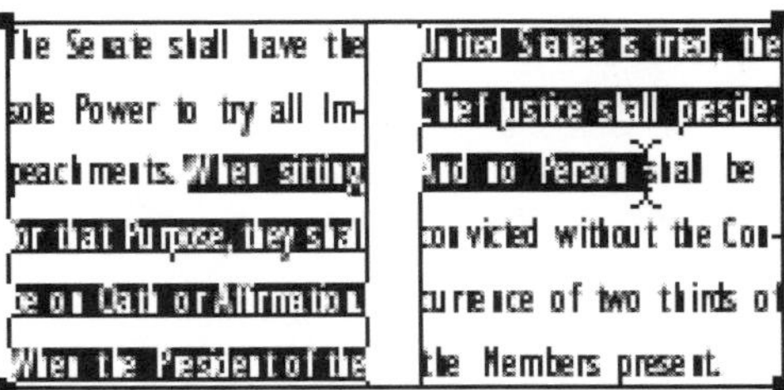

17 *Hold the Shift key and click in a second position to select all the text between.*

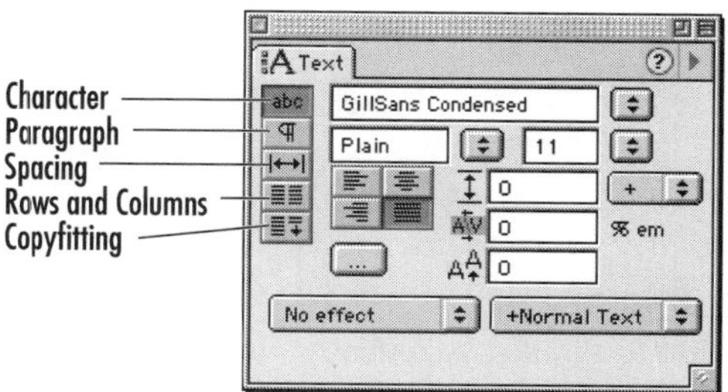

⑱ *The five* **Text inspector icons** *display the different text controls.*

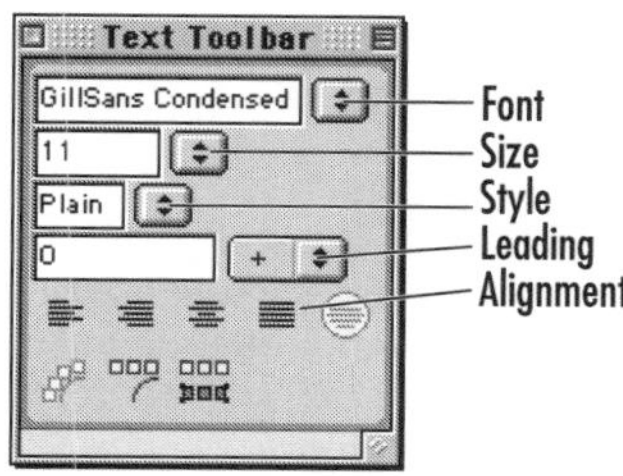

⑲ *The* **Text Toolbar** *icons control some of the text features.*

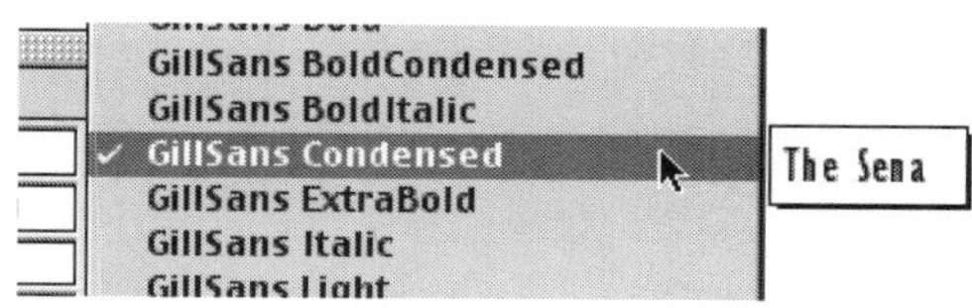

⑳ *You see a preview of the typeface as you choose from the font list.*

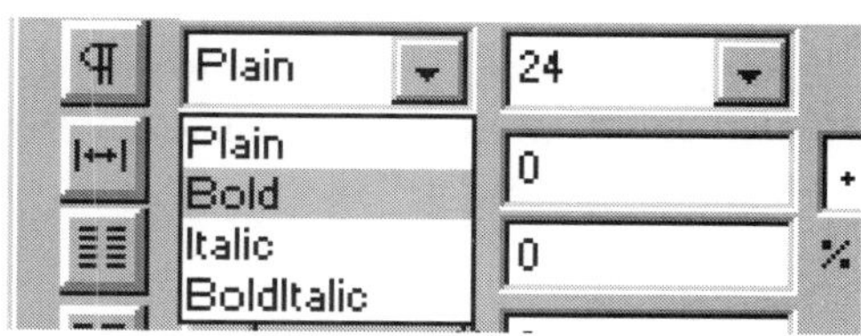

㉑ *The Style controls in the Text inspector.*

Changing Character Attributes

FreeHand gives you several places to change character attributes. The Text inspector contains a full range of all the text attributes.

The Text toolbar contains some of the text attributes. *(For information on customizing the toolbars, see Chapter 32, "Customizing FreeHand.")*

To display the Text inspector character controls:

- Click the Character icon in the Text inspector ⑱.

To change the typeface:

- Choose a typeface from the Font list in the Text inspector or Text Toolbar ⑲.

  or

  Choose **Text > Font** and choose a typeface from the submenu.

TIP If you format without selecting any text, any text you type afterwards will be styled accordingly.

TIP A sample of the typeface is shown next to the Font list in the Text inspector and Text Toolbar ⑳.

To change the style:

- Use the Style list in the Text inspector or Text Toolbar to apply Bold, Italic, or BoldItalic ㉑.

  or

  Choose **Text > Style** and choose a listing from the submenu.

To change the point size:

- Use the Size list in the Text inspector or Text Toolbar to select one of the preset point sizes (22).

  or

  Enter a specific amount in the Size field in the Text inspector or Text Toolbar.

  or

  Choose **Text > Size** and select a size from the submenu.

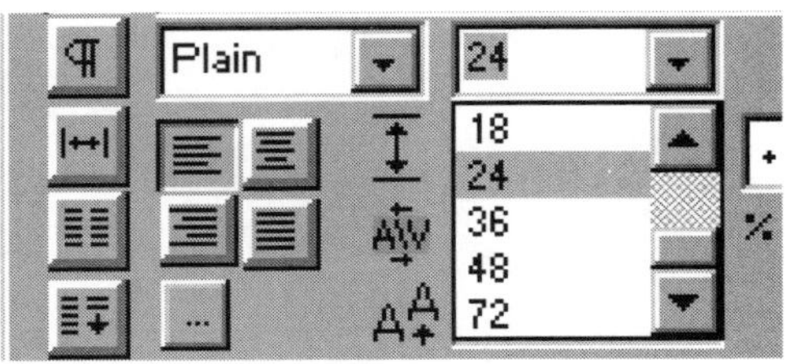

(22) *The* **Point size controls** *in the Text inspector.*

Alignment is the horizontal position of the text within the text block. Strictly speaking, alignment is a paragraph attribute, since it affects the entire paragraph. However you control the alignment in the character area of the Text inspector.

To change the text alignment:

- Click one of the alignment icons in the Text inspector or Text Toolbar to position the text as follows (23):
  - **Left** sets the text to align with the left margin (24).
  - **Centered** sets the text to align at a point between the two margins (24).
  - **Right** sets the text to align with the right margin (24).
  - **Justified** sets the text to align at both the left and right margins (24).

  or

  Choose **Text > Alignment** and select a setting from the submenu.

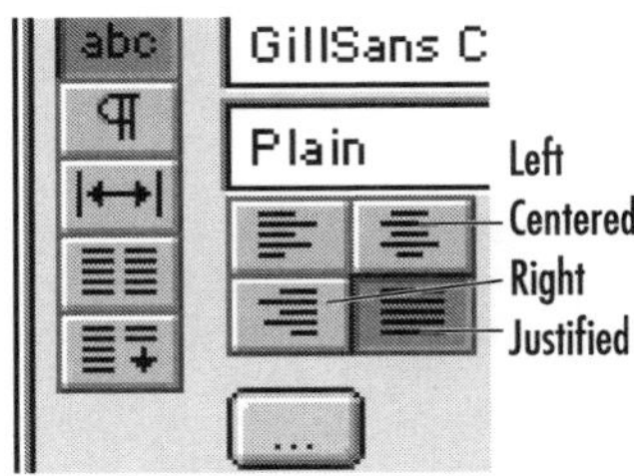

(23) *The* **Alignment icons** *in the Text inspector.*

Left aligned

The Senate shall have the sole Power to try all Impeachments. When sitting for that Purpose, they shall be on Oath or Affirmation. When the President of the United States is tried, the Chief Justice shall preside: And no Person shall be

Center aligned

The Senate shall have the sole Power to try all Impeachments. When sitting for that Purpose, they shall be on Oath or Affirmation. When the President of the United States is tried, the Chief Justice shall preside: And no Person shall be

Right aligned

The Senate shall have the sole Power to try all Impeachments. When sitting for that Purpose, they shall be on Oath or Affirmation. When the President of the United States is tried, the Chief Justice shall preside: And no Person shall be

Justified

The Senate shall have the sole Power to try all Impeachments. When sitting for that Purpose, they shall be on Oath or Affirmation. When the President of the United States is tried, the Chief Justice shall preside: And no Person shall be

(24) *The* **four alignment options** *change how text is positioned in a text block.*

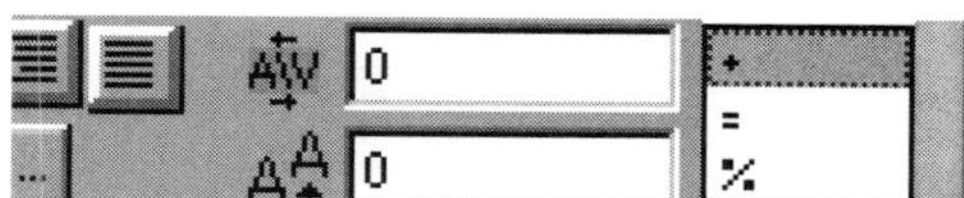

㉕ *The* **Leading pop-up menu** *in the Text inspector.*

Truth
Truth

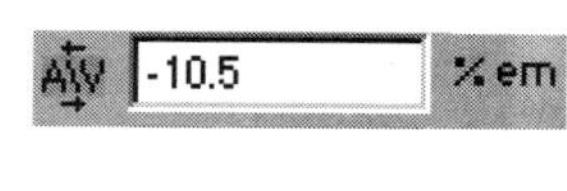

㉖ *A* **Kerning** *value of -10.5 has been applied to the letters and r in the bottom word, decreasing the separation between the letters.*

USA
U S A

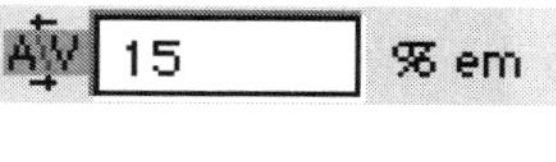

㉗ *A* **Range kerning** *value of 15 has been applied to the letters* **U**, **S**, *and* **A** *in the bottom initials.*

NYC
NYC

㉘ *A* **baseline shift** *of 15 has been applied to the letter* **Y**, *moving it higher than the other letters.*

Leading (pronounced *ledding*) is the amount of space between lines of text.

To change the leading:

1. Use the leading pop-up list to change the leading as follows ㉕:
   - \+ sign adds space between the lines in addition to the space used by the characters.
   - = sign sets an amount of space that does not change if the text size changes.
   - % sign adds an amount of space that is a percentage of the point size of the text.
2. Enter the amount of leading in the leading field.

TIP Drag the top or bottom side handles of a text block to increase or decrease the leading of an entire text block.

To change the kerning:

1. Click between two letters.
2. Enter a value in the Kerning field. Positive values increase the space. Negative values decrease the space ㉖.

To change the range kerning:

1. Drag across the text.
2. Enter a value in the Range kerning field. Positive values increase the space. Negative values decrease the space ㉗.

TIP Drag the left or right side handles to increase or decrease the Range kerning of an entire text block.

TIP Hold down the Opt/Alt key as you drag the left or right side handles to change the Range kerning between words.

To change the baseline shift:

◆ Enter an amount in the Baseline shift field. Positive values raise the text above the normal baseline for the text. Negative values lower the text ㉘.

Setting Paragraph Attributes

Once you have text inside a text block, you can format its paragraph attributes.

To change the paragraph attributes:

- Click the Paragraph icon in the Text inspector. This displays the paragraph options ㉙.

If you want more space between paragraphs, you should use the Above or Below fields to add space before or after the paragraph. You should *not* use extra paragraph returns which can cause problems if you need to copyfit or have others work on your text.

To add space between paragraphs:

- Enter the amount of space you want under Paragraph spacing in the Above or Below fields ㉚.

Ordinarily, text expands to the sides of the text block. The margin indents let you control where the text is positioned in the text block.

To change the margin indents:

- Enter the amount of space as follows in the margin indent fields ㉛:
  - The Left margin indent changes the position of the left margin of a paragraph.
  - The Right margin indent changes the position of the right margin of a paragraph.
  - The First line indent changes the position of the first line of a paragraph.

TIP Use a negative First line indent to create a hanging indent for bullets and numbered lists ㉜.

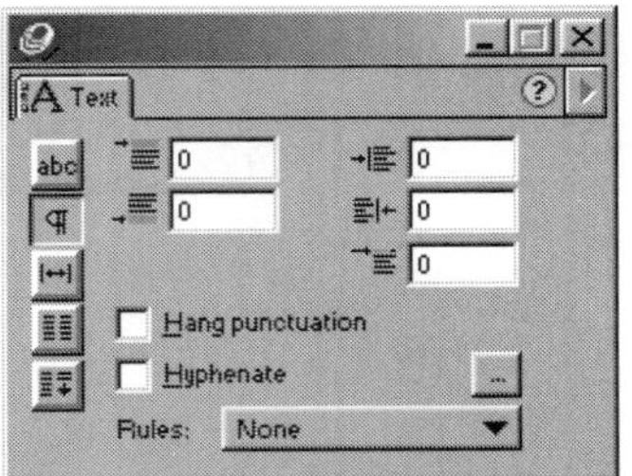

㉙ *The* **Paragraph controls** *in the Text inspector.*

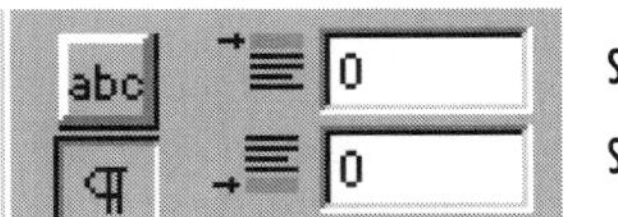

㉚ *The* **Above** *and* **Below fields** *let you add space above or below paragraphs.*

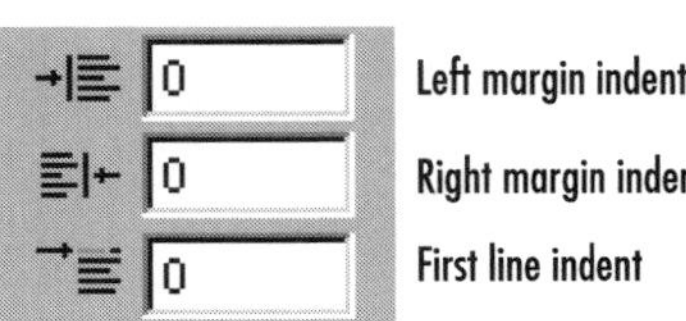

㉛ *The* **Margin indent fields** *let you indent the margins and first lines of a paragraph.*

• Put loyalty to the highest moral principals and to country above loyalty to Government

㉜ *A negative indent applied to the first line moves the bullet outside the left margin.*

> **Text Inset or Margin Indent?**
>
> The Text Inset command *(see page 225)* indents all the text within a text block.
>
> The Margin indent can be applied to individual paragraphs within a text block.

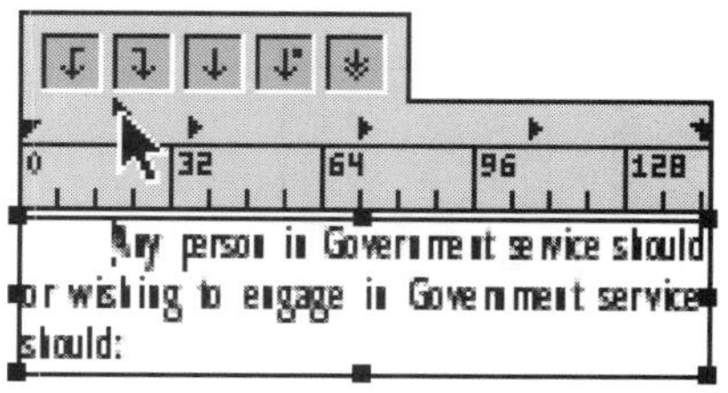

(33) *Dragging the* **indent triangles** *of the text ruler allows you to change margin indents.*

"That to secure these rights, Governments are instituted among Men, deriving their just powers from the consent of the governed."

(34) *An example of* **hanging punctuation.** *Notice how the quotation marks float outside the margins of the paragraph.*

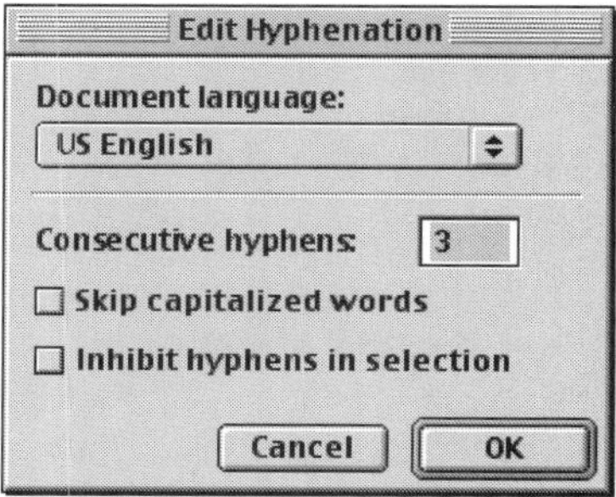

(35) *The* **Edit Hyphenation dialog box.**

FreeHand also lets you use the text ruler to set the margin indents (33).

To change margin indents using the text ruler:

1. Select the text you want to modify.
2. If the text ruler is not visible, choose **View > Text Rulers.**
3. Select the paragraph you want to change.
4. Drag the indent triangles as follows:
   - The bottom of the left indent triangle controls the position of the left margin.
   - The right indent triangle controls the position of the right margin.
   - The top part of the left indent triangle controls the position of the first line.

To create hanging punctuation:

- Select Hang punctuation in the paragraph attributes of the Text inspector. This keeps paragraphs from looking ragged (34).

To turn on hyphenation:

- Click the Hyphenate option in the Paragraph settings of the Text inspector.

To control the hyphenation:

1. Click the Ellipse (...) button in the Text inspector. The Edit Hyphenation dialog box appears (35).
2. Use the pop-up menu to choose the any foreign language dictionaries.
3. To limit the number of consecutive lines that may end with hyphens, enter the number in the Consecutive hyphens field.
4. To prevent capitalized words from being hyphenated, click Skip capitalized words.
5. To prevent a specific word (such as a company name) from being hyphenated, select the text and click Inhibit hyphens in selection.
6. Click OK to apply the settings.

Changing the Spacing Options

Space — the final frontier! Or for FreeHand users: Spacing — the third option in the Text inspector.

To change the spacing attributes:

- Click the Spacing icon in the Text inspector. This displays the spacing options ㉟.

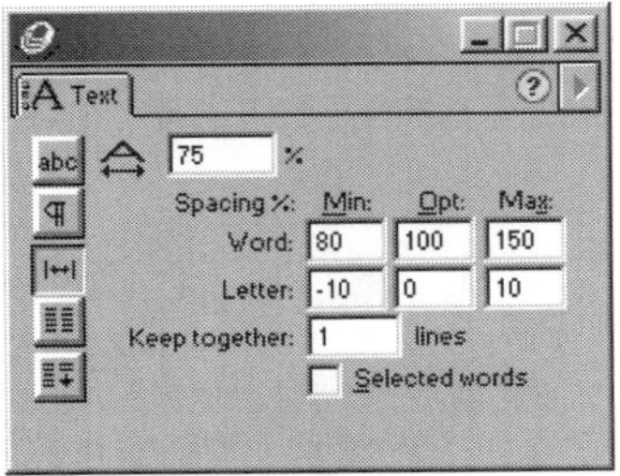

㉟ *The* **Spacing controls** *in the Text inspector.*

Horizontal Spacing is an electronic distortion of the text. Small amounts of horizontal scale are sometimes used to fit a few extra characters into a paragraph.

TIP Extreme amounts of horizontal scaling are unacceptable to professional designers. If you need condensed or expanded type, you should use a typeface that is designed that way.

To change the horizontal scaling of the typeface:

1. Select the text.
2. Enter the amount you want to horizontally scale the text in the Horizontal scale field ㊲. Values lower than 100% compress the text. Values higher than 100% extend the text.

TIP Hold the Opt/Alt key and drag a corner handle to change the horizontal scale of all the text in a text block.

㊲ *A* **Horizontal scale** *value of 75% has been applied to the text, distorting the characters.*

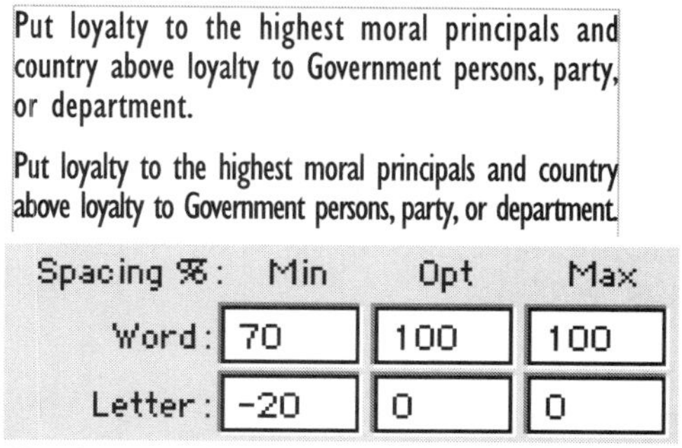

Put loyalty to the highest moral principals and country above loyalty to Government persons, party, or department.

Put loyalty to the highest moral principals and country above loyalty to Government persons, party, or department.

Spacing %:	Min	Opt	Max
Word:	70	100	100
Letter:	-20	0	0

38 *Changing the values for* **Word spacing** *and* **Letter spacing** *compresses the space between letters and words in the second paragraph.*

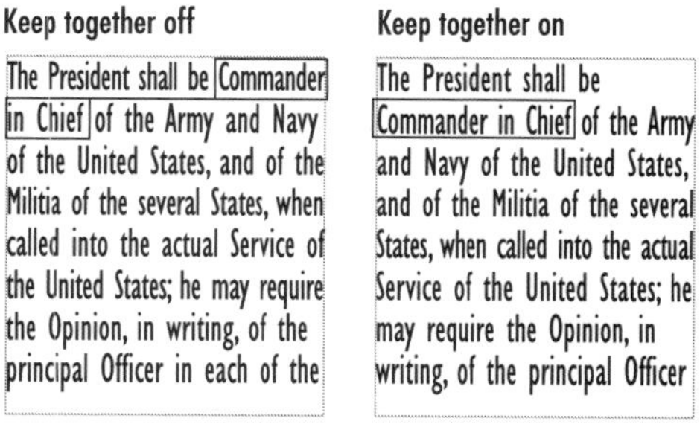

Keep together off

The President shall be Commander in Chief of the Army and Navy of the United States, and of the Militia of the several States, when called into the actual Service of the United States; he may require the Opinion, in writing, of the principal Officer in each of the

Keep together on

The President shall be Commander in Chief of the Army and Navy of the United States, and of the Militia of the several States, when called into the actual Service of the United States; he may require the Opinion, in writing, of the principal Officer

39 *An example of applying* **Keep together selected words** *to keep a phrase on one line.*

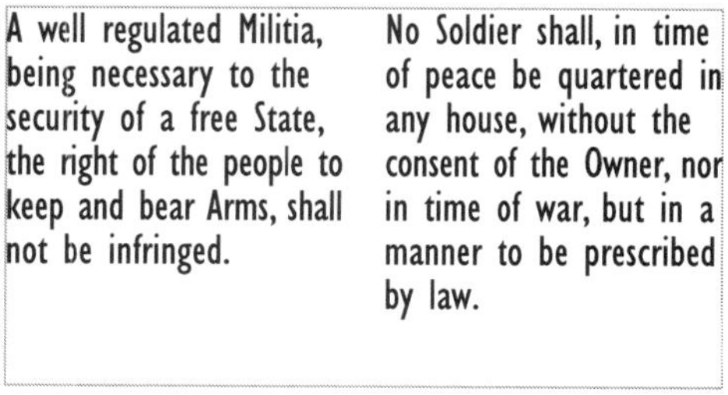

A well regulated Militia, being necessary to the security of a free State, the right of the people to keep and bear Arms, shall not be infringed.

No Soldier shall, in time of peace be quartered in any house, without the consent of the Owner, nor in time of war, but in a manner to be prescribed by law.

40 *An example of applying* **Keep together lines** *to force a paragraph to start in a new column.*

Word spacing controls the space between word. Letter spacing controls the space between character in a word.

To change word and letter spacing:

1. Select the paragraphs you want to change.
2. Set the Word spacing amounts as follows 38:
   - **Min** sets the minimum amount of space FreeHand will allow.
   - **Opt** sets the preferred space.
   - **Max** sets the maximum amount of space FreeHand will allow.
3. Set the Letter spacing amounts as follows 38:
   - **Min** sets the minimum amount of space FreeHand will allow.
   - **Opt** sets the preferred space.
   - **Max** sets the maximum amount of space FreeHand will allow.

Sometimes it is important to keep selected words together. For instance, you may have a title or proper noun that should not be broken across line.

To keep words together:

1. Select the text.
2. Click Keep together: Selected words 39.

You can also force FreeHand to keep the lines in a paragraph together.

To keep lines together:

1. Select the text.
2. Enter the number of lines that you want to keep together in the Keep together: Lines field 40.

Converting Text Case

Once you have text on your page, you may want to convert the case from upper to lower, etc. FreeHand has several sophisticated Convert Case commands.

To apply the Convert Case commands:

1. Select the text to be converted.
2. Choose **Text > Convert Case** and then choose one of the following from the submenu **41**:
   - **Upper** changes all the text to uppercase.
   - **Lower** changes all the text to lowercase letters.
   - **Small Caps** changes the text size to simulate the look of a small caps font.
   - **Title** changes the initial letter of every word to uppercase.
   - **Sentence** changes the initial letter of a sentence to uppercase.

To set the Small Caps appearance:

1. Choose **Text > Convert Case > Settings.** This opens the **Settings** dialog box **42**.
2. Set the Small Caps percentage of point size to whatever amount you want the text reduced for Small Caps.

You can also set certain words that should not be converted using the Convert Case commands. For instance, you would not want the letter USA converted to lowercase.

To set the Convert Case exceptions:

1. Choose **Text > Convert Case > Settings.** This opens the **Settings** dialog box **42**.
2. Click the Add button.
3. Type the word you want to make an exception to the Convert Case command.
4. Check which Convert Case commands should not be applied to that word.

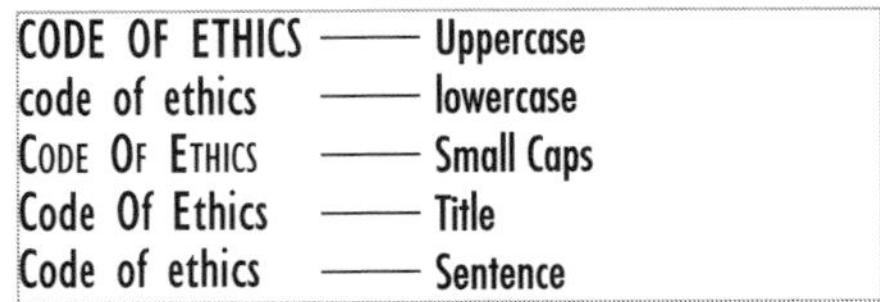

41 *An example of applying the* **Convert Case commands.**

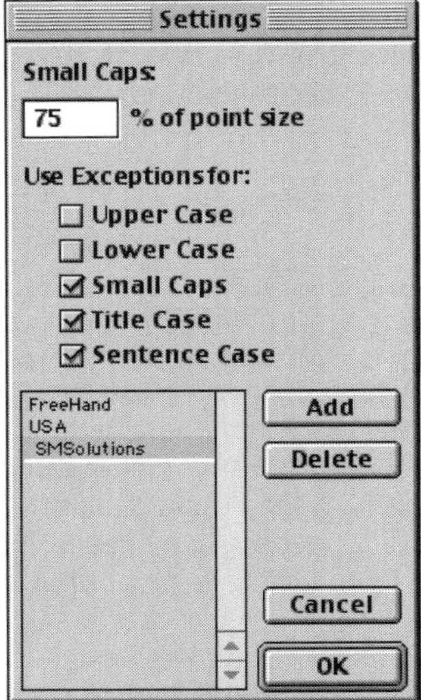

42 *The* **Settings dialog box** *for the Convert Case commands.*

Converting Text Case

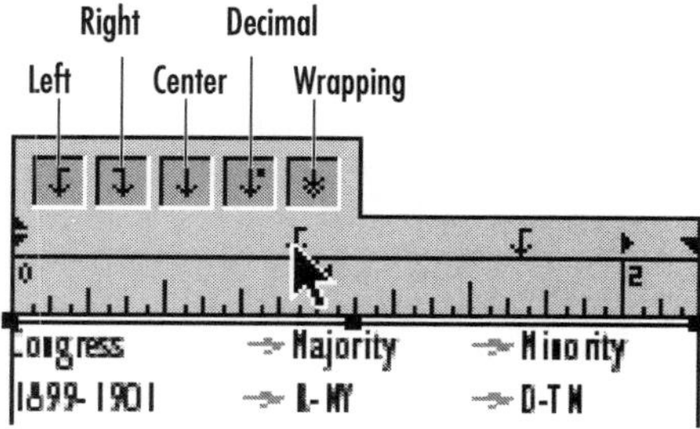

㊸ *To set a tab position, drag a* **tab arrow** *directly to the text ruler.*

Congress	→ Majority	→ Minority
1899-1901	→ R-NY	→ D-TN
1901-1903	→ R-NY	→ D-TN

㊹ *Text set with* **Left alignment tabs.** *Arrows mark where the tab characters were entered.*

→ Congress	→ Majority	→ Minority
→ 1899-1901	→ R-NY	→ D-TN
→ 1901-1903	→ R-NY	→ D-TN

㊺ *Text set with* **Right alignment tabs.**

→ Congress	→ Majority	→ Minority
→ 1899-1901	→ R-NY	→ D-TN
→ 1901-1903	→ R-NY	→ D-TN

㊻ *Text set with* **Center alignment tabs.**

Years	→ Income	→ Expense
1899-1901	→ 2.5M	→ 4.2M
1901-1903	→ 3.05M	→ 1.75M

㊼ *Text set with* **Decimal alignment tabs.**

Sereno E. Payne, R-NY →→	James D. Richardson, D-TN
Sereno E. Payne, R-NY	John Sharp Williams, →→ D-MS

㊽ *Text set with* **Wrapping tabs.**

Working with Tabs

There are two separate parts to working with tabs. The first part is to insert a tab character into the text. This tells FreeHand that the text needs to be aligned at that point.

To insert tab characters in the text:

1. Place the insertion point where you want a tab space to occur.
2. Press the Tab key to insert a tab character into the text.

TIP FreeHand sets default left alignment tabs at half-inch intervals.

The second part to working with tabs is to set the alignment tab stop. FreeHand also offers the ability to align text using five different types of tab stops.

Setting the tabs by dragging:

1. Select the text.
2. If the text ruler is not visible, choose **View > Text Rulers.**
3. Drag the appropriate tab arrow from the top of the text ruler down to the area just above the numbers ㊸. Each of the tabs stops aligns the text in a specific way:
   - Left alignment tabs position the left side of the text at the tab position ㊹.
   - Right alignment tabs position the right side of the text at the tab position ㊺.
   - Center alignment tabs position the center the text at the tab position ㊻.
   - Decimal alignment tabs position a decimal point at the tab position ㊼.
   - Wrapping tabs position the left edge of the text at the tab position. Any text that does not fit into the tab space is moved down into a new line to form a column ㊽.
4. Release the mouse button when the tab arrow is where you want it. The text realigns.

To set the tabs numerically:

1. Double-click any of the tab icons at the top of the ruler. This opens the Edit Tab dialog box 49.
2. Choose the type of tab you want from the Alignment pop-up menu.
3. Enter a number in the Position field for where you want the tab located. This number is in relation to the left side of the text block.
4. Click OK to apply the settings.

49 *The* **Edit Tab dialog box.**

A tab *leader* is a character that repeats to fill the space created by inserting a tab. The table of contents of this book contains tab leaders that fill the space with periods 50.

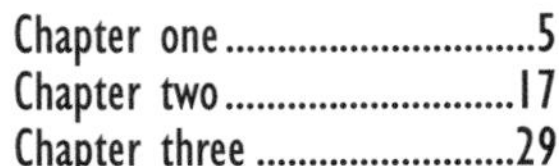

50 *An example of a* **tab leader.**

To set a tab leader:

1. Double-click any of the tab icons at the top of the ruler. This opens the Edit Tab dialog box.
2. Enter a character in the Leader field 51.

   or

   Select a character from the Leader pop-up menu.
3. Click OK to apply the settings.

TIP To change the appearance of a tab leader, double-click the characters in the text and change their size, font, color, and so on.

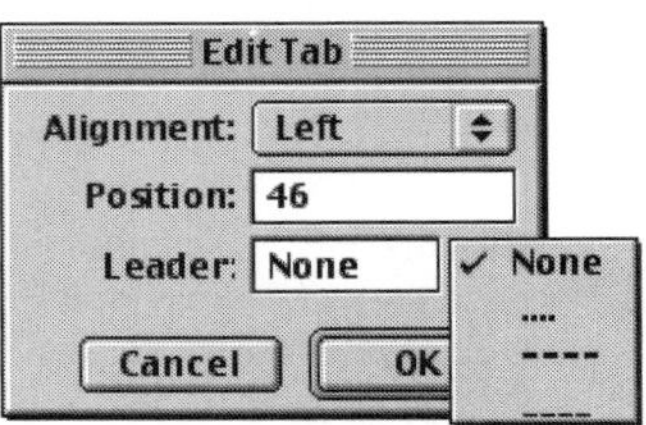

51 *The* **Leader pop-up menu.**

To delete existing tabs:

- Drag the tab arrow down off the ruler and then release.

To move a tab to a new position:

- Drag the tab arrow along the ruler to the position you want.

Columns

Rows

Vertical flow

Horizontal flow

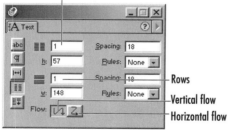

52 *The Rows and Columns controls in the Text inspector.*

January 27 Senate convenes at 12:00	February 14–23 President's Day Recess
April 3–20 Spring Recess	May 22–June 1 Memorial Day Recess

53 *An example of using rows and columns to create a text table.*

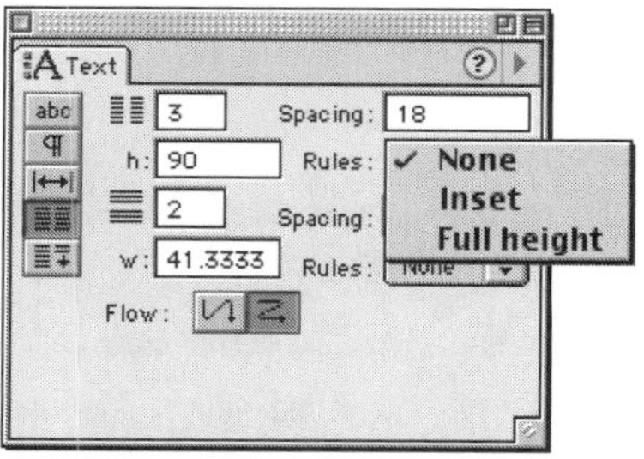

54 *The difference between Full rules (top) and Inset rules (bottom).*

January 27 Senate convenes at 12:00	February 14–23 President's Day Recess
April 3–20 Spring Recess	May 22–June 1 Memorial Day Recess

January 27 Senate convenes at 12:00	February 14–23 President's Day Recess
April 3–20 Spring Recess	May 22–June 1 Memorial Day Recess

55 *Press the Column and Row icon of the Text inspector to see the column and row controls.*

Working with Rows and Columns

FreeHand gives you the ability to divide text blocks into columns and rows.

To create columns and rows:

1. Click the Rows and Columns icon of the Text inspector 52.
2. Set the column controls as follows:
   - Enter the number of columns in the column field.
   - Enter the height for each column in the **h** field.
   - Enter the space between columns in the **spacing** field.
3. Set the row controls as follows:
   - Enter the number of rows in the row field.
   - Enter the width in the w field.
   - Enter the space between rows in the **spacing** field.
4. Click the Flow icon as follows:
   - Horizontal flow fills the columns from left to right and then moves down.
   - Vertical flow fills the rows from top to bottom and then moves to the right.

TIP Rows and columns can be used to create table effects 53.

FreeHand also lets you create rules that fit in the spaces between columns or rows.

To add rules to columns and rows:

1. Apply columns or rows to a text block.
2. Select a rule style from the Rules pop-up menu as follows 54:
   - **Full width** creates rules that cross over the space between columns 55.
   - **Full height** creates rules that cross over the space between rows 55.
   - **Inset** creates rules that break in the spaces between the columns or rows 55.
3. With the text block still selected, use the Stroke Inspector to apply and style the stroke applied to the rule.

Copyfitting Text

If you have multiple columns of text next to each other, you may want the columns to have the same number of lines. You use FreeHand's *copyfitting* commands to adjust your text.

To copyfit text:

1. Click the Adjust Columns icon of the Text inspector (56).
2. Click the Balance option to adjust the columns so there are an equal number of lines in each. This may leave extra space at the bottom of the text block (57).
3. Click the Modify leading option adjust the leading. This increases the leading so that the lines fill the text block (58).
4. To adjust the columns by changing the point size of the text, enter values in the Minimum and Maximum fields. Values below 100 will reduce the point size. Values above 100 will increase it (59).
5. To move the first line down from the top of a column, change the amount in First line leading field.

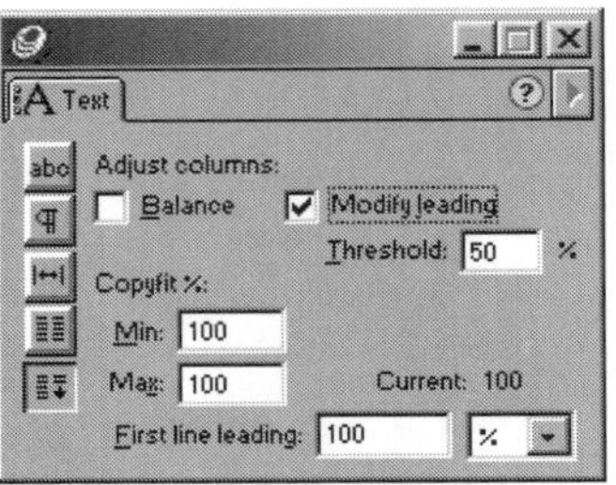

(56) *Click the* **Adjust columns icon** *of the Text inspector to see the copyfitting controls.*

The Senate shall have the sole Power to try all Impeachments. When sitting for that Purpose, they shall be on Oath or Affirmation. When the President of the United States is tried, the Chief Justice shall preside: And no Person shall be convicted without the Concurrence of two thirds of the Members present.

(57) *Copyfitting by* **balancing the columns.**

The Senate shall have the sole Power to try all Impeachments. When sitting for that Purpose, they shall be on Oath or Affirmation. When the President of the United States is tried, the Chief Justice shall preside: And no Person shall be convicted without the Concurrence of two thirds of the Members present.

(58) *Balancing the columns and* **modifying the leading** *to fill the text box.*

The Senate shall have the sole Power to try all Impeachments. When sitting for that Purpose, they shall be on Oath or Affirmation. When the President of the United States is tried, the Chief Justice shall preside: And no Person shall be convicted without the Concurrence of two thirds of the Members present.

(59) *Copyfitting by* **changing the type size** *fills the text block and keeps leading proportional.*

60 *To* link text, *drag from the Link box to another text block or object.*

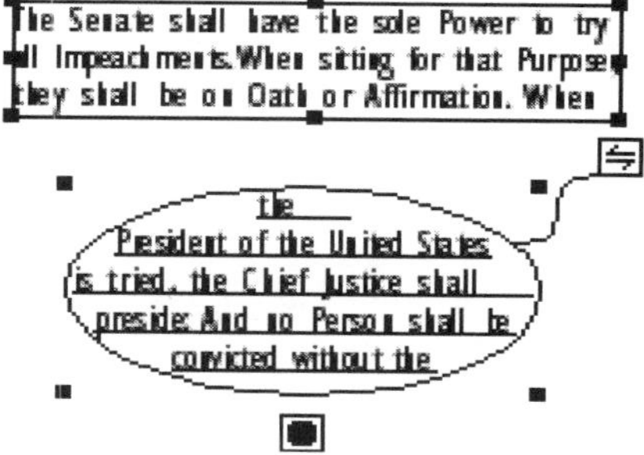

61 *Text linked from a text block to an ellipse.*

Linking Text

While it is very easy to create columns within a text block, you may want to have text flow from one text block to another. Or, you may want your text to flow onto an open path or into a closed path. You can link the text in these ways by using the Link box of the text block.

To link text between objects:

1. Select a text block you would like to link to another object.
2. Using the Selection tool, drag from the Link box of the text block. You will see a wavy line extend out 60.
3. Drag the wavy line onto the object to which you want to link your text 61.
4. Release the mouse button. If you had an overflow of text, the text flows into the new object and you see arrows in the Link box.

TIP If you did not have an overflow, you still see arrows in the Link box. This indicates that if you add text or decrease the size of the first text box, the text will appear inside the new object.

TIP You can link text within a page or across pages.

Importing and Exporting Text

If you are working with long documents, you ought to import the text from a word processing program rather than typing it in FreeHand. To prepare text for exporting, in the word processor save your work in one of two formats:

- **RTF Text** (rich text format) keeps the text formatting.
- **ASCII** (pronounced As-kee) keeps only the characters without any formatting.

To import text:

1. Choose **File > Import** and choose the text file you want to import. Your cursor changes into a corner symbol ❻❷.
2. Position the corner symbol where you want your text to start.
3. If you want your text block to be a certain size on the page, drag the corner symbol to create a rectangle the size you want the text block to be ❻❸.

   or

   If you just want the text on the page, click. A text block is created and filled with text.

To export text:

1. Select the text blocks you want to export. If you select no text blocks, FreeHand exports all the text in the document.
2. Choose **File > Export**. This opens the Export Document dialog box ❻❹.
3. Name the file and specify its destination.
4. Choose one of the following formats:
   - RTF text.
   - ASCII text.

TIP Unlinked text blocks export in their stacking order from back to front, first page to last page.

❻❷ *The* **corner symbol** *indicates that you have text ready for importing.*

❻❸ **Drag the corner symbol** *to size placed text.*

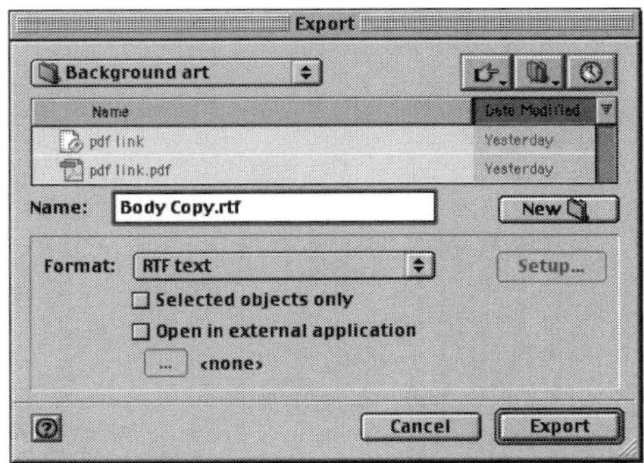

❻❹ *The Export dialog box lets you choose a format to export text.*

TEXT TOOLS 19

Many years ago I wrote copy for print ads and direct mail letters. I'm a pretty fast typist so I wrote my copy directly onto a typewriter.

Many years later, when I switched to writing on a computer, something interesting happened. I was much more likely to spend more time niggling with each little piece of copy.

I would try the copy with one set of words, and then change it to another set. I moved phrases from the top of the copy to the end. I was much more willing to spend time playing with the text — not because I suddenly became more fastidious about what I was writing, but because it was so easy.

Macromedia FreeHand offers you the same tools for editing text.

Using the Text Editor

The Text Editor lets you view and change text all in one place without the formatting.

❶ *The* **Text Editor** *lets you work with text that might be difficult to read on the document page.*

To open the Text Editor:

1. Select the text block or path, or click with the Text tool inside the text.
2. Choose **Text > Editor.** This opens the Text Editor dialog box ❶.
3. Click 12 Point Black to view the type in that point size and color.
4. Make whatever changes you want via the Text menu or the Text Inspector.
5. To see the text changes in the text block or path, click Apply. When you are satisfied with your changes, click OK.

TIP Hold the Opt/Alt key as you click in a text block to open the Text Editor.

To open the Text Editor for a new text block:

- Hold the Opt/Alt key as you click with the Text tool. This opens the Text Editor and creates an auto-expanding text block.

  or

  Hold the Opt/Alt key as you drag with the Text tool. This opens the Text Editor and creates a standard text block.

When vacancies happen in the Representation from any state, the executive authority thereof shall issue writs of election to fill such vacancies. The House of Representatives shall	choose their speaker and other officers; and shall have the sole power of impeachment.

When vacancies happen in the Representation from any state, the executive authority thereof shall issue writs of election to fill such vacancies.	The House of Representatives shall choose their speaker and other officers; and shall have the sole power of impeachment.

❷ *Text before (top) and after (bottom) inserting the* End of Column *character.*

to which the Laws of
Nature and of
Nature's God

to which the
Laws of Nature and
of Nature's God

❸ *Text before (top) and after (bottom) inserting the* End of Line *character.*

We congratulate Ms.
DuPrât on her success.

We congratulate
Ms. DuPrât on her
success.

❹ *Text before (top) and after (bottom) inserting a* Non-Breaking Space *character.*

Space Regular
Space Em
Space En
Space Thin

❺ *Compare the spaces to see how the different types of* spaces *appear.*

Working with Special Characters

Special characters help improve the look of the text or control the flow of the text.

To use the special characters:

1. Place your insertion point where you would like the special character.
2. Choose **Text > Special Characters** and then choose from the submenu.

TIP You can also use keystrokes to insert the characters into your text as you type. *(See the sidebars on the next page.)*

End of Column

Inserts an invisible character that forces the text to the next column or next text block ❷.

End of Line

Inserts an invisible character that forces the text to the next line ❸.

Non-Breaking Space

Inserts a space that does not break across lines ❹.

Em Space

Inserts a space the width of the type size ❺.

En Space

Inserts a space one-half the width of the type size ❺.

Thin Space

Inserts a space that is fixed as 10% of an em in width ❺.

TIP A thin space is often used to add a small amount of space between characters. For instance, I use a thin space on either side of the greater than symbol when I give directions such as **Text > Special Characters.**

Em Dash

Inserts an em dash, that is the length of one em. Used to indicate an abrupt change in thought ❻.

En Dash

Inserts an en dash, that is the length of one-half em ❻. Used to indicate duration.

Discretionary Hyphen

Inserts a hyphen that is visible only if the word breaks across lines.

Invisible characters such as the End of column character do not print and are not visible on your page. However, you can use the Text Editor to view these invisible characters.

To see the invisible character:

1. Open the Text Editor and click the Show Invisibles box.
2. Invisible characters such as spaces, paragraph returns, end of column markers, and tabs show up in the text as gray symbols ❼.

Pop-up menu

Nothing—I meant nothing.

April–July

❻ *Compare how the different types of* **dashes** *appear: (top to bottom) hyphen, em dash, en dash.*

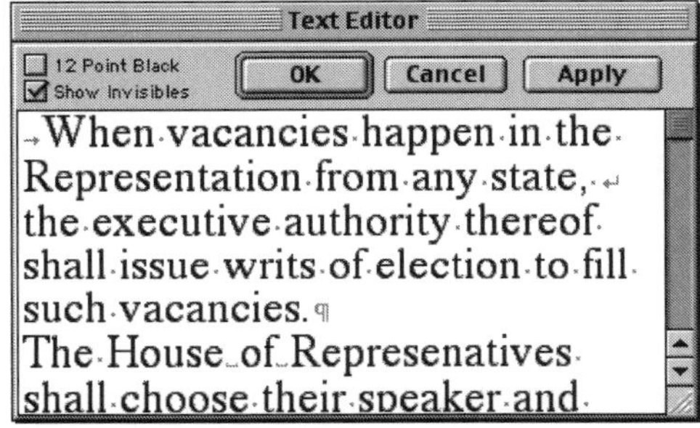

❼ **Show Invisibles** *in the Text Editor let you see the nonprinting characters for tabs, returns, special spaces, and so on.*

Special Characters Keystrokes (Mac)	
End of column	Cmd-Shift-Enter
End of line	Shift-Enter
Nonbreaking space	Alt-Spacebar
Em space	Cmd-Shift-M
En space	Cmd-Shift-N
Thin space	Cmd-Shift-T
Em dash	Alt-Shift-Hyphen
En dash	Alt-Hyphen
Discretionary hyphen	Cmd-Hyphen

Special Characters Keystrokes (Win)	
End of column	Ctrl-Shift-Enter
End of line	Shift-Enter
Nonbreaking space	Alt-Spacebar
Em space	Ctrl-Shift-M
En space	Ctrl-Shift-N
Thin space	Ctrl-Shift-T
Em dash	Alt-1, 5, 1
En dash	Alt-1, 5, 0
Discretionary hyphen	Ctrl-Shift-Hyphen

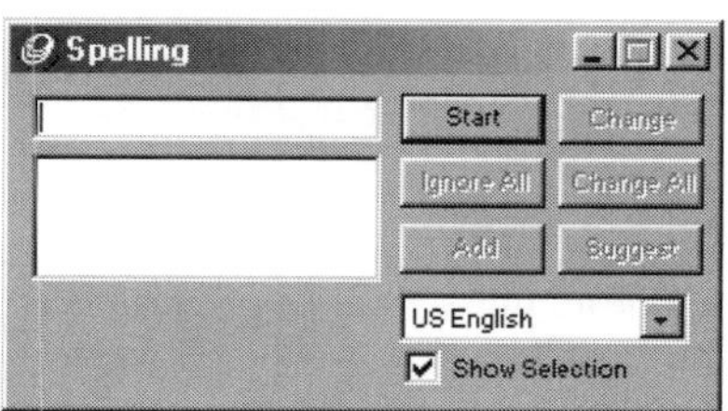

❽ *Click the* **Start button** *to start a spell check.*

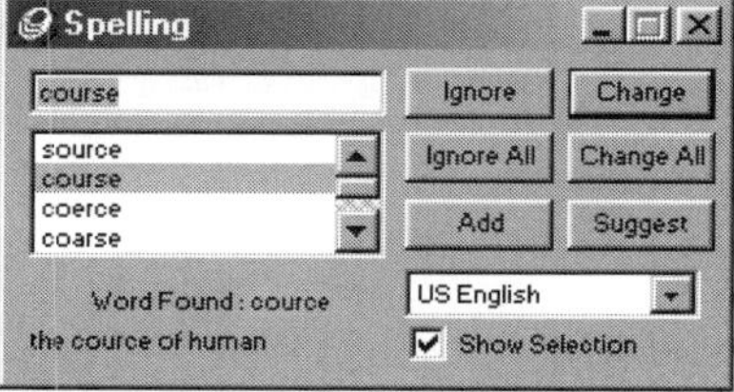

❾ *The* **Spelling checker** *looks for unknown words, capitalization errors, and duplicate words.*

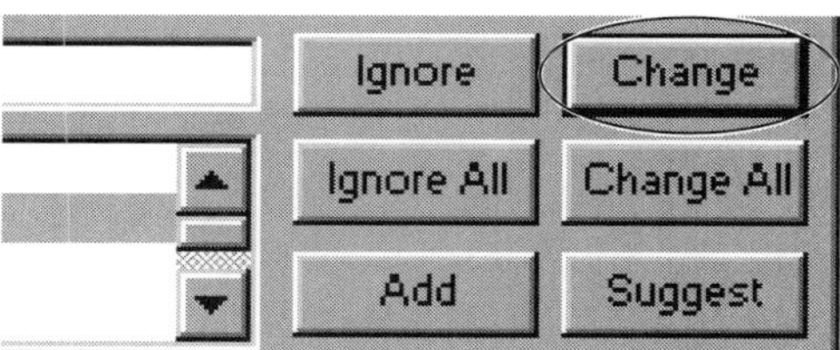

❿ *The* **Change button** *changes the word to one of the suggested alternates.*

Checking Spelling

You may want to make sure the text in your document is spelled correctly. To do so, you can use the spelling checker.

To use the spelling checker:

1. Use the Selection tool to select the text block or path.

   or

   Place your insertion point at the point in the text where you would like the spelling check to start.
2. Choose **Text > Spelling**. The Spelling checker appears ❽.
3. To start checking the spelling of your text, click Start. The spelling checker looks through the text and stops when it finds an error ❾.

TIP If no text blocks are selected, the spelling checker checks the entire document.

4. If the spelling checker finds a word it does not know, it displays the word in the top field. If possible, it shows alternates.

TIP To see the section of text currently being checked by the spelling checker, click Show selection.

TIP The spelling checker is not a grammar checker or a proofreader. It does not find typos such as *He was reel good,* since the word reel is a known word.

To use the Change button:

1. If the original word is incorrect, choose one of the alternates.
2. If none of the alternates are correct, type the correct word and then click Change ❿. The incorrect word is deleted and the correct word is inserted.

Checking Spelling

To use the Change All button:

- If you suspect that other uses of the word are incorrect in the document, choose one of the alternates and then click Change All ⓫.

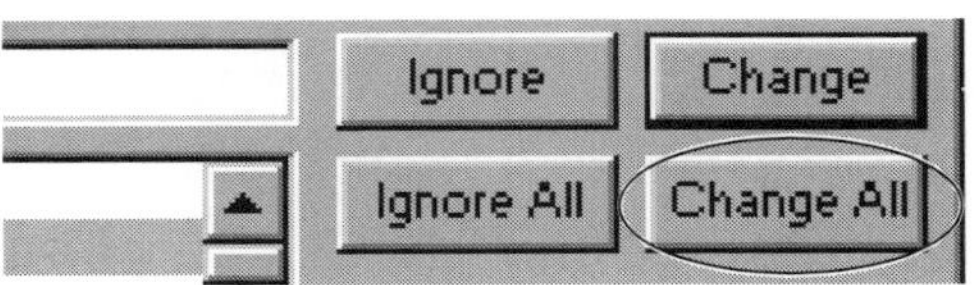

⓫ *The* **Change all button** *changes all instances of the word.*

To use the Ignore button:

- If the original word is correct, click Ignore ⓬. The spelling checker skips over that instance of the word, but stops again if the word is elsewhere in the text chain.

⓬ *The* **Ignore button** *skips the word.*

To use the Ignore All button:

- If all the instances of the original word are correct, click Ignore All ⓭. The spelling checker ignores all instances of that word until you quit that session of FreeHand.

⓭ *The* **Ignore all button** *skips all instances of the word.*

To use the Add button:

- If the original word is correct, click Add ⓮. This adds the word to the spelling dictionary and stops the spelling checker from identifying the word as misspelled in the future.

TIP To change how the spelling checker finds and adds words, change the spelling preferences *(see page 395)*.

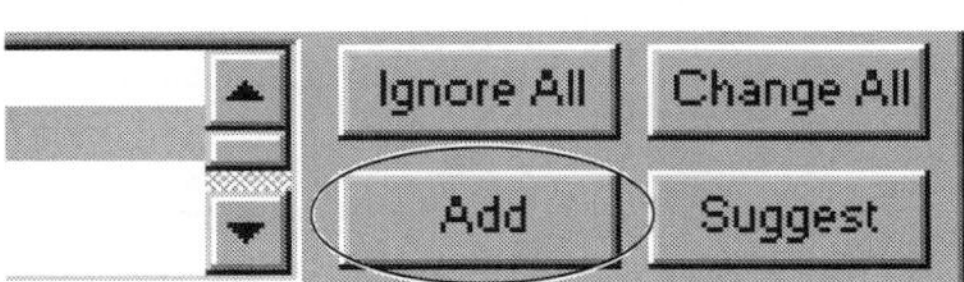

⓮ *The* **Add button** *adds the word to the dictionary that FreeHand uses during a spelling check.*

To use the Suggest button:

- To see the list of suggested words, click Suggest ⓯.

TIP To check the spelling of just a portion of a lengthy text block, use the Text tool to select just that portion and then run the spelling checker.

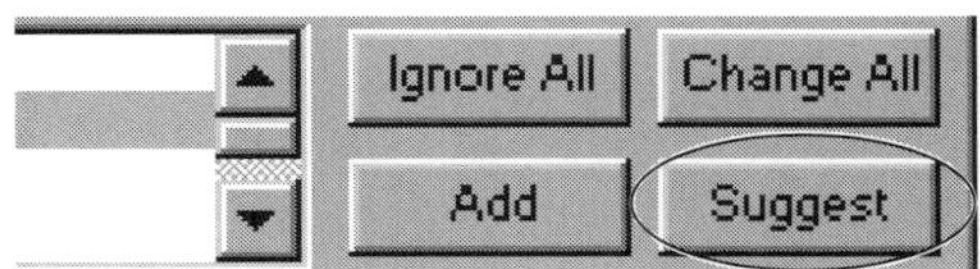

⓯ *Click the* **Suggest button** *to see the list of suggested alternates.*

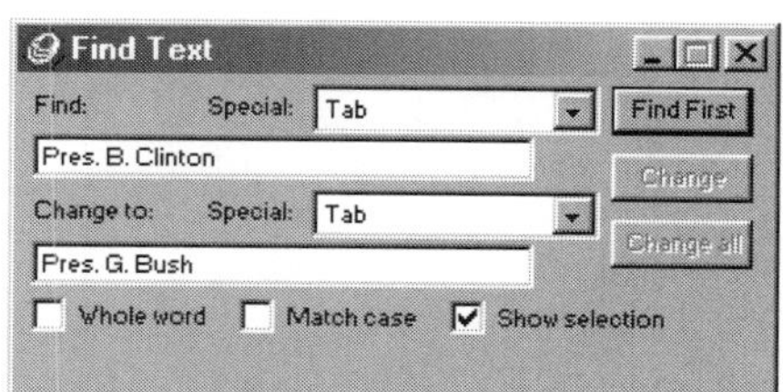

16 *The* **Find Text dialog box** *allows you to search and replace text strings or invisible characters.*

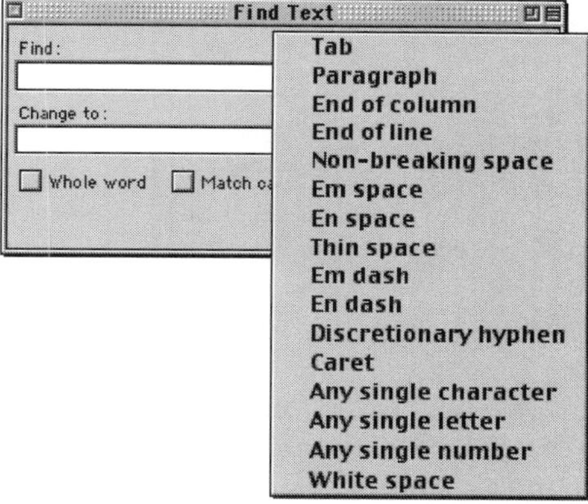

17 *The* **Special pop-up menu** *allows you to insert special characters into the Find and Change to fields.*

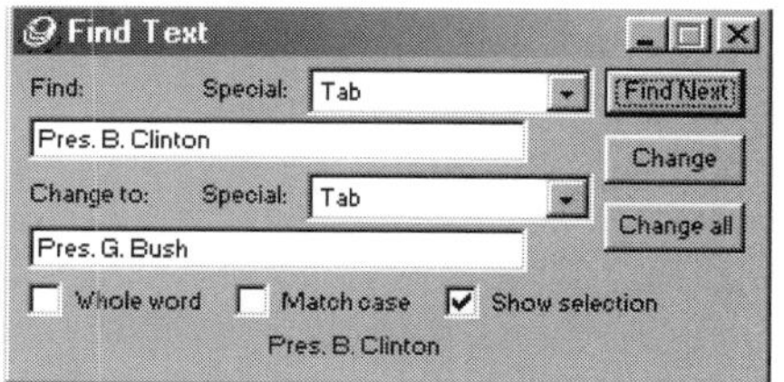

18 *The* **Change and Change All buttons** *allow you to make changes to the text.*

Replacing Text

If you are dealing with long amounts of text, you may need to use FreeHand's Find Text dialog box.

To use the Find Text dialog box:

1. Place your insertion point in the text block, or select the text block or path.
2. Choose **Edit > Find & Replace > Text** to open the Find Text dialog box 16.
3. In the Find field, type the text string you want to search for. In the Change to field, type the text string you want as a replacement.
4. To search for only the word listed, click the Whole word box. If you want to search for the text exactly as typed in uppercase and lowercase, click Match case.
5. Click to open the Special pop-up menus 17. This lets you insert the codes for the special characters into the Find and Change fields.

TIP If you know the codes, you can type or paste them directly into the fields.

6. Click the Find First button to find the first instance of the text string.
7. Click Change to change the text 18.

   or

   Click the Find Next button to find the next instance of the text string.

   or

   Click Change All to change all occurrences of the text string.

TIP To see the text currently being searched by the Find Text dialog box, click Show selection.

Working with Missing Fonts

When you open a FreeHand file that contains text, you need to have the fonts used in the text installed on your machine. If you don't have those fonts, you need to decide how the missing fonts are handled.

To work with missing fonts:

1. Open the FreeHand file. If the fonts are not installed on your machine, the Missing Fonts dialog box appears.
2. Select each font listed in the dialog box.

   or

   Use the Select All button to select all the missing fonts.
3. Click the Replace button. This opens the Replace Font dialog box.
4. Use the Replace with menu to choose a font to replace the missing font ⓳.
5. Use the Text style menu to choose the type style for the font ⓴.
6. Click OK to make the replacement.
7. If necessary, repeat steps 2–6 for any additional missing fonts.

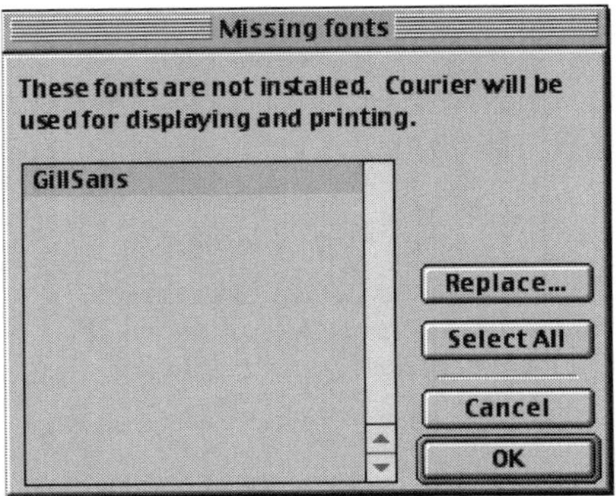

⓳ *The* **Missing Fonts dialog box** *lets you know which fonts are not installed in the system.*

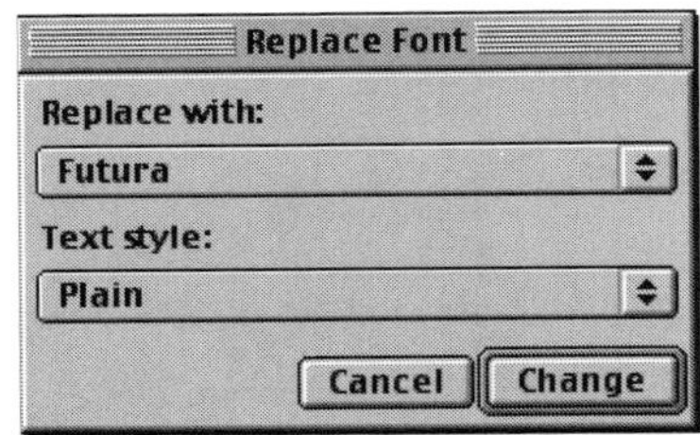

⓴ *Use the* **Replace Font dialog box** *to choose the type face and text style for a missing font.*

TEXT EFFECTS 20

With Macromedia FreeHand, you can create looks for text that would be difficult, if not impossible, to create using an ordinary page layout program. This makes FreeHand an excellent choice for adding special effects to text.

For instance, FreeHand makes it easy to attach text to a path as well as apply special text effects such as highlights and three-dimensional zoom effects.

You can also work with long text to add automatic paragraph rules as wrap text around graphics. So you can also create inline graphics that allow images to become part of the text flow.

Finally, FreeHand lets you convert text into artwork that can be further modified.

Working with Text on a Path

One of the most popular effects in graphic design is to align text to a path. The path can be open or closed, with curve or corner points. The text can even be linked to other paths or text blocks.

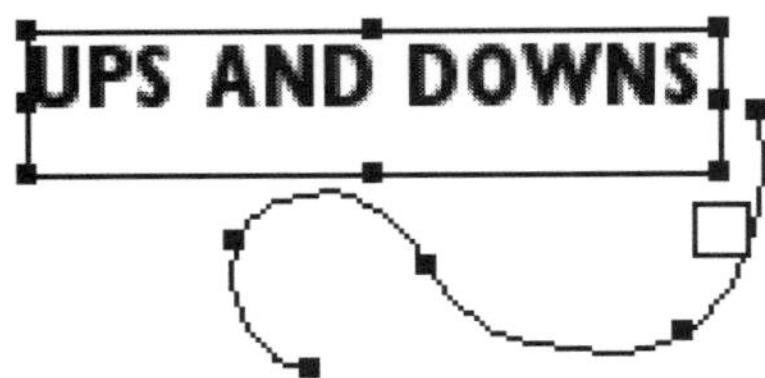

❶ *Text and a path selected.*

To attach text to a path:

1. Select both the text block and the path to which you want the text aligned ❶.
2. Choose **Text >Attach To Path.** The text aligns with the selected path ❷.

❷ *The results of applying the* **Attach To Path** *command.*

TIP If you are aligning text to a closed path, such as an oval, insert a paragraph return in the text to align the text to both the top and bottom of the path ❸.

TIP If the path is not long enough to display all the text, the overflow box fills.

TIP To remove text from a path, select the path and choose **Text >Detach From Path.**

TIP Use the Text tool to select text on the path.

❸ **Insert a paragraph return** *to cause the text to attach to both sides of an ellipse.*

To change the direction in which the text flows:

1. Hold the Opt/Alt key and click with the Pointer tool to select just the path.
2. Choose **Modify > Alter Path >Reverse Direction.** The text flows in the opposite direction ❹.

❹ *The* **Reverse Direction** *command causes the text (top) to change its direction (bottom).*

To move the text along the path:

1. With the Pointer tool, click the path. A small white triangle appears.
2. Drag the triangle to move the text in either direction along the path ❺.

❺ **Drag the white triangle** *next to the text to move the text along the path.*

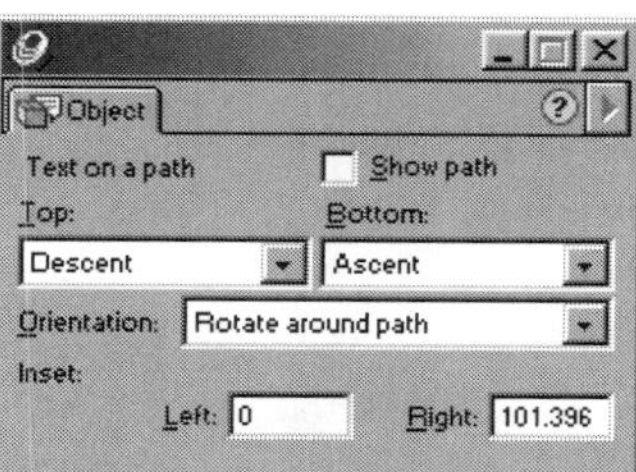

❻ *The* **Text on a path options** *in the Object inspector.*

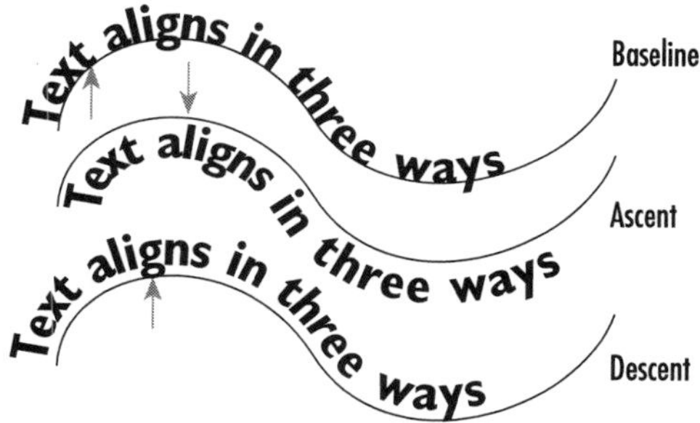

❼ *The ways text can be aligned to a path.*

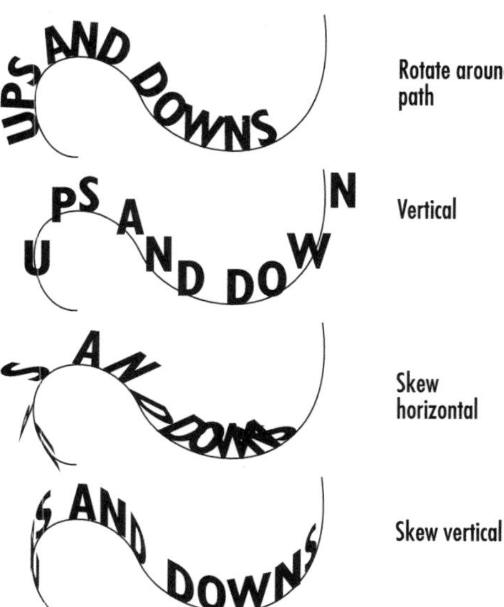

❽ *The ways text can be oriented to a path.*

To change the text alignment:

1. Select the object. The Object inspector shows the Text on a path options ❻.
2. Use the Top and Bottom Text alignment pop-up menus to control where the text sits in relation to the path:
   - **Baseline** puts the baseline of the characters on the path ❼.
   - **Ascent** puts the ascenders, such as the tops of the letter **t** on the path ❼.
   - **Descent** puts the descenders, such as the bottom of the letter **g**, sit on the path ❼.

TIP The Top menu controls text before any paragraph return. The Bottom menu controls text after any paragraph return.

To change the orientation and rotation:

Use the Orientation pop-up menu to change how the the text is oriented to the path.

- **Rotate around path** keeps the text in a perpendicular orientation as it moves around the path ❽.
- **Vertical** makes each character stand up straight no matter how the path curves ❽.
- **Skew horizontal** exaggerates the text's horizontal tilt up to a 90° rotation and distorts the characters shapes as the text follows the path ❽.
- **Skew vertical** maintains a vertical rotation but distorts the characters' shapes as the text follows the path ❽.

To move text numerically:

- Set the amounts in the Left and Right Inset fields.

To display and print the path:

1. Check Show path in the Object inspector.
2. Use the Fill and Stroke Inspectors to style the path.

Special Text Effects

Perhaps some of the greatest unknown features in FreeHand are the special text effects. Quite frankly I've never seen any graphics or page layout program offer anything like these effects.

To apply any of the special text effects:

1. Select the text.
2. Choose the Character options of the Text inspector.
3. Choose one of the special effects from the pop-up menu ❾.
   - **Highlight** creates a color or tint block around the text ❿.
   - **Strikethrough** draws a line that runs across the text ⓫.
   - **Underline** runs a line underneath the text ⓬.
   - **Inline** creates a number of outlines around the text ⓭.
   - **Shadow** adds a drop shadow image behind the text ⓮.
   - **Zoom** adds a 3D perspective effect ⓯.

TIP You can turn the visual display of the text effects on or off by changing your Redraw preferences settings *(see page 397)*.

TIP Text effects may slow your screen redraw. Apply them after you have finished most of your work, or work in the Fast Keyline or Keyline modes.

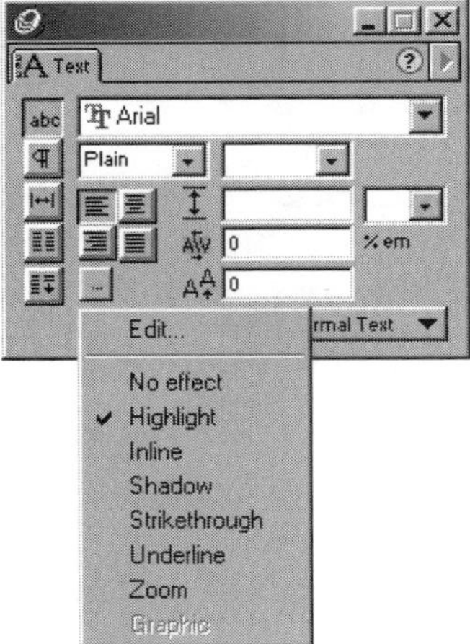

❾ *Use the* **Effects pop-up menu** *of the Text inspector to apply the special text effects.*

We, the people of the United States

❿ *The* Highlight *effect on text.*

We, the ~~folks~~ people of the

⓫ *The* Strikethrough *effect on text.*

establish <u>justice</u>, ensure <u>domestic</u>

⓬ *The* Underline *effect on text.*

GO TEAM USA

⓭ *The* Inline *effect on text.*

We the People...

⓮ *The* Shadow *effect on text.*

⓯ *The* Zoom *effect on text.*

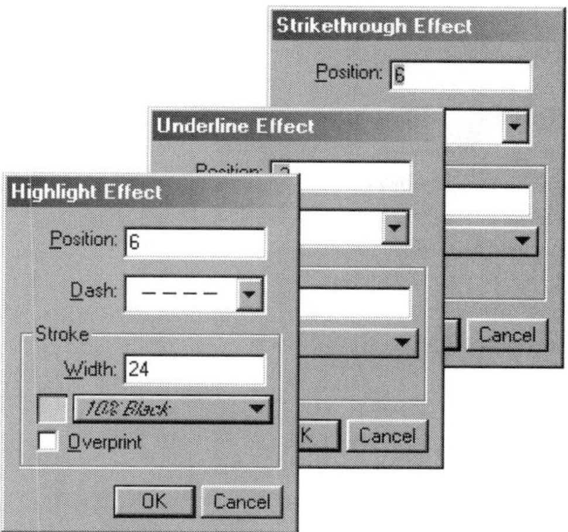

⓰ *The* **Highlight, Underline, and Strikethrough** *effects all have the same settings.*

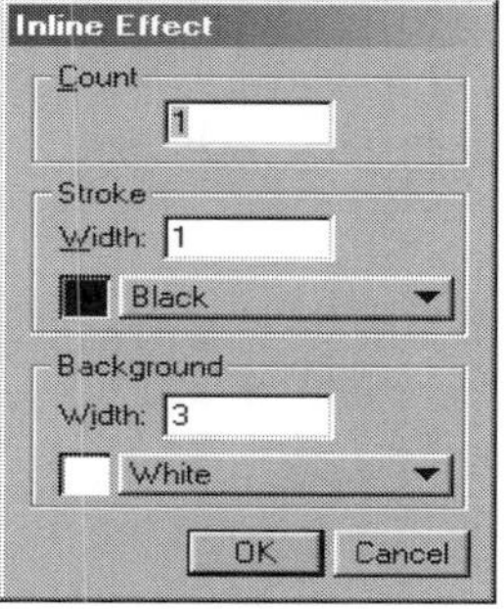

⓱ *The* **Inline Effect** *dialog box*

Highlight, Underline, and Strikethrough effects are actually just variations on the same effect so the settings work the same way for all three.

To edit the Highlight, Underline, and Strikethrough effects:

1. Choose Edit for the selected text. The dialog box appears ⓰.
2. In the Position field, enter the distance from the baseline for the effect.
3. In the Stroke Width field, enter the value of the thickness for the effect.
4. To change the color of the effect, use the color pop-up menu.
5. To apply a dash pattern, choose a pattern from the Dash pop-up menu.
6. Overprinting is one way of compensating for slight misregistrations in the printing process. To allow the effect to overprint the original text, click Overprint.

The Inline effect creates outlines of strokes and colors that surround the text.

To edit the Inline effect:

1. Select the text that has the Inline effect and choose Edit from the pop-up menu. The Inline Effect dialog box appears ⓱.
2. In the Count field, enter the number of sets of outlines you want to surround the text.
3. In the Stroke Width field, enter the width of the stroke.
4. To change the color of the stroke, choose from the color pop-up menu.
5. In the Background Width field, enter the width of the background color that will be between the stroke and the text.
6. To change the background color, choose from the color pop-up menu.

The Shadow effect creates an automatic drop shadow behind the text.

Editing the Shadow effect:

There is no dialog box for editing the Shadow effect. The values of the Shadow effect are fixed. The shadow is always 50% gray. Its position is always down and to the right of the original text.

Zoom creates a 3D effect where the text has one look in the background and changes into another in the foreground.

To edit the Zoom effect:

1. Select the text that has the Zoom effect applied to it and choose Edit from the pop-up menu. The Zoom Effect dialog box appears ⓲.
2. In the Zoom To field, enter the percentage that you want the foreground object to be.

TIP A value of 100% keeps the foreground the same size as the background. A value greater than 100% makes the foreground object larger than the background for a greater perspective effect.

3. In the x and y Offset fields, enter the distance you want to move the foreground object from the original text.
4. To change the color of the background object, use the From pop-up menu.
5. To change the color of the foreground object, use the To pop-up menu.

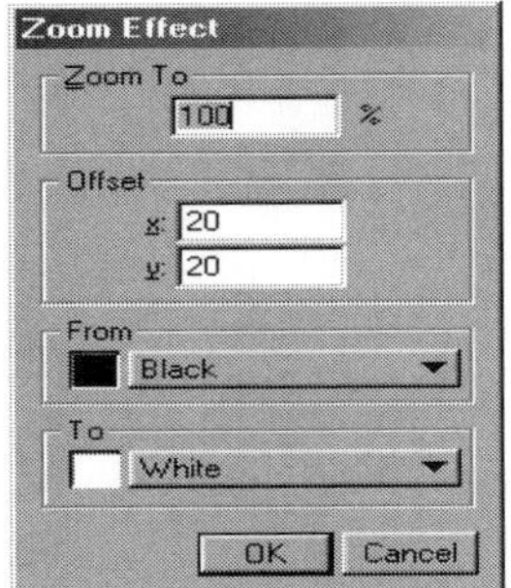

⓲ *The* **Zoom Effect** *dialog box.*

> **True Story**
>
> As you begin to work on the paragraph rules covered on the next page, please remember the following story.
>
> When I first started using computer page layout and graphics programs, I worked at a large ad agency. Each night I would stay late at the office to teach myself how the programs worked.
>
> I didn't have my own computer so I worked on the machine that was for the art directors.
>
> When I got to the menu command that said Rules, I was very frightened. I figured that was where they kept the laws that governed how the program worked. Since I didn't want to mess up the art director's equipment, I steered clear of that command.
>
> It was at least three years later that I discovered what Paragraph Rules did.

Senate Calendar:

January 27 Senate convenes
at 12:00 Noon ET/9:00 am PT

February 14 - 23 President's Day Recess

April 3 - 20 Spring Recess

⓳ **Paragraph rules** *that are aligned to the text.*

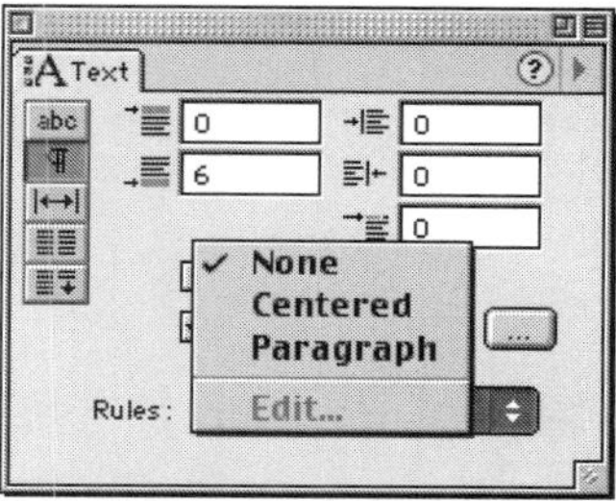

⓴ *The* **Paragraph Rules** *pop-up menu.*

㉑ *The* **Paragraph Rule Width** *controls.*

Paragraph Rules

Rather than use the Line tool, FreeHand lets you create automatic paragraph rules ⓳. The benefit of paragraph rules is that you can add or delete text and the rules reflow with the text. Once again, this is the type of feature found in page layout programs—and hardly ever in illustration programs.

To create paragraph rules:

1. Select the paragraphs where you want the rules.
2. Choose the following from the Rule pop-up menu of the paragraph options of the Text inspector ⓴.
   - **Centered** positions the rule centered on the last line or column.
   - **Paragraph** moves the rule along with the alignment for the paragraph.
3. Make sure Display border is checked in the Object inspector for the text block.
4. Use the Stroke inspector to style the stroke for the rules. The rules appear under the paragraph that were selected.

To edit the paragraph rules:

1. Select the paragraph that you applied rules to.
2. Choose Edit from the Rule pop-up menu. This opens the Paragraph Rule Width dialog box ㉑.
3. Use the % field to set the length of the rule.
4. Choose the following from the pop-up menu:
   - **Last line** extends the rule the width of the last line of text.
   - **Column** extends the rule the width of the column.

Working with Text and Graphics

FreeHand lets you position graphics so that the text automatically flows around the graphic. This is called text wrap.

To wrap text around a graphic element:

1. Select the graphic element you want the text to wrap around.
2. Move the graphic so that it is in the proper position in relation to the text.
3. Make sure the graphic is in front of the text block.
4. With the graphic still selected, choose **Text > Run Around Selection.** This displays the Run Around Selection dialog box ㉒.
5. Click the Runaround on icon to display the Standoff distances fields. The Standoff is the space between the text and the edges of the graphic.
6. Enter the standoff amount for each side of the graphic.
7. Click OK when you are finished. The text automatically flows around the graphic ㉓.

TIP To get more control over the wrap, draw an outline around the object. Do not give this outline a fill or a stroke. Give this object the text wrap. You can then manipulate the outline to create a more precise text wrap.

To change a text wrap:

1. Select an object with a text wrap.
2. Choose **Text > Run Around Selection.**
3. Change the amounts in the Standoff distances fields as necessary.

㉒ *The* **Run Around Selection dialog box** *lets you enter the Standoff distances around an object.*

㉓ *A* Text wrap *around a graphic element.*

We hold these truths to be self-evident, that all men are created equal

㉔ *To create an* **inline graphic,** *select the graphic and choose Copy or Cut.*

We hold these truths to be self-evident, that all men are created equal

㉕ *The* **inline graphic** *as it appears within the text.*

To undo a text wrap:

1. Select an object with a text wrap.
2. Choose **Text > Run Around Selection.**
3. Click the top left icon of the Run Around Selection dialog box.

You can also add inline graphics to text. This lets you create elements, such as ornate letters or logos, that are part of the text. So if the text reflows, the inline graphic flows along with the text.

To create an inline graphic:

1. Create the graphic you want to place inline. Examples of these graphics may be FreeHand objects, text on a path, text blocks, or placed TIFF or EPS images.
2. Use the Selection tool to select the graphic, and choose Copy or Cut from the Edit menu ㉔.
3. Use the Text tool to place an insertion point in the text where you want the inline graphic.
4. Choose **Edit > Paste.** The inline graphic appears and flows along with the text ㉕.

TIP To remove an inline graphic from text, use the Text tool to drag across the graphic as you would a text character. Choose **Edit > Cut** or **Edit > Clear.**

TIP To move the inline graphic up or down on the baseline, drag across the graphic as you would a text character. Change the Baseline shift.

TIP If you select an inline graphic, the Effects pop-up menu displays the words *Graphic Element.* Click Edit and use the Text Wrap dialog box to add more space around the inline graphic.

TIP If you select all the text in a text block, including the inline graphic, and then change the point size of the text, the inline graphic scales up or down along with the text.

So far, all the effects you have created with text have kept the text as text. This means that you can still edit the text. There may be times, however, when you will prefer to convert the text to paths that can be edited as artwork ㉖.

㉖ *Text that has been* **converted to paths** *and manipulated as art.*

To convert text into paths:

1. Use the Selection tool to select the text block or the text on a path you want to convert.
2. Choose **Text > Convert To Paths.**

TIP If you convert text aligned to a path, the path disappears, leaving only the text.

3. To manipulate the individual paths of the characters, choose **Modify > Ungroup** or hold the Opt/Alt key as you click each individual path.

TIP Text that has been converted to paths does not require fonts installed for it to print.

TIP You cannot change the font, spelling, or characters of text that has been converted to paths.

TIP Characters that have holes, such as the letters **A**, **O**, or **B**, are converted as a joined or composite path *(see page 108)*.

TIP Text must be converted to paths in order to use the Paste Inside command to have the text act as a mask *(see page 109)*.

TIP You must convert text to paths in order to apply most of the FreeHand and third-party Xtras that create special effects *(see Chapter 24, "Xtra Tools")*.

STYLES 21

If you have worked in a word processing program or a page layout application, you may have used styles to automate text formatting. Macromedia FreeHand has both text styles and object styles.

So in addition to changing text, you can change the fills, strokes, colors, and other attributes of objects. Using styles, you can change the look of an entire document with just a few actions.

It does take a little preparation to work with styles. You may need to plan the color schemes for your artwork as well as the stroke weights, text formatting, and so on. However, if you have planned your styles well, changes that might have taken hours to fix can be finished in a matter of minutes.

Defining Styles

The easiest way to define a style is by example. This means you can create the object or text and then use it as the reference to define the style.

To define a style by example:

1. Draw an object or type some text.
2. Use the Fill and Stroke inspectors to style the object or use the Text inspector to style the text.
3. With the object or text selected, choose New from the Styles panel submenu ❶.
4. A new style named *Style-1* appears ❷. This style contains all the attributes of the selected object.

TIP Text styles in FreeHand are paragraph styles—that is, they can not be applied to just some of the characters in a paragraph. If you need that type of local formatting, you need to do it manually.

You can also define a style by selecting all its attributes in the various Inspector panels and then defining the style according to those attributes.

To define a style by attributes:

1. Press Tab to deselect all objects and text blocks.
2. Use the various Inspectors panels to choose the object or text attributes you would like for your style.
3. When you are satisfied with the attributes, choose New from the Options pop-up menu of the Styles panel. The new Style is defined from the current state of the panels.

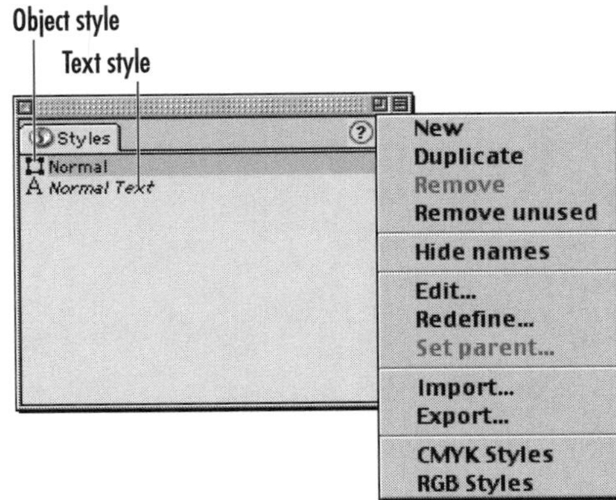

❶ *Select New from the* **Styles panel** *to create a new style based on the currently selected object.*

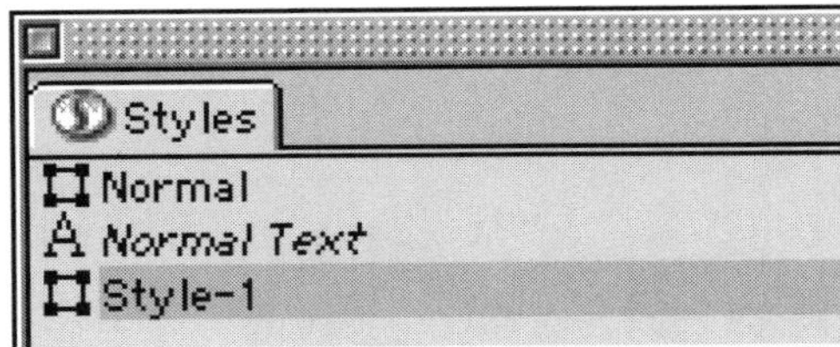

❷ *A new style is created with the name Style-1.*

The Default Normal Styles

Every new document contains two Normal styles. One is an object style; the other is a text style. These are the default styles for new objects and text.

Object styles are shown with a small rectangle symbol. The style name is written in roman text.

Text styles are shown in the Styles panel with an A symbol in front of their name. The style name is written in italic.

You can change the definition of these styles in the document you are working on or in the FreeHand Defaults file *(see page 374)*.

Defining Styles

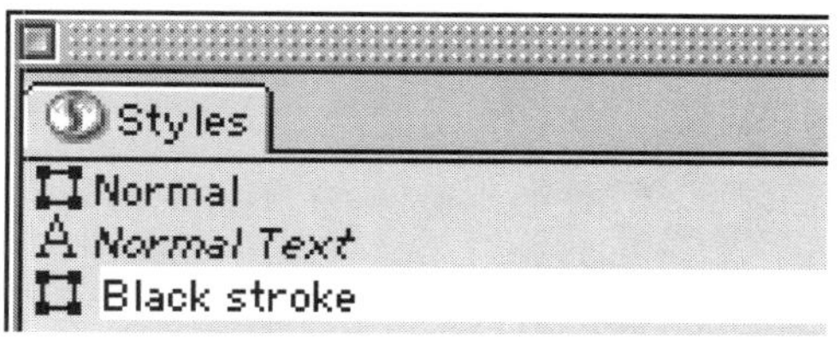

❸ *Highlight a style name to type in a new name.*

When to use Styles

Most of my designer and illustrator friends would never be caught dead applying styles to objects. Their work is much too individual to use the same styled object over and over.

However, my cartographer friends (map makers), use FreeHand's object styles extensively. They define a thick stroke to use as major highways and a thinner stroke for back roads. Then they apply the style to their artwork.

Also, people who use FreeHand to design Web pages use styles to maintain a consistent look for all their pages. That includes working with both object styles and text styles.

I use style extensively when I create long-text documents—especially if I have copy with lots of subheads, lists, and captions.

Once you add a style, it is easy to change the name of the style.

To rename a style:

1. Double-click the name of the style in the Styles panel to highlight the name ❸.
2. Type the new name of the style.
3. Press Return or Enter to apply the new name

To duplicate a style:

1. Choose the style you want to copy.
2. Choose Duplicate from the Styles panel submenu. A new style with the preface *Copy of* appears.

To remove a style:

1. In the Styles panel, click the name of the style you want to delete. Use the Shift key to select any additional styles you want to delete.
2. Choose Remove from the Styles panel submenu. The style is deleted.

TIP If you delete a style that has been applied to objects or paragraphs, those objects or paragraphs keep their attributes.

If you have a long list of styles, some of which are not used in the document, you may want to remove those styles to make it easier to work.

To remove unused style:

- Choose Remove Unused from the Styles panel submenu. All styles not applied to objects or text are removed.

Applying and Editing Styles

Defining styles is dull and boring. The real fun comes from how easy it is to apply complicated formatting using styles.

To apply a style to a selected object:

1. Select as many objects or text blocks as you want.
2. Click the name of the style in the Styles panel. The style attributes are automatically applied.

TIP If you select a text block, styles are applied to all the text in the block. You can apply a text style to an individual paragraph by placing the insertion point anywhere in the paragraph and selecting the style.

To drag a style onto objects:

- Drag the style from the Styles panel onto the object. A style icon indicates you will apply the style to the object ❹.

Once you have applied styles, you can easily edit or redefine a style.

To use the Edit Style dialog box:

1. Select a style that you want to change.
2. Choose Edit Style from the Styles panel submenu. The Edit Style dialog box appears.

TIP If you select an object style, the Edit Style dialog box contains the object attributes ❺. If you select a text style, the dialog box reflects text attributes ❻.

3. Use any of the settings in the dialog box to change the style attributes.
4. Click OK. The style changes are applied.

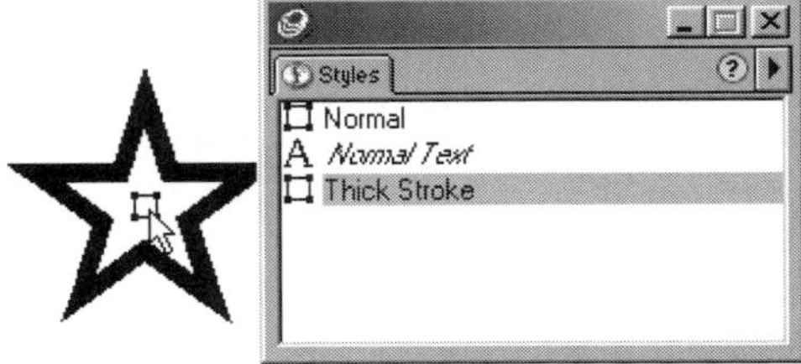

❹ *Styles can also be applied by* **dragging the icon for the style** *onto the object or text.*

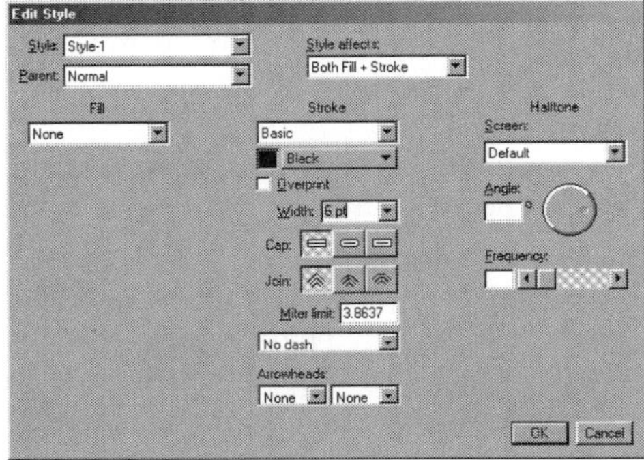

❺ *The* **Edit Style dialog box for objects** *lets you change all the object attributes at once.*

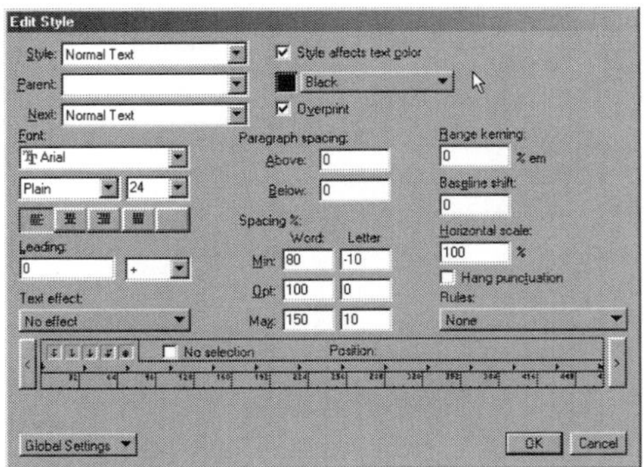

❻ *The* **Edit Style dialog box for text** *lets you change all the text attributes at once.*

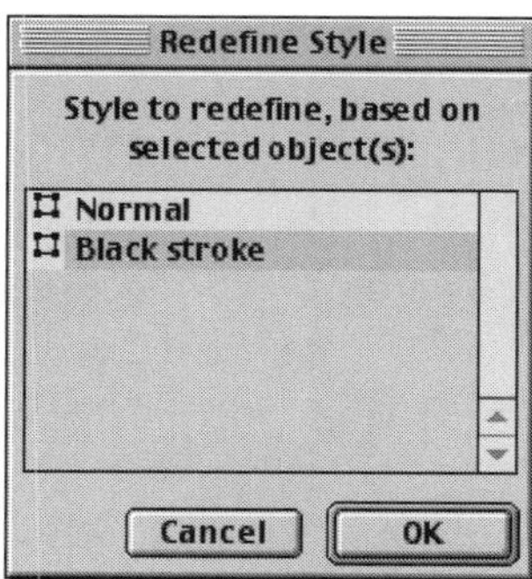

❼ *The* **Redefine Style dialog box** *lets you choose the style to redefine according to the attributes of the selected object or text.*

❽ *The style for these objects was defined with a 50% black fill and a black stroke.*

❾ *Redefining the style to a black fill and white stroke changed all the artwork without selecting any objects.*

The Edit Style dialog box lets you redefine a style using the formatting controls. However, some people find it easier to redefine a style by creating an object that can be used as an example of the new style. The Redefine dialog box lets you change the appearance of a style based on a selected object.

To redefine a style:

1. Use the Inspector panel or Type menu to change an object or text attributes.
2. When you are satisfied with the new attributes, choose Redefine from Styles panel submenu. The Redefine Style dialog box appears ❼.
3. Click the name of the style you want to redefine and then click OK.

TIP If you have an object selected, the Redefine Style dialog box shows object styles. If you have a text block selected, the dialog box shows text styles.

4. All objects that have the style applied to them automatically update with the new attributes ❽–❾.

Using Parent and Child Styles

FreeHand also offers the ability to base one style on another. FreeHand calls the relationship between these styles Parent and Child.

To create Parent and Child styles:

1. Define two object styles or two text styles in the Styles panel.

TIP To make it easier to understand Parent/Child styles, define only one difference (for instance, stroke weight or point size) to the second style.

2. Select the second style and choose Set parent from the Options pop-up menu of the Styles panel. The Set Parent dialog box appears 10.
3. In the Set Parent dialog box, choose the first style as the parent. Click OK. The two styles are now linked as Parent and Child.

TIP One Parent style can have many different Child styles based on it.

Once you have defined Parent and Child styles you will find it easy to make changes to many styles just by redefining the Parent.

To work with Parent and Child styles:

1. Select the Parent style and choose Edit style from the Options pop-up menu.
2. Make whatever changes you want to the Parent style attributes. Click OK.
3. Notice how the changes have been applied to the objects or paragraphs. Only those attributes that are shared by both the Parent and Child styles will change after editing the Parent style 11.

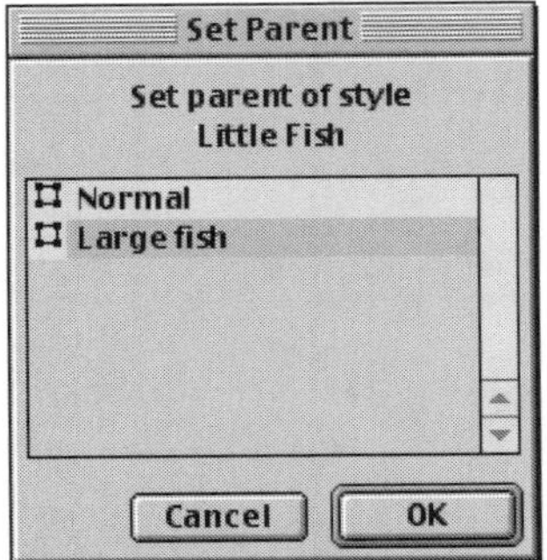

10 *The* **Set Parent dialog box** *allows you to base one style on another.*

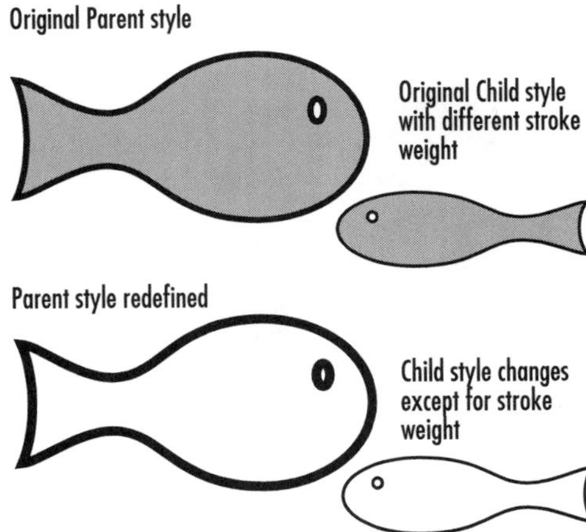

11 *An example of what happens in a* **Parent and Child** *relationship when Parent style is changed.*

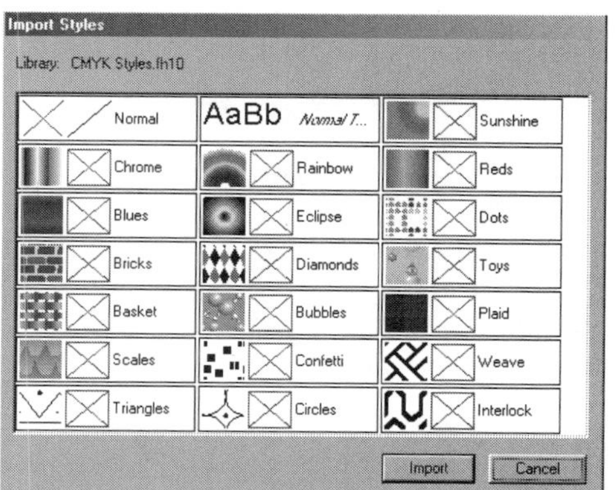

⓬ *The* **Import Styles dialog box** *lets you choose styles from one document to import into another.*

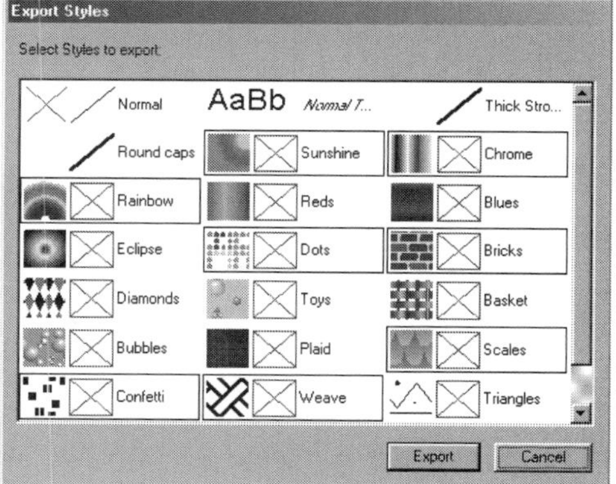

⓭ *The* **Export Styles dialog box** *lets you choose the style in a document to export out.*

Importing and Exporting Styles

You don't have to define new styles every time you open a new FreeHand document. You can easily import styles from other FreeHand documents.

To import styles:

1. Choose Import from the Styles panel submenu.
2. Navigate to find the FreeHand document you want to import styles from.
3. Click Open. The Styles Library for that document appears ⓬.
4. Select the styles that you want to import.
5. Click Import. The styles are imported from one document into another.

TIP FreeHand ships with two files called *RGB Styles* and *CMYK Styles*. You can open these styles by choosing them at the bottom of the Styles panel submenu.

TIP If you copy an object or text with a style and paste it into a new document, the object or text styles appear automatically in the second document.

You can also export styles from a document. This is useful if you want to create a library of just a few of the styles used in a file.

To export styles:

1. Choose Export from the Styles panel submenu. The styles for the document appear ⓭.
2. Select the styles you want to export.
3. Click Export. The Save File dialog box appears.
4. Name the document and file it in the location you want.

TIP If you file the exported styles in the Macromedia Freehand 10: English: Styles folder, the styles will be available at the bottom of the Styles panel submenu.

Displaying Styles

There are two ways to view the Styles panel. One lets you see the names of the styles. The other lets you see a visual representation of the style formatting.

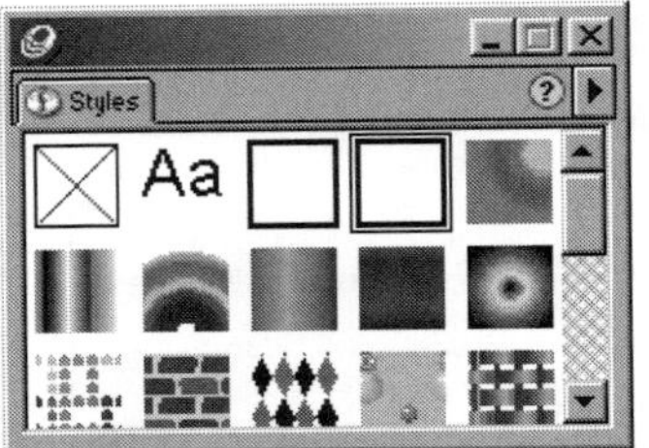

⓮ **Hide names** *shows a visual representation of the styles.*

To view styles visually:

- Choose Hide names from the Styles panel submenu. The display of the Styles panel changes to show visual representations of both the object and text styles ⓮.

To view styles by name:

- Choose Show names from the Styles panel submenu. The display of the panel changes to show the names of the styles.

SYMBOLS 22

Another powerful tool Macromedia FreeHand provides is the Library panel which stores symbols. If you have used Macromedia Flash, you are most likely very familiar with symbols.

Like Flash, symbols in FreeHand not only streamline the use of repetitive elements, they also help minimize the size of the files.

A single symbol can appear many times—each called an instance—in a document. Each instance can be transformed using the tools on the Transform panel.

Each instance refers back to the symbol and is affected by any changes made to the original, much like the Parent and Child relationship for styles.

However, unlike styles, which only control the formatting of an object, symbols also control its shape.

Creating Symbols

Symbols can be made from paths with a variety of strokes and fills, groups, or text blocks.

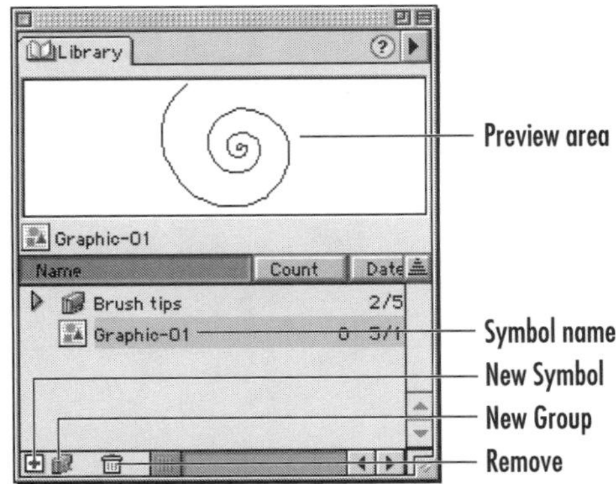

❶ *A new symbol appears in the Library under the name Graphic-01.*

To create a symbol using the menu commands:

1. Select the object you want to convert into a symbol.
2. Choose **Modify > Symbol > Convert to Symbol.** This creates a symbol of the selected object and makes the selected object into an instance of that symbol.

   or

   Choose **Modify > Symbol > Copy to Symbol.** This creates a symbol of the selected object but leaves the selected object unchanged.

TIP New symbols appear in the Library and are given the name Graphic-## ❶.

To create a symbol using the Library:

1. Select the object you want to convert.
2. Choose New Graphic from the Library submenu ❷.

   or

   Click the New Symbol icon at the bottom of the Library. This creates a symbol of the selected object but leaves the selected object unchanged.

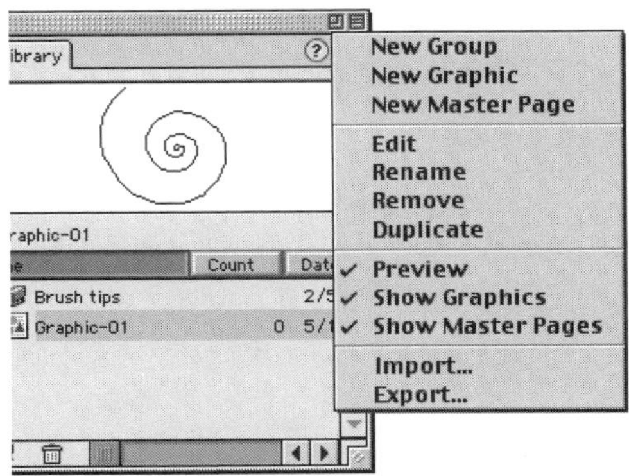

❷ *The* **Library menu** *contains commands for working with symbols*

To duplicate a symbol:

1. Select the symbol you want to duplicate
2. Choose Duplicate from the Library submenu. A new symbol appears with the prefix Copy of before the name.

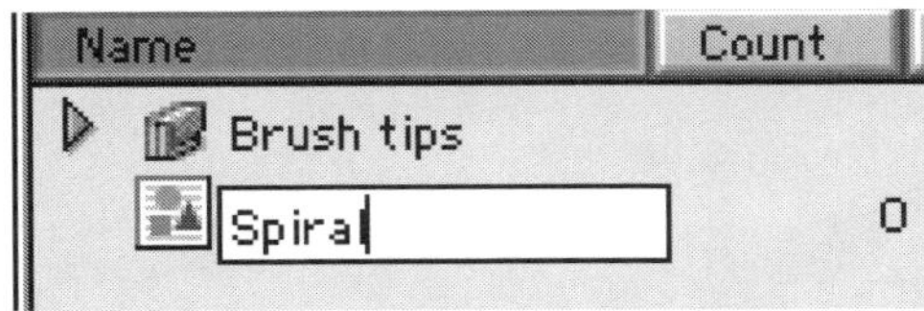

❸ *Highlight the name to type a new name for a symbol.*

To change the name of a symbol:

1. Choose Rename from the Library menu. This highlights the name ❸.
2. Type the new name for the symbol.

TIP You can also double-click to highlight the name.

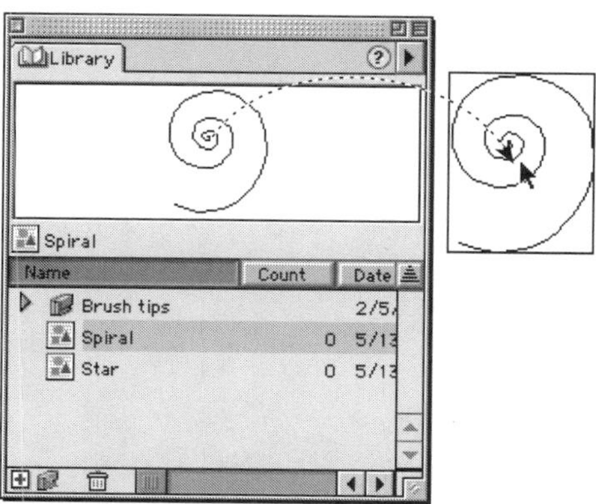

❹ *Drag a symbol from the preview area to create an instance of that symbol.*

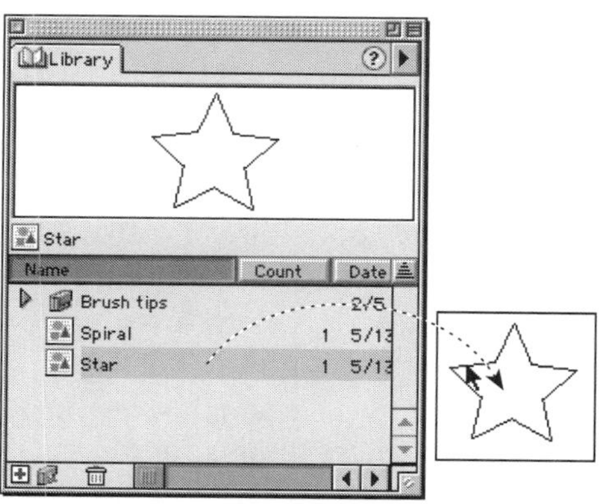

❺ *Drag a symbol from the symbol list to create an instance of that symbol.*

❻ *Instances of the Wheel are used as* **nested symbols** *in the Car symbol. Editing the Wheel changes both instances used in the Car.*

Working with Instances

Once you have a symbol in the Library you can create instances of that symbol and use them in your document.

To create instances of a symbol:

1. Select a symbol from the Library.
2. Drag the symbol from preview area ❹ or from the list ❺ onto the page. This creates an instance of the symbol.

When you have an instance of a symbol on a page, there are some tools and commands you can use on the instance and others that you can't.

Working with Instances

Select	**Yes**	
Subselect		**No**
Modify fill or stroke		**No**
Move	**Yes**	
Resize	**Yes**	
Transform	**Yes**	
Use Freeform tool		**No**
Copy	**Yes**	
Cut	**Yes**	
Paste	**Yes**	
Edit or modify text		**No**

Nesting Symbols

One special technique for working with symbols is to use the instance of one symbol to be part of the artwork for another symbol. This is called nesting symbols ❻. When you nest symbols, you can edit the nested symbol and it changes all the instances in the document—including those instances used in other symbols.

Modifying Symbols

Once you have instances on the page, you can edit the symbols and those edits create changes in all the instances of the symbol.

Once you create a symbol, you edit the graphics that are used in the symbol in the Symbol window ❼.

To open the Symbol window:

1. Select the instance of the symbol you want to edit.
2. Choose **Modify > Symbol > Edit Symbol.**

   or

   Double-click the Preview Area of the Symbol in the Library.

   or

   Double-click the icon of the Symbol in the Library.

   or

   With the symbol selected in the Library, choose Edit from the Library submenu.

To make changes in the Symbol window:

1. In the Symbol window, use any of the tools or commands to modify the object.
2. Click the Auto-Update option to see the changes in the document window as you make the changes to the symbol.
3. Close the Symbol window. The changes are applied to all instances.

TIP You can tell you're working in the Symbol window by the following clues:

- The name of the symbol follows the document name in the title bar
- A symbol icon appears in the title bar.

❼ *The* **Symbol window** *is where you edit the artwork for a symbol.*

Recognizing Instances

Unfortunately there is little difference between the appearance of instances and ordinary artwork.

Here are a few ways to tell if you have selected the instance of a symbol:

An instance of a symbol displays no options for either fill or stroke in the inspectors or the Tools panel.

You can't select any of the points of an instance with the Subselect tool.

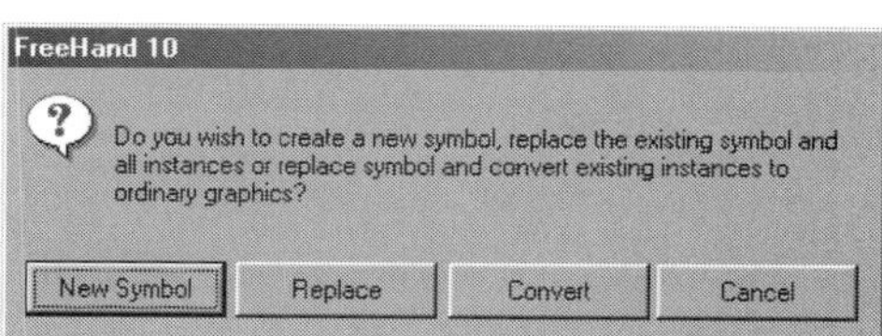

❽ *An alert box lets you control how artwork should be added to the Library.*

❾ *The female icon was replaced by the male icon. Transformations applied to the instances were applied to the new instances.*

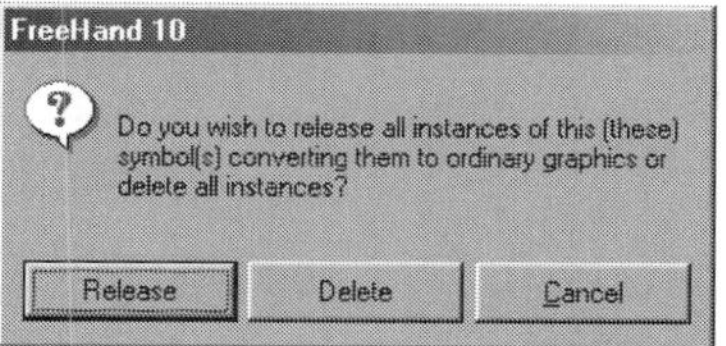

❿ *An alert box lets you control what happens to the instances of a symbol that is removed.*

> **The Two Types of Symbols**
>
> As mentioned earlier, master pages are actually a type of symbol. Although master pages are created using the Document inspector, they are stored in the Library with the other symbols.
>
> The artwork for brushes are also symbols. However, they can be edited and replaced just like the graphic symbols you create yourself.

Although you can't edit an instance, you can release it so that it is an ordinary graphic.

To release an instance:

1. Select the instance.
2. Choose **Modify > Symbol > Release Instance.** This converts the symbol into an ordinary graphic.

You can also have ordinary artwork replace a symbol in the Library.

To replace a symbol:

1. Create the new artwork for the symbol.
2. Drag the artwork onto the name of the original symbol. An alert dialog box is displayed ❽.
3. Click one of the following buttons:
   - **New Symbol** creates a new symbol from the artwork dragged into the Library.
   - **Replace** changes the original symbol to the new artwork. All instances of the symbol are also changed.
   - **Convert** changes the original symbol to the new artwork. All instances of the original symbol are converted into ordinary graphics.

TIP When one symbol replaces another, the new instances inherit any transformations previously applied ❾.

To delete a symbol:

1. Click the name of the symbol.
2. Click the Remove Symbol (trash can) icon in the Library.

   or

   Choose Remove from the Library menu. If the symbol is in use an alert appears ❿.
3. Choose one of the following from the alert dialog box:
   - Convert/Release changes all instances into ordinary art.
   - Delete removes the symbol and its instances.

Organizing Symbols

As you work, you may find it helpful to organize your symbols into different categories. These categories can be for each graphic, category, or page—you decide whatever is right for you.

To create a symbol group:

- Click the New Group icon in the Library.

  or

  Choose New Group from the Library submenu.

To add symbols to a group:

- Drag the symbol from the Library list into the group ⓫.

To open or close a group:

- (Mac) Click the twist triangle in the Library list ⓬.

  or

  (Win) Click the plus or minus signs in the Library list ⓭.

To delete a group:

1. Select the name of the group.
2. Click the Remove (trash can) icon.

   or

   Choose Remove from the Library submenu.

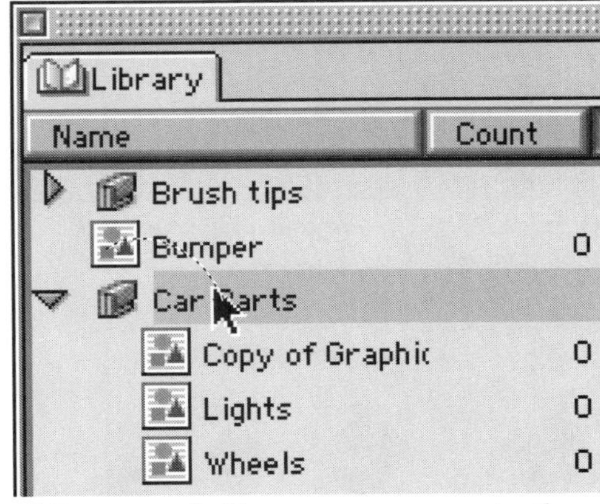

⓫ *Drag a symbol into a group to organize the symbols in the Library.*

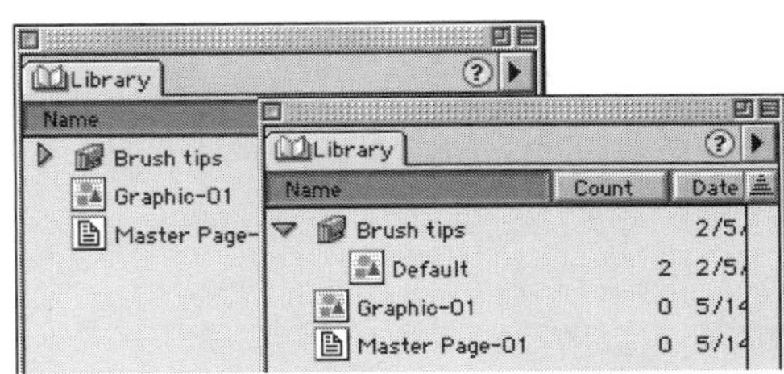

⓬ *(Mac) Use the twist triangle to open and close the groups in the Library.*

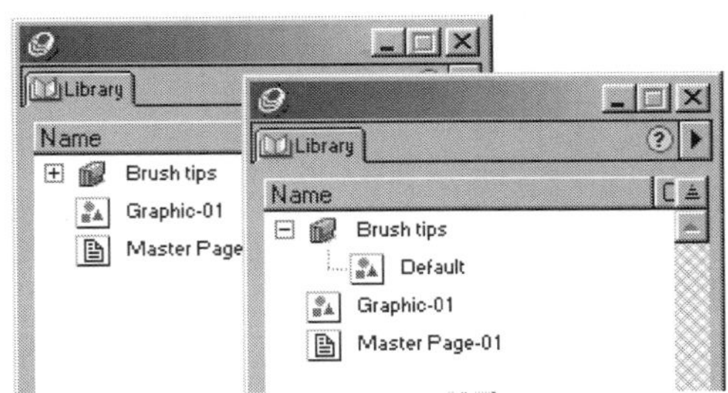

⓭ *(Win) Use the plus or minus signs to open and close the groups in the Library.*

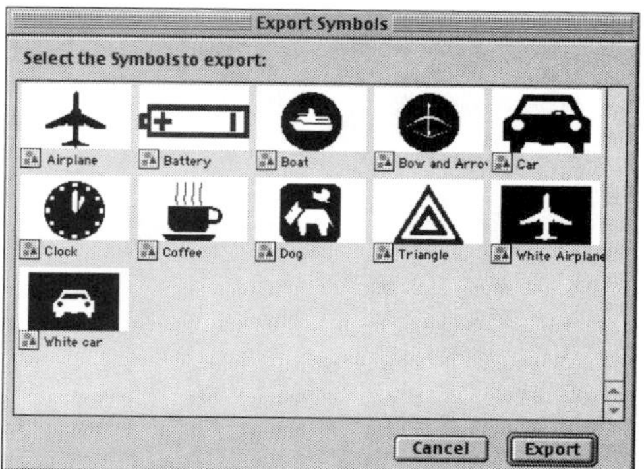

(14) *Choose the symbols you want to export from the* **Export Symbols dialog box.**

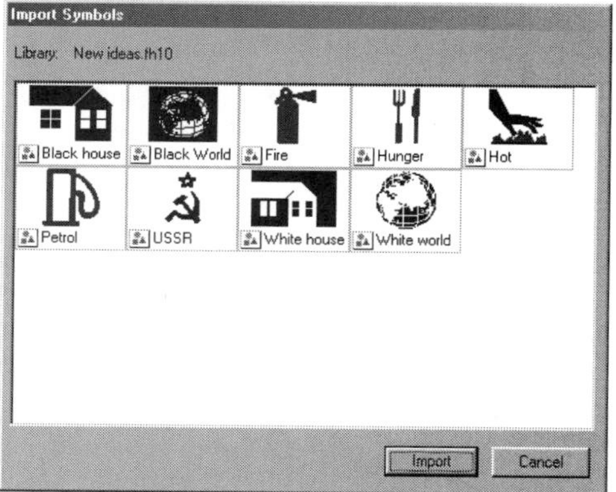

(15) *Choose the symbols you want to import from the* **Import Symbols dialog box.**

Importing and Exporting Symbols

Symbols created in one document can be exported as libraries that can then be opened for use in other documents.

To export symbols:

1. Choose Export from the Options pop-up menu on the Symbol panel. The Export Symbols dialog box opens (14).
2. Select the symbols you want to export.

TIP Use the Shift key to select a range of symbols. Use the Cmd/Ctrl key to select non-adjacent symbols.

3. Click Export. The Save *(Mac)* or Export Symbols *(Win)* panel opens.
4. Assign a name to the library you are creating and click Save.

You can import symbols from any FreeHand document.

To import symbols:

1. Choose Import from the Options pop-up menu on the Symbol panel. The Choose a File navigation dialog box opens.
2. Navigate to the document you want to import symbols from and click Choose/Open. The Import Symbols dialog box opens (15).
3. Select the symbols you want to import.

TIP Use the Shift key to select a range of symbols. Use the Cmd/Ctrl key to select non-adjacent symbols.

4. Click Import. The symbols appear in the Library of the current document.

Changing the Library Display

You also have control of how the Library panel displays symbols.

To change the order of the symbol display:

◆ Click the controls in the Library as follows:

- **Name** arranges the items alphabetically.
- **Count** arranges the items by the number of times they are used in the document ⓰.
- **Date** arranges the items by their creation date.
- The **toggle triangle** reverses the order of the list ⓱.

To hide or show the symbol previews:

◆ Choose Preview from the Library submenu to hide the display of the symbols in the Library. Choose Preview again to show the symbol displays.

To display or hide the graphic symbols:

◆ Choose Show Graphics from the Library submenu to hide the graphic symbols in the Library. Choose Show Graphics again to show the graphic symbols.

To display or hide the master page symbols:

◆ Choose Show Master Pages from the Library submenu to hide the master page symbols in the Library. Choose Show Master Pages again to show the master page symbols.

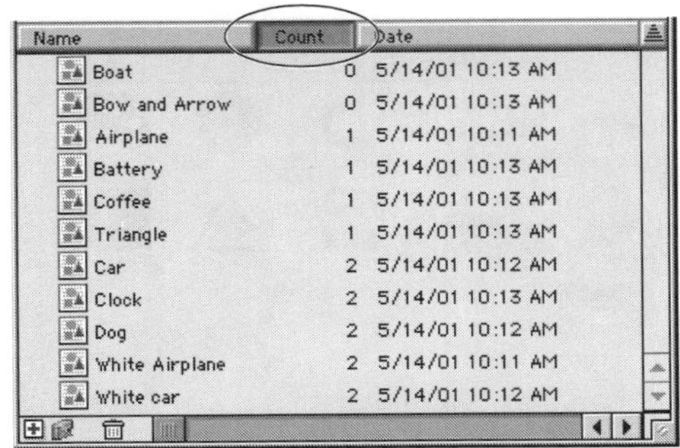

⓰ *Click the* **Count button** *(circled) to order symbols by the number of times they are used in the file.*

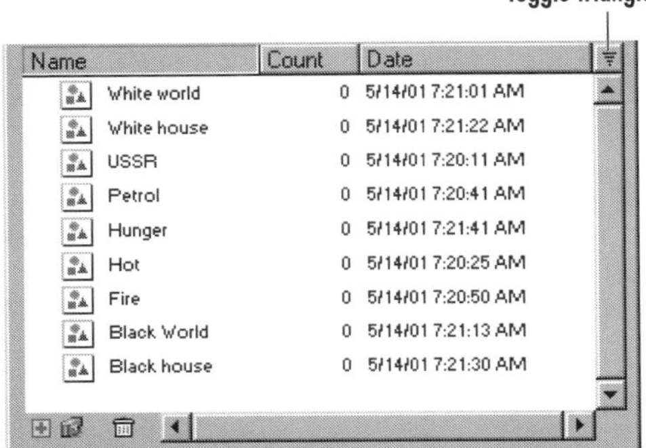

⓱ *Click the Name button and the Toggle triangle to see the items in reverse alphabetical order.*

AUTOMATING FREEHAND 23

As you have seen, styles and symbols let you make changes to many objects at once. Unfortunately both styles and symbols require some advance preparation for them to be helpful.

So what happens if you want to make changes to a file that doesn't have any styles or symbols? Fortunately, there is another way to quickly make changes to objects using the Find & Replace Graphics dialog box.

This chapter is all about automating repetitive tasks and getting your work done as efficiently as possible.

Note: If you are paid by the hour and increased productivity is not important to you, please feel free to skip this chapter entirely.

Finding and Replacing Graphics

This is one of the most sophisticated features of its kind. I know of no other graphics program that lets you search for such a wide range of objects and then change them into something else. For instance, you can find all objects with a certain shape and change them to another without losing the original fill and stroke settings.

To use the Find and Replace Graphics:

1. Choose **Edit > Find and Replace > Graphics.** This opens the Find and Replace Graphics dialog box.
2. Click the Find and Replace tab to open that section ❶.
3. Use the Attribute menu to select those features you want to find ❷. Each attribute displays different choices for the From and To sections. *See the exercises that follow for specifics on how to set each attribute.*
4. Set the Change-in menu as follows:
   - Selection searches through the selected objects.
   - Active page searches through just the current page.
   - Document searches through all the pages and the pasteboard.
5. Set the From choices on the left side of the box to select the features of the objects you want to find.
6. Set the To choices on the right side of the box to select the features of the objects you want to find.
7. Click Change. FreeHand automatically changes the objects from one set of attributes to another.

TIP The number of objects that change is listed at the bottom of the Find and Replace Graphics dialog box.

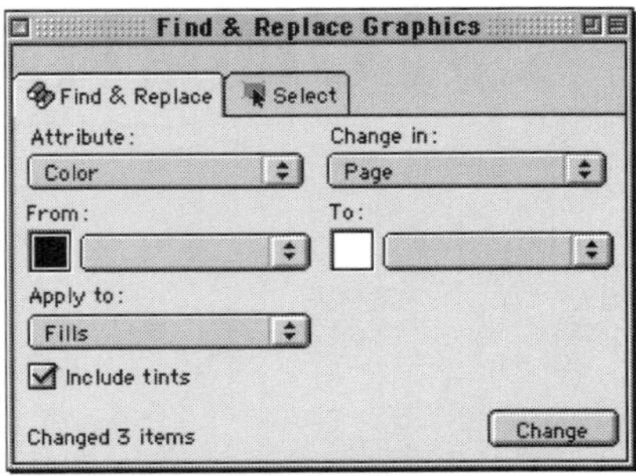

❶ *The* **Find and Replace section** *of the Find and Replace Graphics dialog box.*

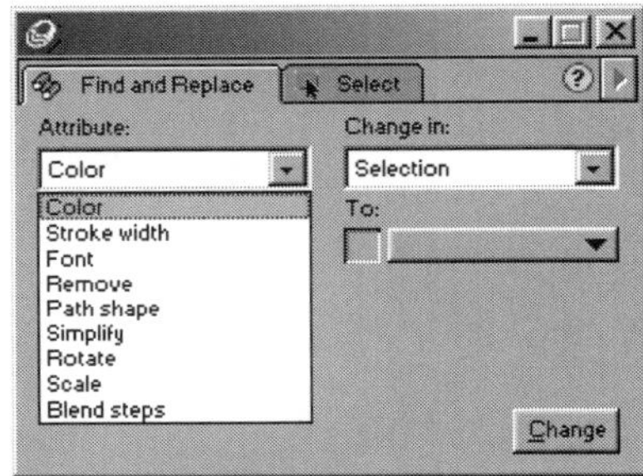

❷ *The* **Attributes choices** *that can be changed using the Find and Replace Graphics.*

> **And (Win) or & (Mac)?**
>
> For some reason, the Find and Replace Graphics features are named *Find and Replace* on the Windows platform, but *Find & Replace* on the Macintosh platform.
>
> Rather than spell out the difference every time I mention the feature, I'll just stick with the *and* version. (This shows no favoritism to the Windows platform, however.)
>
> Why is there a difference in the name of the feature? Beats me.

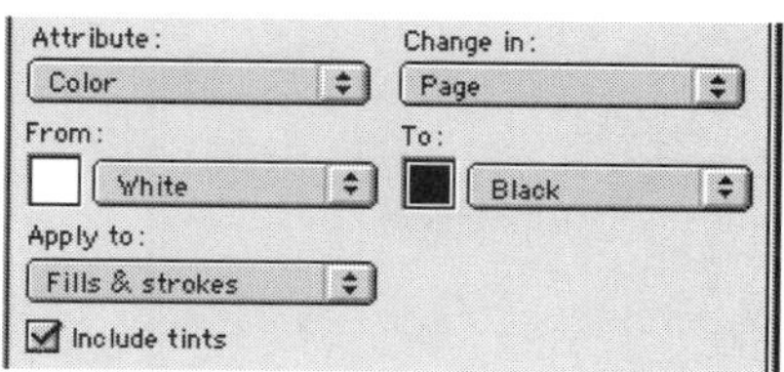

❸ *The* **Color section** *of the Find and Replace Graphics dialog box.*

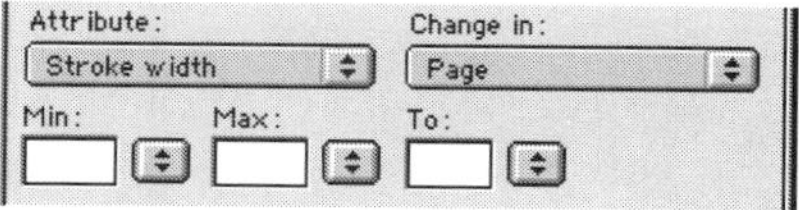

❹ *The* **Stroke width section** *of the Find and Replace Graphics dialog box.*

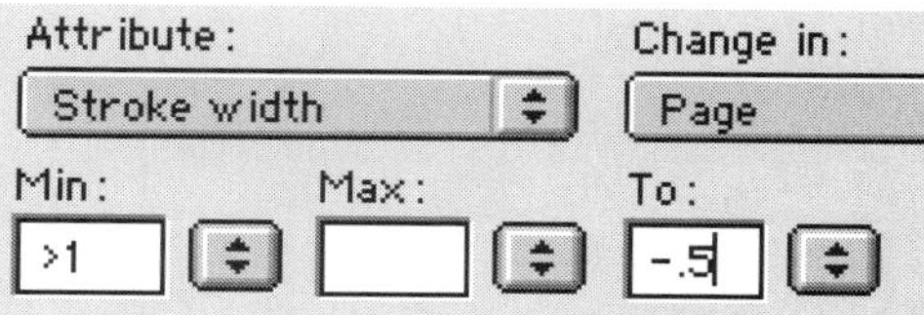

❺ *In this example, FreeHand will find all stroke widths greater than 1 point and decrease their size by .5 points.*

❻ *In this example, FreeHand will find all stroke widths from .5 to 10 points and then decrease them to 50% of their size.*

To set the Find and Replace color attributes:

1. With color selected, set a color under the From side that you want to find ❸.
2. Set a color under the To side that you want to replace.
3. Set the Apply to change only fills, only strokes, or fills and strokes.
4. Check Include tints to include tints of the swatches.

To set the Find and Replace for a specific stroke width:

1. With Stroke width selected, enter a value in the Min field to specify the smallest stroke width to find ❹.
2. Leave the Max field blank.

TIP Use the greater than (>) or less than (<) signs to find strokes larger or smaller than the specified weight ❺.

3. Enter the new stroke width in the To field.

To set the Find and Replace for a range of stroke width values:

1. Enter a value in the Min field to specify the smallest stroke width to find.
2. Enter a value in the Max field to specify the largest stroke width to find.
3. Enter the new stroke width in the To field.

   or

   Use the + or - sign before a number in the To field to increase or decrease all the stroke widths by that amount. For instance, if you enter +2 pt, then all the strokes will be increased by 2 points.

   or

   Use the * sign before a number in the To field to multiply all the stroke widths by that amount ❻. For instance, if you enter *.5, then all the strokes will be changed to 50% of their size.

To set the Find and Replace font attributes:

1. With Font selected, set a typeface in the From side that you want to find ❼.
2. Set a typeface in the To side that you want to replace.
3. Set the style in the From side.
4. Set the style in the To side.
5. Set the point sizes to search for in the Min and Max fields in the From side.
6. Set the point size in the Change field.

TIP Leave the point size fields empty to find all type sizes.

TIP Use the <, >, +, –, or * characters to search for point size amounts and change them using mathematical values.

TIP See the sidebar on page 280 for how to work with text attributes.

To set the Find and Replace remove attributes:

◆ With Remove selected, choose one of the following from the list ❽:
  - Invisible objects deletes all objects with no fill or stroke settings.
  - Overprinting removes any overprint setting applied to fill or strokes.
  - Custom halftones removes any special halftone settings applied to objects *(see page 363)*.
  - Contents removes any objects pasted inside other objects.

To set the Find and Replace path shape attributes:

1. Copy an object that has the same shape as the ones you want to find ❾.
2. With Path shape selected, click the Paste in button in the From side.
3. Copy an object that you want to replace.
4. Click the Paste in button in the To side.

TIP You can paste in instances to change an object into instances of a symbol.

5. Check the Transform to fit original to keep transformations that were applied.

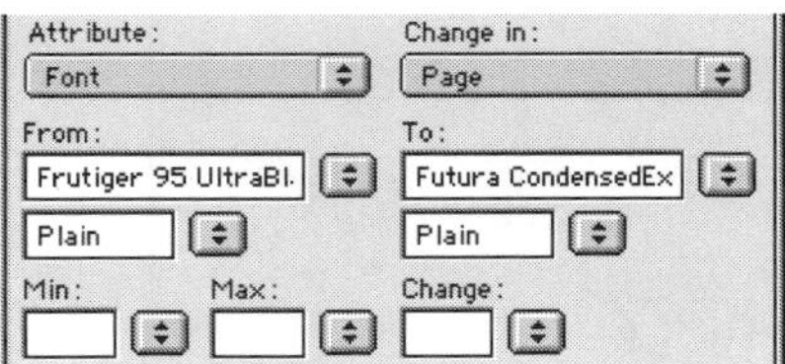

❼ *The* **Font section** *of the Find and Replace Graphics dialog box.*

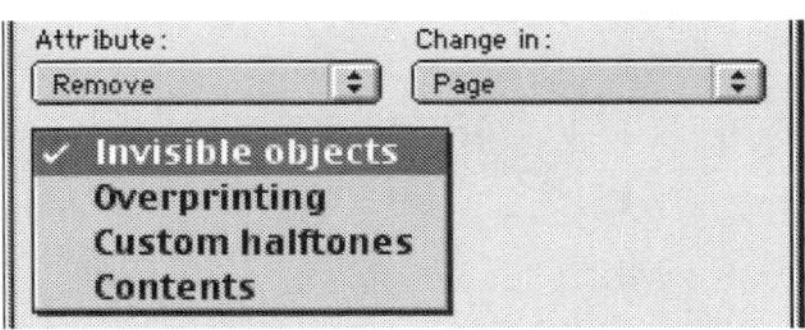

❽ *The* **Remove choices** *of the Find and Replace Graphics dialog box.*

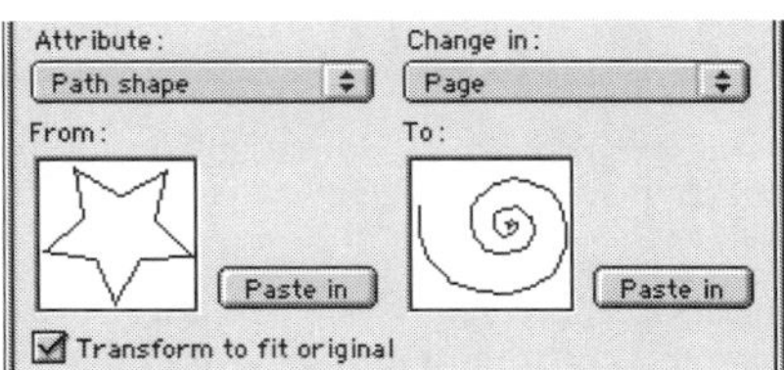

❾ *The* **Path shape choices** *in the Find and Replace Graphics dialog box show the shapes being searched and replaced.*

Tool or Command?

Why is there a special Rotate command in the Find and Replace dialog box? Why not use the Rotation tool?

When you use the Rotation tool on multiple items, the items rotate as a group around a single transformation point. When you use the Find and Replace Rotate on multiple items, the items rotate individually around their center point ⓬.

The same is true for the Find and Replace Scale command.

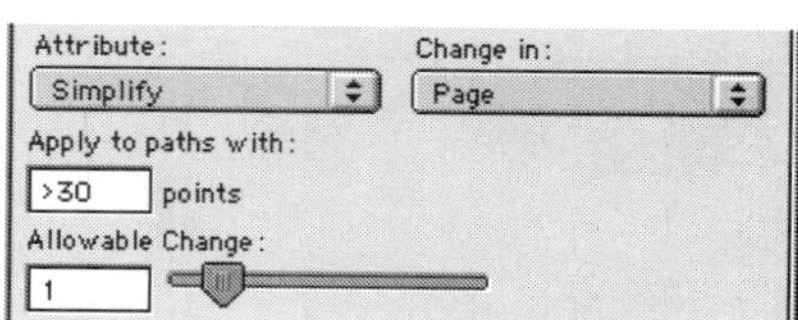

❿ *The* **Simplify options** *of the Find and Replace Graphics dialog box.*

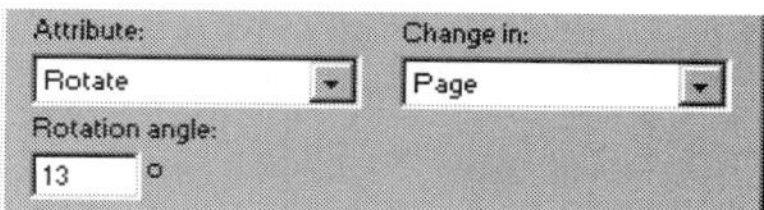

⓫ *The* **Rotation options** *of the Find and Replace Graphics dialog box.*

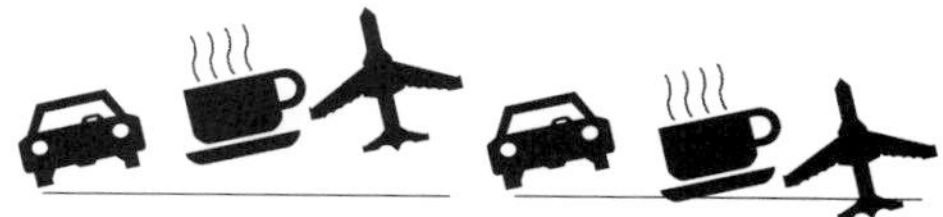

⓬ *The Rotation tool (left) rotates the items as a group. The Find and Replace Rotate command (right) rotates each item individually.*

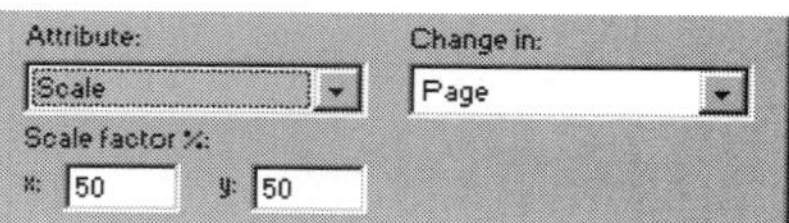

⓭ *The* **Scale options** *of the Find and Replace Graphics dialog box.*

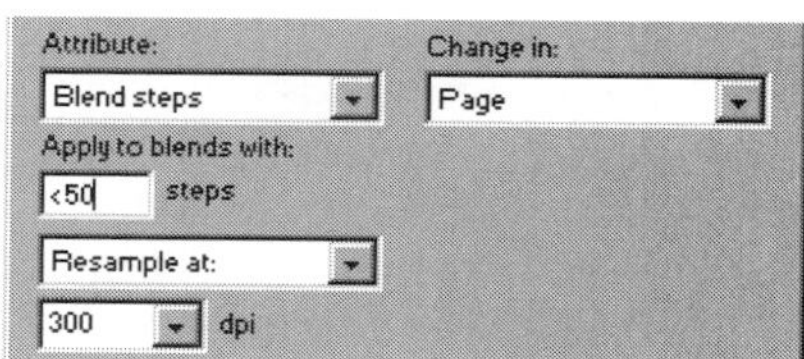

⓮ *The* **Blend steps options** *of the Find and Replace Graphics dialog box.*

To set the Find and Replace simplify attributes:

1. With Simplify selected, enter the number of points in the Apply to path with field ❿.

TIP Use the < or > signs in front of the number to find objects with less than or greater than a number of points.

2. Set the slider to set the amount of simplification to be applied to the object. *(See page 115 for information on using the Simplify command.)*

To set the Find and Replace rotate attributes:

◆ With Rotate selected, enter a rotation amount in the Rotation angle field ⓫.

To set the Find and Replace scale attributes:

1. With Scale selected, enter a horizontal scale amount in the x field ⓭.
2. Enter a vertical scale amount in the y field.

To set the Find and Replace blend steps attributes:

1. With Blend steps selected, enter the number of steps to find in the Apply to blends with field ⓮.

TIP Use the < or > signs in front of the number to find blends with less than or greater than a number of steps.

2. Choose from the following options:
   - **Change** lets you enter a number of steps to change the blend to.
   - **Resample at** lets you set a resolution amount. The blend is then changed so that it looks smooth at that resolution.

Selecting Graphics

The other tab of the Find and Replace dialog box opens the Select panel. Although not quite as powerful as the other side of the panel, the Select commands let you find many more types of objects. Once you have found the objects, you can manually change them, or move them to separate layers, or apply styles to them.

To select objects by attribute:

1. Choose **Edit > Find & Replace > Graphics** to open the Find & Replace Graphics dialog box.
2. Click the Select tab to open that section of the dialog box ⓯.
3. Use the Attribute menu to select those features you want to selected ⓰. Each attribute displays different choices to control what objects are selected. *See the exercises that follow for specifics on how to set each attribute.*
4. Set the Search-in menu as follows:
   - **Selection** searches through the selected objects.
   - **Active page** searches through just the current page.
   - **Document** searches through all the pages and the pasteboard.
5. Click the Add to option to add the selected object to the objects currently selected.
6. Click Find. The objects that fit the search criteria are selected.

TIP The number of objects found in a search are listed at the bottom of the Select Graphics dialog box.

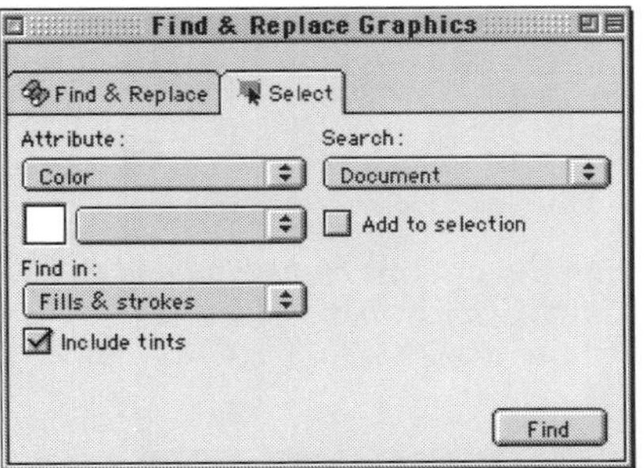

⓯ *The* **Select section** *of the Select Graphics dialog box.*

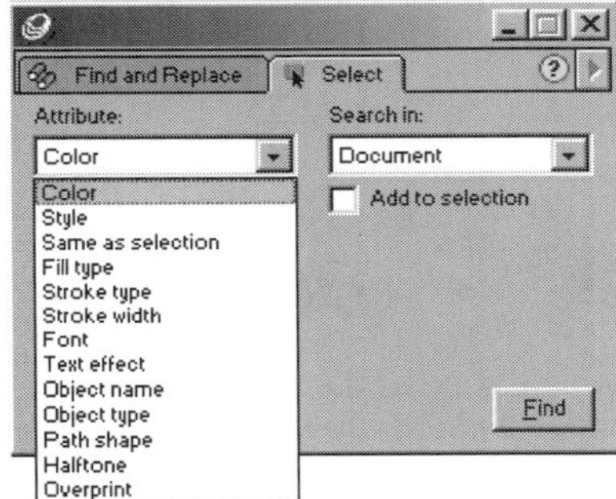

⓰ *The* **Attributes choices** *that can be selected using the Select Graphics.*

Selecting and Replacing Text Attributes

The Find and Replace Graphics and the Select Graphics controls let you search for various text attributes such as font, point size, text effects, and type styles.

However, these commands can not find text attributes that are applied to only some of the text in a text block. They only work if the attribute is applied to all the text in the text block.

If you need to make changes within a text block, you need to use the **Edit > Find and Replace > Text** command *(covered on page 247).*

Selecting Graphics

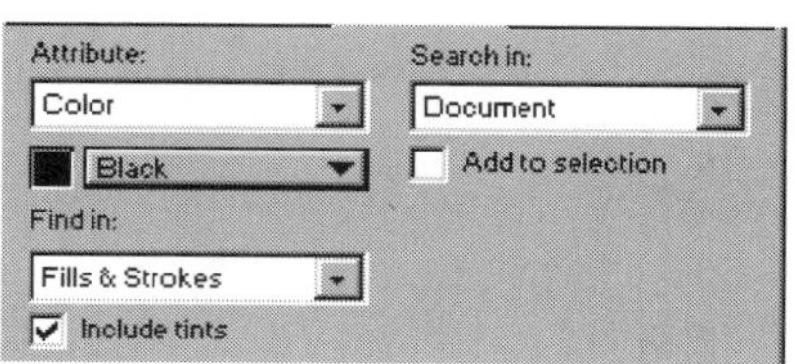

⓱ *The* **Color options** *of the Select Graphics dialog box.*

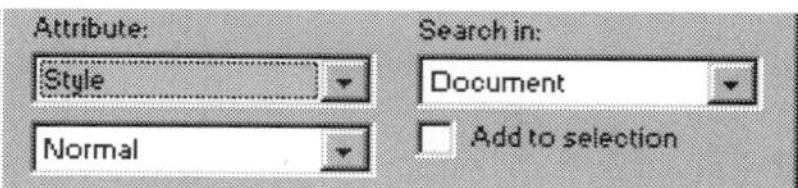

⓲ *The* **Style options** *of the Select Graphics dialog box.*

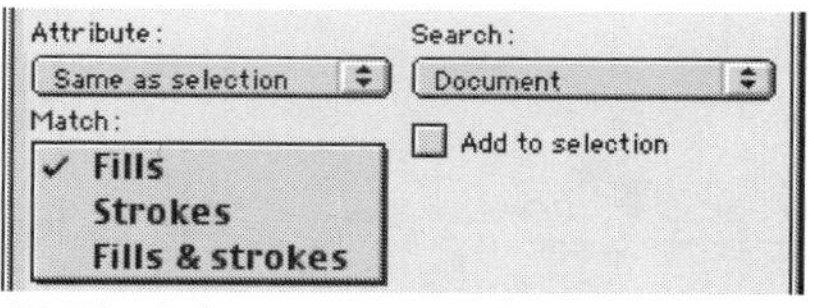

⓳ *The* **Select same as selection options** *of the Select Graphics dialog box.*

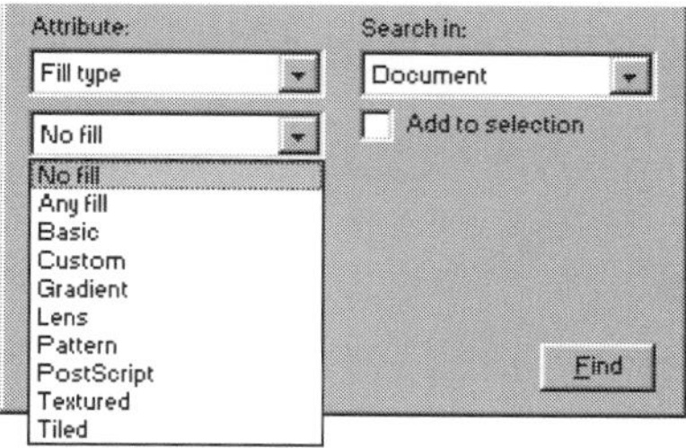

⓴ *The* **Fill type options** *of the Select Graphics dialog box.*

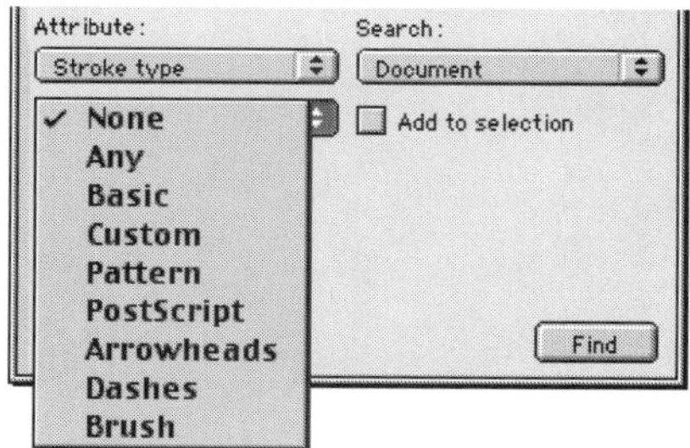

㉑ *The* **Stroke type options** *of the Select Graphics dialog box.*

To set the Select color attributes:

1. With Color chosen, use the list to select a color that you want to find ⓱.
2. Set the Find in list to find only fills, only strokes, or fills and strokes.
3. Check Include tints to include tints of the color:

To set the Select style attributes:

- With Style chosen, use the list to select a style that you want to find ⓲. *(See the sidebar on the previous page for how to work with text attributes.)*

To set the Select same as selection attributes:

1. Select the object that you want to use as the model for the selection.
2. With Same as selection chosen, use the Match list to choose which attributes should be the same in the final selection ⓳.

To set the Select fill type attributes:

- With Fill type chosen, use the list to select the type of fill that you want to find ⓴.

To set the Select stroke type attributes:

- With Stroke type chosen, use the list to select the type of stroke that you want to find ㉑.

To set the Select stroke width attributes:

1. With Stroke width chosen, enter a value in the Min field to specify the smallest stroke width to find ㉒.
2. Enter a value in the Max field to specify the largest stroke width to find.

TIP Leave the Max field blank to select a specific stroke width.

TIP Use the greater than (>) or less than (<) signs to find strokes larger or smaller than the specified weight. *(See the exercise on page 277 on changing stroke width for examples of using these characters.)*

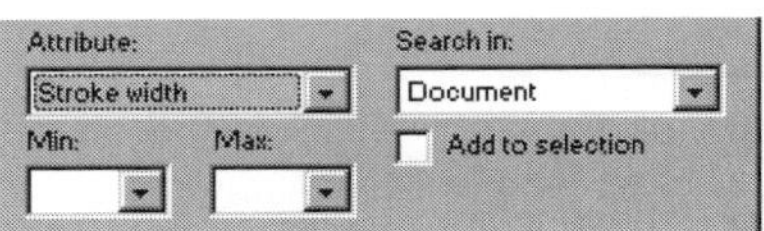

㉒ *The* **Stroke width options** *of the Select Graphics dialog box.*

To set the Select font attributes:

1. With Font chosen, set a typeface that you want to find ㉓.
2. Set the style that you want to find.
3. Set the point sizes to search for in the Min and Max fields in the From side.

TIP Leave the point size fields empty to find all type sizes.

TIP Use the < or > characters to search for point sizes less than or greater than a specific size. *(See the sidebar on page 280 for how to work with text attributes.)*

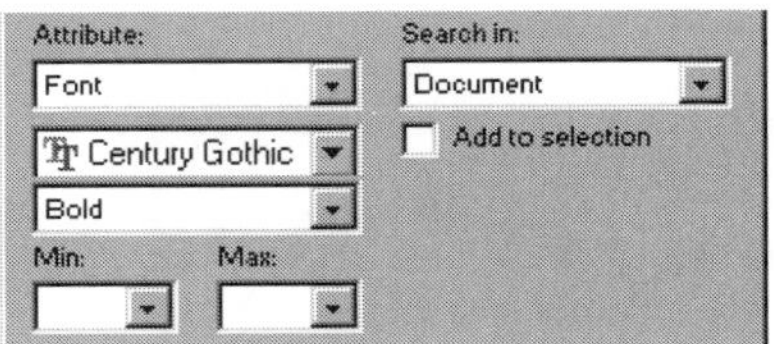

㉓ *The* **Font options** *of the Select Graphics dialog box.*

To set the Select text effect attributes:

- With Text effect chosen, use the list to select the text effect that you want to find ㉔.

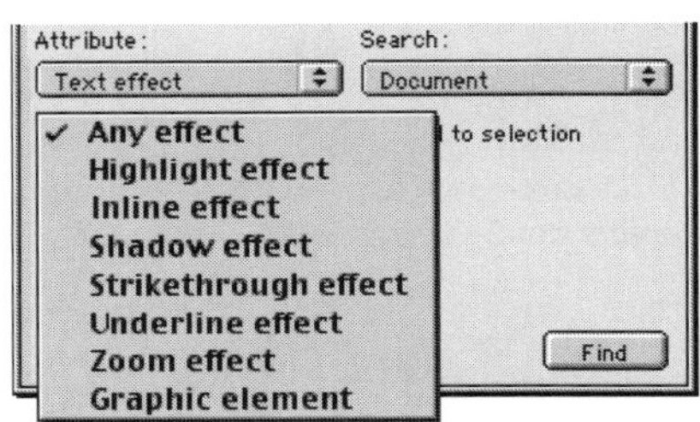

㉔ *The* **Text effect options** *of the Select Graphics dialog box.*

To set the Select object name attributes:

- With Object name chosen, enter the name of the object that you want to find in the object name field ㉕.

TIP The object name is applied using the Set Note command *(covered on page 284)*.

Object name field

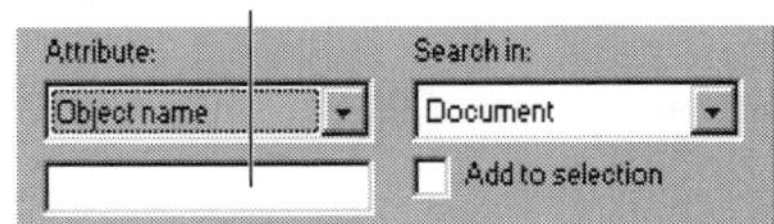

㉕ *The* **Object name options** *of the Select Graphics dialog box.*

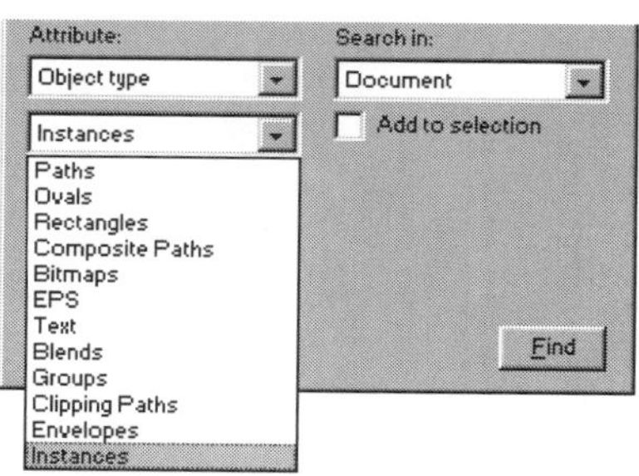

㉖ *The* **Object type options** *of the Select Graphics dialog box.*

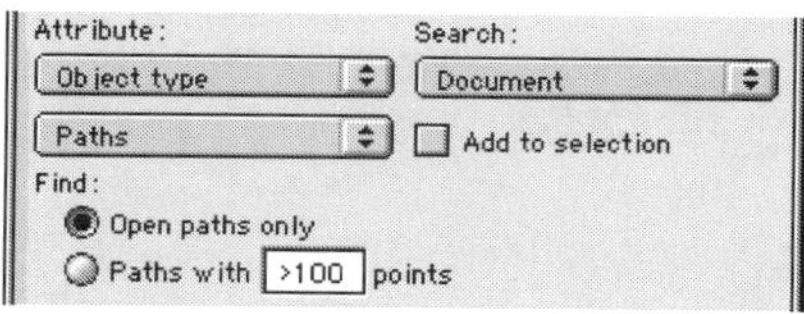

㉗ *The* **Paths options** *in the Object type section of the Select Graphics dialog box.*

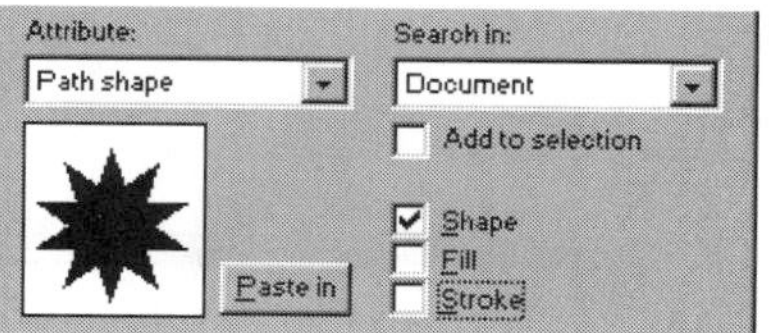

㉘ *The* **Paths options** *in the Object type section of the Select Graphics dialog box.*

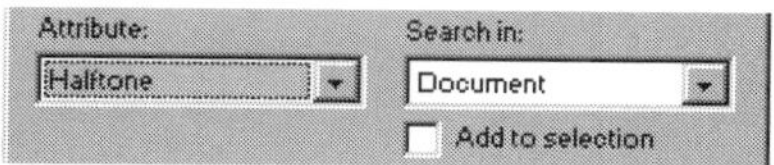

㉙ *The* **Halftone options** *in the Object type section of the Select Graphics dialog box.*

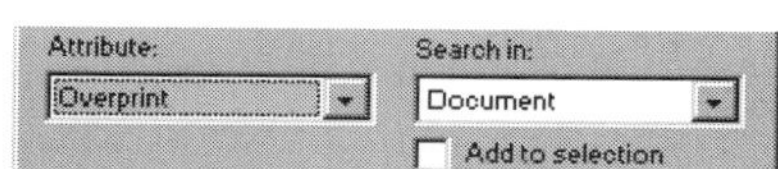

㉚ *The* **Overprint options** *in the Object type section of the Select Graphics dialog box.*

To set the Select object type attributes:

1. With Object type chosen, use the list to choose the type of object you want to find ㉖.
2. If you choose Paths, you can choose to find open paths only or paths with a certain number of points ㉗.

TIP Use the greater than (>) or less than (<) signs to find objects with a larger or smaller number of points.

To set the Select path shape attributes:

1. Copy the path that has the shape you want to find.
2. With Path shape chosen, click the Paste in button ㉘. The path appears in the preview box.
3. Select the options as follows:
   - **Shape** searches for objects with the same shape.
   - **Fill** searches for objects with the same fill.
   - **Stroke** searches for objects with the same stroke.

TIP These options let you search for objects that have a specific shape but may not have the same fill or stroke.

To set the Select halftone attributes:

- Choose Halftone from the attributes list to select all objects that have a custom halftone applied ㉙. *(See page 363 for more information on working with custom halftone screens.)*

To set the Select overprint attributes:

- Choose Overprint from the attributes list to select all objects that have an overprint applied ㉚. *(See page 177 for more information on working with overprinting.)*

Copying and Pasting Attributes

While not as powerful as styles or the Find & Replace Graphics dialog box, there is another way to make changes in graphic attributes quickly.

To use Copy Attributes

1. Select an object with a set of attributes that you want to apply to another object.
2. Choose **Edit > Copy Attributes.**

To use the Paste Attributes:

1. Select the object or objects that you want to change.
2. Choose **Edit > Paste Attributes.** The second object does not change its shape but does change its attributes, such as fill and stroke, to match the first **31**.

31 **Copy Attributes** *was applied with the hat in the left image selected. The hat, pants and shoes of the right image were selected and* **Paste Attributes** *was applied.*

Naming Objects

You can name an object using the Navigation panel.

TIP The primary use of the Navigation panel is to add actions to objects that are used in SWF files. *(For more information, see Chapter 29, "Flash Animations.")*

To name an object:

- In the Navigation panel, enter a name for the object in the Name field **32**.

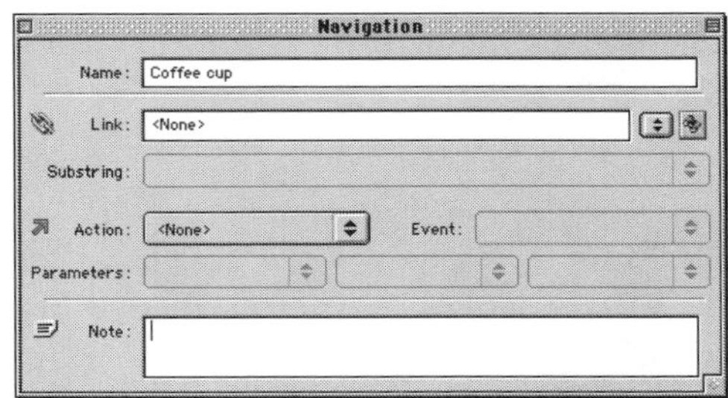

32 *Use the* **Name field in the Navigation panel** *to name an object.*

XTRA TOOLS 24

Xtras are features that are added to the basic Macromedia FreeHand program. When you install FreeHand, the program loads a set of built-in Xtras. These are the Xtras from Macromedia.

You can also buy Xtras from other companies. These are called third-party Xtras. Third-party Xtras are usually more sophisticated than the basic Xtras. For instance, the Avenza MAPublisher Xtra allows you to convert Geographic Information System (GIF) data into FreeHand graphics.

This chapter covers the details of working with the Xtras tools from Macromedia. Some of these tools, such as the Arc and Chart, are covered in other chapters.

Using the 3D Rotation Tool

The 3D Rotation tool applies a combination of transformations to an object as if it were rotated in space. Before you use the 3D Rotation tool, you must set its controls.

❶ *The* **3D Rotation tool** *in the Xtra Tools toolbar.*

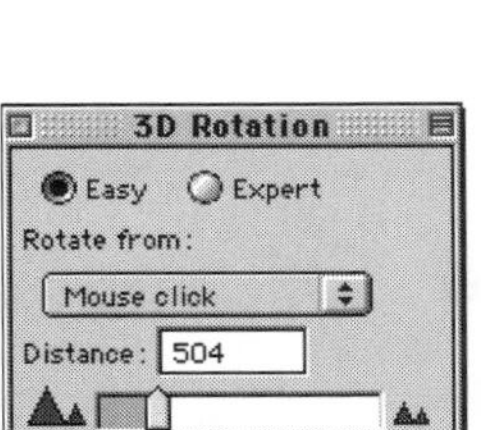

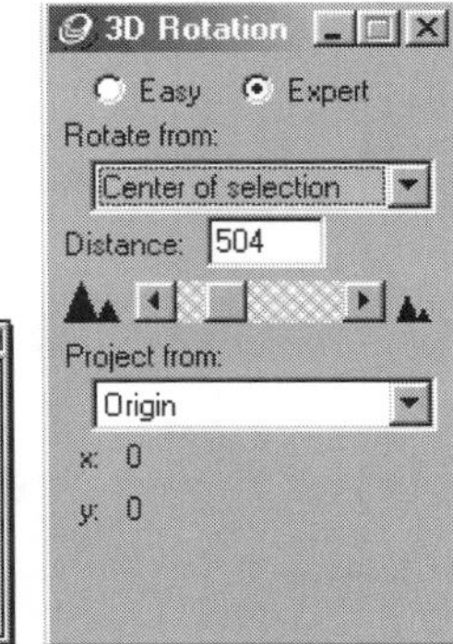

❷ *The* **3D Rotation controls** *in the Easy mode (left) and Expert mode (right).*

To set the 3D Rotation controls:

1. Double-click the 3D Rotation tool in the Xtra tools toolbar ❶. The 3D Rotation controls appears ❷.
2. Use the Rotate from menu to select the point from which the rotation should occur as follows:
   - **Mouse click** sets the rotation pivot point to the position where you click.
   - **Center of selection** makes the point the physical center of the object.
   - **Center of gravity** sets the rotation pivot point to the center of the object when adjusted for uneven shapes.
   - **Origin** sets the rotation pivot point to the bottom-left corner of the bounding box that surrounds the selection.
3. Set a Distance amount for how much distortion occurs during the rotation. For the greatest distortion effect, enter small numbers.
4. In the Expert mode, use the Project from menu to select the projection point (the perspective vanishing point) as follows:
   - **Mouse click** sets the rotation pivot point to the position where you click.
   - **Center of selection** makes the point the physical center of the object.
   - **Center of gravity** sets the rotation pivot point to the center of the object when adjusted for uneven shapes.
   - **Origin** sets the rotation pivot point to the bottom-left corner of the bounding box that surrounds the selection.
   - **X/Y coordinates** sets the projection points from coordinates you enter in the fields.

TIP In the Easy mode, the projection point is set at the mouse click.

Limitations of 3D Rotations

The 3D Rotation tool actually combines several transformations into a 3D effect. However, there is one important part of the 3D Rotation that is missing: Depth.

Unfortunately, the 3D Rotation tool doesn't show you any depth as it moves an object to its side. If you want you can use the Smudge tool (see page 289) to add a very primitive depth to the object.

Also, the 3D Rotation tool isn't as powerful as the perspective grids. So unlike the grid, once you apply the 3D Rotation tool, you can't move the object to a new perspective position.

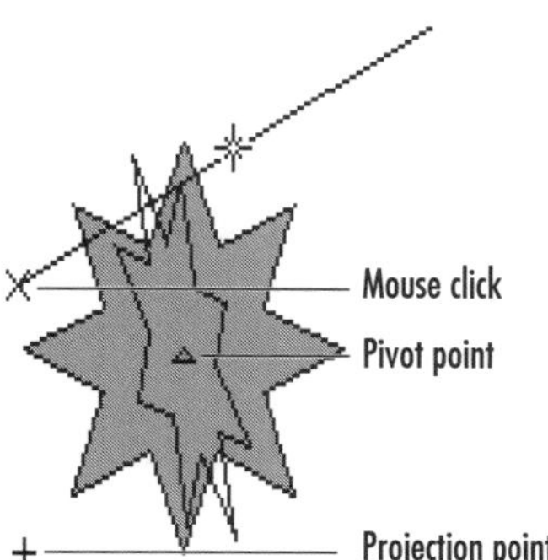

❸ *As you drag with the 3D Rotation tool, a line extends from the mouse click. Drag along the line to control the of distortion.*

❹ *The results of applying the 3D Rotation tool.*

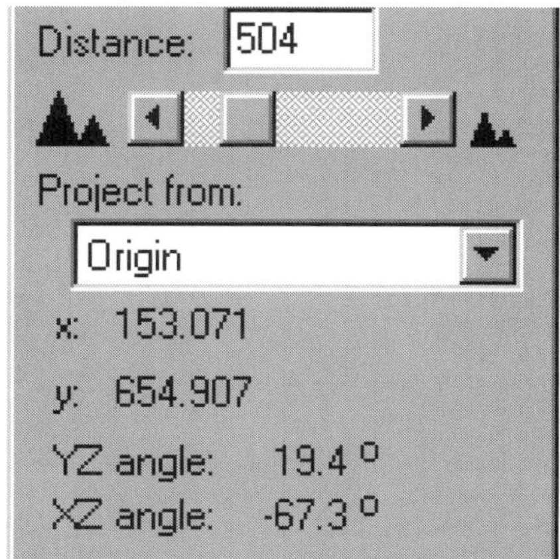

❺ *In the Expert mode, you can view the numeric changes as you drag with the 3D Rotation tool.*

Once you have chosen settings for the 3D Rotation tool, you can then apply it to objects.

To use the 3D Rotation tool:

1. Select the object or objects you want to modify.
2. Choose the 3D Rotation tool.
3. Press and drag the cursor away from this spot. A line extends out. The further along the line you drag, the greater the 3D rotation ❸.

TIP As you press, a preview shows how the object is being modified.

4. When you are satisfied with the rotation, release the mouse button, and the object changes shape ❹.

TIP In the Expert mode, use the 3D Rotation tool panel to track the changes to the object as you drag along the line ❺.

Working with the Fisheye Lens

In photography, a fisheye lens distorts the appearance of photos so that objects seem to be bulging out at the viewer. FreeHand lets you apply the same effect to graphics using the Fisheye Lens tool.

To set the Fisheye Lens tool:

1. Double-click the Fisheye Lens tool in the Xtra Tools toolbar ❻. The Fisheye Lens dialog box appears ❼.
2. Drag the Perspective slider or enter numbers in the Perspective field as follows:
   - **Convex** or positive numbers cause the object to bulge.
   - **Concave** or negative numbers cause the object to be pinched in.

   TIP The preview grid shows you a representation of what the setting will do to the object.
3. Click OK.

To use the Fisheye Lens tool:

1. Select the object you want to modify.

   TIP You must convert text to paths in order to apply the Fisheye Lens tool.
2. Drag your cursor to create an oval over the area you want to distort.

   TIP Hold the Opt/Alt key to create a distortion from the center outward.

   TIP Hold the Shift key to constrain the distortion to a circular shape.
3. Release the mouse button to apply the distortion ❽.

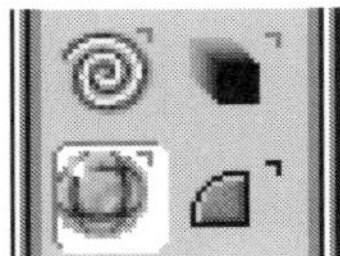

❻ *The* **Fisheye Lens tool** *in the Xtra Tools toolbar.*

Preview grid

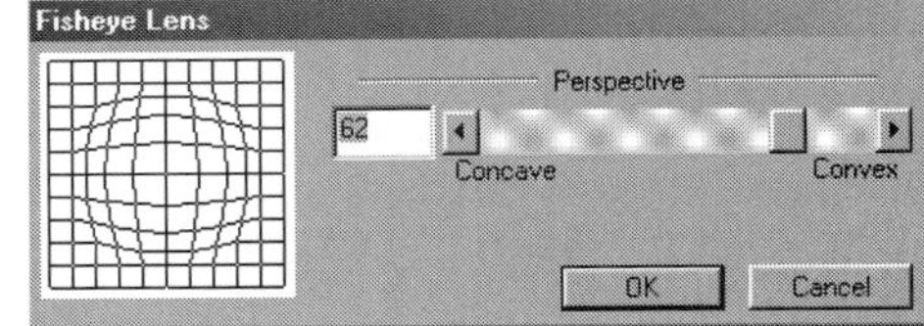

❼ *The* **Fisheye Lens dialog box.**

GAINING WEIGHT?

GAINING WEIGHT?

❽ *The results of applying the* **Fisheye Lens tool.**

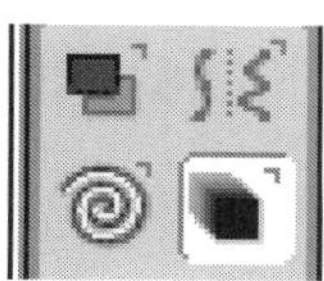

❾ *The* **Smudge tool** *in the Xtra Tools toolbar.*

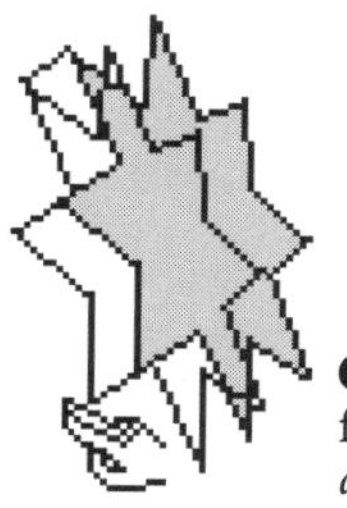

❿ *Dragging with the* **Smudge fingers** *controls the length and direction of the effect.*

⓫ *The results of applying the* **Smudge tool.**

Smudge
Smudge-To Colors
Fill:
Stroke:
Cancel OK

⓬ *The* **Smudge dialog box** *lets you set the colors that the fill and stroke fade into.*

Using the Smudge Tool

The Smudge tool provides you with a quick and easy way to add a soft edge to an object.

To use the Smudge tool:

1. Select the object or objects you want to modify.
2. Choose the Smudge tool from the Xtra Tools toolbar ❾. Your cursor changes into the Smudge fingers.
3. Drag the fingers along the direction the smudge should take. A line extends from the object. That is the length of the smudge ❿.
4. Release the mouse button to create the smudge ⓫.

TIP Spot colors used in a smudge are converted to process.

TIP Hold the Opt/Alt key to create a smudge from the center outward.

TIP The number of steps in a smudge is governed by the printer resolution in the Document inspector. If a smudge looks jagged, undo the smudge, increase the resolution, and then reapply the smudge.

If you are smudging objects over colors, the smudge should fade to those background colors. To do so, you change the smudge colors.

To change the smudge colors:

1. Double-click the Smudge tool in the Xtra Tools toolbar. This displays the Smudge dialog box ⓬.
2. Drag colors from the Color Mixer or Color List into the Fill and the Stroke boxes.
3. Click OK and then apply the smudge as usual.

Working with the Shadow Tool

A more sophisticated version of the Smudge tool is the Shadow tool.

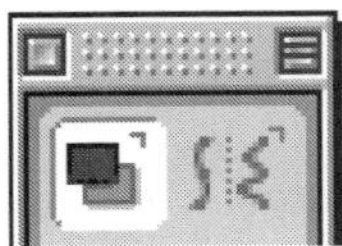

⓭ *The* **Shadow tool** *in the Xtra Tools toolbar.*

To apply a shadow:

1. Select the object or objects you want to modify.
2. Double-click the Shadow tool in the Xtra Tools toolbar ⓭. This opens the Shadow dialog box ⓮.
3. Choose one of the following from the Type menu:
   - **Hard Edge** uses a single object to create a crisp shadow.
   - **Soft Edge** uses a blend to create a shadow with a uniform soft edge.
   - **Zoom** creates a blend that is positioned to create a 3D effect.
4. Choose one of the following from the Fill menu:
   - **Color** lets you choose a specific color for the shadow.
   - **Shade** creates a shadow color that is a darker color of the original object.
   - **Tint** creates a shadow that is a lighter color of the original object.
5. Use the slider for the Color and Tint fills to adjust the lightness or darkness of the shadow.
6. Use the Scale slider to set the size of the shadow element.

TIP Less than 100% makes a shadow that is smaller than the original. Greater than 100% makes a shadow that is larger than the original.

7. Set the x and y offset amounts to position the shadow away from the original.
8. Click OK. The shadow is applied to the object ⓯.

TIP Once you have applied a shadow to an object, you can use the mouse to drag the shadow into new positions.

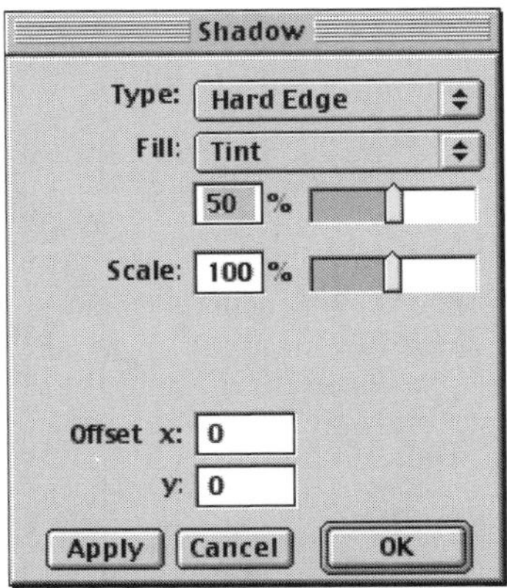

⓮ *The* **Shadow dialog box.**

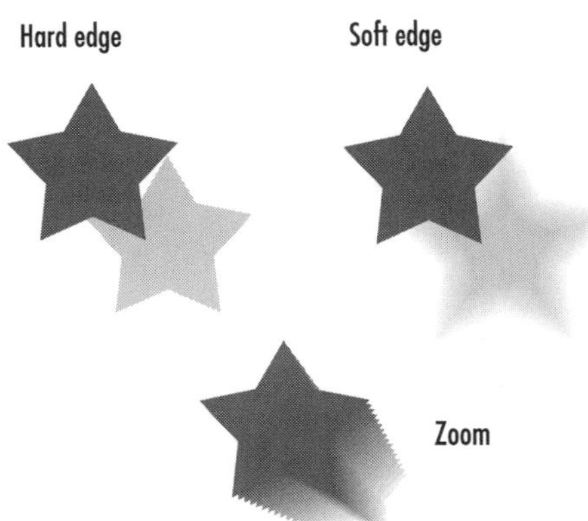

⓯ *The three different* **types of shadows.**

Working with the Shadow Tool

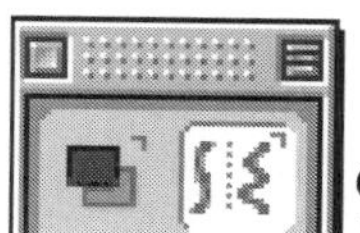

⓰ *The* **Roughen tool** *in the Xtra Tools toolbar.*

Roughen
Amount: 31
Edge: Rough / Smooth
Cancel OK

⓱ *The* **Roughen dialog box.**

NERVOUS — Smooth option

PANICKED — Rough option

⓲ *The results of applying the Roughen tool.*

Using the Roughen Tool

The Roughen tool takes clean, smooth paths and makes them irregular and ragged. This can be very useful in making artwork look hand-drawn, or less "perfect."

To set the Roughen tool options:

1. Double-click the Roughen tool in the Xtra Tools toolbar ⓰. This opens the Roughen dialog box ⓱.
2. Use the Amount slider to increase the number of segments per inch that are added using the tool.
3. Set the Edge options as follows:
   - Rough adds corner points to create the rough edge.
   - Smooth adds curved points to create the rough edge. This creates a less harsh edge to the object.
4. Click OK.

To set the Roughen tool options:

1. Select the object or objects you want to modify.
2. Drag with the Roughen tool along the object. The further you drag, the greater the distortion ⓲.

Using the Mirror Tool

The Mirror tool gives you an interactive way to create multiple rotated and reflected objects.

To set the Mirror tool controls:

1. Double-click the Mirror tool in the Xtra Tools toolbar ⓳. This opens the Mirror dialog box ⓴.
2. Use the Axis pop-up menu to choose the axis as follows ㉑:
   - **Horizontal** reflects the objects from top to bottom.
   - **Vertical** reflects the objects from left to right.
   - **Horizontal & Vertical** reflects the objects both ways at once.
   - **Multiple** reflects the objects around multiple axes.
3. In the Multiple setting, use the slider to control the number of axes the object reflects around.
4. In the Multiple setting, choose the Reflect or Rotate mode.
5. Click OK to apply the settings.

⓳ *The* **Mirror tool** *in the Xtra Tools toolbar.*

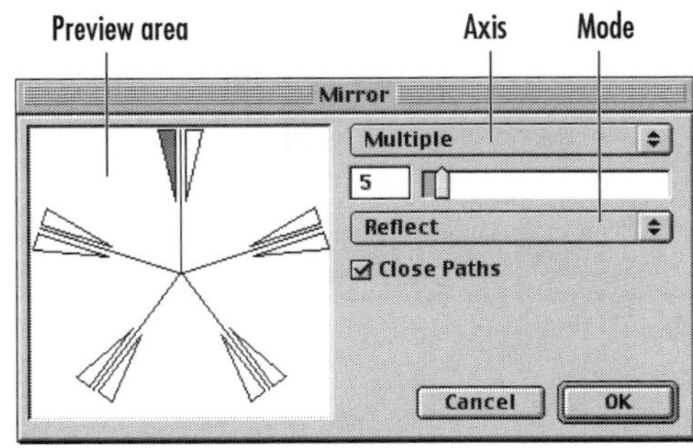

⓴ *The Mirror dialog box.*

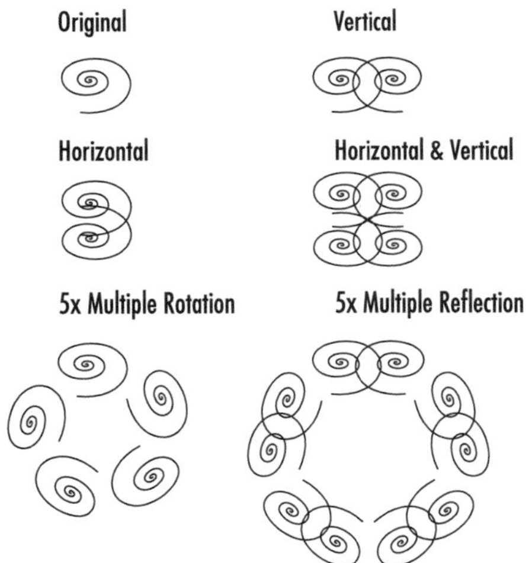

㉑ *The various effects created with the Mirror tool.*

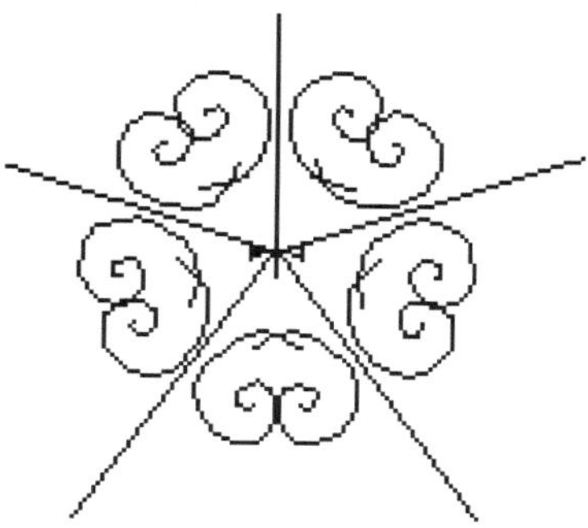

㉒ *Using the Mirror tool shows the line for the axis and a preview of the effect.*

To use the Mirror tool:

1. Select the object you want to reflect. Choose the Mirror tool in the Xtra Tools toolbar.
2. Move the cursor onto the page area and press on the point around which the reflection should occur. A line extends out showing the axis that the object is reflected around ㉒. A preview of the reflection appears.
3. Drag the cursor until you are satisfied with the effect.
4. Release the mouse button to apply the Mirror tool effect.

TIP Tap the left- or right-arrow keys to decrease or increase the number of axes in the multiple setting.

TIP Tap the up- or down-arrow keys to change the Multiple setting from reflect to rotate.

TIP Hold the Opt/Alt key to rotate the angle of the axis.

Working with the Graphic Hose

The Graphic Hose allows you to store objects (including bitmapped images, text, envelopes and symbols) and then drag on the page to paint with those objects. There are two parts to using the Graphic Hose: storing the objects in the Graphics Hose panel and setting the options for painting with the hose.

Objects for the Graphic Hose are stored as sets within the Graphic Hose panel.

To store objects in the Graphic Hose panel:

1. Double-click the Graphic Hose tool in the Xtra Tools toolbar ㉓. This opens the Graphic Hose panel ㉔.
2. Click Hose to display the Hose sets.
3. Choose New from the Sets pop-up menu to add a new set. A dialog box appears where you can name the new set.
4. Copy the artwork.
5. Click Paste in. The artwork appears in the preview window as an object in the Contents pop-up menu.
6. Copy and paste additional artwork into the set. The artwork is added as a new object to the Contents menu.

TIP There is a limit of 10 objects for each set.

TIP Graphic Hose sets are available for any document and other sessions of working with FreeHand.

TIP You can use symbols *(see Chapter 22, "Symbols")* as the elements for the Graphic Hose. This allows you to modify the symbol element and all the objects created by the Graphic Hose update automatically.

㉓ *The* **Graphic Hose tool** *in the Xtra Tools toolbar.*

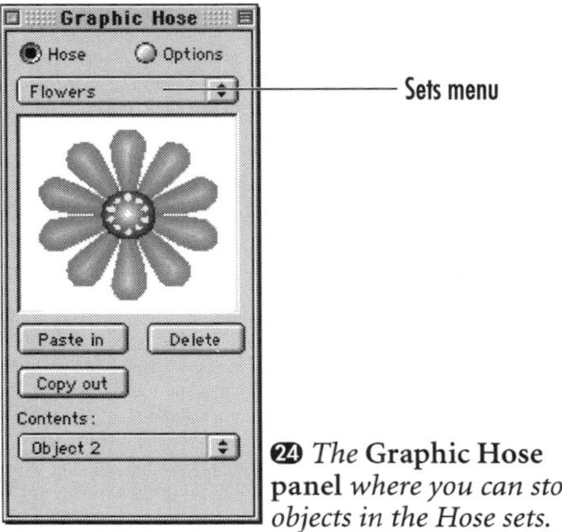

㉔ *The* **Graphic Hose panel** *where you can store objects in the Hose sets.*

How useful is the Graphic Hose?

From the first moment it was introduced, the Graphic Hose has been compared to the scatter brushes found in Adobe Illustrator. Unfortunately, the Graphic Hose came up short in the comparison. Illustrator's brushes not only scattered objects around the page, but they could be edited later to change the objects or their positions.

Today, FreeHand has its own spray brushes that provide the same features. So how useful is the Graphic Hose?

Although I'm sure there are some things that are uniquely suited for Graphic Hose, for the most part it has been replaced by FreeHand's brushes.

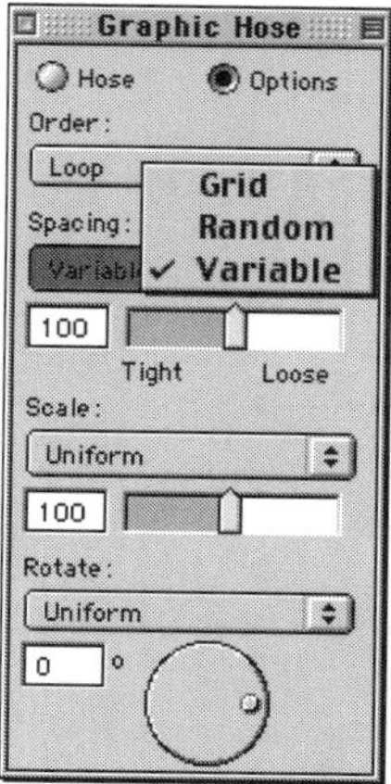

㉕ *The* **Graphic Hose Options** *controls let you change how the objects go on the page.*

㉖ *The original two stars (circled) were used to create the different sized and rotated stars.*

Once you have created Hose sets, you need to set the Options to control how the Graphic Hose applies objects on the page.

To use the Graphic Hose tool:

1. Double-click the Graphic Hose tool in the Xtra Tools toolbar. This opens the Graphic Hose panel ㉕.
2. Click the Options radio button to display the Options controls.
3. Use the Order menu to control the order that objects are placed on the page:
   - **Loop** applies the objects in numerical order.
   - **Back and Forth** applies the objects in forward then reverse order.
   - **Random** applies the objects in no specific order.
4. Use the Spacing menu to control the distance between the objects:
   - **Grid** applies the objects onto a grid with a size you set in the Grid field.
   - **Variable** applies the objects in a spacing that you set as Tight or Loose.
   - **Random** applies the objects with no specific distance between them.
5. Use the Scale pop-up menu to control the size of the objects:
   - **Uniform** sets a certain size for all the objects.
   - **Random** applies the objects in no specific sizes.
6. Use the Rotate menu and angle wheel to control the rotation of the objects.
   - **Uniform** sets one angle for all objects.
   - **Incremental** applies rotations that change in specific increments from one object to the next.
   - **Random** rotates the objects without any order.
7. Once you have set all the options, drag the Graphic Hose on the page to apply the Hose artwork ㉖.

Working with the Bend Tool

The Bend tool applies a distortion to objects to warp the path segments in or out.

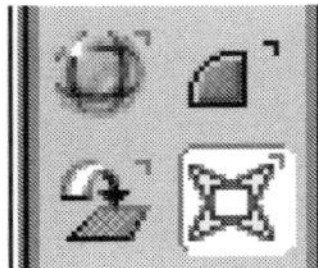

㉗ *The* **Bend tool** *in the Xtra Tools toolbar.*

To set the Bend tool options:

1. Double-click the Bend tool in the Xtra Tools toolbar ㉗. This opens the Bend dialog box ㉘.
2. Adjust the slider or enter an amount in the field to increase or decrease the number of points per inch that are added.
3. Click OK.

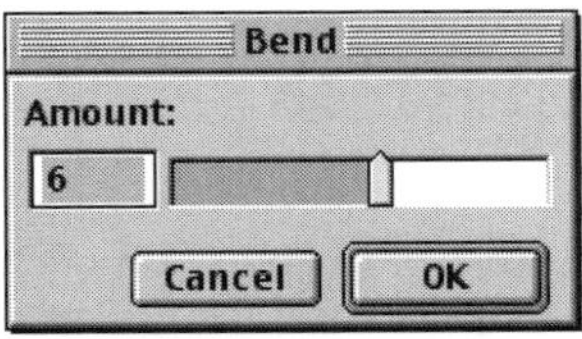

㉘ *The* **Bend dialog box** *allows you to control the number of points per inch that are added during a bend distortion.*

To use the Bend tool:

- With the object selected, drag down to create a rounded bend ㉙.

  or

  Drag up to create a spiked bend ㉙.

TIP The point where you start the drag is the center of the distortion.

TIP The longer you drag, the greater the amount of the bend.

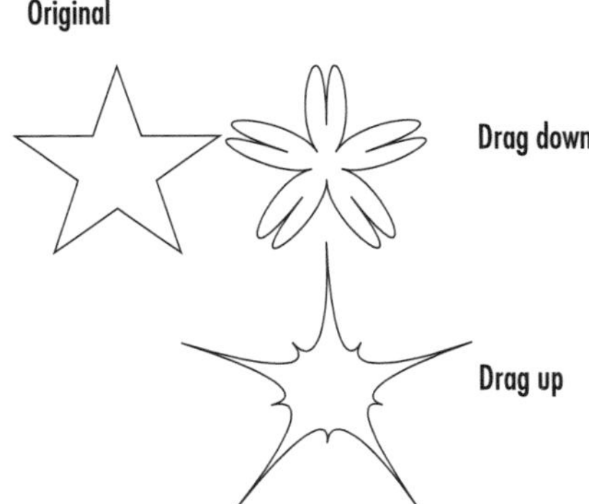

㉙ *The* **results of applying the Bend tool.**

Using third-party Xtras

In addition to the Macromedia Xtras, there are third-party Xtras that you can use within FreeHand. These Xtras allow you to do things you cannot ordinarily do in FreeHand. For instance, VectorTools from Extensis gives you far more control over color than you have using the FreeHand Xtras. Other popular Xtras are KPT Vector Effects from MetaCreations, 3D Invigorator from Zaxwerks, and MAPublisher from Avenza Software. Follow the instructions with the Xtras to install them. After you install them, third-party Xtras are listed either in their own menu or in one of the FreeHand Xtras categories.

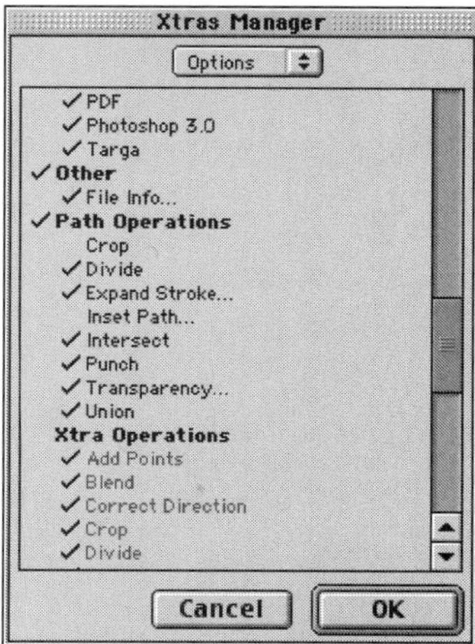

30 *(Mac) Click the checkmark in the Xtras Manager makes the Xtras active or inactive.*

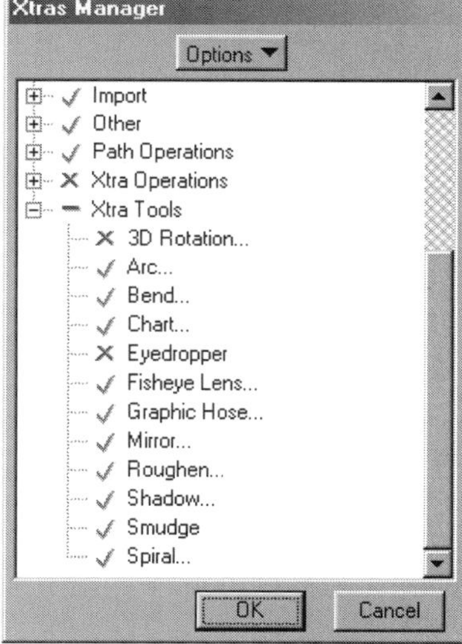

31 *(Win) A checkmark indicates the Xtra is active. An X indicates the Xtra is inactive.*

Controlling Xtras

If you install many third-party Xtras, the Xtras may conflict with each other. FreeHand comes with an Xtras Manager that allows you to turn the Xtras on or off. This can be helpful if you are trying to discover the source of an Xtras conflict or to avoid conflicts.

To use the Xtras Manager:

1. Choose **Xtras > Xtras Manager.** The Xtras Manager dialog box appears 30–31.
2. Click next to each Xtra to make it active or inactive.

   or

   Use the Options pop-up menu to turn all the Xtras on or off.

TIP The Windows Xtra Manager lets you open or close the Xtra categories using the plus or minus signs.

Once an Xtra is used from the Xtras menu, it appears as the Repeat [Xtra] command. This means that the Xtra can be reapplied via a keystroke.

To use the Repeat Xtra command:

- Choose Xtra > Repeat [Xtra]

  or

  (Mac) Press **Command-Shift-+.**

  (Win) Press **Ctrl-Alt-Shift-X.**

CHARTS AND GRAPHS 25

Here's where Macromedia FreeHand gets down to business—creating mathematically correct charts and graphs. Even if you don't understand the mathematics of graphs—and I know few designers who do—you can still create exceptional graphs using FreeHand's charts and graph commands.

Illustration programs such as FreeHand have given many people the tools to translate data into charts and graphs.

Unfortunately, the integrity of the data can be easily compromised when translated into a graphic display. For an excellent study on maintaining graphical integrity in charts, see *The Visual Display of Quantitative Information* by Edward R. Tufte, published by Graphics Press.

Creating Charts or Graphs

To create a chart or graph, you need to open the worksheet and enter the data.

To open the worksheet:

1. Click the Chart tool in the Xtra Tools palette.
2. Drag the + sign cursor to create a rectangle on your work page. (The size of the rectangle determines the size of the chart.) The Chart worksheet appears ❶.

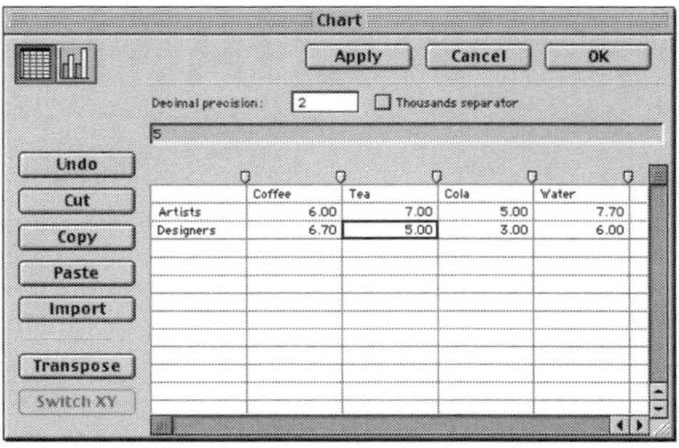

❶ *The* **chart worksheet** *is where you enter data for a chart or graph.*

To enter data:

1. Type the data in the data entry area. This inserts the data into the currently active cell.
2. Press Return or Enter to apply the data to the cell and move to the cell below. Type the data for that cell.
3. Press Tab to apply the data to the cell and jump to the cell to the right.
4. Use the up, down, left, or right arrow keys to move to different cells.
5. Use the Import button to bring tab-delimited text directly into the worksheet.

Once you have entered the data, you need to choose the type of graph or chart you will create.

To style a graph or chart:

1. Click the chart style icon at the top of the Chart window. The worksheet disappears and the styling selections appears ❷.
2. Click one of the six chart type icons: grouped column, stacked column, line, pie, area, and scatter.

TIP To see the effects of changing the style and features of your graph, click Apply at the top of the Chart window.

TIP Use the Subselect tool to select an individual element in a chart.

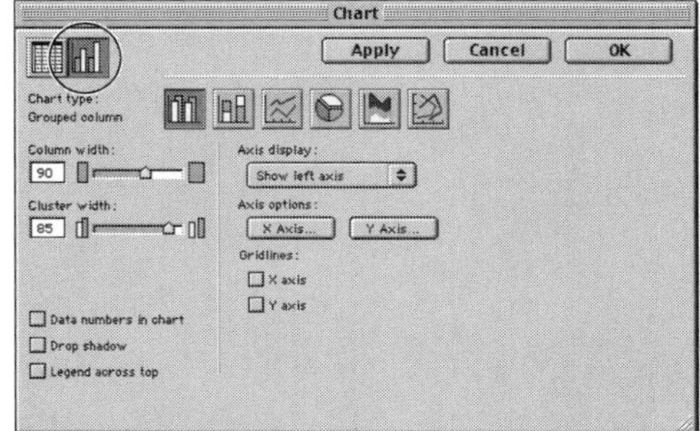

❷ *The* **Style icon** *(circled) switches from the worksheet to the controls for styling charts and graphs.*

❸ *The* grouped column graph *icon.*

❹ *The* stacked column graph *icon.*

❺ *The* line graph *icon.*

❻ *The* pie chart *icon.*

❼ *The* area graph *icon.*

❽ *The* scatter graph *icon.*

When to use a grouped column graph

Use a grouped column graph to compare data ❸. Each bar represents one data cell.

When to use a stacked column graph

Use a stacked column graph to compare the progress of data ❹. Each stacked bar represents one row of data.

When to use a line graph

Use a line graph to compare the trend of data over time ❺. Each line represents a column.

When to use a pie chart

Use a Pie chart to display data as percentages of the total ❻. Each wedge represents one data cell. Each row creates a separate chart.

When to use an area graph

Use an area graph to compare the trend of data over a period of time ❼. Each area represents a column of data. Each column's value is added to the previous column's total.

When to use a scatter graph

Use a scatter graph ❽ to plot data as paired sets of coordinates. Each coordinate represents a row of data containing two cells.

To modify an existing chart:

- Double-click the Chart tool in the Xtra toolbar.

  or

  Choose **Xtras > Chart > Edit.** The Chart worksheet opens.

TIP Don't ungroup a chart or graph, or you will lose the link to the worksheet information.

Formatting Column Graphs

Once you have entered data in the worksheet and picked the style of the graph, you can still modify various elements of the graph. These controls change depending on the type of graph selected.

To change the column width:

1. Click the icon for grouped column or stacked column graphs.
2. To change the width that each column takes up within its cluster, drag the slider or enter the amount in the Column width field ❾.
3. Click Apply to see the effects on the graph ❿.

To change the cluster width:

1. Click the icon for a grouped column or stacked column graph.
2. To change the width of the cluster of the columns, drag the slider or enter the amount in the Cluster width field.
3. Click Apply to see the effects on the chart ⓫.

All the graphs except area graphs let you display the data values in the graph itself.

To show the data values:

- Click the Data numbers in chart checkbox to see those values.

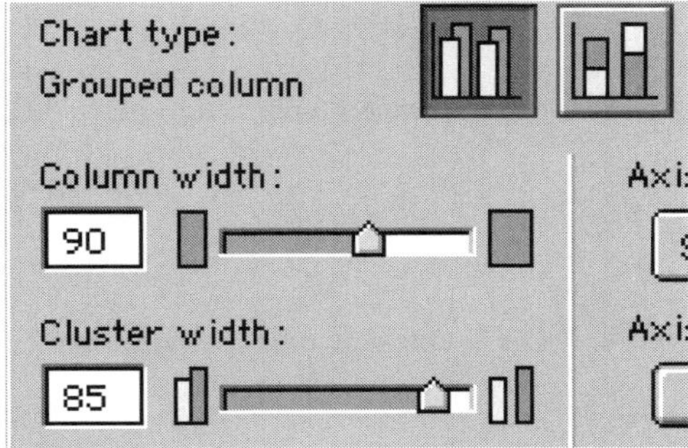

❾ *The controls for* **Column width** *are available for grouped column and stacked column graphs.*

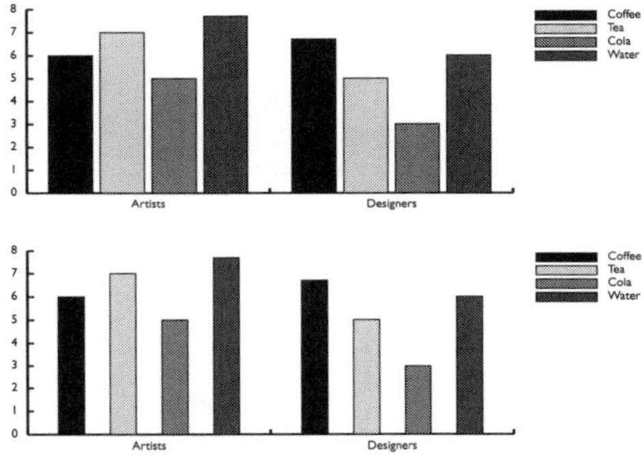

❿ *A* **column width** *of 85 (top) and 50 (bottom).*

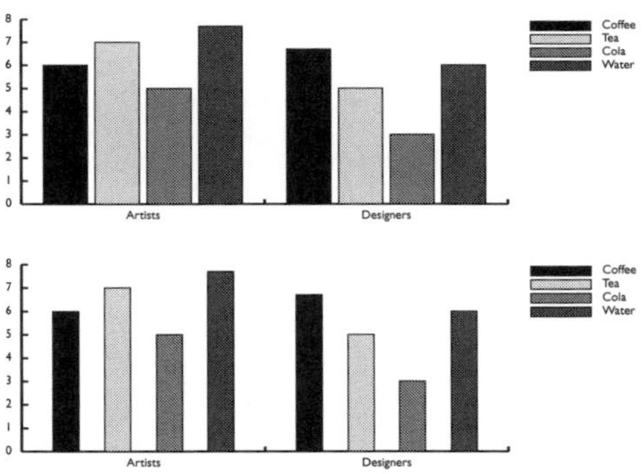

⓫ *A* **cluster width** *of 90 (top) and 50 (bottom)*

Formatting Column Graphs

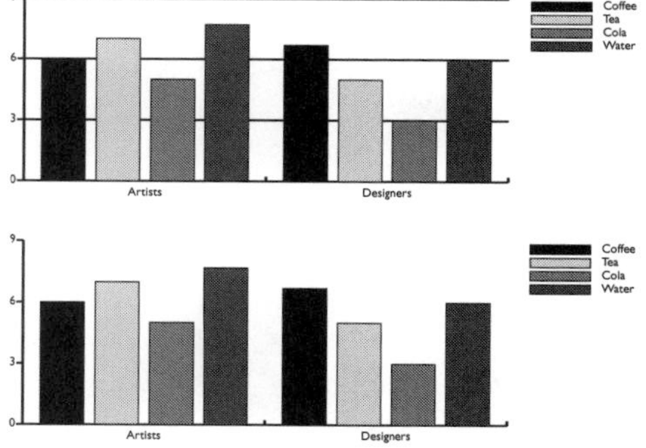

⓬ *X axis* **gridlines** *turned off (top) and turned on (bottom).*

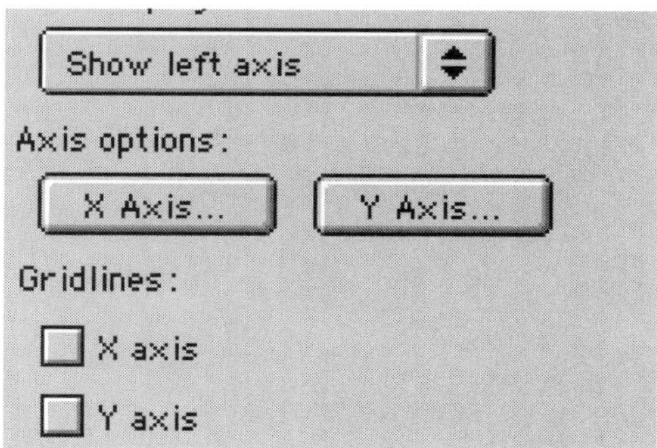

⓭ *The* **Gridlines** *boxes show and hide the* **x** *axis and* **y** *axis gridlines.*

Charts are always created using shades of black. However, you can change the colors applied to the charts.

To color a chart:

- Drag colors onto individual elements.

  or

  Subselect objects and change them through the color list.

TIP you can also use the Find and Replace Graphics dialog box to change each color globally.

All the graphs except line and scatter graphs let you add a drop shadow behind the graph.

To add a drop shadow:

- Click the Drop shadow checkbox to see the effect.

To move the legend:

- Click the Legend across top checkbox.

All the graphs except the pie chart allow you to control whether or not gridlines are displayed along the x or y axis ⓬.

To create gridlines:

1. Check the **x** axis box to display horizontal gridlines.
2. Check the **y** axis box to display vertical gridlines ⓭.

The most powerful part of modifying a column graph is in working with the x (horizontal) axis and the y (vertical) axis. You can modify how numerical values are displayed along an axis; if the axis has no numerical values, the options are grayed out.

To modify the axis values:

1. With a chart selected and the Chart dialog box open, click either the X axis or Y axis buttons under Axis options. The Options dialog box appears ⓮.
2. Under Axis values, click Calculate from data if you want the numbers along the axis to be calculated from the data entered in the worksheet.

   or

   Under Axis values, click Manual to enter your own values for the axis.
3. Choose the following from the Major Tick marks pop-up menu ⓯:
   - **Across axis** positions the tick marks so they straddle the axis.
   - **Inside axis** positions the marks inside the axis line.
   - **Outside axis** positions the marks outside the axis line.
4. Choose the following from the Minor Tick marks pop-up menu:
   - **Across axis** positions the tick marks so they straddle the axis.
   - **Inside axis** positions the marks inside the axis line.
   - **Outside axis** positions the marks outside the axis line.

TIP Many designers like to position the major tick marks across the axis, and the minor tick marks inside the axis.

5. Enter the number of minor tick marks in the Count field.
6. Use the Prefix and Suffix Axis value labels to add a prefix (such as $) in front of the data or a suffix (such as /hour) after the data in the axis.

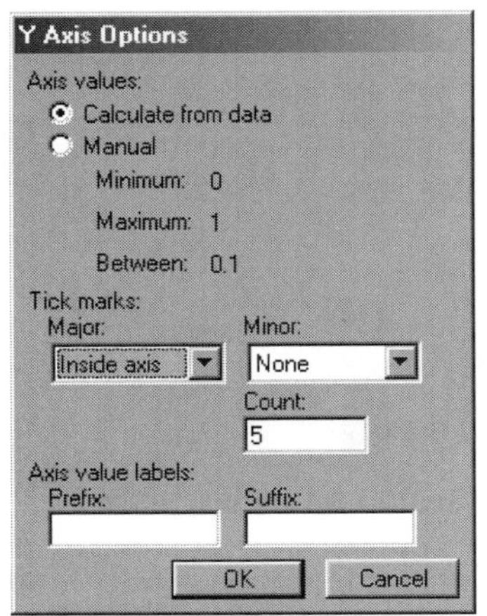

⓮ *The* **Y Axis Options** *dialog box.*

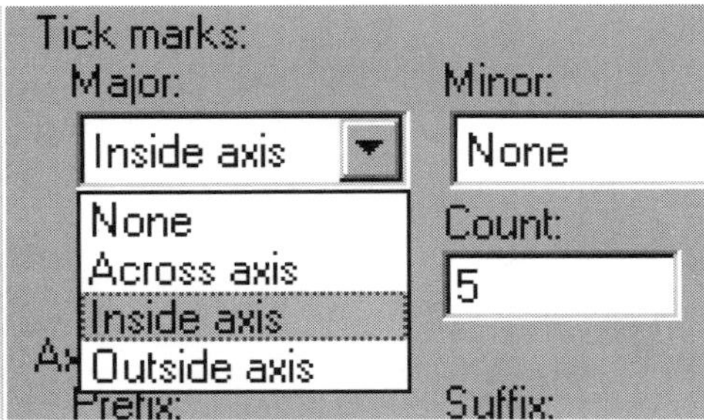

⓯ *The* **Tick marks Options.**

Formatting Column Graphs

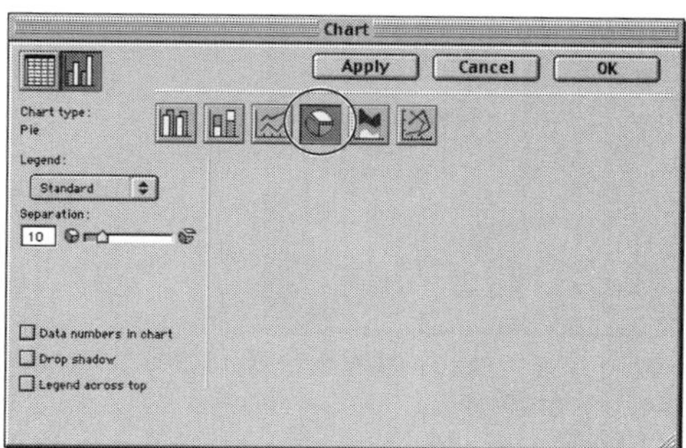

⓰ *Click the* **Pie-chart icon** *(circled) to see the options.*

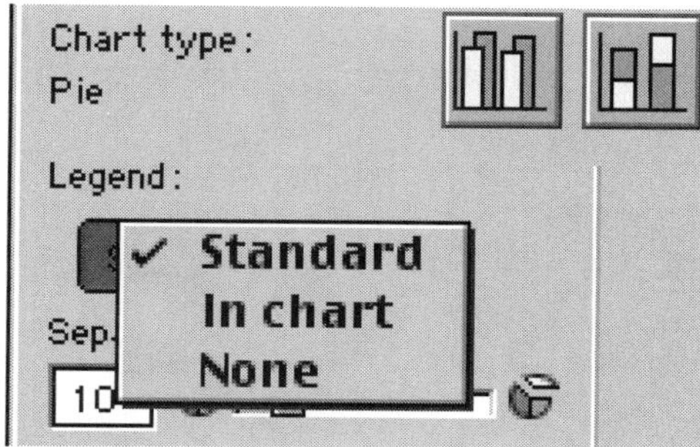

⓱ *The* **Legend options** *for a pie chart.*

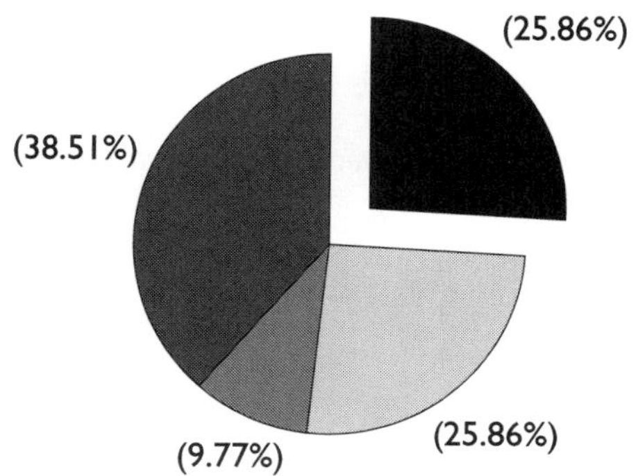

⓲ *A* **Separation amount** *of 28 has moved the black wedge away from the rest of the pie chart.*

Working with Pie Charts

When you create a pie chart, you have special controls for working with the wedges.

To create a pie chart:

◆ Click the pie chart icon in the Chart dialog box. The pie chart options appear ⓰.

To modify a pie chart legend:

◆ Choose the following from the Legend pop-up menu ⓱:
  - **Standard** positions the legend on the side of the chart.
  - **In chart** positions the legend next to each wedge.
  - **None** hides the legend.

The first cell of data creates a wedge that can be moved away from the other segments.

To change the wedge separation:

◆ Drag the slider or enter an amount in the Separation field. This moves the first wedge away from the rest of the chart ⓲.

TIP To enter numbers as labels, not graph data, insert quotation marks around the numbers. For example, the year 1997 would be entered as "1997."

Working with Pictographs

FreeHand also lets you put graphics into the columns of your charts. These graphics, called pictographs, give visual representations of the type of data being shown.

To insert a pictograph in a chart:

1. Find the graphic that you would like to have in the chart.

TIP You can use a FreeHand graphic or an imported file as the pictograph image.

2. Select the graphic and copy it.
3. Select one column of the series to which you want to apply the pictograph.
4. Choose **Xtras > Chart > Pictograph.** The Pictograph dialog box appears.
5. Click Paste in. The copied graphic appears in the preview window ⓳.
6. To repeat the graphic within the column, click the Repeating box. To stretch the graphic within the column, leave the box unchecked.
7. Click OK. The Pictograph replaces the column of the chart ⓴.

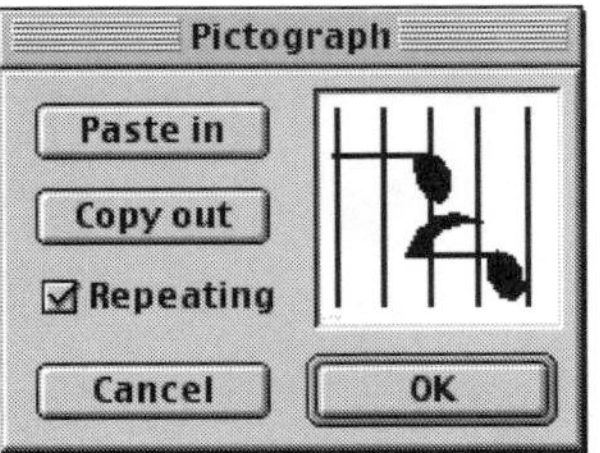

⓳ *The* **Pictograph** *box, where you can paste in the pictograph for a selected series.*

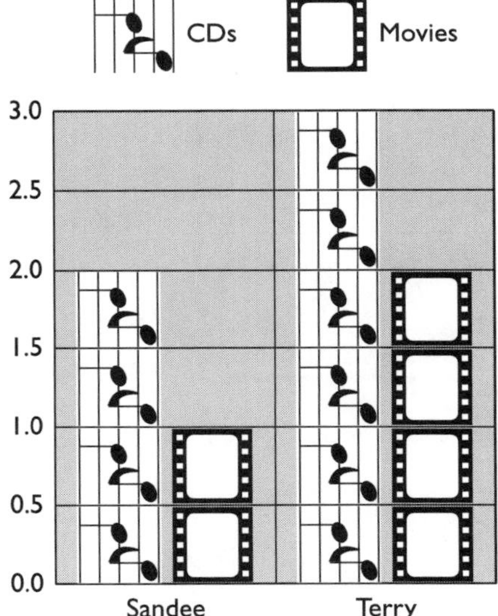

⓴ *An example of a chart that uses pictographs for the columns.*

RASTER IMAGES 26

As mentioned earlier, almost all the objects in Macromedia FreeHand are vector objects. However, the other type of object is called a *raster* or *pixel-based* object.

Raster images are usually scanned photos or graphics from programs such as Corel Painter or Adobe Photoshop. These images can then be imported into a FreeHand document where you can add vector shapes and type to the raster image.

You can also convert FreeHand objects into rasters images. This lets you apply certain filters such as soft blurs that are not available when working with vector images.

Importing Raster Images

FreeHand has several different ways to import raster images into a document.

To import artwork using the File menu:

1. Choose **File > Import.**
2. Use the dialog box to find the image you want to import. The cursor changes into a corner symbol ❶.

TIP If you are going to print your artwork, import a TIFF or EPS file.

3. Click the corner symbol to import the file in its original size.

   or

   Drag the corner symbol to set the image to a specific size ❷.

TIP Unless you have changed the Import Preferences settings, the placed image is only linked to the FreeHand file. You must send the original image along with the FreeHand file for it to print properly.

To import artwork by copying and pasting:

1. Open the file from which you want to import artwork.
2. Select the artwork you want to import and copy it to the clipboard.
3. Bring the FreeHand document to the front and choose **Edit > Paste.**

TIP The artwork is imported as a group which becomes an embedded TIFF when ungrouped. *(See pages 313—314 for understanding embedded images.)*

TIP (Mac) You can drag and drop artwork from applications onto the FreeHand document.

❶ *The* **corner symbol** *indicates that you have a file ready for importing.*

❷ **Drag the corner symbol** *to size a placed image.*

❸ *Drag a corner handle to change the size of an imported image.*

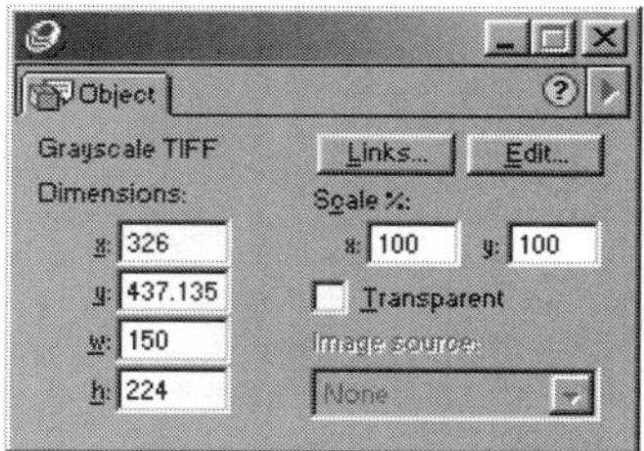

❹ *The* **Object Inspector** *lets you resize images.*

❺ *You can modify raster images with the transformation handles or the transformation tools.*

Modifying Raster Images

Once you have imported an image, there are many ways to modify that image.

To resize raster images by dragging:

1. Place the Pointer tool on one of the corner handles of the raster image.
2. Drag to change the size of the image ❸.

TIP Hold the Shift key to retain the horizontal and vertical proportions of the image.

To resize raster images numerically:

1. With the image selected, open the Object inspector ❹.
2. Use the **Scale %** **x** and **y** fields to change the size of the image.

   or

   Enter the dimensions in the **w** and **h** fields.
3. Press Return or Enter to apply the changes.

To transform a raster image:

1. Double-click the image.
2. Use the transformation handles to rotate, skew or scale the image ❺.

   or

   Use any of the transformation tools (rotating, scaling, reflecting, skewing) to modify the image.

FreeHand also lets you change the color of grayscale or black-and-white TIFF and PICT images.

To colorize a raster image:

1. Select a black-and-white or grayscale image.
2. Drag a color swatch from the Color List or Color Mixer onto the image ❻.

To make a raster image transparent:

1. Select a grayscale image.
2. Click Transparent in the Object inspector. This converts the image to black (or some other color) and transparent and lets objects behind your image show through the clear areas ❼.

TIP The image must be grayscale or the Transparent checkbox will not be active.

FreeHand also lets you change the shade, or lightness and contrast, of grayscale or black-and-white TIFF and PICT images.

To change the shade of an imported image:

1. Select a black-and-white or grayscale image.
2. Click the Edit button in the Object inspector. The Image dialog box appears ❽.
3. Click the controls for Lightness or Contrast.

   or

   Adjust the slider bars.

   or

   Click one of the preset controls.

TIP You can change the shade or color of a portion of an image by putting one of the transparency lens fills over an raster image *(see page 184)*.

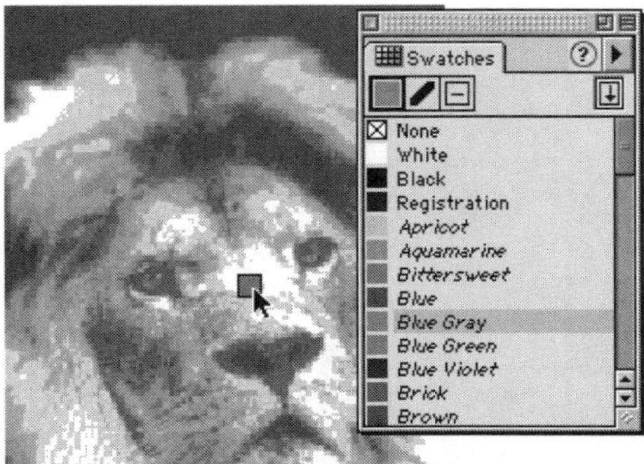

❻ **Drag a color swatch** *onto black-and-white or grayscale TIFF or PICT to colorize the images.*

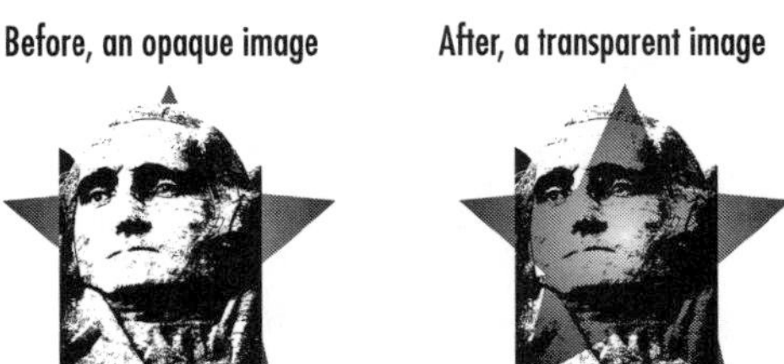

❼ *The results of applying the* **Transparent option** *to a grayscale image.*

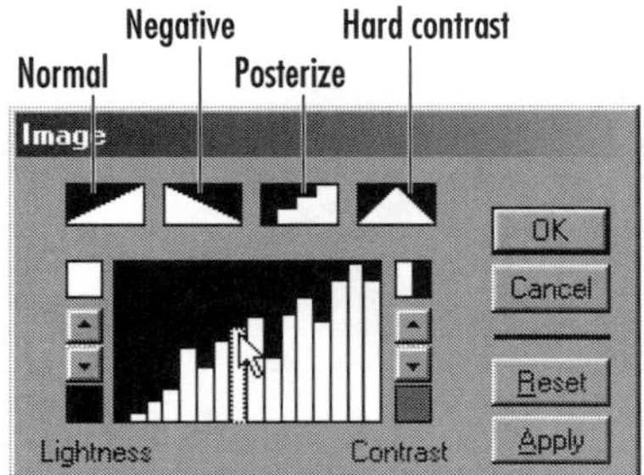

❽ *Drag the bars up or down to change the appearance of the raster image.*

❾ *The* KPT 3 Twirl filter *applied to a placed image.*

You can also use Photoshop-compatible plug-ins within FreeHand to modify raster images.

TIP Only those plug-ins written to the specifications of Photoshop version 3 will work within FreeHand.

To install Photoshop filters within FreeHand (Mac):

- Move or copy the plug-ins (or an alias) into the **FreeHand: English: Xtras folder.**

To install Photoshop filters within FreeHand (Win):

- Move or copy the plug-ins into the **Program Files\Macromedia\FreeHand10\English\Xtras file.**

TIP Photoshop filters appear in the FreeHand Xtras menu with [TIFF] before the name of the Xtra. For instance, a filter might be listed as *[TIFF] Solarize*. This indicates that the filter only works on bitmapped images.

To apply a Photoshop filter to a TIFF image:

1. Select the placed TIFF image.
2. From the Xtras menu, choose the Photoshop filter you want to apply.
3. If a dialog box or a settings box appears, follow the steps necessary to adjust the settings for the filter.
4. Click the prompt to apply the filter to the image ❾.

TIP When you use any Photoshop filters on TIFF images in FreeHand, the result is an embedded TIFF image.

Rasterizing FreeHand Graphics

You might want to convert FreeHand's vector graphics into their pixel-based equivalents. (For instance, you might want to apply a Photoshop filter to the raster file.)

To rasterize an image:

1. Select the vector objects you want to convert.
2. Choose **Modify > Rasterize.** The Rasterize dialog box appears ⑩.
3. Set the resolution to the amount you need.

TIP Most print work use a resolution of 300 dpi. Web graphics need only 72 dpi.

4. Set the anti-aliasing amount. This smooths lines or edges in the image with a slight blur.

TIP High resolutions and high anti-aliasing require more memory for the FreeHand application.

5. Click OK. The objects turn into rasterized art embedded in the file ⑪.

TIP If you are working with Adobe Photoshop, you can copy and paste or drag and drop vectors directly from FreeHand into Photoshop. You then have the option of rasterizing the vectors as pixels or pasting as a vector or path.

⑩ *The* **Rasterize** *dialog box controls how artwork is converted into a pixel-based image.*

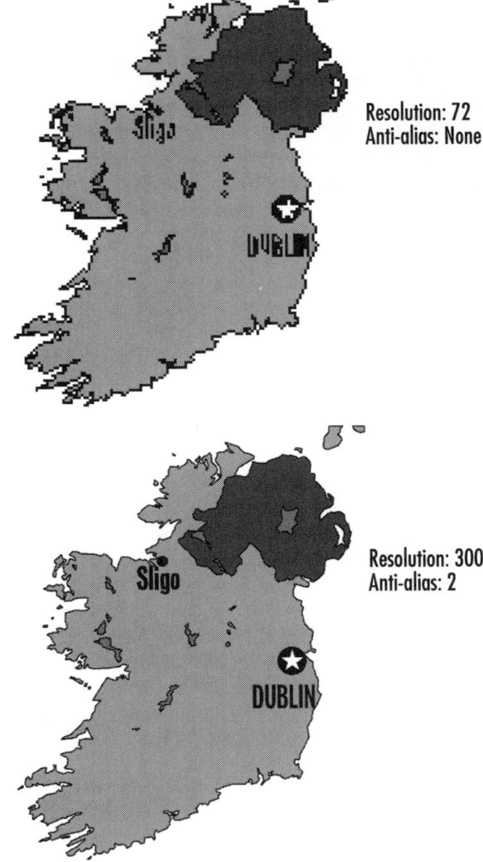

⑪ *Use the Rasterize command at two different resolutions and anti-aliasing amounts.*

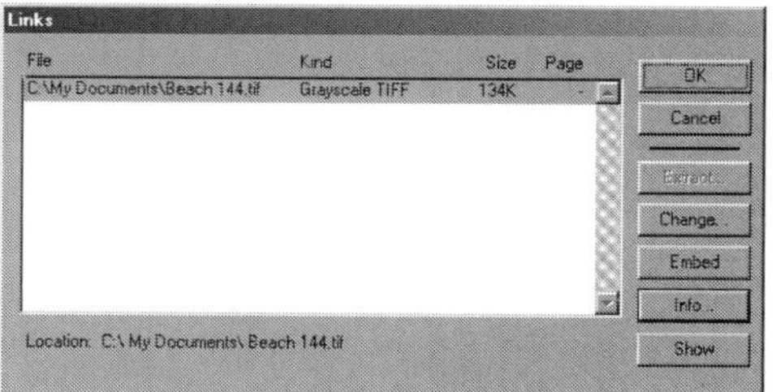

⓬ *The* **Links dialog box** *shows a list of all the imported images in the FreeHand file.*

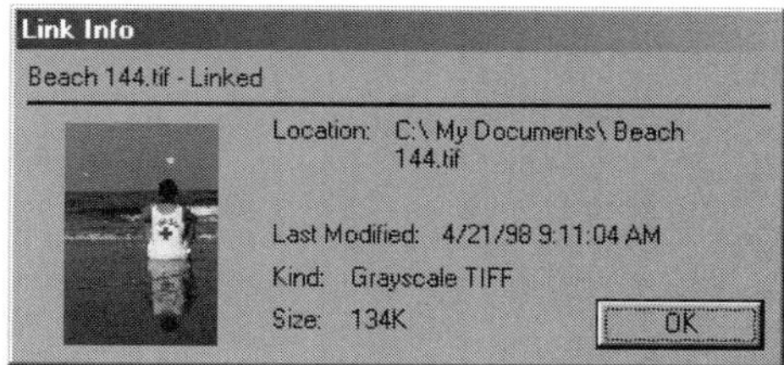

⓭ *The* **Link Info dialog box** *displays the specific information for each linked image.*

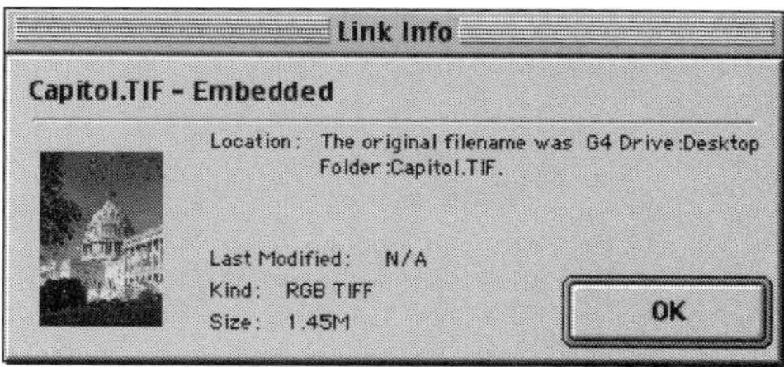

⓮ *The Link Info dialog box shows the former name for embedded images.*

Linking and Embedding Images

As mentioned earlier, the images you import into FreeHand are not actually included in the file. Rather, these images are linked to the original raster file. FreeHand makes it easy to work with linked images.

To view the link information:

1. Choose Edit > Links. This opens the Links dialog box ⓬.

   or

   With the raster image selected, click the Links button in the Object inspector.
2. Click the Info button. This opens the Link Info dialog box which contains the specific information for the imported image ⓭.

Ordinarily, you want to keep raster images linked to their outside file. This helps reduce the size of the FreeHand file. However, if the imported image is small enough, you can embed it in the FreeHand document.

TIP When you embed an image, the FreeHand file contains all the information necessary to print and edit the file.

To embed a linked image:

1. Select the name of the linked image in the Links dialog box.
2. Click the Embed button. FreeHand changes the status of the file from linked to embedded.

TIP The Link Info dialog box displays the information for an embedded image including the original filename ⓮.

Linking and Embedding Images

FreeHand looks for linked images where they were when imported. If you move a linked file, you create a missing link. *(Good-bye!)*

To open a file with a missing link:

1. Open the file. The Locate file dialog box alerts you that the link is missing ⑮.
2. Click the Ignore All or Ignore buttons to open the file without updating the link.

   or

   Navigate to find the missing link file.
3. Click Search the current folder for missing links to update any additional missing links.

You can also update missing links using the Links Info dialog box.

To update a missing link:

1. Open the Links Info dialog box. The missing link is displayed in italics ⑯.
2. Select the missing link entry.
3. Click the Change button. This opens the Open dialog box.
4. Navigate to find the missing link and click Open. This re-establishes the link.

When you rasterize FreeHand elements *(see page 312)*, the resulting image is embedded. Also, when you use a Photoshop filter on a raster image, the result is an embedded image. You can use the Extract command to turn these files into linked images.

To extract an embedded image:

1. Select the image that is embedded in the FreeHand file.
2. Click the Links button in the Object inspector to open the Links dialog box.
3. The Extract button opens the Save (Mac) or Extract Import (Win) dialog box. This lets you choose a name and destination for the extracted image.

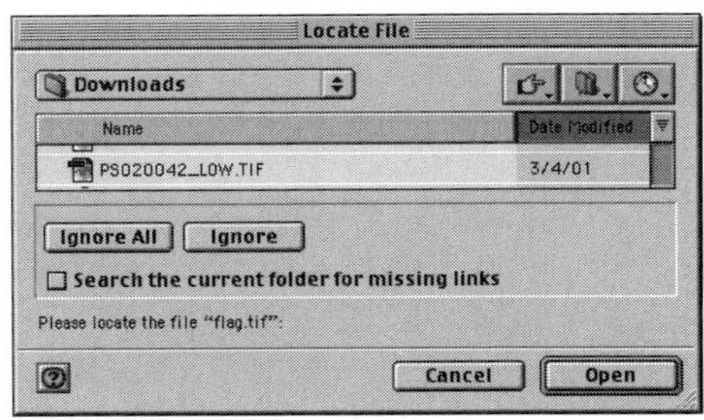

⑮ *Use the* **Locate dialog box** *to re-establish a missing link.*

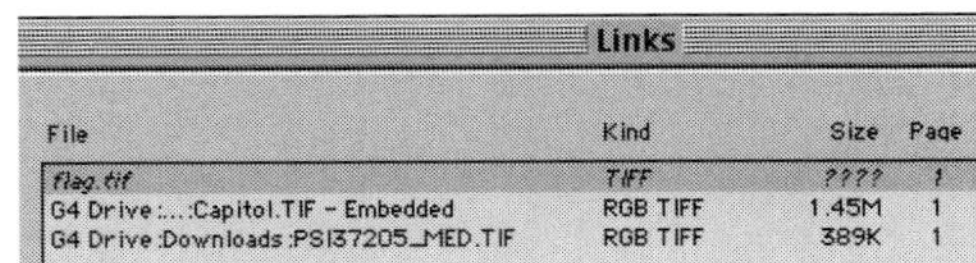

⑯ *The italic typeface and question marks indicate that a imported file is missing its link.*

Linking and Embedding Images

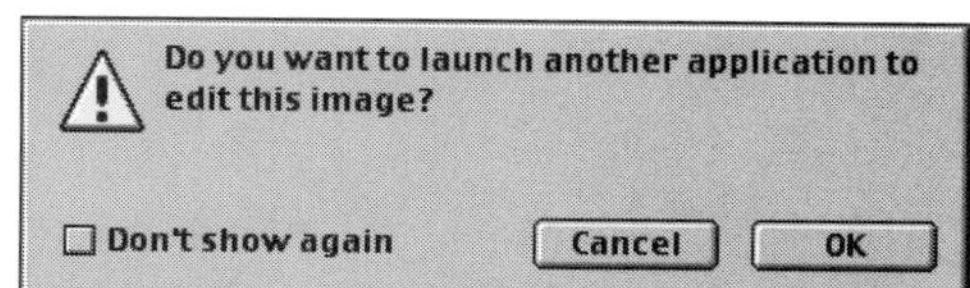

⓱ *This dialog box asks you to confirm that you want to edit the image in another application.*

⓲ *The* **Editing in Progress** *dialog box lets you choose when you have finished editing a file in an external application.*

Editing Raster Images

You can use FreeHand to open the application, such as Macromedia Fireworks or Adobe Photoshop, that created the linked image. This lets you easily modify the image and update it in the FreeHand file.

To edit an image with an external application:

1. Select the image you want to edit.
2. Choose **Edit >External Editor.** A dialog box asks to confirm that you want to open an external application ⓱.
3. Click OK. This opens the image using the application specified in the Object preferences *(see Appendix C).*

TIP If you have not specified an external editing application, a dialog box appears which asks you to choose an application. This application becomes the default until you change it in the Preferences dialog box.

4. When you have completed your edits, save your changes in the external application.
5. Return to your FreeHand document and click Done in the Editing in Progress dialog box to implement your changes or click Cancel to leave the graphic as it was ⓲.

TIP You can also activate the external editing function by holding Opt/Alt key and double-clicking on a graphic.

EXPORTING 27

It's not enough to save files in the Macromedia FreeHand format. Today's designers need to convert files into many different formats.

For instance, you may want to add your FreeHand graphics to Microsoft Word or Microsoft PowerPoint files. If you save in the FreeHand EPS format, you will find that the file doesn't print well to a non-PostScript printer such as an ink-jet printer. So you will need to convert the file into a format that prints well on an ink-jet printer.

You might need to send your file to someone who uses (gasp!) Adobe Illustrator. Fortunately, you can easily change the FreeHand file to the Illustrator format.

Converting FreeHand files from one format to another is called exporting.

Basic Exporting

FreeHand offers you many different ways to convert or export your files into formats that can be read by other applications. Because some formats change the look of your file, pick your format according to your needs.

To export a document:

1. Choose **File > Export.**
2. In the Export dialog box, enter a name for the file and select a location where it will be saved ❶.
3. Choose the format from the Save as Type menu (Win) or the Format menu (Mac).
4. Select the Selected Objects Only option to export only selected objects.

TIP The Selected Objects Only option is not available when exporting to a FreeHand file format.

5. Click Setup to select options for the export file format. *(See the options listed in the next sections for information on the individual export options.)*
6. Click Export.

To open the exported file in another application:

1. Choose **File > Export.**
2. In the Export dialog box, select Open in External Application.
3. Use the dialog box to navigate to the application that will open the image
4. Click OK.

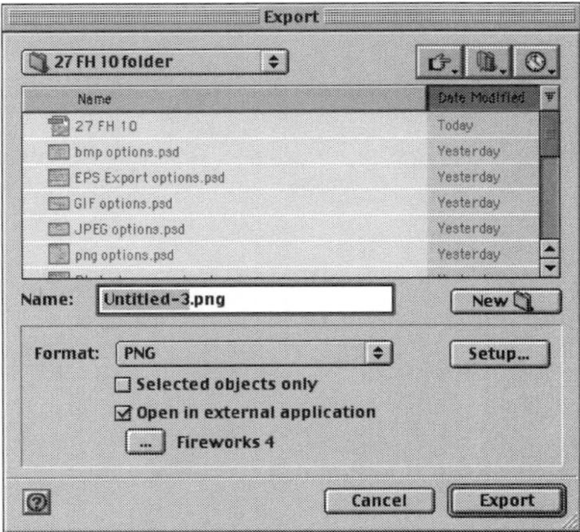

❶ *The* **Export dialog box** *is where you can name and set the format for an exported file.*

> **Export File Formats**
>
> The following are the available export file formats:
>
> **Adobe Illustrator:** Illustrator 1.1, Illustrator 88, Illustrator 3/4, Illustrator 5.5, Illustrator 7.
>
> **Macromedia FreeHand:** FreeHand 5, FreeHand 7, FreeHand 8, FreeHand 9.
>
> **EPS Vector files:** Generic EPS, Macintosh EPS (Win), MS-DOS EPS (Mac), EPS with TIFF Preview (Win), QuarkXPress EPS, DCS2 EPS.
>
> **Other Vector formats:** PICT Paths (Mac), PICT2 Paths (Mac), Windows Metafile (Win), Windows Enhanced Metafile (Win), Macromedia Flash, PDF.
>
> **Raster files:** TIFF, PNG, GIF, JPEG, BMP, Targa, PICT (Mac).
>
> **Adobe Photoshop:** Photoshop 3 EPS, Photoshop 4/5 RGB EPS, Photoshop 5.
>
> **Text files:** ASCII text, RTF text.

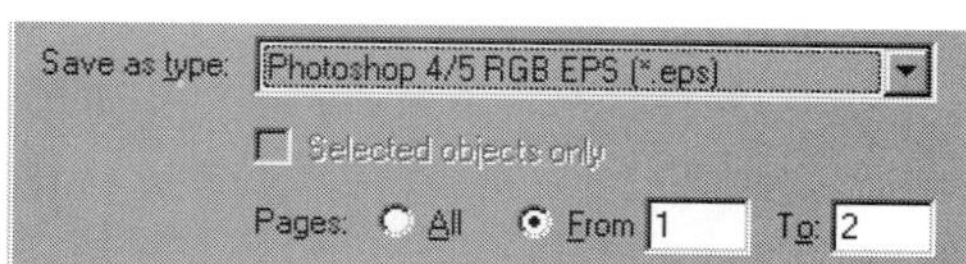

❷ *The* **Pages option** *is available for some export formats in the Windows Export dialog box.*

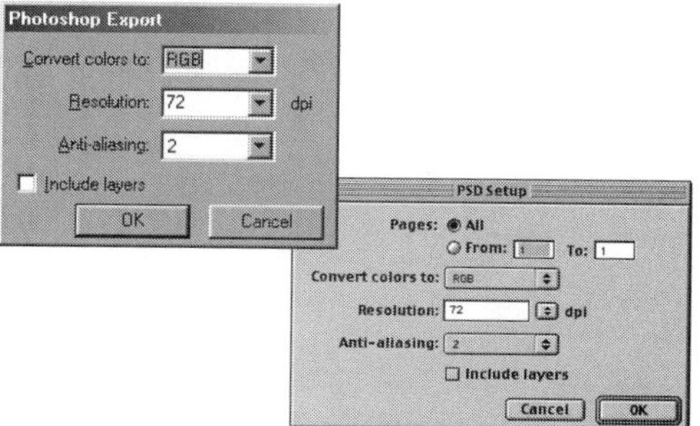

❸ *A significant difference between the Windows (left) and Macintosh (right) export options is that on the Mac the* **Pages option** *is integrated into the Setup dialog box for some export formats.*

Once you have exported a file, you may make some changes to the original FreeHand document. You can then re-export the file without having to go through setting the Export dialog box.

To re-export a document:

◆ Choose **File > Export Again.** FreeHand uses the previous export settings to export a new version of the document.

Because FreeHand is a multi-page program, you have the chance to choose which pages are exported. On the Macintosh platform this is built into the options for each of the file formats. On the Windows platform, this is part of the Export dialog box.

TIP If the file format does not support multiple pages, FreeHand creates individual files for each page.

To set the pages for export (Win):

◆ In the Export dialog box, set the number of pages to be exported as follows ❷:
  - **All** exports all the pages into the selected file format.
  - **From** lets you choose a range of pages to export.

To set the pages for export (Mac):

◆ Use the Setup dialog box for each of the file format to set the number of pages to be exported as follows:
  - **All** exports all the pages into the selected file format.
  - **From** lets you choose a range of pages to export.

TIP Because the Pages option is built into the Macintosh Setup dialog box, there is a distinctive difference between the Windows and Macintosh options for some formats ❸.

Exporting as Raster Images

When you export in the following formats, you convert FreeHand's vector objects into pixel-based illustrations. The TIFF, BMP, PICT, and Targa options are the most basic raster images.

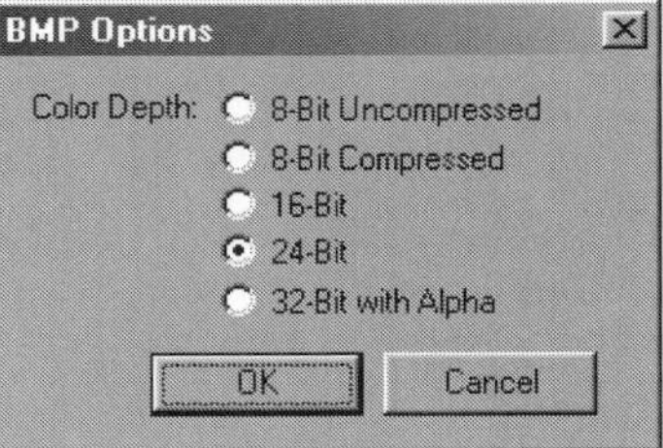

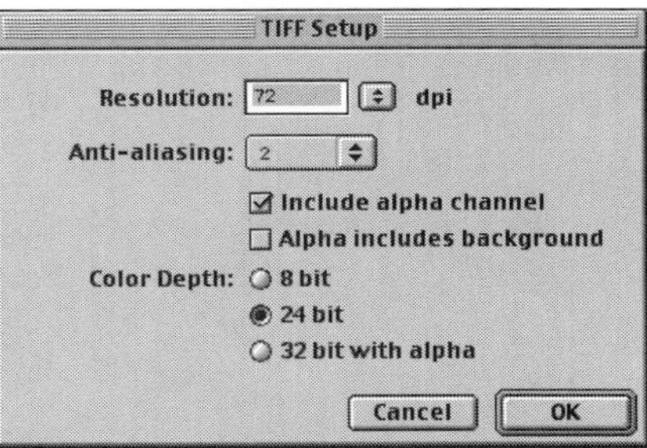

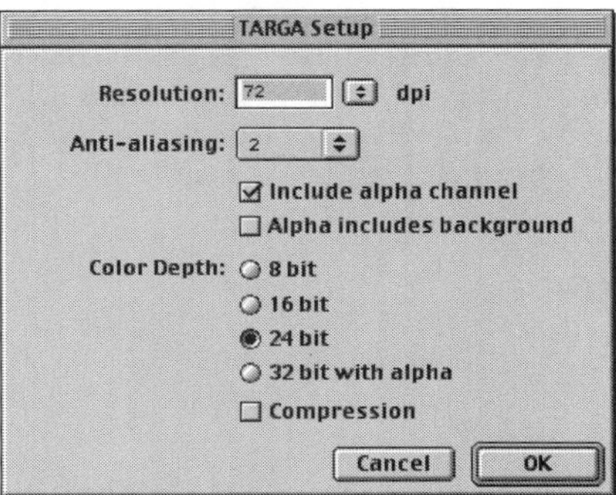

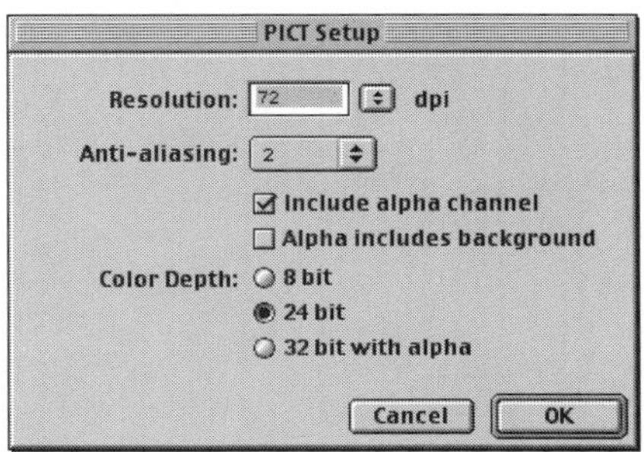

❹ *The* **Setup options** *for exporting BMP, TIFF, Targa, and PICT files.*

To export as BMP, TIFF, Targa, and PICT files:

1. Choose one of the following formats:
   - **BMP** (bitmap) is the most basic pixel format for the Windows platform.
   - **TIFF** (Tagged Image File Format) is the preferred choice for importing into applications that can't accept FreeHand EPS files.
   - **Targa** is widely used in professional video editing.
   - **PICT** is the most basic bitmapped format for the Macintosh platform.
2. Click Setup to open the options or setup dialog box for each format ❹.
3. Choose the resolution. For most print work this is 300 dpi.
4. Choose the amount of Anti-aliasing that smooths the edges of the image.
5. To create an alpha channel that can be used as a mask, click Include alpha channel.
6. To make the alpha channel include the background, click Alpha includes background.
7. Set the Color Depth for how many colors are supported. Higher color depths create larger files.
8. For Targa files, choose the Compression option to make the file smaller.

❺ *The* **Photoshop Export options**.

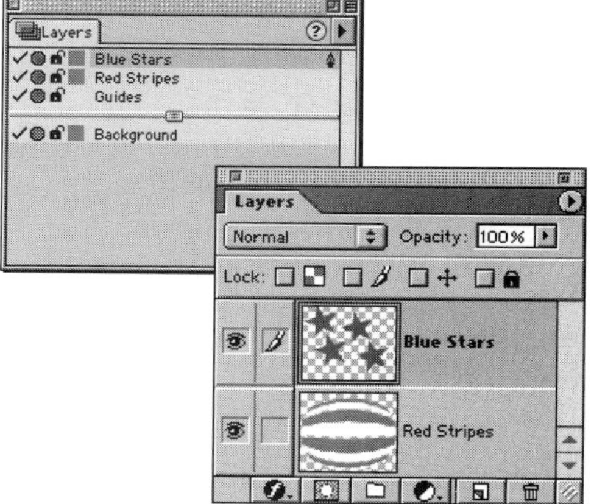

❻ *The* **Include layers** *option for Photoshop export allows you to retain FreeHand layers in the Photoshop file.*

> **Exporting as PNG, GIF, and JPEG**
>
> The other three raster formats, PNG, GIF, and JPEG are primarily used for Web graphics. Their export options are covered in Chapter 28, "Moving to the Web."

FreeHand also lets you export documents in the Adobe Photoshop format. This too converts the vector paths into raster images.

To export as Adobe Photoshop files:

1. Choose one of the following formats:
   - **Adobe Photoshop 3 EPS** saves the image as a Photoshop 3 file. Use this format if it needs to be opened in older versions of Photoshop. The EPS header means it can be imported into a page layout program.
   - **Adobe Photoshop 4/5 RGB EPS** saves the image as a file that can be opened in either Photoshop 4 or 5.
   - **Adobe Photoshop 5** saves the image in the native Photoshop 5 file format. This format gives you additional setup options.
2. If you have chosen Adobe Photoshop 5, click the Setup button. This opens the Photoshop Export dialog box ❺.
3. Use the Convert colors to menu to choose one of the following:
   - **CMYK** creates a 4-channel file that is acceptable for process-color separations.
   - **RGB** creates a 3-channel file that is usually used for Web and multi-media graphics.
   - **Grayscale** creates a single-channel file that is usually used for one color separations.
4. Choose the resolution. For most print work this is 300 dpi.
5. Choose the amount of Anti-aliasing that smooths the edges of the image.
6. Check Include layers to convert the FreeHand layers into the equivalent Photoshop layers ❻.

Exporting as Vector Images

There are quite a few options for exporting as vector files. This is very helpful for placing FreeHand artwork in page layout programs or for working with other applications.

To export as EPS files:

1. Choose one of the following formats:
   - **Generic EPS** saves vectors in an Encapsulated PostScript file without any preview. This is the smallest format but is difficult to work with in page layout programs.
   - **Macintosh EPS** (Win) saves EPS file with a PICT preview.
   - **MS-DOS EPS** (Mac) saves the EPS file with a TIFF preview.
   - **EPS with TIFF** preview (Win) also saves the EPS file with a TIFF preview.
   - **QuarkXPress EPS** saves the file in the best possible format for importing into QuarkXPress.
   - **DCS2 EPS** creates a pre-separated EPS that is usually used with OPI pre-press software.
2. Click the Setup button to select the other options ❼.
3. Choose Include FreeHand document to add the native FreeHand document to the EPS file. This makes it possible to edit the file later using FreeHand.
4. Choose Include Fonts in EPS to add the font information necessary to print the file. *(See the sidebar on this page for an explanation of what including the fonts means.)*
5. Choose the color conversion as follows:
   - CMYK for standard process output and color separations.
   - RGB for use in an image-editing application such as Macromedia Fireworks.
   - CMYK and RGB for print applications with a PostScript RIP such as Illustrator or Photoshop 4 or higher.

❼ *The* EPS Export options.

What does it mean to include fonts?

What does it mean when you include fonts in an exported EPS file?

As discussed in Chapter 19, when you open a FreeHand file that uses fonts that are not installed on your computer, you get a warning dialog box. This lets you know that if you don't have the original fonts in the file, the text will not display correctly unless you change the fonts.

So does that mean that if you include the fonts with an EPS, you don't get any warning? Can you work without installing those fonts?

No, no, no! Absolutely not!

All it means is that there is enough information about the font to *print* the file. But there is not enough information to *edit* the file later.

In order to edit the file you most definitely need to install the proper font.

The Include font option helps those who send their EPS files for placement in newspapers and magazines. Those publications may not have the fonts installed. They can print the file, but they can't open and edit it without the fonts installed.

❽ *The* EPS Setup *for Illustrator 7 files lets you set the color conversion options.*

Working with Other Vector Programs

However, what if you need to send your FreeHand files to someone who uses CorelDraw or Deneba Canvas? Don't panic just because there isn't any export option for CorelDraw or Canvas. Most other vector programs allow you to open Illustrator files.

So, check with the person you're working with and find out if their version of the program can open Illustrator files. Although you may find some special features such as transparency lenses or envelopes are converted to ordinary objects, most likely you will be able to transfer most of the information to the other program.

That's one of the reasons Macromedia has included the Illustrator 1 format. Almost all vector drawing programs can open that basic file format.

Although FreeHand doesn't export in the CorelDraw format, you can *import* uncompressed CorelDraw 7 and 8 files.

You can also save FreeHand files in formats compatible with previous versions of the program. This helps you work with people who do not have FreeHand 10.

To export as FreeHand files:

◆ Choose one of the following formats:
  - **FreeHand 5.x document** for use with FreeHand 5 and 5.5.
  - **FreeHand 7 document** for use with FreeHand 7.
  - **FreeHand 8 document** for use with FreeHand 8.
  - **FreeHand 9 document** for use with Freehand 9.

TIP There are no Setup options for the FreeHand file formats.

Despite a fierce competition between Freehand and Illustrator, Macromedia lets you convert FreeHand files to Illustrator files.

To export as Illustrator files:

1. Choose one of the following formats:
   - **Adobe Illustrator 1.1™** for use with the oldest versions of Illustrator and Macromedia FreeHand. (Ironically, Illustrator no longer exports in this file format.)
   - **Adobe Illustrator 88™** for use with the second version of Illustrator.
   - **Adobe Illustrator® 3** for use with Illustrator 3 (Mac) or Illustrator 4 (Win).
   - **Adobe Illustrator™ 5.5** for use with Illustrator 5.5.
   - **Adobe Illustrator™ 7.x** for use with Illustrator 7.
2. If you choose Illustrator 7, click the Setup button to set the options as follows ❽:
   - CMYK for standard process output and color separations.
   - RGB for use in an image-editing application such as Macromedia Fireworks.
   - **CMYK and RGB** for print applications with a PostScript RIP such as Illustrator or Photoshop 4 or higher.

FreeHand also lets you save documents as Adobe Acrobat PDF (portable document format) files. This file format allows anyone who has the Acrobat Reader application to open your files. In addition, the PDF format compresses files so they take up the smallest amount of space.

To export an Acrobat PDF:

1. Choose PDF from the Format pop-up menu.
2. Click the Setup button to open the PDF Export box ❾.
3. Set the Color Image Compression.
4. Set the Grayscale Image Compression.

TIP Choose None if the PDF file will be used for professional printing. This ensures that all the information is retained in the file.

5. Set the Compatibility choose which version of Acrobat can open the file.

TIP Choose a lower version of Acrobat if you are unsure of what version of Acrobat Reader will be used to open the file.

6. Check which options you want applied to the PDF:
   - **Compress text and graphics** reduces the file size even further.
   - **ASCII format PDF** may be required when sharing PDF files on older networks and e-mail systems.
   - **Editable text format** allows the text to be changed in the PDF.
   - **Export notes** converts any notes added in the Note text box in the Navigation panel into PDF annotations ❿.
   - **Export URLs** converts any URLs as PDF links.
   - **Embed fonts** embeds the fonts used in the file. This ensures the document appears exactly as you created it.

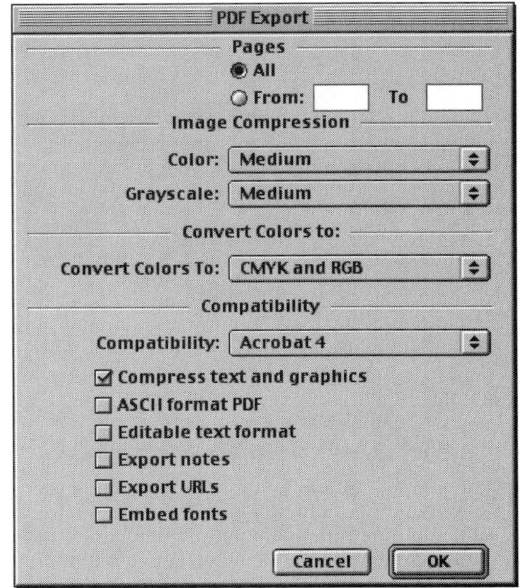

❾ *The* **PDF Export dialog box** *allows you to set the attributes of an Acrobat file.*

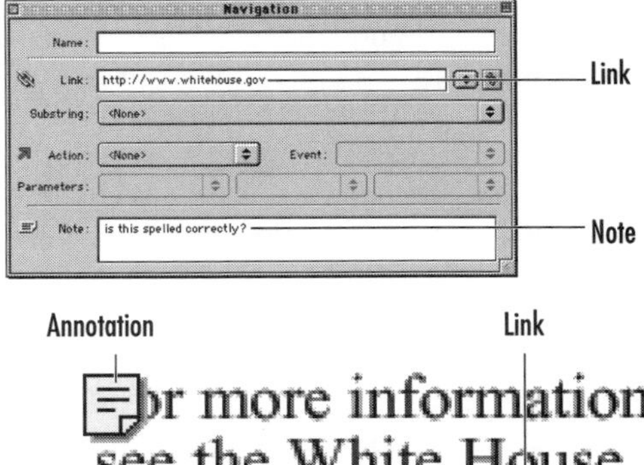

❿ *The* **PDF Export options** *can convert FreeHand notes and links (top) into Acrobat annotations and hyperlinks (bottom).*

⓫ *The* MetaFile Export *dialog box.*

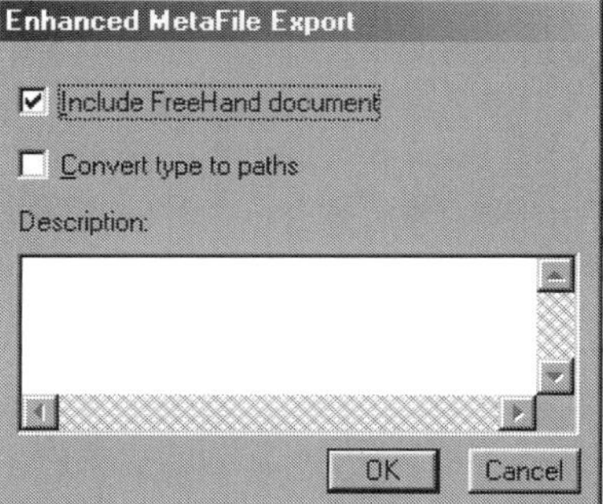

⓬ *The* Enhanced MetaFile Export *dialog box.*

What about Flash?

There's still one more vector file format that FreeHand lets you export—the Macromedia Flash (SWF) format.

SWF is the vector file format that is used for Web graphics, animations, and page layout. It has become one of the most important elements of creating Web pages.

Because working with Flash files is so important, exporting in the SWF format is covered in Chapter 29.

Exporting the Other Vector Formats

The final vector formats are PICT (Paths), PICT2 (Paths), Windows Metafile, and Windows Enhanced Metafile. Quite frankly, these are very specific file formats and most FreeHand users will hardly ever need to use them.

(Mac) To export as PICT (Paths) and PICT2 (paths):

- Choose one of the following from the format menu:
  - PICT (Paths) contains 8-bit color depth.
  - PICT2 (Paths) contains 32-bit color depth.

TIP There is no setup for either PICT format.

(Win) To export as MetaFile and Enhanced MetaFile:

1. Choose one of the following from the format menu:
   - MetaFile contains 16-bit color depth.
   - Enhanced MetaFile contains 32-bit color depth as well as other information.
2. Click the Setup button to select the other options ⓫.
3. Choose Include FreeHand document to be able to re-open the file in FreeHand.
4. Choose Convert type to paths to avoid the need to have the fonts for printing and editing.
5. If you are working with an Enhanced MetaFile, you can add a description of the file that can be used in searching ⓬.

Adding Image Information

FreeHand also lets you add information that can be used when your artwork is part of an Extensis Portfolio image database. This makes it easier to find your artwork in large catalogs.

TIP Sadly, this option is only available on the Mac platform.

(Mac) To add Portfolio information:

1. Choose **View > Portfolio Info.** The Portfolio Info dialog box appears ⓭.
2. Type the keywords in the Keywords field. Use commas to separate the different keywords.

TIP Keywords are usually descriptive labels that can categorize the different uses for the graphic.

3. Type any description of the graphic in the Description field.

TIP Descriptions are usually more lengthy information about the file or its use.

4. Click OK. The Portfolio information is included as part of the file and can be read by the Portfolio application.

TIP To add a preview to your FreeHand file so it can be seen in a Portfolio database, you need to check the Preferences settings for Import/Export *(see Appendix C)*.

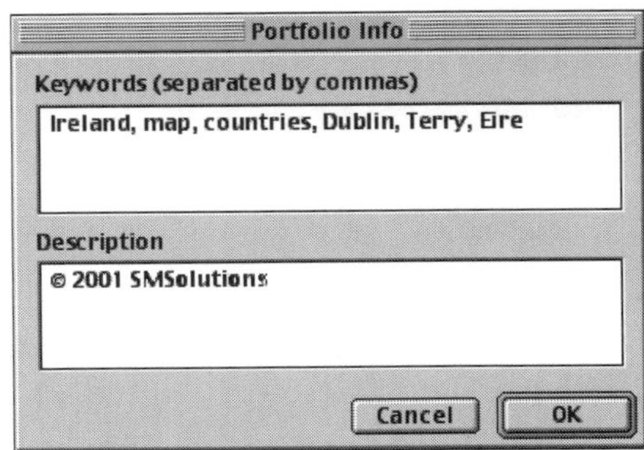

⓭ *Use the* **Portfolio Info dialog box** *to add keywords and descriptions used in a database.*

MOVING TO THE WEB 28

Designers are focusing more and more on publishing to the Web as an alternative to—or even a replacement for—traditional print publishing. Macromedia FreeHand has moved to accommodate them by incorporating many features for creating Web graphics and Web pages.

FreeHand lets you choose those colors that are specially designed to look their best when viewed on various computer monitors. It also lets you export your graphics in the special formats that are viewed in Web browsers.

Finally Macromedia has created a direct route to converting your FreeHand graphics into HTML, *(HyperText Markup Language)* the *lingua franca* of the Internet.

Note: As handy as FreeHand's Web features are, they are not a substitute for programs such as Macromedia Fireworks or Macromedia Dreamweaver. Rather, FreeHand's Web features are handy for those occasions when you need to convert a print brochure into a set of Web pages—not to design an entire Web site.

Working with Web-safe Colors

In the early days of the Web, the people behind Netscape put together a set of 216 colors that were able to be seen on both Macintosh and Windows monitors that could display 256 colors. These are now called the Web-safe colors.

Although most people today can view more than just 256 colors, some people still insist on using only the Web-safe colors in their Web pages. FreeHand gives you two ways to pick colors from the Web-safe set.

To choose Web-safe colors:

- Click the Fill or Stroke color box in the Tools panel. The default listing shows the Web-safe colors ❶.

To import Web-safe colors:

1. Use the Swatches panel menu to choose the Web Safe Color Library. The library appears containing the 216 Web colors ❷.
2. Select the colors you want in your document *(see page 169)*.

TIP Web pages take less time to display if you design with a small number of colors.

3. Click OK. The colors you have selected appear in the Colors List ❸.

TIP The Web-safe colors are identified with both their hexadecimal codes and their RGB values. The hexadecimal codes are the tags used by the HyperText Markup Language (HTML) to designate Web colors.

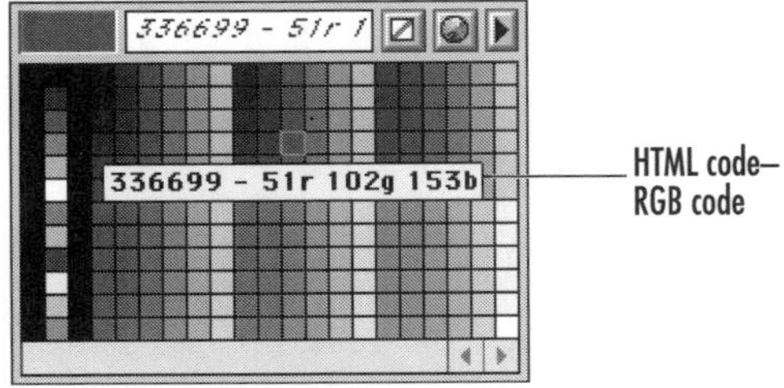

❶ *The Web-safe colors are displayed in the Fill and Stroke color box.*

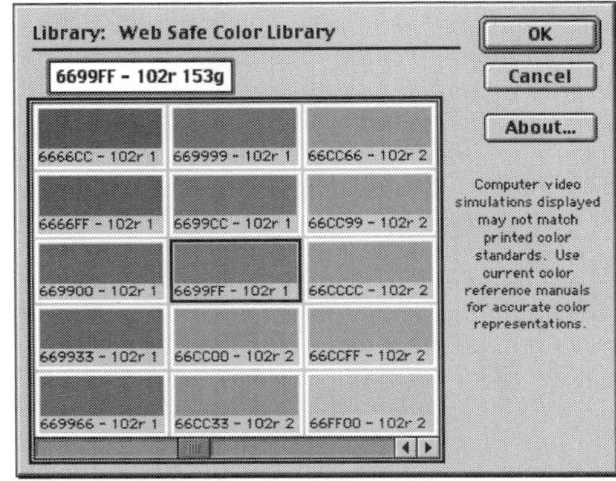

❷ *The Web Safe Color Library lets you choose up to 216 colors that can be used for Web graphics.*

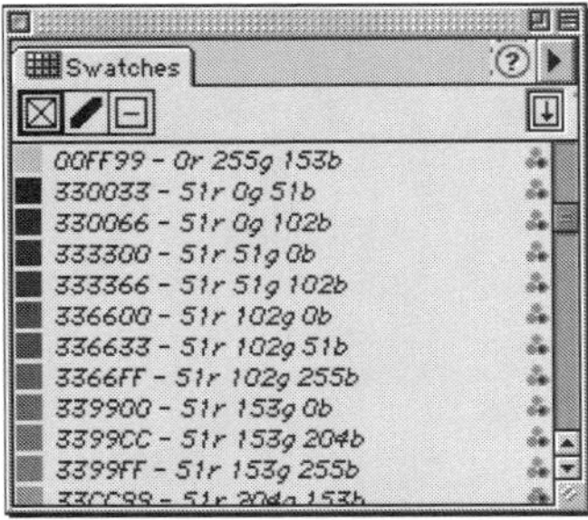

❸ *Web-safe colors are displayed in the Colors List with their hexadecimal codes as well as their RGB values.*

❹ *A* **blend between Web-safe** *colors creates non–Web-safe colors between the original colors.*

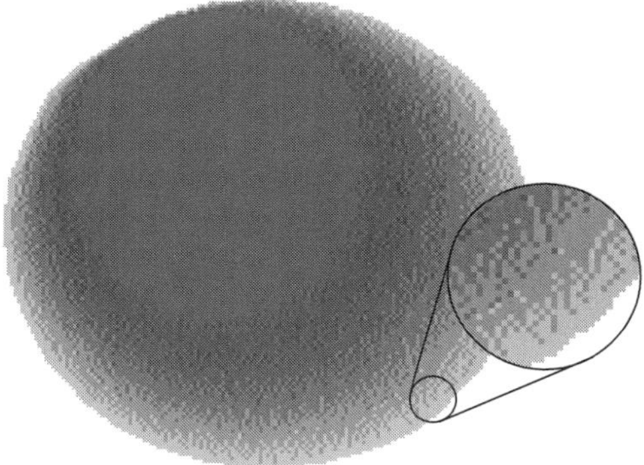

❺ *With* **Dither turned on,** *the area between the original Web colors has a speckled look as the colors mix many Web-safe colors together.*

❻ *When a blend is converted with* **Dither turned off,** *the intermediate steps abruptly change from one Web-safe color to another.*

Blending Web-safe Colors

If you insist on using only Web-safe colors, your best best is not to use any blends or gradients. Both blends and gradients will create colors outside the range of the Web-safe colors.

When you convert a gradient or blend to a GIF, you need to decide how the colors in the intermediate steps are handled ❹. One way is to dither the intermediate colors. Dithering is the process that makes a few colors look like more. For instance, a dither between red and yellow means that dots of red are next to dots of yellow. An even mix between the red and yellow dots appears orange. More red than yellow appears red-orange. More yellow than red appears yellow-orange.

Dithering is the best way to preserve the look of blends in Web graphics ❺. Dithering is usually not acceptable for solid colors and should be turned off when exporting those graphics.

When colors are not dithered, they are converted to the closest Web-safe color. This may mean that a deep red turns brown or a light green turns dark. When you are working with flat colors, this is acceptable unless the color shift causes two colors you intend to be distinct to resemble each other too closely.

When blends or gradients are not dithered, there are abrupt changes in each step of the blend ❻. This usually looks unacceptable; turn dithering on when exporting graphics with gradients or blends.

My own personal feeling is that since so many people have monitors that can display millions of colors, it is no longer sucha a big deal to limit yourself to the Web-safe colors.

Exporting as Web Graphics

FreeHand lets you export your files in three popular Web formats. This means you can convert a print logo into a Web graphic. *(For more information on exporting, see Chapter 27, "Exporting.")*

To export a file for the Web:

1. Create the artwork you want to turn into a Web graphic.
2. Choose **File > Export.** This opens the Export Document dialog box ❼.
3. Choose one of the following from the Save as type menu:
   - **GIF** is usually for images with flat color.
   - **JPEG** is used for photographs or images with many blends or gradients.
   - **PNG** is not often used. Choose it only if you are sure your viewers will have the proper browsers.
4. Click the Setup button. On the Windows platform, this opens the Bitmap Export Defaults dialog box ❽. On the Macintosh platform, these options are part of the setup for each of the file formats.

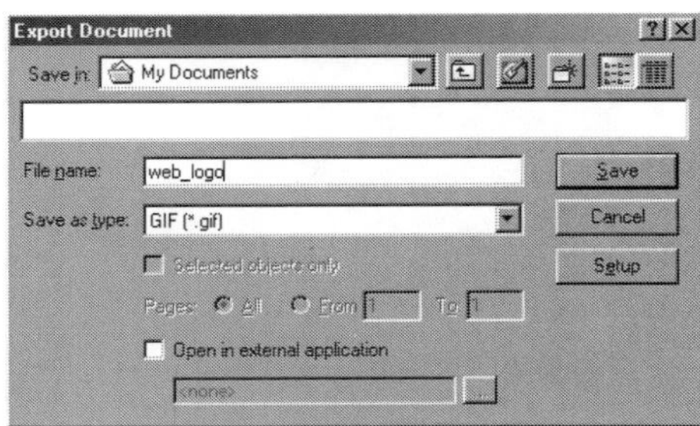

❼ *The* **Export Document dialog box** *lets you save files in common Web formats.*

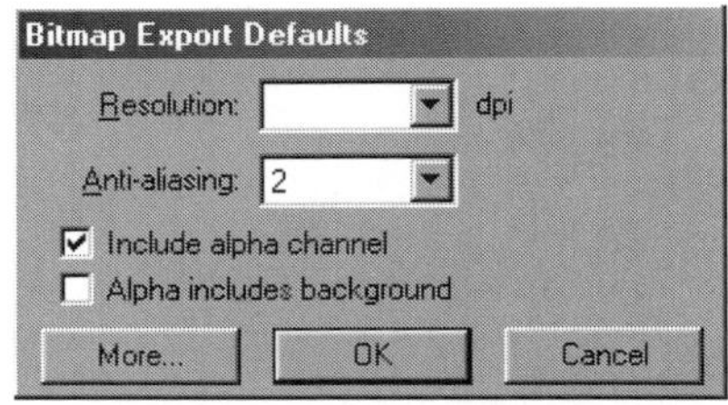

❽ *(Win) The* **Bitmap Export Defaults dialog box** *allows you to set the overall options for exporting files into different Web formats.*

(Win) To set the Bitmap Export Defaults options:

1. Set the Resolution. For Web graphics, this is usually 72 dpi.
2. Use the Anti-aliasing pop-up menu to control how much softening of the image is applied. *(For more information on anti-aliasing, see page 312.)*
3. To create an alpha channel that can be used as a mask for your image, check Include alpha channel.
4. To include the background area in the alpha channel, check Alpha includes background.
5. Click the More button to open the options for each of the bitmapped formats.

Naming Web Graphics

Both the Windows and Macintosh platforms give you much freedom in how to name a file. They allow a file name with spaces, upper-and lower-case letters, and really long file names.

If you're like me you may have files with names like *Final copy of the Second logo. eps.*

Unfornately many Web pages are hosted on Unix systems that have much stricter file formats. So if you save your files for the Web, you may need to limit your names to all lower case letters and no spaces. This means a name such as final_logo.gif

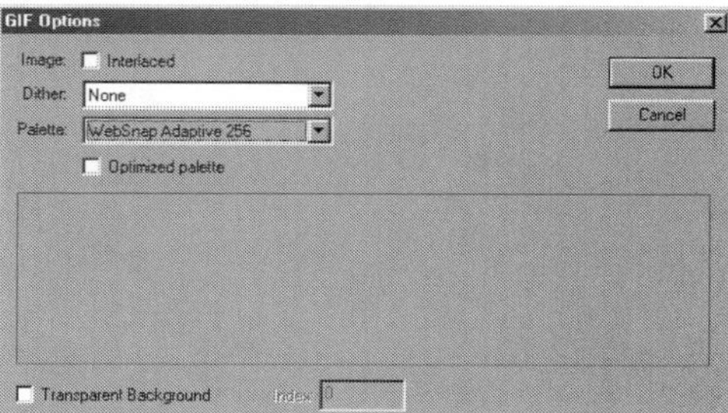

❾ *The* **GIF Options** *let you control how the image is displayed on the Web.*

> ### GIF Palette Options
>
> GIF images can have up to 256 colors. However, you have a great deal of choices as to which colors to include in the color palette.
>
> - **Exact Palette** creates a color palette with only the colors used.
> - **WebSnap Adaptive 256, 128, or 16** creates a color palette that is converted to the closest Web-safe color equivalent.
> - **WebSafe 216** includes the standard 216 Web-safe colors.
> - **64 colors, 32 colors, or 16 colors** lets you quickly select preset Web-safe color palettes.
> - **Macintosh System** uses the 256 colors native to the Macintosh OS.
> - **Windows System** uses the 256 colors native to the Windows OS.
> - **3-3-2** uses the palette of the original FreeHand GIF Import Export Xtra.
> - **Grays** uses a palette of 256 grayscale colors.
>
> You don't have to use all 256 colors. Fewer colors make smaller GIF files.

Once you have set the bitmapped attributes, you then need to set the options for the specific file format you have chosen. One of the most common formats for Web graphics is the GIF format. *(GIF is pronounced as "gif" because I don't like peanut butter on the Web.)*

To set the GIF export options:

1. (Win) Click More in the Bitmap Export Defaults dialog box.

   or

   (Mac) Click More in the GIF Setup dialog box. The GIF Options dialog box opens ❾.
2. Use the Palette pop-up menu to choose one of the palette options described in the sidebar on this page:

   TIP You can install Photoshop color palettes files (.act) in the Palettes folder within FreeHand 10:English:Palettes.
3. Use the Dither menu to select the amount of dithering applied to colors. None applies no dithering. High applies the most.

   TIP Turn off the Dither option if you have detailed artwork or text that needs to be clearly visible.
4. For Image, select Interlaced to create an image that appears almost immediately in a rough form and then gradually becomes clearer.
5. Select Optimized Palette to create the smallest file with the least number of colors. This automatically removes unused colors from the palette.

   TIP To create a GIF image with a transparent background, see the exercise on the following page.

FreeHand lets you create a transparency in a GIF based on the object's outlines. The Exact and WebSnap Adaptive palettes do not support transparency.

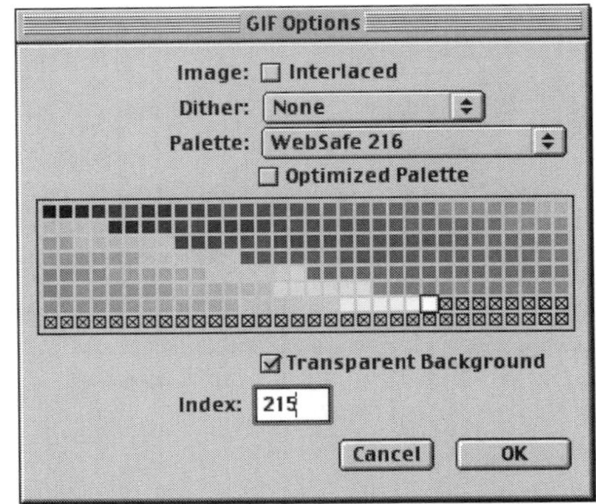

⑩ *When you choose* **Transparent Background** *the palette colors appear so you can set which color is transparent.*

To apply a transparent background:

1. Select Transparent Background in the GIF Options dialog box. The Index color palette appears along with the Index field ⑩.

TIP Each color used is represented by a small color square. The small squares with an X indicates unused colors.

2. Click a color swatch to define which color should be transparent.

   or

   Enter its number in the Index field.

TIP If you select Transparent Background, be sure you also choose Include Alpha Channel in the Bitmap Export Defaults or GIF Setup dialog boxes.

TIP If you choose a transparent background color, make sure the color is not used inside the image or that part of the image will also be transparent ⑪.

⑪ *The Transparent Background option (right image) lets the background of the Web page be visible without a white rectangle.*

Working with Fireworks, a dedicated Web graphics program

A terrific as FreeHand is, it is actually very primitive when it comes to converting artwork into Web graphics. One of the reasons is that you can't see what the different palettes and compression options do to your file. You have to export them, and then view them in a Web browser.

Fortunately, there is a terrific program that is totally dedicated to creating Web graphics—Macromedia Fireworks.

Fireworks not only gives you exceptional control when you create GIF, JPEG, or PNG files; it also gives visual feedback of how the final exported file will appear on the Web.

Even better, you can simply drag FreeHand objects right into Fireworks. Of course, if you do work with Fireworks, you should get the *Fireworks 4 Visual Quickstart Guide* by Sandee Cohen. *(Hey, that's me!)*

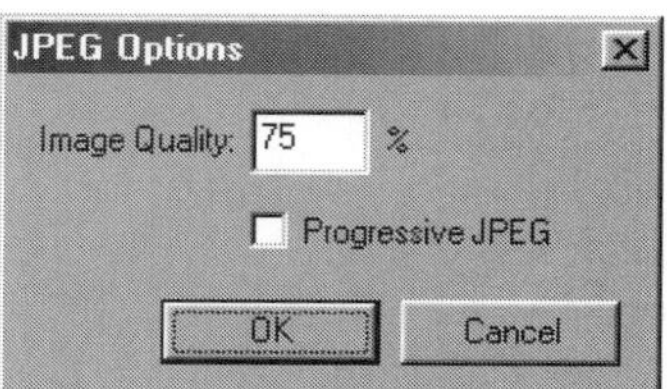

⓬ *JPEG Options let you control the quality of your image and how the image is displayed.*

⓭ *The PNG Setup dialog box lets you control the image colors and how the image is displayed.*

Another format used on the Web is the JPEG (pronounced "Jay-peg") format. This is primarily used for photographic images or images with lots of blends or gradients.

To set the JPEG options:

1. (Win) Click the More button in the Bitmap Export Defaults. This opens the JPEG Options dialog box ⓬.

   or

   (Mac) Click Setup in the Export dialog box. This opens the JPEG Setup dialog box which contains the Bitmap Export options as well as the JPEG Options.
2. Enter a percentage for Image Quality. Low quality settings create smaller files. High quality settings create larger files.
3. Click Progressive JPEG to create an effect similar to the Interlaced GIF.

The last format is the PNG (pronounced Ping) format. This format has applications in both Web graphics and printing.

TIP PNG files require a plug-ins to be viewed in most Web browsers. However, PNG files are helpful to get FreeHand graphics into applications such as Microsoft PowerPoint.

To set the PNG options:

1. (Win) Click the More button in the Bitmap Export Defaults. This opens the PNG Options dialog box ⓭.

   or

   (Mac) Click Setup in the Export dialog box. This opens the PNG Setup dialog box which contains the Bitmap Export options as well as the PNG Options.
2. Choose the options for the color bit depth. High bit depths are for print work.
3. Click Interlaced PNG to create an effect similar to the Interlaced GIF.

Adding URL Links

One of the most important features of a Web page written in HTML is its ability to include URL links. Links let the reader click on a word or phrase or an image and go to another location, either on the current Web site or on a totally different site. Links also let the reader send e-mail or download files.

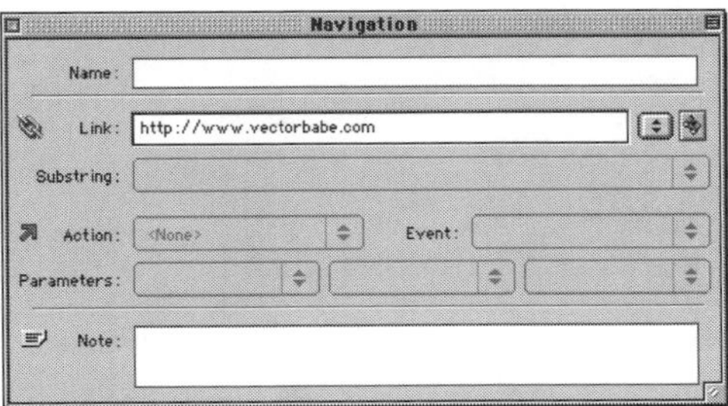

⓮ *Use the* **Link field** *of the Navigation panel to add URLs to graphics.*

To add a URL to an object:

1. Select the object that you want to apply the link to. This can be a path or text block.
2. In the Navigation panel, type the URL address in the Link field ⓮.

   or

   If you have already added the link to that document, use the Link menu to choose the link.

   or

   If you are working with multiple pages, use the pop-up menu to choose a link to another page ⓯.

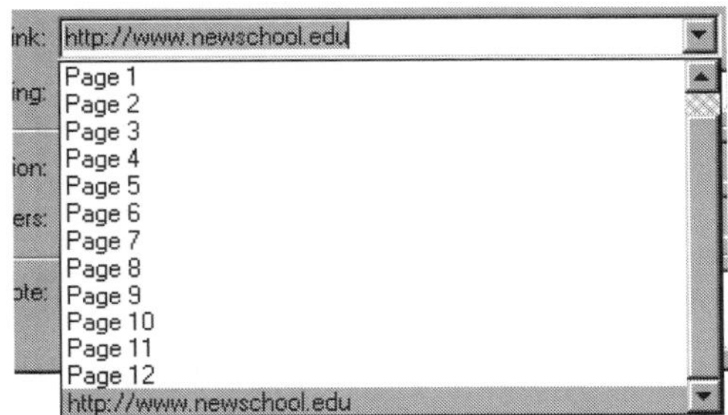

⓯ *Use the* **Link menu** *to add links from one page to another.*

TIP You can create invisible hotspots in your document by creating paths with no stroke and a lens fill with the opacity set to 0. This will allow you to link to a specific area of an image.

Links can also be added to selected text within a text block.

To add a URL to selected text:

1. Use the Text tool to highlight the text that you want to apply the link to.
2. Use the Link menu or field to add a URL link to the text. The selected text appears in the Substring field.

URL link choices

The three most common URL links are http, mailto, and ftp.

http: Stands for HyperText Transfer Protocol, used when you want to access a Web site. For example, **http://www.vectorbabe.com** is my Web site.

mailto: This URL is used to send e-mail. For example,you can use the link **mailto:sandee@vectorbabe.com** to send me e-mail.

ftp: This stands for File Transfer Protocol. This lets people download files. A sample URL link would be **ftp://ftp.vectorbabe.com/sandee.sit.**

⓰ *The* **Find button** *(circled) in the Navigation panel lets you find objects that have a specific link attached.*

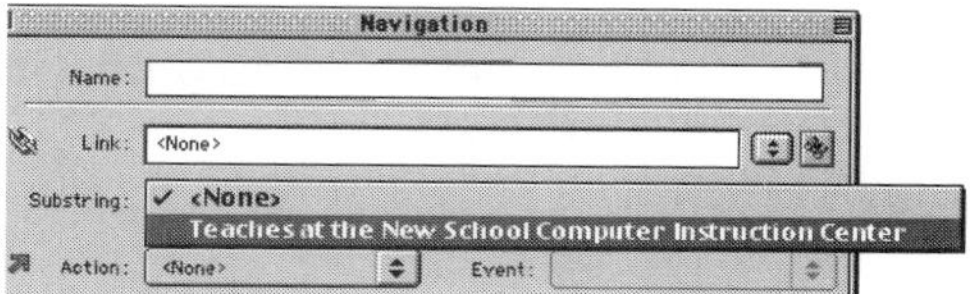

⓱ *The* **Substring menu** *in the Navigation panel lets you find text that has a specific link attached.*

To search for an object with a specific link:

1. In the Navigation panel, enter a URL in the Link field.

   or

   Select a URL from the Link menu.
2. Click the Find button in the Navigation panel ⓰.
3. All objects in the current document that are linked to the URL are selected in the Document window.

The Find button only finds objects or text blocks that have the link applied to the entire object. You use the Substring menu to find selected text that has a link applied to it.

To find selected text with a specific link:

1. With the Text tool, click inside the text block. If there is a link within the block, the Substring menu becomes active.
2. Choose the Substring listing from the menu ⓱. The text that contains the link becomes highlighted.

Once you have selected all the objects with a specific link, you can easily change the URL information.

To update a URL for all the objects linked to it:

1. Deselect all objects in the document.
2. In the Navigation panel, select the URL you want to update from the Link menu.
3. Click the Find button to the right of the Link text box.
4. Modify the URL in the Link text box as needed. The URL is updated for all objects linked to it in the current document.

Creating HTML Pages

Billions of years ago Web pages were created by hand-coding the text and HTML instructions in word-processing applications. Then someone got the clever idea that they could convert FreeHand documents into HTML pages. Of course, this doesn't make FreeHand a substitute for professional Web layout programs such as Macromedia Dreamweaver. But it does make it easy to convert a small brochure or print project into Web pages ⑱.

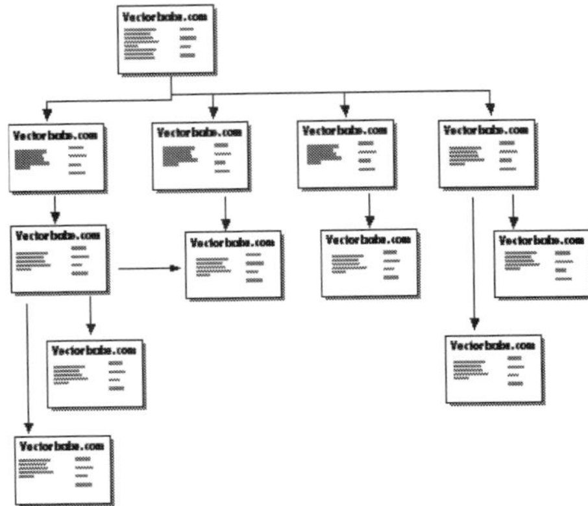

⑱ *The multi-pages of a FreeHand document can be converted into Web pages. The arrows were manually added to show the links between pages.*

To convert a document to HTML:

1. Select **File > Publish as HTML.** This opens the HTML Output dialog box ⑲.
2. Choose a setting from the HTML Setting menu.

   or

   Click the Setup button to create a new one. *(See the following exercise for how to create a new HTML setup.)*
3. Check Show Output Warnings if you want the HTMLOutput Warnings screen to display warnings of possible problems with the export of the file to HTML.
4. Check the View in browser or HTML Editor checkbox if you want the file to open immediately in an browser such as Internet Explorer or Netscape Navigator.
5. Select a browser or HTML editor from the pop-up menu.

   or

   Click the Browse button to choose a Web browser using the navigation dialog box.
6. Click Save as HTML. FreeHand creates the HTML file in the folder selected as the document root in the HTML Setup dialog box. The images are placed in a subfolder within that folder.

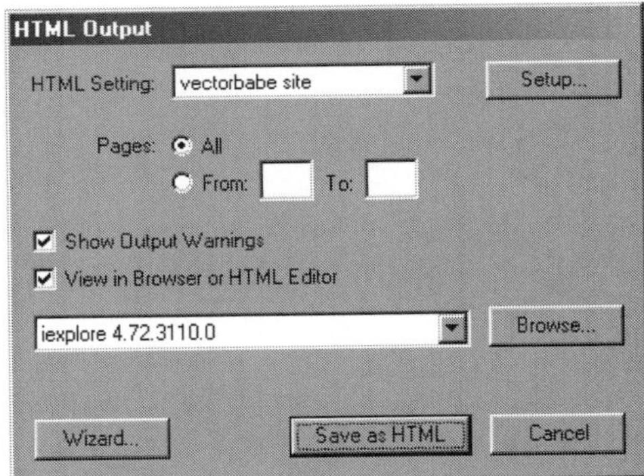

⑲ *The* **HTML Output dialog box** *for creating Web pages from FreeHand files.*

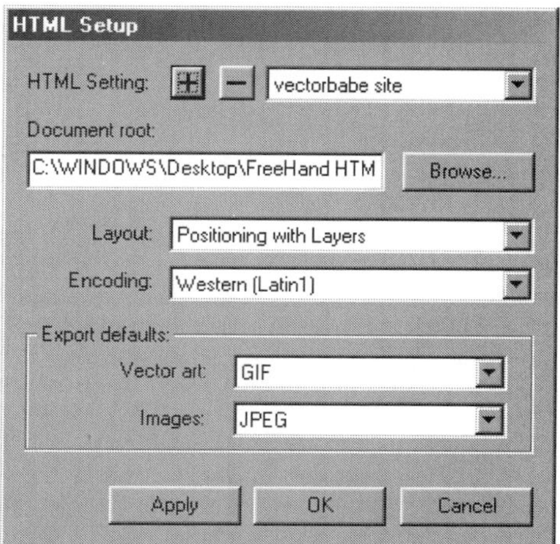

⑳ *The HTMLSetup dialog box controls specific elements of the HTML conversion.*

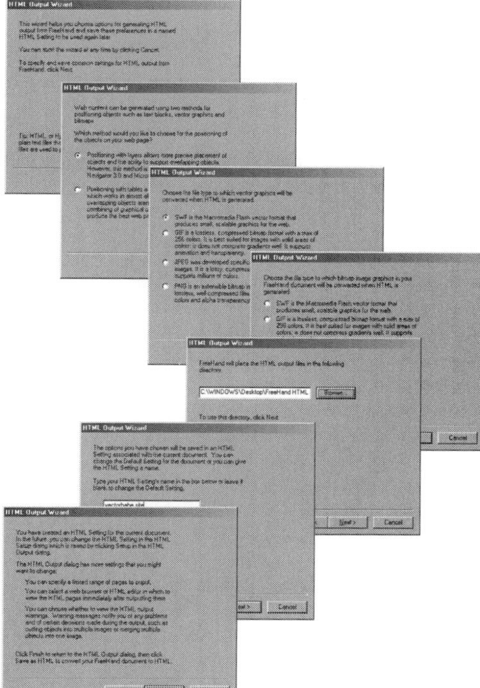

㉑ *The* **HTML Export Output Wizard** *(Win) or the* **HTMLOutput Assistant** *(Mac) guide you through the process of setting up the creation of an HTML file.*

Rather than go through all the setting controls every time you create HTML pages, you can save the settings under one name.

To create an HTML setting:

1. In the HTML Output dialog box, click Setup to open the HTML Setup dialog box ⑳.
2. Click the + button to create a new setting. Give it a name and click OK.
3. Use the Document root menu to choose the folder/directory in which you want to save the HTML files.

   or

   Click the Browse menu to choose a new folder.
4. Use the Layout menu to choose one of the following:
   - **Positioning with Layers** uses Cascading Style Sheets to make a very precise equivalent of the layout.
   - **Positioning with Tables** uses a less precise mode to convert the layout.
5. Use the Encoding menu to choose the language for the page.

TIP Leave this set to Western (Latin 1) unless you have a very good reason to do otherwise.

6. Choose one of the following as the Export defaults for Vector art and Images:
   - **GIF** creates GIF images.
   - **JPEG** creates JPEG files.
   - **PNG** creates PNG graphics.
   - **SWF** creates SWF (Flash) images.
7. Click OK to accept all your preferences.

TIP Click the Assistant (Mac) or Wizard (Win) button to let FreeHand help you through the setup process with short explanations of the each step ㉑.

To check the HTMLOutput Warnings:

1. Choose **Window >Xtras > HTMLOutput Warnings** to open the HTMLOutput Warnings window ㉒.
2. Click either Scan Page or Scan Document. FreeHand displays a list of potential problems with the export to HTML.
3. Click each problem in the list. FreeHand selects the item so that you can decide if or how you want to change it.

TIP Some of the items listed as HTML output warnings may not have any impact on the Web page you create; experience will help you evaluate which ones need to be dealt with and which can be safely ignored.

TIP If you have checked the View in browser or HTML Editor checkbox in the HTMLOutput dialog box, the file opens and you will be able to see what the exported HTML file looks like ㉓.

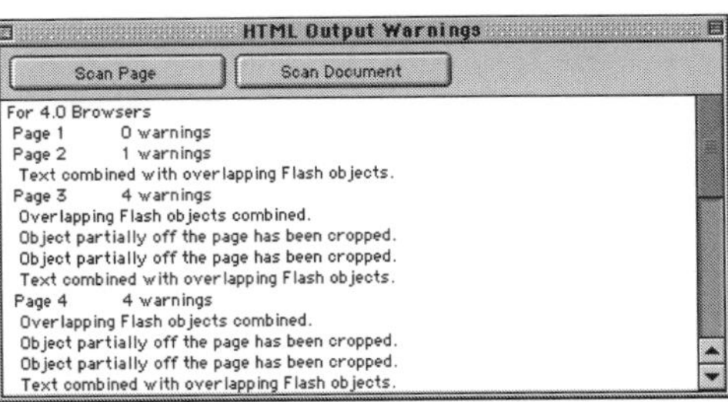

㉒ *The* **HTML Output Warnings** *window lists possible problems in the document before you create the HTML pages.*

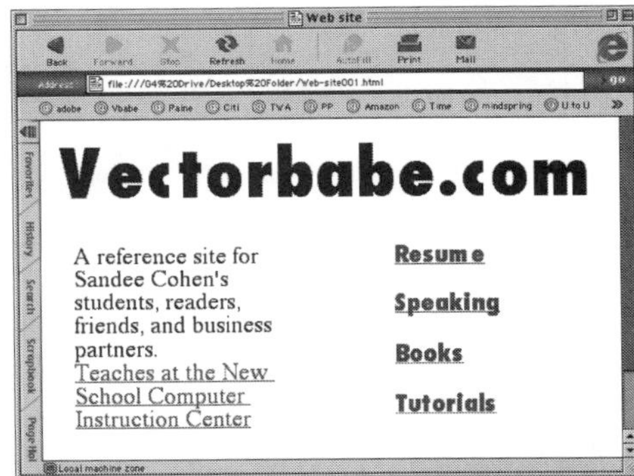

㉓ *The HTMLfile can be viewed in a browser or HTML editor.*

FLASH ANIMATIONS 29

One of the most exciting developments in Web design has been the addition of Flash movies and Flash Web sites. Flash movies are much smaller than GIF animations which means they can run far longer than GIF files. They don't even have to be movies, *per se.* Instead of playing all the frames of a movie at once, you can start and stop each frame one at a time. This makes the Flash movies behave like individual Web pages.

Unfortunately, Flash doesn't have many of the sophisticated drawing tools that Macromedia FreeHand has. There's no enveloping, no perspective, no power duplicating, and none of the special effect Xtras. So many Flash designers start by using FreeHand to layout their projects and then bring the files into Flash.

FreeHand makes it easy to copy and paste or export into Flash. You can even add basic Flash navigational elements to move from page to page. And you can create animations by sending objects and text to layers.

This makes FreeHand the best choice of vector program for use with Flash.

Pasting into Flash

The easiest way for a designer to work with both Freehand and Flash is to copy FreeHand artwork and paste it into a Flash frame. Or, if you have the monitor space, you can drag and drop artwork from one application into another.

TIP Before pasting into Flash, set the Export preferences to convert colors to CMYK and RGB for the clipboard formats *(see page 395)*.

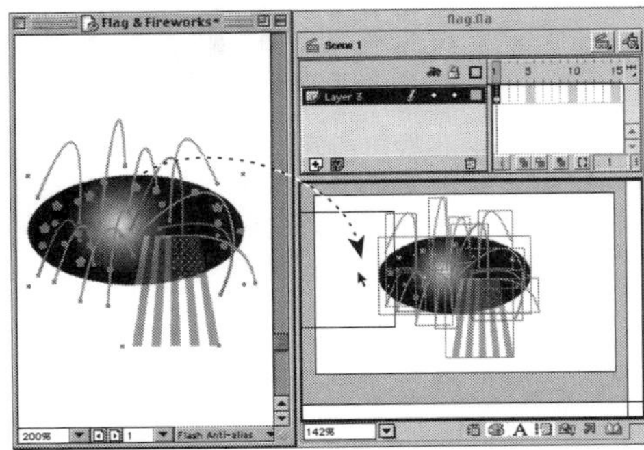

❶ *You can easily* **drag and drop** *FreeHand artwork into Flash documents.*

To paste into Flash files:

1. Select the FreeHand object or objects.
2. Copy the objects.
3. Switch to make the Flash file active.
4. Paste. The FreeHand objects are imported into the Flash file.

TIP Unlinked text blocks become Flash text objects.

TIP Linked text blocks or text on a path are converted into paths.

TIP Vector-based objects become a group that can be ungrouped and edited like any other Flash element.

TIP Bitmaps become a single grouped object just like imported bitmaps. You can break apart pasted bitmaps or convert pasted bitmaps to vector graphics.

To drag and drop into Flash files:

1. Position the windows so you can see both the FreeHand and Flash files.
2. Select the FreeHand object or objects.
3. Use the Pointer tool to drag the FreeHand objects into the Flash window ❶.
4. When you see the rectangle box appear in the Flash file, release the mouse. The FreeHand artwork is imported into the Flash file.

FreeHand features supported in Flash files

The following FreeHand features will be kept when imported into Flash.

- Basic strokes and fills. However square endcaps will be changed to round endcaps.
- Transparency lens fills remain transparent upon export. Other lens fills are changed.
- Gradient fills except the contour gradient.
- CMYK or RGB TIFFs and embedded images (JPEG, GIF, PNG).
- Blended paths.
- Composite paths, including text converted into paths.
- Clipping paths containing vector path image files.
- Text blocks. However, text on a path is converted to objects.
- Arrowheads.

Use the Flash Anti-alias preview to see how your artwork will appear when imported into Flash.

Creating Layer-based Animations

As much as I enjoy creating simple Flash animations in FreeHand, I know that there is far more power and sophistication in Flash itself. However, FreeHand does have a few techniques to convert blends, text, text on a path, groups and brushes into animated sequences ❷.

❷ *The type of objects that can be animated (from top to bottom): text, text on a path, blend, blend on a path, group of objects, and brushes.*

To prepare artwork for animation:

1. Set text as a single line of type or attach the text to a path *(see page 250)*.

   or

   Create a blend or attach a blend to a path *(see page 219)*.

   or

   Group individual items in the order that you would like them to appear.

   or

   Brushes must be released and ungrouped as many times as necessary until each individual symbol is selected. Then the individual symbols should be grouped into one object.
2. If you want an object to appear throughout the animation, place the artwork on a non-printing background layer ❸ *(see page 156)*.

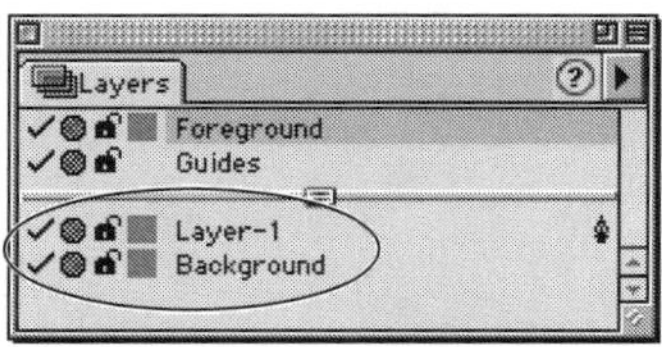

❸ *The* **non-printing layers** *(circled) hold the artwork that is seen throughout the animation.*

One way to create Flash animations is to put objects on their own layers so that each layer acts like a movie frame. Although you could manually place each object on its own layers, it is much easier to do it automatically.

To create an animation sequence using layers:

1. Select the artwork to be animated.
2. Choose **Xtras > Animate > Release to Layers.** The Release to Layers dialog box appears ❹.
3. Use the Animate menu to choose one of the following:
   - **Sequence** releases each object individually to separate layers.
   - **Build** creates a stacking effect by copying the objects in sequence to separate layers.
   - **Drop** copies the objects to all layers but omits one object in sequence from each layer.
   - **Trail** copies and releases objects to the number of layers you specify. Objects are copied incrementally to the specified number of layers.
4. If you have chosen Trail, use the Trail By field to specify the number of layers on which objects will be copied.
5. If desired, select Reverse Direction to release the objects in reverse stacking order and animate the sequence in the opposite direction.
6. Select Use Existing Layers to release objects to existing layers, beginning with the current layer.

TIP Deselect Use Existing Layers to create new layers for the objects that are released.

7. If you have chosen Use Existing Layers, you can also select Send to Back to release the objects to the back of the stacking order.
8. Click OK. The objects appear on new layers ❺.

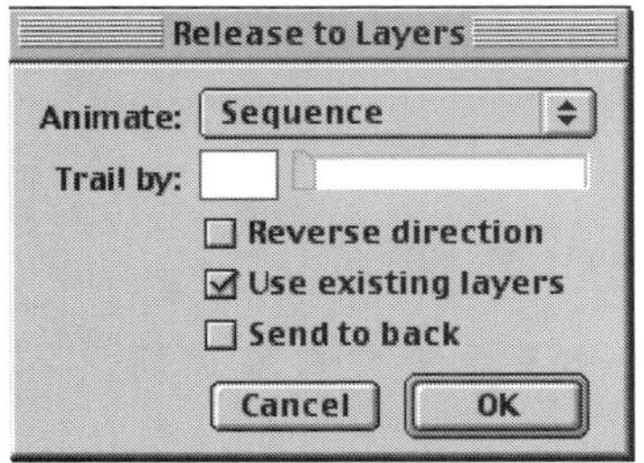

❹ *The* **Release to Layers dialog box** *gives you several choices as to how objects are animated.*

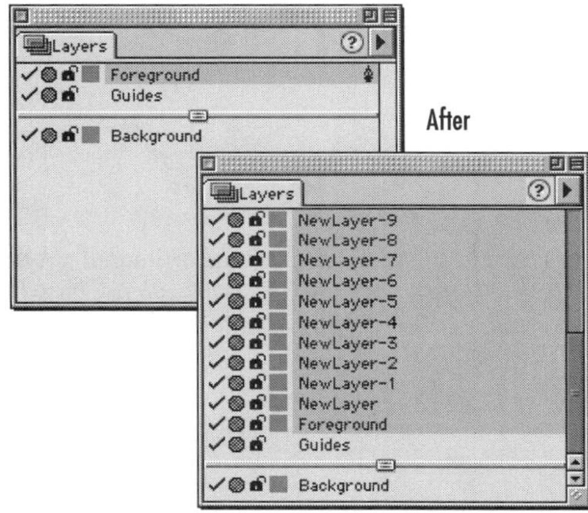

❺ **New layers are created** *after you apply the Release to Layers command.*

Animation Choices

The four animation choices make different movie effects.

- **Sequence** creates shows one element at a time.
- **Build** adds an element to the previous one.
- **Drop** creates the effect of each element dropping into place.
- **Trail** displays the new elements as the previous elements disappear.

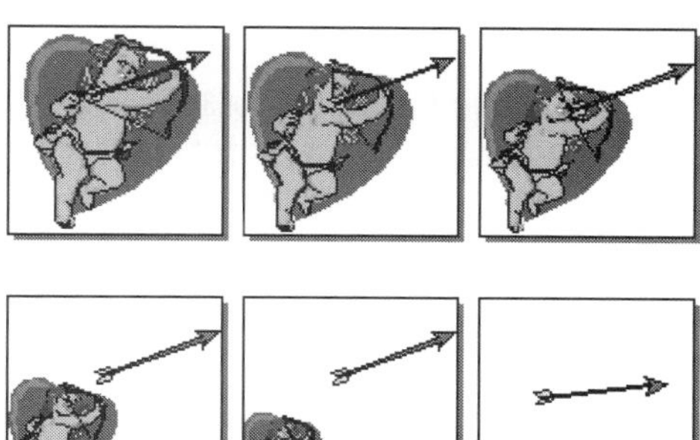

❻ *Individual pages can be used to layout a page animation.*

❼ *The common elements for this page animation come from the master pages.*

Creating Page-based Animations

You're not just limited to working with layers to create animations. You can use the document pages as the individual frames of an animation. The benefit of this method is that you can easily visualize the animation as you work.

To manually create a page animation:

1. Create your first frame's artwork on a page.
2. Duplicate the page and modify the artwork on that duplicate page.
3. Continue to duplicate pages and modify the artwork. Each page of the document becomes a frame of the animation ❻. You can then export the file as an animation. *(See page 250 for steps on how to export the file as an SWF movie.)*

To use master pages to create a page animation:

1. Create the master page or pages that contain the artwork.
2. Create as many child pages based on those master pages ❼.
3. Add individual elements to each page.

   or

   Use the Release child page command in the Document inspector panel. This releases the objects on the page from the master page symbols *(see Chapter 4, Working With Pages)*.
4. Select and modify the individual elements on each page.

Page- and Layer-based Animations

Finally, you can create animations that use both pages and layers as the animation frames ❽. The pages act like different scenes that you jump to, while the layers act like different frames.

To create page- and layer-based movies:

1. Apply the elements for the first scene on the first page.

   TIP To view the elements throughout the scene, place them on a non-printing layer.

2. Apply the elements for each frame to individual layers. These are the elements that change during the scene.
3. Apply the elements for the next scene to the next page.
4. Apply the elements for each frame to the individual layers. These are the elements that change during the scene.

   TIP Objects on each layer are seen only on the page that is displayed. So one layer can contain frames for different scenes.

   TIP You must have at least one element on a printing layer in order for any non-printing layers to be visible during the animation.

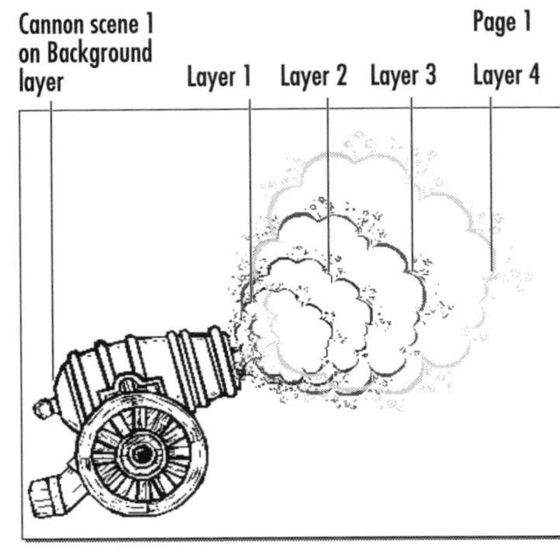

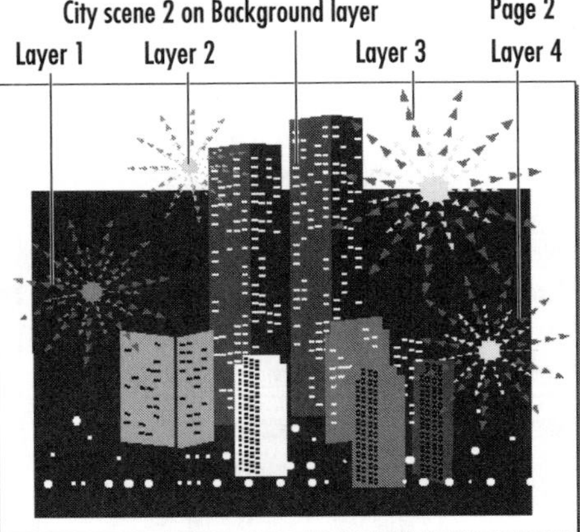

❽ *An example of how using both pages and layers can create an animation.*

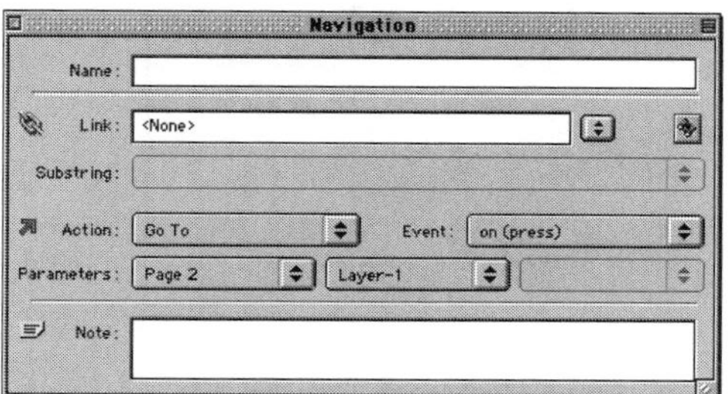

❾ *Use the* **Navigation panel** *to add Flash actions to objects.*

> ### Assigning Flash actions
>
> Although there are fewer actions in FreeHand, they are similar to the actions in Flash.
>
> - **Go To** jumps to a frame or scene.
> - **Play** and **Stop** control how the movie starts and stops.
> - **Print** specifies which frames users can print directly from the Flash Player.
> - **Full Screen** displays the movie in the Flash Player in full-screen mode, rather than normal mode.
> - **Start/Stop Drag** makes a movie clip draggable when an event happens, and stops the behavior when the opposite event occurs.
> - **Load Movie** and **Unload Movie** load and unload additional movies when the current movie is playing.
> - **Tell Target** controls other movies and movie clips that were loaded into the current movie with the Load Movie action.
>
> TIP FreeHand allows only one level of loaded movies; thus you can assign only one movie to load at a time.

Adding Flash Actions

Movies don't necessarily have to move—that is, you can go through a movie by manually advancing each frame. That sort of Flash movie is considered a series of Web pages. If you want you can add objects that act as buttons to advance a movie, print a page, or stop the playback.

To assign actions to artwork in FreeHand:

1. Select the object or objects to which you want to assign actions.

   TIP Objects must have a fill or stroke to create the area that can be manipulated.

2. In the Navigation panel, use the Action menu to select an action ❾. *(See the sidebar on this page for details on the actions.)*
3. Use the Event menu select the event that will trigger the action.

   TIP For Start/Stop Drag, the Event menu is disabled.

   TIP Depending on the action, you may need to set some or all of the Parameters menus.

4. If you selected Go To, Print, Load/Unload Movie, or Tell Target, use the first Parameters menu to select from the list of current document pages.
5. If you select Go To or Print, use the second Parameter menu to specify which part of the document should be displayed or printed.
6. If you select Tell Target, select an action from the second Parameter pop-up menu to control playback of another movie: GoTo, Play, Stop, or Print.
7. If you select GoTo or Print in step 6, use the third Parameter menu to specify which part of the document should be displayed or printed.

Flash Actions in Action

Here's a little explanation that can help you understand how the Flash actions work in Freehand.

The movie starts as a two-page Free-Hand file ⑩. The first page has all its objects on a non-printing layer. This is so those objects can be seen at all times.

The second page has the artwork for the cannon on a non-printing layer. Each puff of smoke for the blast is on its own printing layer. The printing layers create the effect of the cannon firing.

The Load Movie action with Page 2 as its parameter was applied to the *See the Cannon* button. When this button is clicked, the cannon appears on top of the first page ⑪.

The Start/Stop Drag action was applied to the cannon artwork. This allows the viewer to move the loaded movie around the page ⑫.

The Tell Target action with Page 2 as its parameter and Play as its event was applied to the *Shoot the Cannon* button. When this button is clicked, the smoke layers play as an animation.

The Tell Target action with Page 2 as its parameter and Stop as its event was applied to the *Stop the Blast* button ⑬. When this button is clicked, the smoke layers stop playing.

The Animation in the Movie Settings was set for Layers so that the smoke movie could play. Autoplay was turned off so that the movie would not start on its own.

When the movie was exported, there were actually two SWF files created: one for the buttons; another for the cannon movie.

⑩ **An interactive movie** *starts with two separate pages.*

⑪ *The* **Load Movie action** *lets the viewer add the Page 2 movie on top of Page 1.*

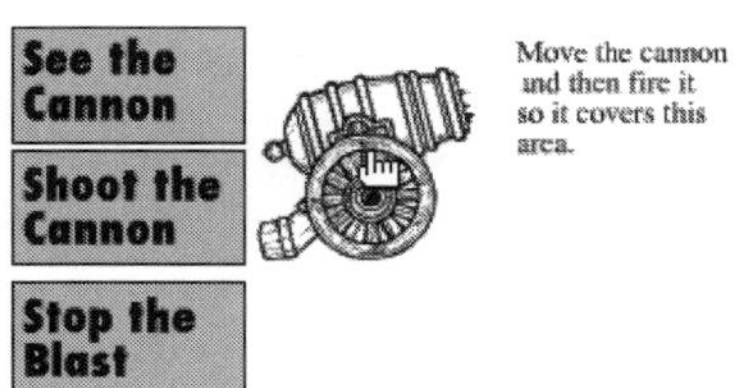

⑫ *The* **Start/Stop Drag action** *lets the viewer move the Page 2 movie around Page 1.*

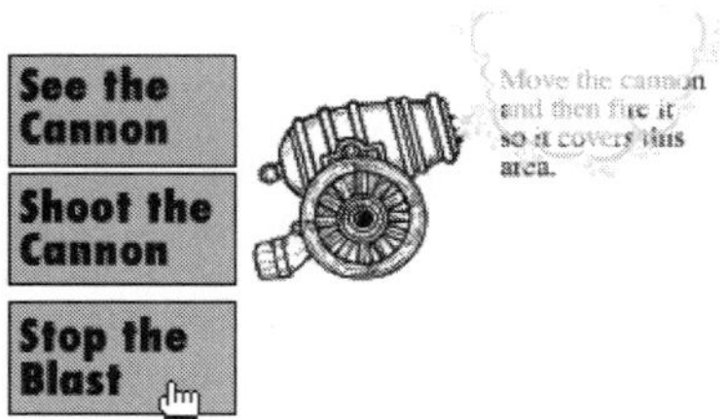

⑬ *The* **Tell Target action** *lets the viewer play or stop the Page 2 movie.*

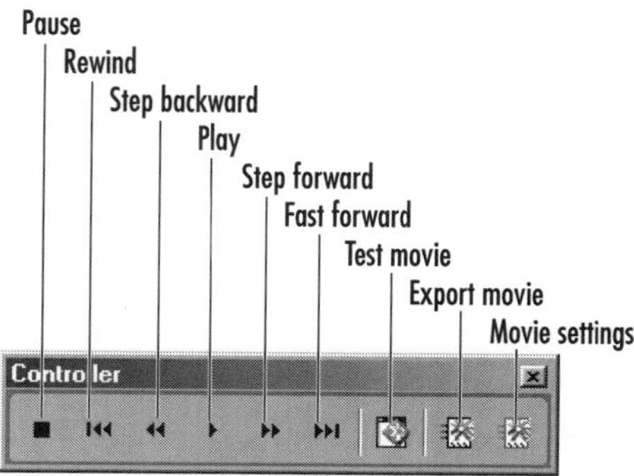

⓮ *Use the* **Controller panel** *to work with Flash movies.*

⓯ *The* **Flash player icon** *in the title bar indicates you are previewing the Flash movie.*

www.freehandsource.com

I would like to thank Ian Kelleigh for his help in describing how actions work on the preceding two pages.

Ian is the brains behind the Web site www.freehandsource.com. This unofficial Web site is one of the best resources for anyone who is learning FreeHand.

It also has history about all the different versions of FreeHand, online tips, and files you can download to see how the magic is created. The site also contains some excellent Flash training.

Testing and Controlling Movies

Once you create an animation, you will most likely want to see if it is running correctly. You may also want to change the settings that control how the movie runs. Fortunately you can test your movies within FreeHand.

To test a movie:

1. Choose **Control > Test Movie.**

   or

   Click the Test Movie button in the Controller toolbar ⓮. FreeHand processes the movie which opens in a separate window.

   TIP The Flash Player icon appears at the top of the test movie document ⓯.

   TIP The Test Movie command opens the move in the Flash player window. You then need to play the movie to see the animation.

2. To play the movie choose **Control > Play.**

   or

   Click the Play button in the Controller.

3. To stop the movie, choose **Control > Stop.**

   or

   Click the Stop button in the Controller.

4. To move one frame at a time, choose **Control > Step Forward** or **Control > Step Backward.**

   or

   Click the Step forward or Step backward buttons in the Controller.

5. To move to the start of the movie, choose **Control > Rewind.**

   or

   Click the Rewind button in the Controller.

6. To jump to the end of the movie click the Fast Forward button in the Controller.

To modify the movie settings:

- Choose **Control > Movie Settings.**

  or

  Click the Movie Settings button in the Controller. This opens the Movie Settings dialog box.

There are three different areas in the Movie Settings dialog box ⓰. The first area, Objects, controls the appearance of the FreeHand objects, text frames, and raster images that are exported into the Flash format. The second area, Frames, controls the actual animation of the movie. The final area, Publish, controls how the Flash file is created.

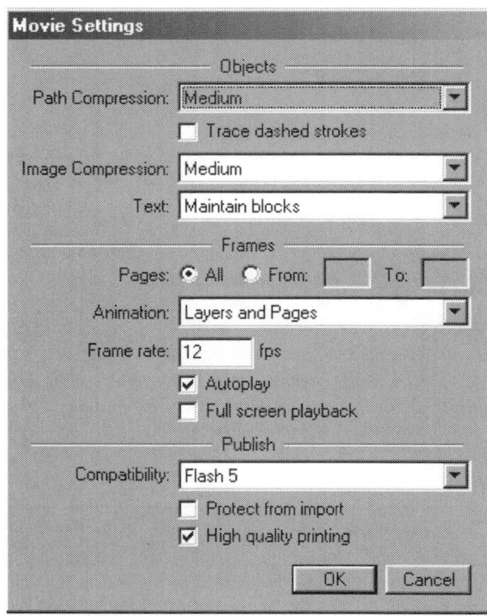

⓰ *Use the* **Movie Settings dialog box** *to control the appearance, behavior, and format of the exported SWF file.*

To set the Objects controls:

1. Use the Path Compression menu to control the precision used to convert FreeHand paths to Flash paths.

   TIP No compression is the most precise. Maximum compression creates the smallest files.

2. Use the Image Compression menu to control the compression of bitmapped images.
3. Choose one of the following from the Text menu to control what happens to text blocks.
   - **Maintain blocks** keeps all the text for editing in Flash.
   - **Convert to Paths** converts the text to artwork.
   - **None** deletes the text from the file.

   TIP The Convert to Paths option creates a slightly smaller Flash file but makes the text uneditable.

> **Flash or SWF: what's the difference?**
>
> Strictly speaking, there are no Flash files on the Web.
>
> A Flash file (.fla) is the native file format created by the Macromedia Flash application. You don't post those files on the Web.
>
> What most people call Flash movies on the Web are actually Shockwave Flash files (.swf). This is the file format that FreeHand exports as Macromedia Flash (SWF).
>
> However, the Flash application doesn't open SWF files. If you want to work with those files within Flash, you need to choose **File>Import** from within Flash. However, that option may often chop up the file into pieces that are difficult to work with.
>
> Ironically, Flash itself can not import FreeHand files. You need to save the FreeHand file in the Illustrator format. Flash can then import that file—and maintain the layers.
>
> A better option for working with Freehand artwork within Flash is to use the simple Copy and Paste or Drag and Drop.

To set the Frames controls:

1. Use the Pages options to choose which pages are part of the animation.
2. Choose one of the following from the Animation menu:
   - **Pages** exports each page as a Flash frame in one SWF file. The layers of each page make up the entire image for that frame.
   - **Layers** exports each page as a separate SWF file, with the layers of each page as separate frames in the each SWF file.
   - **Layers and Pages** exports a single SWF file that contains all the FreeHand document content. All layers of the first page are converted to frames. Then all the layers of the second page are converted to frames, and so on.
   - **None** exports each page as a separate SWF file.

   TIP Guides layer and hidden layers are not seen in the animation.
3. Set the Frame rate. The default is 12 and creates reasonably smooth movement.
4. Check the Autoplay option if you want your animation to automatically start.
5. Check Full screen playback to have the movie automatically expand to fill the monitor screen.

To set the Frames controls:

1. Use the Compatibility menu to choose which version of the Flash Player is necessary to play the final file.

   TIP The Flash 5 player provides the most features. Older versions of the Flash Player are more widely distributed.
2. Check Protect from import to prevent others from downloading the file.
3. Check High quality printing to allow the Flash file to be printed using its full resolution. If not selected, the file prints at screen resolution.

Exporting a Flash (SWF) File

Once you have all the movie settings to your liking, it is a simple step to export the SWF file. If you are in the Flash Player window for the Test Movie command, you can easily export the movie at the current settings.

To export a SWF file from the Flash Player:

- Choose **Control > Export Movie.**

  or

  Click the Export Movie button in the Controller. This opens the Export dialog box where you can name the exported file and save it to a location 17.

TIP The Flash movie is exported using whatever settings are currently active in the Movie Settings dialog box.

You can also export an SWF file directly from the FreeHand document.

To export a SWF file from the FreeHand window:

1. Choose **Edit>Export.** This opens the Export Document dialog box 18.
2. Choose Macromedia Flash (SWF) from the format list.
3. Click the Setup button. This opens the Movie Settings dialog box.
4. Make any necessary changes to the Movie Settings dialog box and click OK.
5. Name the exported file and save it to a location.

17 *When you export from the Flash Player, the* **Export Movie dialog box** *only requires you to name the file and choose a destination.*

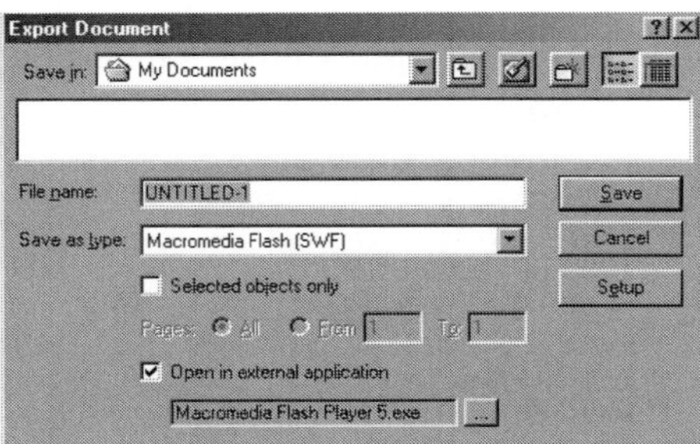

18 *When you export from the FreeHand document, you open the regular* **Export Document dialog box.**

BASIC PRINTING 30

When I first started using illustration programs, print was the ultimate goal. You either printed to a low-end desktop printer in your own office or you sent your work to a high-end service bureau or a print shop to be printed on a professional imagesetter.

Nobody ever thought that you could turn FreeHand files into Web pages, much less Flash movies. In fact, today there are people who work extensively in FreeHand and never see their work in print.

Fortunately there are still many others who want to hold a hard copy printed version of their artwork. Some of them need to print only to their own office printer. This chapter is for them.

The others are interested in sending their files to professional service bureaus and print shops. They need to read this chapter and then go on to the next chapter.

Setting the Basic Print Options

For most basic printing, there are just a few options that you need to set. For instance, you may simply want to set the number of pages that you need to print.

To set the number of copies and print range (Mac):

1. Choose **File > Print.** The Print dialog box appears ❶.
2. If it is not active, choose the General setting from the top menu in the printer dialog box.
3. In the Copies field, enter the number of copies you want to print.
4. In the Pages section, choose All to print all the pages in your document.

   or

   Enter the range of pages. If you want to print only one page, type that page number in both the From and To fields.
5. Click OK to print the file.

TIP The Mac Print dialog box may look different if you have different printer software.

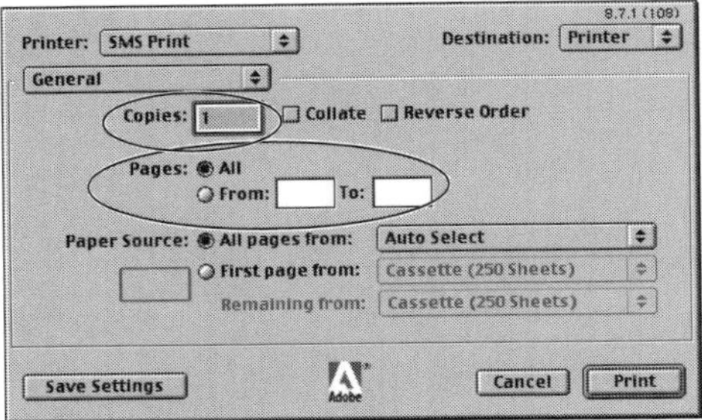

❶ *The* **General menu of the Print dialog box** *lets you choose the page and copies options for the Macintosh platform.*

To set the number of copies and print range (Win):

1. Choose **File > Print.** The Print dialog box appears ❷.
2. In the Output section, enter the number of copies you want to print.
3. In the Print Range options, choose All to print all the pages in your document.

   or

   Choose Current page to print the active page in the document window.

   or

   Choose Pages and enter specific page numbers to print only certain pages.
4. Click OK to print the file.

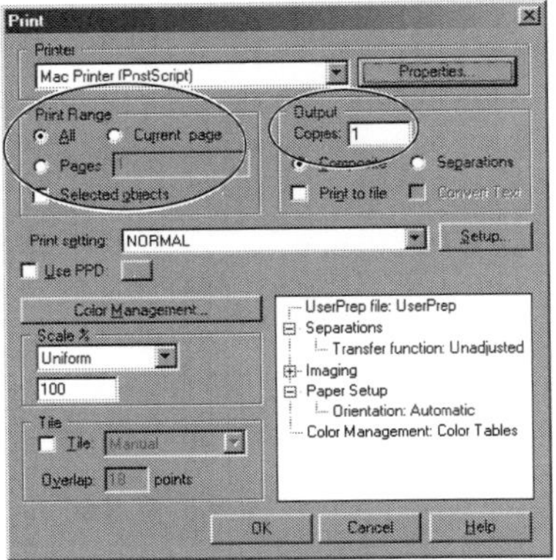

❷ *The* **Print Range** *and* **Output sections** *of the* **Print dialog box** *lets you choose the page and copies options for the Windows platform.*

> **Do you have a PostScript printer?**
>
> Before you print your document, determine what kind of printer you will be using. If your printer is not a PostScript device, the Custom, Textured, and PostScript fills and strokes do not print. If you are in doubt as to the type of printer you have, check the documentation that came with the printer.

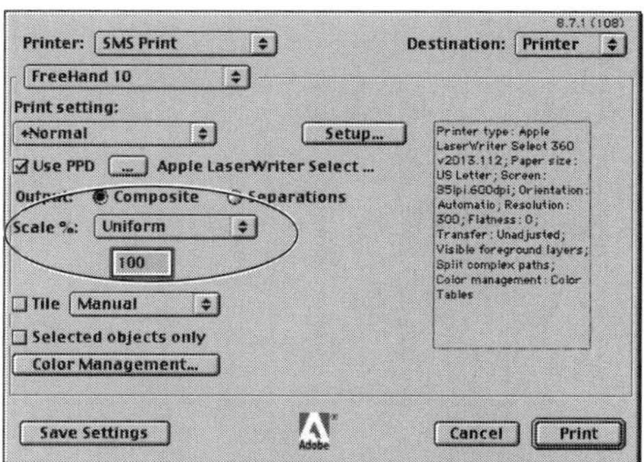

❸ *(Mac) The* **Scale % of the Print dialog box** *lets you change the size of the printed file.*

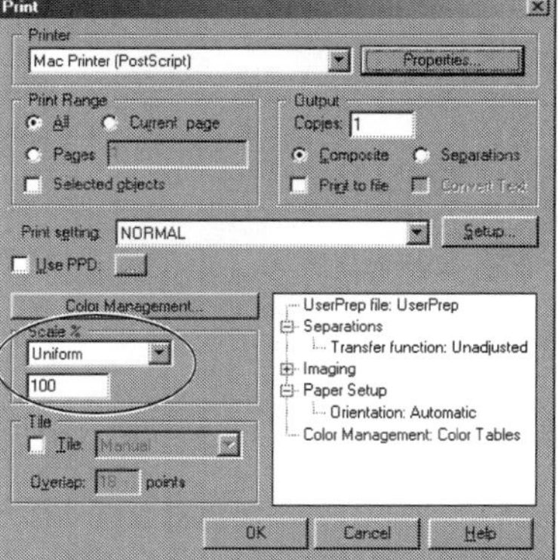

❹ *(Win) The* **Scale % of the Print dialog box** *lets you change the size of the printed file.*

To scale as you print (Mac):

1. If it is not active, choose the FreeHand setting from the top menu in the printer dialog box.
2. Choose one of the following from the Scale menu ❸:
   - **Uniform** scales the artwork without distorting it.
   - **Variable** scales the artwork with different amounts for the **x** and **y** dimensions.
   - **Fit on paper** changes the size of your illustration so that it fits on the paper.

TIP The Fit on paper option is very helpful when using the Print Area tool to print many different pages.

3. If you have chosen Uniform or Variable, enter the amounts in the percentage field.

To scale as you print (Win):

1. In the Print dialog box, choose one of the following from the Scale menu ❹:
   - **Uniform** scales the artwork without distorting it.
   - **Variable** scales the artwork with different amounts for the **x** and **y** dimensions.
   - **Fit on paper** changes the size of your illustration so that it fits on the paper.

TIP The Fit on paper option is very helpful when using the Print Area tool to print many different pages.

2. If you have chosen Uniform or Variable, enter the amounts in the percentage field.

FreeHand uses the PPD (PostScript Printer Description) information for the page setup. To set choices such as paper size and orientation, select the correct PPD for your printer.

To select the PPD:

1. In either the Printer dialog box or the Print Setup dialog box, click on Use PPD.
2. Click the ellipsis (…) button to find the list of PPDs that are installed.
3. Find the PPD for your printer and click Open. The information from that PPD is shown in the Print Setup box.

Most likely you will always want to print a *composite* image of your file ❺. This is an image that combines all the colors together into one image. However, if you want you can print separations. That gives you a individual print for each of the ink colors that are used to create the file ❻.

To set the basic separations options:

◆ If your illustration has color in it, choose Composite or Separations.

TIP You can print to separations to make sure you have set your document up properly for different color plates. Each piece of paper that is printed counts as a color plate in your document. Too many plates means you have probably defined too many spot colors.

❺ *A* **Composite print** *displays a combination of all the colors.*

❻ **Separations** *print each individual color of the image.*

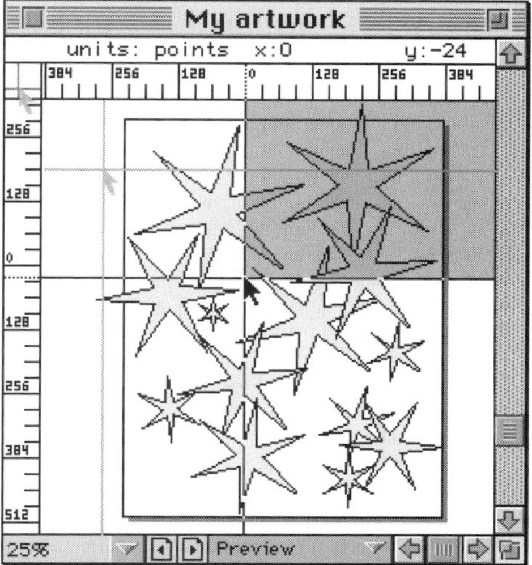

❼ **Drag the zero point** *from the ruler to set the position of the page for Manual tiling. (The shaded area shows the portion of the page that will print.)*

Printing Custom Selections

Just as you can print a selected range of pages, you can also print selected object on the page.

To print selected objects:

1. Select the objects you would like to print.
2. In the Print dialog box, click Selected objects only.
3. Set any of the other options and print as usual.

If your artwork is bigger than the paper in your printer, you won't be able to fit the illustration on one page. *Tiling* is a technique that lets you break up your illustration onto many pieces of paper that you can assemble to form the larger illustration.

To set the tile options:

1. In the Print dialog box, select the Tile.
2. Choose one of the following the from Tile options:
   - Manual lets you manually choose which where the tile breaks should appear.
   - Automatic sets each of the tile breaks automatically.
3. If you choose Auto, choose how much overlap you want between each page.

To manually tile an illustration:

1. In the document, move the zero point from the ruler down onto the artwork ❼.

TIP The zero point sets the artwork above and to the right of that point to print.

2. In the Print dialog box, set the Manual tile option and print that portion of the artwork.
3. Set a new zero point and print that next portion of the artwork.
4. Repeat step 3 as many times as is necessary to print the entire illustration.

In addition to printing selected items, you can also print within a selected area. This is extremely helpful if you would like to create thumbnails of a large number of pages or print items that are off the page.

❽ *The* **Print Area cursor** *lets you choose the specific area to be printed.*

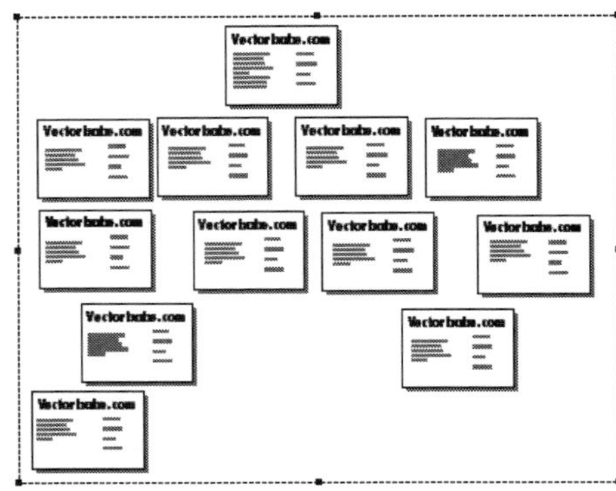

❾ *The* **Print Area handles** *let you define a specific area to print.*

To print a selected area:

1. Choose **File > Print Area**. This displays the Print Area cursor ❽.
2. Drag the Print Area cursor around the area that you want to print. A box with handles appears ❾.
3. Use any of the handles to adjust the area within the box.
4. When you are satisfied with the size of the area, double-click inside the box with the Print Selection cursor ❿. This opens the Print dialog box.
5. Set the Print dialog box controls as usual.

TIP If you have selected a large area to be printed, you may need to set the Scale options to Fit on paper.

❿ *Double-click with the* **Print Selection cursor** *to finalize the area to be printed.*

ADVANCED PRINTING 31

Even if you don't actually print to an imagesetter, you still need to understand the controls in the advanced printing options. They will help you understand any instructions that your print shop or service bureau may ask you to do to the file.

You also need to know how to prepare your file so that it can be sent out for high-end printing.

Some of this information is less for designers, illustrators, and graphic artists. However, if you're a designer working on your own, think of this chapter as your introduction to production trouble-shooting.

If you work in a large organization, you may have a production manager whose job it is to set up your files for final output. Don't be lazy just because you have someone else to check production. Take the time to ask questions and learn something about production. You never know when you'll be out on your own without a large staff to back you up.

Using the Print Setup Controls

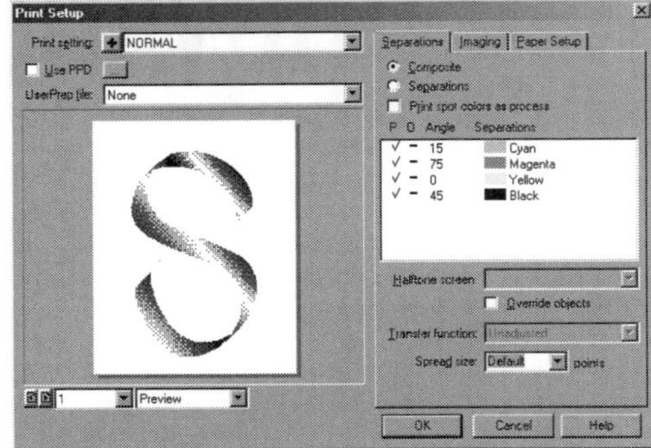

❶ *The two sides of the* **Print Setup dialog box.**

To open the Print Setup:

1. Choose **File > Print** to open the Print dialog box.
2. Click the Setup button. This opens the Print Setup dialog box ❶.

The left side of the Print Setup box shows a preview of the artwork to be printed. You can make some modifications to the artwork in this box.

To control the Print Setup preview:

1. In the Print Setup dialog box, use the page number pop-up menu to control which pages are visible.
2. Use the preview pop-up menu to choose one of the following preview options ❷.
   - **Preview** displays the artwork with all the fills, colors, and so on.
   - **Keyline** shows just the paths that define the objects without the fills, colors, and so on.
   - **X-Box** fills the preview area with an **X** that indicates the page.

   TIP If your artwork is extremely detailed, you may find it faster to view the print preview in the Keyline or X-Box modes.
3. Drag to move the artwork to different positions in the Print Preview area.

   TIP If you have moved the preview artwork, click the area just outside the print preview to restore it to the original position.

❷ *The left side of the* **Print Setup dialog box** *contains the Preview controls.*

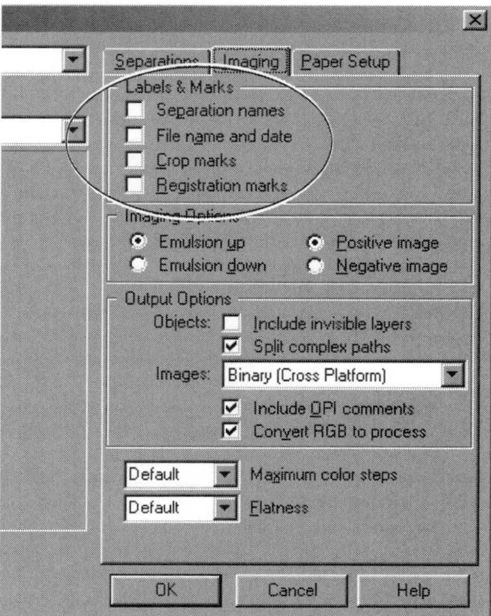

❸ *Click the boxes for each of the Labels & Marks to have those marks printed around the artwork.*

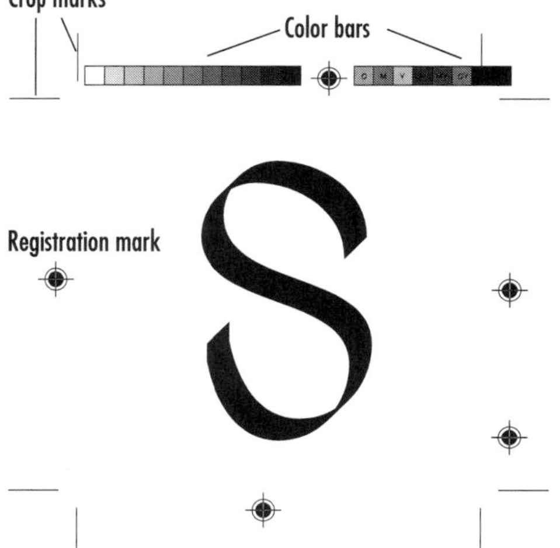

❹ *Artwork printed with* **Crop marks** and **Registration marks** *selected.*

Setting the Imaging Options

When you print a file, the print shop that will be printing the job may ask you to add certain labels and marks around your artwork. Rather than create these marks manually, FreeHand can automatically add them.

To add labels and marks:

1. In the Print Setup dialog box, click the tab for Imaging. The Labels & Marks options appear on the right side of the dialog box ❸.
2. Click Separation names to add a label with the name of the color plate that is printed.
3. Click File name and date to add the name of the file, page number, and date and time that the file is printed.
4. Click Crop marks to add the marks that indicate the trim size of the artwork.
5. Click Registration marks to add registration marks and color bars that are necessary for printing multiple colors.

TIP The labels and marks appear in the Print Setup preview only if the page size for the FreeHand document is smaller than the paper size selected in the print setup ❹.

The imaging options control the look and direction of the images when printed. This is used when creating film to create a negative of the image and control its direction.

To choose the imaging options:

1. In the Print Setup dialog box, click the tab for Imaging. The Imaging Options appear on the right side of the Print Setup dialog box ❺.
2. Choose one of the following emulsion options:
   - **Emulsion up** prints the file so that the emulsion is up.
   - **Emulsion down** prints the file so that the emulsion is down.

TIP These two settings are controlled by the requirements of your print shop and matter only when preparing to print film.

3. Choose one of the following color options.
   - **Positive image** is used for printing to paper.
   - **Negative image** is used for printing to film.

TIP Negative image is the usual choice when printing to film separations, but check with your printer to be sure.

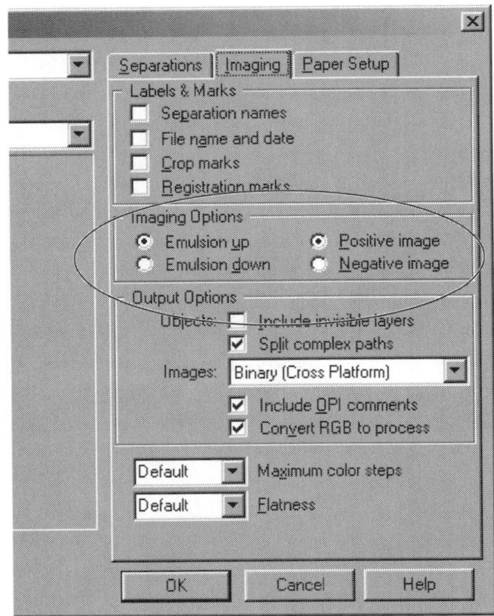

❺ *Click the* **Imaging options** *to control the color and direction of the image.*

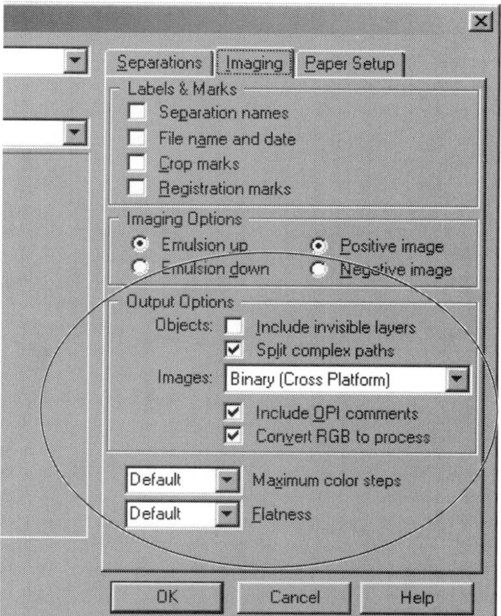

❻ *The* **Output options** *control the aspects of a FreeHand file and exported images.*

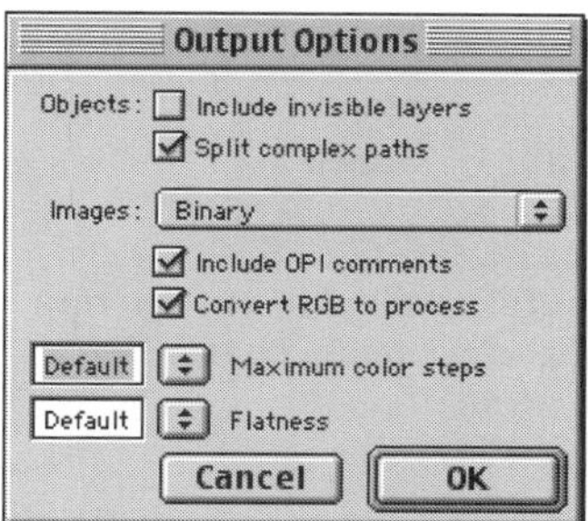

❼ *The* **Output Options dialog box** *let you set the output options without using the Print command.*

FreeHand offers various options for printing to a PostScript device. These options stay with the file when it is saved or exported as an EPS file *(see pages 23 and 322).*

To set the Output Options:

1. In the Print Setup dialog box, click the tab for Imaging. The Output Options appear ❻.

TIP You can also set the Output Options by choosing **File > Output Options** ❼.

2. Check Include invisible layers to print objects that are on hidden layers. Otherwise those layers do not print.
3. Check Split complex paths, to automatically split long paths.

TIP Modern printing software is less likely to need this option.

4. Choose one of the following from the Images menu:
   - **Binary** or **Binary** (**Macintosh**) is used for printing on the Macintosh platform.
   - **Binary** (**Cross Platform**) is used for both Macintosh and Windows.
   - **ASCII** is used only for the Windows platform or if you have trouble outputting on the Macintosh platform.
   - **None** is for when using an OPI system.
5. Select Include OPI comments if TIFF images will be replaced during prepress.
6. Choose Convert RGB to process if you have RGB TIFF in the file.

To set the Maximum Steps:

- Leave this field set for Default. If you have trouble printing, use the pop-up menu to set a lower number in the Maximum color steps field.

To set the Flatness:

- Leave this field set for Default. If you get a limitcheck error when printing, enter a number from 1 to 100 in the Flatness field.

Setting the Separations Options

The Separations options control how the colors of your file print when outputting your work to separate pieces of film.

To choose the Separations options:

1. In the Print Setup dialog box, click the tab for Separations ❽.
2. If you want all the colors to print together, click Composite.
3. To separate the colors to different plates, click Separations.
4. Click Print spot colors as process to override the settings for spot colors.
5. To prevent a color from printing, click its checkmark in the **P** column to delete the checkmark for that color.

To set the overprint options:

1. In the separations options, click the O column. The Overprint Ink dialog box appears ❾.
2. Choose one of the following:
   - On sets all instances of that color to overprint.
   - Threshold specifies what tint of that color or higher will overprint.
   - Off turns off overprinting.

TIP A checkmark in the **O** column of the indicates that the ink is set to overprint. A diamond indicates that the ink is set to overprint at a threshold level.

To set the screen angle:

1. Click the angle column for that color. The Screen Angle dialog box appears ❿.
2. Enter the angle you want for that color and click OK.
3. Repeat for each color.

TIP Consult with your print shop before you adjust the screen angles, screen frequency, or overprinting options.

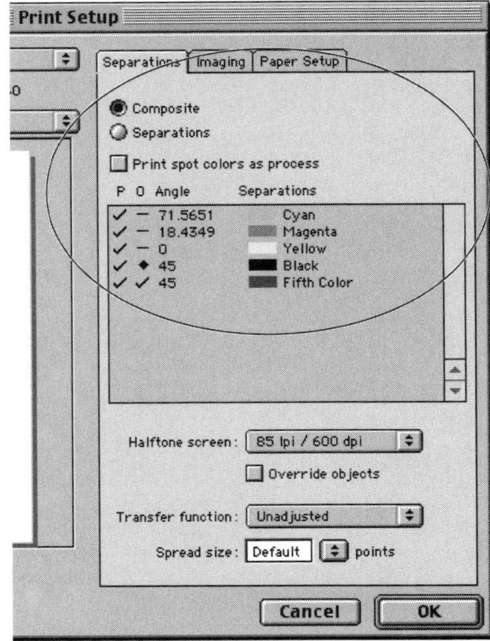

❽ *The* **Separations** *controls.*

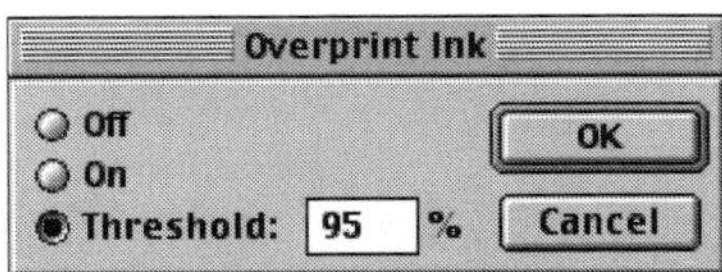

❾ *The* **Overprint Ink dialog box** *lets you turn on overprinting or set an amount at which overprinting will occur.*

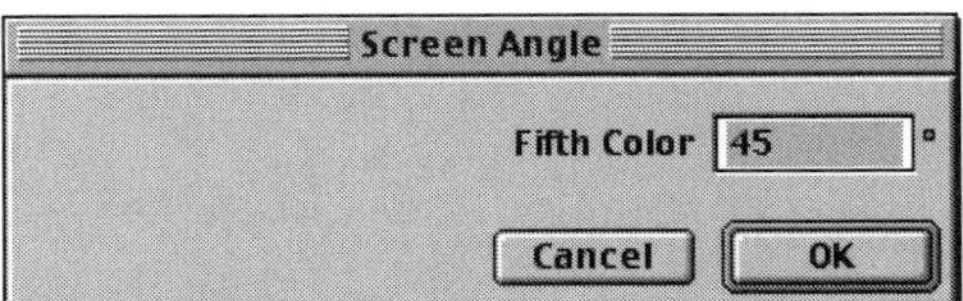

❿ *The* **Screen Angle dialog box** *lets you set the angle at which a color's screens will be printed.*

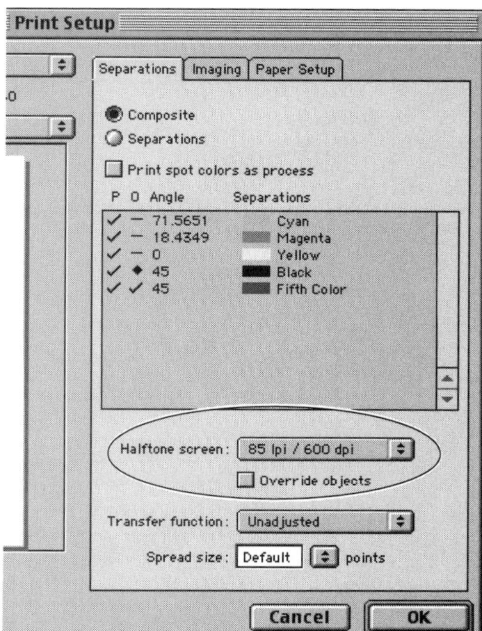

⓫ *The* **Halftone screen** *controls.*

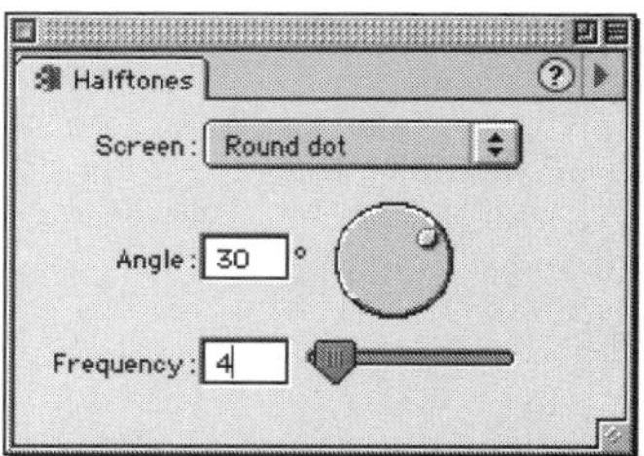

⓬ *The* **Halftone panel** *lets you change the halftone screen for individual objects.*

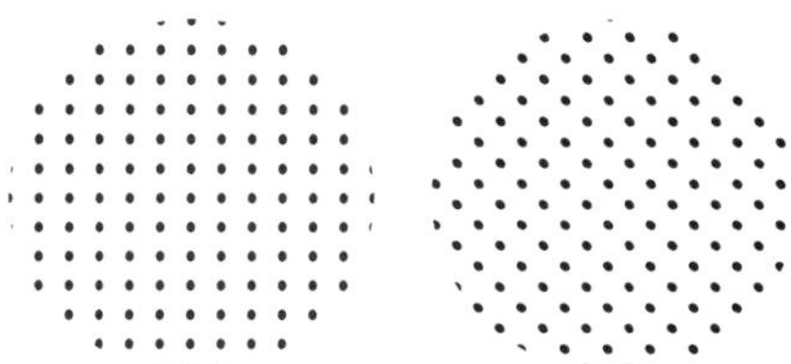

⓭ *The difference between a screen angle of zero degrees (left) and 45 degrees (right).*

If your artwork has any screened objects, you may want to set the halftone screen.

To set the halftone screen:

1. Select the printer's PPD.
2. Open the Separations options.
3. Use the Halftone screen pop-up menu in the Separations options to choose from the list of common screens for your output device ⓫.
4. To override any halftone screens set for individual objects, click Override objects.

TIP If you print to a laser printer and find banding in your blends, lower the screen frequency to around 35 lpi (lines per inch) or 40 lpi. While the screened artwork may look a little "dotty," this should reduce the banding.

In addition to setting the halftone screen for the entire illustration, you can set the halftone screen for individual objects.

To set the halftone screen for individual objects:

1. Select the object whose halftone screen you want to set.
2. Choose **Window > Panels > Halftone.** The Halftone panel appears ⓬.
3. Choose the shape of the screen dot from the Screen pop-up menu.
4. Enter the angle of the screen in the Angle field or rotate the wheel to set the screen angle. If no value is set, the default angle of 45 degrees is used ⓭.
5. Enter the frequency (lines per inch) of the screen in the Frequency field or use the slider to set the number. If no value is set, the default of the output device is used.

The Transfer function controls the dot gain for screened images.

To set the Transfer function:

- With the Separations tab selected in the Print Setup dialog box, select one of the following from the Transfer function menu ⓮:
  - **Unadjusted** is used if you are printing to a specially calibrated output device.
  - **Normalize** is used if you are printing to an ordinary laser printer.
  - **Posterize** is used if you want to speed the printing and do not mind sacrificing quality. This reduces the number of levels of screens.

In addition to the Trap Xtra *(see page 174)*, FreeHand has a global trapping option called spread.

To choose the spread size:

- In the Spread size field, enter the amount that you want basic fills and strokes to expand ⓮. This compensates for misregistrations in the printing. Before you enter any amount, talk to the print shop where the artwork will be printed.

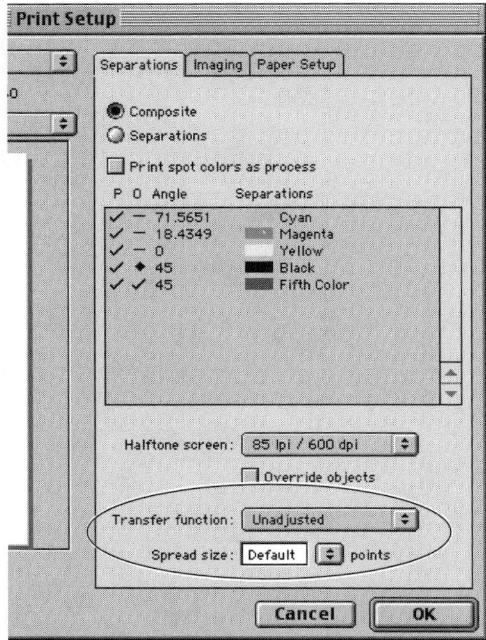

⓮ *The* **Transfer function and Spread size** *controls.*

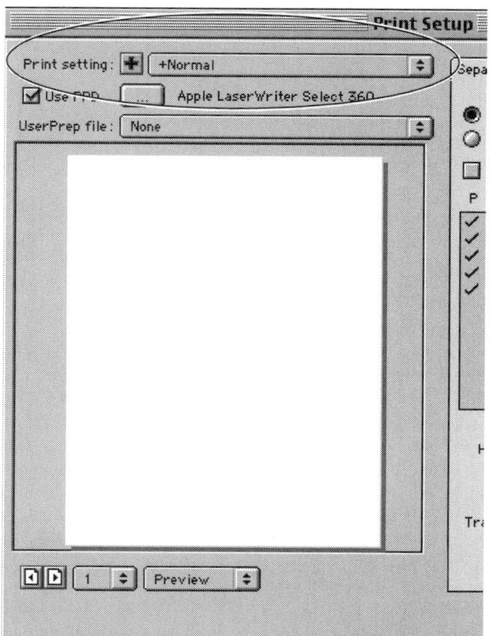

⓯ *The* **Print setting controls** *allow you to save and apply preset print options.*

Saving Print Settings

If you are working with a specific print shop, they may give you a complete set of instructions as to how to save your file. You may want to reapply those settings without going through all the Print Setup controls. FreeHand lets you save all the print options so you can easily apply them to other work.

To save print settings:

1. Set all the print options the way you want the file to print.
2. Click the + sign next to the Print Settings pop-up menu ⓯. A Save dialog box appears.
3. Use the Save dialog box to name and save the file in the PrintSet directory. This adds the preset to the pop-up menu.

To apply print settings:

- Choose a setting from the Print Settings menu.

Collecting for Output

If you send your document to be printed by someone else, it is handy to have a record of all the information about the file. FreeHand provides you with a very sophisticated report for all your documents.

To create a document report:

1. With the document open, choose **File > Report**. The Document Report dialog box appears ⑯.
2. Click the categories listed on the left side of the Document Report dialog box. Each one of these categories then displays a different set of Options. *(See the sidebar on the next page for a list of the options for each category.)*
3. Click each of the Options for each category to indicate which information you want listed.
4. Click Report (Mac) or OK (Win) to see the Document Report Viewer ⑰, where you can read the complete document report.
5. Click Save to create a permanent text file of your report.

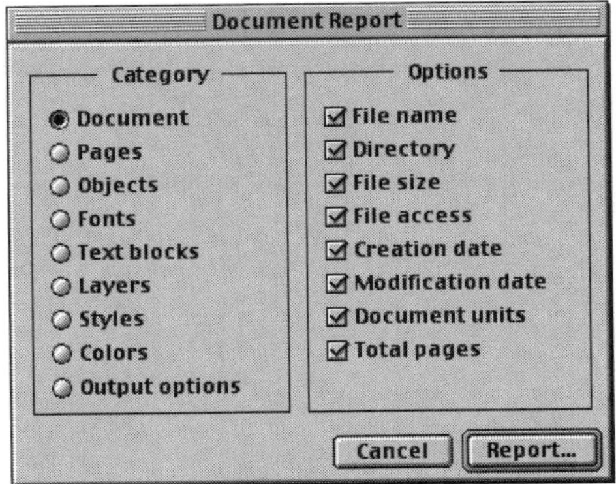

⑯ *The* **Document Report dialog box** *lets you select the information to be included in the document report.*

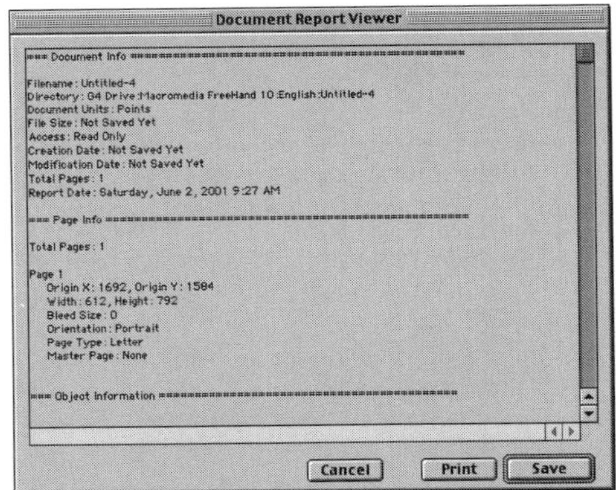

⑰ *The* **Document Report Viewer** *lets you read the report, save it as a text file, or print it.*

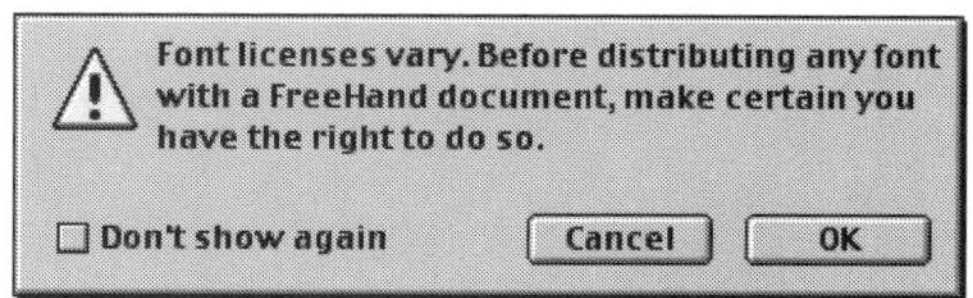

⓲ *The alert box that appears as part of the Collect For Output process.*

⓳ *The files assembled by the Collect For Output command.*

Information in each report category

Document: File name, Directory, File size, File access, Creation date, Modification date, Document units, Total pages

Pages: Page location, Dimensions, Bleed size, Orientation, Page type

Objects: Set Note, Halftone, Place file

Fonts: Font name, Font PS name, Font file format, Font style, Font size

Text: Blocks Fonts used, Color used, Bounding box, Line count, Paragraph count, First line

Layers: Foreground layers, Background layers, Visibility, Editing color, Access, Preview status

Styles: Graphics styles, Text styles

Colors: Named colors, Separations

Output Options: Invisible layers, Split paths, Image date, Convert image, Max color steps, Flatness

Unless you have your own high-resolution imagesetter, you must transfer your work onto a floppy disk or some type of removable media such as a Zip disk. You then send the disk or cartridge to a service bureau that will output the file. You must send certain files along with your FreeHand file. Rather than collect these file manually, the Collect For Output feature automates the process.

To use the Collect For Output command:

1. Choose **File > Collect For Output**. An alert box appears warning you that you should find out whether or not you have the rights to distribute fonts ⓲. Click OK.

   TIP Click Don't show again to stop the alert from appearing.

2. The Document Report dialog box appears *(see previous page)*. Click each of the Options for each category to indicate which information you want listed. Click OK.
3. Choose a destination for the report and files, such as a folder on the current drive or a removable cartridge. Click Save.
4. FreeHand collects all the files necessary to print the document ⓳. This includes the original FreeHand file, linked graphics, the document report, fonts, the printer user prep, and printer driver (Mac).

CUSTOMIZING FREEHAND 32

Assemble a group of Macromedia FreeHand users in the same room and you're going to get a very diverse group of people.

For instance, those who have been working with FreeHand for many years can't stand the idea of someone changing a single keystroke.

Others who work extensively with a particular feature, such as the Xtra tools, may want them to be added to the Tools panel.

Others may have migrated over to FreeHand from another program such as Adobe Illustrator, CorelDraw, or QuarkXPress. They may want to make FreeHand work similarly to those programs.

Finally, someone just might want a different page size to come up each time them open a new document.

Fortunately FreeHand gives you a wealth of opportunities to customize the program.

Changing the Toolbars

Each of the toolbars comes with different themes—the main tools, xtra tools, xtra operations, and so on. However, you can easily customize each toolbar with whatever commands you would like.

To open the Customize Toolbars dialog box (Win):

1. Choose **Edit > Keyboard Shortcuts**. The Customize dialog box appears.
2. Click the Toolbars tab to open the controls for the Toolbars ❶.

To open the Customize Toolbars dialog box (Mac):

◆ Choose **Window > Toolbars > Customize**. The Customize Toolbars dialog box appears ❷.

To add an icon to a toolbar:

1. Open the toolbar that you want to customize.
2. Open the Customize Toolbars dialog box as explained in the previous exercises.
3. Open the categories on the left side of the Customize Toolbars dialog box to find the command that you want to add to a toolbar.
4. Select the command. The icon for the command highlights on the right side of the dialog box.
5. Drag the icon for the command onto the toolbar.

TIP In addition to the toolbars listed under the **Window > Toolbars** menu, you can drag icons onto the Tools panel ❸.

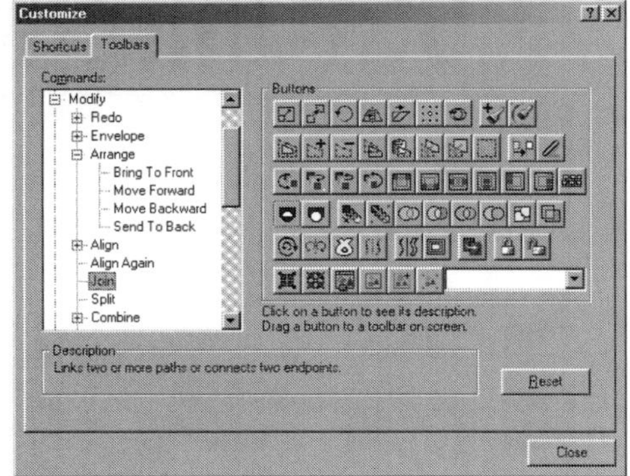

❶ *The Windows* **Customize Toolbars dialog box** *lets you add commands to the toolbars.*

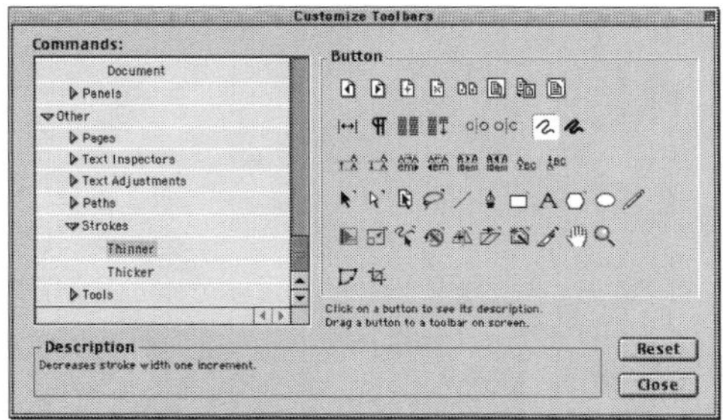

❷ *The Macintosh* **Customize Toolbars dialog box** *lets you add commands to the toolbars.*

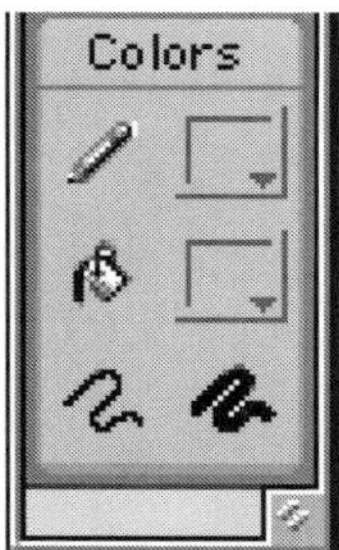

❸ *An example of how the icons to decrease or increase the stroke weight appear when added to the Tools panel.*

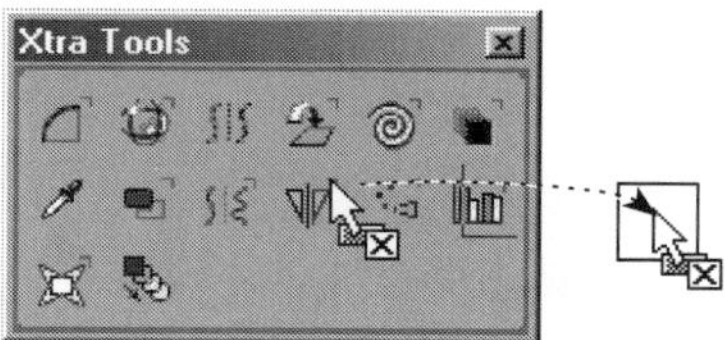

❹ *You can* **drag an icon off** *a toolbar.*

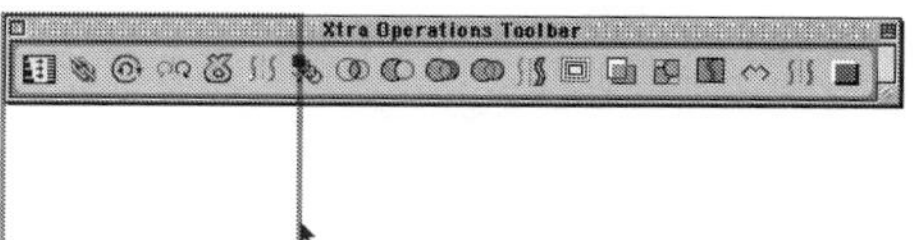

❺ *Drag the corner to* **resize a toolbar.**

To delete icons from the toolbars:

- With the Customize Toolbars dialog box open, drag an icon off any toolbar ❹.

  or

  Hold the Cmd/Alt key and drag an icon off a toolbar at any time without opening the Customize Toolbars dialog box.

To add icons from one toolbar to another:

- With the Customize Toolbars dialog box open, drag an icon off one toolbar onto another.

  or

  Hold the Cmd/Alt key and drag an icon off one toolbar onto another without opening the Customize Toolbars dialog box.

To change the shape of toolbars:

1. Position the Pointer over the corner of a toolbar.
2. Drag the toolbar to the new shape ❺.

Modifying the Keyboard Shortcuts

FreeHand lets you customize the keyboard shortcuts that are assigned to commands. This allows you to add shortcuts to commands or to change the shortcuts so they match other programs.

To customize keyboard shortcuts (Mac):

1. Choose **Edit > Keyboard Shortcuts.** The Customize Shortcuts dialog box appears ❻.
2. Use the categories on the left side of the dialog box to find the command that you want to customize.
3. Click the command. The current shortcut keys, if any, appear in the Current shortcut keys area.
4. Type the keyboard shortcut that you want for the command.
5. If the shortcut is assigned to another command, that command appears after the words *Currently Assigned to.* Type a new command or change the conflicting shortcut.
6. Click Assign to set the shortcut.
7. Repeat the steps to assign additional commands or click the Close button to return to the work page.

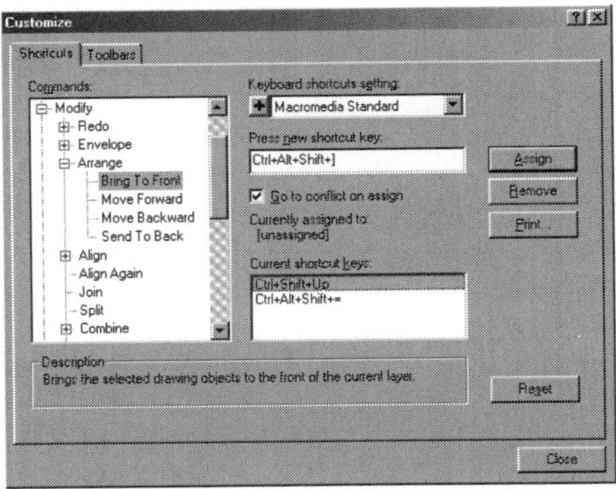

❻ *The* **Customize Shortcuts** *dialog box.*

Preset Shortcuts

The following are the preset shortcuts that are available. Where indicated, some shortcuts are available only for the Windows or Macintosh versions of FreeHand.

Authorware 4

CorelDRAW 6 (Mac)

CorelDRAW 7 (Win)

Fontographer 4.1 (Mac)

FreeHand 8

FreeHand 9

Illustrator 6 (Mac)

Illustrator 7

Macromedia Standard

PageMaker 6 (Mac)

Photoshop 4 (Mac)

QuarkXPress 3.3

QuarkXPress 4

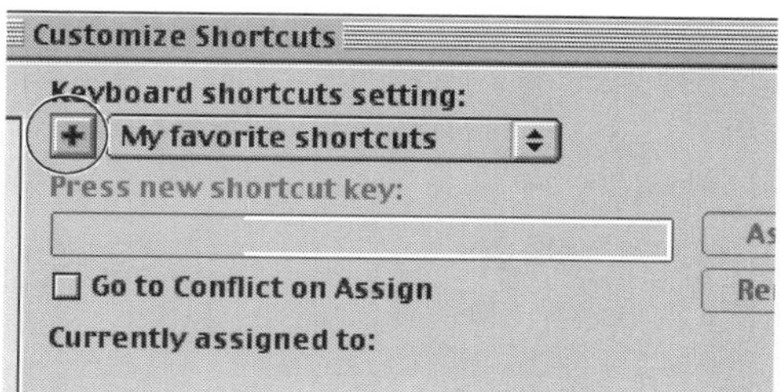

❼ *Click the plus sign (circled) to add a custom keyboard setting.*

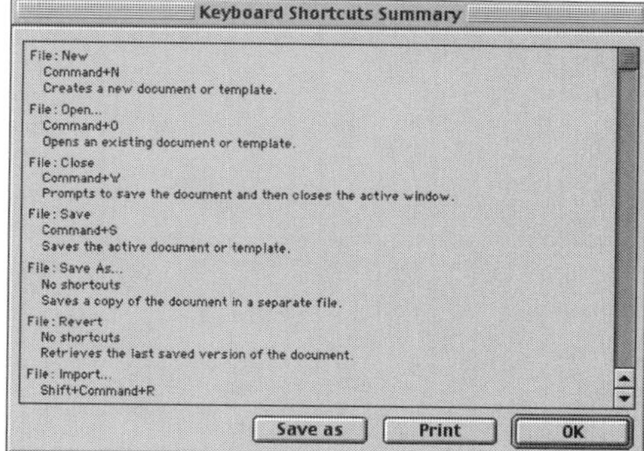

❽ *The* **Keyboard Shortcuts Summary** *contains a list of all the keyboard shortcuts.*

What is the Macromedia Standard?

The set of shortcuts that is active when you first install FreeHand is called the Macromedia Standard set.

This set uses slightly different shortcuts from previous versions of FreeHand.

It was created for those who use applications such as Macromedia Flash or Macromedia Dreamweaver.

If you have used previous versions of Freehand, you may be more comfortable using those presets. However, if you work with other Macromedia products, you may be more comfortable working with the Macromedia Standard set.

Once you have created a set of shortcuts, you can save that set as a preset that you can choose at any time.

To save a custom preset:

1. Click the plus sign next to the Keyboard shortcut settings menu ❼.
2. Use the dialog box to save the preset as a file in the Macromedia FreeHand 10: English: Settings: Keyboard folder. This lists the setting along with the other presets.

If you are used to working in other programs, you can change the shortcuts to match the keystrokes of other programs.

To apply the preset shortcuts:

1. Use the Keyboard shortcut setting pop-up menu to display the list of preset shortcuts.
2. Choose from the list of presets and then click Assign.

You can also print out a list of the keyboard shortcuts to hang next to your computer screen.

To print the keyboard shortcuts:

1. Click the Print button. The Keyboard Shortcuts Summary dialog box appears that displays all the shortcuts ❽.
2. Click the Print button to print the list of shortcuts.

   or

3. Click the Save As button to save the list as a text file.

TIP This text file can be imported into a page layout program and formatted as desired. *(See Appendix A for a printout of all the default shortcuts that ship with FreeHand.)*

Changing the Defaults File

Defaults are the settings that you have when you open a new FreeHand document. Default settings include such things as the units of measurement, the colors in the Swatches panel, if the rulers are visible, page sizes, number of pages, and so on.

To create a new defaults file:

1. With FreeHand open, choose New from the File menu. An untitled file opens.
2. Create a new document, changing the preferences and settings to your specifications ❾.
3. Choose **File > Save As.** The Save dialog box opens.
4. Navigate to the folder/directory English within the FreeHand folder/directory.
5. Save the file under a unique name.

To choose the new defaults file:

1. Choose **Edit > Preferences.**
2. Click the Document category. *(See the next section on specifics of choosing the preferences.)*
3. Type the name of the defaults file you created in the previous step in the New document template field ❿. The new defaults file now controls all new documents.

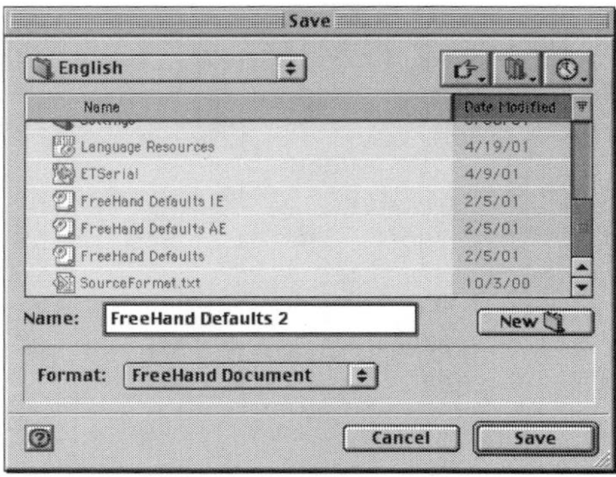

❾ *Save a new document as the FreeHand Defaults file.*

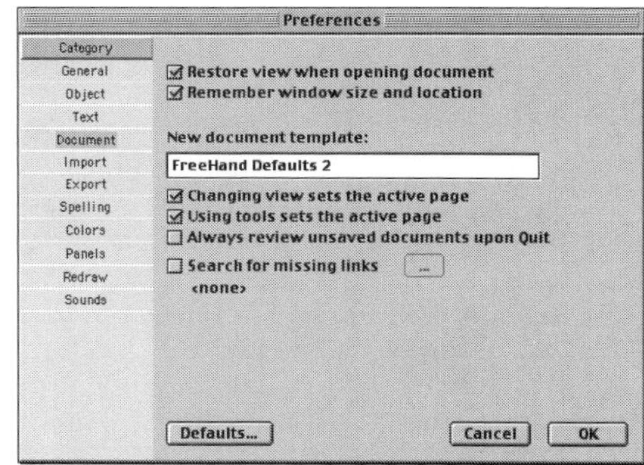

❿ *Use the New document template field to type in the name of the document to be used as the FreeHand Defaults file.*

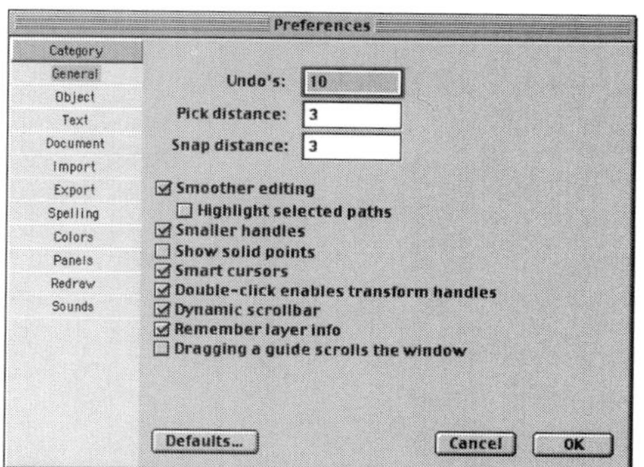

⓫ *The* **Macintosh Preferences** *settings with the categories controlled by a list on the left.*

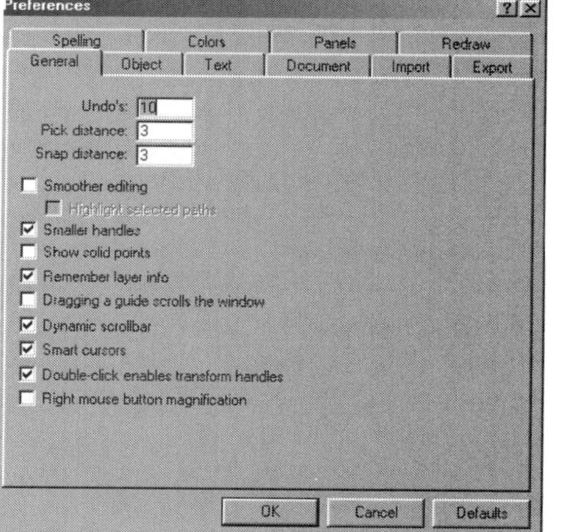

⓬ *The* **Windows Preferences** *settings with the categories controlled by the tabs on the top.*

Setting the Preferences

Preferences control the entire application. This means that any changes you make to the Preferences settings will be applied to all documents—past, present, and future.

To change the preferences (Mac):

1. Choose **Edit > Preferences.** The Preferences dialog box appears ⓫.
2. The preferences settings are divided into 11 categories on the left side of the Preferences dialog box.
3. Click the category you want to control and change the settings as needed.

To change the preferences (Win):

1. Choose **Edit > Preferences.** The Preferences dialog box appears ⓬.
2. The preferences settings are divided into 10 categories shown as tab settings at the top of the Preferences dialog box.
3. Click the category you want to control and change the settings to suit the way you work.

TIP For a complete list of each of the preferences and how they affect working with FreeHand, see Appendix C.

KEYBOARD SHORTCUTS

Working with keyboard shortcuts is probably the fastest way to work on a computer in any application. FreeHand offers a wealth of keyboard shortcuts for almost all the menu commands as well as many non-menu items.

As explained in Chapter 32, you can change the keyboard shortcuts to fit your own particular work habits. This may be to make Freehand work similarly to another program that you are used to. It may be to add a shortcut to a command that doesn't have a shortcut.

If you change your keyboard shortcuts, you can print a copy of those changes to use as a reference.

This appendix lists the default keyboard shortcuts in FreeHand. If you have not made any changes to your settings, you will find that this list matches how Freehand works on your computer. If you have changed your settings, you can use the Print command in the Customize dialog box to print your own list.

Macintosh Keyboard Commands

The following are the default keyboard shortcuts. These are the abbreviations used:

Cmd = Command key
Opt = Option key
Left = Left arrow key
Right = Right arrow key
Down = Down arrow key
Up = Up arrow key
Space = Spacebar
Num = Keypad number
Key = Keypad
> = Increase
< = Decrease

File menu commands

New	Cmd+N
Open...	Cmd+O
Close	Cmd+W
Save	Cmd+S
Save As...	Cmd+Shift+S
Import...	Cmd+R
Export...	Cmd+Shift+R
Print...	Cmd+P
Quit	Cmd+Q

Edit menu commands

Undo	Cmd+Z
Redo	Cmd+Y, Cmd+Shift+Z
Cut	Cmd+X
Copy	Cmd+C
Paste	Cmd+V
Cut Contents	Cmd+Shift+X
Paste Inside	Cmd+Shift+V
Duplicate	Cmd+Opt+D
Clone	Cmd+Shift+D
Select All	Cmd+A
Select All In Document	Cmd+Shift+A
None	Cmd+D
Find & Replace Graphics	Cmd+F
Preferences...	Cmd+U

View menu commands

Fit Selection	Cmd+Opt+0
Fit To Page	Cmd+Shift+W
Fit All	Cmd+0
Magnification: 50%	Cmd+5
Magnification: 100%	Cmd+1
Magnification: 200%	Cmd+2
Magnification: 400%	Cmd+4
Magnification: 800%	Cmd+8
Preview	Cmd+K
Fast Mode	Cmd+Shift+K
Toolbars	Cmd+Opt+T
Panels	F4, Cmd+Shift+H
Page Rulers Show	Cmd+Opt+R
Text Rulers	Cmd+/
Grid: Show	Cmd+Opt+G
Snap To Grid	Cmd+Opt+Shift+G
Guides: Show	Cmd+;
Guides: Lock	Cmd+Opt+;
Guides: Snap To Guides	Cmd+Shift+;
Snap To Point	Cmd+'

Modify menu commands

Scale...	Cmd+F10
Rotate....	Cmd+F13
Reflect...	Cmd+F9
Skew...	Cmd+F11
Transform Again	Cmd+,
Bring To Front	Cmd+Shift+Up
Move Forward	Cmd+Up
Move Backward	Cmd+Down
Send To Back	Cmd+Shift+Down
Align... Top...	Cmd+Opt+4
Align... Right	Cmd+Opt+3
Align... Center Horizontal...	Cmd+Opt+5
Align... Center Vertical...	Cmd+Opt+2

Align… Bottom…	Cmd+Opt+6
Align… Left	Cmd+Opt+1
Align Again	Cmd+Opt+Shift+A
Join	Cmd+J
Split	Cmd+Shift+J
Blend	Cmd+Shift+B
Join Blend To Path	Cmd+Opt+Shift+B
Rasterize…	Cmd+Opt+Shift+Z
Lock	Cmd+L
Unlock	Cmd+Shift+L
Group	Cmd+G
Ungroup	Cmd+Shift+G
Convert to Symbol	F8

Text menu commands

Size: Smaller	Cmd+Shift+,
Size: Larger	Cmd+Shift+.
Style: Bold	Cmd+B
Style: Italic	Cmd+I
Style: BoldItalic	Cmd+Opt+Shift+O
Highlight…	Cmd+Opt+Shift+H
Strikethrough…	Cmd+Opt+Shift+S
Underline…	Cmd+Opt+Shift+U
Align: Left	Cmd+Opt+Shift+L
Align: Right	Cmd+Opt+Shift+R
Align: Center	Cmd+Opt+Shift+C
Align: Justify	Cmd+Opt+Shift+J
Editor…	Cmd+Shift+E
Run Around Selection…	Cmd+Opt+W
Flow Inside Path	Cmd+Shift+U
Attach To Path	Cmd+Shift+Y
Convert To Paths	Cmd+Shift+P

Special characters

Em Space	Cmd+Shift+M
En Space	Cmd+Shift+N
Thin Space	Cmd+Shift+T
Discretionary Hyphen	Cmd+-

Control menu commands

Test Movie	Cmd+Return

Xtras menu commands

Repeat Last	Cmd+Shift+=

Window menu commands

New Window	Cmd+Opt+N
Tools	Cmd+7
Library	F11
Inspectors: Stroke	Cmd+Opt+L
Inspectors: Fill	Cmd+Opt+F
Inspectors: Text	Cmd+T
Layers Panel	F2, Cmd+6
Styles Panel	Shift+F11, Cmd+3
Swatches Panel	Cmd+F9
Color Mixer	Shift+F9, Cmd+Shift+C
Align Panel	Cmd+Opt+A

Other commands

Previous page	Cmd+Page Up
Next page	Cmd+Page Down
Character Inspector	Cmd+T
Text Inspectors: Spacing	Cmd+Opt+K
Text Inspectors: Paragraph	Cmd+Opt+P
Text Inspectors: Copyfit	Cmd+Opt+C
Strokes Thinner	Cmd+Opt+Shift+,
Strokes Thicker	Cmd+Opt+Shift+.

Text adjustment commands

Move to Previous Word	Cmd+Left
Move to Next Word	Cmd+Right
Move to Start of Sentence	Cmd+Key 7
Move to End of Sentence	Cmd+Key 1
Move to Start of Story	Cmd+Home
Move to End of Story	Cmd+End
Select Previous Word	Cmd+Shift+Left
Select Next Word	Cmd+Shift+Right
Select to Start of Sentence	Cmd+Key 8

Command	Shortcut
Select to End of Sentence	Cmd+Key 2
Select to Start of Story	Cmd+Shift+Home
Select to End of Story	Cmd+Shift+End
Delete Previous Word	Cmd+Shift+Delete
Delete Next Word	Cmd+Shift+Del
>Leading	Cmd+Key +
>Leading Lesser	Cmd+Opt+Key +
<Leading	Cmd+Key -
<Leading Lesser	Cmd+Opt+Key -
>Kerning 1%	Cmd+Opt+Right
<Kerning 1%	Cmd+Opt+Left
>Kerning 10%	Cmd+Opt+Shift+Right
<Kerning 10%	Cmd+Opt+Shift+Left
>Baseline Shift	Cmd+Opt+Up
<Baseline Shift	Cmd+Opt+Down
>Horizontal Scale	Cmd+Key 6
<Horizontal Scale	Cmd+Key 3

Tools commands

Command	Shortcut
Select	Shift+F10
Line	Shift+F4
Pen	Shift+F6
Rectangle	Shift+F1
Text	Cmd+Shift+F9
Polygon	Shift+F8
Ellipse	Shift+F3
Pencil	Shift+F5
Scale	F10
Rotate	F13
Reflect	F9
Knife	Shift+F7
Bezigon	Shift+F2

Windows Keyboard Commands

The following are the default keyboard shortcuts. These are the abbreviations used:

Ctrl = Ctrl key
Alt = Alt key
Left = Left arrow key
Right = Right arrow key
Down = Down arrow key
Up = Up arrow key
Space = Spacebar
Num = Keypad number
Key = Keypad
> = Increase
< = Decrease

File menu commands

Command	Shortcut
New	Ctrl+N
Open...	Ctrl+O
Close	Ctrl+W
Save	Ctrl+S
Save As...	Ctrl+Shift+S
Import...	Ctrl+R
Export...	Ctrl+Shift+R
Print...	Ctrl+P
Exit	Ctrl+Q

Edit menu commands

Command	Shortcut
Undo	Ctrl+Z
Redo	Ctrl+Y, Ctrl+Shift+Z
Cut	Ctrl+X
Copy	Ctrl+C
Paste	Ctrl+V
Cut Contents	Ctrl+Shift+X
Paste Inside	Ctrl+Shift+V
Duplicate	Ctrl+Alt+D
Clone	Ctrl+Shift+D
Select All	Ctrl+A
Select All In Document	Ctrl+Shift+A
Select None	Ctrl+D

Find And Replace: Text	Ctrl+Shift+F
Find And Replace: Graphics	Ctrl+F
Preferences...	Ctrl+U

View menu commands

Fit Selection	Ctrl+Alt+0
Fit To Page	Ctrl+Shift+W
Fit All	Ctrl+0
Magnification: 50%	Ctrl+5
Magnification: 100%	Ctrl+1
Magnification: 200%	Ctrl+2
Magnification: 400%	Ctrl+4
Magnification: 800%	Ctrl+8
Preview	Ctrl+K
Fast Mode	Ctrl+Shift+K
Toolbars	Ctrl+Alt+T
Panels	F4
Show Page Rulers	Ctrl+Alt+R
Text Rulers	Ctrl+/
Show Grid	Ctrl+Alt+G
Snap To Grid	Ctrl+Alt+Shift+G
Show Guides	Ctrl+;
Lock Guides	Ctrl+Alt+;
Snap To Guides	Ctrl+Shift+;
Snap To Point	Ctrl+'

Modify menu commands

Redo: Scale...	Ctrl+F10
Redo: Rotate...	Ctrl+F2
Transform Again	Ctrl+,
Bring To Front	Ctrl+Shift+Up
Move Forward	Ctrl+Up
Move Backward	Ctrl+Down
Send To Back	Ctrl+Shift+Down
Align: Top	Ctrl+Alt+4
Align: Bottom	Ctrl+Alt+6
Align: Center Horizontal	Ctrl+Alt+5
Align: Center Vertical	Ctrl+Alt+2
Align: Left	Ctrl+Alt+1
Align: Right	Ctrl+Alt+3
Align Again	Ctrl+Alt+Shift+A
Join	Ctrl+J
Split	Ctrl+Shift+J
Blend	Ctrl+Shift+B
Join Blend To Path	Ctrl+Alt+Shift+B
Rasterize...	Ctrl+Alt+Shift+Z
Lock	Ctrl+L
Unlock	Ctrl+Shift+L
Group	Ctrl+G
Ungroup	Ctrl+Shift+G
Convert to Symbol	F8

Text menu commands

< Size	Ctrl+Shift+,
> Size	Ctrl+Shift+.
Bold	Ctrl+B
Italic	Ctrl+I
BoldItalic	Ctrl+Alt+Shift+O
Highlight...	Ctrl+Alt+Shift+H
Strikethrough....	Ctrl+Alt+Shift+S
Underline...	Ctrl+Alt+Shift+U
Align: Left	Ctrl+Alt+Shift+L
Align: Right	Ctrl+Alt+Shift+R
Align: Center	Ctrl+Alt+Shift+C
Align: Justified	Ctrl+Alt+Shift+J
Em Space	Ctrl+Shift+M
En Space	Ctrl+Shift+N
Thin Space	Ctrl+Shift+T
Editor...	Ctrl+Shift+E
Run Around Selection...	Ctrl+Alt+W
Flow Inside Path	Ctrl+Shift+U
Attach To Path	Ctrl+Shift+Y
Convert To Paths	Ctrl+Shift+P

Control menu commands

Test Movie	Ctrl+Enter

Xtras menu commands

Repeat	Ctrl+Shift+=

Window menu commands

New Window	Ctrl+Alt+N
Tools	Ctrl+7
Library	F11
Stroke Inspector	Ctrl+Alt+L
Fill Inspector	Ctrl+Alt+F
Text Inspector	Ctrl+T
Layers Panel	F2
Styles Panel	Shift+F11
Swatches Panel	Ctrl+F9
Color Mixer	Shift+F9
Halftones Panel	Ctrl+H
Align Panel	Ctrl+Alt+A
Transform Panel	Ctrl+M

Other menu commands

Previous Page	Ctrl+Page Up
Next Page	Ctrl+Page Down
Paragraph Text Inspector	Ctrl+Alt+P
Spacing Text Inspector	Ctrl+Alt+K
Copyfit Text Inspector	Ctrl+Alt+C

Text adjustment commands

Select Next Word	Ctrl+Shift+Right
Select to Start of Sentence	Ctrl+Num 8
Delete Next Word	Ctrl+Shift+Del
>Horizontal Scale by 5%	Ctrl+Num 6
<Horizontal Scale by 5%	Ctrl+Num 3
Strokes: Thinner	Ctrl+Alt+Shift+,
Strokes: Thicker	Ctrl+Alt+Shift+.

Tools commands

Select	Shift+F10
Line	Shift+F4
Pen	Shift+F6
Rectangle	Shift+F1
Polygon	Shift+F8
Ellipse	Shift+F3
Freehand	Shift+F5
Scale	F10
Reflect	F9
Skew	Ctrl+F11
Knife	Shift+F7
Bezigon	Shift+F2

FILL & STROKE DISPLAYS

As shown in chapters 14 and 15, there are some fills and strokes that you can apply to objects but can't preview on screen. These are the Custom fills, Textured fills, and Custom strokes. This is because those fills and strokes are based on the PostScript language.

However, since they do not display onscreen within FreeHand, it is difficult to use them properly. This chapter provides a printout of those fills and strokes so that you may find it easier to work with them.

It also provides a printout of the Pattern fills and strokes. These do appear onscreen. However, there are so many of them, I thought it would be helpful to have them all printed so you can see what they look like. (Remember, the Pattern fills and strokes are not recommended for PostScript print output.)

Custom Fills

The ten Custom fills appear onscreen as a series of Cs in the artwork. The examples below show how each Custom fill prints at its default settings. The gray circles show which of the Custom fills allow background objects to show through their transparent areas.

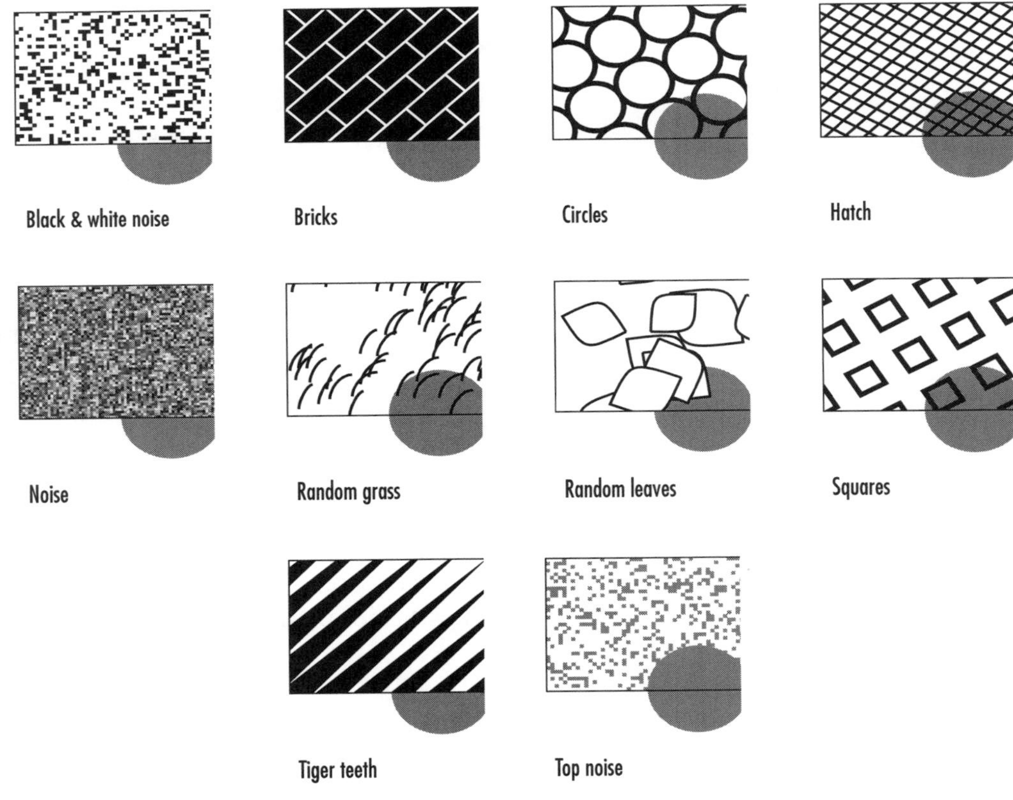

❶ *The* ten Custom fills *at their default settings*

Textured Fills

The nine Textured fills appear onscreen as a series of Cs in the artwork. The examples below show how each Textured fill prints at its default settings. The final example shows how only the fill responds to a change in color.

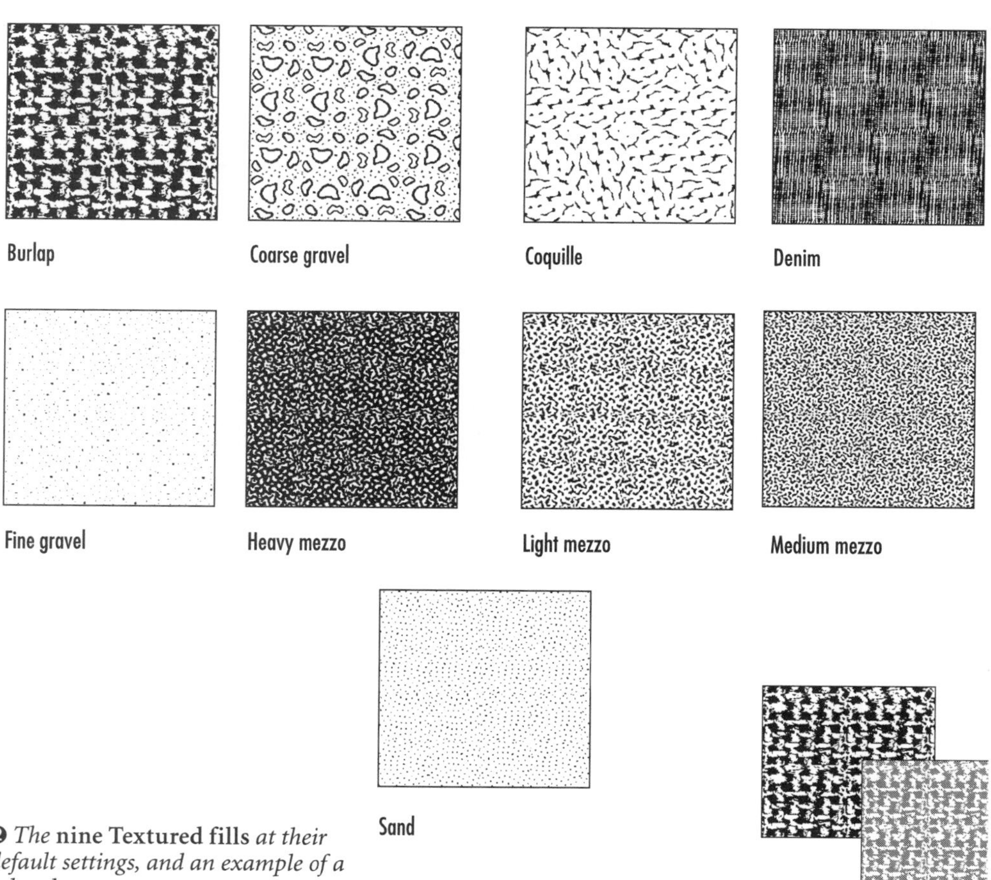

❷ *The* **nine Textured fills** *at their default settings, and an example of a color change*

Pattern Fills and Strokes

The Pattern fills and strokes are bitmapped patterns that appear onscreen and print as shown below. In addition to these default settings, each of the patterns may be inverted or have its pixels edited one by one.

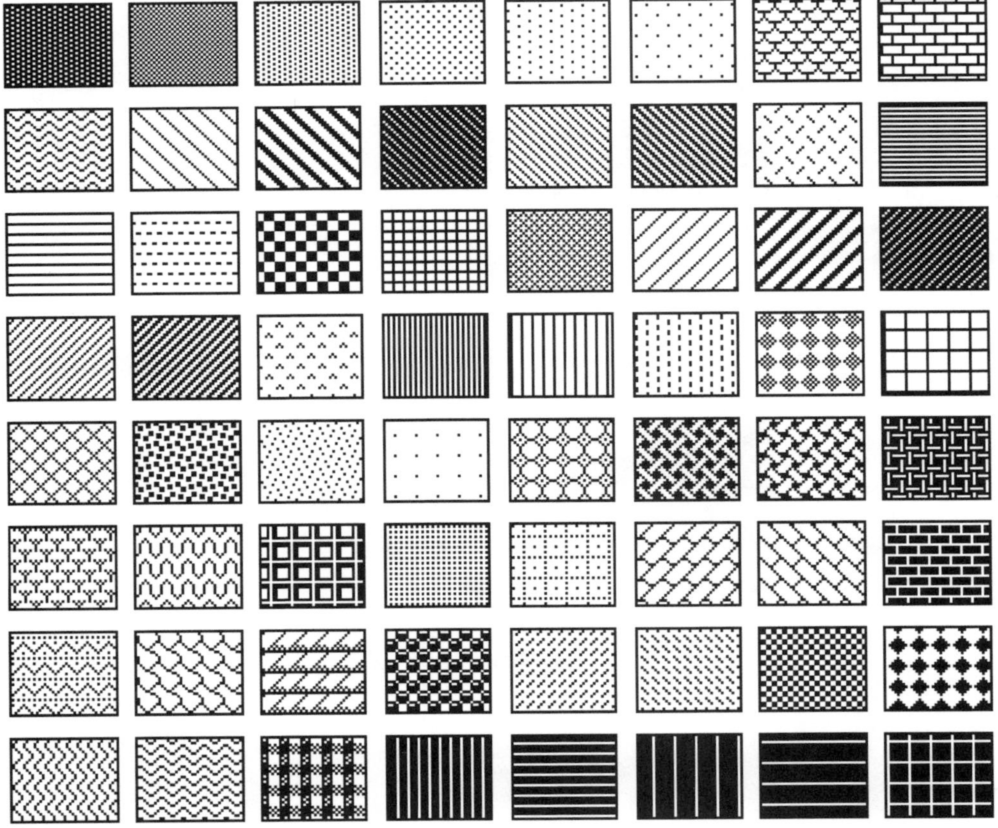

❸ *The* 64 Pattern fills and strokes *at their default settings*

Custom Strokes

The 23 Custom strokes appear onscreen as solid strokes. The examples below show how each of the fills will print at its default settings. The gray circles show how the white areas react with backgrounds—either staying white or becoming transparent.

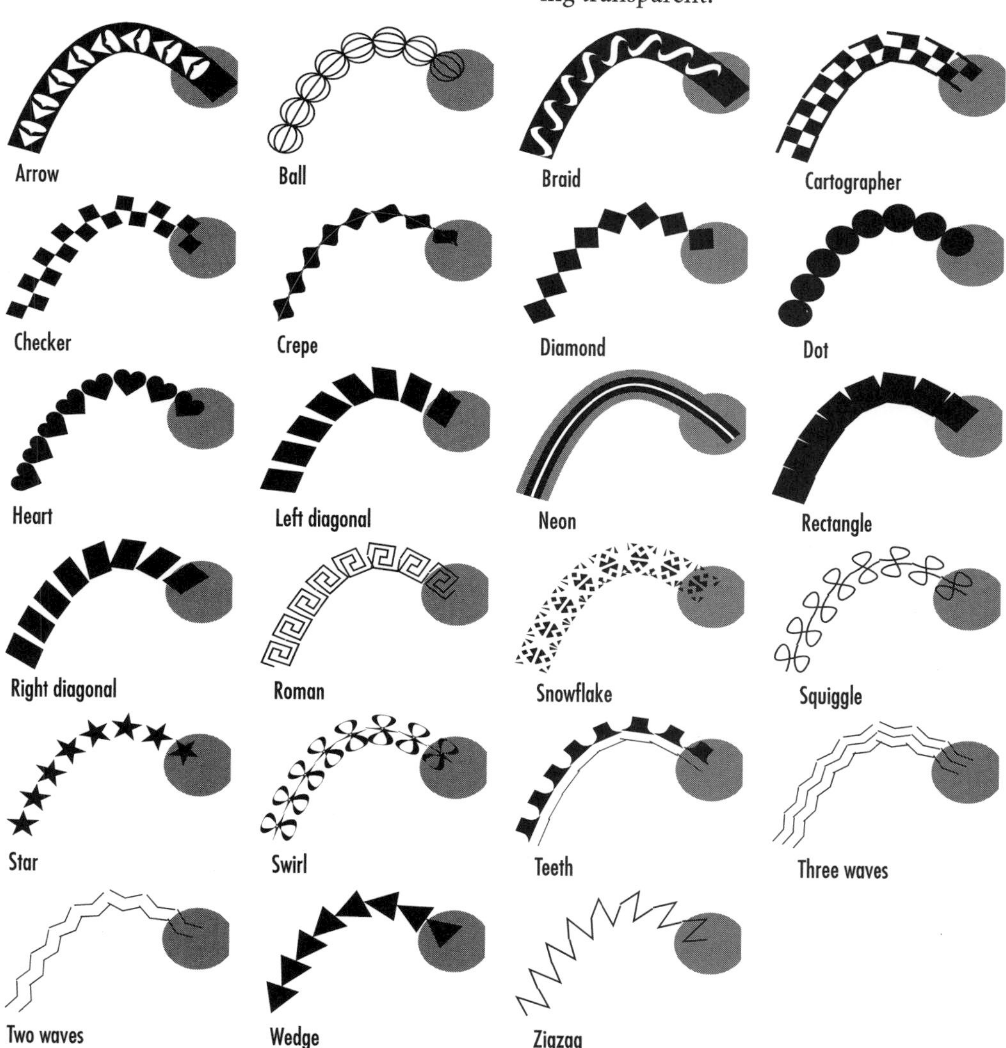

❹ *The* 23 Custom strokes *at their default settings*

APPENDIX

PREFERENCES C

Just because Macromedia FreeHand installs with certain settings doesn't mean you have to keep them the way you found them. FreeHand gives you a wealth of choices as to how your application operates.

In addition to the custom toolbars and keyboard commands covered in Chapter 32, FreeHand gives you many different preference settings for working with the program.

Some of these preferences are just cosmetic—that is, they only affect the look and feel of how you work with the program.

Other preferences are more substantial and can change the way files are exported or copied.

Some of the preferences cover very esoteric actions. If you don't understand what a preference setting does, it's best to leave it the way it was set during installation. That default setting is almost always the way most people will need to work.

General Preferences

Undo's lets you set the number of actions that can be reversed.

Pick distance controls, in pixels, how close the cursor has to come to manipulate a point.

Snap distance controls how close the cursor has to come when snapping one object to another.

Smoother editing allows faster screen redraw of objects on the page but uses more memory ❶.

Highlight selected paths displays paths and points in the color of the layer they are on ❶.

Smaller handles changes how the control handles of points are displayed ❷.

Show solid points reverses how FreeHand displays selected and unselected points. When this option is off, selected points are hollow. When it is on, selected points are solid ❸.

Smart cursors changes how the cursors for the tools are displayed ❹.

Double-click enables transform handles gives you the transformation handles when you double-click on an object *(see page 136)*.

Dynamic scrollbar lets you see your artwork as you drag the scrollbars of the window.

Remember layer info means an object copied and pasted from one document to another will be pasted onto the same layer it originally had.

Dragging a guide scrolls the window means that if you drag a guide into a ruler, you move to a different section of the artwork.

Right mouse button magnification (Win) allows you to click-drag with the right mouse button pressed to define an area to be enlarged.

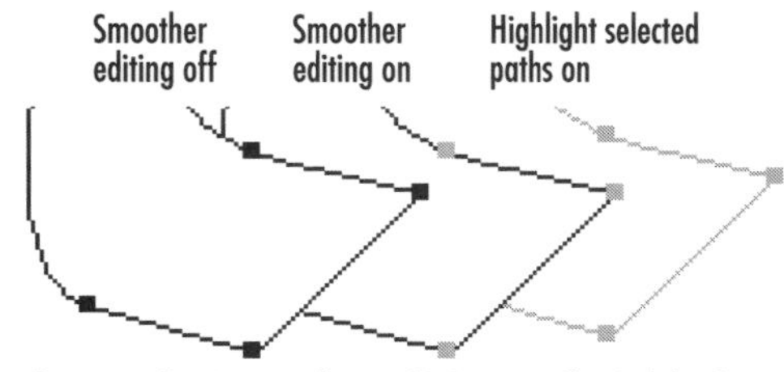

❶ *How the* **Smoother editing** *and* **Highlight** *preferences affect the display of points and paths.*

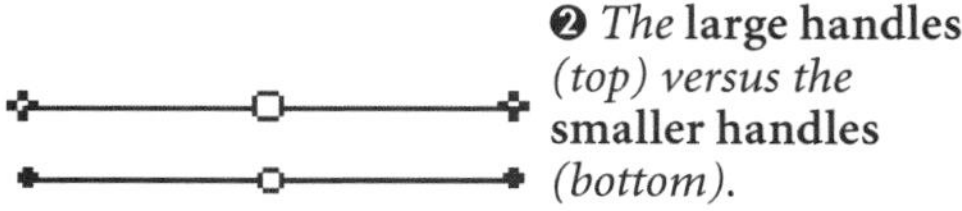

❷ *The* **large handles** *(top) versus the* **smaller handles** *(bottom).*

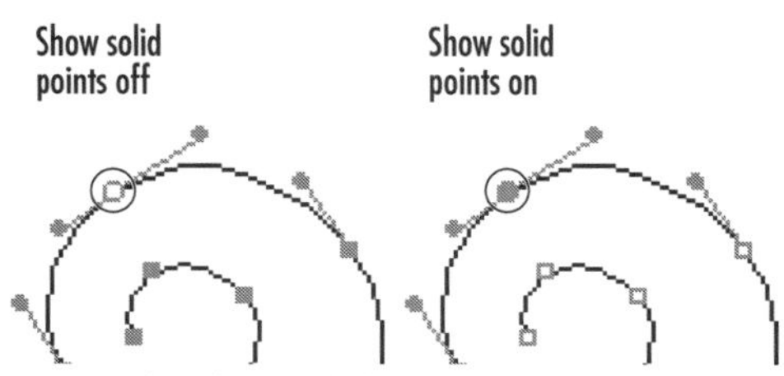

❸ *How the* **Show solid points setting** *changes the display of the selected point (circled).*

❹ *The Smart cursors on (top) versus Smart cursors turned off (bottom).*

Object Preferences

Changing object changes defaults means that if you change an object's fill or stroke, the next object has those attributes.

Groups transform as unit by default means that all items in a group transform together, but this may result in unwanted distortions.

Join non-touching paths means when you Join non-touching objects, FreeHand draws a line between the two nearest points.

Path operations consume original paths means that when you apply path operations commands, the original paths are deleted.

Opt/Alt-drag copies paths controls whether holding the Opt/Alt key while dragging or transforming creates a duplicate of the object.

Show fill for new open paths allows you to see the fill in open paths. Only those paths drawn after changing this preference display the fills.

Warn before launch and edit controls whether the External Editor automatically opens when you double-click imported files.

Edit Locked Objects allows the stroke and fill attributes of locked objects to be modified. Also text within a locked text block can be modified.

External Editor menu selects the application that opens when you double-click imported files.

Default line weights field controls the sizes, in points, in the Stroke Widths submenu.

Auto-apply style to selected objects controls how an object is used to define a new style.

Define style based on selection means that a style takes its attributes from the selected object.

Text Preferences

Always use Text Editor means that the Text Editor appears when you click with the text tool.

Track tab movement with vertical line means a line extends through the text when tab stops are placed on the ruler ❺.

Show text handles when text ruler is off lets you see the text block handles even if the text ruler is turned off ❻.

New text containers auto-expand means that if you click to create a text block, the text block will expand as you type.

Text tool reverts to Pointer causes the Text tool to change to the Pointer tool when it is moved outside the text block.

Display Font Preview shows a representation of the font when you choose it in the font menus ❼.

"Smart quotes" and its pop-up menu allows you to have FreeHand substitute typographer quotes or guillemets instead of plain tick marks ❽.

Build paragraph styles based on controls whether styles are defined by the first paragraph or the shared attributes of the text block.

Dragging a paragraph style changes controls whether the whole text block or a single paragraph changes when you drag a style icon.

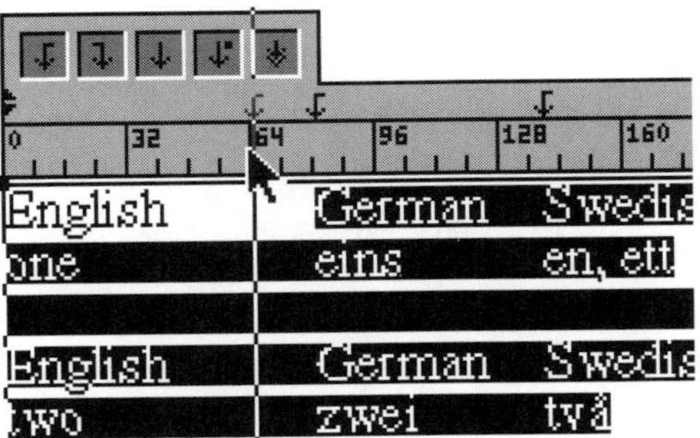

❺ *A line extends through the text to mark the tab location when* **Track tab movement with vertical line** *is turned on.*

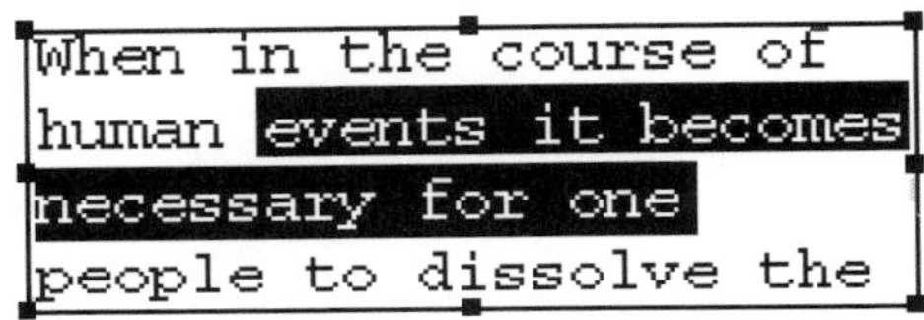

❻ *Working in a text block with the* **Show text handles when text ruler is off** *option turned on.*

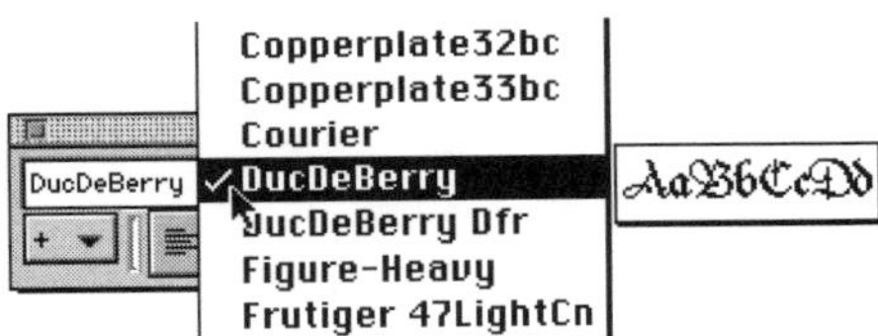

❼ *Turning on* **Display Font Preview** *lets you see a representation of the font when the cursor passes over the font name.*

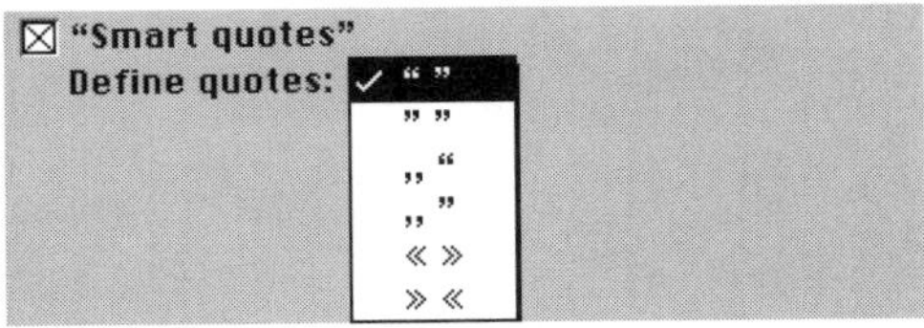

❽ *The various choices for* **Smart Quotes.**

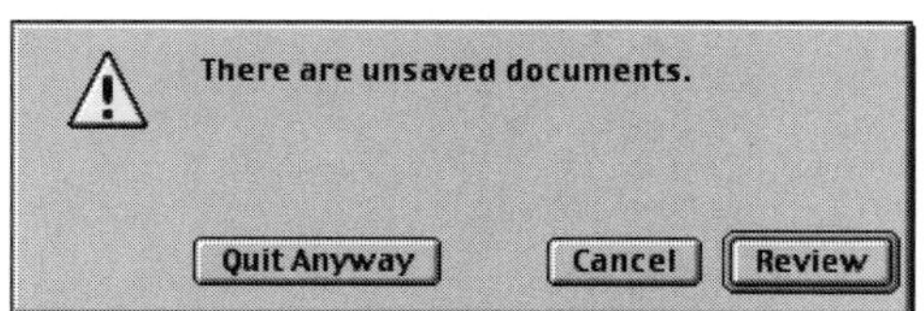

❾ *The* **unsaved documents** *dialog box.*

Document Preferences

Restore last view when opening document prompts FreeHand to remember the last view of a document before it was closed.

Remember window size and location prompts FreeHand to remember the size and position of the window that holds the file.

New document template lets you change the file that FreeHand uses for the defaults file.

Changing the view sets the active page means that as you scroll or change pages, the page that comes into view will be the active page.

Using tools sets the active page means that if you use a tool on a page, that page is active.

Always review unsaved documents upon Quit means that you will be presented with a dialog box prompting you to save each unsaved document when you quit ❾.

Search for missing links (Mac) lets you set which folder to search through for graphics that have lost their links to the original image.

Import Preferences

Convert editable EPS when imported means that, when possible, placed EPS files are converted to objects that you can select.

Embed images and EPS upon import means that the information necessary to print those graphics is embedded directly in the FreeHand document—not linked.

Convert PICT patterns to grays (Mac) converts the bitmapped patterns from MacDraw Pro and Canvas into a gray color.

DXF import options (Mac) control how objects are converted from the DXF format when they are imported into FreeHand.

PDF import options control how objects are converted from the PDF format when they are imported into FreeHand.

Clipboard paste format (Win) controls which formats FreeHand imports from the clipboard.

Export Preferences

Save file thumbnails creates a preview of the artwork, visible in the **File > Open** dialog box.

Bitmap export lets you set the default attributes for exporting files in bitmapped format.

Bitmap PICT previews (Mac) changes the preview of files exported to programs such as QuarkXPress or Adobe PageMaker. This means faster redraw.

(Mac) **Include Portfolio preview** means that a preview is created for the program Extensis Portfolio.

UserPrep file field lets you choose the file FreeHand looks for when printing.

Override Output Options when printing (Mac) lets you choose between binary and ASCII image data. Your files print faster if you choose binary.

Clipboard output/copy formats controls the information on the Clipboard when you switch to another application.

Convert Colors/EPScolor space lets you save your colors in the various formats.

Spelling Preferences

Find duplicate words controls whether the checker finds errors such as "the the."

Find capitalization errors controls whether the checker finds mistakes such as "Really? how did that happen?"

Add words to dictionary exactly as typed means that case-sensitive words such as "FreeHand" or "QuickStart" are entered with capitalization intact.

Add words to dictionary all lowercase means the words are not case sensitive.

Colors Preferences

The boxes for **Guide color or Grid color** open color pickers where you can choose the colors for guides and grid dots.

Color List shows Container color means that when a text block is selected, the Fill color shows the color of the text block.

Color List shows Text color means that when a text block is selected, the Fill color in the Color List shows the fill color of the text, not the block.

Auto-rename [**changed**] **colors** means that the names of colors automatically change when their CMYK or RGB values change.

Color Mixer/Tints panel uses split color well allows you to compare any changes to a color in the Color Mixer with the original color.

Dither 8-bit colors (Mac) improves how colors are displayed onscreen if you are working on a monitor with only 256 colors.

Color management gives you options for how colors are displayed onscreen.

Panels Preferences

Remember location of zipped panels allows a panel to occupy one location when zipped, and a different, unzipped location.

Show Tool Tips shows explanations of what the icons in the toolbars mean when your cursor passes over them ⑩.

Clicking on a layer name moves selected objects means you do not have to use the options pop-up on the layer panel to change the layer an object inhabits.

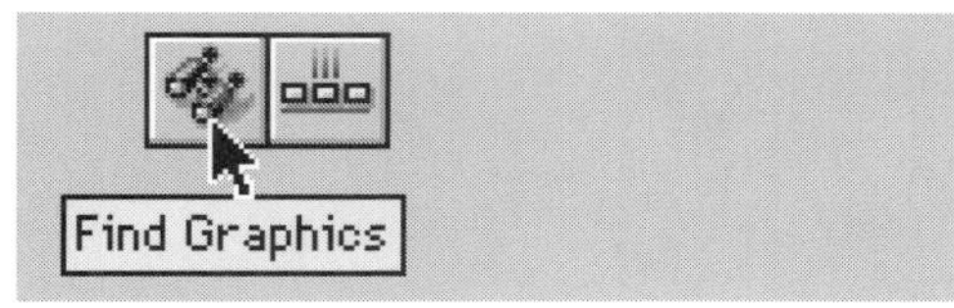

⑩ *Showing the* **Tool Tips.**

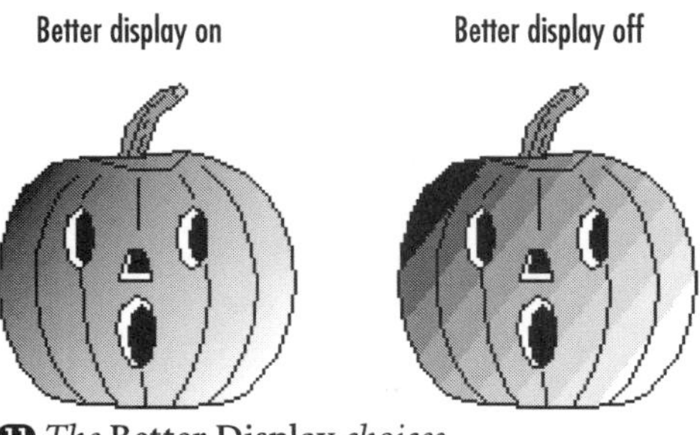

⑪ *The* **Better Display** *choices.*

Full-resolution preview

Low-resolution preview

⑫ *Two of the Smart image preview resolution choices.*

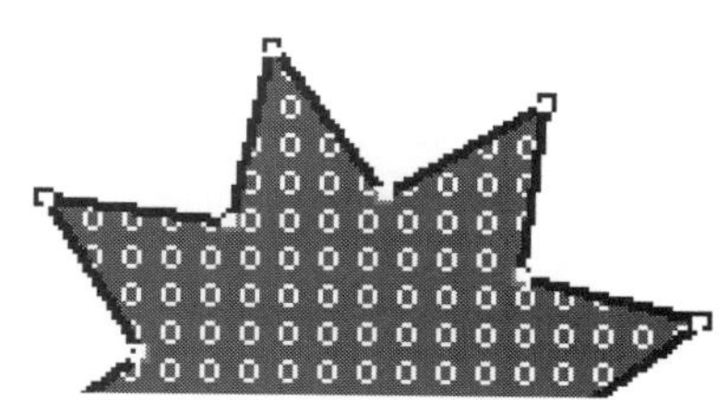

⓭ *The* Os *indicate that the fill overprints.*

When in the course of
human events it becomes

⓮ *An example of* Greeked text *(top) and visible text (bottom).*

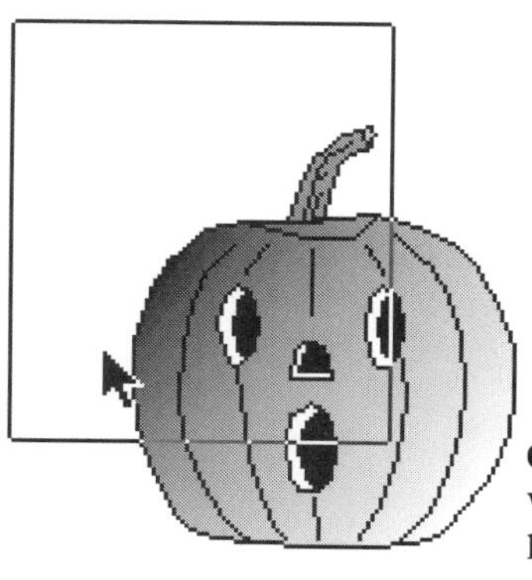

⓯ *Dragging* without a preview.

⓰ *Dragging* with a preview.

Redraw Preferences

Better display means that Graduated and Radial fills are displayed in smoother blends ⓫.

Display text effects means that special effects such as Inline and Zoom are visible.

Redraw while scrolling means that you see your artwork as you scroll instead of after you finish scrolling.

Smart image preview resolution lets you choose low-, medium-, high-, or full-resolution previews of TIFF images ⓬.

Display overprinting objects means that **Os** aresdisplayed when an object is set to overprint ⓭.

Image RAMcache (Win) controls the amount of RAM set aside for the import of images from other applications.

Greek type below controls the size at which text is *greeked* or displayed as a gray band ⓮.

Preview drag field controls how many items are displayed as a preview as they are moved or transformed ⓯–⓰.

TIP Press and release the Opt/Alt key as you drag to see a preview of all the items regardless of how the preferences are set.

Sounds Preferences (Mac)

FreeHand lets you hear sounds when you snap to different objects such as grids, points, and guides. The pop-up menu next to each action lets you choose the sound for that action.

None turns off the sound.

Play lets you preview the sound.

Snap sounds enabled turns on the sounds for all the choices.

Play sounds when mouse is up plays the sound whenever the cursor passes over the object, even if the mouse button is not pressed. (Very noisy!)

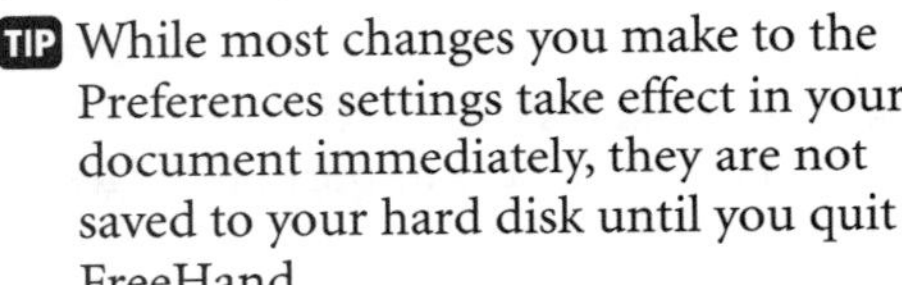

TIP While most changes you make to the Preferences settings take effect in your document immediately, they are not saved to your hard disk until you quit FreeHand.

INDEX

A

B

C

Index

Index

D

E

G

H

I

J

K

L

M

N

Index

O

P

R

S

T

U

V

W

X

Y

Z